ANGLO-SAXON ENGLAND

F. M. STENTON

THIRD EDITION

Oxford   New York

OXFORD UNIVERSITY PRESS

Oxford University Press, Great Clarendon Street, Oxford OX2 6DP

Oxford   New York

Athens Auckland Bangkok Bogota Buenos Aires Calcutta
Cape Town Chennai Dar es Salaam Delhi Florence Hong Kong Istanbul
Karachi Kuala Lumpur Madrid Melbourne Mexico City Mumbai
Nairobi Paris São Paolo Singapore Taipei Tokyo Toronto Warsaw

and associated companies in
Berlin Ibadan

Oxford is a registered trade mark of Oxford University Press

First published 1943
First issued as an Oxford University Press paperback 1989
Reissued in new covers 1998

British Library Cataloguing in Publication Data

Data available

Library of Congress Cataloging in Publication Data

Stenton, F. M. (Frank Merry), 1880–1967.
Anglo-Saxon England.
(Oxford history of England; v. 2).
Reprint. Originally published: Oxford [England]:
Clarendon Press, 1971.
Bibliography: p.
1. Great Britain—History—Anglo-Saxon period,
449–1066.   2. Anglo-Saxons—History.   I. Title.
II. Series: Oxford history of England; 2.
DA152.S74   1989   942.01   88–25347
ISBN 0–19–282237–3 (pbk.)

10

Printed in Great Britain by
Cox & Wyman
Reading, England

PREFACE TO THE THIRD EDITION

WHEN my husband died on 15 September 1967 he left this third edition of his book unfinished, although he had been working on it for some years. He had had an interleaved copy of the book bound for him in our university bindery and had made a number of corrections, but had not succeeded in systematically bringing it up to date. He had however, written one long paragraph on Domesday Book to replace the end of the chapter on that subject. He had a notebook which for years was his constant companion, even on holidays, into which he wrote occasional comments and listed books and articles which he wished to include in the Bibliography and noted subjects which he wished to revise. I was distressed to think that his task would have to be left unfinished. But Professor Dorothy Whitelock, who had been a close friend since her youth, offered to go through the notebook and the papers he left behind him to see whether she could, with my help, finish it for him. He had himself come to the conclusion that there was less he wanted to change than he had at first thought. Some things he no longer wished to change: some he felt that the time had not come to change. Of these Sutton Hoo was one. He knew that some at least of what he had written over twenty years ago about coins was out of date, particularly in view of the immense amount of new work on the Anglo-Saxon coinage which has been done under the leadership of Mr. C. E. Blunt and Mr. Michael Dolley. The Sylloge of Coins of the British Isles, produced under the aegis of the British Academy, was a main intellectual interest of my husband in recent years. *Anglo-Saxon Coins*, edited by Mr. Dolley and presented to my husband on his eightieth birthday, as well as giving him very great pleasure, contained much which should be reflected in *Anglo-Saxon England*; Mr. Blunt's article on the coinage of Offa is a case in point. But the physical effort of making the necessary changes was more than he could face. Both Mr. Blunt and Mr. Dolley were ready to help, but none of us wished to upset the balance of the book. Its author, from the time he took his first degree in 1902, always had the Anglo-Saxons and

Anglo-Scandinavians in the background of his mind, even when he might seem to have been engaged on matters far distant from them. This book is the result of a lifetime's work by a scholar who was meticulous in his choice of words. We all agreed with Miss Whitelock's suggestion that where a necessary change could be made by using a phrase or sentence from his own notes, made either for the revision of *Anglo-Saxon England* or for a lecture on an Anglo-Saxon subject, it should be made, but no change should be made for the sake of change. In some places my husband's words are not altered although numismatists have made suggestions contrary to his statements; for there seems reason to believe that the new views which they express may not be finally accepted. Where he had himself written in a new footnote or altered the wording of a passage, no indication of this is made in the volume, but footnotes or new sentences by other hands are put in square brackets. At first I thought of adding the initials of the writer, but in reading the book through I found it a tiresome distraction. In general those in the Anglo-Saxon period are Miss Whitelock's. The numismatic alterations of the early part are Mr. Blunt's and of the later period Mr. Dolley's. Some of the notes are mine. Miss Whitelock assures me, and Professor Darlington agrees with her, that although there have been advances in some aspects of the Anglo-Saxon field covered by this book, they have generally corroborated what my husband wrote, and hence the book requires little change and practically no correction. Although some writers have differed from certain opinions they have not refuted him. Professor Darlington and I take a similar view about the post-Conquest period.

When the new rooms of the British Numismatic Society at the Warburg Institute were opened on 23 April 1958 my husband was invited to give the first address to the society and chose as his subject 'The Anglo-Saxon Coinage and the Historian'. Fortunately a typed copy of the lecture was made, so that it has been possible to revise it for printing in the forthcoming volume of his *Collected Papers*. It is an important paper, for it makes a new and persuasive suggestion about the date when and the reason why Offa's new coinage was issued.

My husband had wanted to re-write the section of this book about the ceorl, a subject on which he did a good deal of work in preparation for a lecture he gave in the University of

Cambridge at the invitation of Miss Whitelock soon after her election to the Elrington and Bosworth Professorship. Unfortunately he did not type or write all the lecture, but most of it could be reconstructed from his notes either made for the lecture itself or for re-writing that part of *Anglo-Saxon England*. Miss Whitelock suggested that we should reconstruct the lecture to the best of our ability and print it under the title of 'The Thriving of the Anglo-Saxon ceorl' in the volume of his *Collected Papers*, giving references to the paper in this edition of the book. She made herself responsible for typing it and putting in the footnotes.

To the three scholars I have mentioned, Professor Whitelock, Mr. Blunt, and Mr. Dolley, I, who am neither a Saxonist nor a numismatist, owe an immense debt of gratitude. To Miss Whitelock, in particular, I am grateful for continued support and encouragement, for care in going through the book with a view to noting places where change might be necessary and where new editions of old authorities should be referred to, and for her support in not making changes where we both felt sure that my husband would not have wished it. Only a Saxonist of the highest standing could have done what she has done: only a close friend would have taken so much time from her own work to do it.

I should add an expression of my gratitude to the general editor of the series, Sir George Clark, who thought it was time that a table of Contents was added, as in all the other volumes of this series, and helped me to make it.

DORIS MARY STENTON

Whitley Farm Park, Reading
17 May 1968

NOTE TO SECOND EDITION

I HAVE used the reissue of this book as an opportunity for necessary corrections of fact and wording, the insertion of a few significant details omitted from the first edition, and reference to some important studies published since 1943. No general revision of the text has been attempted at any point.

1946

F. M. S.

PREFACE

IT is impossible to give a precise date for the beginning of this volume. Its first sections relate to the situation in Britain immediately preceding the emergence of the earliest English kingdoms, and are mainly concerned with racial movements too vaguely reported to be brought within any exact chronological scheme. It is not until the second half of the sixth century that an outline of continuous English history begins to appear. In round figures the year 550 may be taken as the point from which the volume starts. In political history the central interest of the following centuries is the evolution of an effective monarchy, covering all England, and overriding all the differences of race and custom which separated the various English peoples from one another, and the English people as a whole from the Scandinavian colonists of the North and East. The volume ends with the death of William the Conqueror, who in twenty years had transformed this immemorial Germanic kingship into a pattern of feudal sovereignty.

In social and religious, as in political history, the year of the Conqueror's death may reasonably be taken for the close of a period. The form imposed on English society by centuries of obscure development had been displayed by the Domesday Survey of the previous year. In ecclesiastical history the death of King William ended a unique phase of intimate association between lay and spiritual authority in the government of the English church. In the organization of church and state, as in the vaguer sphere of social relationships, the Conquest had brought about an introduction of ideas which were to revolutionize English thought on public questions. But the revolution itself belongs to a later age.

The writing of Anglo-Saxon history is complicated by two main difficulties. One of them arises from the character and the uneven distribution of the original authorities for the period. The continuity of history is apparent in the *Historia Ecclesiastica* of Bede and in many sections of the *Anglo-Saxon Chronicle*. But there are numerous points at which the only clue to the course of events is given by incidental sources of information such as letters and charters. On other occasions—some of them important—the significance to be attached to an episode turns on the interpretation that is given to a particular Old English word or phrase. The chronology of the period has been studied intensively, but there remains an embarrassing number of incidents of which the date has not yet been fixed. Under these conditions it is impossible to avoid an extensive use of footnotes and references, and, from time to time, the discussion of questions on which no certainty can now be reached.

The second difficulty arises from the fact that most Old English personal names passed out of use during the early Middle Ages and are therefore unfamiliar at the present time. Most of these names are very old, and in successive periods of Old English history appear in different forms, produced by phonetic developments or by changes in the method of representing sounds in writing. Many names appear in different forms in different Old English dialects, so that even in records of the same date there is no consistency in their recorded spellings. In a general history it would obviously be impossible to reproduce these variations. In this volume the few Old English names which still survive, such as Alfred, Athelstan, Edward, and Edgar, appear in their modern shape. The others are represented by the simplest or the best known of their genuine Old English variants. Scandinavian names, which often caused difficulty to English clerks, appear in the forms which are either most familiar or most easily intelligible.

The preparation of this volume has extended over many years, and many people have helped me to carry it through. To all of them I offer my sincerest thanks. Among them the General

Editor of this series has given me valuable advice both on general questions and on points of detail. Mr. L. C. Loyd has allowed me to draw upon his unrivalled knowledge of early Norman genealogy. Miss A. M. Kirkus has supplied me with a detailed analysis of the massive Lincolnshire Domesday. Professor Bruce Dickins has read the proofs of the volume, and his minute accuracy has saved me from much inconsistency and error. To Mr. Kenneth Sisam I am indebted for long-continued encouragement, and for invaluable notes on the sections which deal with Old English learning and literature. I must take full responsibility for the volume as it now stands, but I cannot overstate my gratitude to these scholars for the generosity with which they have placed their learning at my service. To the staff of the Clarendon Press I owe thanks for the rapidity with which they have printed the book, and for their skill in dealing with my corrections in proof. That the book ever reached the stage of proof is due entirely to my wife. I owe to her the conditions which have permitted so long drawn out an under-taking, and I have discussed with her every page of typescript as it was produced. The index to the book, which she compiled, is no more than her final contribution to a volume which she has made possible. In all but formal dedication, the book is hers.

F. M. S.

Whitley Park Farm, Reading
27 August 1943

CONTENTS

III. ANGLIAN NORTHUMBRIA

IV. THE CONVERSION OF THE ENGLISH PEOPLE

V. THE ENGLISH CHURCH FROM
THEODORE TO BONIFACE

VI. LEARNING AND LITERATURE IN EARLY ENGLAND

VII. THE ASCENDANCY OF THE MERCIAN KINGS

VIII. THE AGE OF ALFRED

IX. THE STRUCTURE OF EARLY ENGLISH SOCIETY

X. THE CONQUEST OF SCANDINAVIAN ENGLAND

XI. THE DECLINE OF THE
OLD ENGLISH MONARCHY

XIII. THE TENTH-CENTURY REFORMATION

XIV. ENGLAND BEFORE THE CONQUEST

1. THE PEASANTS AND THEIR LORDS

XV. THE LAST YEARS OF THE OLD ENGLISH STATE

XVI. THE NORMAN CONQUEST

XVII. THE NORMAN SETTLEMENT

XVIII. THE REORGANIZATION OF THE
ENGLISH CHURCH

EPILOGUE. THE ANGLO-NORMAN STATE

LIST OF MAPS

ABBREVIATIONS

B.N.J. = British Numismatic Journal.

C.D. = Codex Diplomaticus Aevi Saxonici, ed. J. M. Kemble.

Councils iii = Haddan and Stubbs, *Councils and Ecclesiastical Documents relating to Great Britain and Ireland,* vol. III (1871).

C.P. = Preparatory to Anglo-Saxon England being the Collected Papers of Frank Merry Stenton.

C.S. = Cartularium Saxonicum, ed. W. de G. Birch.

D.B. = Domesday Book, 2 vols., 1783.

E.H.R. = English Historical Review.

E.P-N.S. = English Place-Name Society.

H.E. = Bede, Historia Ecclesiastica, ed. C. Plummer.

M.G.H. = Monumenta Germaniae Historica.

R.S. or (R.S.) = Chronicles and Memorials of Great Britain and Ireland ('Rolls Series').

V.C.H. = Victoria History of the Counties of England.

The capital letters (A–F) which are sometimes used in references to the *Anglo-Saxon Chronicle* indicate the different manuscripts of that work, and are explained below, pp. 689–91.

I

THE AGE OF THE MIGRATION

ETWEEN the end of Roman government in Britain and the emergence of the earliest English kingdoms there stretches a long period of which the history cannot be written. The men who played their parts in this obscurity are forgotten, or are little more than names with which the imagination of later centuries has dealt at will. The course of events may be indicated, but is certainly not revealed, by the isolated or incidental references to Britain made by writers of this or the following age. For the first time in five centuries Britain was out of touch with the Continent. Contemporaries in Gaul, who might have told something of its history, were preoccupied with their own troubles. Britain was lost to the Roman Empire, and its fortunes were of little interest to men whose own civilization was at stake.[1]

At first their attention was called to Britain intermittently by eccentric movements of opinion within the British churches. Twice during the fifth century a recrudescence of British Pelagianism caused Germanus, bishop of Auxerre, to visit Britain. The account of his life, which was written by a younger contemporary, shows that in 447, the date of his second visit, the Britons of the south had not yet become the subjects of barbarian masters. But with the departure of Germanus Britain definitely passes outside the range of recorded history. British traditions current in the sixth century placed the invitation of 'Saxon' adventurers to Britain for the defence of the land—the first in the series of events which led to the Saxon conquest of the south—in the years between 446 and 454. Archaeological discoveries have shown that permanent English settlements were founded in Britain during, if not before, the last quarter of the fifth century. But archaeological evidence is an unsatisfactory basis for an absolute chronology, and even if the British traditions may be trusted, they do not indicate the rate at which

[1] The condition of Britain in the fifth century is discussed in vol. i of this *History*, chapter xix, and by R. H. Hodgkin, *History of the Anglo-Saxons*, ed. 3, chapter ii.

events moved between the first coming of the Saxons and their establishment of permanent kingdoms. And the English traditions of the Conquest, around which discussion is still playing, reveal no more than fragments of a story which was ill-remembered, and moves by decades rather than by years.

The story can be regarded either as an epilogue to the history of Roman Britain or as a prologue to the history of Saxon England. In either case, the foundation of all inquiry into its details is a tract on the miseries of Britain written a little before the year 547 by a British monk named Gildas.[1] It is a work of exhortation and bitter reproach; the greater part of it is a mosaic of quotations from scripture, and the historical information which it gives is quite incidental to its real purpose of calling the British rulers of its author's day to repentance. But it gives a coherent impression of a possible sequence of events. They begin with an appeal for help against unnamed barbarians sent by the Britons to the consul Aëtius, then commanding the Roman forces in Gaul. Aëtius gave no help, but the Britons defended themselves, and the barbarians, that is, apparently the Picts and Scots, left the province. This recovery was followed by a civil war, a pestilence, and another series of barbarian raids, which led a certain British 'tyrant' to introduce a body of Saxons into Britain for the defence of the land. Gildas does not name the tyrant, but traditions which go back at least to the seventh century give him the name Vortigern. Three ships' companies of Saxons came at his invitation, and were soon joined by larger forces. They served their British employers for what Gildas describes as a long time, but at last a dispute about their rations led to a revolt, in the course of which they ravaged the whole island as far as the western sea.

The towns of the province were destroyed, and life in the south of Britain became utterly intolerable. But it was re-established when the mercenaries had returned to their own country, and the British defences were reorganized under a man of Roman race, named Ambrosius Aurelianus, whose descendants in the second generation were still ruling somewhere in Britain when Gildas was writing. For a time there was a struggle on equal terms between the Britons and new invading forces, but it was ended by a British victory won at a place,

[1] *De Excidio et Conquestu Britanniae,* ed. Mommsen (Monumenta Germaniae Historica. Auctorum Antiquissimorum, xiii. 1).

not now to be identified, called Mons Badonicus. The phrase in which Gildas attempts to give the date of this battle is obscure, but places it a little before or after the year 500. To Gildas the battle was a turning-point in history, for it gave to the Britons a respite which, when he wrote his book, had already lasted for at least forty years.

His narrative implies that an ordered society existed in southern Britain at this time. He definitely contrasts present prosperity with former calamities, although he states that the cities of Britain were not inhabited as before, and that the land was troubled by civil wars between contending kings. There is, indeed, no primary authority other than Gildas for the British recovery which followed the battle of Mons Badonicus, and he ignores the permanent Germanic settlements for which there is archaeological evidence in many parts of eastern, central, and southern England. But his references to the deserted towns of the province and to the kings who were continually fighting with one another, are confirmed in many different ways. There is at present no conclusive evidence that the organized life of any Romano-British town survived the severance of its communications in the troubles of the fifth century. Two at least of the kings whom Gildas mentions by name reappear in the pedigrees of ancient Welsh royal houses. The inscribed stone which marked the grave of one of these kings is still preserved.[1] There is every reason to believe that the continuity of urban life in Britain had long been broken when Gildas wrote, and that monarchy was already an established institution.

It is remarkable that Gildas ignores the British leader whose legendary fame was to carry the struggle between Saxons and Britons into the current of European literature. Gildas has nothing to say of Arthur, whose claim to an historic existence rests upon the ninth-century compilation of the Welsh scholar Nennius, and upon the observation of an earlier Welsh poet that a certain warrior, though brave, 'was not Arthur'.[2] The silence of Gildas may suggest that the Arthur of history was a less imposing figure than the Arthur of legend. But it should not be allowed to remove him from the sphere of history, for Gildas was curiously reluctant to introduce personal names into his

---

[1] R. H. Hodgkin, *History of the Anglo-Saxons*, ed. 3, p. 179 and plate 30.
[2] On this poem, the *'Gododdin'* of Aneirin, see below, p. 77.

writing. This habit of mind helps to explain the meagreness of the information which he gives about Britain in his own day. The purpose of his work compelled him to mention by name those British kings whose flagrant sins invited commination. It also made him dilate upon—it may have made him exaggerate—the miseries of the British race in the generation before his own. But a king who sinned in moderation had no interest for Gildas, and a description of Britain in an age which had known neither judgements nor deliverances would have been quite irrelevant to his design. He had no concern with the instruction of future generations, and it is as dangerous as it is easy to argue from his silences. In particular, it is unwise to regard the names of the kings who attracted his denunciation as an index to the extent of the territory which was still British in his day. His longest and most intense invective is devoted to the greatest of contemporary rulers, Maelgwn of Gwynedd, lord of Anglesey. He addresses exhortation to Constantine of Dumnonia, a kingdom of which the memory survives in the name Devon—to a certain Cuneglassus, whose kingdom is unnamed, and to Votiporix, the foolish tyrant of the Demetae, who inhabited the south-western parts of Wales. A fifth king, reproved under the name of Aurelius Caninus, is otherwise unknown. The fact that three of these five kings belonged to the extreme west of south Britain should not be strained to imply that the whole centre was then deserted, or in English occupation. There were certainly British kings of whom Gildas takes no account. He writes nothing about any king of Strathclyde, though it is possible that he was a native of that region. He ignores the ancient kingdom of Powys, and he makes no obvious reference to the ancestors of Kings Coinmail, Condidan, and Farinmail, who were reigning to the east of the lower Severn late in the sixth century.[1] He was a prophet, not a historian; he wrote with passion, and the world which he addressed was small.

It was also a world in isolation. No Frankish writer adds anything to the narrative of Gildas. But the relations of Theudebert, king of the eastern Franks, with the court of Justinian brought north-western Europe for a moment within the view of Byzantine scholars. Shortly after the middle of the sixth century, Procopius of Caesarea, the most brilliant member of an

[1] Below, p. 29.

illustrious company, inserted a chapter about Britain as a parenthesis into his history of Justinian's wars against the Goths in Italy.[1] The chapter consists of a brief description of Britain and its peoples, a romantic story about a war between a young king beyond the Rhine and the daughter of a king of the *Angiloi*, and an account of certain marvels related about the island. To many scholars the story and the marvels, which include a fantastic description of the ferrying of disembodied souls from Gaul to Britain, discredit Procopius' remarks about the races dwelling there. On the other hand, the marvels come as an afterthought at the end of the chapter, the story which forms its centre shows a knowledge of Germanic custom which can only have been acquired from a barbarian informant,[2] and the preliminary description of Britain is set out in a way which proves that it was derived from Frankish visitors to Constantinople. Its most interesting portion is a statement that Britain was inhabited by three races named *Angiloi*, *Frissones*, and Britons, each ruled by its own king. Each race was so fertile that it sent large numbers of men, women, and children every year to the land of the Franks, who planted them in the emptier parts of the Frankish territory. Through this migration the king of the Franks had come to assert a claim to Britain itself, and had included certain of the *Angiloi* in a recent embassy to Constantinople in order to impress the reality of his claim upon the emperor. The passage is obviously an extreme simplification of a very complex situation. But it is nearly two hundred years earlier than the *Historia Ecclesiastica* of Bede, and more than three hundred years earlier than any extant manuscript of the *Anglo-Saxon Chronicle*. It was written by a man of alert and curious mind, in a position to be acquainted with those who knew the facts, and its implications, which are very important, deserve at least to be tested.

In part, it is undoubtedly correct. It contains a clear reference to the British migration which at this time was turning the peninsula of Armorica into Brittany.[3] It is also certain that the *Angiloi* of Procopius were the people known among themselves as *Engle*, and to Latin writers as *Angli*. There is no earlier reference to their settlement in Britain, but there is evidence

---

[1] *De Bello Gotthico*, iv. 19.   [2] H. M. Chadwick, *The Heroic Age*, pp. 97–9.

[3] The general tendency of the available evidence suggests very strongly that this migration took place in the first half of the sixth century. Cf. W. H. Stevenson, *E.H.R.* xiv (1899), pp. 44–5.

from archaeology and place-names that it was already in progress. The Frisians, who are obviously represented by the *Frissones* of Procopius, are not generally considered to have taken any important part in the Germanic invasions of Britain. On the other hand, linguistic analysis has established a fundamental connection between English and Frisian which is the first certain fact in English history. The Frisian language shared in all the more important sound-changes which distinguish English from German on the one hand and from the Scandinavian languages on the other.[1] English and Frisian are in fact collateral branches of a common linguistic stock, and there can be little doubt that the differences between the later forms of these languages arose after the period of the English migration to Britain. In view of this connection, it becomes highly probable that the *Frissones* of Procopius were Frisian migrants from the coastal lands west of the lower Elbe, whose descendants, amalgamated with other races, appear in later descriptions of the English peoples under the wider and vaguer name of Saxons.

But the chief interest of the passage lies in the statement that not only the Britons but the *Angiloi* and the *Frissones* were crossing in great numbers from Britain to the Continent. If it is at all near the truth, it means that the English penetration of the south had been checked, some, and perhaps many, years before the middle of the sixth century. No Germanic race ever took to the sea without some urgent reason, and a reverse migration of English peoples to the Continent at this date would imply that the invaders had outgrown their first settlements and abandoned the attempt to find new ones. That such a situation was possible is clear from the narrative of Gildas. Whatever may have been the English frontier after the battle of Mons Badonicus, it cannot have been materially extended against the Britons during the long peace which followed. Historically, the statement of Procopius is important because, if it can be trusted, it shows that after the war the invaders were restricted to a territory which gave them no adequate opportunity of providing for a growing population by the establishment of new inland colonies. It becomes, in fact, a warning against the assumption that the war left the English in possession of the centre as well as the east and south-east of Britain.

[1] H. M. Chadwick, *The Origin of the English Nation*, pp. 61-4.

If it stood alone, this statement could easily be dismissed as a rationalization of the travellers' tales which happened to reach an author living at the other end of Europe. It is brought within the sphere of history by an independent Germanic tradition of a migration of English peoples from Britain to the Continent in the first half of the sixth century. The oldest version of this tradition[1] was written down by a monk of Fulda a little before the year 865, when it was already regarded as an ancient story. It asserted that the ancestors of the continental Saxons sprang from the *Angli* of Britain. Being compelled to find new land for settlement, they crossed the ocean to Germany, landed at Haduloha—the modern Cuxhaven—at a time when Theuderich, king of the Franks, was at war with the Thuringians. When he learned that the immigrants were anxious to settle in Germany, Theuderich invited them to join him, and after the Thuringian war gave them land to the north of the river Unstrut in the territory which he had conquered. It is impossible to accept this legend as a complete account of the origin of the continental Saxons. The differences between their language and the Anglo-Frisian dialect from which English is descended go back to a time far beyond the Thuringian wars of Theuderich. On the other hand, there is some evidence that a language closely related to Old English was once spoken in the districts assigned to the migrant 'Saxons' by the legend, and the name of the canton Engilin between the Unstrut and the Saale points to an early settlement of Angles in this quarter.[2] What is more remarkable is the curious agreement between this legend, which has all the appearance of a genuine popular tradition, and Procopius' account of the migrations from Britain to the Continent. In each case the motive for the migration was the necessity of finding new regions for settlement. The establishment of the 'Saxons' by Theuderich in conquered lands beyond the Unstrut reads like an illustration of Procopius' statement that the Franks planted the immigrants in the more deserted parts of their own territory. There is also a general agreement between Procopius and the monk of Fulda as to the period in which these migrations took place. Theudebert, king of the Franks, to whose relations with Justinian Procopius owed whatever he knew of affairs in Britain, reigned from 534 until 548. He is known to have boasted to Justinian of the number of peoples under his rule, and he was undoubtedly the Frankish king who, according to Procopius, used the migrations from Britain into Frankish territory as proof of his lordship over the island. The Thuringian war of Theuderich can be precisely dated to the year 531, some thirty years after the barbarian penetration of Britain had been checked by the battle of Mons Badonicus.

Coincidences like these raise at the least a strong presumption that some migration of the kind described by Procopius actually took place. Intrinsically it is by no means improbable. The communications which are known to have passed between the Frankish and Byzantine courts give a simple explanation of the way by which it might have come to Procopius' knowledge. His account of the migration agrees with the situation within Britain described by the contemporary Gildas, and is reinforced by the early and independent tradition preserved at Fulda. Nothing but a consistent series of adverse local traditions would justify the rejection of a contemporary statement thus supported. And the English traditions of the conquest of southern Britain, confused as they are, imply a sequence of events in which the movements recorded by Procopius have a natural place.

It is unfortunate that the greatest of Anglo-Saxon historians, writing at a time when these traditions were still alive, regarded them as irrelevant to his purpose. Bede was in touch with men who could have told him much about the origins of the English kingdoms. His pupil Egbert, archbishop of York, was a member of the Northumbrian royal family. Ceolwulf, king of the Northumbrians, to whom Bede sent a draft of the *Historia Ecclesiastica* for revision, was particularly interested in the deeds and sayings of the illustrious Englishmen of the past. In view of Bede's relations with the Northumbrian court, it is highly dangerous to reject anything that he offers as a statement of historical fact. But he had a scholar's dislike of the indefinite, and traditions of events to which no date or circumstance could be assigned fell outside his conception of history. To Gildas' account of the coming of the 'Saxons' he added the statements that their leaders were said to have been Hengest and Horsa, sons of Wihtgils, son of Witta, son of Wecta, son of Woden; that Horsa was killed in battle by the Britons; and that his monument was still shown in the east of Kent. He gave the name of Vortigern to the British king who invited them to Britain, and placed their arrival in the reign of the emperors Marcian and Valentinian III, which he considered to run from 449 to 456. Later in his book, when tracing the genealogy of Æthelberht, the first English king to become a Christian, he observes that the kings of Kent in his own time were known as the 'Oiscingas', because Œric, Hengest's son, from whom they were descended, had borne the surname Oisc. Most of this information probably came to Bede from learned friends in Kent, and there is no reason to doubt its accuracy. But in its austerity it represents a point of view from which traditional stories only become matter for the historian when they can be brought into relation to the genealogies of kings or the established framework of secular chronology.

Bede's chief contribution to the history of the Anglo-Saxon invasions is a statement of what he believed to be the relationship between the invaders and the various English peoples of his own day.[1]

They came from three very powerful nations of the Germans; that is, from the *Saxones*, *Angli*, and *Iutae*. Of the stock of the *Iutae* are the *Cantuarii* and *Uictuarii*; that is, the race which holds the Isle of Wight, and the race in the country of the West Saxons which is still called *Iutarum natio*, established over against the Isle of Wight. From the *Saxones*; that is, from the country now called the land of the Old Saxons, came the East Saxons, South Saxons, and West Saxons. From the *Angli*; that is, from the country called *Angulus*, which is said to have lain deserted from that time to this between the countries of the *Iutae* and *Saxones*, are sprung the East Angles, Middle Angles, the whole Northumbrian race—that is, the people living to the north of the river Humber—and the other peoples of the *Angli*.

Recent work in related studies suggests that this famous analysis over-emphasizes the distinction between the various peoples of whom the English nation was composed. It is dangerous, for example, to assume that the features which distinguish one Old English dialect from another go back to the age of the migration.[2] The study of English place-names has not yet established any fundamental distinctions between the

---

[1] *Historia Ecclesiastica*, i. 15.
[2] H. M. Chadwick, *The Origin of the English Nation*, pp. 64–9.

local nomenclature of Anglian, Saxon, and Jutish territory.[1] As evidence for the continental origins of the English people the differences between the heathen cultures of Anglian and Saxon England,[2] though real, are less significant than the resemblances. Kent in the heathen time was distinguished from other parts of England by the prevalence of a far more elaborate culture, closely related to that of the Frankish Rhineland, but at present it seems to be an open question whether it should be regarded as native to the original English settlers of Kent or as the result of later intercourse between that region and the Continent. In regard to social structure and agricultural practice there is at least no obvious difference between Anglian and Saxon England; though Jutish Kent, again, is distinguished by customs which, like its material culture, point to an early connection between its inhabitants and the men of the Rhineland. The idiosyncrasies of Kentish culture and custom undoubtedly suggest that the Jutish settlers of that region had passed through experiences in which other invaders did not share. But they do not outweigh the linguistic evidence that the men whose settlements formed the original English kingdoms all belonged to a single group of closely related Germanic nations.

This does not mean that Bede's analysis of the English people should be disregarded. It satisfied a king of the Northumbrians in an age when kings were accustomed to listen to heroic verse covering all the nations of the Germanic world. It was the work of a cautious scholar, who had known eminent persons and was in communication with friends in many different parts of England. Its precision in regard to the obscure race of the Jutes, who had not given their name to any English kingdom, proves the care with which it was written. But it is not a mere piece of scholarly reconstruction. Titles of kings and bishops, recorded before the date of Bede's work, show that different English peoples actually regarded themselves as Angles or Saxons. It was not as a result of any deliberate theory that two adjacent peoples came to be known respectively as East Saxons and East Angles. Names like these stood for a real, if faded, memory of origins. In representing the *gens Anglorum* as a

[1] *Transactions of the Royal Historical Society*, 4th Series (1940), pp. xxii, 6–15. My husband's papers quoted henceforward are referred to as C.P. with the page references.

[2] For the archaeology of the period a general reference may be made here to the first volume of this *History*, book v, by J. N. L. Myres.

composite people drawn from three distinct Germanic nations
Bede was reflecting the common opinion of his time, and the
vitality of tradition makes it very unlikely that this opinion was
fundamentally mistaken.

The early history of these nations is enveloped in the obscurity
which overhangs all Germany in the age of national migration.
The best material for this history, the *Germania* of Tacitus, the
Geography of Ptolemy, the *Natural History* of Pliny, comes from
the first or second century. For the next two hundred years the
nations of Germany were involved in a movement which carried
them to distant seats, and created new confederacies which
caused the adoption of new racial names. Fragments of their
history can be learned from the episodes which brought them
within the knowledge of Roman writers. Other fragments,
often strangely disguised, were preserved in poems which survived into an age when men made common use of writing.
Tradition could preserve a genealogy for many generations.
But it is only an imperfect story which can be recovered from
materials like these, and there are irrecoverable passages of
crucial importance in the early history of the Angles, Saxons,
and Jutes.

Of these nations the Saxons are the least obscure. Tacitus
does not mention them, but Ptolemy, probably following a lost
authority of the late first century, places them on the neck of the
Cimbric peninsula, in the modern Holstein. They had appeared
in the narrow seas before the end of the century, and two hundred years later Roman writers regarded them as the typical
German enemy. It is probable that the Saxons of Latin literature were in reality the kindred peoples of the whole country
between the original Saxon settlements in Holstein and the
Weser or the Ems. Over all this country, from Slesvig to the
modern Holland, the furniture of heathen burials, especially
the pottery, shows the prevalence of the same general culture.
It is a true barbaric culture, untouched by the Roman influences which were already affecting the life of even the eastern
Franks. To the Roman world of the fifth century the Saxons
were outer barbarians.

To a contemporary observer early in that century it may well
have seemed that if ever the Saxons were able to obtain a permanent settlement within the empire it would be in Gaul
rather than in Britain. Gaul was the richer province, and its

coastal defences seem to have been less formidable than those of the *Litus Saxonicum per Britanniam*. Even after the middle of the century, when the imperial defence of Britain had long come to an end, the Saxons still attempted to establish themselves to the south of the Channel, and indeed came near to the occupation of at least the northern third of Gaul. In 463 under their King Eadwacer they took possession of Angers, to be dislodged by Childerich, king of the Franks, acting as an ally of the empire. It is in every way possible that the stream of Saxon invaders was diverted from Gaul to Britain by the extension of Frankish power along the south coast of the Channel in the reign of Clovis.[1] After the defeat of Syagrius in 486 the Franks were definitely the masters of northern Gaul, and there was no opportunity for the settlement of other Germanic peoples. The course of events in Gaul thus supplies a reason, independent of British or English tradition, for believing that the beginnings of Saxon settlement in Britain belong to the last decades of the fifth century. This continental evidence is important, for it is in these decades that Gildas by implication places the struggle which preceded the battle of Mons Badonicus. It is more remarkable that when the compilers of the *Anglo-Saxon Chronicle* came to write down the traditions of the English settlement, they placed the foundation of Sussex and Wessex, the two Saxon kingdoms with which alone they concerned themselves, in precisely the same period. It would be straining probability to assume that this triple coincidence is a mere accident. It may be of little help towards establishing the precise chronology of the earliest Saxon kingdoms in Britain, but it certainly suggests that a genuine memory of the date at which they arose was preserved into historic times.

Unlike the Saxons and Jutes the Angles are definitely mentioned by Tacitus. They formed in his time part of the great confederation of peoples bearing the common name of *Suevi*. They were associated with six other small nations in the cult of the goddess Nerthus—mother earth—whose sanctuary was in an island in the ocean. As Tacitus is known to apply the name *Mare Suebicum* to the Baltic, his Ocean should probably be identified with the North Sea. In any case, his language suggests that the *Angli* were a maritime people. On the other hand, Ptolemy, the only other ancient writer who mentions the Angli,

[1] As was suggested by W. H. Stevenson in *E.H.R.* xiv (1899), p. 41.

describes them as an island tribe, seated to the west of the middle Elbe. In obedience to Ptolemy, a succession of scholars has placed the Angli in north central Germany. But the passage in which he refers to the Angli is confused in itself, and conflicts alike with geographical probability and English tradition. The oldest fragment of that tradition, incorporated in the poem called *Widsith*, recites how Offa, king of *Angel*, drew between his people and the *Myrgingas* a boundary *bi Fifeldore*, which the *Engle* and *Swæfe* held thenceforward. There is good reason for thinking that the *Fifeldor* of the poem is an alternative poetical name for the river Eider.[1] But the strongest evidence for the northern origin of the Angles is the narrative of a voyage from Oslo Fiord to Slesvig which King Alfred prefixed to his translation of the history of Orosius.[2] After the narrator has described how Jutland and many islands lay on the starboard for the last two days of the voyage, Alfred interpolates the remark that the Angles dwelt in those islands before they came hither to this land. On a point like this, Alfred, who was saturated in English traditions, is an authority of the first order. Even if it stood alone, his evidence would establish a strong probability that the Angles had lived in Jutland and the neighbouring islands before the migration to Britain.

But there is other evidence which points in the same direction. The archaeology of Anglian burials on English soil suggests that the Angles were the most northerly of the three nations which Bede recognized in England. The practice of cremation, which was being abandoned in the fifth century by the Germans living near the Roman frontier, was widely prevalent among the Anglian invaders of Britain. In Saxon England it was becoming obsolete at the date of the earliest known interments, and it has left hardly any trace among the burials of Jutish Kent. The cruciform brooches which often accompany Anglian burials but are rare in Saxon territory, and the specifically Anglian sleeve clasps, are derived from northern prototypes. When all allowance has been made for the fragmentary nature of the archaeological evidence, its general trend seems clear, and consistent with the tradition preserved by Bede and King Alfred.

---

[1] R. W. Chambers, *Beowulf, an Introduction*, p. 35 *n.*; Kemp Malone, *Widsith*, p. 144. The *Myrgingas* are not mentioned again, and no convincing explanation of their name has been given.

[2] ed. H. Sweet, Early English Text Society, p. 19.

The nation which appears in Bede's Latin under the name *Iutae* was among the obscurest of all Germanic peoples. It is ignored by most continental writers, and although it is mentioned in two Old English poems the context throws little light on its relations with other tribes, or on the situation of the lands which it inhabited. In a letter to the Emperor Justinian, Theudebert, king of the Franks, included a nation which he called *Saxones Eucii* among the peoples of whom he claimed to be lord,[1] and a generation later a Frankish poet placed the *Euthiones* between the Danes and the Saxons in a list of nations which had been made to feel the power of the Frankish king Chilperich.[2] Each of these passages points to a close connection between the Jutes and the Saxons, which appears again in the later history of Wessex, but neither tells anything definite about its nature. To this vague suggestion the references to the continental Jutes in Old English poetry only add the unconnected facts that Heremod, an early Danish king, had lived in exile among them; that Finn, the most famous of early Frisian kings, had taken a large body of them into his service; and that, as a people, they had once been ruled by a king named Gefwulf. No independent Jutish traditions have been preserved, and modern opinion as to the region from which the Jutes migrated to Britain varies between Jutland and the country east of the lower Rhine.

In his description of the origins of the English people, Bede states that *Angulus*, the ancient home of the *Angli*, lay between the countries of the Saxons and the Jutes. As English traditions suggest that by *Angulus* Bede meant the district now known as Angeln in Slesvig, it would seem that he regarded the Jutes as the northern neighbours of the Angles. Many scholars, following Bede, have derived the name Jutland from the *Iutae*, a derivation implying that the Scandinavian peoples which have inhabited this region since the early sixth century adopted the name of its former inhabitants. Although difficult, it is not impossible to establish a connection between the Old English name of the Jutes and the Scandinavian *Jótar*, from which the name Jutland is derived, but it is difficult to imagine any process by which the name of a people vacating its territory could be adopted by a supplanting race. The evidence which points to an early connection between the Jutes of Kent and the Franks of

[1] Bouquet, *Recueil*, iv. 59.   [2] Venantius Fortunatus, *Carmina*, ix. i. 73.

the Rhineland greatly increases the difficulty of believing that the Jutes came to England from Jutland. Whatever may be the significance of the archaeological side of this evidence, the social system of Kent, as it is revealed in the very early Kentish laws, is definitely of Frankish character, contrasting at essential points with both Saxon and Anglian custom. The affinities between the field-systems of Kent and the Rhineland give another clue which points in the same direction. Where all is obscure, it seems most probable that Bede was mistaken in the position which he gave to the pre-migration Jutes, and that it was not from the western fiords of Jutland but from the mouths of the Rhine that they descended upon England.

In the absence of any guidance from Bede, later writers who wished to trace the early history of the English kingdoms were thrown back upon the disassociated traditions preserved in verse, in the genealogies of kings, and in occasional memoranda set down by ecclesiastical persons in a later age. It is a collection of such traditions which gives unique importance to the ninth-century work known as the *Anglo-Saxon Chronicle*. In its present form this work consists of a series of annals written in English, intended to give a West Saxon reader of King Alfred's time an outline of history. It begins with the invasion of Britain by Julius Caesar, gives a rapid sketch of world-history down to the accession of Marcian and Valentinian III in 449, and becomes an original authority with a long succession of entries in which its compiler set down what he knew about the English conquest of Kent, Sussex, and Wessex. So late a work would be of little value for the history of the fifth and sixth centuries if the occasional preservation of an archaic case-ending or a pre-Alfredian form of a proper name did not show that it incorporates ancient matter. The foundation of the work was a set of West Saxon annals, possibly written in Latin,[1] which came down to the middle of the eighth century. The curious fact that the entries relating to the English conquest tend to be spaced out at intervals of four or eight years suggests that they were derived from notes inserted retrospectively into chronological tables devised for the finding of Easter, for in these tables the margin was divided into isolated spaces by recurrent indications

---

[1] The possibility is suggested by certain turns of phrase—in particular, the recurrent *on þære stowe þe is gecueden*, which reads like, and may well be a translation of, *in loco qui dicitur*.

of leap year.[1] The influence of the Easter-table is very evident in the earliest Frankish annals, which were imitated from English models, and it is highly probable that the English traditions of Hengest and Cerdic were first committed to writing within this incongruous framework.

The authority of Bede is behind the statement that Hengest and Horsa, invited by Vortigern, came to Britain in the time of the emperors Marcian and Valentinian. Their later history was a matter of tradition, not record, and there are indications that, in part at least, it had been handed down in alliterative verse. They are said to have arrived in 449—a date derived from Bede—at the shore called Ypwines fleot, and to have fought with Vortigern, six years later, at a place named Agæles threp. Horsa was killed in this battle, and Hengest and 'Æsc' his son thereafter 'took to the kingdom'. In 457 Hengest and Æsc fought with the Britons at a place called Crecgan ford, and killed four thousand men. The Britons then left Kent, and fled in great fear to London. In 465 Hengest and Æsc fought with the Britons near Wippedes fleot, killed twelve British chiefs, and lost one of their 'thegns' named Wipped. In 473 they fought again with the Britons at a place of which the name is not preserved, taking uncountable spoils, and compelling the Britons to flee before them like fire. Nothing more is said about Hengest in the *Chronicle*, but under the year 488 it is stated that Æsc became king, and remained king of the Kentishmen for twenty-four years.

After the initial year 449 the dates assigned to these events are unlikely to represent anything more authoritative than the conjectures of an annalist writing some three hundred years after the wars of Vortigern and Hengest. There are also traces in the annals of a still later hand which has substituted the intelligible Æsc for the archaic Oisc as the name of Hengest's son. But there is no reason to doubt that they represent a genuine tradition of the war through which Kent became English. That they are much older than the ninth century is shown by the extreme difficulty of identifying the place-names which occur in them. Ypwines fleot can only mean Ebbsfleet, and it is possible that Agæles threp means Aylesford, though it is impossible to trace any regular connection between the ancient

---

[1] W. H. Stevenson in *E.H.R.* xiv (1899), p. 41. On the significance of the Easter table in the development of the chronicle see R. L. Poole, *Chronicles and Annals*, c. i.

and modern forms of the first name, and the second identification turns on the assumption that the familiar word *ford* had been substituted for the unintelligible *threp* before the tenth century. The other names in the series present even greater difficulty. The common identification of Crecgan ford with Crayford depends on the bare possibility that all extant manuscripts of the *Chronicle* go back to an original in which the name was misrepresented, and Wippedes fleot looks like a name created to denote the stream where the thegn Wipped was killed rather than a name in common use. These names must have been taken over by the original West Saxon annalist as an integral part of an ancient tradition, and it is greatly to his credit that he did not translate them into forms intelligible to himself or his readers.

It is, nevertheless, probable that the fame of Hengest as the first invader of Britain distorted the memory of subsequent events. Early as the Hengest tradition undoubtedly is, it does not outweigh the fact that the later kings of Kent derived the name of their family from Oisc and not from Hengest.[1] The application of the name *Oiscingas* to the Kentish royal house raises a strong presumption that it was Oisc rather than Hengest who founded the kingdom of Kent. The historic Hengest is best regarded as a chief of very noble descent who brings his own retine from over sea to Britain, enters the service of a British king, revolts, and fights various battles which open the way to an occupation of Kent by men of his race in the next generation. He belongs to the history of Britain rather than to that of England.

In the *Chronicle* the story of Hengest is linked to the beginnings of West Saxon history by three annals devoted to the conquest of Sussex. They begin with the statement that in 477 Ælle and his sons Cymen, Wlencing, and Cissa landed with three ships' companies at a place called Cymenes ora, where they killed many Britons and drove others into the wood called Andredes leag. A battle between Ælle and the Britons by an unknown stream called Mearcredes burna is placed under the year 485, and an entry under 491 states that Ælle and Cissa besieged Andredes cester and killed all who were inside it, so that not one Briton was left. Three of these place-names can be identified. The sea has covered the site of Cymenes ora, but

---

[1] Bede, *Historia Ecclesiastica*, ii. 5.

later references to the place show that it lay immediately to the
south of what is now Selsey Bill. Andredes cester represents the
Roman fort of Anderida, adjacent to Pevensey, and the 'wood
called Andredes leag' means the Sussex Weald.[1] Although each
of these annals represents a separate piece of tradition, the
series as a whole suggests that the English conquest of Sussex
proceeded slowly from west to east against a steady British
resistance. The massacre which followed the storming of
Anderida does not imply a war of extermination in the open
country, but the extreme rarity of British place-names in Sussex
points to English colonization on a scale which can have left
little room for British survival.

The general character of the English place-names in the
county points to the same conclusion. No other group of local
names reflects more clearly the primitive speech of English
peasants. These archaic words occur in all parts, and their
appearance in the Weald shows that some rudimentary forms
of English life had arisen there within a few generations of the
invasion. Between the South Downs and the sea, along the
rivers which pierce the Downs, and in the broken country east
of Pevensey, an early settlement is proved by many names which
originally denoted neither villages nor natural features but
groups of persons. Names of this type, of which Beeding,
Malling, and Patching are examples, had been familiar to the
English peoples before their migration to Britain, and wherever
in England they occur in large numbers, they point to a settlement which was in progress by the early part of the sixth
century.[2] The communities represented by these names varied
in size between the inhabitants of a single farm and the men
of what Anglo-Saxon writers describe as a *regio* or province.[3]
The people whose name survives in Hastings remained for
centuries a race apart. Fifty years before the Norman Conquest
the *Hæstingas* and the South Saxons were still regarded as two
separate folks.[4] Both the place-names and the field-systems of

[1] In the 9th century (*Chronicle* under 893), and doubtless in the 6th, the Weald
was connected by continuous woodland with the forest district of south-west
Hampshire. In the 11th century, part, if not the whole, of the New Forest still
bore the name Andred (*Place-Names of Sussex*, English Place-Name Society, vol.
vi, p. 1).

[2] These names form the subject of a detailed study by E. Ekwall (*English Place-
Names in -ing*, Lund 1923 [ed. 2, 1962]), a work which establishes their archaic
character and therefore their value as evidence of early settlement.

[3] These *regiones* are discussed below, pp. 293-7.   [4] Below, p. 208.

the rape of Hastings have features which suggest, though they do not prove, that the district was colonized from Kent. It may not be through chance that the traditions preserved in the *Chronicle* refer exclusively to the country west of Anderida.

These traditions, unlike most of their kind, underestimate the importance of their central figure. Ælle, whom they represent as a leader of no more than local reputation, is described by Bede as the first of seven kings who were recognized as the overlords of all the English peoples south of the Humber. On such a point the authority of Bede is conclusive, and whatever the precise significance of Ælle's overlordship may have been, there can be no doubt that for a time he was the leader of the whole English movement against the Britons of the south. If the dates assigned to him in the *Chronicle* are even approximately correct, he was separated by more than half a century from Ceawlin, king of Wessex, his successor in Bede's list of overlords. There is no means of checking the dates in the *Chronicle*. But the tradition which placed Ælle in the last quarter of the fifth century agrees with Gildas' description of Britain in the years before the battle of Mons Badonicus, and the long interval between his overlordship and that of Ceawlin strengthens the impression given by Procopius that the English advance against the Britons was suspended for at least a generation after that battle.[1]

In the reign of King Alfred, when the *Chronicle* assumed its present form, information about the origins of the West Saxon kingdom could be obtained from three distinct sources. The oldest of them was a genealogy tracing the descent of the kings of Wessex back to Woden,[2] and in one version,[3] beyond Woden to a figure of primitive Germanic mythology named Sceaf. The stages between Woden and the historic kings of Wessex form a poem composed according to strict rules of alliteration for the pleasure of some West Saxon king of the heathen time. Less ancient than the genealogy, but older than the reign of Alfred, is a list of the kings of Wessex,[4] prefaced by the important statement that Cerdic and Cynric his son landed in 494 at

[1] H. M. Chadwick, *The Origin of the English Nation*, pp. 14–15.

[2] On the character of this and other early English genealogies see R. W. Chambers, *Beowulf*, pp. 195 ff. [and K. Sisam, 'Anglo-Saxon Royal Genealogies', *Proceedings of the British Academy*, xxxix (1953), pp. 287–348].

[3] Preserved in the *Chronicon* of Æthelweard [ed. A. Campbell, p. 33].

[4] Prefixed to the oldest manuscript of the *Chronicle* (MS. A) and printed in all editions of that work. [See Sisam, op. cit., pp. 294–7.]

a place called Cerdices ora, and conquered the kingdom of Wessex about six years after their landing. Finally, there existed a body of tradition about the landing of different groups of invaders, their wars with the Britons, and the deaths of important leaders. The Alfredian *Chronicle* is itself the oldest authority for these traditions, but Old English phrases which point to a Latin original, a tendency to arrange events at intervals of four years, and an occasional linguistic archaism suggest that they had formed part of the eighth-century annals which the Alfredian chronicler used as the basis of his own work. There is no material variation between different texts of the *Chronicle* in regard to the annals which relate to the conquest of Wessex. But in the late tenth century a West Saxon ealdorman named Æthelweard, translating the annals from English into Latin, inserted under the year 500 the curious sentence 'Cerdic et Cinric occidentalem circumierunt partem Brittanniae quae nunc Uuest Sexe nuncupatur'.[1] In these uncouth words he was trying to say that Cerdic and Cynric conquered Wessex in the year 500. It is possible that he derived this statement from the preface to the early West Saxon list of kings. But he introduces no other extraneous annals into his translation, and it is far more probable that an annal to this effect stood under the year 500 in the very ancient version of the *Chronicle* which he is known to have possessed.

The annals may be translated as follows:

495 Two chiefs, Cerdic and his son Cynric, came to Britain with five ships in the place called Cerdices ora, and fought with the Britons the same day.

501 Port and his two sons Bieda and Mægla came to Britain with two ships in the place called Portes mutha, and killed a young British man, a very noble man.[2]

508 Cerdic and Cynric killed a British king called Natanleod, and five thousand men with him. That land was afterwards called Natan leaga as far as Cerdices ford.

514 The West Saxons, Stuf and Wihtgar, came to Britain with

---

[1] [*The Chronicle of Æthelweard*, ed. A. Campbell, p. 11.]
[2] This annal has often been dismissed as a fabrication based on the place-name Portsmouth. It is a plausible view, but it does not explain the appearance of the names Bieda and Mægla, it takes no account of the other evidence for Port as an Old English personal name, and it offers no reason for the invention of the annal. That *mutha* could be combined with a personal name is proved by the compound *Eadgylses mutha* which occurs in a charter relating to the Isle of Wight (*C.S.* 392).

three ships in the place called Cerdices ora, and fought with the Britons and drove them into flight.

519 Cerdic and Cynric took the kingdom, and in the same year they fought with the Britons where it is now called Cerdices ford.

527 Cerdic and Cynric fought with the Britons in the place called Cerdices leaga.

530 Cerdic and Cynric took the Isle of Wight, and killed a few men in the place called Wihtgaræsbyrg.

534 Cerdic died, and his son Cynric ruled for twenty-six years, and they gave the Isle of Wight to their nephews Stuf and Wihtgar.

544 Wihtgar died, and was buried at Wihtgarabyrg.

552 Cynric fought with the Britons in a place called Searobyrg and drove them into flight.

556 Cynric and Ceawlin fought with the Britons at Beranbyrg.

560 Ceawlin became king of the West Saxons.

It is clear that these annals should not be regarded as a piece of consecutive history. They represent traditions preserved, not for their historical importance, but because their recital had once interested a barbarian audience. Under such conditions, many events of far-reaching significance passed entirely out of memory because they were not accompanied by any incident of which a poet could take advantage. If, for example, the compiler of the annals says nothing about the circumstances under which the West Saxons reached the Thames valley, the reason may well be that these circumstances were as obscure to him as they are today. He arranged the few facts which he possessed in what seemed to him an intelligible order, but his work should not be criticized as if it represented a deliberate selection of the most important incidents in the history of the Saxon conquest. His outlook was confined to the limited range covered by a casual series of traditions which had gathered round the early kings of Wessex. They told him little beyond stories of landings, battles, and deaths of kings, and he did not try to supplement them even by information which must have been a matter of common knowledge. He ignores the fact, recorded by Bede, that the West Saxons were originally called *Gewisse*.[1] He describes Cynric as the son of Cerdic, and

---

[1] Nothing definite can be said about the derivation of this name. It was obsolete in England already in Bede's time, but it survived among the British peoples, and it was revived as a piece of antiquarian decoration in the charter-styles of the later Old English kings.

associates Cerdic with Cynric in entry after entry in defiance of the statement of the West Saxon genealogy that Cynric was the son, not of Cerdic, but of Cerdic's son Creoda. The traditions which he recorded were often blurred and sometimes discrepant with one another, and it is certainly fortunate that he made no attempt to reduce them to an artificial harmony.

Occasional discrepancies are natural in a long series of traditions handed down in heroic verse. In an age before writing was used for the preservation of a story, its form, and much of its content, were determined by the interaction of poet and audience. A single story could be told in many different ways. The central place in a narrative could be given to different actors at different times, and the names of persons could be inserted, omitted, or even changed in accordance with the mood of the moment or convenience in alliteration. A later writer, dependent on such materials, was always in danger of regarding two versions of the same story as the record of two separate incidents. In the annals which relate to the West Saxon invasion there are various features which point to such a duplication of events. The wording of the annal for 514 strongly suggests that it represents a tradition of the landing of the West Saxons in which Stuf and Wihtgar, not Cerdic and Cynric, played the leading part. If so, there at once arises a suspicion that the battle of Cerdices leaga, thirteen years after the landing of Stuf and Wihtgar, may be no more than a duplicate of the destruction of Natanleod and his army thirteen years after the landing of Cerdic and Cynric. When the evidence of the early West Saxon list of kings is compared with that of the annals, the theory of a double tradition of the West Saxon invasion becomes something more than a conjecture. It has always been difficult to accept the statement of the annals that Cerdic and Cynric 'took the kingdom' in 519, for as it stands it seems to imply that they had been fighting for twenty-four years before their position was assured. But it becomes intelligible as a misplaced variant of the tradition, recorded in the regnal list, that they conquered Wessex about six years after their arrival. Above all, when allowance has been made for the existence of duplicate entries, these fragments of West Saxon history cease to conflict seriously with the narrative of Gildas. It is true that they do not mention the battle of Mons Badonicus, which on any theory must have checked the advance described in the regnal list as a conquest of Wessex. But at least it is no longer necessary to believe that the West Saxon tradition of the invasion intrudes a protracted war on the mainland of southern Britain into the peace by which, according to Gildas, that battle was followed.[1]

It is not with Gildas, but with Bede, that these traditions are at variance. In his description of the races which inhabit Britain Bede definitely assigns Kent, the Isle of Wight, and the mainland districts over against it, to the people whom he calls *Iutae*. In another part of his work he observes incidentally that the *Homel ea*—the Hampshire river Hamble—runs through this 'Jutish' territory. Even without this explicit statement, there would be no doubt that the Isle of Wight was settled by men who in culture were closely allied to the Jutes of Kent.[2] The objects recovered from the burial-places on the island downs show the distinctive features of Kentish grave-furniture. The Jutish occupation of the opposite mainland has not yet been confirmed by archaeology, though it is suggested by some curious points of resemblance between the place-names of this country and those of Kent.[3] But it is placed beyond doubt by the remarkable statement of an Anglo-Norman historian that William II died 'in the New Forest, which in English is called Ytene'.[4] This name represents the genitive plural of a nominative *Yte*, which is the late West Saxon form of Bede's *Iutae*. Its survival proves not only that the New Forest had once been Jutish land, but that its inhabitants preserved the memory of their origin for many generations.

There was also an aristocratic tradition of this settlement. Asser, King Alfred's biographer, records that Oslac, father of Osburg, the king's mother, was of Jutish origin, derived from Stuf and Wihtgar, Cerdic's nephews. This statement, which

---

[1] There is no evidence to show whether the conquest of the Isle of Wight, which the annals assign to 530, belongs to this or to an earlier period. In any case, it lay outside the range of Gildas' interests.

[2] For the most recent account of this connection see J. N. L. Myres, *Oxford History of England*, i. 364–6.

[3] In particular, by the use of the element *ing*, in the singular, to form a local name from a personal name, an adjective, or a common noun. Such names are common in Kent, and there are a number of clear examples in south Hampshire, such as Swathling and Nursling. They are rare in every other part of England except Berkshire, where they may well be due to colonists from earlier settlements along the Hampshire coast. On names of this type see E. Ekwall, *English Place-Names in -ing*, [ed. 2, pp. 8–20, 91–3]; F. M. Stenton, *C.P.*, pp. 271–3.

[4] Florence of Worcester, *Chronicon ex Chronicis*, ii. 44–5.

clearly represents a court tradition of Osburg's ancestry and race, is good evidence that Stuf and Wihtgar were Jutes, and therefore of the tribe to which Bede attributes the settlement of southern Hampshire and the Isle of Wight. That a Saxon chief such as Cerdic should have Jutish nephews is by no means improbable under the conditions which prevailed in the fifth century. Intermarriage between two Germanic races was common, and Stuf and Wihtgar may well have been the sons of Cerdic's sister and a Jutish noble. But it is evident that the early history of Wessex was more complicated than would be gathered from the bare record of events preserved in the *Chronicle*. If Cerdic and his men were Saxons—and tradition is unanimous on this point—the establishment of a Jutish people in southern Hampshire implies that he and his followers left the lands of the original conquest in the possession of allies, and themselves passed on in search of adventure or of other country for settlement. His later history is unknown, and speculation is very dangerous. Some of his people may have returned to the Continent in the way described by Procopius. Others, presumably, settled in the country between the northern boundary of the mainland Jutes and the woodland which separated the districts afterwards known as Hampshire and Berkshire. But the centre of the powerful West Saxon kingdom of the late sixth century undoubtedly lay in the region immediately to the south and west of the middle Thames. Archaeological evidence shows that Saxon settlements had been founded in this country even before the traditional date of Cerdic's invasion. Among many possibilities, it seems on the whole most probable that by war or negotiation Cerdic made himself the lord of this district and distributed his followers among its existing settlers.

No name which only comes into history through the medium of half-remembered tradition can ever be much more than a centre of conflicting theories. The name Cerdic, which is both rare and obscure, has sometimes been regarded as a mere figment derived from the place-names Cerdices ora, Cerdices ford, and Cerdices leaga, which occur in the traditions of the West Saxon invasion. This theory involves the improbable assumption that three separate place-names, each containing the same anomalous personal name, existed before these traditions were written down, in the small area to which they relate. But the most serious objection to any view which would regard Cerdic as a fiction founded on place-names is his position in the genealogy of the West Saxon Kings. He was undoubtedly regarded as the founder of the West Saxon dynasty in an age when a claim to rule in Wessex rested on descent from the original head of the West Saxon royal house. The assumption that the poets who first recited the West Saxon royal genealogy evolved an ancestor for their patrons out of three obscure place-names conflicts with all that is known of the attitude of a Germanic aristocracy towards matters of descent. It may be added that no one inventing an ancestor for these kings would have been likely to give him so singular a name as Cerdic. It does not correspond to any known English name, and in the opinion of most scholars it represents the Old Welsh name *Ceretic*. If such an origin is ever conclusively established, it will compel a reconstruction of the relations between Saxons and Britons in the age immediately preceding the migration. It will raise the question whether the Saxon raiders of fifth-century Britain, like the Scandinavian raiders of ninth-century Ireland, did not sometimes take their wives from among the peoples whose land they visited, and give to their sons names current among their mother's kin. But it will not disprove the historical existence of Cerdic, nor depose him from his place at the head of the West Saxon royal line.

The obscurity of the period through which the shadowy form of Cerdic moves is mainly due to the narrow outlook of the poets who preserved its traditions. Their business was to praise the ancestors of great men, and they had little concern with the movements of peoples in which a modern student is chiefly interested. It would never be gathered from the meagre tale of disconnected events recorded in the *Chronicle* that Saxon settlements had been established in the valley of the middle Thames by at latest the beginning of the sixth century. But archaeological evidence to this effect comes from several sites and takes various forms. The early objects which accompanied Saxon burials at Frilford, Reading, and East Shefford indicate a Saxon settlement which falls outside the sequence of events recorded in the *Chronicle*. On several sites in Berkshire, such as Milton near Didcot and Lowbury Hill, there is an association of Romano-British and Saxon remains which goes far to prove a virtual continuity of occupation from one age into the other.

At Sutton Courtenay on the Thames, the site of a primitive
Saxon village has yielded, among other early objects, an equal-
armed brooch, of a type characteristic of north-western Germany, which can safely be referred to the fifth century. The
date at which these settlements came into being cannot be
fixed at all closely, but there can be no serious doubt that they
are both earlier than and independent of the invasion led by
Cerdic.

Their origin is still an open question. It is possible that they
arose from a movement of Saxon peoples up the Thames.
The early Saxon settlements of Surrey and Kent west of the
Medway were certainly founded by invaders who used this
obvious water-way. But the early Saxon culture of Berkshire
has features suggesting that the settlers whose life it represents
reached the middle Thames, not by following the river, nor
overland from Hampshire, but from the north-east, along the
line of the Icknield Way.[1] The rivers which find a common
estuary in the Wash offered easy access from the sea into the
heart of the midlands, and there is varied evidence of an Anglo-
Saxon settlement, not later than the year 500, in the districts
opened to the invaders by the Welland, Nene, Ouse, and Cam.
In the opinion of many archaeologists, the points of resemblance
between the culture introduced by this settlement and the
culture revealed by excavation on sites in Berkshire are at once
too definite and too various to be the result of chance. Up to
the present, no site between the middle Thames and the upper
Lea has yielded objects which can definitely be referred to the
late fifth or the early sixth century, and until this gap has been
reduced, the theory that the Saxons of Berkshire descended on
the Thames from the north-east will never be established. But
the archaeological evidence which points to this conclusion
cannot be ignored in any attempt to understand the conditions
under which the historic West Saxon kingdom came into
being.

The historical evidence tells neither for nor against the view
that this kingdom represented the coalescence of two bodies of
invaders, one entering Britain from the Channel and the other
from the Wash. But it clashes uncompromisingly with any
theory which implies that the country between the upper Lea
and the Thames was occupied continuously by Saxon settlers

[1] This view was first set out by E. T. Leeds, *History* (1925), x. 97 ff.

from the late fifth century into historic times. If the traditions preserved in the *Chronicle* correspond, even approximately, to the facts, this country was in British hands in the year 571, when a certain Cuthwulf is said to have captured the four towns of Limbury above Luton, Aylesbury, Bensington, and Eynsham, after a battle with the Britons at a place called Bedcan ford. No annal in the early sections of the *Chronicle* is more important than this, and there is none of which the interpretation is more difficult. The site of the battle cannot be identified with any assurance, for it is very difficult to establish any connection between the Bedcan ford of the annal and the early spellings of the place-name Bedford. The name Cuthwulf, borne by the Saxon leader, alliterates with West Saxon royal names like Cerdic, Cynric, and Ceawlin, but his place in the West Saxon royal family is quite uncertain. These are minor difficulties, which do not affect the credibility of the annal. The discussion which has centred upon it turns, not on its details, but on the historical situation which it seems to presuppose. An annal which implies that the downs above Luton were British in 571 means that four generations after the traditional date of Hengest's landing, the Britons were still holding ground within forty miles of London. There is nothing in any literary source which makes this implication incredible; but it conflicts with the impression of a rapid conquest of the midlands which most historians have derived from the narrative of Gildas. On geographical grounds, though by no means impossible, it is somewhat unlikely that at this late date a belt of unreduced British territory should have separated the Saxon settlements west of the middle Thames from those of Cambridgeshire and Bedfordshire. It is not surprising that many scholars have been disposed to deny the historical character of this annal, or at least to regard it as a misplaced tradition of events which were already remote in the year 571.

But the mere difficulty of interpreting the entry is an insufficient reason for separating it from its context. The general agreement of the early annals with Gildas and of the later annals with Bede makes it very unlikely that any intervening event has been misdated by as much as a generation. In particular, it is almost incredible that the battle of Bedcan ford, which was one of the most important events in the whole series, should have been placed out of its proper sequence.

Its significance is another question, and one to which no final answer can yet be given. But the evidence for a migration of Germanic peoples from Britain in the first half of the sixth century raises something more than a bare possibility that the battle of 571 meant, not the conquest of lands which had always been British, but the recovery of territory won in the first energy of the Saxon invasion and lost after the defeat at Mons Badonicus. It can at least be said that on this view the two chief objections which have been brought against the annal disappear.[1] It ceases to imply that the British occupation of the plain beneath the Chilterns was unbroken for a century and a half after the severance of Britain from the empire. And it no longer conflicts with the archaeological evidence for an early connection between the Saxons of Berkshire and the original settlers in the valleys of the Ouse and Cam.

The battle of 571 was an isolated episode in the history of the West Saxon peoples, and the country which it opened to their settlement was never firmly attached to the West Saxon kingdom. Geographically, it is an extension of the great plain of central England, which was gradually annexed by the rulers of the north-midland Anglian people known as the Mercians. In the seventh and eighth centuries there was continual warfare between the kings of Wessex and Mercia for the possession of these lands, and in the end the Mercian kings retained them. It was not in this quarter, but towards the west, where they had no rivals of their own race, that the West Saxons won the territory which made them a great people. According to the *Chronicle*, their westerly expansion began in 552, when Cynric, the head of their dynasty, defeated the Britons at Old Sarum. Four years later, Cynric and Ceawlin his son defeated the Britons again at Barbury castle, a prehistoric fortification above the prehistoric Ridge Way, five miles south of Swindon.[2] These victories carried the West Saxons permanently beyond the field of Cerdic's wars, and within a few years their history begins to take on a more substantial form. The first of their kings whose

---

[1] The case for this view was much strengthened in 1954, when J. N. L. Myres pointed out that certain distinctive types of fifth-century pottery appear both in the north of East and Middle Anglia and in the Saxon coastlands west of the Elbe (*The Antiquaries Journal*, xxxiv (1954), pp. 201–8).

[2] The *Chronicle* states that the battle was fought *æt Beran byrg*. The identification of this site with Barbury castle is well borne out by the medieval forms of the latter name collected in *Place-Names of Wiltshire* (E.P.-N.S.), pp. 278–9.

claim to existence does not depend on the traditions of his own court is Ceawlin son of Cynric, who succeeded his father in 560, and is placed by Bede next to Ælle of Sussex among the overlords of the southern English peoples.

But it is as the leader of his own people against the Britons that Ceawlin becomes an important figure in English history. Under the year 577 the *Chronicle* states that 'Cuthwine and Ceawlin fought with the Britons at a place called Deorham, and killed three kings, Coinmail, Condidan, and Farinmail, and took three "chesters", Gloucester, Cirencester, and Bath'. This is one of the few annals in this section of the *Chronicle* which raise no difficult problems of identification. Deorham is undoubtedly the modern Dyrham, six miles north of Bath. The three British kings are otherwise unknown, but their names are represented in archaic forms, which certainly come from a written source much older than the Alfredian chronicle. The historical importance of the battle has always been recognized. It opened the valley of the lower Severn to Saxon colonists, and thus separated the Britons of the south-west from those who lived to the north of the Bristol Channel. Like the battle of Bedcan ford, the battle of Dyrham placed the Saxons in possession of territory which they were unable to hold. Long before the end of the seventh century, the English settlers of the Severn valley had passed under Mercian lordship. But the loss of this country by the West Saxon kings of a later age does not affect the importance of the battle of 577 as an episode in the expansion of the English peoples against the Britons.

For the next seven years the annals tell nothing about Ceawlin. Then, under the year 584, there occurs an enigmatical entry which probably conceals as much as it records. 'In this year Ceawlin and Cutha fought with the Britons in the place called Fethan leag, and Cutha was killed, and Ceawlin took many towns and innumerable spoils of war, and returned in anger to his own country.' A wood called *Fethelée*, mentioned in a twelfth-century document relating to Stoke Lyne in north-east Oxfordshire, bore the only name so far observed which corresponds to the *Fethan leag* of the *Chronicle*, and it is highly probable that the battle was fought in the immediate neighbourhood of this place.[1] If so, it seems clear that Ceawlin, whose people were already well established by the upper and

[1] C.P. pp. 278–9.

middle Thames, was moving northwards towards the conquest of the uplands above the head-waters of the Great Ouse. But there is at least a strong probability that the war of 584 ended in a Saxon disaster which the compiler of the annals saw fit to ignore. A king did not usually come home in anger after winning innumerable spoils of war. It may well have been this reverse which ended Ceawlin's overlordship of the southern English. There is no record of any further Saxon advance in his reign, and there were signs that before its close his kingdom was beginning to disintegrate. In 591 a certain Ceol, whose relationship to Ceawlin is uncertain, began a reign which is said to have lasted for six years. In 592 the annals record that there was great slaughter at Woddesbeorg or Wodnesbeorg—probably the tumulus now called Adam's Grave overlooking the Vale of Pewsey—and that Ceawlin was driven out. Finally, in 593 it is stated that Ceawlin 'perished', together with a certain Cwichelm and Crida, who are otherwise unknown. It is obvious that Ceawlin's reign ended in confusion and disaster. But it is no less clear that in his day he had been the leader of the advance through which the English peoples became the masters of southern Britain.

The obscurity of the period which begins with the landing of the first Saxon invaders is a commonplace of history. Its details are lost, and the materials from which alone its course can be inferred are fragmentary and sometimes obscure. Nevertheless, it is possible to exaggerate their incoherence. Gildas, Procopius, and the early traditions of the West Saxon court agree in suggesting that the English conquest of southern Britain was accomplished in two phases, separated by a considerable interval in the early part of the sixth century. Both Gildas and the tradition of a conquest of Wessex close to the year 500 imply that the greater part of southern England was overrun in the first phase of the war. Gildas claims for the Britons a victory which gave them peace from external enemies for more than a generation, and the traditions of the West Saxons suggest that after their early advance they were thrown back on to the settlements which they had founded immediately after their first landing. Procopius describes a migration of English peoples to the Continent in the first half of the century which can only mean that for a time the invaders had abandoned the attempt to find new lands in Britain. The Fulda tradition of a landing of

Saxons from Britain at Cuxhaven in 531 indicates that these migrations had begun within a few years of the British victory recorded by Gildas. They are not mentioned by any English authority, but the period within which they must have fallen coincides with a significant gap in the traditions of Wessex, Kent, and Sussex. The memory of Creoda, Cerdic's son, was only preserved in an alliterative genealogy; the kings of Kent between Oisc, the son of Hengest, and Æthelberht, St. Augustine's protector, are no more than names; and there is no record of any South Saxon king for nearly two centuries after the time of Ælle. Finally, the West Saxon traditions imply that the second phase of the conquest began in the south immediately after the middle of the sixth century, proceeded very slowly at first, and then culminated in a twofold advance which carried the Saxons as far as the Lea towards the east and as far as the Severn towards the west. Regarded singly, each of the authorities which have been quoted has its own weakness. Gildas was writing polemic, not history; Procopius had little interest in the condition of the lost province of Britain; the Fulda tradition was not written down until three centuries after the event which it records; and the traditions preserved in the *Chronicle* are only memoranda derived from verse in praise of ancient kings. But it may at least be claimed that when four independent authorities agree in suggesting a single coherent story, it is unlikely to be very far from the truth.

II

THE KINGDOMS OF THE SOUTHERN ENGLISH

THE most important fact in the history of the earliest English kingdoms is the clear distinction which was maintained for more than two centuries between the peoples established respectively north and south of the Humber. It is reflected in the language of many formal documents written by men for whom the titles of kings and the names of peoples represented at least an approximation to political facts. As early as the year 672 the different English peoples beyond the Humber are collectively described in a solemn record[1] as *Nordanhymbrorum gens*—the nation of the Northumbrians. No formal document ever speaks of the Southumbrians,[2] but the Anglian, Saxon, and Jutish peoples who lived between the Humber and the Channel are often brought together in early charters as the *Sutangli*, or southern English.[3] The distinction does not coincide with any difference of race or culture. The Angles of Northumbria and Mercia were of the same stock, and their dialects are closely related. It is also unlikely that the Anglian invasion of the north was much later than that of the midlands. Extensive settlements had been founded in central and eastern Yorkshire before the middle of the sixth century, and it is at least probable that the invasion had begun before the end of the fifth.[4] At present

[1] The Acts of the Council of Hertford, *H.E.* iv. 5. The form of the name shows that it was derived from popular speech, and was not the invention of the notary who wrote the Acts, or of Bede, who copied them into his history.

[2] That the name *Suthanhymbre* was in use before the tenth century is made probable by its appearance in certain notes and annals which are found in MSS. D and E of the *Chronicle*, and must have been present in the lost version from which both manuscripts are derived (Plummer, *Two of the Saxon Chronicles Parallel*, ii, pp. lxviii–lxxi). Under 449, for example, MS. E represents Bede's statement that many royal lines were descended from Woden by the remark *Fram þan Wodne awoc eall ure cynecynn and Suðanhymbra eac.* In this passage the name *Suðanhymbre* covers all the southern English peoples, in contrast to the Northumbrians. It was obviously written in Northumbria. The name appears elsewhere in these manuscripts but it tends to be restricted to the Mercians, and looks like the survival of an earlier usage which was no longer clearly understood.

[3] As in *C.S.* 154, which speaks of the provinces *quae generale nomine Sutangli dicuntur.*   [4] J. N. L. Myres, *Oxford History of England*, i. 418–19.

it seems most probable that the origin of the distinction lies in the circumstances of the invasion rather than in its date. Until the early part of the seventh century the independent British kingdom of Elmet[1] stretched westwards for many miles from the marshes at the head of the Humber, and separated the Angles of the northern midlands from those of the plain of York. In an earlier age this kingdom must have been a serious obstacle to any military co-operation between the invaders of northern and southern Britain. In particular, it must have kept the Northumbrian invaders apart from any of the early confederacies formed among the southern peoples by leaders such as Ælle and Ceawlin. The particularism which at a later time distinguished the Angles beyond the Humber may well be due to the isolation of their ancestors in the age of the migration.

Whatever its origin, the distinction between the English peoples north and south of the Humber profoundly affected their early history. From the age of the migration down to the Danish wars of the ninth century the peoples south of the Humber were normally subject to the authority of a common overlord. He was generally one of their own number, though in the seventh century three Northumbrian kings successively secured a recognition of their lordship from the various kings of the south. Conversely, a southern king whose supremacy was admitted everywhere between the Humber and the Channel might attempt to extend his authority over the Northumbrians also. But the difference between the normal subjection of the southern peoples to a single overlord and the occasional creation of a dominion which covered all England was never forgotten by early writers. It is clear, for example, that Bede regarded the English peoples of his day as falling, politically, into two great divisions, and in various passages he emphasizes the fact that the Humber was the traditional boundary between them. In the first book of his *Ecclesiastical History* he describes Æthelberht of Kent as a most powerful king, 'who had extended the boundaries of his dominion as far as the great river Humber, by which the southern and northern peoples of the English are separated'. In a more famous passage, introduced in order to place Æthelberht in his proper historical setting, he not only reasserts the importance of the Humber as a political boundary, but names the early kings who had once held lordship throughout the country to the south. The list begins with Ælle of the South Saxons, and continues through Ceawlin of the West Saxons and Æthelberht of Kent to Rædwald of the East Angles. He is followed by three Northumbrian overlords, Edwin, Oswald, and Oswiu, with whom the list closes—apparently because Bede wished to avoid the anti-climax of carrying it beyond the great name of Oswiu, who had ruled over Picts and Scots as well as over Northumbrians and the southern English. But it is clear from other evidence that Wulfhere, king of the Mercians, was supreme in the south for some years before his death in 674.[1] Sixty years later Bede expressly states that all the English provinces south of the Humber were subject to Æthelbald, king of the Mercians. And the supremacy of Offa, Æthelbald's successor, determined the whole character of English history in the last third of the century.

Either through prejudice, or, more probably, through the mechanical following of Bede, the only other ancient writer who made a similar list also omitted the Mercian overlords who succeeded Oswiu. After recording the rise of Egbert of Wessex to supremacy in southern England the ninth-century compiler of the *Chronicle* gives what purports to be the series of Egbert's predecessors in that dignity. He recites Bede's list of the first seven overlords of the southern English, and then, in defiance of recent history, adds the statement that Egbert was the eighth. But his inaccuracy is more than compensated by his preservation of the English title applied to these outstanding kings. Writing of the year 829 he states that 'King Egbert conquered the kingdom of the Mercians and all that was south of the Humber, and he was the eighth king who was Bretwalda.'[2] In structure, this famous title resembles innumerable laudatory epithets familiar in early English verse, such as *beah-gifa*, 'bracelet giver', or *dæd-fruma*, 'deed doer'. It should probably be translated 'Britain ruler', for in the eighth century the position which it denoted could be represented by the style *Rex Britanniæ*.[3] 'Bretwalda' is not a formal style, accurately

---

[1] See p. 85.

[2] The *Bretwalda* of MS. A of the *Chronicle* seems to be a contracted form of the word, which appears in other manuscripts as *Brytenwalda* (MS. B), *Bretenanwealda* (MS. C), *Brytenwealda* (MSS. D. E), *Brytenweald* (MS. F). The form in MS. C suggests that the second element in the compound was *anwealda*, 'sole ruler'.

[3] *C.S.* 154, on which see F. M. Stenton, 'The supremacy of the Mercian kings', *C.P.*, pp. 53–6. This equation is against the view, in itself attractive, that *Brytenwalda* contains the Old English adjective *bryten* 'wide' and means 'wide' or 'great ruler'.

expressing the position of its bearer; still less is it a deliberate invention founded on historical fact. It belongs to the sphere of encomiastic poetry, and its origin should be sought in the hall of some early king, like Ælle or Ceawlin, whose victories entitled him, in that uncritical atmosphere, to be regarded as lord of Britain. It therefore falls into line with the other evidence which points to the Germanic origin of the earliest English institutions. It should not be regarded as a barbarous imitation of imperial dignity, nor can it express, what some have read into it, the supremacy of an English overlord over British kings. It arose among Germanic invaders whose position in Britain was insecure, and in its origin it was clearly a defiance of British chiefs rather than the assertion of a claim to lordship over them. The most remarkable feature of its history is its survival under the conditions of a later age. It is difficult now, and it must have been no less difficult in the ninth century, to explain a custom which gave the title 'ruler of Britain' to the head of a confederacy of the southern English peoples. But it carries at least a dim suggestion of the time when such a confederacy under Ælle of Sussex had been overrunning southern Britain in the years before the battle of Mons Badonicus.

The position of the English in Britain was still insecure more than a century after the time of Ælle, and their earliest confederacies were undoubtedly created by military necessity. There was always a military element in the relationship between the overlord of the southern English and his dependent kings. But as the possibility of an overwhelming British revival becomes more remote, the overlord begins to appear as the patron rather than the leader of his dependants, and the association of the southern English peoples gradually assumes a political character. Before the end of the seventh century the overlord was dealing with his subject kings very much as he dealt with the hereditary nobility of his own country. His safe-conduct ran throughout their lands, and he could transfer provinces from one of them to another. It was always wise for an under-king to obtain the overlord's consent to important grants of land. In 635, when the king of the West Saxons gave Dorchester on Thames to his bishop, the king of the Northumbrians was associated in the grant as overlord. Above all, between the overlord and each of his dependent kings there existed the personal relationship of lord and man. In the eighth century,

Offa, king of the Mercians, who emphasized every power which a recognized supremacy gave him, expressed his view of this relationship in the most uncompromising of terms. Egbert II, king of Kent, had granted certain lands to one of his ministers, who gave them to the monastery of Christ Church at Canterbury. Offa took possession of them, 'saying it was wrong that his *minister* should have presumed to place land which his lord had given him under the authority of another, without his lord's testimony'.[1] No doubt, the common men of the subject kingdoms lived their lives without much interference from their king's overlord. He certainly took tribute from them, but he left them to apportion its incidence among themselves, and he was not otherwise interested in the deliberations of their upland moots. But over the kings who had become his men he had authority such as they themselves exercised over their own followers. It was his duty to settle disputes between them and to avenge their wrongs. And on great occasions he would require them to place themselves and their retainers under his command in war.

No confederacy of this period survived the king who had brought it into being. There was no convention that an underking must give his allegiance to his dead lord's son, or adhere to a lord whose luck had deserted him. Nevertheless the historical importance of these confederacies is very great. No other institution did so much to prepare the way for the ultimate unity of England. In their normal state of subordination to some greater lord the lesser kings of southern England gradually lost the power of independent political action. In the eighth century, under two strong Mercian overlords, England south of the Humber was rapidly developing into a single state, of which the ancient kingdoms of Sussex, Essex, Kent, and Lindsey were no more than provinces. The development was arrested by the succession of weaker kings in Mercia. But the first step had been taken towards the creation of the kingdom of all England foreshadowed nearly two hundred years before, when three Northumbrian kings had successively been recognized as overlords throughout the south.

---

[1] *C.S.* 293. In 811 Archbishop Wulfred of Canterbury, referring to another estate to which his church had a similar claim, stated that Offa had confiscated it 'as though it were not lawful for Egbert to grant lands in perpetuity by a written instrument'. *C.S.* 332.

The chief factor which delayed the emergence of such a kingdom was the remarkable number of separate dynasties between which England was divided. On the Continent most of the peoples which settled within the Roman empire gave unquestioned pre-eminence to a single royal family. A kingdom might be partitioned among coheirs—the early history of the Franks in Gaul is largely the record of such divisions and their consequences—but its integrity was not compromised by the existence of independent dynasties claiming the allegiance of individual tribes within the nation. Unlike Gaul, Spain, and Italy, Britain was invaded, not by tribes under tribal kings, but by bodies of adventurers, who according to their own traditions were drawn from three distinct Germanic peoples. Most of them came from the remoter parts of the Germanic world, where kingship was less a matter of political authority than of descent from ancient gods. Respect for such descent, like the religion with which it was associated, survived even a migration across the North Sea, and meant that any leader who could claim this divine ancestry might hope to establish himself as the king of some portion of the nation to which he belonged. In course of time many of the small kingdoms thus founded lost their independence. Before the end of the seventh century most of the lesser midland princes had become the men of the kings of the Mercians; Lindsey had become a mere province in dispute between the kings of Mercia and Northumbria; and Cædwalla, king of Wessex, had exterminated the dynasty which had once ruled in the Isle of Wight. Nevertheless there still survive in ancient manuscripts the genealogies of eight separate royal families which had once ruled simultaneously in England.

Two of these families had ruled over the Northumbrian peoples known in the seventh century as the *Dere* and *Bernice*, and to modern writers as the Deirans and Bernicians. The other six all belonged to the country south of the Humber, and were associated with the people known as the *Lindisfaran*, who lived in Lindsey, between the Humber and the Witham, the *Mierce*, or Mercians, of the Trent valley, the East Angles, the East and West Saxons, and the *Cantware*, or men of Kent.[1]

[1] The genealogies of all these dynasties except those of the East and West Saxons are given by the early ninth-century manuscript printed by Sweet, *The Oldest English Texts*, pp. 169–71. The two Saxon genealogies are printed on p. 179 of that

Long as it is, this list is incomplete. It omits the royal families of Sussex and the Isle of Wight, where independent kingdoms are known to have survived until late in the seventh century, and it ignores several important peoples such as the Middle Saxons, whose original independence is at least probable. But even as it stands it shows a congestion of dynasties in southern England to which there is no parallel in western Europe.

In the south the Kentish, South Saxon, and West Saxon dynasties preserved a dim tradition of the way in which their kingdoms came into being. Beyond the Humber the Britons of Strathclyde remembered some incidents of their struggle with their Bernician enemies, and the origin of the Deiran kingdom is carried back far into the sixth century by the famous story of the play which Gregory the Great made with the name of Ælle the first Deiran king. But in the intervening country all is obscure. The distribution of heathen burial-grounds roughly defines the region occupied by the midland Angles before their conversion to Christianity, and the objects recovered from such sites enable a general distinction to be drawn between districts of early and late settlement. The study of place-names is beginning to yield results by which the archaeological evidence can be supplemented. But there is no tradition of incident, and therefore no means of determining the rate at which the conquest proceeded, or of giving historical substance to the names of ancient kings preserved in genealogies. It is only with the appearance of definite kingdoms in this country towards the beginning of the seventh century that it comes within the sphere of history.

It is especially unfortunate that no traditions have come down from the peoples of the Trent valley who formed the original kingdom of the Mercians. They first appear early in the seventh century, under a king named Cearl, of unknown ancestry, whose existence was only remembered because he gave his daughter in marriage to Edwin, the exiled heir of the royal house of Deira.[1] The marriage proves that the Mercians were independent of the Northumbrian kingdom then ruled by

work from a manuscript of King Alfred's time. A version of the Bernician, Deiran, Kentish, East Anglian, and Mercian pedigrees, annexed to the *Historia Brittonum* of Nennius, is printed in Mommsen's edition of that work in the *Monumenta Germaniae Historica*, pp. 202–6. [See K. Sisam, *Proceedings of the British Academy*, xxxix (1953), pp. 287–348.]

[1] *H.E.* ii. 14.

Æthelfrith of Bernicia, Edwin's enemy, and there is no reason to doubt that they formed part of the southern confederacy led by Æthelberht of Kent. But they only emerge from obscurity some years later, with the rise to power of a noble of their royal family named Penda, who for nearly a generation after the year 632[1] was the central figure in English history. Throughout his career, which ended with his death in battle in 654, Penda was the enemy of every Northumbrian king who tried to bring the peoples of southern England under his lordship. He was himself a great fighting king of the kind most honoured in Germanic saga; the lord of many princes, and the leader of a vast retinue attracted to his service by his success and generosity. Many stories must have been told about his dealings with other kings, but none of them have survived; his wars can only be described from the standpoint of his enemies, and the stages by which he came to power are unknown.

The outstanding fact in the history of the Mercian kingdom is the unique eminence of the family to which Penda and at least eight of his successors belonged. It is the one dynasty which spans the gulf between the English peoples of historic times and their continental ancestors. The Mercian kings claimed to be descended from Woden through Offa, king of Angel—presumably Angeln in Slesvig—one of the chief heroes of Germanic legend, in which he was long remembered as 'the best of all mankind between the seas'. It is probable that the first of the race to reach Britain was Offa's great-grandson Icel, who in the eighth century seems to have been regarded as the founder of the Mercian royal family.[2] There is no reason to doubt that an historical basis underlies this genealogy. In its oldest form it is derived from a text written before the end of the eighth century,[3] and it agrees with the meagre materials by which it can be tested. Above all, if it is fundamentally true, it becomes possible to understand the commanding position held in central England by the historic Mercian kings, and in particular their success in bringing the various peoples of the

---

[1] Below, p. 83.

[2] H. M. Chadwick, *The Origin of the English Nation*, pp. 15–16.

[3] [Zimmer's contention (*Nennius Vindicatus*, 1893) that the list was already part of the *Historia Brittonum* at the end of the seventh century has been shown to be mistaken by K. Sisam, op. cit., pp. 293–4. He concludes that it was incorporated into this at the end of the eighth century or in the first half of the ninth, and that it was in existence by the last decade of the eighth century.]

midlands into a single state. They certainly did not owe their influence to the importance of their own ancestral kingdom. If archaeological evidence can be trusted, the heathen Mercians were heavily outnumbered by the heathen Middle Angles, who were their south-eastern neighbours. But the power and influence of their kings are intelligible if, as their genealogy asserts, they were descended from the men who had ruled the whole Anglian race before its migration to Britain.

The tribal name *Mierce*, from which a convenient territorial name 'Mercia' has been derived, means 'boundary folk'. In the seventh century the Mercians appear as a people of 12,000 households, occupying the whole country from the lower Trent to the forests of the western midlands. It is clear that the people as a whole had come to adopt a name which originally described the portion of the race in contact with its British enemies. Already in the heathen age, the Angles of the northern midlands, following the course of the Trent, had reached the water-parting between the Trent and Severn. The names Wednesbury and Wednesfield—'Woden's fortress' and 'Woden's plain' —prove that the country above the head-waters of the Tame had been sacred ground in the heathen time. The boundary from which the Mercians took their name may well have been the belt of high land connecting the hills of Cannock Chase with the forest of Arden. To the west of this belt, along the streams which flow to the Severn, there stretched forests which bore British names, such as Morfe and Kinver, and even in the eighth century had not yet been divided out among English settlers. Immediately to the east lay the country which formed the centre of the historic Mercian kingdom, and contained Lichfield, the seat of its bishopric, and Tamworth, the chief residence of its kings.

No early documents have come down from the churches of the Trent valley, and little is known about the primitive organization of the peoples along its course. In the seventh century they were divided by the river into the North Mercians, of 7,000 households, and the South Mercians, of 5,000.[1] The origin of the division is uncertain, but it has an artificial appearance, and it was probably introduced for the more convenient distribution of public burdens among the various folks of which the Mercian people was composed. Only one of these

[1] *H.E.* iii. 24.

folks can now be identified. A charter of 849 which refers to the district south-west of Birmingham mentions the boundary of a folk called *Tomsætan*, that is the dwellers by the river Tame.[1] They appear in another document which shows that they were ruled by their own ealdorman, or local governor, and that their country contained the monastery of Breedon on the Hill in north Leicestershire.[2] As it is more than thirty miles in a straight line from Birmingham to Breedon, it is clear that the Tomsætan occupied a territory comparable in extent with an average county of the present day. It is perhaps of greater interest that their name points to a funda-mental resemblance between the early units of local adminis-tration in Mercia and Wessex. The Tomsætan of the Tame valley are unlikely to have differed materially in organization from the Wilsætan of the Wylye valley, whose territory formed the nucleus of Wiltshire.

Nothing is known of the stages by which the Mercians ex-panded from their original settlements over the country to the north and west. But there are two provinces of the later Mer-cian kingdom which clearly represent important phases in this movement. To the north of the Mercians of the Trent valley a folk of 1,200 households, known as the *Pecsætan*, was sparsely distributed over the Peak district of what afterwards became Derbyshire. Its origin is carried back into the heathen time by the barrow-interments of that age which have been discovered in the hills west of the upper Derwent. But the objects thus discovered belong, as a whole, to the later generations of the heathen period; the place-names of this country have few early features; and the beginnings of its settlement should probably be referred to the latter part of the sixth century. The folk who gave its name to the second of these two provinces—the *Wreocen-sætan* of the country around the Wrekin—may well have been of still later origin. It comprised 7,000 households, and it must have formed one of the more important divisions of the historic Mercian kingdom. But no heathen burials have been discovered in its territory, and none of the place-names which arose from its settlement need be earlier than the seventh century. It can hardly have been before the age of Penda that the Mercians of the upper Trent began to occupy the broken country which separated them from the plains along the upper Severn.

[1] *C.S.* 455.   [2] *C.S.* 454.

The original Mercian kingdom included many different kinds of country, most of them unattractive to early settlers. Neither the heavy clays west of the lower Trent, the sandy expanses of Sherwood forest, the wolds of south Nottinghamshire, nor the broken country between the Derwent and Erewash, can have invited settlement so long as land could be obtained elsewhere. From the distribution of heathen burial-grounds it is clear that the first Mercian settlements were made in the valley of the Trent or a little way up the course of its tributaries. None of them has produced objects which need be dated earlier than the middle of the sixth century, or imply more than a modest standard of barbaric culture. The archaeological evidence leaves, in fact, no serious doubt that the penetration of the northern midlands from the Humber was later, and for a long time less thorough, than the penetration of the eastern and central midlands from the Wash. If, as is more than probable, the ancestors of the later Mercian kings had played a part in the wars of the fifth century, it was as the leaders of war-bands rather than as the kings of a people permanently settled on the land.

To the south-east of the Mercians the uplands of central England and the valleys of the rivers which converge on the Wash were occupied by the congeries of folks known as the Middle Angles. Unlike the Mercians, from whom Bede is careful to distinguish them, the Middle Angles have left abundant evidence of their heathen culture. It was varied in character, including 'Saxon' elements of which the origin is still under discussion. The objects which illustrate it give the impression of a settlement which had begun before the end of the fifth century and continued without interruption into historic times. The name of the Middle Angles, which clearly refers to their position between the East Angles and the Mercians, strongly suggests their original independence, and the suggestion is confirmed by their ecclesiastical history. In the age of the Conversion it was only the fewness of priests that prevented the Middle Angles from receiving a bishop of their own. The diocese of Leicester, which was finally established in 737, was a belated recognition of their existence as a separate people. On the other hand there is no trace of any dynasty peculiar to the Middle Angles and ruling over all of them. They had fallen under Mercian lordship before the middle of the seventh century, when Penda placed Peada his son over them, 'because he was an excellent youth, and worthy of a king's name and dignity'. Their previous history is unknown; but their common name and the looseness of their association suggest that they represent an early alliance of related peoples, who had migrated separately from the Continent and among whom no single family had ever risen to permanent supremacy.

Many of these peoples are mentioned by Bede, or in the ancient tribute-list of the Mercian kings which is generally known as the Tribal Hidage.[1] But in the tenth century the kings of Wessex carried out an administrative reorganization of central England which obliterated earlier divisions, and there are few Middle Anglian peoples whose names can be placed with confidence upon a modern map. Among those whose position is known, the *Cilternsætan*, a folk of 4,000 households, occupied the plain beneath the Chilterns; the *Gifle*, of 300 households, inhabited the Ivel valley in south Bedfordshire; the *Hicce*, also of 300 households, have left their name to the town of Hitchin; and the *Gyrwe*, divided into two folks, each of 600 households, lived in and on the western edge of the Fens. Little is known about Middle Anglia under the Mercian kings, but an incidental reference by Bede to a *princeps* of the South Gyrwe suggests that each of the Middle Anglian folks was ruled by a separate ealdorman. As the Tribal Hidage mentions nearly twenty separate folks who from their position in the list seem to belong to Middle Anglia, it is unlikely that Bede was guilty of much exaggeration when he stated that Penda was accompanied to his last battle by thirty *duces regii*, or ealdormen.

The great block of woodland which formed the medieval forest of Arden prevented the Middle Angles from expanding at an early date continuously across England from the Wash to the Severn. Between Arden and the Chilterns there were few physical obstacles to their settlement, but the southern part of this country was open to penetration from the south-west as well as the north-east. It remained for centuries in dispute between the kings of Wessex and Mercia, and tradition, probably rightly, attributed its conquest from the Britons to a member of the West Saxon royal house.[2] On the north of the upper Thames the country amenable to early methods of cultivation was interrupted by many stretches of woodland, of which the

---

[1] Below, pp. 295–7.   [2] Above, p. 27.

most westerly is still called Wychwood Forest.[1] This name is
the only surviving memorial of the people known as the *Hwicce*,
who in the seventh century occupied the territory now represented by Gloucestershire, Worcestershire, and the western half of
Warwickshire. They were regarded as distinct alike from West
Saxons, Middle Angles, and Mercians, and in the organization
of the English church carried through by Archbishop Theodore,
their country was formed into a separate diocese, of which the
bishop's seat was fixed at Worcester. The Mercian kings who
became their lords believed them to include 7,000 tribute-
paying households—an estimate which ranks them with the
East and South Saxons, the *Wreocensætan*, and the men of
Lindsey. So large a people must have comprised a considerable
number of small folks, and ancient charters relating to the
territory of the Hwicce mention the *Pencersætan* of the country
south-west of Birmingham,[2] the *Stoppingas* of the country around
Wootton Wawen,[3] and the *Usmere* who lived in the woods to
the east of Kidderminster.[4]

Like the Cilternsætan, from whom they were separated by
Wychwood and the forests adjacent to it on the east, the Hwicce
were a people of mingled Anglian and Saxon stock. Six miles
to the north-east of Worcester the curious name Phepson records
the former presence of a group of settlers who derived their
origin from the Middle Anglian people known to Bede as
Feppingas. To the south of Phepson a stream called Whitsun
Brook derived its name from the *Wixan*, a people who appear
in the Tribal Hidage in close association with the *Gyrwe* of the
Fens. These names reinforce the archaeological evidence which
points to the settlement of a people of Anglian culture in the
Avon valley in the sixth or early seventh century, and their
character suggests that the northern part of the territory of the
Hwicce may have come into English occupation through the
migration of organized communities from the Anglian country
to the east. But the southern part of this territory—the country
around the Roman centres of Gloucester and Cirencester—
was undoubtedly acquired from the Britons by conquest, and
through a battle won by a Saxon, not an Anglian, king. There
is nothing in the evidence supplied by archaeological discoveries
or place-names which contradicts the opinion that the valley of

[1] First mentioned in a charter of 840, where it appears as *Huiccewudu* (*C.S.* 432).
[2] *C.S.* 455.   [3] *C.S.* 157.   [4] *C.S.* 154, 220.

the lower Severn first came into English possession as a result of Ceawlin's victory at Dyrham in 577.

It is probable that this country was held by Ceawlin and his successors throughout the next half-century. But under the year 628 the *Chronicle* states that Cynegils, king of Wessex, and Cwichelm his son 'fought with Penda at Cirencester and came to an agreement with him there'. There can be little doubt that this agreement gave to Penda Cirencester and the lands along the Severn which Ceawlin had conquered in 577. It was not until 632 that Penda became king of the Mercians, and in 628, for all that is known to the contrary, he may have been merely a landless noble of the Mercian royal house fighting for his own hand. But there is every reason to believe that it was he who first brought the Angles and Saxons of the middle and lower Severn under a single lordship, and that the under-kingdom of the Hwicce which is known to have existed within a generation of his death was in fact his creation.[1]

The numerous early charters which relate to the Severn valley give some indication of the way in which the Hwicce were governed under their Mercian overlords. A series of local rulers, of whom the earlier describe themselves as *reges* and the later as *reguli*, can be followed from the third quarter of the seventh century until the last quarter of the eighth. It begins with two brothers named Eanfrith and Eanhere, who are mentioned by Bede, without any title, as the rulers of the Hwicce shortly before 675, and it is continued by a certain Osric, whom Bede describes as king of the Hwicce in a passage relating to the last decade of the century. Bede generally reserves the title *rex* for independent rulers, but in a narrative of the foundation of Gloucester abbey, which seems to rest on materials older than Bede himself,[2] Osric and a brother named Oswald are described by King Æthelred of Mercia as two *ministri* of noble race— a phrase showing that whatever rank may have been theirs by birth, they owed their authority to his gift. In the seventh and eighth centuries the distinction between a king, an under-king, and a thegn set in charge of a province by his lord was blurred

---

[1] The dual origin of the Hwicce makes it very unlikely that any local family can have possessed an inherent right to rule over the whole people, and strongly supports the view that the later *reges*, *reguli*, and *duces* who reigned among them were set in power by the kings of the Mercians.

[2] *C.S.* 60. On this narrative see W. H. Stevenson, *Asser's Life of King Alfred*, (1904), p. 155.

by the recurrent subjection of all the southern English rulers to an overlord whose powers over their lands and men were very wide. But in the course of time the writers of formal documents gradually evolved a terminology which approximated to political facts, and as part of this process they worked their way towards an accurate description of the position filled by the rulers of the Hwicce. A little before the year 700 a certain Oshere, who seems to have been Osric's successor, had styled himself 'king of the Hwicce' without any qualification.[1] Some forty years after his death his real position was defined by an archbishop of Canterbury, who described him as *comes*, or retainer, of Æthelred, king of the Mercians, and *subregulus*, or under-king, of the Hwicce.[2] Oshere was succeeded in his kingdom by four of his sons, and in 736 one of them attests the oldest original Mercian charter as 'under-king and retainer of Æthelbald king of the Mercians'.[3] But in 736 the archaic conception of a king or under-king who was also a member of a lord's household was itself becoming obsolete, and the last of these early rulers of the Hwicce—three brothers who held the throne jointly under Offa of Mercia—ignore the association with an overlord's court which their ancestors had regarded as an especial honour. They assert, and even emphasize, the shadow of kingship that belonged to them. In 777 one of them styles himself 'under-king of the Hwicce by the dispensation of the Lord'.[4] But in the same charter King Offa, his overlord, expressed the realities of his position by calling him 'my under-king, ealdorman, that is, of his own people of the Hwicce'.

Beyond the Hwicce the plain of Herefordshire north of the Wye and the broken country of south Shropshire were occupied by a people known as the *Magonsætan*. Their settlement probably represents the last phase of the original Anglian advance against the Britons of Wales, for the river Wye alone separated them from a country which remained in Welsh possession until the Norman Conquest. Hereford, which was the seat of their early bishops, still had the character of a border fortress in the eleventh century. There is some reason to think that towards the west they occupied more land than their descendants could retain, for English place-names of an early type occur sporadically beyond the frontier drawn in the eighth century by Offa's Dyke. The history of this remote people

[1] *C.S.* 85.   [2] *C.S.* 156.   [3] *C.S.* 154.   [4] *C.S.* 223.

would be utterly obscure were it not that certain women of their reigning family became eminent in the religious life. Soon after the middle of the seventh century, Merewalh, their ruler, married Eormenbeorg, a lady of the Kentish royal house, who founded the monastery of Minster in Thanet, where Mildthryth, her daughter, was abbess before the year 691. Another daughter, named Mildburg, founded a monastery at Much Wenlock in her own country, and a third daughter, named Mildgyth, lived as a nun at Eastry in Kent. The fame of these women meant that some traditions of their origin were preserved, and the little that is known of their family relationships was written down before the Norman Conquest. From what was then collected it appears that Merewalh had a brother named Mearchelm and a son named Merefin—names which alliterate not only with one another but with the name of the Magonsætan themselves.[1] These details point to the existence of a local dynasty, and their significance is confirmed by independent evidence that at some period before the middle of the eighth century the Magonsætan were ruled by a *regulus* named Mildfrith,[2] whose name continues the alliteration. Whatever may have been the position of this dynasty among the noble families which found a common centre in the Mercian court, its solidarity was expressed with remarkable consistency in the names of the men and women who belonged to it.

It is unlikely that the under-kings of the Hwicce and the Magonsætan, or any of the Middle Anglian princes, could claim that descent from ancient gods in which the essence of early Germanic kingship lay. They could intermarry with families thus descended. Tondberht, *princeps* of the South Gyrwe, married a daughter of the king of the East Angles, and Æthelwalh, king of the South Saxons, married a daughter of Eanfrith of the Hwicce. But Anglo-Saxon royalty was never a closed caste, and the fact that such marriages were possible does not prove that the local rulers of the midlands represented families

---

[1] In the tenth century it was said that Merewalh was a son of Penda, king of the Mercians (*Liber Vitae of Hyde Abbey*, ed. W. de G. Birch, p. 84). But a statement of this kind in so late a text has little, if any, authority. The fact that no names beginning in M occur in the elaborate genealogy of the Mercian kings makes it in the highest degree unlikely that Merewalh was Penda's son. The further fact that the names current in the family alliterate with the name of the Magonsætan suggests very strongly that they had a claim to rule in their own right over this people, and that originally they were independent of the Mercian kings.

[2] William of Malmesbury, *Gesta Pontificum*, [*R.S.*] ed. Hamilton, p. 299.

entitled to authority by divine descent. In status, the rulers of
the Hwicce were probably typical members of their class, and it
seems clear that though their family was noble their territorial
position depended on the favour of the Mercian kings. It is at
least certain that in historic times none of these rulers is known to
have asserted himself against his overlord. The power of the Mercian kingdom in the seventh and eighth centuries rested on the
combination into what was in effect one state of the Mercians,
the men of the country between the original Mercia and the
British border, the Magonsætan, the Hwicce, and the Middle
Angles.

It was natural that a king who was the lord of this vast region
should attract to his court other kings, of equal birth but fewer
resources. From an early time—perhaps even from the fifth
century—a dynasty which traced its descent from Woden ruled
in the district between the Humber and the Witham which now
forms the Parts of Lindsey in the county of Lincoln. But none
of the kings of Lindsey played an independent part in Anglo-
Saxon politics, and after a period in which it was doubtful
whether a Northumbrian or a Mercian overlord would secure
their allegiance, they became permanently attached to the
circle of local rulers dependent on the Mercian court. Apart
from the last of the line—a king named Aldulf who appears in
attendance on Offa of Mercia between 787 and 796—the kings
of Lindsey are mere names. But some of the names have an
archaic appearance, and the first element of the name Cædbæd,
which has the fourth place below Woden in their genealogy, is
clearly derived from the Celtic name-stem *cad*, 'battle', and
suggests the possibility that a British strain entered the family
at a very early date.[1] The dynasty has, in fact, the appearance
of a survival from the age of individualistic adventure which
preceded the migration of the English peoples to Britain.

In the ninth century Lindsey was colonized by the rank and
file of a Danish army, and its earlier history is very obscure.
Like the territories of the Hwicce and Magonsætan, Lindsey was
formed into a diocese by Archbishop Theodore, but the succession of its bishops was ended by the Danish invasion, and the
site of their cathedral is unknown. A Scandinavian division of
the country into three ridings replaced its Anglian organization

---

[1] See F. M. Stenton, 'Lindsey and its Kings', *C.P.*, pp. 127–35.

by folks, and much of its Anglian local nomenclature was over-
laid by Danish place-names resulting from the Danish occupation. Up to the present, archaeological discoveries have thrown
little light on the beginnings of Anglian settlement in Lindsey,
but it is carried back to the early part of the sixth century by
numerous place-names ending in -*ingham* and by the three
archaic names Barlings, Beckering, and Minting which occur
within a radius of four miles a little distance to the east of
Lincoln. Few Celtic names have survived the successive conquests of Lindsey by Angles and Danes. But the hint of early
intercourse between Angles and Britons given by the name of
King Cædbæd is strengthened by the fact that Lindsey itself
is a British name, and is turned into certainty by the adoption
into common speech of the Roman compound *Lindum Colonia*
which has become the modern Lincoln.

Lindsey is one of the few early English kingdoms of which
the boundaries can be drawn with some approach to precision.
On the north and east it was bounded by the Humber and the
sea. On the west it included the low hills between the Don and
the Trent which form the Isle of Axholme, and the patches of
habitable land which are surrounded by the moors of Hatfield
Chase. In country like this, no definite frontier line was either
possible or necessary. But to the south of the Isle of Axholme
the Trent formed a natural boundary between Lindsey and
Mercia up to the point near Torksey at which the river was
joined by the Roman canal known as the Foss Dyke. At this
point the boundary turned towards the east, running at first
along the Foss Dyke, and then below Lincoln along the Witham,
to the fens which lie behind the coast.[1] In early times the
districts to the south of the Foss Dyke and the Witham, which
have been known since the eleventh century as Kesteven and
Holland, belonged, not to Lindsey but to Middle Anglia. The
early ecclesiastical history of this country connects it definitely
with Mercia.[2] Guthlac, the founder of Crowland abbey,
belonged to the Mercian royal house, and it was Headda,

---

[1] The most northerly division of Holland—the wapentake of Skirbeck—lies to
the north of the Witham, but it is not unlikely that in early times it was a delta
between two arms of the river.

[2] The connexion comes out very clearly in the life of the Mercian saint Werburh,
who was the head of many monasteries, but is particularly associated with Hanbury
in Staffordshire and Threckingham in Kesteven. J. Tait, *Cartulary of Chester Abbey*,
i, pp. viii–xiv.

bishop of Lichfield, who dedicated Guthlac's new church a few years before 706.[1]

The fenland which stretches for many miles to the south and east of Crowland played an important part in early English history, for it prevented the Mercian kings from making East Anglia a Mercian province. From time to time individual East Anglian kings, like all of their kind in southern England, were compelled to acknowledge Mercian supremacy. But a Mercian invasion of their territory was made difficult by the impassable country which lay between East Anglia and the Mercian provinces of the north-eastern midlands, and the Mercian kings never obtained in East Anglia the unchallenged ascendancy that was theirs in Lindsey. The name of the first East Anglian king is uncertain. The fact, recorded by Bede, that the kings of East Anglia were known collectively as the *Wuffingas* suggests very strongly that their dynasty was founded by the king named Wuffa who appears in their genealogy as the grandfather of Rædwald, the fourth on Bede's list of the overlords of the southern English. It must be left an open question whether this evidence is outweighed by a tradition, which seems to have been written down in the late eighth century, that Wehha, Wuffa's father, was the first king 'who reigned in Britain over the East Angles'.[2] In any case the fact that Rædwald was reigning as late as the year 616 seems to imply that the kingdom had not come into being much before the year 500.

The objects recovered from the ordinary burial-grounds of East Anglia, though numerous, include nothing of pre-eminent quality. They seem to indicate a culture of the normal Anglian type, little touched by extraneous influences. But the recent excavation of an undisturbed ship burial at Sutton Hoo above the estuary of the Deben near Woodbridge has yielded materials[3] which throw the archaeology, not only of East Anglia, but of Anglo-Saxon England, into a new perspective. No trace was found of the body of the man in whose honour these objects were brought together. It is on the whole most probable that he

---

[1] [*Felix's Life of Saint Guthlac*, ed. B. Colgrave, p. 144.] The significance of this consecration has sometimes been missed through the confusion of Headda of Lichfield with his contemporary Hæddi of Winchester.

[2] Nennius, *Historia Brittonum*, ed. Mommsen, p. 203. On the date see p. 39 n. 3 above.

[3] They are described and their significance is indicated in *Antiquity*, xiv. 1–87 (March 1940).

perished at sea or in battle far from his own land, and that the
mound with its grave-furniture should be regarded as a memorial rather than an interment. His name is unknown, but the
value of the articles dedicated to his memory shows that he
must have been a king, and the fact that they were deposited,
certainly in the first half, and probably in the first quarter, of
the seventh century makes it possible to identify him provision-
ally with Rædwald, the East Anglian overlord of the southern
English.[1] In this connection it is significant that the place of
burial is within four miles of Rendlesham, where the East
Anglian kings of this period are known to have had a residence.

Many of the articles are of a kind commonly, or at least
occasionally, associated in other rich interments of this age—
sword and sheath, shield, helmet, spear-heads, bronze bowls of
more than one type, wooden buckets ornamented with decorative metal-work, horns with silver mounts. The notable feature
of these objects is the remarkable elaboration of their adorn-
ment. More curious in themselves are a number of articles to
which no parallels have been found elsewhere in England.
They include a massive whetstone, ornamented with bronze
terminals; a large iron object, decorated at salient points with
representations of bulls' heads, which has been explained as a
portable flambeau; a five-stringed instrument of music; a purse
with a golden frame containing forty gold Frankish coins; and a
leather bag with silver handles. Fragments of chain mail and
extensive remains of textile fabrics are of great interest as
illustrations of industrial craftsmanship. But the outstanding
feature of the discovery is the large number of objects in the
precious metals which it includes. No such treasure has been
found in any other English burial, and few treasures which are
at all comparable have been found in any part of the whole
Germanic north. Apart from their intrinsic value, which is very
great, the gold objects are made highly important by the excellence and the unusual character of their decoration. The
technical accomplishment which they show is in every way
remarkable, they are undoubtedly of English workmanship,

[1] [In 1959 in 'The East Anglian Kings of the Seventh Century' in *The Anglo-
Saxons*, ed. P. Clemoes, pp. 50–2, Sir Frank accepted the view then current that the
Merovingian coins belonged to about 650–60, and thus dissociated the memorial
from Rædwald. He considered that it might commemorate Æthelhere, who was
killed at the Winwæd in 654. But since then the dating of the coins has been
questioned and the matter is still *sub judice*. Excavation continues at the site.]

and as pieces of design they are virtually independent of all other schools of ornament which have hitherto been identified in England. At the very least, they prove that Kent was not the only heathen kingdom in which the decorative arts were practised with brilliant success. The interest of the silver objects is of another kind. They comprise a large dish, a fluted bowl, bearing a conventionalized female profile embossed in low relief, a nest of nine small bowls, two spoons, and a small ladle. None of these pieces can well be of English manufacture, and the large dish bears four control stamps which show the monogram of Anastasius, emperor of Constantinople from 491 to 518. The whole group of pieces gives a strong impression of an eastern provenance, though apart from the dish, it is not yet possible to refer the individual specimens to any particular country of origin.

It will be long before the archaeological implications of this astonishing discovery have been worked out convincingly in detail. But two general conclusions already seem permissible. The first is that historians have underestimated, or at least understressed, the amount of movable wealth that was at the disposal of a great seventh-century English king. In the magnificence which to early peoples symbolized power, the man commemorated in the Sutton Hoo burial could have held his own with any prince in the Germanic world. It is no longer possible to regard the culture of the Anglo-Saxon courts as a stunted and poverty-stricken version of the environment which surrounded the barbarian kings of larger peoples. In the second place, the discoveries greatly enlarge the range of the contacts known to be possible to Englishmen of the early seventh century. The way in which an English king could have acquired the eastern silver found at Sutton Hoo will never be fully known. But it is in every way probable that this silver came to him through trade rather than plunder. No ancient authority ever hints at any large-scale raiding from England in this period. The discoveries at Sutton Hoo, like the traces of eastern influence on early English sculpture, should probably be taken as indications of peaceful, if sporadic, intercourse between England and the countries of the further Mediterranean.

East Anglia is not one of the districts in which the archaeological evidence for a fifth-century settlement is most striking. But the evidence is steadily increasing, and it is supported by innumerable place-names of early type. There is no part of England in which there are more place-names pointing to an original settlement by communities, and many of these place-names contain personal names which can only be explained by reference to continental parallels. Other names contain words, unrecorded elsewhere in England, which had belonged to the common vocabulary of the North Sea peoples. The local nomenclature of East Anglia as a whole gives the definite impression of a self-contained people whose ancestors had migrated to England independently of other peoples before the end of the fifth century.

At the middle of the sixth century the East Angles were probably the most powerful people in southern England. Norfolk and Suffolk form a territory much larger than either Kent or Sussex—larger, even, than Wessex before the great expansion of Ceawlin's time. Outside this region the early East Anglian kingdom certainly included the Isle of Ely, which in Bede's time was supposed to contain 600 households, and may well have extended into Cambridgeshire as far as the Devil's Dyke, which formed the boundary of the medieval diocese of Norwich. It was not strange that Rædwald, king of the East Angles, was able to make himself the overlord of all the southern English peoples. But after the consolidation of the Mercian kingdom no East Anglian king was of much account outside his own country. Three East Anglian kings were killed by Penda, and by the end of the century the kingdom had fallen into an obscurity so dense that even the royal succession is not exactly known.

On passing from Anglian into Saxon territory, from East Anglia into Essex, the obscurity deepens. No East Saxon king was of more than local importance; and although an early Saxon occupation of Essex is proved by place-names of a primitive type, no other part of south-eastern England has yielded so little archaeological evidence of its condition in the heathen age. The chief interest of early East Saxon history lies in the genealogy of the royal house. Every early English king tried to secure that the name of his son should fall into an alliterative series with the names of his ancestors, but the kings of Essex observed this custom with unusual persistency. Sigered, the last of the line, was the son of Sigeric, son of Selered, son of Sigeberht, son of Sigebald, son of Selefrith, son of Sigefrith, son of Seaxa, son of Sledda. Historically, the genealogy is important because in its oldest version it descends from a pair of names—Gesecg Seaxneting—which connect the kings of Essex with the gods of continental heathenism. *Seaxneting* contains an English form of *Saxnot*, the name of a god still worshipped by the continental Saxons of the eighth century. Whatever traditions may lie behind the appearance of his name at the head of the East Saxon royal genealogy, it proves at least that the kings of Essex believed themselves to represent a stock in which the other English dynasties had no part. They alone claimed another god than Woden as their ancestor.

At the beginning of the seventh century London is known to have been their chief town, and it is probable that the whole of the district now called Middlesex was then, as later, a province of their kingdom. But it would be very unsafe to assume that this association was of long standing. The Middle Saxons bore a name that carries a strong suggestion of original independence. Names which refer to the position of a people between two great divisions of the same race are unlikely to have been given to the men of a subordinate province, and there is a strong probability that for some generations after their settlement the Middle Saxons formed, if not a single kingdom, at least an independent group of closely related folks. It is also probable that the present county of Middlesex was only a part of their territory. To the north-west of London there is no natural obstacle to settlement until the foot-hills of the Chilterns are reached, and for most of its course the northern boundary of Middlesex represents nothing more ancient than the southern limit of the franchises of St. Alban's abbey. As an organized people the Middle Saxons have no history, but among the obscure folks of whom they were composed, the *Geddingas*, *Gillingas*, and *Mimmas* of Yeading, Ealing, and Mimms bore names which may well go back to the age of the migration, and the *Gumeningas* of the place known in the eighth century as *Gumeninga hearh*, and now as Harrow, possessed the most impressive site of heathen Germanic worship in the whole of England.

The Middle Saxons are first mentioned by name early in the eighth century, and there is no doubt that at this time their territory was bounded on the south by the Thames. But there is evidence which suggests very strongly that at an earlier time Surrey had been one of their provinces. The name Surrey

means 'southern district'. It is strictly parallel to the name
Eastry, which denoted the most easterly of the primitive divisions of mainland Kent, and it is most easily explained as a
survival from a time when the Saxons settled on either side of
the Thames above London were regarded as a single people.
Like the Saxons of Middlesex, the Saxons of Surrey have no
independent history. Their country was in dispute between
the kings of Wessex and Kent as early as the year 568, when
Ceawlin, king of Wessex, defeated Æthelberht, king of Kent,
and drove him into his own land. At different periods in the
seventh century Surrey appears as a province of Kent, Wessex,
and Mercia, and the only one of its early rulers who is known by
name—a certain Frithuwald, who gave a great estate to Chertsey abbey with the consent of Wulfhere, king of Mercia[1]—looks
like an under-king appointed by a superior lord rather than the
representative of a local dynasty. The only certainty in the
early history of Surrey is the fact that its settlement had begun
before the appearance of organized kingdoms in the Thames
valley. The Saxon burial-grounds at Croydon, Beddington,
and Mitcham are among the most ancient in the whole Thames
basin, and the place-names Eashing, Godalming, Tyting, and
Woking; Getingas, the ancient name of Cobham; and Binton
in Seale, formerly Bintungas, show that the Wey valley was a
region of primary Saxon settlement.

More difficult, and in many ways more interesting, questions
are raised by the history of London in this period. In the
absence of contemporary record some scholars have represented London as a city which preserved through all the confusion of the English migration an essential continuity of
organized life. Others have considered that with the disappearance of the economic factors which had created the
Roman city, its life ended and its site lay derelict. It is becoming increasingly difficult to hold either opinion without qualification. There are no features in the constitution of Saxon
London which suggest a Roman origin, and the traces of Roman
law which some have seen in the later customs of the city will
not bear a close examination. On the other hand, the history of
many Roman towns in Gaul shows that the disappearance of
the street plan of Roman London, which is the chief argument
for the desertion of the city, has little significance. It is possible

[1] C.S. 34.

that London may still have been recognizable as a Roman city for centuries after the collapse of Roman government. Many Roman buildings may have been standing in various phases of decay, and traffic may have been moving along many Roman ways in 839, when Bishop Helmstan of Winchester wrote that he had recently been consecrated 'in the illustrious place, built by the skill of the ancient Romans, called throughout the world the great city of London'.[1]

But the starved and barbarized existence which is all that can be attributed to London in the age of the Anglo-Saxon invasions cannot be regarded as true continuity of life. The peculiar importance of Roman London had been due to its function as a distributing centre for goods coming from the Continent to Britain. In the eighth century Saxon London was described by Bede, in words appropriate to its Roman predecessor, as the market-place of many peoples coming by land and sea. But in the earlier of the intervening centuries there had been a long period in which the geographical position of London had little if any economic significance. Apart from the possibility of buying cheap slaves there can have been little to bring the foreign trader to London in the first half of the sixth century, when south-eastern Britain was occupied by loosely compacted bands of invaders, still unsure of their future in the island. It was not until the Anglo-Saxon colonists of southern England had found a settled way of life that the natural advantages which had made London a great Roman city could come again into play.

All that has survived from sixth-century London to the present day is a series of small objects, accidentally discovered, which prove the bare fact that there were people of an Anglo-Saxon culture living in the city towards the close of this period. But it is clear from Bede's narrative of Augustine's mission that when Æthelberht of Kent founded St. Paul's cathedral for Augustine's companion Mellitus, London was already the seat of a considerable population with a will of its own. It was the conservative heathenism of the men of London which frustrated this first attempt to establish a local bishopric. In view of their attitude it is hard to believe that any tradition of Roman Christianity still persisted in the city, or that traders from the romanized lands of Gaul had played any important part in the

[1] *C.S.* 424.

revival of its life. It is significant that the only evidence for the external relations of London in the seventh century connects the city, not with the Frankish kingdom, but with the heathen of the Frisian coast. Among the barbarous silver coins [sceattas] which then circulated in England a considerable number are inscribed with the name of London. Many of these pieces have been found on ancient habitation-sites in Holland, and form the earliest indication of trade between any part of England and the Continent. The Frisians were the most adventurous of early Germanic traders, and there can be little doubt that their intercourse with England, which is illustrated by these coins, was already of long standing when the first of them were struck.

In the early history of London the local rulers within whose territory the city had arisen play an insignificant part in comparison with the great kings who from time to time became supreme in southern England. It was not the local king of Essex but his overlord, Æthelberht of Kent, who founded the first Saxon Cathedral in London. For the next seventy years the history of London is almost a blank, but at the end of this time Wulfhere of Mercia, as overlord of the southern English, was in a position to sell 'the see of the city of London' to an exiled West Saxon bishop who had sought his court. The power of the Mercian kings in London seems to have survived the general collapse of the Mercian supremacy which followed Wulfhere's death. In 740 Æthelbald, king of the Mercians, released to the bishop of Rochester the toll which the king and his predecessors had taken in London from a ship belonging to the bishop's church—a transaction which carries the Mercian control of the port of London back to the beginning of the eighth century. It is, in fact, probable that under Mercian overlordship the kings of Essex had possessed little authority in London beyond that which belonged to them as the natural protectors of their own men living there. In any case, it is certain that they were not the only kings with property within the city. There is contemporary evidence that in 686 the kings of Kent possessed a hall in London to which any Kentishman who had bought cattle in the city might summon the vendor to give warranty of the sale.

These complex conditions make it difficult to form any definite impression of the government of London under its Mercian overlords. But it is at least clear that they favoured the preservation of local liberties. They create, in fact, a distinct possibility that some of the privileges which the men of London claimed in the twelfth century may have been inherited from the traders whose settlement had founded the Saxon city. The few documents which relate to Anglo-Saxon London throw no light on any of these privileges. But the most remarkable of the series—the right of hunting over the country roughly defined by the Chilterns, the southern and western boundaries of Surrey, and the river Cray—has at least the appearance of high antiquity, and was undoubtedly a matter of immemorial custom in the Norman period. The region thus defined does not correspond to any political or administrative division which is known to have existed in historic times. But it is not unlikely that the country over which the men of London hunted under the Norman kings represented the territory which had belonged to the Middle Saxons in the age when they were still a separate people.

Each of the three peoples between whom the south coast of England was divided preserved some memory of its origins. The traditions which relate to the founding of the Kentish, South Saxon, and West Saxon kingdoms form an important part of the material for the history of the English conquest of Britain.[1] In the case of Kent and Wessex, the men who are most prominent in these traditions are connected by an ancient thread of genealogy with the kings who afterwards appear in these countries. But no royal genealogy has descended from the South Saxon kingdom, and nothing is known of the history of Sussex between the fall of Anderida in 491 and the baptism of a king named Æthelwalh shortly before 675. Æthelwalh himself only appears in history for a moment, and little would be known about his successors but for a series of charters connected with the Saxon cathedral of Selsey. They are only preserved in poor copies, but they bring out the important fact that in the late seventh and early eighth centuries many kings were reigning simultaneously in Sussex. The earliest of these charters, made by a king named alternatively Nothelm and Nunna, is witnessed by another king named Watt.[2] A second charter of King Nunna is witnessed by a king and queen named Æthelstan and Æthelthryth who are otherwise unknown;[3] and a king named Æthelberht, who is equally obscure, is mentioned in another charter of the same period.[4] There is no means of

[1] Above, pp. 15 ff.   [2] C.S. 78.   [3] C.S. 132.   [4] C.S. 145.

knowing whether all or any of these kings claimed descent
from Ælle, but the broken alliteration of their names suggests
that they represented a number of separate local dynasties
rather than different branches of a dominant royal family.

The marsh and woodland which lay between the South
Saxons and the Jutes of Kent separated one of the most primitive from the most advanced of early English peoples. The
chronology of the different types of Kentish culture is still
unsettled, but there is no doubt that in the late sixth century
the applied arts were practised in Kent with more general
accomplishment than in any other English kingdom. It is also
clear that the distinctive culture of Kent is closely related to
that of the Frankish Rhineland, and that there are features in
the later social and agrarian organization of Kent which seem
to descend from a Frankish origin. These facts are most simply
explained on the theory that the Jutes of Kent had lived in or
on the fringe of Frankish territory for some time before their
migration to Britain. It is at least suggestive that the only piece
of evidence which throws any clear light on the relations of the
continental Jutes with other peoples reveals them as the dependants, if unwilling dependants, of the Frankish monarchy.
Between 561 and 584 Chilperich, king of Soissons, is described
as the lord by conquest of a people known as the Euthiones, who
are shown by their name to have belonged to the same nation as
the Jutes of Kent, and clearly represent the remnant of this
nation which had not taken part in the migration to Kent. It
was probably in order to bring their insular kinsmen into a
more definite relationship to the Merovingian dynasty that at
about this period Bertha, daughter of Chilperich's brother
Charibert, king of Paris, was given in marriage to Æthelberht,
king of Kent.

In the sixth century the king of a small people who married
into a great family became its dependant. None of the Frankish
kings contemporary with Æthelberht would have regarded him
as an equal. The view of their relationship taken by the greatest
ruler in the west is expressed in the letter by which Gregory the
Great commended Augustine and his companions to Theuderich, king of Orleans, and Theudebert, king of Metz. 'After
Almighty God has adorned your kingdom with the uprightness
of faith and made it eminent among other peoples in the integrity of the Christian religion, we have good reason to believe

that you wish your subjects in every respect to be converted to that faith in which you, their kings and lords, stand.' It is easy to read too much into the phrasing of a papal letter. The description of Theuderich and Theudebert as the lords of the people to whom Augustine was going may be the language of compliment rather than fact. There is no evidence that Æthelberht ever became, by a formal act, the man of any Frankish king. But his treatment of Augustine and his companions is a good illustration of the conduct expected from an under-king towards strangers sent him by his lord.

Whatever may have been the relations between Æthelberht of Kent and the kings of the house of Clovis, there is no doubt that his own lordship was recognized for a time throughout southern England. His name stands third in Bede's list of the kings who had successively ruled all England south of the Humber. He may have held this position for nearly thirty years, for his predecessor, Ceawlin, king of Wessex, won no battles after 584, and his successor, Rædwald of East Anglia, was not fully recognized as overlord till Æthelberht himself died, in 616. His supremacy was the dominant fact in English politics at the beginning of the seventh century. But it is through the laws which he issued for his own kingdom of Kent that Æthelberht enters into general history. They belong to the period following his reception of Christianity, and one motive for their enactment was the necessity of providing appropriate penalties for offences against God and the Church. But there is remarkably little that is specifically christian in the detail of the code, and despite Bede's statement that Æthelberht composed his dooms 'after the Roman manner', they show no sign of Roman influence. It is unlikely that they owed anything definite to any model, and their general affinities lie, not with any law-book of the Western Empire, but with the *Lex Salica*, the great code which Clovis had issued for the Salian Franks. Even so, the affinities are in subject-matter and not in form; the Salic law is a far longer text than the ninety brief sections into which Æthelberht compressed his laws, and primitive as is the content of the Salic law, it was written in Latin. The laws of Æthelberht were written in English and are of unique interest as by far the earliest body of law expressed in any Germanic language.

None of Æthelberht's successors ever won a position of equal influence among the princes of southern England. Eadbald, his son, who reigned from 616 until 640, was still a heathen at his accession. He married his father's widow, and according to Bede, was punished by fits of intermittent madness. The Roman mission to Kent nearly expired at the beginning of his reign, but he was brought before long to accept Christianity and repudiate his unlawful wife. For the rest of his life he appears as a Christian king, lax in imposing conformity on his people, but causing no scandal by his own conduct. He was something more than a local Kentish ruler. He gave his sister in marriage to Edwin, king of the Northumbrians, and although the parentage of his second wife has not been ascertained, there seems no doubt that she belonged to the Frankish royal house. It is a curious fact that the date of his death, unnoted by any English writer, is recorded in the annals of the church of Salzburg. The Frankish affinities of the Kentish court can still be traced in the next generation. Two children of Eorcenberht, Eadbald's son and successor, bore Frankish names—a son named Hlothhere, who ultimately became king of Kent, and a daughter named Eorcengota, who lived as a nun at Faremoutiers-en-Brie. But a somewhat remote connection with the decadent Frankish royal house of the seventh century brought no material strength to an English king, and Eorcenberht and his successors are insignificant figures in comparison with their contemporaries in the midlands and the north.

Eorcenberht died in a pestilence which visited England in 664, and Egbert, his eldest son, reigned after him until 673. During at least a part of his reign Egbert must have been recognized as king in Surrey as well as in Kent, for there is almost contemporary evidence that he was the original founder of Chertsey abbey.[1] But in the next generation Kent itself was often divided between two or more kings, and was harried several times by expeditions from Mercia or Wessex. Until 684 Hlothhere, Egbert's brother, ruled over the whole kingdom, but late in that year an army from Sussex invaded Kent at the instigation of Eadric, Egbert's eldest son, and in February 685 Hlothhere died of wounds received in battle. On Eadric's death in the summer of 686 the kingdom fell apart between a number of obscure kings, of whom one, at least, was the man of Æthelred, king of Mercia. It was reunited in or soon after 690 by Eadric's

[1] C.S. 34.

younger brother Wihtred, who reigned until 725, with no rival in his own country, and apparently without acknowledging the king of any other country as his lord.

Two out of the three surviving codes of Kentish law belong to this period. In a prologue to the earlier of these codes its contents are described as the enactments by which Hlothhere and Eadric, kings of Kent, enlarged the law made by their ancestors. They show a somewhat elaborate development of legal procedure. But they seem to recognize a title to nobility which is derived from birth and not from service to a king, and the men who direct the course of pleas in popular assemblies are not the ministers of a king but 'the judges of the Kentish people'. The laws of Hlothhere and Eadric are less archaic in language than the laws of Æthelberht, but they give the same impression of a primitive form of Germanic society, little affected by the growth of royal power or aristocratic privilege.

The second of these codes was issued by King Wihtred in an assembly of the Kentish nobles and clergy held at Bearsted late in 695. Apart from four final clauses it relates exclusively to matters of ecclesiastical interest. In this respect, and in its character as a legislative act, it differs fundamentally from the collection of secular enactments informally attributed to Hlothhere and Eadric. The main immediate object of Wihtred's code was to provide penalties for unlawful marriages, heathen practices, and the neglect of fasts and holy days, and to define the process under which accused persons might establish their innocence by oath. But as an historical document its chief interest lies in the privileges which it gives to the church and its leading ministers. The church is declared free from taxation, the oath of a bishop, like the oath of a king, is declared incontrovertible, and the church receives the same compensation as the king for violence done to dependants. Within ninety years the church which Æthelberht had taken under his protection had become a power all but co-ordinate with the king himself in the Kentish state.

Long after Wihtred's time the traditions of Augustine and the kings who had protected his church placed Kent apart from other English kingdoms. At the end of the eighth century an English scholar living in Gaul addresses a letter to 'the imperial kingdom of the people of Kent', and recalls the great religious teachers of its past, the wisdom and high rank of its kings, and the courage and just judgements of its former rulers.[1] But in the slow movement towards political unity which is the essential history of England in the seventh and eighth centuries, Kent like every other small and self-contained kingdom fell into insignificance. The future was with the kings who could enlarge their territory and reward their followers at the expense of the British peoples towards the west and north. In southern England, only the kings of Mercia and Wessex had this opportunity, and Wessex is the only kingdom of which, in outline, the growth can still be traced.

At the beginning of the seventh century the West Saxons, under a king named Ceolwulf, were in occupation of Berkshire, Wiltshire, and the extreme north of Somerset. They held the north and centre of Hampshire, and it is probable that the overlordship of their kings was generally recognized by the Jutes of the south. Little can be said of the stages by which they moved towards the west, for most of the fighting in their advance occurred at places which cannot now be identified.[2] There is no evidence as to the date of their occupation of Dorset; but no heathen burial-grounds of their race have yet been discovered in the county, and a large number of its British inhabitants undoubtedly survived the Saxon conquest. The place-names of Dorset, regarded as a whole, are remarkable for the frequent use of British river-names as names of English settlements, and suggest that the Saxon occupation of the country belongs to the seventh rather than the sixth century. The place-names of Somerset have a similar character, and there is definite evidence that the east of that county was still British in 650. Under the year 658 the *Chronicle* states that Cenwalh, king of Wessex, fought with the Britons *æt Peonnum* and drove them in flight as far as the river Parret. There seems no doubt that the battle was fought near Penselwood on the edge of Somerset and Wiltshire, and it has always been regarded as opening the east of Somerset to English settlement, and establishing the Parret as the Saxon border. In reality, the battle may well have been followed by the English conquest of all Somerset, for the fact

---

[1] *Monumenta Alcuiniana*, ed. Jaffé, pp. 369–71.

[2] Under 614 the *Chronicle* notes that the West Saxon kings Cynegils and Cwichelm fought with the Britons 'on Beandune', where more than two thousand Britons fell. This battle must have marked an important phase in the Saxon advance, but it cannot be brought into the general history of the time until a satisfactory identification of 'Beandun' has been made.

that the West Saxons pursued the Britons as far as the Parret does not mean that the victors adopted the river as their political boundary. The place-names of the country beyond the Parret suggest that it had passed into English occupation long before the end of the seventh century, and it is probable that the victory of 658 carried the Saxons at least as far as the hills which form the natural boundary between Somerset and Devon.

The kingdom of Dumnonia, of which the memory survives in the name Devon, was an ancient and still important British power. In the sixth century one of its rulers had attracted the unfavourable notice of Gildas, and at the end of the seventh Aldhelm, the most learned of West Saxon abbots, was at great pains to bring the king and clergy of Dumnonia to a right opinion on the question of the date on which Easter should be celebrated.[1] The kingdom was still in existence as late as 710, when Geraint, Aldhelm's correspondent, its last recorded king, is known to have been attacked by the kings of Wessex and Sussex in combination. On the other hand, the West Saxons were already in possession of at least the eastern portion of the kingdom twenty years before this date. Exeter had come into their hands before the last decade of the seventh century; for according to the oldest life of St. Boniface a monastery under an English abbot existed in the city at a date which cannot be later than 690.[2] Whatever its circumstances, it is at least clear that the Saxon conquest of Devon was followed by an extensive movement of population westward from regions already settled. The place-names of Devon are essentially English, varied in character, and pointing to a rapid occupation of new territory both by peasant communities and by aristocrats with their followers. Although Celtic place-names survived the conquest in considerable numbers, they remain as exceptions, distributed over the county in a way which shows that the English settlement was equally thorough in its eastern and western portions. And in the centre of the county even the local names of Dartmoor are mainly English.

In the eighth and ninth centuries these lands of later acquisi-

---

[1] The letter which he wrote for this purpose is addressed 'Domino gloriosissimo occidentalis regni sceptra gubernanti . . . Geruntio regi, simulque cunctis Dei sacerdotibus per Domnoniam conversantibus'. *Aldhelmi Opera*, ed. R. Ehwald (M.G.H.), pp. 480–1.

[2] *Monumenta Moguntina*, p. 433.

tion were clearly distinguished from the ancient Wessex of Berkshire, Hampshire, and Wiltshire. In 705 they were formed into a separate diocese with its bishop's seat at Sherborne. Aldhelm, its first bishop, died in 709. When recording his death the oldest manuscript of the *Chronicle* states that he was bishop 'to the west of the wood'; the manuscript which is next in date calls him bishop 'to the west of Selwood'; and Æthelweard, the first translator of the *Chronicle*, states that his diocese was commonly known as Selwoodshire.[1] Selwood appears again as a boundary in the ninth century; a great English army levied in 893 is said to have included men 'from every fortress east of the Parret, both east and west of Selwood'. All that is now left of Selwood is a narrow stretch of wooded country along the border of Somerset and Wiltshire, to the east of Frome and Wincanton; but the existence of much medieval woodland towards the south-east suggests that in the eighth century there was little open country between Selwood proper and the forests of southern Hampshire. To the Welsh of the ninth century Selwood was known as Coit Maur—the great wood.[2] Throughout the eighth century the real strength of the West Saxon kingdom lay in the country beyond this barrier. Berkshire, Wiltshire, and northern Somerset were repeatedly invaded from the north, and the West Saxons were never secure in the occupation of their lands beyond the Thames. Southern Hampshire was a land of Jutish settlement; and the distinction between Jutes and Saxons, noted by the Northumbrian Bede, was certainly not forgotten by the men of the Meon and Itchen valleys. Wessex between Selwood and the Tamar was a wide and varied country, lying off the most obvious lines of invasion, and including no discernible centres of alien population, such as the Jutes of Hampshire and the Britons of southern Northumbria. The later kings of Wessex possessed a large demesne in this country, and the branch of the royal house from which they were descended was established there long before the end of the seventh century. The oldest West Saxon charter of which a good text has survived records a grant of land for religious purposes at Fontmell in Dorset by Cenred, father of King Ine and of Ingeld, King Alfred's ancestor.[3] In the ninth century it

---

[1] *The Chronicle of Æthelweard*, ed. Campbell, p. 21.
[2] *Asser's Life of King Alfred*, ed. Stevenson, p. 45.
[3] *C.S.* 107.

was in Wessex beyond Selwood that Alfred gathered forces for his great offensive against the Danes, and it was there that the Alfredian chronicle probably came into being.[1]

It is hard to disentangle the genealogical relationships which connected the various West Saxon kings of the seventh century. For the first half of that century Wessex was one of the least important of English kingdoms. Bede knew little of its history, and although the *Chronicle* gives what purports to be the complete succession of its kings, the pedigrees which it assigns to different members of the royal house are often inconsistent with each other. The history of the kingdom is further complicated by the fact that in the seventh century the royal title could be borne by two or more persons at the same time. Bede records that in 626 Cwichelm, 'king of the West Saxons', plotted the murder of Edwin, king of Northumbria, but there is no doubt that Cynegils, Cwichelm's father, was head of the West Saxon royal family in that year. There may be a genuine tradition behind the statement in a late version of the *Chronicle* that Edwin killed five kings in the invasion of Wessex by which he avenged this plot.[2] It is often uncertain whether the appearance of two simultaneous kings in Wessex points to an actual division of the kingdom, or to a custom which gave the name of king to all active members of the royal house. On the other hand, it seems certain that throughout this period one member of the family was always regarded as overlord of the whole kingdom, and that such lesser lordships as existed in Wessex all arose from his grant. One definite example of such a gift is recorded by the *Chronicle* under the year 648, when King Cenwalh gave 'three thousands' of land by Ashdown—the line of the Berkshire Downs—to Cuthred his kinsman. This archaic description of the land tells nothing definite as to its extent,[3] but a comparison with other passages in which land is measured in 'thousands' shows that it represented a province rather than a mere estate. In the next generation there is definite evidence that such provinces existed. Shortly after 680 Somerset was subject to a

[1] F. M. Stenton 'The South-Western element in the Old English Chronicle' *C.P.*, pp. 106–15.

[2] *Chronicle*, MS. E. The entry was probably inserted into the text of the *Chronicle* in Northumbria at some date not much later than the early part of the tenth century. For such additions see above, p. 32, n. 2.

[3] On the method of reckoning by 'thousands' see Stevenson, *Asser's Life of King Alfred*, pp. 154–5.

certain Baldred who is called *patricius* by Aldhelm[1] but, if the text of a somewhat questionable charter can be trusted, gave land to Glastonbury as a king.[2] The earliest historians of Abingdon abbey attributed the foundation of that house to a 'king of the West Saxons' named Cissa, and place him in the late seventh century.[3] The antecedents of Baldred and Cissa are unknown; but they enter into history in a way which shows that the unity of the West Saxon kingdom was only superficial in their time.

In West Saxon tradition two kings in succession stand out as overlords of the whole people in the central decades of the seventh century. Cynegils, the first of them, was believed to have reigned from 611 until 643. Little is known of him beyond his acceptance of Christianity in 635, but it was probably in his time that the lands along the lower Severn which Ceawlin had conquered passed from West Saxon under Mercian lordship. The enmity between the West Saxon and Mercian royal houses, thus foreshadowed, became more definite in the next generation. It was stimulated by a personal quarrel of a king familiar in Germanic legend. Cenwalh the son of Cynegils, who had married and then repudiated one of Penda's sisters, was driven from his kingdom by Penda and compelled to live among the East Angles for three years. Wulfhere, Penda's son, made large encroachments on Cenwalh's territory. In the last years of his reign, Wulfhere was in firm occupation of the district, once West Saxon, which lies at the northern foot of the Chilterns.[4] He had previously conquered and given to Æthelwalh king of Sussex the Isle of Wight and at least the eastern portion of the opposite mainland.[5] It is clear that Cenwalh was never the equal of his formidable Mercian contemporaries, but he was among the most important of the lesser kings of his time, and he was known outside his own country. He appears, somewhat unexpectedly, in Northumbrian history as the close friend of

[1] *Aldhelmi Opera*, ed. R. Ehwald (M.G.H.), p. 503.

[2] *C.S.* 61; Ordnance Survey Facsimiles of Anglo-Saxon Manuscripts, II, *Marquis of Bath*, i. It is written in what appears to be an eleventh-century hand, but there are indications that its writer was trying to imitate the script of a more ancient document.

[3] F. M. Stenton, *The Early History of the Abbey of Abingdon*, pp. 9–18.

[4] It was from Thame in Oxfordshire that he issued the charter for Chertsey abbey which is represented by *C.S.* 34.

[5] *H.E.* iv. 13.

Alhfrith son of king Oswiu,[1] and as the helper of Benedict
Biscop, the founder of Wearmouth and Jarrow.[2]

There is a remarkable divergence between Bede and other
authorities about the course of events after Cenwalh's death in
672. According to Bede, the West Saxon kingdom was divided
between a number of under-kings, and remained in that condition for approximately ten years. According to the *Chronicle*,
Cenwalh was succeeded by his widow Seaxburg, who reigned
for one year, and was followed successively by two distant
members of the royal house—Æscwine, who reigned from 674
until 676, and Centwine, whose end is not recorded. The
difference cannot be reconciled, and has sometimes been considered to discredit the authority of the *Chronicle* for the seventh
century. But Aldhelm of Malmesbury, who was contemporary
with Centwine, describes him as a strong king who ruled the
kingdom of Wessex successfully for many years, gave large
endowments to newly-founded churches, and defeated unnamed enemies in three great battles.[3] As the *Chronicle* was
clearly accurate in including Centwine among the kings of all
Wessex, it becomes probable that its statements about Seaxburg
and Æscwine are also derived from a good tradition.

Like his predecessors, Centwine applied himself to the extension of his kingdom towards the south-west, and the statement of the *Chronicle* that in 682 he 'drove the Britons as far as
the sea' probably marks a stage in the English conquest of
Devon. Expansion in this quarter was necessary if the kings of
Wessex were to maintain their dignity and revenue, for the
Mercian hold upon their northern provinces was growing
stronger. Between 675 and 685 a Mercian bishopric was established at Dorchester on Thames, where the first bishops of
Wessex had sat. Its life was short, but its foundation shows that
Mercian authority was recognized for the time being to the
north of the middle Thames. There is some evidence that even
the lands to the south of the river, where the centre of the
West Saxon kingdom had once lain, had passed under Mercian
lordship in this period. In local tradition the name of Æthelred of Mercia is associated with the foundation of Abingdon

[1] Eddi, *Vita Wilfridi* c. 7.
[2] Bede, *Historia Abbatum* c. 4.
[3] *Aldhelmi Opera*, ed. R. Ehwald (M.G.H.), pp. 14, 15. Aldhelm's statement
that Centwine *imperium Saxonum rite regebat* proves that he was the overlord of the
whole West Saxon kingdom.

abbey in a way which suggests that he held authority in the surrounding country in the period following Cenwalh's death.[1] Mercian influence is still more evident in the earliest charters which come from the abbey of Malmesbury. According to these documents, Aldhelm, the virtual founder of that house, received lands at Tetbury in south Gloucestershire and Long Newton in north Wiltshire from Æthelred himself in 681.[2] Four years later he received a large estate at Somerford Keynes, four miles south of Cirencester, from Berhtwald, a nephew of Æthelred, who confirmed the gift.[3] There is no evidence that Centwine himself ever accepted Æthelred as his lord, but he was clearly the lesser of the two kings, and his chief interests probably lay in Wessex beyond Selwood, where he was a generous benefactor to the newly refounded abbey of Glastonbury.[4]

The orientation of West Saxon history was abruptly changed in the next generation. In 685, according to the *Chronicle*, a young member of the royal house named Cædwalla 'began to contend for the kingdom'. His name, which is an anglicized form of the British Cadwallon, points to a British strain in his ancestry, but nothing definite can be said of its origin,[5] and it was in virtue of a male descent from Cerdic that he claimed to be king. His branch of the royal family had never produced a king of all Wessex, but its head had as good a title to that position as Æscwine or Centwine, and Cædwalla had been compelled to live in exile during his predecessor's reign. Like other young exiles of royal birth Cædwalla collected a band of companions and fought for his own hand. He harried Sussex and killed Æthelwalh, its king. But he was driven out by two of the dead king's ealdormen, and he was still a landless adventurer when he began his attempt to secure the West Saxon kingdom.

His reign of three years was a time of incessant war, producing little permanent result, but creating a tradition which materially affected later West Saxon history. Secure in Wessex itself, he seems to have formed the ambition of adding all south-eastern England to his kingdom. He invaded the Isle of Wight

---

[1] F. M. Stenton, *The Early History of the Abbey of Abingdon*, p. 10.

[2] *C.S.* 58, 59.   [3] *C.S.* 65. See also below, p. 151.

[4] J. Armitage Robinson, *Somerset Historical Essays*, pp. 29–30.

[5] In view of the fact that no British names occur in any other branch of the West Saxon royal house, the name is unlikely to be connected with the British associations of the family implied, according to most scholars, by the name of the ancestral Cerdic.

and set himself to exterminate its inhabitants and replace them by settlers from the mainland. The two boys who represented the island dynasty fled into the Jutish country west of the Solent, and were there captured and killed by his orders. He made himself master of Sussex and killed one of the two ealdormen who had driven him from the country after his earlier invasion. His power in Surrey is proved by a charter through which he devoted Farnham and the surrounding country to religious uses.[1] In Kent, which he invaded in 686, he secured at least a partial recognition as king. There is evidence that he founded a monastery at Hoo between the Thames and Medway estuaries. But in 687 the Kentishmen burned Mul his brother with twelve companions, and their own royal line was restored soon afterwards. Local loyalties were as yet too strong to allow a single dynasty to hold so many ancient kingdoms, and of all this territory the Isle of Wight alone remained permanently to Cædwalla's successors. But his career indicated the direction in which the West Saxon kingdom was ultimately to be enlarged.

Throughout these years, Cædwalla, although an associate and patron of churchmen, had never received baptism. It seems clear that his delay was due to the simple reverence in which he held the Christian mysteries[2]—Bede states that he wished for the singular honour of baptism at Rome itself, and for an early death thereafter. He was still a young man, but he had led a life of incessant violence; he had been severely wounded during his harrying of the Isle of Wight, and he was plainly conscious of approaching death. He left England, probably in the summer of 688, and can be traced on his way to Rome at Samer near Calais where he gave money for the building of a church,[3] and at the court of Cunipert, king of the Lombards.[4] On Easter day 689 he was baptized at Rome in the presence of the pope, who received him from the font and gave him the baptismal name of Peter. Ten days later he died,

---

[1] C.S. 72.

[2] Cædwalla's postponement of baptism does not imply that he had previously been in any hesitation between heathen and Christian beliefs, and gives no ground for describing him as a heathen. It is an illustration of the custom which in the seventh century still allowed an individual, unbaptized in infancy, to decide the circumstances of his formal admission into the church.

[3] [Vita sancti Vulmari, Acta Sanctorum, July, v, p. 86.]

[4] [Pauli Historia Langobardorum, vi. 15 (M.G.H. ss. rer. Langobardam, p. 169).]

still wearing the white clothes of the newly baptized, and the archbishop of Milan wrote an epitaph for him,[1] describing in verse the position which he had abandoned for religion and the circumstances of his baptism, and recording in prose his burial in the fourth consulate of the Emperor Justinian II and the second year of Pope Sergius.

Ine, his successor, was the most important king of Wessex between Ceawlin and Egbert, but the course of events in his reign is remarkably obscure. The *Chronicle* seems to be a contemporary authority for this period; but most of the annals of which it consists stand in isolation and refer to persons and events otherwise unknown. Under 715, for example, it records a battle at Wodnesbeorg[2] above the Vale of Pewsey between Ine and Ceolred, king of the Mercians, but gives no indication of its result, and under 722 it inserts the remarkable but by no means luminous statement that Queen Æthelburg 'destroyed Taunton, which King Ine had formerly built'. There is a real danger of treating as fact the fiction with which medieval writers embroidered statements like these, and thus giving to Ine's history a colour and substance for which there is no ancient authority.

But even without passing outside the range of contemporary materials it is clear that Ine was a statesman with ideas beyond the grasp of any of his predecessors. If not the originator, he was the effective supporter of the process which in his day was creating an organized church in Wessex out of a number of isolated monasteries and mission stations. He founded the see of Sherborne for the better government of the churches west of Selwood. The first West Saxon synods of which there is definite evidence belong to his reign, and the oldest record of such a body which has survived shows that it met by his advice and under his presidency.[3] The same quality is shown in the code of West Saxon law which has carried Ine's name into the general history of England. For its date it is a lengthy document, covering a wide range of human relationships, entering

[1] The epitaph is an important piece of evidence for the cultivation of Latin verse in late seventh-century Italy, F. J. E. Raby, *History of Secular Latin Poetry in the Middle Ages*, i. 159.

[2] For this site see above, p. 30.

[3] Willibald, *Vita Sancti Bonifatii*, ed. Jaffé, *Monumenta Moguntina*, p. 439: 'Regnante Ine Westsaxonum rege subitanea quaedam incuberat . . . necessitas et statim synodale a primatibus aecclesiarum cum consilio predicti regis servorum Dei factum est concilium.' A little later, the king is represented as addressing the synod.

much more fully than any other early code into the details of the agrarian system on which society rested, and marked by a definite purpose of advancing Christianity.[1] It is not a tariff of offences, but the result of a serious attempt to bring together a body of rules governing the more complicated of the questions with which the king and his officers might have to deal. It is the work of a responsible statesman, capable of bringing his clergy and nobles into deliberation on the blending of ancient custom and new enactment in an elaborate body of law. It stands for a new conception of kingship, destined in time to replace the simple motives which had satisfied the men of an earlier age. There is historical propriety in the fact that Ine's laws were copied out by King Alfred as an appendix to the great code with which the continuity of English legislation begins.

The character of Ine's reign is made more remarkable by the insecurity of his position. The circumstances of his accession were anomalous. Cenred, his father, was still alive, and, indeed, appears as one of his chief advisers in the prologue to his laws, written in or shortly before 694. Primitive Germanic custom may well have allowed a son to secure the kingship of his people during the lifetime of an unambitious father, but there is no English parallel to the case of Ine and Cenred. Whatever its explanation, it illustrates the fact that kingship in Wessex was a personal, not an hereditary, dignity. Each of the kings who had followed Cenwalh had belonged to a different branch of the royal house, and supremacy in Wessex was clearly open to any representative of any line which could claim descent from Cerdic. Throughout his reign Ine was thrown into difficult relations with other kings by the activities of possible rivals. In 705 the reception of West Saxon exiles by the king of Essex caused serious trouble. In 721 Ine killed a certain Cynewulf whose name suggests descent from the West Saxon royal house. In the following year the flight of an exile named Ealdberht into Surrey and Sussex caused Ine to invade the latter kingdom, and in 725 he killed Ealdberht in the course of a second invasion. Even at the end of Ine's reign there was clearly no obvious successor to his position. In 726 he resigned his power and left

---

[1] Shown, in particular, by the assignment of more than ordinary value to the oath of a communicant. Wihtred of Kent was legislating in the same spirit at the same time.

England in order to die at Rome. Bede, recording his departure, says vaguely that he 'commended his kingdom to younger men', and it ultimately passed to a certain Æthelheard, whose connection with the royal family is quite uncertain.

Despite the existence of enemies of his own house, Ine remained the strongest king in southern England throughout his reign of thirty-seven years. In the early part of this period he seems to have held a position comparable with that of Cædwalla in the south-east. In 694 he compelled the Kentishmen to pay a great treasure as compensation for the burning of Cædwalla's brother Mul. He was certainly regarded as king in Surrey early in his reign, when he could speak of Eorcenwald of London, whose diocese included that province, as 'my bishop', Bede states that, like Cædwalla, he kept Sussex under subjection for a long time, and as late as 710 he caused Nunna, king of Sussex, who is described as his kinsman, to join him in an attack on Geraint, king of Dumnonia. It was probably in his time that the West Saxons completed the conquest of Devon, for in 722 his people were fighting, though unsuccessfully, on the river Hayle in Cornwall.[1] It is uncertain whether he ever recovered any of the ancient West Saxon possessions to the north of the Thames, but there is no doubt that he held the country immediately to the south of the river. One of the few genuine charters which have come from his time shows him granting land at Streatley on Thames and elsewhere in that neighbourhood for the foundation of a monastery.[2] The land which he acquired in the south-west was never lost, but he was unable to maintain the position which he had held in his earliest years among the other kings of the south. Before the end of the reign, Sussex and Surrey had become hostile countries, where West Saxon exiles might find support. It is to the nature of his rule in Wessex itself that Ine owes his place in history.

[1] [Annales Cambriæ, s.a. 722.]   [2] C.S. 74.

III

ANGLIAN NORTHUMBRIA

A T the end of the sixth century there were two distinct Anglian kingdoms in England beyond the Humber. In the far north a people known as the *Bernice*, after some fifty years of precarious existence on the coast, had recently become a formidable enemy to the older Celtic kingdoms along the Clyde and Forth. Within a generation they were to spread over the whole country between the Forth, the Solway, and the Tees, but in the year 600 they were still fighting on no more than equal terms with the other northern peoples, and their chief stronghold was the rock of Bamburgh. It is probable that the country to the south was already theirs, and it is possible that they had already crossed the water-parting between Tyne and Solway. But there is no archaeological evidence of their presence at this date in either Durham or Cumberland, and although there are place-names which suggest that the Anglian occupation of these regions began in the sixth century, their rarity gives the impression that the settlers of this period can only have been few.

The second Northumbrian kingdom was smaller but more ancient. In the centre and east of what is now Yorkshire a number of Anglian peoples had been settled for more than a century before the year 600. They were known collectively as the *Dere*, and their name, which is derived from the British word *deifr*, 'waters', suggests that their first settlements had been founded along the rivers which converge upon the Humber. Archaeological evidence seems to imply that they had reached York by the year 500, and further north, the place-name Ripon represents a tribal name of archaic character which may well go back to the fifth century. Their expansion towards the west was long delayed by the Britons of Elmet, and it was not until the third decade of the seventh century that they can have begun to settle in the valleys of the Aire or Wharfe. The distribution of their recorded burial-places suggests that in the heathen time they were settled most thickly in the neighbourhood of the Yorkshire Wolds, beneath which, in the plain around Beverley, the name Dera wudu preserved the memory of their common woodlands until the age of Bede.

When these kingdoms first appear, late in the sixth century, each is associated with a dynasty claiming a separate descent from Woden.[1] The Bernician royal house traced its divine ancestry through Bældæg, the son of Woden, to whom the West Saxon kings also ascribed their origin. The coincidence is interesting, even if it is only due to the deliberate invention of a poet in the service of some West Saxon or Bernician king. The Deiran royal pedigree runs up to Woden through names which do not enter into other genealogies. The two families were clearly of equal ancestry, and much of early Northumbrian history turns on their rivalry. But except for the sixteen years between 616 and 632, the Bernician house was always the more important. Ælle, the first recorded king of Deira, is only a name, and there was an ancient tradition that on his death in 588, Æthelric of Bernicia acquired his kingdom. There is no doubt that Æthelfrith, Æthelric's son, who reigned in Bernicia from 593 until 616, married Ælle's daughter and reigned in Deira for the latter part of this period. It was the Bernician dynasty which first brought the two Anglian peoples of the north into a single kingdom.

Beyond Ælle, there is not even the vaguest tradition of Deiran history. The origins of the Bernician kingdom are less obscure. Early in the ninth century a British scholar named Nennius brought into one volume a miscellaneous collection of all the materials that he could find for the history of the struggle between his race and its Anglo-Saxon enemies. The analysis of his work has shown that he possessed, among other texts now lost, a life of St. Germanus, which is of more value for folklore than for history, a list of the cities of Britain, and the genealogies of the kings of Bernicia, Deira, East Anglia, Kent, and Mercia. The genealogies are glossed with occasional historical notes, and are followed by what amounts to an outline of northern history in the period between the foundation of the Bernician kingdom in 547 and the fall of Penda, king of Mercia, in 654. It is still uncertain whether the notes and outline were composed by Nennius himself, or taken by him from some older work, but the information which they give seems to include some fragments of

[1] The pedigree of each dynasty is given in the ninth-century set of genealogies printed by Sweet, *The Oldest English Texts*, pp. 169–70.

genuine tradition, and they agree with what may be inferred from other evidence as to the general course of events in the north.

In particular, they agree with the English tradition of the date at which the Bernician kingdom came into being. According to Bede, who was probably following an ancient list of Bernician kings, Ida, the first of the line, began to reign in 547. The arrangement of Nennius' work implies that Dutigern, the British king who opposed Ida, was a contemporary of Maelgwn of Gwynedd, the Maglocunus of Gildas, who died in that year. None of the incidents mentioned by Nennius can be dated by external evidence, but there are no intrinsic discrepancies in his story. In language borrowed from Gildas he states that now the 'citizens' and now the enemy were victorious. He records that in the time of Theodric, Ida's son, the English were besieged in Holy Island for three days and nights, and that four British kings, Rhydderch the lord of Strathclyde among them, made war on Hussa, the fifth of Ida's successors. His narrative gives the impression that for a generation after Ida's time the Angles of Bernicia could do little more than hold their fortified positions on the Northumbrian coast, and it therefore helps to explain the remarkable scarcity of archaeological information about Bernician origins. If in the late sixth century the Bernician leaders could be thrust back and held in Holy Island, it is not surprising that few Anglian burial-grounds of the heathen age have been discovered in the interior of the country.

The continuous history of Northumbria, and indeed of England, begins with the reign of Æthelfrith, son of Æthelric and grandson of Ida, king of Bernicia.[1] His life, like that of his West Saxon contemporary Ceawlin, ended in a disaster. Nevertheless, he was the real founder of the historic Northumbrian

---

[1] For the next 150 years the framework of this history is supplied by the *Historia Ecclesiastica* of Bede. The chronology of the account which follows is based on the convincing argument of R. L. Poole that Bede considered the year to begin in the September before Midwinter—that is at the annual change in the number of the 'Indiction', by which years were commonly reckoned in and before his time (*Studies in Chronology and History*, pp. 38–53). W. Levison (*England and the Continent*, pp. 265–79) has argued that Bede began each new Incarnation year on 25 December. Bede's numerous indications of date cannot be brought into perfect consistency on either system. But the reckoning from September removes all the more serious chronological difficulties raised by his work. Its consequences are sometimes important. The battle of Hatfield, for example, which Bede dates 12 October 633, should be dated, in modern terms, 12 October 632.

kingdom, and he was remembered as the first great leader who had arisen among the northern Angles. To Bede it seemed that no English king had been more successful in winning land for the settlement of his own people, or in bringing British tribes under tribute.

The initiative in this warfare was not always in his hands. The most famous of Old Welsh poems tells the story of a disastrous assault on a place which can reasonably be identified with Catterick by a force of young British warriors sent out by the ruler of the country round Edinburgh.[1] The poem does not mention Æthelfrith, but yields chronological indications which point with sufficient clearness to his time. The poet may well have exaggerated the importance of this episode. But his description of the equipment with which the young men were provided, and of their long training in the lord's household, gives the impression of a British court which in the late sixth century was still a wealthy and aggressive power.

Beyond the northern Britons a small kingdom had been founded in Argyll by settlers from Ireland, early in the fifth century. Their descendants had always kept in touch with their Irish kinsmen, and throughout the sixth century their kings seem to have regarded the king of Ulster as their lord. Under Aedan mac Gabrain, who became their king in 574, they suddenly appear as a formidable people. One of his expeditions harried the Britons settled along the middle Forth, and another is said to have reached the Orkneys. At the turn of the sixth and seventh centuries the advance of the Bernicians brought them within raiding distance of Aedan's country, and in 603 he attacked them. He had been joined by many Gaels from Ireland, and the son of the king of Ulster is said to have fought in his army. But Æthelfrith defeated him at a place in English territory called Degsastan,[2] and thenceforward the Britons of Strathclyde remained the only serious rivals of the Angles of Bernicia for the possession of the Scottish lowlands.

The place which Æthelfrith holds in general history is due

---

[1] The early date and historical value of this poem, the 'Gododdin' of Aneirin, has lately been shown in an edition, with an introduction in Welsh, by I. Williams (Cardiff, 1938). His results are conveniently summarized in two articles in *Antiquity* by K. Jackson (March 1939) and C. A. Gresham (September, 1942).

[2] Generally identified with Dawston in Liddesdale. But an Old English *Degsastan* would normally have become Daystone, and the identification of the site is best left an open question.

less to his northern wars than to an expedition which he made
at a later time towards the south-west. Between 613 and 616 he
attacked and defeated the Britons at Chester. From Welsh and
Irish sources it appears that the British leader, who is not named
by Bede, was Solomon son of Cynan, king of Powys, the region
between the upper Severn and the Dee. Before the battle
Æthelfrith's men, by his orders, slaughtered a host of British
monks who had come from the monastery of Bangor Iscoed to
pray for a British victory. Apart from this massacre, Bede has
little to tell of the battle, and there is nothing to suggest that he
regarded it as in any sense a turning-point in history. To most
modern writers the battle has far greater significance. It is
usually regarded as the event which brought the English to the
shore of the Irish sea, and separated the Britons of Wales from
their compatriots to the north. That the separation had occurred
before Æthelfrith's death is certain, but there is no adequate
reason for regarding it as a result of the battle of Chester. From
the moment when the westward expansion of the Bernicians
first became possible, more than twenty years before that battle,
the valleys of the Tyne and Irthing offered a well-defined line
of advance to the lowlands around Carlisle. There is no direct
evidence as to the date at which the Bernicians reached the
Cumbrian coast. But there are enough ancient place-names in
Cumberland and Lancashire to suggest that Æthelfrith could
have ridden from the Solway to the Mersey through territory
in the occupation of his own people.[1]

Æthelfrith's victory at Chester did not mean that the surrounding country was added to his kingdom. Within three
years, or less, any designs which he may have formed against
the Britons of Powys were ended by his overthrow at the hands
of his English enemies. Towards the end of a long exile, part
of which he had spent with British hosts, Edwin, son of Ælle,
the heir of the Deiran kingdom, took refuge with Rædwald,
king of the East Angles. Æthelfrith demanded that Edwin
should be killed or surrendered, but Rædwald was persuaded by
his wife that a man of honour could not betray his guest, and
in the end resolved to bring him back to his own kingdom.
Rædwald had recently become supreme in England south of the

[1] On the Lancashire evidence see Ekwall, *The Place-Names of Lancashire*, pp. 231–
2. The significance of the ancient Anglian names of Cumberland is indicated by
F. M. Stenton, *C.P.*, pp. 279–80.

Humber, and the war which followed is the first recorded trial of strength between a king of the Northumbrians and an over-lord of the southern English confederation. It was decided in the summer or early autumn of 616 by a battle fought on the southern border of Deira, near the point at which the river Idle is crossed by the Roman road from Lincoln to Doncaster. Æthelfrith, who had been unable to bring all his men together, was defeated and killed, and his sons fled into exile. Edwin was accepted as king in Bernicia as well as Deira, and within a few years he had succeeded Rædwald as overlord of all the English peoples south of the Humber.

Edwin's overlordship marks an important stage in the move-ment of the English peoples towards unity, for it first brought the southern kingdoms into definite association with Northum-bria. He is described by Bede as more powerful than any earlier English king, and although the king of Kent never became his man, he was undoubtedly the head of the greatest confederation which as yet had arisen in England. But it was a confederation of a barbarian type, and its basis was the mere allegiance of individuals. In his position, as in all the recorded incidents of his life, Edwin was a typical king of the Heroic Age. Some vague traditions of Roman custom may have reached him. According to Bede, a standard-bearer rode before him on his longer journeys, and as he passed through the streets he was preceded by a banner of the kind 'which the Romans call *tufa*, and the English, *thuuf*'. He was in touch with the world outside Britain. He married a daughter of Æthelberht of Kent and Bertha of Paris, and the connection thus established with the Merovingian dynasty was recognized at its courts. Neverthe-less, in character and environment he belonged to the world depicted in Old English heroic poetry. Like other heroes, he had travelled far as an exile, and had known his life to depend on the conflict between honour and interest in the mind of a protector. He secured his father's kingdom through the help of a stronger king, and made himself in time the lord of other kings. He moved over the country surrounded by retainers ready to give their lives for him. One of the most famous stories preserved by Bede tells of the devotion of Edwin's thegn, Lilla, who inter-cepted the blow aimed at his lord by a murderer from Wessex. The tale is impressive in Bede's Latin, but it would have been told much better in Old English verse. The last scene in Edwin's

life had the same epic quality, for he fell in battle on the border
of his kingdom, one son fell before him, another son fled to
his father's enemy, and a faithful thegn carried the children
remaining to the royal line into a distant land. The confederation which Edwin founded foreshadowed a kingdom of all
England, but he stands in history as a great king of the age of
national migrations rather than as the predecessor of Offa or
Alfred.

Northumbrian writers of the next century attributed to Edwin
a vague lordship over the whole of Britain, and it is not impossible that, at one time or another, British, Pictish, and Irish
kings may have come to his court. Nothing is known in detail
about his dealings with the northern peoples, and there is no
record of any territory won from them in Edwin's time. But
there is at least the authority of Nennius for the statement that
to the south of his own country he conquered Elmet and expelled 'Certic' its king.[1] The ultimate reduction of this British
outpost was inevitable as soon as the Angles of the north had
spread in force beyond the Pennines, but the immediate cause
of its fall seems to have been a feud between its king and Edwin.
Bede records that Hereric, the son of an unnamed nephew of
Edwin, had been driven into exile by Æthelfrith of Bernicia,
and had died of poison while the guest of a certain Cerdic, king
of the Britons. It is probable that Certic of Elmet was identical
with Hereric's host, and that the conquest of Elmet, which was
the one permanent result of Edwin's wars, was in fact his
revenge for a kinsman's death.

His wars against other British peoples were remembered
more clearly. From a combination of English and Welsh
authorities it appears that in the latter part of his reign he took
possession of the Isle of Man, invaded North Wales, conquered
Anglesey, and besieged Cadwallon king of Gwynedd in Priestholm, off the eastern point of the island. His invasion of
Gwynedd was answered by a British invasion of Northumbria
which showed that the latent strength of the British kingdoms
was much greater than would be gathered from the general
drift of their recent history. In 632 Cadwallon, who had found
an English ally in Penda, as yet merely a warlike noble of the
Mercian royal house, struck across England to the Northumbrian border, where he was met by Edwin at an unknown spot

[1] *Historia Brittonum*, ed. Mommsen, p. 206.

in the region now called Hatfield Chase. Edwin and Osfrith
his son were killed, his army was scattered, and Cadwallon with
Penda's help set himself to a deliberate devastation of all
Northumbria.

The kingdom immediately fell apart into its two fundamental
divisions of Deira and Bernicia. Osric, a cousin of Edwin,
maintained himself as king in Deira until the summer of
633, when Cadwallon destroyed him and his army. Bernicia
reverted to the family of its ancient kings. Eanfrith, son of
Æthelfrith, who first made a bid for the kingdom, was killed
within a year, when he visited Cadwallon to beg for peace. But
in the last weeks of 633 his brother Oswald, at the head of a
small army, defeated and killed Cadwallon near Rowley Burn
in the wild country south of Hexham, and as the deliverer of
the whole Northumbrian people, he was immediately accepted
as king in Deira as well as in Bernicia.

These events changed the course of British as well as English
history. Cadwallon was the only British king of historic times
who overthrew an English dynasty, and the British peoples
never found an equal leader. He was followed in Gwynedd
itself by a king not of royal race, and although his line was
afterwards restored, its later members were insignificant.[1] In
England, Edwin's defeat meant not only the collapse of the confederation which he had founded but the extinction of his branch
of the royal house. Eadfrith, his eldest surviving son, surrendered to Penda, and was killed at his court. Wuscfrea and Yffi,
his infant son and grandson, were sent to his wife's kinsman,
Dagobert I, king of the Franks, but died soon afterwards in
Gaul. There were still men in Northumbria who traced their
descent from the kings before Ælle, but of Edwin's own family
there only remained a daughter named Eanflæd, who ultimately married Oswiu, brother of Oswald, the victor of 633.

More important on a long view than the overthrow of the
house of Edwin was the appearance of a new power in the
midlands. The language in which Bede describes Cadwallon's
enterprise leaves no doubt that his ally Penda, though descended from the royal family of the Mercians, only became their
king after Edwin's defeat in 632.[2] If it had not been for Penda's

---

[1] J. E. Lloyd, *History of Wales*, i. 188–90.

[2] 'Rebellavit . . . Caedwalla rex Brettonum, auxilium praebente illi Penda, viro
strenuissimo de regio genere Merciorum, qui et ipse ex eo tempore gentis eiusdem

resistance, a loosely compacted kingdom of England under Northumbrian rule would probably have been established by the middle of the seventh century. But he was still new to his kingdom when Cadwallon and his army were destroyed in 633, and it was long before he could meet Oswald on equal terms. For the next eight years Oswald ruled over both Deira and Bernicia. Through his mother, who was Ælle's daughter, he was descended from older Deiran kings, and he was himself the head of the Bernician royal house. For most, if not the whole of his reign, he was overlord of all the English kingdoms south of the Humber, and Bede describes him as lord of all the nations and provinces of Britain, whether British, Pictish, Irish, or English. A miracle-story told by Bede[1] shows that Oswald's direct authority in Sussex covered not only his Northumbrian companions but also the native population of the province. His position may have been exaggerated in retrospect, for he was a great Christian king, who had been honoured as a saint for two generations when Bede wrote his history. But there is no need to question Bede's statement of his supremacy within England, and the scarcity of recorded incident between 633 and 641 is really a sign that his overlordship was effective. He married a daughter of Cynegils, king of Wessex, and his one recorded act of authority in the south is his confirmation of the grant of Dorchester on Thames by Cynegils to the first bishop of Wessex.

On 5 August 641 Oswald was defeated and killed by Penda at a place which Bede calls Maserfelth, probably, though not certainly, to be identified with Oswestry in Shropshire. Nothing is recorded of the events which led up to the battle, nor of its incidents beyond the tradition that Oswald was heard to pray for the souls of his army as his enemies closed in on him. His death at heathen hands was followed almost at once by his popular recognition as a saint and martyr, and his cult spread rapidly and far. There is much in his career to justify the instinct which remembered him as a saint rather than a king. As the protector and disciple of the men who established Christian-

---

regno annis xx et ii varia sorte praefuit' (*H.E.* ii. 20). This careful statement clearly outweighs the observation in the *Chronicle* under 626 that Penda had the kingdom for 30 years—presumably from that date—and was 50 years of age when he began to reign. These figures, which in any case are too neat to carry conviction, were challenged effectively on chronological grounds by H. M. Chadwick, *The Origin of the English Nation*, pp. 16-17.

[1] *H.E.* iv. 14.

ity in the north, Oswald left a permanent impression on English history. His political supremacy, like all of its kind, was an artificial creation which ignored the traditions of the different subject peoples, and there were regions where it was long resented. Half a century after his death, when his niece Osthryth, queen of the Mercians, wished to translate his relics into the monastery of Bardney in Lindsey, its inmates refused to receive them, 'because, although they knew him to have been a saint, they pursued him, dead, with ancient enmities, as one sprung from another province who had taken rule over them'. As Bede tells the story,[1] they were brought to accept him at last by the appearance of a column of light which shone over Lindsey from the cart where his relics lay. But the survival of resentments so strong that they could only be appeased supernaturally helps to explain the fact that the supremacy of Oswald, like that of Edwin before him, could be destroyed in a single battle.

Oswald's fall left Penda the most formidable king in England. There is no evidence that he ever became, or even tried to become, the lord of all the other kings of southern England. But none of them can have been his equal in reputation, and in many battles none of them ever defeated him. In the north each of the two ancient divisions of the Northumbrian people chose its own king on Oswald's death. Bernicia passed to Oswiu, Oswald's brother, and Deira, to Oswine, son of the ephemeral king Osric whom Cadwallon had killed in 633. In 651 Oswiu, hoping to reunite the kingdoms, invaded Deira, compelled Oswine to take to flight, and brought about his death. But the Deirans then chose for their king a son of Oswald, named Æthelwald, who placed himself under Penda's protection, and for the next three years Deira was, in effect, a Mercian province. Of Oswiu's own sons, the elder was married to a daughter of Penda, and the younger was a hostage at Penda's court. Oswiu himself was always regarded by Penda as a personal enemy, and in 654, after at least two previous raids over Bernicia, Penda determined to make an end of him.

Bede states that Penda had thirty 'legions' with him on this expedition, and mentions incidentally that Æthelhere, king of the East Angles, was present in the army. Nennius, who preserved a confused tradition of the war, brings out the important

[1] *H.E.* iii. 11.

fact that Penda was accompanied by many British princes—
Cadafael of Gwynedd among them. According to Bede, Oswiu,
reduced to the last extremity, tried to buy peace from Penda
with a great treasure, which was refused. According to Nennius, Oswiu, who was besieged in a fortress called Iudeu,
surrendered all the treasures in that place to Penda, who then
distributed them among his British allies. These statements
cannot be reconciled; and all that is certain about the campaign
is the fact that Oswiu and his army, after coming near to destruction, won one of the decisive battles of Anglo-Saxon history.
It was fought by an unknown stream called Winwæd, somewhere in the country round Leeds. On the eve of the battle,
Oswiu, in despair at the thought of the odds against him,
promised to devote his infant daughter to God's service, and to
assign twelve estates to religious uses if he obtained victory. In
the event, Æthelwald of Deira, who had been the invader's
guide, kept aloof from the battle; Penda and Æthelhere of East
Anglia were killed, and Cadafael of Gwynedd escaped ignominiously to his own land.[1]

Through this victory Oswiu became the overlord, not only
of the Mercians, but of all the southern English peoples. There
is no definite evidence of his authority in any of the smaller
kingdoms; but Sigeberht, king of Essex, is known to have been
his friend, the East Angles were kingless for the moment, and
Cenwalh of Wessex, whom Penda had once driven into exile,[2]
is unlikely to have resisted the king who had destroyed his own
enemy. For a short time Mercia itself was dismembered. The
Mercian peoples south of the Trent were given to Penda's son,
Peada, king of the Middle Angles, who had married Oswiu's
daughter. Mercia north of the Trent seems to have been annexed outright to Northumbria, and on the murder of Peada
in the spring of 656, his whole kingdom passed to Oswiu and
was ruled by his officers. For more than a year Mercia and
Middle Anglia formed a province of the Northumbrian kingdom, but towards the end of 657 three Mercian ealdormen
produced a son of Penda named Wulfhere, whom they had kept
in hiding since his father's death, and proclaimed him king of
the Mercians. Their revolt destroyed Oswiu's overlordship in

---

[1] [See J. O. Prestwich, 'King Æthelhere and the battle of the Winwæd', *E.H.R.*
lxxxiii (1968), pp. 89–95.]

[2] Above, p. 67.

southern England. For the rest of his reign, which ended in 670, he appears as a great Northumbrian king, interested in the spread of Christianity throughout England, and willing to co-operate with southern kings for the good of the church, but looking towards the north for the enlargement of his kingdom.

In the meantime, by slow degrees, Wulfhere son of Penda had made himself supreme in southern England. He is not included in Bede's list of the southern overlords, but there can be no doubt as to the range of his power. By 665 the kings of Essex had become his subjects, and his kingdom had been extended to the middle Thames. By 670, when Oswiu died, it is probable that the whole of southern England was under Wulfhere's lord-ship, for in 674[1] he invaded Northumbria at the head of an army drawn from all the southern English peoples.[2] He was defeated by Ecgfrith, Oswiu's son, and the confederation which he had formed was dissolved. Lindsey was detached from the Mercian complex of dependent kingdoms and annexed to Northumbria. It is possible that for a short time Ecgfrith, like each of his three predecessors, was recognized as overlord in Mercia itself. But his supremacy, if ever admitted, left no impression on Mercian history. In 678 he was defeated in a battle near the Trent by Æthelred, Wulfhere's brother, and Lindsey became once more a Mercian province. The battle of the Trent proved to be one of the decisive incidents in early English history, for Ecgfrith never again attempted to conquer any part of southern England, and his successors were kept from adventures in the south by new dangers which threatened their northern border.

In the sixth century the Britons of Strathclyde had been the most formidable of the northern peoples with whom the English came into contact. By the reign of Ecgfrith their territory had been reduced within narrow limits. On the East the English possessed the whole southern coastline of the Firth of Forth. Dunbar was the head-quarters of a Northumbrian ealdorman, and the lands between the Lammermoors and the Esk belonged to an English monastery at Tyninghame. A large Anglo-Irish community had been established at Melrose for a generation,

---

[1] [On this date see P. Hunter Blair, 'The *Moore Memoranda* on Northumbrian History', *The Early Cultures of North-West Europe*, ed. Sir Cyril Fox and Bruce Dickins, pp. 254–5.]

[2] Eddi, *Vita Wilfridi*, c. xx.

and there is record of St. Cuthbert's preaching in Teviotdale. The central hills of southern Scotland may well have been a debatable land. The Britons were certainly the masters of lower Clydesdale, and it is possible that towards the south they still possessed Kyle and the other districts which now form Ayrshire. On the other hand, it is improbable that Galloway or any part of the Solway coast was in their hands. Within fifty years of Ecgfrith's death, Whithorn, the most famous church of Galloway, had become the seat of an English bishopric, and one of the greatest of Northumbrian crosses had been erected at Ruthwell near Dumfries. Throughout this period the Northumbrian kings had been on the defensive against enemies in the north, and none of them can have been free to engage in wars of conquest with the Britons of the west. It is probable that when Ecgfrith died, and indeed for a generation before his time, the Britons beyond the Solway were confined to the territory which could be protected by short expeditions from their chief fortress, the rock of Dumbarton, the ancient Alcluith.

The Irish of Argyll had never found another chief like Aedan. In the seventh century they were generally subject to one or other of the stronger northern peoples, and their importance in the history of the time rests on their possession of the sanctuary of Iona. Apart from Strathclyde and Galloway, where traditions of Kentigern and Ninian were preserved, the whole of northern Britain was subject ecclesiastically to this great church. It was the foundation of Columba, who had evangelized the northern Picts in the sixth century. Its monks had sheltered Oswald while Edwin was king in Northumbria; he had been baptized while among them, and Christianity had been restored in his kingdom by members of their community. Through Iona and its dependent churches some knowledge of affairs in northern Britain reached Ireland, so that Irish annals form a main source of information about the history of the Picts, and preserve a broken outline of the course of events in Northumbria. But to Bede and the other English writers of his time no king of Argyll except Aedan seemed to play a part that was worth recording.

Already by the time of Edwin the expansion of Anglian territory had made the Bernicians the neighbours of the Picts. In the age of Bede the Firth of Forth separated the races; but Bede's generation had seen a great retrocession of English territory, and it would be hard to draw the English boundary as it existed at the middle of the seventh century. The internal history of the Pictish nation is utterly obscure. In the sixth century it had been divided into two races separated by the central Highlands,[1] and the distinction was still remembered in the age of Bede.[2] But the Picts of the seventh century normally appear as a single people; and there is some evidence that in the second half of this period a single king was recognized by all the Picts between the English border and Caithness. In any case, there is no doubt that the Picts with whom the English came into contact formed a definite kingdom, and not a mere congeries of tribes. The succession to this kingdom was governed by ancient customs which attracted the curiosity of Bede, and from time to time created singular relationships between the royal family and the kings of other peoples. According to Bede the Picts were accustomed to choose a king from the female rather than the male line of the royal stock when the succession to the kingdom was in doubt.[3] At different periods in the seventh century the Picts were ruled by British, English, and, apparently, by Irish kings. For a short time at the middle of the century Talorcan, son of Eanfrith, son of Æthelfrith of Bernicia, was their king. He was followed by two kings whose names suggest an Irish origin, and in 672 the kingdom passed to Bruide mac Beli, the son of a king of Strathclyde, who ruled for twenty-one years and made himself the strongest power in the north.[4]

There can be no doubt that Oswiu and Ecgfrith annexed much Pictish territory to the Northumbrian kingdom, and that Ecgfrith in his later years was recognized as overlord by the Irish of Argyll and the Britons of Strathclyde. In describing the Celtic reaction in the north which followed Ecgfrith's death in 685, Bede carefully distinguishes between the Irish and Britons, who had been Ecgfrith's subjects, and the Picts on whose land he had been encroaching. 'The Picts', he says, 'regained their land which the English had held; and the Irish who were in Britain, and part of the Britons, regained their liberty.' There

---

[1] There is no adequate evidence for the view that Galloway was a Pictish country. The statement in the anonymous life of St. Cuthbert (ed. B. Colgrave, p. 82) that the saint journeyed from Melrose *ad terram Pictorum ubi dicitur Niuduera regio* has often been taken to imply the existence of Pictish communities in the country along the Dumfriesshire river Nith. But the context, which shows that Cuthbert came to the *Niuduera regio* by sea, makes the identification impossible.

[2] *H.E.* iii. 4.   [3] *H.E.* i. 1.

[4] See *The Problem of the Picts*, ed. F. T. Wainwright, Nelson (1955).

is no evidence as to the nature of Ecgfrith's rule over the Irish and Britons, but in 684 he sent an army to Ireland which devastated part of the kingdom of Meath. It is possible that this expedition was intended to intimidate tribes which might have supported the Irish of northern Britain. To the Picts Ecgfrith appeared as an open and dangerous enemy. Early in his reign, he and a Northumbrian ealdorman named Beornhæth invaded their territory and suppressed what seems to have been a rising of the whole Pictish nation. In 685, against his friends' advice, he led a raiding army far into the land of the Picts. Like many later invaders of Scotland, he was enticed into dangerous country by an enemy which continually gave ground to him. On 20 May 685 he and his army perished near Forfar, at a place which Irish and English writers respectively call Duin Nechtain and Nechtanesmere.[1]

This disaster marks the end of the English ascendancy in northern Britain. King Bruide, the victor of Nechtanesmere, died in 693, but the advantage in the northern war remained with his people. The Northumbrian border was in serious danger through the reign of Aldfrith, Ecgfrith's brother and successor. The first sign of an English revival came in 711, when a Northumbrian ealdorman named Beorhtfrith defeated a Pictish army in the central plain of Scotland near the middle Forth. It is probable that this event, which is recorded by Irish, Northumbrian, and West Saxon authorities, prevented any further expansion of the Picts towards the south. In 731, when Bede ended his *History*, there was peace between Picts and Angles, and, apparently, an understanding about the line of their common boundary.

The defence of Northumbria after the battle of Nechtanesmere had rested on Aldfrith, son of Oswiu, its king, who reigned from 685 until 704. On his work as ruler Bede passed the judgement that he re-established his ruined kingdom nobly, though within boundaries narrower than before.[2] Whatever may have been the condition of his border provinces, he gave security to the ancient churches of Northumbria. The oldest piece of English historical writing now extant, an anonymous life of St. Cuthbert, was written at Lindisfarne in his time, and refers to him as 'Aldfrith, who now reigns peacefully'.[3] His

---

[1] *The Problem of the Picts*, ed F. T. Wainwright, Nelson (1955).
[2] *H.E.* iv. 24.   [3] *Two Lives of Saint Cuthbert*, ed. B. Colgrave, p. 104.

defence of his kingdom, which was his elementary duty, proved
to be a signal service to European culture. The learning and
scholarship of the Northumbrian monasteries in the age of
Bede were made possible by the work of Aldfrith in the critical
years following the battle of Nechtanesmere. In the cultivation
of letters and learning which preceded the supreme Northumbrian achievement, the king himself took part. Throughout his
early life it must have seemed highly improbable that he would
ever succeed to the kingdom. His birth was illegitimate, and he
was educated for the priesthood. It would seem that he was
sent to school in Wessex; for Aldhelm, abbot of Malmesbury,
who had been brought up in that house, afterwards wrote to
him in terms implying their early intimacy.[1] Malmesbury was
then a centre of Irish influence; and it is probable that Aldfrith
there acquired the scholarship of Irish pattern which remained
to him throughout his life. Before his accession he spent many
years in study among the Irish themselves; he was living at
Iona in the year before his brother's death, and he was long
remembered in Ireland as a writer of Irish verse. His learning
was commemorated by writers as dissimilar in outlook as Bede,
Eddi, St. Wilfrid's biographer, and Alcuin, the intimate of
Charlemagne. Alcuin describes him as *rex simul et magister*, and
there is no doubt that his interest in learning survived the
troubles in which his reign began. It was after his accession
that Aldhelm of Malmesbury, in remembrance of early friendship, dedicated to him the work on Latin metres which is known
as the epistle to Acircius. He caused Adamnan's book on the
Holy Places to be copied for use in Northumbria, and gave
a considerable estate to the monastery of Wearmouth for a
treatise on cosmography which the founder of that house had
bought at Rome. He was undoubtedly one of the most learned
men in his own kingdom, and it is probable that his influence on
the development of Northumbrian learning was much greater
than appears on the surface of history. He is the most interesting
member of the remarkable dynasty to which he belonged, and
he stands beside Alfred of Wessex among the few Old English
kings who combined skill in warfare with desire for knowledge.

After his death the character of Northumbrian history begins
to change. The Bernician royal family survived until at least
the beginning of the ninth century, and until 759 every king

[1] *Aldhelmi Opera*, ed. R. Ehwald (M.G.H.), pp. 61–2.

who obtained general recognition in Northumbria belonged to one or other of its many lines. But thenceforward the succession of kings belonging to the ancient dynasty was repeatedly broken by kings of whose descent nothing is known. Pretenders of this type had begun to appear early in the century. Aldfrith himself left at least two sons, of whom the eldest was of sufficient age to rule, but a noble unconnected with the royal house was able to maintain himself as king for a few months in 705. Incidents like this became more frequent as time went on, and their effect on the monarchy was disastrous. For a hundred years after the death of Aldfrith no Northumbrian king was ever secure among his own people.

But the political confusion of Northumbria did not destroy Northumbrian civilization. The life of the northern schools was unaffected by the rise and fall of kings. It was in the second half of the eighth century that the Northumbrian learning of an earlier age came to full influence abroad. Alcuin, the scholar who was the chief agent in its transmission, had made the school of York illustrious before he passed, in 782, from England to the court of Charlemagne. It is more difficult to estimate the condition of lay society. It is clear that the traditional loyalty of the retainer towards his chief was weakening, and that evil men could seize and for a time retain the crown. Nevertheless, the age could show both virtuous kings and loyal retainers. King Alhred, who reigned from 765 until 774, did all that was in his power to help the English mission in Germany. Ælfwald, 'the just and pious king', who reigned from 779 until 788, upheld the standards of a Christian life among his people. The spirit of the primitive retainer was still alive in Torhtmund, the minister of King Æthelred, who slew the king's murderer and was introduced by Alcuin to Charlemagne as 'King Æthelred's faithful servant, a brave man of proved loyalty, who has valiantly avenged his lord's blood'.[1] It is a superficial view which dismisses the Northumbrian history of this period as a mere record of treason and murder.

The Northumbrian revolutions of the eighth century would have been impossible if any single branch of the royal house had been regarded as indefeasibly entitled to the kingship. But in every English kingdom the mere fact of royal descent gave a title to rule, and in Northumbria the configuration of the country

[1] *Monumenta Alcuiniana*, ed. Jaffé, p. 619.

made rebellion easy. Deira, or at least the original Deira of the eastern Wolds and the central plain, is in structure a detached fragment of southern England. But the great mass of the Pennines and the central hills of southern Scotland which are its continuation gave a distinctive character to the life of western Deira and of all Bernicia. Even in the habitable country between the mountains and the eastern or the western sea, the poverty of the soil under ancient methods of cultivation meant that a vast estate was necessary for the support of a nobleman's rank. It was therefore possible for a few disaffected lords to withdraw a wide region from the king's obedience, and the difficulties of Northumbrian travel were so great that a royal army could not easily be concentrated for their suppression. Between the east and west of the kingdom, the Pennines formed a barrier, passable at many points, but everywhere hindering the movement of large masses of men. For forty years after the destruction of the Northumbrian kingdom by the Danes, an English aristocracy was able to maintain itself in independence beyond the mountains.[1] There was no part of England where the physical obstacles to government were so formidable as in Northumbria, and nowhere else was it so difficult for a king to be forewarned against the movements of his enemies.

Osred son of Aldfrith, who began to reign in 705 at the age of eight, was regarded by his illustrious contemporary St. Boniface as a worthless youth who led an evil life and violated the ancient privileges of the Northumbrian church.[2] Bede, who had welcomed him to the throne as a new Josiah, mature in spirit though not in years,[3] is austerely silent about his later conduct, and records his murder in 716 without any comment. He stands out most clearly in a Northumbrian poem of the early ninth century,[4] where he appears as a wild and irreligious young king, who regarded the nobles of his country as his enemies, killed many of them, and compelled others to take refuge in monasteries. The three kings who followed him were milder, and at least one of them was overweighted by his duties. The dedicatory sentences of Bede's *Ecclesiastical History* have given immortality to the obscure king Ceolwulf, who reigned from 729 until 737. But the *Historia Ecclesiastica* ends on a note of

---

[1] Below, p. 320.   [2] *S. Bonifatii et Lulli Epistolae*, ed. Tangl, pp. 152–3.
[3] *Bedas metrische Vita Sancti Cuthberti*, ed. Jaager, p. 100.
[4] Æthelwulf, *De Abbatibus* [ed. A. Campbell, pp. 4–7].

anxiety; Bede, who honoured the king for his religion and his interest in the past, clearly mistrusted his political capacity, and may well have foreseen the retirement from the world with which his reign ended.

The decay of the kingdom, which Bede foresaw, was arrested by Eadberht, Ceolwulf's successor, who was the last Northumbrian king to lead effective expeditions beyond the northern border. An early campaign against the Picts led to no result worth record; apparently because Æthelbald, king of Mercia, had invaded Northumbria in Eadberht's absence. But in 750 Eadberht conquered Kyle and other regions from the Britons of Strathclyde, and in 756, in alliance with the king of the Picts, he attacked Alcluith, the British capital, and imposed terms on its defenders. In his own country a rising on behalf of Offa son of Aldfrith seems to have been easily suppressed; Offa was taken from the church at Lindisfarne half dead with hunger, and the bishop of that see was imprisoned at Bamburgh. Throughout the whole of Eadberht's reign his brother Egbert was archbishop of York, and to Alcuin, writing with local knowledge, the years of their joint rule seemed in retrospect a golden age. In 758, when Eadberht withdrew from affairs to live as a clerk in his brother's minster, the Northumbrian kingdom was stronger and its boundaries were wider than at any time since the disaster of Nechtanesmere.

Within a year it was thrown into confusion by the first of a new series of revolutions. In the summer of 758 Oswulf, Eadberht's son, was killed by his own retainers, and before the end of 759 a noble named Æthelwald and surnamed Moll became king. There is no evidence to connect him with the royal family, and the statement of a Northumbrian annalist that he was 'chosen king by his own people' suggests that he was carried into the kingship by the local feeling of some province in which he had been the leading magnate.[1] After six years allegiance was withdrawn from him in favour of a descendant of Ida named Alhred. Unlike the kings immediately before him, he plays a small but distinctive part in the general history of his time. The mission of St. Willehad, which led to the foundation

---

[1] *a sua plebe electus* (*Continuatio Bedae*, ed. Plummer, *Bedae Opera Historica*, ii. p. 363). The phrase shows that Æthelwald was raised to the throne by a popular movement. The word *plebs* was often used as a Latin synonym for the Old English *folc*.

of the archbishopric of Bremen, was authorized by an assembly
of Northumbrian bishops and clergy summoned by Alhred,[1]
and a letter has survived in which he commends his kinsmen
and friends to the prayers of Lull, archbishop of Mainz, and
asks him to assist the messengers whom he has sent to Charles,
king of the Franks.[2] But in 774 he was deprived of his kingdom
by what seems to have been a formal act of his nobles and household,[3] and after a flight to Bamburgh he disappeared into the
land of the Picts.

On his deposition Æthelred, son of Æthelwald Moll, was
received as king against the will of many Northumbrian nobles.
During the next five years four of his enemies are known to have
been betrayed into the hands of his friends and killed by his
orders. But in 779 he was expelled from the kingdom by a
grandson of Eadberht named Ælfwald, who reigned until 788.
Ælfwald was remembered as a 'just and pious king', and his
death, which was the result of a private conspiracy, was followed
by a grievous degeneration of morals in the north.[4] He was the
last Northumbrian king for whom any ancient writer expressed
admiration. His successor, Osred son of Alhred, was driven
from the country within a year, and Æthelred came back from
exile. Alcuin, who had known him, and welcomed his restoration, had no respect for his behaviour as a king,[5] and regarded
the sack of Lindisfarne by the Northmen in 793 as the beginning
of judgements about to fall on Northumbria because of the
violence, the contempt of justice, and the evil lives of its rulers.
Alcuin's words leave no doubt as to the general character of his
reign, and the Northumbrian annals which relate to his time
show that he was a treacherous and merciless enemy. It is
clear that he was never at ease in his kingdom, and it was
probably in order to obtain an ally who could protect him that
in 792 he married a daughter of Offa, king of the Mercians.
For nearly four years after his marriage he seems to have reigned
in peace. But in 796 he was murdered by a band of conspirators

---

[1] *Vita Sancti Willehadi* (Langebek, *Scriptores Rerum Danicarum*, i. 344).

[2] *S. Bonifatii et Lulli Epistolae*, ed. Tangl, pp. 257–8.

[3] 'consilio et consensu suorum omnium, regiae familiae ac principum destitutus
societate' (*Symeonis Monachi Opera*, ii. 45).

[4] *Monumenta Alcuiniana*, p. 181.

[5] At the end of 790 he wrote to the abbot of Corbie that he had not found the
new king's mind such as he either expected or desired (*Monumenta Alcuiniana*,
p. 172).

led by one of his nobles, and Northumbria fell into virtual anarchy.

Through Alcuin the Frankish court was well acquainted with Northumbrian affairs. To Charlemagne the murder of a king by men who owed him allegiance was the most atrocious of crimes. On the news of Æthelred's death he broke out into an invective against the whole Northumbrian people, whom he described as traitors, murderers of their lords, and worse than heathen.[1] In the event the murder led to a close, if temporary, association between the Frankish and Northumbrian courts, for Eardwulf, the king who ultimately emerged from the confusion in the north, placed himself under Charlemagne's protection.[2] He was at first so far successful that in 801 he was able to invade Mercia, where King Cenwulf had been entertaining his enemies. Peace was made between the kings on equal terms by the mediation of English bishops and nobles.[3] But in the spring of 808 Eardwulf was driven from his kingdom, and owed his life to certain emissaries of Charlemagne, who brought him to the emperor's court at Nymwegen. He had already been in correspondence, not only with the emperor, but with Pope Leo III, and after receiving an assurance that Charlemagne would support him, he passed on to Rome. The pope, who had learned of these events at first hand from England, as well as by letter from Charlemagne, declared himself in Eardwulf's favour, and an English deacon in the pope's service accompanied him on his return to the emperor's court. Before the end of the year he crossed to England, attended by the deacon from Rome and by two Frankish abbots dispatched by Charlemagne, through whose representations he was received again as king. None of these transactions are mentioned by English writers, and no details are known of the political situation from which they arose.[4] But they show at least that Charlemagne, confronted

---

[1] *Monumenta Alcuiniana*, ed. Jaffé, p. 290.

[2] He had not been implicated in the murder of Æthelred, and in 798 was himself attacked by the conspirators, *Symeonis Monachi Opera*, R.S. ii, p. 59.

[3] Ibid. ii, p. 65.

[4] The only authorities which mention them are the *Annales Regni Francorum* under 808 and 809, and two letters addressed by Leo III to Charlemagne in 808 (*Councils*, iii, pp. 562–4). The *Annales* give the bare sequence of events. The letters bring out the important point that the pope and the emperor were each in close communication with Northumbria, but they are allusive in regard to the situation in that country, and throw no light on the reasons for Eardwulf's expulsion. In 797 Alcuin had written to a Mercian nobleman that he feared that Eardwulf would soon lose

across the Channel by the formidable power which Offa of Mercia had created, welcomed the opportunity of intervening in the affairs of northern England.

With the return of King Eardwulf the series of Northumbrian revolutions comes to an end. He died in power, in or before 810, and Eanred, his son, seems to have kept the Northumbrian aristocracy in obedience for the next thirty years.[1] Under him the political isolation of Northumbria, broken for a few years in the previous generation, becomes complete once more. There is no local record of his reign, and the one event which brings him into general history is his submission to Egbert of Wessex in 829. Nevertheless, his kingdom comprised more than half of what was then England. After all the disorders of the eighth century, Northumbria was still a single state, and in the age of Eanred, as in the age of Bede, the Firth of Forth was its northern boundary. Its scholars were respected on the Continent, and the little that remains to illustrate their work[2] shows that they honoured the memory and were faithful to the traditions of the great men before them. The continuity of Northumbrian scholarship, like the integrity of the Northumbrian kingdom, had survived half a century of dynastic revolutions.

his kingdom because he had put away his wife and ostentatiously taken another woman in her place (*Monumenta Alcuiniana*, p. 350). But this was eleven years before he was actually driven out.

[1] Northumbrian tradition, best preserved by Symeon of Durham (*Opera*, R.S. i, p. 52) interpolated the two years' reign of a certain Ælfwald between Eardwulf's expulsion and Eanred's succession. There is some evidence from coins for the existence of a Northumbrian king named Ælfwald at approximately this time. But although a king of this name may have been recognized in Northumbria on Eardwulf's flight, his power must have ended with Eardwulf's restoration, which is placed under 808 by the contemporary Frankish annals.

[2] In particular the great necrology, generally known as the *Liber Vitae* of Durham, which was written at Lindisfarne in the first half of the ninth century.

IV

THE CONVERSION OF THE ENGLISH PEOPLES

THE heathen background of Old English history is impenetrably vague.[1] The names of the chief divinities of English worship have been preserved and a few specific practices have been recorded by historians anxious to condemn them. Writers concerned with the saints of the Conversion could not avoid an occasional reference to the temples, idols, and priests of heathenism, and the principal scientific work of the pre-Danish period—the *De Temporum Ratione* of Bede—records a few pieces of information about the chief festivals of the heathen year. As a collection of isolated facts, the English contribution to the general stock of knowledge about Germanic paganism is by no means negligible. But it is indefinite at almost every crucial point, it is often coloured by scriptural reminiscence, and it affords no more than the faintest of clues to the nature of the beliefs which lay behind observances.

In recent years the range of the materials for the study of Old English heathenism has been narrowed in one direction and enlarged in another. In much that has been written about the subject in general, and about the gods of English heathenism in particular, scholars have drawn somewhat freely upon the abundant material which has survived from heathen Scandinavia. But the connection between English and Scandinavian heathenism lies in a past which was already remote when the English peoples migrated to Britain. Much of the Scandinavian evidence has a sophisticated cast, and the danger of using it for the illustration of primitive English beliefs is steadily becoming clearer. It is equally dangerous to use the magical literature of the tenth and eleventh centuries as a line of approach towards the English pagan fore-world, for there is

[1] The most recent account of Old English heathenism is that of E. A. Philippson, *Germanisches Heidentum bei den Angelsachsen* (Leipzig, 1929). The evidence from place-names, which has greatly increased since 1929, is described by B. Dickins in *Essays and Studies by members of the English Association* x.x (1934) and by F. M. Stenton, see *C.P.*, pp. 281–97.

the strongest probability that Scandinavian influence has played upon the fragments of ancient tradition which it incorporates. On the other hand, modern work on English place-names has made an unexpectedly large contribution to the store of facts which relate directly to native heathenism. Many of these facts amount to little more than evidence that a particular site was a primitive cult-centre. Cumulatively they are important because they prove the strength of heathen feeling and give local definition to the heathen scene.

The most important of the literary sources of information about Old English heathenism is the section of the *De Temporum Ratione* in which Bede names and describes the months of the Anglo-Saxon year.[1] Some of the names are etymologically obscure, and were possibly as unintelligible to Bede as they are today. But his occasional misinterpretation of a name does not affect his credibility when he states that a particular heathen festival had been associated with a particular season. According to Bede, the heathen year began on 25 December, and certain ceremonies which he did not attempt to describe caused the following night to be named *Modra nect*, 'the night of the mothers'. The last month of the Old Year and the first month of the New were both comprised under the name *Giuli*, the modern Yule, a name so old that its meaning is quite uncertain. *Solmonath*, the name of the second month, is described by Bede as 'the month of cakes, which they offered in it to their gods'. Most scholars reject this explanation, for no English word *sol*, meaning cake, is known, but although Bede seems to have proposed a wrong derivation of the name, his statement about a festival at which cakes were offered to the gods may well be founded on a genuine tradition. The third and fourth months, according to Bede, were named respectively after the goddesses Hretha and Eostre; the fifth was called *Thrimilci*, 'because cows were then milked three times a day'; the sixth and seventh were brought together under the name *Litha*, another ancient word, which apparently meant simply 'moon'; and the eighth was called *Weodmonath*, 'the month of weeds'. The ninth month was known as *Halegmonath*, 'holy month', or, as Bede renders the name, 'the month of offerings', a phrase which points unmistakably to a heathen festival held

---

[1] The very difficult questions raised by these names are indicated and discussed by M. P. Nilsson, *Primitive Time-Reckoning*, pp. 292–7.

at the end of harvest. *Wintirfyllith*, the name of the tenth month, is connected by Bede, probably rightly, with the appearance of the first full moon of winter. *Blotmonath*, the name of the eleventh month, which means 'month of sacrifice', arose, according to Bede, 'because they devoted to their gods the animals which they were about to kill'. The explanation gives what is by far the earliest reference to the practice of killing off superfluous stock for winter food, and the name shows that the custom, with a naïve economy, was made a sacrificial occasion. For all the obscurity of some of these names and the neutral character of others, it is clear that there was a strong element of heathen festivity at the base of the Old English calendar.

The personal divinities mentioned in Old English sources range from gods and goddesses honoured among all Germanic peoples to figures which have names but no attributes. Two of these names are known only because they occur in Bede's list of Old English months. He states that the English called their third month *Hrethmonath* after their goddess Hretha and their fourth month *Eosturmonath* after their goddess Eostre, 'for whom they were accustomed to hold festivals at that season'. Neither name can be explained, and neither appears in any other mythological system. Some scholars regard the goddesses Hretha and Eostre as fictions, invented by Bede in order to give a meaning to the unintelligible names *Hrethmonath* and *Eosturmonath*. But other divinities which have never been called in question bear equally obscure names—there is at least no obvious explanation of Erce, the Old English name of Mother Earth—and the popular recognition of goddesses named Hretha and Eostre is strongly supported by the fact that it is reported on Bede's authority. It is incredible that Bede, to whom heathenism was sin, should have invented a heathen goddess in order to explain the name of the month of Easter.

Several lines of evidence suggest that the principal gods of heathen English worship were the common Germanic deities Tiw or Tig, Thunor, and Woden. The cult of the fertility goddess Frig is sufficiently proved by the occurrence of her name in the Old English *Frigedæg*, the modern Friday. But no place of her worship has yet been identified with complete certainty, and her name was not used in the formation of English personal names. Seaxneat, the ancestor of the kings of Essex, was presumably honoured by their subjects, though the place-names which arose among them contain no trace of him. But Woden, Thunor, Tiw, and Frig are the only deities whose individualized worship in England is beyond dispute.

The worship of Tiw, the pre-eminent war-god of the Germanic peoples, is well attested in England. Like Woden, Thunor, and Frig, he belonged to the company of deities from whom the days of the Old English week were named. His own name forms the first element of a small number of early personal names, such as Tiuwald and Tiowulf. It has for some time been generally agreed that the village-name Tuesley in Surrey and the Old English boundary-names Tislea in north Hampshire and Tyesmere in north Worcestershire denoted centres of his worship. It is now known that his name also enters into the village-name Tysoe in south Warwickshire. The name means 'Tiw's hill-spur' and clearly refers to one of the projections which issue at this póint from the escarpment above the plain known since at least the seventeenth century as the Vale of the Red Horse. It is not improbable that the vale derived its name from the figure of a horse cut into the hill-side as a symbol of Tiw. In any case, his association with one of the most commanding sites in the southern midlands is an impressive testimony to the importance of his cult.

The worship of Thunor, the thunder-god, has left many more traces in local names. The occurrence of a *Thunores hlæw*—'Thunor's mound'—in Thanet, and of a *Thunres lea*—'Thunor's grove'—near Southampton, proves the existence of his cult among both the eastern and western divisions of the Jutish people. No names which point unequivocally to his worship have been found in Anglian territory, a fact which may be partly due to the rarity of Old English charters relating to this district. But among the Saxon peoples he seems to have been the most generally honoured of all gods. In Wessex his cult is represented in the boundary-names Thunres feld near Hardenhuish in Wiltshire—the most westerly heathen site in England —and Thunres leah in east Hampshire. In Surrey it gave rise to the names Thursley in the Wey valley and Thunderfield near Reigate; in Sussex to the boundary-name *Thunorslege* near Bexhill; in Essex to the place-names Thunderley in the north and Thundersley in the south, and the hundred-names Thurstable —'Thunor's pillar'—on the coast and Thunreslau on the Suffolk border. Thundridge in Hertfordshire—'Thunor's ridge'—is an outlying piece of evidence for his cult in what was probably Middle Saxon country.

The traces of Woden's cult are scattered still more widely. In Kent they occur in the village-names Woodnesborough near Sandwich and Wormshill on the eastern slope of the Downs near Sittingbourne. In Essex, where they have vanished from the modern map, they can be seen in the ancient field-names *Wodnesfeld* in the north of the county and *Wedynsfeld* in the south-west. There was an important centre of his worship above the vale of Pewsey in Wessex, where the great earthwork called *Wodnes dic*, or Wansdyke, runs between sites once known as *Wodnes beorg*, 'Woden's barrow', and *Wodnes dene*, 'Woden's valley'. There seems to have been another centre of the same kind in the heart of Mercia, marked by the place-names Wednesbury, 'Woden's fortress', and Wednesfield, 'Woden's open country', above the head-waters of the Tame. Elsewhere in Anglian territory there are isolated signs of his cult in Wensley, 'Woden's grove', the name of a village overlooking the Derwent in the Peak of Derbyshire, and in the hundred-name *Wodneslawe*, 'Woden's mound', in the east of Bedfordshire. As memorials of popular heathenism these names give a useful indication of the general English attitude towards the god who was claimed as an ancestor by most English kings. They bring him out of the aristocratic mythology in which dynastic traditions wrapped him, down to his holy places in the countryside. They show that he was worshipped by common men belonging to each of the three principal races of which the English nation was composed.

The popular element in his cult is brought out even more clearly by the fact that, so far as is known, he was the only god to whom the English peoples applied an alias. In Old Norse mythology, which gave him the habit of appearing as a wanderer in disguise, he often appears under the by-name *Grímr*, a name which literally meant a masked person. There is no direct evidence for this usage in England, but it is placed beyond serious doubt by the frequent association of the name Grim with eminent natural features, and earthworks felt to be supernatural. The conception of Woden as the maker of works beyond mortal power was clearly present to the men who called the greatest earthwork of northern Wessex *Wodnes dic*. The name *Grimes dic*, or Grimsdyke, which is borne by many ancient earthworks in southern England belongs to the same order of ideas.

The case for the vitality of Old English heathenism does not rest entirely on the facts which attest the worship of individual gods. Modern work on English place-names has identified a large number of sites which were undoubtedly centres of heathen worship, but to which the name of a particular god was never attached. The best of the evidence comes from names containing the Old English words *ealh*, 'temple', *hearh*, which in place-names seem to have the meaning 'hill sanctuary', and *weoh*, 'idol', 'shrine', or 'sacred precinct'. *Ealh* is rarely found in local names, but it forms the first element in the name of Alkham near Dover, and in Ealhfleot, an early name of the channel connecting Faversham with the sea. *Hearh* occurs in the names Harrowden in Bedfordshire, Harrowden in Northamptonshire, Harrowden in north Essex, Arrowfield Top in east Worcestershire, and Peper Harow in Surrey. In *Gumeninga hearh*, the oldest form of the name of Harrow on the Hill, it appears in a more significant context, for the name means 'the holy place of the Gumeningas', and shows that the tribal sanctuary was known in pre-Christian England.[1] *Weoh*, the commonest of these heathen elements, was also the most widely distributed. To the south of the Thames it forms the name of Wye in Kent, which must have been a sanctuary as well as an administrative centre of the early Jutes. It is compounded with *leah*, 'grove', in the South Saxon place-names Whiligh and Whyly, in Willey in the west of Surrey, and in Wheely Down in the east of Hampshire. Farther to the west it occurs in Weyhill, where it originally stood alone, and in the ancient Wiltshire field-names *Wedone* near Damerham and *Weoland* near Wootton Bassett. Beyond the Thames it is combined with *dun*, 'hill', in Weedon Beck and Weedon Lois in Northamptonshire and in Weedon near Aylesbury; with *leah*, again, in Weoley in north Worcestershire, *Welei*, a lost village-name in north Hertfordshire, and Weeley near the coast of Essex; with *wiella*, 'spring', in Wyville in Kesteven; and with *ford* in Weeford on the Staffordshire section of Watling Street. Near the Humber the locative plural of the word forms the name of Wyham between

[1] [This is implied also by the name *Besingahearh*, where Ceadwalla issued in 688 a charter (*C.S.* 72) concerning Farnham, Surrey. This charter includes the name *Cusanweoh*, mentioned below.]

Grimsby and Louth, which must have been a principal sanctuary of the men of Lindsey. Apart from these examples there are two cases of exceptional interest in which it forms the second element of a compound name. One of them is the name Patchway near Stanmer in Sussex, which means the *weoh*, or shrine, belonging to an individual named Pæccel. The other is the name of an outlying property belonging to Farnham in Surrey, which appears in the seventh century as *Cusan weoh*, and means the shrine of a man named Cusa. It seems clear from these names that a heathen shrine might have an owner. It would be easy to exaggerate their significance. But they provide the only evidence which has yet appeared in England to support the view that there were heathen precedents for the rights of ownership claimed by the first lay founders of English churches.

The distribution of these heathen names is curiously irregular. More than nine-tenths of them fall within an area which could be indicated on a map by lines drawn from Ipswich to Stafford, and thence due south to the Channel. No heathen names have so far been found in Northumbria; they are very rare between the Humber and the Welland; and there is no certain example in East Anglia. For the present it must be left an open question whether their rarity in this country is due to the lethargy of popular heathenism, to changes in nomenclature brought about by later Danish settlement, or to the deliberate obliteration of heathen memorials by unusually zealous Christian kings. What the surviving names establish beyond all doubt is the strength of heathenism in the centre and south-east of England. Many passages in the history of the Conversion become clearer in their light. The difficulty with which the East Saxons were brought to accept Christianity is made more intelligible by the numerous heathen sites in their kingdom. The heathen sanctuaries of Wessex provide an admirable illustration of Bede's statement that Birinus, meaning to preach in the remoter parts of England, remained in the south to combat the strong paganism of the Gewisse. On the wider question of the conditions which governed the work of the Roman mission to England, the evidence of these names is of peculiar significance. It shows that, throughout the country in which Augustine and his companions laboured, heathenism was still a living religion when it met the Christian challenge.

The challenge was long delayed. So far as is known the

British clergy made no attempt at the conversion of the invaders who had expropriated their kinsmen.[1] It was on the Continent or in northern Britain that the wandering Irish monks of the sixth century satisfied their desire for religious adventure, and there is no trace of any Irish missionary in England at a date earlier than the coming of Augustine. No evangelist came, or was likely to come, to England from the Gaul of Gregory of Tours. For the greater part of the sixth century the church of Rome, from which decisive action came at last, had been compelled to concentrate its energy upon the maintenance of its own independence. The heathenism which confronted the mission of Augustine was rooted in the soil by the practice of generations.

The dispatch of this mission by Gregory the Great, in 597, gave effect to a design which had lain in his mind for twenty years. In the seventh century it was believed that his attention had been called to England by a conversation with certain English youths at Rome while Benedict I was pope—that is, between 574 and 578. There is no need to reject this famous story,[2] for it contains nothing that is improbable, and it belongs to the oldest stratum of tradition about Gregory's life. According to this tale Gregory himself wished to attempt the conversion of the English, and was only prevented by the protests of the Roman citizens. The opportunity never returned, for under Pope Benedict's successor Gregory was occupied at first by a legation to Constantinople, and afterwards by the charge of his own monastery at Rome. He was elected pope in 590, and it was not until he had been in office for six years that he was free to make definite plans for an English mission.

Although the Northumbrian tradition may be substantially true, it does not give the full explanation of Gregory's interest in heathen England. The future of the Roman see itself was

---

[1] [The prolonged hatred felt by the British clergy for the Saxons is shown in the letter which Aldhelm wrote before 705 to Geraint, King of Dumnonia, for he says that the clergy across the Severn in Dyfydd will not associate with the English in church, nor eat from the same dishes. They even throw the remnants of a shared meal to the dogs, and scour the dishes as being contaminated. See *Aldhelmi Opera*, ed. R. Ehwald (M.G.H.), p. 484.]

[2] The tale has been made familiar by Bede, but its oldest form is the version preserved in *The earliest life of Gregory the Great by an anonymous monk of Whitby*, ed. B. Colgrave, University of Kansas (1968), pp. 90–3. The life was written in Northumbria on the basis of current tradition. At the points where it differs from Bede its statements generally seem preferable.

uncertain in the late sixth century.[1] It was still dependent on the eastern empire, and it was threatened with imminent danger from the new Lombard power in Italy. The ancient churches of Gaul and Spain were governed with little reference to Rome, and ascetic Irish pilgrims were bringing a new and incalculable element into the religious life of the West. It was doubtful for how long the great traditions of the Roman see would secure respect for its supremacy in a world where conditions were a tacit denial of claims to universal authority, spiritual or secular. That Gregory's attention was first called to Britain by a simple desire for the conversion of its heathen inhabitants need not be doubted. But Gregory was in the succession of ancient Roman statesmen, and could not have been indifferent to the political advantages that would follow from the reunion of a lost province of the empire to the church of its capital. He died when the success of his enterprise was still uncertain, but his statesmanship found its justification at last in the conversion of the southern Germans and the reorganization of the Frankish church by Englishmen acutely conscious of the debt in religion which their nation owed to Rome.

The man whom Gregory chose as leader of the mission to Britain was the prior of his own monastery of St. Andrew on the Coelian Hill at Rome.[2] Augustine of Canterbury owes his place in history to his association with Gregory, for the conception of the mission was the pope's, the organization at the pope's command made it possible, and the measure of success which it attained was due to his encouragement and instruction. His letters are the chief materials for its history, for Augustine's followers left his life unwritten, and the traditions of his time had grown faint when Bede collected them in the eighth century. All that is known of the beginnings of the enterprise is contained in Bede's statement that in the fourteenth year of the Emperor Maurice, Pope Gregory sent Augustine the servant of God and with him many other monks fearing the Lord to preach the word of God to the English race. The fourteenth year of Maurice ran from August 595 to August 596, and the expedition

[1] S. J. Crawford, *Anglo-Saxon Influence on Western Christendom*, pp. 1–17.
[2] The fundamental authorities for the mission of Augustine are the letters of Gregory the Great and the narrative of Bede, which is itself founded on materials of this kind. From time to time doubts have been expressed about the authenticity of individual letters, but the attack has not been convincing at any point. The documentary sources are conveniently brought together in *Councils*, iii. 5 ff.

probably started early in the latter year. At some point in southern Gaul the mission halted, the monks recoiled from the thought of meeting a barbarous and infidel race whose language they did not know, and sent Augustine back to Rome to beg release. Gregory's action at this crisis saved the mission from an ignominious end. It is probable that Augustine's authority over his companions had not hitherto been precisely defined. Gregory, in a letter of encouragement addressed to the monks, stated that he had appointed Augustine to be their abbot, and proceeded to make the papal sanction behind the mission evident to all with whom it might come into contact. In a series of letters which still survive he commended it to individual Gaulish ecclesiastics whose support might be useful, and to Arigius patrician of Burgundy, the Frankish kings Theuderich of Burgundy and Theudebert of Austrasia, and their grandmother Queen Brunhild. The letters in this series which have been fully copied bear a date corresponding to 23 July 596, and Augustine must have left Rome to rejoin his monks in Gaul soon afterwards. Henceforward the mission was assured of respect throughout Gaul, and early in 597 Augustine landed in Thanet with about forty companions.

Even at this early date the beginnings of political intercourse had been established between Kent and the Frankish kingdoms. Before 588 Æthelberht, king of Kent, had married Bertha, daughter of Charibert, the Frankish king reigning at Paris.[1] The marriage does not seem to have aroused much interest in Gaul—to Gregory of Tours Æthelberht is simply 'the son of a certain king in Kent'—but a Frankish bishop named Liudhard had accompanied the queen to Britain, and Christian observances must have been followed within the king's household for at least nine years before Augustine's landing. Neither the queen nor her bishop seems to have made any attempt to explain their religious practices, and in 597 Christianity was still a strange and therefore sinister religion to the king himself. The story that Æthelberht, afraid of the strangers' magic, insisted on meeting Augustine and his companions under the open sky looks like a genuine tradition. The interview, which took place in Thanet, convinced him of their honesty, and although he refused to abandon at once what he and the whole English race had hitherto believed, he gave them a dwelling-place in

[1] Above, p. 59.

Canterbury, supplied them with food, and allowed them to preach their religion. They on their part lived a simple communal life in Canterbury, using for their services an ancient church on the east of the city, dedicated to St. Martin, which the queen had been accustomed to visit. The first stage in their mission ended when Æthelberht himself accepted Christianity. From him they received an appropriate seat in the city, and the beginnings of an endowment in land. The number of converts increased, though not as yet overwhelmingly, and Augustine could begin to restore ancient churches and build new ones.[1]

Up to this time the mission had consisted of a band of monks united by common obedience to the authority of Augustine, their abbot. By the autumn of 597 it had become necessary to provide for the permanent organization of the newly founded church. Before the end of the year, with the pope's approval, Augustine received episcopal consecration in Gaul from 'the bishops of the Germanies'. Soon after his return he sent two members of the mission, Laurentius the priest and Peter the monk, to Rome with an account of what had been achieved and a request for instruction on a number of practical questions which were certain to arise in the future. His own account of the mission has not survived, but in the summer of 598 the pope told the patriarch of Alexandria that Augustine had reported the baptism of more than ten thousand converts on the Christmas day after his consecration. Despite this evidence of success it was not until the summer of 601 that Gregory replied to Augustine's questions, urgent though some of them were. In the interval Gregory had been occupied with the negotiations for the peace of 599 between the eastern empire and the Lombards, and with the affairs of the papal patrimony. His health was bad throughout these years; in June 600 he wrote that for nearly two years he had scarcely been able to rise for three hours on festivals for the service of the Mass. It is not strange that he was slow in preparing what amounted to a code for the government of a new ecclesiastical province.

The reply which came at last was elaborate and detailed.

---

[1] The distinction between the work of building and repairing churches is clearly marked by Bede (*H.E.* i. 25). His language, which implies that a considerable number of Romano-British churches could still be recognized in Augustine's time, is important as evidence that whatever may have been the circumstances of the Jutish occupation of Kent, it was not carried out with devastating violence.

More than half of it relates to the morals of the laity and their behaviour in regard to the church and its services. The beginnings of a marriage law appear in sentences which allow two brothers to marry two sisters who are not of their near kin, forbid the marriage of first cousins, and denounce the heathen practice of marriage with a stepmother. The theft of church property is discussed with moderation; the church must inquire in each case whether the thief can support himself or not, and must never demand more than simple restitution of what has been stolen. On this point Gregory was asking much less than the king was prepared to give; the laws of Æthelberht begin with the sentence 'God's and the Church's property twelve-fold'. The same moderation appears in Gregory's instructions on matters of strictly ecclesiastical importance. Augustine is allowed to compile an eclectic liturgy, incorporating such usages of the Roman, Gallican, or other churches as he might consider most profitable. In words which almost suggest impatience Gregory dismisses Augustine's scruples at the thought of consecrating a bishop without the presence of other bishops. He is reminded that he is the only bishop in the church of the English, and is asked how often bishops come from Gaul whom he could invite as witnesses of consecrations. He is instructed to consecrate bishops to sees so placed that intercourse may be easy, and then to ask three or four bishops to join him in each consecration. On the vital question of the relations between Augustine and the bishops of Gaul and Britain Gregory writes with deliberate precision. The British bishops are explicitly placed under Augustine's authority for instruction and correction. It is ruled, on the other hand, that Augustine can have no authority over the bishops of Gaul, for from ancient times Gregory's predecessors had granted the pallium to the bishop of Arles, and their precedent must be followed. If, however, Augustine should be in Gaul, he should join with the bishop of Arles in the correction of offending Gallic ecclesiastics, but as a matter of Christian duty, not of right. The situation thus created would in any case be delicate, and Gregory was careful to define Augustine's position in a separate letter to the bishop of Arles.

For the moment, however, the external relations of the church were less important than its internal organization. The first of all Augustine's inquiries had related to the manner of life which, as bishop, he should adopt for his clergy, and the administration of the revenue drawn from the offerings of the faithful. There can be little doubt that Augustine was already established in the seat of his bishopric at Canterbury, an ancient church within the city which he dedicated *in nomine Sancti Salvatoris*. In any case, Gregory's reply gives contemporary evidence as to the nature of the community gathered there under the first archbishops. The way of life which he prescribed was communal but not monastic. His writings show that in his mind the obligations of the monastic life were such that no one bound to the service of a church could properly bear them, and to him the work which Augustine's companions had undertaken undoubtedly freed them from the responsibility of keeping their former rule. It would be enough if henceforward they lived in common with their bishop, supported as a community by the revenues at his disposal. On the other hand, it was essential to provide for the training of a native clergy, and it is probable that the community at Canterbury already included, besides its senior members, youths and even children preparing for admission to holy orders. To such candidates, as they approached a suitable age, it was usual to offer the option of marriage, and the married clerk of or below the grade of lector had an important place in the organization of a sixth-century cathedral church. Augustine was directed to make provision of clerks of this type, keeping them under ecclesiastical rule, but assigning a separate stipend to each on marriage.

Gregory's *responsa* are closely connected in date and subject with an important document defining the relative position of the two metropolitan sees required by his conception of the future church of the English. The document implies, though it never states, that Augustine or his immediate successor will remove his seat from Canterbury to London at a suitable opportunity. Augustine is directed to consecrate twelve bishops who will remain subject to him, and consecrate his successor in their synod. He is also directed to send a bishop to York, who, if the people of those parts accept Christianity, shall consecrate twelve other bishops and be their metropolitan, though he and they shall be subject to Augustine's authority. After Augustine's death the see of York shall be independent of Augustine's successors; each successive metropolitan of York and London shall receive the pallium from the pope, and their precedence shall be determined by seniority of consecration. This arti-

ficial division of Britain into two equal provinces is most easily
intelligible as an attempt to reproduce in the ecclesiastical
sphere the distinction between the kingdoms subject to the overlord of the southern English and independent Northumbria.
It never approached realization. The southern archbishop
obtained his twelfth suffragan when the diocese of Leicester
was founded in 737, but the removal of his seat to London had
been prevented by delay in the conversion of the East Saxons,
and then by respect for Augustine's church. An archbishopric
was not permanently established at York until 735; Hexham,
Lindisfarne, and Whithorn were its only suffragan sees, and this
meagre number was afterwards reduced owing to the decline
of the Northumbrian kingdom. But the scheme, though im-
practicable, was never forgotten, and Gregory's intention that
the two English archbishops should have co-ordinate authority
was the foundation of the case for independence put forward
by later archbishops of York.

In the summer of 601 Laurentius and Peter returned to
Britain as leaders of a second mission, bringing a pallium for
Augustine, the pope's scheme for the future constitution of the
church of the English, his replies to Augustine's questions, and
less formal letters to the archbishop, King Æthelberht, and
Queen Bertha. By this time the ultimate conversion of Kent
seemed to be assured. Kent was the most civilized, and probably
the most populous, of all the English kingdoms, and in 604 a
second Kentish see was established in a church built by Æthelberht at Rochester, with Justus, a member of the recent mission,
as bishop. The same year was also marked by a precarious
advance into territory beyond the sphere of Æthelberht's direct
rule. He was overlord of the southern English, and Saberht,
king of the East Saxons, was his sister's son. London was the
chief town of the East Saxons, and on the highest ground within
the city Æthelberht built a church in honour of St. Paul, where
Mellitus, another member of the mission of 601, was established
as bishop. Although nothing definite is known as to the constitution of the early cathedrals of London and Rochester, it
seems safe to assume that they followed the model of Canterbury, and that although each cathedral was served by many
men who had once made a monk's profession, neither was a
monastery. The only English monastery known to have been
founded in Augustine's time was that of St. Peter and St. Paul

outside the east wall of Canterbury, where Peter the companion of Laurentius became abbot, and Augustine himself, who did not live to consecrate its church, was buried.

The one serious reverse of Augustine's career belongs to the period between 601 and 604. In granting authority to Augustine over the British churches, Gregory was attempting to deal with a situation which he did not understand and could not control. It is significant that in his own relations with British ecclesiastics Augustine laid no special stress on his claim to their obedience. On two occasions he engaged in conference with British bishops and learned men in order to secure their co-operation with his mission. He tried to bring them into conformity with Roman practice in regard to such matters as the computation of Easter and the ritual to be observed in baptism, but he was prepared to compromise on lesser differences, and it was as the interpreter of Roman custom that he claimed respect. Bede, who is the only authority for these interviews, has preserved a tradition that the second conference failed because Augustine did not rise when British ecclesiastics approached him. But an anecdote never tells the whole truth about a complicated issue, and there were many reasons besides Augustine's possible failure in courtesy for a breach between the Roman mission and the British churches. The obstacles to his success lay even deeper than the conservatism which had developed through generations of British isolation and the hatred of a retreating for an advancing race. The most illustrious saints of Wales belong to the sixth century. They had devoted themselves to the foundation of monasteries, and their traditions were sacred to their disciples. The Roman mission, which required the abandonment of ancient customs by the British clergy, had little to offer of which they felt the need. The pupils of a great ascetic like St. David could have had little sympathy with the humane Italian monasticism in which Augustine and his companions had been trained.

Augustine died on 26 May in an unknown year between 604 and 609. It is easy to emphasize the limitations of his success, his failure to conciliate the British clergy, and occasional signs of weakness in his conduct, and to conclude that he was a man of meagre personality associated almost accidentally with a great historical movement. He certainly cannot be given a high place among the leading missionaries of the Dark

Ages. There is no sign in his history of the strength and passion which distinguished Willibrord or Boniface. Without the advice and support of Gregory the Great he would have accomplished nothing. But no one who possessed Gregory's confidence should be dismissed as negligible by a modern writer, and Augustine's mission was faced with its own peculiar difficulties. Unlike later missionaries of Germanic stock he was attempting the conversion of a people whose culture he did not understand. In the background of his mission stood the hostile clergy of an ancient church suspicious of his ultimate designs and conscious of justification for refusing their help. Under the conditions which governed his activities it was a notable achievement to secure the establishment of Christianity in one English kingdom and to provide for the training of a clergy who would continue his work.

Few remains of the churches which he founded are visible today. His cathedral has been obliterated by later building on its site. But the foundations of the church which served his suburban monastery of St. Peter and St. Paul have been recovered by excavation, and fragments still survive of two adjacent churches of the same period. These churches are built to a general plan which is repeated in the original cathedral of Rochester and in two later Kentish churches of the seventh century, one serving a house of women at Lyminge, the other a house of men founded at Reculver in 669.[1] Each of these churches ended towards the east in a circular apse, generally separated from the nave by a triple arcade, and in each of them, except perhaps Rochester, the main building was flanked by chambers of a kind devised for the keeping of sacred vessels, but often used in later times for the burial of eminent persons connected with the foundation. The plan of these churches was derived from Italy, and surviving fragments show a technical skill in the use of Roman brick which proves that they were the work of foreign, and probably Italian, builders. Outside Kent the only building which plainly belongs to this group is a church built of re-used Roman stone-work for Cedd, bishop of the East Saxons, at Bradwell on Sea, the site of the Roman fort of Othona. The oldest churches of Northumbria were influenced by Gallic rather than Italian models. Between Humber and Thames there are few remains of any building earlier than the tenth century. But the greatest English building

[1] *Chronicle, sub anno.*

of the pre-Danish period, the monastic church of Brixworth, though far larger in scale than Augustine's churches, belongs in character and the essentials of its plan to the Roman tradition which he introduced.[1]

For nearly half a century after Augustine's death the succession of St. Gregory's disciples was maintained at Canterbury. Shortly before he died Augustine consecrated Laurentius his successor. Already in the fifth century such consecrations had been forbidden by the pope in synod, and Augustine's act can only be justified as an attempt to avoid confusion in his church. It is possible that the position of Laurentius was regarded as uncanonical at Rome, for he never received the pallium.[2] His recognition by his fellow-bishops in England is proved by his association with Mellitus of London and Justus of Rochester in a letter exhorting the bishops and abbots of the Irish to accept the Roman Easter-computation. The letter is interesting as the earliest piece of evidence for contact between the Roman mission and Irish ecclesiastics. It shows that the contact was unfriendly, for the writers state that an Irish bishop named Dagan, who had lately come into Britain, refused to join them in either food or lodging. Little else is recorded about the pontificate of Laurentius beyond unsuccessful negotiations with the British clergy. Communication was maintained with Rome. Bishop Mellitus of London was present at a Roman synod held by Boniface IV on 27 February 610, and returned with letters from the Pope to Laurentius and King Æthelberht. But there is no sign of any expansion of the English church; Rædwald, king of the East Angles, was induced by Æthelberht to accept baptism, but none of his people followed him, and the ceremony led to nothing but the introduction of a Christian altar into one of his heathen temples. The Kentish church itself nearly expired after the death of its protector Æthelberht in 616.

Twenty years after Augustine's landing the Kentish court was not yet wholly Christian. The new king, Eadbald, son of Æthelberht and Bertha, had never received baptism, and openly turned to heathen ways.[3] In Essex little had been accomplished

[1] On the southern English churches of this period see A. W. Clapham, *English Romanesque Architecture before the Conquest*, pp. 16–38.

[2] The Roman attitude towards the situation in England is discussed briefly but suggestively by T. Nicklin, *E.H.R.* xxviii (1913), p. 556.

[3] According to Bede he married his father's widow, who, presumably, was also a heathen. The date of Queen Bertha's death is unknown.

beyond the conversion of King Saberht. On his death his three
sons, still heathen, drove Mellitus from their kingdom because
he refused to give them the eucharistic bread which he used to
give to their father. Mellitus and Justus of Rochester fled to
Gaul, and according to tradition Laurentius would have
followed them but for a special visitation from St. Peter. The
story went that Eadbald was brought to accept Christianity by
the archbishop's account of his experience. In any case, the
king's mind changed before long; Justus returned to Rochester,
and the church in Kent was once more secure under royal
protection. In Essex the pagan reaction was stronger. Mellitus
never returned to London, and nearly forty years passed before
another bishop could be consecrated for the East Saxons.

By remaining in his see Laurentius had preserved the continuity of the church in Kent. Upon his death, probably in
619, Mellitus succeeded him, and when he died, in 624, Justus
was translated from Rochester to Canterbury. Within three
years he was succeeded by a certain Honorius, who is described
by Bede as 'one of the disciples of St. Gregory'—a phrase which
implies that he had been a member of one of the two original
Roman missions. He lived until 652, but in the expansion of
English Christianity which marks these years he and his church
of Canterbury played at most a secondary part. There was no
longer any danger of a reversion to heathenism in Kent. King
Eadbald, who reigned until 640, became a respectable Christian
ruler. He ultimately married the daughter of a Frankish king,
and was remembered as a benefactor of churches. Eorcenberht,
his son, was the first English king to order the destruction of
idols throughout his kingdom. The church of Canterbury was
honoured for the traditions which had already gathered around
it, and the metropolitan dignity of its head was recognized
at Rome. But it had lost the initiative in the conversion of the
English peoples long before the death of the last archbishop
who had known Augustine.

Before its energy declined it had secured one remarkable success in the temporary conversion of Northumbria and Lindsey.
In 625, while Justus was archbishop, Edwin, king of the Northumbrians, married Æthelberg, daughter of Æthelberht of Kent.
Edwin promised that his wife's religion should be respected,
and that he would consider the question of changing his own
beliefs. Accordingly a certain Paulinus, who had come to

England with the mission of 601, was consecrated a bishop at Canterbury and sent north with Æthelberg. Within a few weeks of their marriage the king and queen received admonitory letters from Pope Boniface V. But many months passed before Edwin was brought to the point of baptism, and Northumbrian tradition gave a dramatic air to the final collapse of his resistance. The story ran that Edwin, when in peril at Rædwald's court, had been visited by a stranger, who had assured him of safety and a future kingdom in return for a promise of obedience when a man resembling the visitor should ask for it, and give an appointed sign. In Bede's version of the story Paulinus was divinely inspired to remind Edwin of his promise and claim its fulfilment. In the floating tale on which Bede's narrative was founded[1] Edwin seems to have identified Paulinus himself with the stranger. The facts behind the story are indiscoverable. But it is evidence of a very early tradition that Edwin regarded his baptism as the satisfaction of a debt of honour for the deliverance of his youth.

After yielding to Paulinus Edwin summoned a council of his 'friends, princes, and counsellors', so that if they agreed with him they might all be baptized together. In his account of the debate which followed Bede assigns parts to representatives of heathenism, but he does not, and indeed could not, allow them to put forward any rational statement of the heathen case. The chief of the king's priests, named Coifi, is made to declare the futility of his religion at the outset, on the ground that while none of the king's men had been more assiduous in the cult of the gods, many had received greater rewards. This naïve confession is followed by the famous speech of an unnamed noble, dwelling on the darkness of all that comes before or after life, and comparing human existence to the flight of a sparrow through a lighted hall 'from winter tó winter'. Paulinus then set out the elements of the Christian faith, and Coifi, declaring that now for the first time he had learned the truth, asked the king that temples and altars which had been honoured without profit should immediately be burned. Coifi, to defy the law that a priest must never bear arms nor ride except on a mare, borrowed weapons and a stallion from the king, rode to a temple at Goodmanham, twenty miles from York, and, in the

---

[1] *The earliest Life of Gregory the Great by an anonymous Monk . . . of Whitby*, ed. B. Colgrave, pp. 98–101.

presence of a crowd which thought him mad, threw his lance into the building and called on his companions to burn it. On the eve of Easter, 627, Edwin was baptized at York in a wooden church, dedicated to St. Peter, which he had built for the occasion.

A rapid, if superficial, extension of Christianity followed in the north. Paulinus received a seat for his bishopric in York, where Edwin began to build a church for him which was still unfinished when the northern mission was interrupted in 632. His work in the open country was based on the royal villages which were the centres of local administration. He spent thirty-six days with the king and queen at Yeavering in Bernicia, catechizing and baptizing incessantly from morning till evening. He baptized many converts in the Swale at Catterick, and built the only local church of his mission in the king's village of Campodonum in the neighbourhood of Leeds. Before long his success had reached a point at which the establishment of a second archbishopric seemed possible. On 11 June 634 Pope Honorius I addressed letters to King Edwin and Archbishop Honorius of Canterbury, recognizing the metropolitan position of Paulinus by sending a pallium for him, together with one for Honorius, so that when either metropolitan died, his successor could be consecrated by the survivor. The difficulty of communication between England and Rome, which the pope mentioned as the reason for this concession, is illustrated by the fact that Edwin had been dead and Paulinus a fugitive for a year and eight months before these letters were written.

Early in his northern mission Paulinus turned aside to attempt the conversion of Lindsey, then under Edwin's overlordship. His first convert was a certain Blæcca, who is described as *praefectus*, that is, apparently, king's reeve, of Lincoln. As was usual in these early missions, a bishop's church was built as soon as possible in the chief town of the people whose conversion was in progress. By 627 Paulinus had come to possess a church in Lincoln, in which he consecrated Honorius, the new archbishop of Canterbury.[1] Nothing is known about Lindsey for the next half-century, and it is possible that the work of Paulinus may have been more permanent there than in Northumbria.

[1] At the moment Paulinus was probably the only bishop in England. In any case, as bishop of York, he was the proper person to consecrate the elect of Canterbury.

It is certain that in Lindsey, as further north, he brought large crowds to baptism, and a description of his appearance has come down from one whom he had thus baptized in the Trent 'near the city called Tiowulfingacæstir'.[1] He was remembered as a tall figure, slightly bent, with black hair, a thin hooked nose, and an emaciated face. It is a testimony to the possibilities of oral tradition that Bede, who had received these details at second hand, was able to compose in 731 a portrait of a man sent to Britain by Gregory the Great.

Edwin fell at Hatfield on 12 October 632, Northumbria was devastated by Cadwallon and his Mercian allies, and Paulinus escaped to Kent, where he received the vacant bishopric of Rochester. With his flight the church which he had founded came to an end. His work had been done too quickly to be permanent under adverse conditions. Its utter collapse suggests that there may have been wisdom in the unadventurous policy of Augustine and his successors, and that the gradual spread of religious instruction from a few centres was a surer method of advancing Christianity than the undiscriminating reception of converts. The flight of Paulinus did not mean the end of Northumbrian Christianity, for his deacon James, the one heroic figure in the Roman mission, remained in the north and worked there for more than a generation. But the permanent establishment of Christianity in that region was the achievement of Celtic monks with whom the school from which Paulinus came had little sympathy, and it was only after much controversy that continental influences prevailed once more in the north.

The fall of Christianity in Northumbria was balanced by its introduction into East Anglia. The initiative in this country was taken by Sigeberht its king, who had lived in Gaul as an exile and had been baptized there. For help in the task of establishing a church he looked to Canterbury, and it was from Archbishop Honorius that he obtained a bishop. A Burgundian named Felix, who had already received episcopal consecration in Gaul, had recently placed himself at the archbishop's disposal for missionary work in England. Honorius sent him to Sigeberht, who gave him a seat in Dunwich for his bishopric. The future of the church was secured by the foundation of a

---

[1] Which can safely be identified with Littleborough in Nottinghamshire (*Place-Names of Nottinghamshire*, E.P-N.S., pp. 35–6).

school for which Felix obtained teachers such as there were in
Kent—an important illustration of the educational activities in
which the real strength of the Kentish mission lay. It is clear
that the East Anglian church was organized from the beginning
on continental lines, but its development was complicated by
Celtic influences which must have penetrated deeply into its
life. Within at most a few years from the coming of Felix, the
king was visited by a very eminent Irish ascetic named Fursa,
whom he allowed to settle in a deserted fortress, probably,
though not certainly, to be identified with Burgh castle in
Suffolk. As the ultimate source of the copious medieval literature devoted to the portrayal of the other world, Fursa has an
important place in the history of culture. His own vision was
conceived in East Anglia, where there long survived a tradition
of him sitting in a thin shirt during a hard winter, and sweating
as he told what he had seen. Towards the middle of the century
he migrated to Gaul, where he died, but his East Anglian
monastery survived his departure for some years in the charge
of Folian, his brother. There is no record of any conflict between the Irish and the continental strain in East Anglian
Christianity. So far as can be seen, the East Anglian church
formed a well-knit community. It kept its members Christian
in evil times, and the succession of its bishops was maintained
until the outbreak of the Danish wars. In Botulf of Icanhoh it
produced a monastic saint whose house was regarded as a
pattern of the religious life.[1] But it never produced a chronicler,
and the details of its history are lost.

While Felix was working in East Anglia another independent
missionary was beginning the conversion of the West Saxons.
Birinus, their first bishop, is a shadowy figure, for Bede knew
little about West Saxon history, and Birinus had no successor of
his own training to hand down the tradition of his work. His
name suggests that he was of Germanic stock, but his mission
was undertaken on the advice of Pope Honorius I, and the
Church which he founded was presumably organized on an
Italian model. He came to Britain intending to preach in the

---

[1] According to the anonymous life of Abbot Ceolfrith of Wearmouth (ed. C.
Plummer, *Venerabilis Bedae Opera Historica*, i. 389) he visited East Anglia shortly
after 669 'ut uideret instituta Botuulfi abbatis, quem singularis uitae et doctrinae
uirum . . . fama circumquaque uulgauerat'. The site of Botulf's monastery of
Icanhoh is unknown.

midlands, where no teacher had preceded him, and with this object he received episcopal consecration from Asterius, archbishop of Milan from 630 to 640. Finding the West Saxons among whom he landed intensely heathen, he remained with them and, according to the *Anglo-Saxon Chronicle*, baptized their king Cynegils in 635. King Oswald of Northumbria, who was about to marry a daughter of Cynegils, acted as his godfather, and the two kings jointly gave the *civitas* of Dorchester on Thames to Birinus as a seat for his bishopric. The baptism of Cynegils did not mean the conversion of the whole royal house of Wessex. His eldest son and grandson soon followed him, but Cenwalh, his second son and successor, was still a heathen in 645 when Penda and the Mercians expelled him from Wessex. His ultimate conversion was due to the influence of his host, Anna, king of the East Angles. If an important member of the royal house delayed so long before accepting Christianity it is unlikely that Birinus secured any general conversion of the West Saxon people. The foundation of his church at Dorchester may well have been his principal achievement.

Although the missions of Felix and Birinus had not arisen from within the church of Canterbury its influence must have been increased by the foundation of two new bishoprics in the south. During these years Christianity was restored in the north by men who were indifferent, if not hostile, to the primacy of any episcopal church.[1] The overthrow of Cadwallon at the end of 633 was followed by the re-establishment of the Northumbrian kingdom under Oswald son of Æthelfrith of Bernicia. While Edwin was king Oswald had lived in exile, and had received Christianity from the monks of Iona, 'the chief of nearly all the monasteries of the northern Irish and of all the monasteries of the Picts'. As soon as he was secure in power Oswald sent to Iona for a bishop, and before the end of 634 a company of monks under a leader named Aidan had reached Northumbria. They settled for security on the tidal island of Lindisfarne, where Aidan died in 651, and their monastery remained for nearly thirty years the seat of the only bishopric in Northumbria.

[1] For the literature bearing on the Irish share in the conversion of England and on the Irish contribution to the learning and culture of the Dark Ages a general reference may be made to J. F. Kenney, *The Sources for the Early History of Ireland*, vol. i. See also L. Gougaud, *Christianity in Celtic Lands*, pp. 201–6.

Within twenty years Aidan and his followers had re-established Christianity in the north. Their work had all the characteristics of a Celtic missionary enterprise. The original community at Lindisfarne lived in gaunt austerity. It was left for Aidan's successor to build a church suitable for a bishop's seat, and a timber structure, roughly thatched, was all that he attempted. Aidan himself was an ascetic evangelist, utterly indifferent to the dignity of a bishop, but influencing men of all ranks by his humility and devotion. He was intimate with Northumbrian kings and nobles, and honoured by churchmen in the south,[1] but his achievement was due to the popular veneration in which he was held. The importance of his aristocratic friendships lay in the religious foundations which they made possible. He and his companions were monks, and the monastic note runs through all their work. Already in his lifetime communities of religious women had begun to appear beyond the Humber. Heiu of Hartlepool, the first Northumbrian woman to take the veil, received it from Aidan, and it was he who persuaded Hild, the greatest of all English abbesses, to follow religion in her own country, and not, as she had proposed, in Gaul. In their general conception of the religious calling, and especially in their tendency towards asceticism, the monastic communities founded by Aidan differed widely from those of the Roman pattern. But his own moderation was remembered, and there is nothing grotesque in the tradition of his life.

On many points of ecclesiastical order the Irish church to which Aidan belonged differed from the prevailing custom of the West. It was distinguished by peculiarities of liturgy and ritual, and by an elaborate system of penitential discipline. In organization it was monastic rather than territorial; the bishop's function was ministerial, and authority rested with the abbot of the chief monastery in each tribe. The Irish method of consecrating bishops differed from continental practice, and its validity was questioned by ecclesiastics trained in other schools. The exact nature of the Irish tonsure is unknown, but its difference from the Roman fashion was evident. Above all, in its method of determining the date of Easter, the Irish church was governed by principles which differed fundamentally from

[1] In particular, by Honorius of Canterbury and Felix of Dunwich. [See Bede, *H.E.* iii. 25.]

those accepted at Rome or in the English churches founded under Roman influence.[1]

To Bede, who admired Aidan greatly, it seemed that his one error was his refusal to abandon the Irish system of Easter computation. Under Aidan's successor Finan (651–61), who like himself had been a monk at Iona, a dispute on this point between the adherents of Roman and Irish usages divided the whole Northumbrian church. For personal reasons, the court was interested in the question. King Oswiu favoured the custom which had been followed at Iona when he had lived there as a youth in exile. His wife, who was a daughter of King Edwin, had been educated in Kent after her father's death, and adhered to the system accepted by her teachers. Among the Northumbrian clergy an Irish scholar named Ronan, who had studied in Gaul and Italy, induced many of his fellows to accept the Roman computation, and engaged in a bitter controversy with the bishop.

In spite of these troubles the episcopate of Finan was marked by a notable extension of Christianity south of the Humber through priests sent out by the Northumbrian church. In 653 Peada, son of Penda king of the Mercians, then ruling the Middle Angles under his father, was baptized by Finan on his marriage with Alhflæd, Oswiu's daughter. Penda, firm in his own heathenism, allowed his son to introduce four priests into the territory under his rule, and the conversion of central England began with their coming. No details of their work are known, but soon after Penda's death in the autumn of 654 Diuma, the one Irishman of the four, was consecrated by Finan to a see which appears to have comprised Mercia, Middle Anglia, and Lindsey. The first bishops of this great diocese seem to have had no permanent seat, and the establishment of a church at Lichfield for the bishop of the Mercians belongs to the age of Archbishop Theodore. Before the retirement of the last Celtic bishop of Lindisfarne in 663 Diuma had been followed in his own diocese by three bishops in succession, the first of them Irish in birth and training, the second an Englishman of Irish education, the third, also an Englishman, of unknown antecedents. There is no trace of any intercourse between these bishops and the see of Canterbury, and there can

[1] On the difficult questions connected with the Irish and Roman systems of Easter reckoning see Kenney, op. cit., pp. 210–17.

be little doubt that all of them regarded Lindisfarne as the church to which they owed obedience.

The Northumbrian mission can hardly have begun its work in central England before one of its members left it for a separate enterprise. The flight of Bishop Mellitus from London in 616 had postponed the conversion of the East Saxons for a generation. Shortly after the middle of the century Sigeberht, king of Essex, was persuaded by Oswiu to receive baptism, and the restoration of Christianity among the East Saxons became possible. Towards this end Oswiu recalled to Northumbria Cedd, one of the four members of the recent mission to the Middle Angles, and sent him to Essex with another priest as his companion. Cedd was of English birth, but the influence of his Celtic training is apparent throughout his life. It was to Finan of Lindisfarne that he reported the result of his early work in Essex, and Finan, with two other Irish bishops, consecrated him bishop of the East Saxons. As bishop, Cedd had no fixed seat, no early writer brings him into connection with London, and his life, like that of innumerable Irish missionaries, was divided between travel and residence in monasteries of his own foundation. There still survives one remarkable memorial of his work in Essex in the church which he built in the Roman fort of Ythancæstir, at the northern end of the promontory between the rivers Crouch and Blackwater;[1] a desolate site, closely resembling that which the Irish Fursa had chosen for his monastery on the Suffolk coast in the previous generation. In later life Cedd often visited Northumbria; he became intimate with Æthelwald, the under-king of Deira, and he thus obtained a site for a monastery at Lastingham, in a fold of the Yorkshire Moors. The ritual fast, extending over an entire Lent, by which Cedd purified this site, is a singular illustration of the Celtic strain in northern Christianity. To the end of his life Cedd remained bishop of the East Saxons, among whom he established a regular ministry of priests and deacons and founded many churches, but it was to Lastingham that he retired for death in 664.

The history of the southern churches in this period is extremely obscure. The death of Archbishop Honorius in 652 ended the succession of Augustine's companions in the see of Canterbury. He was followed by a West Saxon, named in

[1] Above, p. 111.

religion Deusdedit, who died in 663. There is no evidence that Deusdedit had any authority outside Kent, and the primacy of his church must have been in virtual abeyance.[1] The most remarkable figure among the southern bishops of the time was Agilbert, second bishop of the West Saxons, whose strange career touches the history of both the northern and southern English churches. He was a Frank by birth, who had studied in southern Ireland under teachers following the Roman system of Easter-reckoning, and had received episcopal consecration in Gaul, probably in preparation for work as a missionary in England. Towards the middle of the century he arrived in Wessex and attached himself to King Cenwalh, from whom he received the episcopal seat originally given to Birinus at Dorchester on Thames. But in time the king grew weary of his outlandish speech and 'subintroduced' into Wessex another bishop, named Wine, who, like Agilbert, had been consecrated in Gaul, but was of English birth. In or soon after 660 the king set Wine as bishop in Winchester. Agilbert thereupon abandoned his see at Dorchester, and in 667 or 668, after obscure wanderings, he obtained the bishopric of Paris, which he held for at least twelve years.

Between his departure from Wessex and his appearance in Paris Agilbert played an important part in the crisis which was distracting the Northumbrian church. The strength of the Roman party in the north had grown during the later years of Bishop Finan. It was joined by Oswiu's son Alhfrith, sub-king of Deira, under the influence of his friend Cenwalh, king of Wessex, who might be arbitrary in his dealings with bishops, but was a firm supporter of Roman usages. Among the Northumbrian clergy a new generation was rising, without personal knowledge of the conditions which had prevailed before the coming of Aidan, and conscious from early life of the dignity and immemorial traditions of the Roman church. To men of this generation the conservatism of Lindisfarne meant a deliberate refusal to acknowledge the clear teaching of scripture and history. The future of the Northumbrian church was to be in their hands, but they could do little to change its practices until the spread of their opinions had forced the question on the king's attention.

He was slow to act. Finan, who died in 660, was followed by

[1] His one recorded act is the consecration of a bishop of Rochester.

a third bishop from Iona, named Colman. It was not until the autumn of 663 that the questions in debate were at last referred to a synod. The assembly met at a place called Streoneshalh, which since the eleventh century has been identified, probably correctly, as Whitby. In 663 it was the site of an important monastery of which a kinswoman of King Oswiu, named Hild, was abbess. The men who answered the king's summons represented every phase in the history of the northern church. They included James the deacon, a survivor from the days of Paulinus, and Cedd, bishop of the East Saxons, the most eminent of Aidan's pupils. Bishop Colman spoke for the Celtic party. The Roman party had no such obvious representative. Bishop Agilbert, who was visiting Northumbria, attended the synod, and was, in fact, the senior ecclesiastic present. The king regarded him as the leader among the advocates of Roman usages. But since he would have needed an interpreter, he left the statement of his case to a Northumbrian enthusiast for Roman ways named Wilfrid, who had spent five years studying the religious customs of Italy and Gaul, and at the time of the synod was ruling a community of like-minded persons at Ripon.

So far as is known the debate was confined to the central question of the method which should be followed for the determination of Easter. Colman claimed that his usage was sanctioned by the authority of St. John among the apostles, and of Anatolius among the doctors of the church; by the practice of those who had sent him to Northumbria as bishop, and by the tradition of St. Columba. Wilfrid challenged the rules which governed the Celtic Easter-reckoning, but the power of his argument lay in his emphasis on the folly of resistance to the unique authority of St. Peter, inherited by his church, and obeyed by all Christians except a part of the inhabitants of the two last islands of the Ocean. The appeal to St. Peter's authority allowed the king to close the debate in a way which suggests that his own decision had been made before it began. His famous declaration that, as between St. Peter and St. Columba, he would obey St. Peter, to whom the keys of heaven had been granted, is often regarded as the statement of a new conviction. Bede records it without comment. But Eddi, Wilfrid's biographer, who was even better placed for knowing the facts about the synod, notes that the king gave his judgement with a smile.[1]

---

[1] *Subridens*, Eddi, *Vita Wilfridi*, c. xx.

After the decision Colman retired at once to Iona, and then passed over to Ireland. Many of his Irish clergy followed him, and thirty English monks of his obedience founded a settlement on Inishboffin off Mayo, which conformed in time to Roman usages, attracted recruits from England, and received a succession of English bishops in the eighth century. Colman was succeeded at Lindisfarne by a bishop of the southern Irish consecration but probably of English birth, named Tuda, who was already known in Northumbria as an adherent of the Roman party. Tuda died soon after his appointment, and before the end of 664 the vast Northumbrian diocese was divided. Lindisfarne ceased for a time to be a bishop's seat. On Colman's departure and at his request its remaining monks were placed under the rule of Eata, abbot of Melrose, who had been a pupil of St. Aidan, but was prepared to accept the Roman Easter-reckoning. A large district in western Deira was assigned as a diocese to Wilfrid, whose church at Ripon became its cathedral. The rest of Northumbria was placed under Ceadda, brother of Cedd, the bishop of the East Saxons, whose seat was fixed in York. These changes made a tentative advance towards the realization of St. Gregory's plan for the organization of northern England, but their effect was delayed by the unhappy condition of the southern churches. Wilfrid and the party to which he belonged questioned the validity of episcopal orders conferred by bishops of British or Irish consecration. After the death of Archbishop Deusdedit, Wine of Winchester, according to Bede, was the only bishop in England against whose orders this objection could not be brought. Ceadda of York, who had been trained under Celtic influences, was content to receive consecration from Wine, with whom two British bishops were associated. But Wilfrid, the precisian, went to Gaul, and was consecrated at Compiègne by twelve Gaulish bishops, of whom his former master Agilbert was one.

The historical importance of the synod of Whitby is beyond question. It decided an issue which was paralysing the Northumbrian church with sterile controversies. It made easier the unification of the English church by Archbishop Theodore, and it made possible the Northumbrian contribution to the English missionary enterprise of the next generation. The leaders on both sides have often been blamed for failing to keep their sense of proportion. But it would be unreasonable to

expect churchmen of passionate convictions to show academic
detachment about the date of their chief festival, and in fairness
to the disputants it should be remembered that each party was
alive to the wider issues behind its arguments. To the victors
the persistence of the Irish ascetics in their ancient ways meant
a deliberate rejection of Roman authority, and indifference to
the advantages of conformity with the general body of Christians. To the Celts submission on the central question of the
Easter-reckoning meant disloyalty to the teaching of their
fathers. The Easter controversy was arid, but it was not fought
out over trifles.

There is little profit in trying to assess the relative importance
of the Irish and continental influences in the conversion of the
English. The Roman victory of 663 did not cause a general
departure of Irish clergy from England.[1] Many features of
Irish Christianity, such as its asceticism and its insistence on
penitential discipline, profoundly affected the later development of the English church. Even in regard to an earlier time,
the spheres of Irish and continental missionary enterprise
cannot be closely defined. The conversion of the Middle Angles
was begun under Irish influence, but there is no discernible
Celtic strain in the early history of Medeshamstede, better
known as Peterborough, the greatest monastery of this region.
The conversion of the West Saxons was begun by continental
missionaries, and Cenwalh, their king, was an upholder of
Roman customs, but long before his death an Irish scholar
named Maildubh had founded a notable centre of religion
and learning at Malmesbury. The Irish Fursa should be remembered beside the Burgundian Felix in any account of
the conversion of the East Angles, and even in regard to Kent,
the centre of all Roman influence in England, it is unwise
to ignore the Irish bishop Dagan who refused communion
with Laurentius and his companions. The strands of Irish
and continental influence were interwoven in every kingdom,
and at every stage of the process by which England became
Christian.

They can be clearly distinguished in the life of the saint who
has always symbolized the northern church of the seventh
century. Every historian has been conscious of the Celtic

---

[1] On the position in the north after the council see J. A. Duke, *The Columban
Church*, pp. 101–6.

influence behind the career of Cuthbert of Lindisfarne.[1] The
community at Melrose, which he joined as a novice in 651,
represented the traditions of Irish monasticism. Eata, its abbot,
had been one of the twelve original English pupils of St. Aidan.
The whole of Cuthbert's life as a monk—as guest-master of a
colony sent out from Melrose to Ripon, as prior of Melrose,
and, after 664, as prior of Lindisfarne—was spent under Eata's
authority. In his later retirement on Farne Island Cuthbert
was supported, and at first maintained, by the monks of Lindisfarne, where Eata had now become bishop.[2] His intimacy with
Eata was such that soon after his own election to the bishopric of
Hexham in 684 he prevailed with Eata to exchange sees with
him in order that he might return to Lindisfarne. Through
Eata there passed to Cuthbert a living memory of the first
Irish mission to Northumbria, and through Cuthbert its spirit
survived for twenty years the defeat of the Celtic party at the
council of Whitby. In his cultivation of the ascetic life, and in
the evangelistic journeys through which he impressed Christianity on the imagination of a barbarous people, Cuthbert belongs
to the world of ancient Irish saints.

But he was never an uncompromising upholder of Celtic
usages. His earliest biographer records that he was tonsured
after the Roman model.[3] On the question of the Easter-reckoning he must at first have taken the Celtic side. He and Eata,
his abbot, were evicted from Ripon shortly before 663 in order
to make room for a company of monks led by Wilfrid, the rising
advocate of the Roman computation. But neither Eata nor
Cuthbert can have been intransigent on this issue. Eata was
set soon afterwards as abbot over the monks of Lindisfarne who
accepted the Roman reckoning, and before long he invited
Cuthbert to serve under him as prior. By the end of his life
Cuthbert had come to regard the conservatives of the Irish
party as wanton disturbers of the peace of the church. In his
last message to the monks of Lindisfarne he enjoined them to
avoid communion with those who err from the Catholic unity
by keeping Easter at an improper time, or by a perverse way of

---

[1] The chronology of Cuthbert's life presents many difficulties, and the only
fixed points seem to be his entry into Melrose in 651, his migration to Lindisfarne
in 664, his election as bishop late in 684, followed by his consecration on 26 March
685, and his death on 20 March 687.
[2] Below, pp. 135–6.
[3] *Two Lives of Saint Cuthbert*, ed. B. Colgrave, p. 76.

living.[1] In his later years Cuthbert clearly realized that the future of religion in England depended on the maintenance of ecclesiastical order. As prior of Lindisfarne he set himself to restrain the more eccentric forms of private devotion by designing a code suitable for common observance.[2] He accepted the metropolitan authority of the archbishop of Canterbury, and it was in obedience to a synod in which the archbishop presided that he left his retirement to become a bishop.[3] In his attitude towards his new and unwelcome duties he showed that he had passed far beyond the ministerial conception of a bishop's office which prevailed in the Irish church. He considered that as bishop he was directly responsible for the state of religion in his diocese. His presence at Carlisle as a bishop, attended by a company of priests and deacons on 20 May 685[4] shows him engaged in a visitation of the diocese of Hexham within two months of his consecration on 26 March. The record of his short episcopate is a mere tissue of miracles, but it shows him preaching and administering confirmation to the rustics of the central hills, and visiting members of the king's household on their isolated estates. Aidan had travelled still more widely a generation before. But, unlike Aidan, Cuthbert moved over the country at the head of a retinue appropriate to his rank, and he was praised for maintaining a bishop's dignity.[5]

There can be no doubt that the attitude of each local king determined the date at which Christianity reached his people. But except for brief intervals, England south of the Humber formed a primitive kind of confederacy under a common overlord, and too little attention has been given to the influence of this overlordship on the progress of the conversion. The influence might well be adverse; the stagnation of the Kentish mission in the later years of Archbishop Laurentius is due in part to the dubious attitude of Rædwald, the new overlord of the southern English. But the relationship between lord and man required that an under-king should visit his overlord's court, and the visits of under-kings to overlords like Edwin and Oswald must have carried some elementary knowledge of the new religion into regions which no missionary had yet explored. Intercourse of this kind helps to explain the remarkable fact that

---

[1] Ibid., pp. 282–4. [2] Ibid., pp. 94–6. [3] Ibid., p. 110.
[4] The day of the battle of Nechtanesmere. Ibid., pp. 122, 242–8.
[5] Ibid., p. 110.

at the middle of the seventh century men sprung from kingdoms as yet newly converted or wholly heathen were qualified for the highest ecclesiastical office. The West Saxon Deusdedit was consecrated archbishop of Canterbury twenty years after the coming of Birinus, and Sussex remained heathen for a generation after 655, when the South Saxon Damian was consecrated bishop of Rochester. The examples of Damian and Deusdedit show that Bede and his successors, in treating the expansion of English Christianity as the gradual winning of kingdom after kingdom, have only told part of a complex story.

The concentration of the protagonists at Whitby on causes of division within the church can easily be allowed to obscure the fact that England was still not wholly Christian. There was no serious danger of any general relapse into heathenism. Apart from Sussex, where a heathen folk was incuriously watching a little community of Irish monks at Bosham, every English kingdom now contained the seat of a bishopric. In East Anglia, Northumbria, and Wessex Christianity had been established at court and preached in the country for at least a generation, and the continuity of the church in Kent had never been completely broken since Augustine's time. But it is significant that between 670 and 690 Archbishop Theodore found it necessary to appoint penances for those who sacrificed to devils, foretold the future with their aid, ate food that had been offered in sacrifice, or burned grain after a man was dead for the well-being of the living and of the house. It is still more significant that he was asked for his ruling whether altars might be hallowed or masses said in churches where heathen were buried, for the fact that such a question could be put indicates the survival of heathenism among the higher orders of society. It is also clear that this survival was not merely the result of conservatism in remote parts. In Kent itself, a generation after King Eorcenberht had ordered his people to destroy their idols, the laws of Wihtred contain provisions against offerings to devils. There is no doubt that Christianity was the dominant religion throughout England in 664. But it is equally certain that the older beliefs of the English people, though driven underground, were still alive.

Note on the Date of the Synod of Streoneshalh

The synod of Streoneshalh is placed by Bede in the year 664, that is in the year running from September 663 to September 664. To determine the part of the year in which the synod met it is necessary to consider Bede's chronology for the pontificate of Archbishop Deusdedit of Canterbury. According to Bede, Archbishop Honorius died on 30 September 653, that is 652 according to modern reckoning. His see was vacant for a year and six months. Deusdedit was consecrated on 26 March in a year which can only be 654. Bede states in one place that he died on 14 July in a year marked by an eclipse which is known to have occurred on 1 May 664, by the pestilence which broke out not long after the synod, and by the secession of Bishop Colman from Lindisfarne. The last three events can all be assigned to the year September 663–September 664. But in another place, the accepted text of the *Historia Ecclesiastica* states that Deusdedit sat at Canterbury for 9 years 4 months and 2 days, which will place his death on 28 July 663, that is before the year 664 can have been considered to begin on Bede's system of computation. The discrepancy as to the day of his death cannot be reconciled. But the Moore manuscript of the *Historia Ecclesiastica* when recording the length of his duration originally read *menses vii*, not *menses iiii*, and this reading is supported by at least two other manuscripts of good authority. The acceptance of this reading will place the date of Deusdedit's death on 28 October 663, which Bede would regard as falling within the Year of Grace 664. As Deusdedit is known to have died soon after the conclusion of the synod, its meeting should probably be assigned to the end of September or the beginning of October 663.

V

THE ENGLISH CHURCH FROM
THEODORE TO BONIFACE

THE five years following the council of Whitby form the most critical period in the history of the Anglo-Saxon church. Its ultimate unity had been made possible by King Oswiu's decision. But the men who were to realize this ideal were as yet untried in responsible positions, and for the moment the mere continuance of organized Christianity in England was uncertain. At the very time of the council England, like much of western Europe, was being swept by a pestilence, which removed many leaders of the clergy, depopulated whole monasteries, and produced a widespread reversion to heathenism. The East Saxons, whose bishop Cedd died in the plague, relapsed in a general panic. Individual bishops like Jaruman of Mercia laboured outside their own dioceses to prevent apostasy, and although few monastic communities seem to have escaped the plague, most of them survived it. But the whole organization of the church in England was rapidly disintegrating in these years; it was becoming difficult to maintain an ordered succession of bishops, and the see of Canterbury itself was vacant.

Archbishop Deusdedit, who had sat at Canterbury since the spring of 654, had been overshadowed by stronger men in other sees. But the tradition of Augustine always prevented Canterbury from becoming a mere local diocese, and Oswiu, king of Northumbria, was associated with Egbert, king of Kent, in the task of finding a new archbishop. In 667 the two kings, in accordance with the choice and consent of the church of the English people, selected Wighard, a priest of the late archbishop's *familia*, for this office. His first duty was to be the consecration of new bishops to vacant sees, and it was probably to prevent any future question as to his authority that he was sent to Rome for consecration by the pope himself. He was able to present his credentials to the pope, but died of the plague immediately afterwards with nearly all his companions. At the moment the papacy was passing through a time of grave depression; Pope Vitalian had recently been made to feel his subjection to the Eastern Emperor, and policy as well as the necessities of the English church indicated that the pope should himself provide an archbishop for the English. He first approached Hadrian, a learned monk of African origin who was abbot of a monastery near Naples. Feeling himself unworthy of this office, Hadrian proposed in his place a monk of greater age, named Andrew, belonging to a neighbouring house. Andrew's ill health prevented him from undertaking a bishop's duties, and in his stead Hadrian presented to the pope another monk of his acquaintance named Theodore, a native of Tarsus, sixty-six years of age, then living in Rome with a great reputation as a scholar, philosopher, and divine.

This remarkable nomination proved to be the prelude to a new period in the history of the Anglo-Saxon church, but at the time the pope naturally doubted its wisdom. Theodore had acquired his learning in the East, in an age when bitter theological controversies were separating the eastern from the western churches. He was a monk of eastern tonsure, and the discipline with which he was familiar differed in character, as in origin, from the monastic life of the West. Superficially there can have been little to suggest that this aged scholar from Asia Minor was fitted for the task of restoring Roman order in a distracted northern church, and the success of his rule in England was partly due to the conditions which the pope attached to his appointment. Abbot Hadrian, who knew the routes across Gaul, and could provide an escort from the men on his own property, was required to accompany Theodore to England, and to instruct him in Catholic doctrine, so that he should not introduce any Greek perversities into the teaching of his church. In the event, Hadrian remained with Theodore in England, accompanied him on his first visitation of his province, and afterwards, as abbot of the monastery of St. Peter and St. Paul outside Canterbury, worked beside him as a teacher. Theodore owed the completeness of his achievement in England to the constant support of a man at least his equal in learning, who was insistent, like himself, on the adoption of Roman usage and the recognition of Roman authority.

Towards the close of 667 Theodore was ordained subdeacon. On 26 March 668, when he had substituted the Roman for the eastern tonsure, he was consecrated archbishop by the pope. On 27 May he began his journey to Britain, accompanied by Abbot Hadrian and by Benedict Biscop, a friend of Wilfrid of Ripon and a leader of the Roman party in the Northumbrian church, who had been studying the monastic life at Lerins, its Mediterranean centre. The travellers became separated in Gaul. Hadrian was detained for a time by Ebroin, mayor of the palace in Neustria, who suspected him of being an agent of the emperor, sent to work in Britain against Frankish interests. Theodore was allowed to live with Agilbert, bishop of Paris, who was one of Ebroin's partisans. It was clearly from Agilbert that Theodore derived the intimate knowledge of English conditions with which he entered on the government of his province. After a long delay he was enabled to continue his journey by the intervention of Egbert, king of Kent, whose reeve brought him with Ebroin's leave to Quentavic at the mouth of the Canche. After a short illness he crossed to Kent, and reached his church of Canterbury on 27 May 669, a year after his departure from Rome.

His first undertaking was a visitation of his province, in which he enjoined the clergy to adopt the Roman Easter-reckoning and observe a canonical method of life. Before the end of the year he had begun the task of establishing a regular diocesan episcopate in England. At the time of his visitation there was no bishop in Wessex, Mercia, East Anglia, or at Rochester. The only bishop in office between the Humber and the Channel was Wine, the successor of Agilbert as bishop of the West Saxons. He had recently abandoned his see after a dispute with King Cenwalh, and bought the bishopric of London from Wulfhere, king of Mercia. North of the Humber Wilfrid, with his seat at Ripon, was acting as bishop in western Deira, and Ceadda was ruling the rest of the Northumbrian diocese from York. On his first visitation Theodore took exception to Ceadda's orders, and removed him from York, where he was succeeded by Wilfrid, who now became bishop of all Northumbria. Out of respect for Ceadda's humility Theodore supplied whatever defect existed in his orders, and soon afterwards sent him as bishop to the Mercians, among whom he fixed his seat at Lichfield. Within the year Theodore had established bishops at Rochester and Dunwich, and in 670, at the request of the king and people of Wessex, he consecrated Leuthere, nephew of Agilbert, to the see of Winchester. By the autumn of 672 ecclesiastical order was so far restored in England that Theodore could summon a general council of the whole English church.

This assembly, which met at Hertford on 26 September 672, did not include the whole English episcopate. Only four of Theodore's suffragans appeared in person. If the simoniacal Wine of London received a summons, he ignored it. Wilfrid of York was content to send proctors. The strength of the council lay in the 'many masters of the church', who, as Bede says, knew and loved the canonical decrees of the fathers. The canons proposed by Theodore secured the individual bishop against the invasion of his diocese by other bishops, empowered him to check the migration of his clergy, and ruled that his precedence should be determined by the date of his consecration. Monks were forbidden to leave their monasteries without their abbot's licence, and bishops were forbidden to trouble monasteries or take away their possessions. The method of determining Easter was defined, and it was agreed that a synod should be held each year on 1 August at a place called Clofeshoh, which has not yet been identified. The problems raised by the institution of Christian marriage among a half-converted people were covered by a canon forbidding incest, the abandonment of wives for any cause except adultery, and the remarriage of those who had so offended. On all these canons there seems to have been agreement, but a proposal that the number of bishops should be increased as the number of converts grew was postponed for future discussion. Collectively these canons, each of which was derived from older sources, amount to little more than an assertion of the elementary principles necessary to any regular system of ecclesiastical administration. They have a more general importance because they were put out by a body which represented the entire church of the English peoples. For nearly seventy years, from the arrival of Theodore to the elevation of the see of York into an archbishopric in 735, the whole English church acknowledged a single archbishop and was capable of united action. The synod of Hertford was the first occasion on which that unity found practical expression. It is easy to exaggerate the political influence of an ecclesiastical council on a people by no means wholly Christian, but the synod of 672 can fairly be regarded as marking a definite stage in the process which wore down the separatism of the different English kingdoms.

By its reserve on the question of creating new dioceses the council of Hertford laid a direct responsibility on the archbishop. Of the seven English sees existing in 672 Canterbury and Rochester were small, London was only of moderate extent, and Dunwich, although it could be divided with profit, was not beyond the energy of a single bishop. But the sees of Winchester, Lichfield, and York represented three large and composite kingdoms, and the question of their division was urgent. The political disunion of England gave Theodore no opportunity of dealing with the problem as a whole. He was compelled to wait on events, and his success was naturally incomplete. There is no evidence that he ever attempted to divide the see of Winchester. In the latter part of his life conditions were unfavourable for the endowment of a second bishopric in western Wessex, and he was the friend of Hæddi, who succeeded Leuthere at Winchester in 676. He provided for the division of the East Anglian see by supplying its aged bishop with two coadjutors, each of whom afterwards became bishop of an independent diocese, one sitting at Dunwich and the other at North Elmham in Norfolk. In regard to the graver problem of the great Mercian diocese Theodore's action was more decisive. Lindsey, which had formed part of the original diocese of Lichfield, was conquered by Ecgfrith of Northumbria in 674, and came under the authority of the bishop of York. In 677, when Theodore was at last able to divide the Northumbrian see, he formed Lindsey into a separate diocese, which survived the reconquest of this region by Æthelred of Mercia in 678. Before 680 Theodore had created the diocese of Worcester for the Hwicce of the Severn valley, and that of Hereford for their western neighbours the Magonsætan. There are also traces of an attempt, which cannot be precisely dated, to found new bishoprics in the southern provinces of the Mercian kingdom. The series of bishops of Leicester, serving the Middle Anglian dependencies of Mercia, begins in Theodore's time,[1] although the see was not permanently established until 737. Bede refers

[1] *Councils*, iii. 128–9. The position of Leicester as the see of the Middle Angles is well brought out by two documents issued in the Council of Clofeshoh on 12 October 803. One describes bishop Werenberht as *Meditanorum* [*sic*] *Anglorum episcopus*, the other as *Legorensis civitatis episcopus*. *C.S.* 309, 312.

incidentally to a certain Ætla who became bishop of Dorchester on Thames in this period,[1] and his appointment probably represents the temporary provision of a bishop for the West Saxon lands beneath the Chiltern range, which the Mercian kings had recently conquered. Theodore was plainly unable to complete the ecclesiastical organization which he had designed for the Mercian provinces, but the creation of three permanent sees in this region remains a notable achievement.

Theodore's opportunism is most clearly seen in his dealing with the Northumbrian situation, which led directly to the first appeal by an English ecclesiastic to the see of Rome. Between 669 and 677 Wilfrid ruled the whole Northumbrian church.[2] He became in these years an outstanding figure in the secular as well as the ecclesiastical life of the North. The heads of innumerable monasteries placed themselves under his protection or made him the heir of their possessions; he acquired many great estates, and his household became a school where young nobles received their military education. He was the spiritual director of the Northumbrian queen Æthelthryth, and obtained from her a site at Hexham on which he founded a great monastery. His fall from power was an indirect result of his relationship with the queen, for he incurred the ill will of King Ecgfrith, her husband, by encouraging her desire for the religious life. After her departure from the world into the monastery of Coldingham Ecgfrith married a second wife who became Wilfrid's bitter enemy, and excited her husband to jealousy of his wealth, the number of his monasteries, and the magnificence of his military following. The exact course of events is obscure at this point, but Wilfrid was ultimately deprived of his bishopric and his property and expelled from Northumbria. Theodore, with whom the interest of the Northumbrian church outweighed the claims of ecclesiastical order, accepted the king's decision, visited the north, and proceeded to the division of Wilfrid's see. Before the end of 677 he had consecrated three bishops in Wilfrid's place. A monk from Whitby, named Bosa, was ordained bishop of Deira. His seat was placed in Wilfrid's principal church of York, where he

[1] *H.E.* iv. 23.

[2] On the chronology of Wilfrid's life after 669, the circumstances of his appeals to Rome, and his position in England at different periods, a general reference may be made to the chapter on St. Wilfrid and the church of Ripon in *Studies in Chronology and History* by R. L. Poole (1934), pp. 56–81.

established a communal way of life and a continuous routine of service for his clergy.[1] Eata, prior of Lindisfarne, Cuthbert's friend and teacher, was ordained bishop of Bernicia, with the choice of a seat in Lindisfarne or in Wilfrid's monastery of Hexham. The third see was created for the unstable Northumbrian province of Lindsey.

Between February and September 677 Wilfrid left England to state his case before the pope. He moved southward very slowly. He was driven by a storm on to the Frisian coast, and spent the winter of 677 in preaching to the heathen of that region, an episode which marks the beginning of English missionary enterprise in the Netherlands. Resuming his journey in the following spring, he stayed for a time with Dagobert II, king of the Austrasian Franks, and then with Perctarit, king of the Lombards. It is probable that he spent the greater part of the year 678 with the two kings. On reaching Rome, he found Pope Agatho acquainted with the matter in dispute by letters from Theodore, and in October 679 a council of fifty-three bishops met at the Lateran for its settlement. Its decision was that Wilfrid should be restored to his see, that the bishops who had replaced him should be removed, and that with the advice of a local council he should choose others in their place, whom Archbishop Theodore should consecrate. The council seems, in fact, to have aimed at a compromise, restoring Wilfrid to his seat in York, but approving Theodore's policy of dividing the Northumbrian see. It avoided blaming Theodore for acquiescing in Wilfrid's expulsion, but it was clearly of the opinion that Wilfrid had been treated harshly. It is significant that in addition to a copy of the council's decision he received from the pope a separate privilege, confirming him in the possession of his monasteries at Hexham and Ripon, of which the former had been offered as an alternative seat to the new bishop of the Bernicians.

Wilfrid's case formed only part of the English business which came before the council of October 679. An isolated record of another session of the same council shows that the general state of the English church was also under consideration. According to this document a dispute which only papal authority could appease had arisen between Archbishop Theodore and the bishops of his province. The dispute was probably

---

[1] Alcuin, *De Sanctis Eboracensis Ecclesiae*, Monumenta Alcuiniana, pp. 107–8.

connected with Theodore's policy of increasing the English episcopate, for the council appears to have decreed that twelve bishops, including the archbishop of Canterbury, were sufficient for the English province. No later forger is likely to have made a Roman council depart so widely as this from the Gregorian constitution of the English church; and the document has probably preserved a genuine record of a decision actually taken at Rome in the autumn of 679.[1] It certainly agrees with what is known of the condition of the English church in that year. There seem to have been precisely twelve bishops in England at this time, and the dispute which had arisen over the division of the Northumbrian see is likely to have predisposed the council against any advance beyond this number. There is no other evidence of a general disagreement between Theodore and his bishops, but some years previously Theodore had deposed Bishop Wynfrith of Lichfield for an act of disobedience which may well have been a symptom of wider opposition to the archbishop's policy. There were innumerable occasions of friction in the reorganization of a national church.

Meanwhile, the policy of the Eastern Emperor had led to the summoning of the second ecclesiastical council known to have been held in England under Theodore's primacy. In 678 the Emperor Constantine Pogonatus, wishing to obtain the decision of a general council against the Monothelite heresy, had asked Pope Donus to send representatives from his church to Constantinople. The death of Donus left the responsibility of action to his successor Agatho, who made plans for convening a council of bishops in Rome, and in the meantime obtained declarations of catholic orthodoxy from other churches. In England this declaration was made by a council held at Hatfield on 17 September 679, under the presidency of Theodore, who alone among western ecclesiastics had seen the whole course of the Monothelite controversy in the East. The Roman council met on 27 March 680, and Bishop Wilfrid, who had remained in Rome for the meeting, attested its confession of faith as bishop of York and legate of the synod of Britain—a style which seems to imply an unrecorded commission from the Council of Hatfield. The controversies which troubled the English church did not affect its dogmatic unity.

On Wilfrid's return to England in the summer of 680 he

---

[1] Spelman's *Concilia* i. 158 and *Councils* iii. 133-5.

brought his case before a Northumbrian council, producing an authenticated copy of the judgement of the Roman synod in his favour, and apparently the papal bull confirming Ripon and Hexham to him. But the council showed no respect to Wilfrid or his documents, and went to the length of ordering his arrest. After an imprisonment which may have lasted for as long as nine months, he left Northumbria, spent some uneasy weeks in Middle Anglia and Wessex, and at last found refuge with Æthelwalh, the Christian king of the heathen South Saxons. Within the next five years Wilfrid and a band of followers had converted the South Saxons, and Wilfrid had received from their king the estate at Selsey, which afterwards became the seat of the South Saxon bishopric. Towards the close of this period Æthelwalh was killed by the West Saxon exile Cæd-walla. Wilfrid thereupon attached himself to Cædwalla, and on his conquest of the Isle of Wight in 686 received a quarter of the whole island from him. Its inhabitants were still heathen, but before Wilfrid could undertake their conversion it became possible for him to return to Northumbria, and he entrusted his property in the island, and the responsibilities which it carried, to Beornwine, his sister's son. In less than a generation the last of the heathen English tribes had accepted Christianity.

There is no sign that Theodore had intervened between Wilfrid and his enemies at the Northumbrian council of 680. The papal judgement in Wilfrid's favour could not be carried out against the king's will. Ecclesiastical penalties could not wisely be invoked against a king who was the only protector of the northern church, and Ecgfrith remained implacable until his death. In this situation, Theodore used Wilfrid's expulsion as an opportunity for a further division of the Northumbrian sees. He founded a new bishopric at Abercorn for the Picts who were Ecgfrith's subjects, placed a second Bernician bishop in Wilfrid's church of Hexham,[1] and translated the bishop of Lindsey, recently expelled from his see by the king of Mercia, to Wilfrid's original diocese of Ripon. These changes were adequate as an immediate solution of the problem caused by Wilfrid's exile, and they were accepted by the whole Northumbrian church. On the other hand, Theodore, whom the Roman

[1] Under circumstances which are nowhere explained, Tunberht, the new bishop, was 'deposed' before the end of 684. To fill the vacancy thus created Cuthbert was consecrated bishop of Hexham on 26 March 685.

church had sent to Britain, cannot have been content with a settlement which involved the rejection of papal mandates; and his conduct shows that he sought the opportunity for a compromise which would at least bring back Wilfrid honourably into the north. The death of King Ecgfrith in 685 removed the most obdurate of Wilfrid's enemies, and in 686 Theodore and Wilfrid were reconciled at London in the presence of a company of bishops.

To Theodore the reconciliation was part of a general preparation for approaching death. He expressed sorrow for yielding to the kings who had deprived Wilfrid of his possessions, and, if Wilfrid's biographer can be trusted, proposed him to the assembled bishops as his own successor. Wilfrid, referring this proposal to a larger council, only asked that Theodore should announce the reconciliation to his friends and request them to restore some part of the property of which they had unjustly deprived him. Theodore thereupon wrote letters to Aldfrith, the new king of Northumbria, to Aldfrith's sister, the abbess of Whitby, and to King Æthelred of Mercia, asking them to make peace with Wilfrid as he himself had done. Before the end of 686 Wilfrid had returned to Northumbria. But the ecclesiastical settlement of 680 was not affected by his arrival. Bosa seems to have remained bishop of York from his appointment in 677 until his death in 705. St. Cuthbert, appointed bishop of Hexham in 684, had exchanged sees with his friend Eata of Lindisfarne, and continued to be bishop of the latter diocese until he retired from the world in 687. The see of Hexham had been vacated by Eata's death shortly before Wilfrid's return, but Bede states that Eata was succeeded at once by John, commonly called John of Beverley, who remained at Hexham until he was translated to York in 705. On the other hand, so far as can be seen, Ripon, Wilfrid's original church, was without a ruler at the moment[1] and he resided there as bishop for the next five years, governing the see of Lindisfarne as a mere administrator when it was left vacant by St. Cuthbert's death in March 687. Superficially the Northumbrian church was at peace when Archbishop Theodore died on 19 September 690.

He lives in history as a great ecclesiastical statesman, who gave unity and organization to a distracted church. Historians

[1] On the situation at Ripon see Poole, *Studies in Chronology and History*, pp. 71-2.

have always emphasized the importance of his practical achievements—the councils which he held and the bishoprics which he founded. But the men of the next generation honoured him also as a legist, who could show the bearing of both Greek and Roman practice on English problems.[1] He himself was not an author, nor save in the most general sense a legislator, but the routine of his office made him a judge. Soon after his death his disciples made collections of the penances which he had appointed for offences against morality, for heresy, heathen observances, and behaviour of a sort forbidden to Christians. Through their work his decisions, themselves affected by earlier Irish custom, came to influence the whole penitential system of the West, and in particular that of the churches established in Germany by English missionaries of the next generation. In England they formed the basis of a penitential order which survived the Norman Conquest.

The latter part of the work commonly known as Theodore's *Poenitentiale* is a separate collection of canons, primarily relating to the internal order of the church, but often impinging on the sphere of secular law.[2] The ecclesiastical canons, though a fundamental authority for the state of the church in Theodore's day, have less general interest than the sentences in which he tries to bring the religious conception of marriage into relation with the life of his people. He was compelled to admit a variety of causes which might lead to the dissolution of a marriage, and he was by no means rigid in regard to the circumstances under which one or other party might marry again. He allowed remarriage after five years to a husband or wife whose partner had been carried off into hopeless captivity. Contradictory opinions are attributed to him on the question whether the return of the captive should dissolve the second marriage, and there is a note of uncertainty in his definition of the conditions under which a husband or wife whose partner entered religion should be free to marry again. But he was unequivocal in allowing remarriage to a man whose wife, despising him, and refusing reconciliation, abandoned him for five years. He only

[1] The text printed in *Councils*, iii. 173–204 under the title *Poenitentiale Theodori* contains virtually all the matter which represents a genuine tradition of Theodore's judgements and teaching. The history of its transmission is extremely complicated. The conclusions which seem best established are summarized by F. de Zulueta, *E.H.R.* xlv (1930), pp. 645–7.

[2] *Councils*, iii. 190–203.

imposed a year's delay on a woman, not previously married, whose husband had been condemned to penal slavery. The whole tenor of his canons shows his anxiety that a moral life should not be made impossible for those whose marriages were broken by disaster. He had the humanity of a man who had known many countries and the customs of many churches.

Theodore found no early biographer, and there are many aspects of his work to which no ancient writer draws attention. It is, for example, unlikely to be through chance that the oldest English charters of which the authenticity is beyond question come from the time when Theodore was reorganizing the English church. The solemn charter of pre-Conquest England is derived from the private charter of the later Roman empire.[1] The members of Augustine's mission were no doubt familiar with documents of this type, and various medieval manuscripts have preserved a small group of charters purporting to record gifts by Æthelberht or Eadbald of Kent to churches of Augustine's foundation. But the formulas in which these instruments are drafted are of a Frankish, not a Roman type, and each of them shows features which must have been inserted at a later time.[2] In any case, there is no evidence for the use of the charter in England during the fifty years between Laurentius and Theodore, and the permanent introduction of the written instrument as a means of recording a grant of land can reasonably be attributed to Theodore and his companions. Few records of any kind have survived from the first ten years of Theodore's archiepiscopate; but the oldest English charter preserved in a contemporary text is dated in May 679,[3] and it supports the authenticity of several slightly earlier documents expressed in similar formulas, but only known through later copies. By the date of Theodore's death the practice of confirming gifts by charter was spreading somewhat rapidly among the southern English rulers. At the end of the seventh century a long series of such documents was evidence of the permanence

---

[1] As was established conclusively by W. H. Stevenson, *E.H.R.* xxix (1914), p. 695.

[2] These charters are discussed by Margaret Deanesly in *Trans. R. Hist. Soc.* xxiii. 53–68 [but see W. Levison, *England and the Continent in the Eighth Century*, pp. 174–233]. It is perhaps most probable that the records on which they were founded were not charters in the precise sense of the word, but notices of gifts entered in gospel-books or other volumes.

[3] *C.S.* 45; *Facsimiles of Ancient Charters in the British Museum*, i. 1.

which Theodore's rule had given to English ecclesiastical institutions.

Theodore's death was followed by a long vacancy in his see. Nothing more is heard of his proposal that Wilfrid should succeed him, but it can hardly have been rejected without reference to a synod, and consequent delay. It was not until 1 July 692 that the vacancy at Canterbury was filled by the choice of Berhtwald, abbot of Reculver. For reasons which are unknown he sought consecration in Gaul and received it a year after his election from the archbishop of Lyons. Berhtwald was in no sense comparable to his great predecessor, but he maintained the authority of his see and increased the number of his suffragan bishops. The series of bishops of Selsey begins in his time, and in 705 he consecrated Aldhelm, abbot of Malmesbury, to a see established at Sherborne for Wessex beyond Selwood. In Kent he was associated with a king who was prepared to grant remarkable privileges to ecclesiastical institutions. The laws of King Wihtred, issued apparently in 695, grant complete freedom from taxation to the church; and in a later Kentish council the monasteries founded by the king or his ancestors are declared free from secular lordship, so that each community may henceforward choose its own head, subject only to the bishop's consent. But the most remarkable proof of Berhtwald's influence and authority is given by a letter addressed to him by Waldhere, bishop of London, in 704 or 705.[1] The bishop states that he has been invited to a council shortly to be held at Brentford for the settlement of disputes between the kings of Essex and the king of Wessex, in which ecclesiastical persons are involved. His presence is needed because the kings have promised to observe whatever form of agreement he and the West Saxon bishop may devise. But he cannot go to the council without the archbishop's leave, because in a synod of the previous year it had been agreed that there should be no intercourse with the West Saxons until they had obeyed the archbishop's decree touching the consecration of bishops—a clear reference to the long-delayed division of the West Saxon diocese. He promises to do whatever the archbishop may order in regard to this meeting, and he adds that he has recently refused the invitation of Cenred, king of Mercia, to a council summoned to deal with the 'reconciliation' of a certain Ælf-

[1] *C.S.* 115; *Facsimiles of Anglo-Saxon Charters in the British Museum*, i. 5.

thryth because he did not know the archbishop's mind in the matter. This document, which is the first letter known to have been written by one Englishman to another, gives a curious illustration of the confused relations of the southern English kings at a moment when they had no common overlord. It shows the influence which a bishop might exert as a mediator at such a time, and the respect of the lay world for the bishop's office. But the letter is even more important as evidence of the strength of the tradition which Theodore had established. The idea of a centralized church had survived a dangerous vacancy in the see of Canterbury.

For ten years after Berhtwald's election the complete realization of this idea was prevented by the attitude of Bishop Wilfrid. He had never reconciled himself to the position which he had accepted in 686, and during the vacancy of the see of Canterbury he raised again his claim to the whole Northumbrian diocese. King Aldfrith was insistent that he should observe Theodore's settlement of the Northumbrian church, and expelled him from Northumbria in 691. For the next eleven years Wilfrid lived under the protection of Æthelred, king of Mercia, administering the whole Mercian diocese for a time, and then, apparently, confining himself to its Middle Anglian provinces. His position in Mercia was dignified; he founded many monasteries in that country, and he was King Æthelred's friend. But he had not yet abandoned the hope of returning to Northumbria as bishop of York, and in 699 or 700 he brought his suit by proxy before Pope Sergius I. The pope referred the question to an English synod, and in 702 King Aldfrith held a council at Austerfield, on the southern border of Northumbria, where Wilfrid opened his case to an assembly which included Archbishop Berhtwald and most of the bishops of his province.

Only one account of the proceedings at Austerfield has survived, and the course of events is far from clear. But it is certain that Wilfrid's claim was bitterly resented, and that an influential part of the council wished to bring about his ruin. His opponents were naturally exasperated by his persistence in asserting claims which if accepted would unseat every bishop in the north, and by his obvious contempt for the judgement of an English council. An uneasy consciousness that he had a real case against them is unlikely to have moved them in his favour.

After an angry debate, in which it was proposed that Wilfrid should be deprived of all his property in Mercia as well as Northumbria, the council agreed to leave him in possession of Ripon, on the impossible condition that he should confine himself within the precincts of the monastery and lay aside the office of a bishop. It was inevitable that he should appeal again to Rome; and after entrusting his interests to King Æthelred of Mercia he set out with a small following, excommunicated by his Northumbrian enemies. According to one of his companions he travelled on foot from the coast of northern Gaul to Rome, followed by messengers from Archbishop Berhtwald carrying letters of accusation against him. The pleading which followed extended over four months in the early part of 704. Wilfrid requested that effect should be given to Pope Agatho's decree restoring him to the see of York, or, at least, that Ripon and Hexham should be restored to him. To the charge of contumacy towards the archbishop and the council of Auster-field he replied that while refusing a preliminary demand for his unconditional submission, he had promised to accept any judgement which was in accordance with the canons and the decree of Pope Agatho. In view of this reply the synod declined to go further with the case without fuller knowledge of what had happened at Austerfield. But after an adjournment certain members of the synod suddenly introduced the irrelevant circumstance that Wilfrid had subscribed to the Roman confession of faith against the Monothelites in 680, and out of respect for his age and eminence the synod proceeded to a decision. On the technical ground that it could not decide the suit until Wilfrid's accusers had appeared in person at Rome, it ordered Archbishop Berhtwald to hold a synod in England for its settlement, and enjoined the kings of Northumbria and Mercia to keep in mind the decrees which Pope Agatho and his successors had issued on Wilfrid's behalf. It was a decision which settled nothing; but it safeguarded the archbishop's authority, appeased Wilfrid, and opened the way to a compromise. Wilfrid was more than seventy years of age; he passed through a dangerous illness in the course of his return to England, and in the end he abandoned the dream of a restoration to the see of York. King Aldfrith, with whom no compromise was possible, died in December 704, and within a year Wilfrid was restored to his churches of Ripon and Hexham by the judgement of a synod held by Archbishop Berhtwald near the river Nidd. After four years of peace he died in 709 in his Middle Anglian monastery of Oundle.

Despite abundant information about Wilfrid's career it is hard to form an impression of his personality. His life was written by Eddi, his chanter, who saw nothing but malice in opposition to his hero, and was capable of distorting facts in his honour. Bede, who was in sympathy with most of Wilfrid's ideals, treats him with a curious detachment, and he was opposed by many persons whose motives are beyond criticism. He was certainly one of the greatest men of his generation. He combined the passion of an evangelist with a natural power of leadership, and he could move among the rulers of his day as one of their own kind. But his abilities were thwarted by his identification of his own interests with the cause of religious order, and for all his insistence on the universal authority of the Roman church he remained essentially an individualist. The ultimate significance of his work lies in the achievements which he claimed for himself at the council of Austerfield— the eradication of the Irish teaching about the reckoning of Easter and the shape of the tonsure, the introduction of a method of chanting in accordance with the practice of the primitive church, and the establishment of the rule of St. Benedict in England.

It does not seem that Wilfrid ever raised the general question of the relation of the northern churches to the see of Canterbury, and he should not be regarded as standing for the ecclesiastical independence of Northumbria. The organization of the Northumbrian church was still rudimentary in his time, and its development was delayed by the controversies to which he was a party. But the idea of a northern archbishopric was never forgotten, and its realization gradually became possible as men of a younger generation came into power. Early in 731 the death of Archbishop Berhtwald removed the last ecclesiastic of high rank who had known the time of confusion before the coming of Theodore. He was succeeded by Tatwine, a Mercian abbot, who died in the summer of 734. In the following year, probably before the consecration of Tatwine's successor, Egbert, bishop of York, received an archbishop's pallium from Pope Gregory III. The elevation of the see of York into an archbishopric destroyed the constitutional unity of the English church. In later centuries the ecclesiastical independence of the north increased Northumbrian separatism, and formed a serious obstacle to the political unity of the English people. But the men who secured independence for their church were not concerned with its political consequences. To them, the establishment of an archbishopric at York was a step towards an increase in the number of Northumbrian bishops. Egbert of York, who was known to realize the importance of this work, belonged to the Northumbrian royal family, and might therefore hope to overcome local resistance to the foundation of new sees. An archbishop's pallium would give him power for this end over the whole Northumbrian church, and enable him to found new dioceses without waiting for authorization from Rome. In the end, this policy failed. Northumbria fell into political disorder, and endowments could not be found for the new sees. Archbishop Egbert was the most eminent English ecclesiastic of his generation; but his fame rests on his work for the instruction of the Northumbrian clergy, and in particular on the great school which he founded at York.

After the creation of the see of Leicester in 737, the diocesan organization of the English church was unchanged for many years. Its development had been arrested in the north, where four dioceses covered all Northumbria.[1] But the southern province contained thirteen dioceses[2] which, with few exceptions, were of moderate extent, and even in Northumbria episcopal supervision was a reality. These dioceses had been founded under various influences, and there was no uniformity in the constitution of the bodies which surrounded the several bishops in their cathedrals. At Lindisfarne and Hexham the bishop was the head of a monastery. At Canterbury Augustine had established a body of clergy who lived together but were unbound by any monastic rule.[3] Traces of a similar constitution

[1] Ripon had ceased to be a bishop's seat on Wilfrid's death. Thenceforward, York remained the only bishopric in Deira. Northumbria beyond Tees was divided between the bishoprics of Lindisfarne and Hexham until approximately 731, when a new diocese was founded at Whithorn for the congregations which had recently come into being in the country afterwards known as Galloway (*H.E.* v. 23). The succession of its bishops can be traced downwards into the ninth century. The see of Abercorn, founded by Theodore for the Picts under Northumbrian overlordship, became extinct after the battle of Nechtanesmere.

[2] Canterbury, Rochester, Selsey, Winchester, Sherborne, London, Leicester, Worcester, Hereford, Lichfield, Lindsey, Dunwich, Elmham.

[3] Above, pp. 107–8.

have been observed at Worcester[1] and Rochester.[2] The earliest
description of the cathedral community at Winchester defines it
as a group of priests, deacons, and clergy.[3] Even at Canterbury
the archbishop's clergy had abandoned the habit of communal
residence by the early part of the ninth century, when it was
reimposed by a reforming archbishop.[4] In the tenth century the
clergy attendant on the cathedrals of Worcester and Winchester
had ceased to form a communal society and were replaced by
monks. On the eve of the Norman Conquest most cathedral
churches which were not definitely monastic seem to have been
served by clergy who were maintained out of a common
revenue, but lived in separate houses. In most cases this system
seems to represent the abandonment of communal life by a body
of secular clergy rather than the secularization of a community
which was originally monastic.

In the age of Theodore and Bede the men who insisted on the
foundation of new bishoprics were not concerned with mere
matters of organization. The state of religion in any part of
England depended on the activity of its bishop. Only a minority
of the clergy ever rose to the priesthood, and the division of a
diocese into parishes, each under the spiritual charge of its
own priest, was still a remote ideal in the early eighth century.
In Bede's opinion preaching was the first duty of a bishop; and
the ordination of priests was a means of bringing instruction
and the sacraments to districts which the bishop himself could
not reach. Even St. Cuthbert, whose desire was for a life of
solitary meditation, entered on a course of incessant travel as
soon as he had undertaken the office of a bishop. In the eighth
century the bishop still took an important part in every stage of
the process by which admission was gained into the Christian
community. He was the principal instructor of candidates for
baptism, he frequently administered that rite, and he alone
could complete it by confirmation. A bishop's infirmity meant
that a whole generation might fail to obtain access to the sacraments of the church. Bishop Daniel of Winchester, who had

[1] J. Armitage Robinson, *St. Oswald and the Church of Worcester*, pp. 8–11.
[2] See R. A. L. Smith, *E.H.R.* lx (1945), pp. 289–99.
[3] In 858 Bishop Swithun granted Farnham to King Æthelbald of Wessex 'cum
consensu et licentia eiusdem æcclesiæ congregationis, hoc est presbiteris diaconibus
et omni clero consentientibus'. *C.S.* 495.
[4] Margaret Deanesly, 'The Familia at Christchurch, Canterbury'; *Essays in
Medieval History presented to Thomas Frederick Tout*, pp. 1–13.

once been an exemplary bishop, became blind towards the close of his life, and the tradition of the multitude of children who had died without baptism in his time had passed to the Continent before the end of the century.[1]

It was only by slow degrees that the religious life of the English village community became centred upon a church served by a resident priest. Already in the seventh century, the parish as a local unit appears in the earliest life of St. Cuthbert, which describes a vision seen by the saint as he was staying in a *parrochia* called Osingadun belonging to the abbess of Whitby.[2] But the general establishment of a parochial system was impossible until kings and their companions had been persuaded to build and endow churches on their estates, and the impulse to this work spread very gradually from the higher to the lower ranks of the nobility. The general evolution of the Old English parish is represented in outline by the classification of churches recognized by late Old English law[3]—the 'head minster', or cathedral, the 'ordinary minster', the lesser church with a graveyard, and the 'field church'. The head minster, in which a bishop had his seat, stands apart from all other churches. The 'ordinary minster' of this series is the 'old minster' of other texts, the *matrix ecclesia* of medieval documents. Most of these churches were royal or episcopal foundations, and traces of their original dignity often survived far into the middle ages. In many, perhaps in most cases, the lesser church arose within the original parish of the *matrix ecclesia*, and the memory of its origin was often preserved by a pension from its priest to the rector of the parish from which its territory had been withdrawn. The field church, in its turn, arose for the benefit of a community established on lands newly brought under cultivation. In its essential features the parochial system of the middle ages represents the gradual foundation of new churches within the territory dependent on the primitive minster.

The word *mynster* is the Old English form of the Latin *monasterium*, and there is no doubt that many ancient parish churches actually represent early monasteries which have disappeared without other trace. The missionary impulse was

---

[1] *S. Bonifatii et Lulli Epistolae*, ed. Tangl, p. 249.

[2] *Two Lives of Saint Cuthbert*, ed. B. Colgrave, p. 126; cf. *Review of English Studies*, xvi (1940), pp. 462.

[3] Set out in the Laws of Æthelred II (vii, c. 5. 1) and Cnut (1, c. 3. 2).

strong in early English monasticism, and the foundation of a monastery was a natural means of spreading Christianity among a backward people. There is definite evidence that the monastery of Breedon in Leicestershire was founded in order to bring teaching and baptism to the men of the surrounding country.[1] On the other hand, it should not be assumed that the description of a community as a *monasterium* necessarily means that its members were monks. In the eighth century and even later the word was often applied to a church served by a group of clergy sharing a communal life, and it is through this usage that the greater parish church came to be described as a minster. So far as can be seen, the earliest English parishes were large districts served by clergy from a bishop's *familia*, grouped round a central church. Such communities, which would certainly have been described as *monasteria* by early writers, were in effect replicas of the cathedral bodies in which their members had been trained. No records of these communities have survived, but Old English documents occasionally contain references to religious bodies, obviously of high antiquity, which do not seem to be monastic in any precise sense of that word. Some at least of them may well represent the clergy of primitive upland minsters.

Despite the importance of the ancient 'minster', most parish churches of the early middle ages belonged to the Old English class of 'lesser churches'. Normally, these churches had been founded, not by kings or bishops, but by lay noblemen. Throughout the Old English period the founder of such a church regarded it as his property, which would yield an income to him and his heirs. The origin of lay patronage in England lies in the custom which allowed the founder of a church to appoint its priest; and it was only by slow degrees that the priest came to acquire a body of rights which could be enforced against the lord who had appointed him. Even in the eleventh century, although the priest was secure against arbitrary dispossession, his economic position was unsatisfactory. By virtue of an agreement with his patron he was often subject to a payment amounting to a very considerable part of the income attached to his church. Four hundred years earlier his predecessor had supported life on the part which his lord allowed him in the offerings of newly converted parishioners,

[1] *C.S.* 841.

on the produce of whatever share in the village arable had been allotted to his church, and on a tithe which was purely a voluntary payment. The lord who had founded his church could do virtually whatever he pleased with it. He could bury his heathen kinsmen in it, remove it from one place to another, or even destroy it, though in that case Theodore enjoined that its timbers should be used for some other religious purpose.[1] The bishop's right of institution, through which the parish priest ultimately secured economic independence, is not asserted in any English document earlier than the decrees of the council of Clofeshoh in 746.[2]

Even at the end of the eighth century many Christian communities of long standing were still unprovided with any form of church. Archbishop Theodore had allowed priests to say mass 'in the field'. A century later the life of St. Willibald, written by a nun of West Saxon origin, represents it as an English custom that on the estates of many lords there was no church, but only a cross raised on high for the daily service of prayer. The history of the standing cross in England is carried back to Theodore's time by a sentence in his book of canons enjoining that when a church has been removed to another place a cross should be erected on the site of the vanished altar.[3] Within a century of Theodore's arrival a succession of sculptors, working chiefly in Northumbria and northern Mercia, had produced a series of crosses decorated with sculpture of a quality unapproached elsewhere in Europe. Nothing definite is known about their teachers or the sources of their art, though there is reason to think that the vine-scroll which is the most distinctive of their many decorative motives came to them from Italy. In any case, their fertility in design and their mastery of the fantastic suggest that their work represents a sudden release of native artistic power which may have been assisted, but was never controlled, by motives supplied by foreign craftsmen. Naturally, they were more successful in design than in the representation of the human figure. Even so, the figure sculpture on their greatest works, the crosses of Bewcastle in Cumberland and Ruthwell in Dumfriesshire,[4] though lapsing into crudities of detail, preserves an essential dignity, and an isolated

---

[1] *Councils*, iii. 190. [2] Ibid. 365. [3] Ibid. 190.
[4] For a minute review of the evidence bearing on the date of these crosses see G. Baldwin Brown, *The Arts in Early England*, v, pp. 102–317.

fragment of their sculpture at Reculver is marked by almost classical poise and restraint. The conditions which produced their work are as obscure as its artistic antecedents.[1] Some of these crosses were certainly raised as memorials to the dead. A cross now at Durham, on which the vine-scroll appears in its simplest form, is generally believed to have marked the grave of Acca, bishop of Hexham, who died in 740. A much weathered inscription seems to record that the Bewcastle cross commemorated Alhfrith son of Oswiu and his wife Cyneburg, Penda's daughter. But in view of the rarity of such inscriptions it is probable that most crosses of this period were intended to mark sites of worship on which not even a 'field church' had yet arisen.

Few parish churches of the seventh or eighth century have left remains which can now be identified.[2] Only one—the church of Escombe by the middle Wear—still survives in its entirety. Its areal dimensions are small, but its height, and the strength of a chancel arch composed of vast through-stones, make it a work of austere dignity. At Corbridge on Tyne, an important seat of the early Northumbrian kings, the tower and nave of a large church which probably ranked as an 'ordinary minster' belong to this period. Occasionally, as at Kirby Hill near Boroughbridge and Britford near Salisbury, decoration of an early type carries the foundation of a particular parish church back to the eighth or even the seventh century. More rarely, documentary evidence establishes a case for the high antiquity of a church with few distinctive features. In 685 Berhtwald, nephew of Æthelred king of Mercia, granted forty hides at Somerford Keynes near the upper Thames to Abbot Aldhelm for the support of the monks of Malmesbury.[3] The modern church of this place incorporates a megalithic doorway surmounted by an arch cut out of a single stone and ornamented by narrow parallel mouldings. As Aldhelm is known to have been a builder of churches, there is at least a presumption that this doorway represents a church built by his orders for the peasantry on his new estate. This presumption in turn supports other evidence suggesting that the ruined chapel of Heysham near Morecambe, which was entered by a doorway of the same type, was built in the seventh or

[1] A. W. Clapham, *English Romanesque Architecture before the Conquest*, pp. 62–9.
[2] For these churches see A. W. Clapham, op. cit.   [3] *C.S.* 65.

eighth century. Apart from these few examples, every church which can reasonably be referred to this period seems to have been built for men or women following a communal if not a monastic life. Neither the fragments of Augustinian churches in Kent, the later work in the same tradition at Brixworth and Bradwell on Sea, the archaic porch and tower of Monkwearmouth, nor the eighth-century friezes at Breedon in Leicestershire tell anything directly about the buildings around which the parochial organization of the English church was originally centred.

Even in its most rudimentary form, this organization necessitated some permanent provision for the support of the parish church and its priest. An income derived from the voluntary offerings of primitive farmers was highly unstable, and at a very early date the priest was admitted into agricultural partnership with the village community which he served. The amount of his holding can only be inferred from later evidence. In the parts of England where ancient arrangements were undisturbed by Danish settlement, and particularly in Wessex and western Mercia, the glebe of an ordinary parish church seems as a rule to have approximated to two yardlands. On the other hand, the ancient 'minsters' of this region, represented in the middle ages by the churches of large royal and episcopal manors, were usually endowed more generously. Few of them seem to have possessed less than an entire hide, and some possessed very considerable estates. It is probable that these differences of endowment go back to a very remote period. The ordinary parish church—the 'lesser church' of pre-Conquest law—had never needed more than an endowment which would support a single priest. The 'minster' had originally been the church of a religious community.

The first document which enumerates the more general sources of ecclesiastical revenue is an ordinance of King Athelstan,[1] commanding his officers to see that churches receive their plough-alms, *cyric-sceat*, and *sawol-sceat*—the church-scot and soul-scot of later documents. None of these payments was a novelty in Athelstan's time, and the whole series may well go back to the seventh century. Soul-scot, indeed, may well represent a heathen custom turned to Christian uses. In

[1] I Athelstan, c. 4. Tithe is also mentioned in this ordinance, but the king does not indicate its destination.

the eleventh century the phrase could be used to cover all the property, whether land or chattels, which a testator devoted to religious purposes. In its primitive sense it meant a portion of the dead man's goods offered for the welfare of his soul by his open grave to the priest of his parish church. There is a significant resemblance between such gifts made on such occasions and the grave-furniture which had once accompanied heathen burials. The custom prevailed throughout England, and survived the middle ages themselves. The medieval mortuary or corpse-present, which usually consisted of the dead man's second best chattel, was often rationalized as a payment for neglected tithes, but there is no doubt that it represented an attenuated form of the archaic soul-scot.

Unlike soul-scot, which arose as a voluntary offering, plough-alms and church-scot were taxes imposed by higher authority. Plough-alms consisted merely of a penny paid within a fortnight after Easter in respect of each plough-team working in a parish. The burden of church-scot varied from place to place, but it was never negligible and it was sometimes extremely heavy. It first appears in Ine's laws,[1] which provide that it shall be paid at Martinmas, and that a defaulter shall forfeit sixty shillings to the king and pay twelve times the sum originally due from him. It was levied on all free men in proportion to the amount of each man's holding, and like the tithe, with which it has sometimes been confused, it was a payment in kind. The church-scot from a holding generally consisted of a number of measures of grain, it often included one or more hens, but money rarely entered into it. Old English terms of measurement are generally obscure, and it is not easy to translate ancient definitions of church-scot into modern quantities. In the eleventh century, church-scot in Worcestershire seems to have been levied at the rate of a horse-load of grain on the 'hide',[2] the unit which represented the holding of a primitive peasant family. But Worcestershire was a county dominated by ancient churches, and it is unlikely that church-scot was often levied at so high a rate as this. In Northamptonshire at this date the church-scot of a large village might well amount to

[1] cc. 4, 61.
[2] D.B. i, ff. 174, 175b. On the 'hide' as a unit of tenure and assessment see below. pp. 279, 646–7. [One may note that in a Winchester lease of an eight-hide estate in 871–7 eight church-scots are excluded from the exemption from burdens. See Robertson, *Anglo-Saxon Charters*, No. XIV.]

no more than a single quarter of wheat or rye. Long before the close of the Old English period, the incidence of this charge had plainly ceased to bear any close relation to agrarian facts.

Although all free householders were subject to this payment, there were many parish churches which never received it. In the tenth century it was reserved to the 'old minsters' which had been the churches of primitive parishes. Churches built at a later date within the limits of these parishes had no claim to church-scot from their own parishioners unless some agreement to this end had been made with the clergy of the old minster. Traces of this custom often complicated the finance of a medieval parish. Before the Norman Conquest the church of Fawsley in Northamptonshire had received the church-scot from the two hundreds attached to the king's manor in that place.[1] Henry I gave the church of Fawsley to Daventry priory, and in the fourteenth century it was still receiving church-scot from nine separate parishes in virtue of his gift. Like other ecclesiastical revenues of high antiquity, church-scot was occasionally secularized. In the eleventh century the burgesses of Derby were paying twelve thraves of corn, which obviously represented their church-scot, to the king each year at Michaelmas.[2] But exceptions like this do not affect the interest of the payment as the fundamental endowment of the ancient 'minsters' with which the English parochial system began.

It was only by slow degrees that tithe came to replace church-scot as the financial basis of this system. In the seventh century the payment of tithe was a religious duty, incumbent as a matter of conscience on all Christians. But it was not yet enforced by secular penalties, and within limits, which were by no means rigid, a man was free to devote his tithe to whatever religious purpose attracted him. The maintenance of a priest was only one, and hardly the most important, of the objects to which tithe might be assigned. Theodore, whose canons are the earliest authority for the history of tithe in England, ruled that tithe could lawfully be given only to the poor, to pilgrims, and by laymen to their churches. Naturally, he regarded it as desirable that a lord who built a church should assign at least a part of his tithe to the support of its priest. But he was clearly anxious that the multiplication of private churches should not lead to a complete diversion of tithe from other objects. He was

[1] Cott. MS. Claud. D xii, f. 105. [2] D.B. i, f. 280.

careful to provide that, although tribute should be paid to
the church according to the custom of the country, the poor
must not suffer wrong in regard to tithes or any other matters.[1]
Tithe, to him, was part of the general revenue of the whole
church rather than a means of supporting the clergy of individual parishes.

Three centuries later, tithe had become a legal obligation,
and the state was attempting to regulate the distribution of its
proceeds. The change had come about very slowly. In 786 a
legatine council at Clofeshoh enjoined the payment of tithe on
all men,[2] but although the principal English rulers of the time
had acquiesced in this injunction, there is no sign that they ever
tried to put it into effect. Tithe only enters into Alfred's laws
as an element in the Mosaic law, which he translated as a model
of legislation, but neither attempted nor wished to impose on
his subjects. It was not until the tenth century that any English
ruler ventured to appoint penalties for refusal to pay tithes.
Edgar, at whose court ecclesiastical influence was very strong,
was the first king who introduced provisions for the enforcement
of tithe into a code intended to be valid throughout England.[3]
The provisions are both elaborate and severe.[4] They direct the
reeves of the king and the bishop and the priest of a defaulter's
parish to seize a tenth of his tithable property for the local
church, to assign another tenth to the defaulter himself, and to
divide the remaining eight parts between the defaulter's lord
and the bishop. It is not unlikely that this process represents an
ideal rather than a practical course of action, but its inclusion in
a general body of law shows that the king has at last undertaken
the responsibility of compelling his subjects to pay their tithes.

Other passages in the same code show that tithe was becoming reserved to the use of parish churches. Pilgrims and the
poor have fallen out of sight. The king assumes that most
tithe-payers will be parishioners of an 'old minster', and he
begins by ordering that in such a case the ancient church shall
receive tithe from the whole of its territory as the plough goes
over the demesne farms of thegns and the lands of their free

---

[1] *Councils*, iii. 203.   [2] Ibid. 456–7.

[3] The code often quoted as 'Edward and Guthrum's Peace' (Liebermann,
Gesetze, i, pp. 128–35), which appoints secular penalties for failure to pay tithe,
really comes from the reign of Æthelred II; D. Whitelock in *E.H.R.* lvi (1941),
pp. 1–21.

[4] Laws of Edgar II, 3; 3. 1.

tenants. But he also recognizes that lords have been building churches on their estates, and he provides that where a grave-yard is annexed to such a private church, its owner may give a third of his own tithe for its support, paying the other two-thirds to the old minster to which his property had once been subject parochially. If a lord possesses a church without a grave-yard—the 'field church' of other documents—he must support his priest out of the property remaining to him after the old minster has received its full tithe. Traces of these provisions can be discerned in the ecclesiastical custom of the Norman period. Most lords of this age seem to have regarded their manorial churches as entitled to one-third of their demesne tithes, and many ancient minsters were still drawing tithe, as they drew church-scot, from distant parishes which had once lain within their ecclesiastical jurisdiction. On the other hand, the Norman lord of a village, unlike the thegn of Edgar's laws, was free to give two-thirds of his demesne tithes to any religious object which pleased him, without regard to the vested interests of any ancient minster. Such tithes formed an important part of the endowments of the new English monasteries of the twelfth century. It is, in fact, probable that even in Edgar's reign lords had a wider discretion in the assignment of their tithes, and those of their men, than would be gathered from the precise regulations laid down in his laws. The right of a lord to build a church and endow it with tithe was fully recognized in the last years of the Old English state. In 1086 a Derbyshire jury de-clared that a certain pre-Conquest lord could provide himself with a church on his land or in his 'soke' without anyone's licence, and pay his tithe wherever he wished.[1]

The ecclesiastical dues of which tithe and church-scot were the chief amounted collectively to a serious charge on the re-sources of the old English peasantry. In good times they could be borne, if not always easily, at least without distress. Times of war or famine suspended the operation of ecclesiastical finance, as they suspended the whole course of economic life. Between these extremes there were many occasions when the payment of church-scot or tithe must have deprived a peasant household of meagre reserves stored up for bad years ahead. By the tenth century the whole power of the state was at the service of the church for the exaction of its dues, and ancient

[1] D.B. i, f. 280.

penalties for default were repeated by kings with a new administrative system at their command. The formidable twelve-fold penalty prescribed by Ine for failure to pay church-scot can be traced through the laws of Æthelred II and Cnut, and is recorded as a matter of local custom by the Domesday jurors of Worcestershire. It would be unjust to assume that the church was harsh in its insistence on its dues, but they certainly made against the economic independence of the peasant.

The development of a parochial system is the central thread of English ecclesiastical history in the generations following the arrival of Theodore, but it is virtually ignored by contemporary writers. They regarded the foundation of parish churches as only one among a bishop's many duties, and found nothing remarkable in the negotiations with kings and nobles by which this end was brought about. Historians of this period have always tended to concentrate attention on the men and women who established the monastic life in England, on the nature of their discipline, and on the history of the monasteries which they founded. It is a natural tendency; for the monastic ideal influenced the whole character of the early English church, and the cultivation of learning in individual monasteries was destined to affect the general history of letters in western Europe. But it is also true that the great age of early English monasticism, brilliant as were its achievements, was comprised within a century, and that most of the monasteries which perished in the first Danish raids on England had little distinction either of life or learning. In the general history of the English church the monasteries of this period are of less significance than the obscure parish churches which remained as the permanent basis of English ecclesiastical organization.

Every ecclesiastical statesman of the seventh century regarded the monastic order as essential to the life of the church. At the very beginning of English Christianity, Augustine had founded a monastery close to his cathedral church of Canterbury. Nevertheless, the very remarkable development of English monasticism in the seventh and eighth centuries was not due to the deliberate policy of ecclesiastical rulers. It expressed a popular impulse towards a new way of living, which the leaders of the church in this period might influence, but could never entirely control. Roman and Irish teachers were agreed upon the merit of the monastic life and the sanctity of the profession through which it was entered, and amid innumerable diversities of practice the monasteries founded under Celtic and Italian influences shared in the last resort the same ideal. It was an ideal which could be expressed in many different forms. Accidents of temperament and circumstance decided whether a man would seek absorption in a community under another's rule, found a monastery on his own land, or lead a contemplative life in isolation. The political circumstances of the time contributed to the movement. At least one important Northumbrian monastery was founded by a noble driven from active life by an unfriendly king.[1] St. Guthlac, whose cell in the fens of Middle Anglia became the nucleus of Crowland abbey, left the world as a young man because he suddenly realized the futility of the life of incessant warfare imposed on him by his descent from ancient kings.[2] But the motive of escape from a violent world will not explain the enthusiasm with which men and women of all classes entered religion. Willibrord, the apostle of Frisia, was the son of a Northumbrian *ceorl* who late in a quiet life left his family, built an oratory at the mouth of the Humber, and became at last the head of a small religious community grouped around a church established with the aid of kings and nobles.[3] It was the appeal to the imagination of the ordinary man which gave vitality to early English monasticism.

In the seventh century the founder of a monastery was free to determine the rule by which he and his companions would live. There was a real danger that this freedom might degenerate into eccentricity, for there was a strong vein of asceticism in the English conception of the monastic life. It is a proof of Wilfrid's essential statesmanship that he saw in the humane rule of St. Benedict the means by which the various forms of individual devotion could best be directed to a common end. Most of the early evidence for the adoption of St. Benedict's rule in England is associated with Wilfrid's circle. On the other hand, religion had been introduced into England by monks trained in the Benedictine tradition, and a church which owed its foundation to Gregory the Great was bound to revere the monastic saint whom Gregory regarded as his master. Long before Wilfrid's death the Benedictine rule was observed

---

[1] Æthelwulf, *De Abbatibus*, ed. A. Campbell, pp. 5–9.
[2] *Felix's Life of Saint Guthlac*, ed. B. Colgrave, pp. 82–3.
[3] Alcuin, *Vita Sancti Willibrordi*, i. 1.

in many houses with which he had never been connected. Aldhelm of Malmesbury, whose influence was very powerful in southern England, describes St. Benedict as establishing the course of the monastic life, and assumes that a religious community will normally be following his rule.[1] It was certainly observed by the community at Nursling which St. Boniface joined in the first years of the eighth century.[2] On the other hand, it does not seem that the Irish monks who founded the Northumbrian church attached pre-eminent authority to any single form of monastic order. There is, for example, no evidence for the observance of the rule of St. Columbanus in England. At Lindisfarne, the headquarters of the original Irish mission, no common rule of any kind seems to have been observed before the priorate of St. Cuthbert, but before the end of the seventh century the monks of that house had accepted the Benedictine rule as a supplement to the precepts which Cuthbert had composed for their predecessors.[3]

To early ecclesiastical historians the rule observed in a particular house was of little interest in comparison with the reputation of its founder or the circumstances of its foundation. The information which has been preserved on these subjects is often inadequate, but it shows at least the variety of the conditions under which the earliest English monasteries arose. A notable part in their creation was played by men who deliberately planned the foundation of organized communities equipped for every activity permissible to men or women following the religious life. Wilfrid undoubtedly followed this ideal, and it was pursued with greater concentration by his contemporary Benedict Biscop, who from the first intended that his monasteries of Wearmouth and Jarrow should be centres of learning as well as religion.[4] Owing to the difficulty of managing scattered properties from one single centre, a founder could rarely bring all his resources to bear on the endowment of a single monastery. An enthusiast for the monastic order usually established a number of separate houses, each ruled under his own supervision by a local provost or abbot. Wilfrid, whose monasteries were scattered over all England between the Tyne

[1] *Aldhelmi Opera*, ed. R. Ehwald (MGH), pp. 268–9; 390.
[2] *Willibaldi Vita Sancti Bonifatii*, ed. Jaffé, *Monumenta Moguntina*, pp. 435–6.
[3] *Two Lives of Saint Cuthbert*, ed. B. Colgrave, pp. 94–7.
[4] Below, pp. 184–5.

and the Channel, governed them through abbots responsible
to himself. Aldhelm, who had founded monasteries at Frome
and Bradford on Avon while he was abbot of Malmesbury,
kept the control of all his houses in his own hands, and was
persuaded by his monks to remain their ruler after he became
bishop of Sherborne.[1] Similar federations naturally arose when
the head of a great monastery was asked to send a group of his
monks to found a new house on a distant site, with the result
that the influence of a famous monastic centre sometimes extended far beyond the boundary of the diocese in which it lay.
In the seventh century, monks were sent from the monastery
of Medeshamstede—afterwards known as Peterborough—to
Breedon in Leicestershire, Woking and Bermondsey in Surrey,
Hoo in Kent, and probably Brixworth in Northamptonshire.
Each of these colonies was subject to the ultimate authority of
the abbot of Medeshamstede, and its muniments were sent there
for preservation.[2] Little is known of these early federations,
but their existence corrects the impression of extreme individualism produced by most of the evidence for the first phase
of English monastic history.

Nevertheless, the typical monastery of this period was an
independent house—the creation of a founder who did not feel
himself compelled to imitate any particular form of religious
organization. An infinite range of experiment was possible
within the simple conception of a monastery as a community of
persons under a vow of religion. A whole family, for example,
might agree to devote itself to the religious life, build a church
for its common services, and obtain recognition as a monastery
from kings and bishops. The practice could easily be abused.
In England the lands which supported a religious community
were exempt from most kinds of secular service, and there was
an obvious temptation for the head of a family to evade his
duties to the state by converting his household into a pseudo-
monastery. At the end of his life Bede was seriously alarmed at
the danger into which his country was falling through the withdrawal of land from the service of the state for the benefit of
monasteries which were often of doubtful character. In a
letter to Bishop Egbert of York, written in 734,[3] he advocates

---

[1] C.S. 114.

[2] F. M. Stenton, 'Medeshamstede and its Colonies', pp. 179–92.

[3] Venerabilis Bedae Opera, ed. Plummer, i. 414–17.

the resumption of the grants which had been made to such houses.[1] But the family monastery had originally expressed a genuine religious impulse, and the ideas which lay behind it affected the whole course of early English monasticism. Already before the age of Bede, the idea that men and women might be associated in the religious life had created a number of double monasteries which were eminent in learning as well as devotion. In the seventh century the double monastery was known in every western country, and its English form probably represents a combination of Irish and continental usages. The institution was firmly established in England before the arrival of Theodore, who disapproved of it on principle, but accepted it as the custom of the land. None of the leading English churchmen of the time shared Theodore's scruples. Aldhelm dedicated his longest work to a group of nuns belonging to the double monastery of Barking. Wilfrid and Cuthbert were friends of Æbbe, abbess of a similar house at Coldingham, and Boniface encouraged the foundation of double monasteries in Germany.

Most of the evidence which proves the association of men and women in a double monastery is preserved accidentally in narratives written for some other purpose. The existence of a double monastery at Repton is only known because St. Guthlac learnt the principles of the monastic life under its abbess. The double constitution of the original monasteries at Ely, Much Wenlock, and Bardney is only revealed in a similar incidental way. The double monastery was obviously a normal feature of the earliest English monasticism, and, indeed, it is doubtful whether any houses for women only were ever founded in this period. No detailed description of life in a double monastery has survived, and it is impossible to form a clear impression of the relations between the two communities of which such institutions were composed. The strictness with which these relations were controlled can safely be inferred from the good repute of these houses. Only one of them—

[1] There is some evidence that the archbishop's brother Eadberht, who became king of Northumbria in 737, tried to reduce the number of monasteries in his kingdom. A letter of Pope Paul I, addressed jointly to the king and the archbishop, complains that the king had given to one of his nobles three *monasteria* which an abbess had recently granted to an abbot (*C.S.* 184; *Councils*, iii. 394–5). The pope, relying on the abbot's statement, calls on the king to restore these monasteries. Nothing is known about their character. But the archbishop, whom Bede had once instructed, was plainly aware of the king's action, and there can be little doubt that Bede himself would have approved of it.

Coldingham, isolated above the sea in the far north of Bernicia —is known to have given grounds for scandal. At Wimborne, the largest house of the kind in Wessex, the separation of men and women was almost complete; each community had its own church, and the abbess who was head of the whole monastery gave orders to her monks through a window. But in other double houses monks and nuns might be associated in the services of a common church, and Aldhelm, in a poem on a West Saxon double monastery, uses words which seem to be describing monks and nuns reading and chanting in alternation. At Whitby the personality of the great Abbess Hild dominated the whole life of a large congregation of men and women, and the eminence of many monks trained in that house was undoubtedly due to her teaching. There was, in fact, no dominant type of double monastery, and the only feature common to all these houses was the rule of an abbess over the whole community.

Many of these abbesses were women of the highest rank. Hild of Whitby was a kinswoman of Oswiu, king of Northumbria, and Ælfflæd, her successor, was his daughter. Wimborne was founded by two sisters of Ine, king of Wessex. Æthelthryth, the foundress of Ely, and Seaxburg her successor, were daughters of Anna, king of the East Angles.[1] Mildburg, abbess of Wenlock, and Mildthryth, abbess of Minster in Thanet, were daughters of Merewalh, king of the Magonsætan. Women of this type exercised an influence on the life of their time to which there is nothing parallel in later history. Most of their houses perished in the Danish invasions of the ninth century, and the double monastery had fallen out of favour before English monasticism was restored in the age of Dunstan. Few of the houses then founded for women were of more than local importance, and their abbesses are shadowy figures in comparison with the women who ruled the double monasteries of the seventh and eighth centuries. No woman in the middle ages ever held a position comparable with that of Hild of Whitby.

The obvious importance of religious leaders like Hild or Benedict Biscop tends to distract attention from the innumerable men and women who lived monastic lives under conditions of

---

[1] Æthelberg, their sister, became abbess of the Merovingian double house of Faremoutiers-en-Brie.

little dignity or independence. The ordinary layman who founded a monastery in the seventh or eighth century regarded himself as the lord of the community which he had brought into being, managed the property which accrued to it, and appointed its head, if he did not himself assume that office. These rights sometimes descended for generations in the founder's line. By virtue of his descent, Alcuin, the confidant of Charlemagne, inherited the monastery which St. Willibrord's father had founded at the mouth of the Humber more than a century before.[1] The lord of a monastery had a direct interest in the conduct of its inmates. The laws of Alfred provide for the situation which might arise if anyone entrusted property to 'another man's monk' without the consent of the monk's lord.[2] They also allow the 'lord of the church' to receive part of the money exacted for the offence of taking a nun from a monastery without the leave of the king or the bishop.[3] Lordship of this kind was profitable to its possessor, and many monasteries which had once been independent were appropriated by aggressive local magnates. In unquiet times a monastery must often have been tempted to place itself under the power of a noble who could protect it. In 803 a synod of the southern province, in obedience to a papal mandate, expressly forbade monasteries to choose secular persons as their lords.[4] But there can be no doubt that in the last resort the lay lord of a monastery represented a popular feeling that the founder of a religious institution, whether a monastery or a simple church, might fairly derive temporal advantage from his good work.

The monasteries founded in the seventh century often failed to attract congregations which could maintain a full religious life. Many of them expired after a few years of precarious existence, and it was then an open question whether their possessions should be retained for religious uses or reabsorbed into the property of the founder's kin. The bishops of the eighth century were always anxious to prevent the secularization of ecclesiastical property, and through their influence the endowment of a derelict monastery was often given to another house or annexed to a cathedral church. Here, as in all issues affecting the monastic institution, it was the work of the bishops of

---

[1] Described by Alcuin himself as 'cellula . . . cui ego . . . legitima Deo donante successione praesideo'; *Monumenta Alcuiniana*, p. 40.
[2] c. 20.   [3] c. 8.   [4] *C.S.* 312, a contemporary text.

THE ENGLISH MISSIONS TO THE CONTINENT

this period to secure what had been accomplished by the en-thusiasm of an earlier age. The relations between bishop and monastery were governed by a few elementary principles which were never challenged in the pre-Alfredian period. In a privi-lege issued by Pope Constantine for the monasteries of Woking and Bermondsey they are expressed in a simple statement to the effect that the bishop should inquire into the matters 'which belong to canonical order', and that the abbot, the *prepositus*, and the elders of the community should control its property and expenditure.[1] In practice, it was for the bishop to see that the course of the religious life was observed in all the monasteries of his diocese, to provide for the maintenance of their services by raising selected members of each congregation to the diaconate and priesthood, and to consecrate the person chosen by each community to be its head. Beyond these official duties lay the responsibility of defending the possessions of each monastery against secular encroachment. No monastery of the eighth century could have afforded to question the authority of the bishop who was its only disinterested protector.

The main features of the ecclesiastical order which has been described naturally reappear in the churches founded in this period by Englishmen abroad. Long before primitive heathen-ism was dead in England itself, individual Englishmen were working as missionaries in the lands from which their ancestors had come to Britain. All of them were monks, and it was through the foundation of monasteries that Christianity was ultimately established in Frisia and in western and central Germany. On the other hand, all the leaders in this movement were either trained in, or influenced by, the tradition of a centralized church which had been created by the work of Theodore. They all looked forward to the establishment of a regular diocesan episcopate, and the monasteries which they founded were intended to serve as permanent centres of religious instruction, subject to the authority of the bishop in whose diocese they lay. The community of interest between the bishop and the monks within his jurisdiction determined the whole character of the English achievement in Frisia and Germany.[2]

---

[1] *C.S.* 133, discussed by F. M. Stenton in *C.P.*, pp. 185-8.

[2] Described with abundant detail in W. Levison's *England and the Continent in the Eighth Century*, pp. 45-93. There is an illuminating survey in *Anglo-Saxon Influence on Western Christendom* by S. J. Crawford, pp. 32-71.

In the winter of 677 Wilfrid had visited Frisia in the course of his first appeal to Rome, and according to his biographer laid the foundation of the faith in that country. But whatever immediate success Wilfrid may have won, the Frisians were wholly heathen twelve years after his visit, and the movement which led to their conversion owed nothing beyond its origin to him. Its real founder was a Northumbrian scholar named Egbert, who after many years of learned retirement in Ireland formed the design of attempting the conversion of the Frisians and Saxons. He was prevented—supernaturally, as Bede believed—from undertaking the work himself, and the succession of English missionaries in Frisia begins with one of his companions named Wihtberht, who preached there to an irresponsive people for two years, shortly before 690. When his failure was evident, Egbert collected a band of twelve monks for a more extended mission. The most distinguished of them, and the only priest in the company, was Willibrord, a Northumbrian monk who had just completed twelve years of study in Ireland after a youth spent in Wilfrid's monastery of Ripon. It is with Willibrord's name that the expedition is always associated, but he does not seem to have been its original leader. As soon as its future was secured, Willibrord went to Rome to secure relics for the new Frisian churches and to obtain the pope's blessing on the enterprise. During his absence, or immediately after his return, his companions chose a certain Swithberht as their bishop, who received consecration in England from Wilfrid in 692 or 693. He was established in a seat at Wijk bij Duurstede under Frankish protection, but before long he departed in order to preach to the Boruhtware of Westphalia. His work there was undone by a Saxon invasion, and he then retired to the island of Kaiserswerth in the Rhine, where he built a monastery which his heirs still possessed in the time of Bede. On Swithberht's withdrawal from Frisia, Willibrord became the unquestioned head of the mission, and for more than forty years its direction was in his hands.

Recent political changes helped him to succeed where others had failed. At the battle of Tertry in 687, Pippin, mayor of the palace in Austrasia, had made himself supreme throughout the Frankish kingdom. He could therefore act decisively against the dangerous Frisian neighbours of the eastern Franks, and within ten years he had conquered all Frisia south and west of the Yssel. Realizing that the establishment of Christianity would strengthen his control of that country, Pippin took the mission under his patronage. In 695 he sent Willibrord to Rome with an embassy which asked the pope to consecrate him bishop to the Frisians. The embassy was welcomed at Rome as a sign that the great Austrasian house which dominated the Frankish kingdom wished to enter into direct relations with the papacy. On 21 November 695, Pope Sergius I ordained Willibrord to a charge which covered the whole Frisian nation, and then invested him with the pallium as a symbol of his metropolitan rank, and as an indication that he had authority to institute new bishoprics within his province. The pope was clearly influenced by the knowledge that Gregory the Great had given the pallium to Augustine, and his own action became a precedent for the gift of the same symbol to the rulers of the missionary provinces which afterwards arose in Germany.

In the early part of his mission Willibrord risked his life to little purpose in remoter parts. He explained his religion to Radbod, king of the Frisians, in the heart of his own country, baptized converts in the holy spring of Heligoland, and even taught for a time among the Danes. But his permanent achievement was the creation of an organized church in Frankish Frisia. Pippin gave him a place for his bishop's seat adjacent to the port of Utrecht. The site was dangerously near the border of the independent Frisians, who occupied it for at least three years in the time of confusion after Pippin's death in 714. But it was ultimately recovered by Charles Martel, his son, and Willibrord worked from this centre throughout the latter part of his life, founding monasteries and parish churches, training pupils for the clerical order, and destroying symbols of heathenism. To the end he remained in close association with the rulers of the Franks, and he died in 739 in a monastery which he had founded and placed under Pippin's protection at Echternach in the centre of Austrasia.

His work had been authorized by a papal commission, and it was made effective by Frankish support. Each of these factors reappears in the life of his younger contemporary, Boniface, the legate of the pope in Germany and the organizer of the Frankish church. Willibrord had shown that the sustained effort of a few individuals might found a new church among the heathen. Boniface worked on a far greater scale, establishing religion and suppressing heresy among the Germanic peoples subject to the Franks, and bringing the Frankish rulers themselves to the point of initiating reform in their own churches. Nevertheless, the two men had much in common. Each regarded himself as the pope's minister, and realized that alliance with the secular power was necessary if whole peoples were to be brought into the catholic church. Each owed the permanence of his achievement to the support of his countrymen, and in particular to the strain of evangelistic fervour which English monasticism had acquired from earlier Celtic teachers. It was the work of Willibrord which first provided a continental field where this devotion could be expressed, and to this extent he may be regarded as making possible the greater career of Boniface.

Willibrord and all the earliest English missionaries to the continent were Northumbrians by birth. Boniface, whose native English name was Wynfrith, was a West Saxon from the country beyond Selwood. He was born shortly before 675, and placed as a boy in a monastery at Exeter. After some years he migrated to a house at Nursling in Hampshire, where he devoted himself to learning and became head of the monastic school. In 716, with two or three companions, he left his monastery and made his way to Frisia. Radbod, the heathen king of the independent Frisians, had recently recovered the country south of the Yssel from the Franks; Willibrord's mission was suspended, and in the following year Boniface returned to Nursling. In 718, after declining election as abbot of that house, he resolved to place himself at the disposal of the pope for work among the heathen. Bishop Daniel of Winchester gave him commendatory letters, and in the spring of 719 he visited Rome and received a general commission as evangelist from Pope Gregory II. He began to preach in Thuringia, but on hearing of Radbod's death he joined Willibrord in Frisia and remained with him for nearly three years. At the end of this time he resumed his German mission, refusing consecration as an assistant bishop in Frisia, and was so successful that he found it necessary to ask the pope for guidance in the organization of the new church. The pope summoned him to Rome, and on 30 November 722 consecrated him bishop to the Germans and gave him letters of commendation to Charles Martel. For the next ten years he worked in Hesse and Thuringia, destroying heathen sanctuaries, suppressing false teachers, and founding churches. He had never lost touch with English life, and the success of his German mission was largely due to the numerous Englishmen who now came over to help him.

In 732 Pope Gregory III recognized his achievement by the gift of an archbishop's pallium. He was still a regional bishop without any permanent seat, and it was not until 747 that he adopted the ancient church of Mainz as his cathedral. But his mission had prepared the way for the introduction of a regular diocesan organization into southern Germany, and in 738, after a third visit to Rome, the pope authorized him to begin this work. His authority as archbishop and papal legate in Germany was not confined to the churches of his own foundation, and his first undertaking was the revival of episcopal government in Bavaria. In 739 he divided the duchy into the dioceses of Salzburg, Regensburg, Freising, and Passau; consecrating new bishops for the first three of these sees, and assigning Passau to a German ecclesiastic who had already received consecration from the pope. A few years later he was able to establish bishoprics among the tribes converted by his own mission. Before 742 he had founded sees at Würzburg, Büraburg near Fritzlar, and Erfurt. The first bishops of Würzburg and Erfurt were Englishmen, and a cousin of Boniface named Willibald, famous for his travels in the East, was established in a fifth Bavarian see at Eichstätt. Other Englishmen were used by Boniface as assistant bishops without any specific local responsibilities. Little is known about them, but there is reason to think that Leofwine, who appears in 747 among a group of bishops attendant on Boniface, is identical with the English missionary Lebuin who worked among the Frisians in the next generation, and was afterwards honoured as a saint at Deventer.

The death of Charles Martel in 741 enlarged the sphere and to some extent changed the character of Boniface's work. As a political realist Charles had encouraged the conversion of the peoples adjacent to the Frankish border. But he had always behaved as the autocratic master of the church in his own country; he had regarded papal politics with complete detachment, and he would never have admitted that Boniface had acquired any authority over the Frankish clergy in virtue of his general commission as papal legate in Germany. Through his personal influence with Carloman and Pippin, Charles's sons, Boniface became the leading ecclesiastic in the Frankish kingdom, and his work led directly to a change in the whole character of the relations between the Frankish rulers and the papacy. In the ten years which followed Charles's death, the support of Carloman and Pippin allowed Boniface to initiate a general reform of the discipline and organization of the Frankish church. He began the work under the patronage of Carloman, who helped him to hold synods of the East Frankish clergy in 742 and 743. He held a West Frankish synod at Soissons in 744, and in the following years Carloman and Pippin enabled him to convene more general councils, which included clergy from each of the two great divisions of the Frankish kingdom. Pippin continued to support the work of reform after Carloman had retired from the world in 747. Throughout the whole course of his dealings with the Frankish church Boniface maintained an unbroken correspondence with Rome, and through his attitude the more responsible members of the Frankish episcopate came to realize that, in the last resort, the pope was the only power which could protect them against aristocratic aggression and give permanence to their reforms. For political reasons, Pippin was compelled to acquiesce in this extension of papal influence over the Frankish church. He was the real ruler of the Frankish kingdom, but the ancient Merovingian dynasty still survived, and its dispossession in his favour could be sanctioned by the pope alone. He was rewarded for the abandonment of his father's policy in 751, when Boniface consecrated him king of the Franks, with the approval of Pope Zacharias.

The reform of the Frankish church affected the whole history of western Europe. It made possible the Carolingian renaissance of the next generation, and it brought the Frankish rulers into intimate relations with the papacy, which led to the Italian campaigns of Pippin and ultimately to the overthrow of the Lombard kingdom by Charlemagne. But to Boniface himself the holding of councils and the enforcement of discipline upon the Frankish clergy were official duties which interrupted the real work of his life, the conversion of the heathen races outside the Frankish dominion. Throughout the years of his activity in the Frankish kingdom he was constantly preoccupied with the establishment of churches on the border of the heathen country to the east and the maintenance of the clergy who had come from England to serve them. In 752 he was prevented from writing a letter of greeting to the new pope Stephen II by the necessity of restoring more than thirty churches recently destroyed by heathen Saxons. At last, when conscious that his life was nearly over, he felt himself free once more to undertake a mission to a people wholly heathen. Early in 754, with a company of priests, deacons, and monks, he passed beyond the range of Frankish protection into Frisia beyond the Yssel. The mission was successful at first, but the mass of the Frisian people persisted in its old beliefs, and on 5 June 754, at Dockum near the Frisian coast, Boniface and more than fifty of his companions were massacred by a heathen band.

On the surface, this astonishing career seems to belong to continental rather than English history. The work of Boniface profoundly influenced the relations of church and state in both France and Germany, and contributed materially towards the extension of papal authority over all the churches of the West. Nevertheless, to the end of his life Boniface regarded himself as a member of the Anglo-Saxon church from which he had sprung. He maintained a constant correspondence with its rulers, consulted with them about the holding of ecclesiastical councils, and asked their advice on questions of discipline. His work for the establishment of learning in the churches of his foundation depended on the teachers who joined him from England, and it was to England that he turned for the books which he needed. Above all, it was through the men and women of English descent who worked with him in Germany that the English tradition of an organized church under the ultimate authority of the pope passed to the countries converted under his leadership. When all allowance has been made for the part played by Boniface in the ecclesiastical politics of the Frankish kingdom, he remains essentially the leader of an Anglo-Saxon mission to the heathen of Germany.

Its history is illustrated by the most remarkable body of correspondence which has survived from the Dark Ages. The correspondence between Boniface and the papal court, which formed the nucleus of the collection, is an authority of the first importance for the ecclesiastical history of the eighth century. But the collection was soon extended to include many informal letters from men and women connected with Boniface by ties formed in his youth. These letters, which introduce a strong vein of personal interest into the series, make it valuable evidence as to the state of English learning in this period. Boniface himself wrote Latin with ease and power, and his letters have an important place in the history of early medieval literature. None of his English correspondents was his equal as a master of Latin composition. But the letters which came to him from England show a competence in writing which proves that men and women of every rank in the Anglo-Saxon church were touched by a genuine Latin culture. The collection is too small to give a full impression of the learning of Boniface's English correspondents, but Virgil, Augustine, and Jerome are occasionally quoted, and there are many signs of the influence of Aldhelm's characteristic style. Most of the writers belonged to southern England, and their literacy proves the high quality of the education which could be obtained in Kentish or West Saxon monasteries in the age of Bede.

The Anglo-Saxon culture in which Boniface had been trained was naturally reproduced in the churches founded under his influence. The great abbey of Fulda, which he founded in 744, was entrusted to the rule of his leading German follower, but formed from the first a centre of English influence on the border of Hesse and Thuringia. The learning of the Irish scholars who had preceded Boniface in Germany had been intensely individualistic, and many of their disciples had developed opinions irreconcilable with catholic doctrine. To Boniface, the establishment of English scholars in German monasteries was a means of preventing the peoples under his supervision from falling into heresy. As a direct result of his policy, English learning rapidly came to extend beyond the monasteries newly founded by English missionaries to older houses like St. Gall and Reichenau, where Irish traditions had always been strong. Books which had a special interest for Englishmen were multiplied in such houses, and some of the oldest materials for English history have only been preserved in copies made there. The English style of handwriting was used in their *scriptoria*. For more than a generation after the death of Boniface this English strain coloured, and at many points dominated, German learning, and its influence extended far beyond the sphere of purely religious knowledge. One of the fixed points in the historiography of the Frankish kingdom is the derivation of the earliest

Frankish annals from English models introduced into Germany before the close of the eighth century.

The distinctive feature of the educational work of Boniface is the extent to which it depended on the help of women. He had been trained in a church which allowed them unusual influence, and he realized the service which the double monastery could render to the advancement of sacred learning. More than one English abbess regarded him as a spiritual adviser, and asked for his sympathy with her troubles—the oppressions of kings and ealdormen, the distress of a kinsman hated by his king, or the uncertain fate of a sister said to be in prison at Rome. It was primarily through such personal relationships that Boniface attracted women from England into his mission. Their number was considerable; but few of them are more than names, and little is known of the churches, such as Kitzingen and Ochsenfurt, over which they were set. The outstanding figure among them was Leofgyth, a pupil of Eadburg, abbess of Minster in Thanet, and the daughter of a West Saxon friend of Boniface named Dynne. Boniface invited her into Germany from Wimborne, where she had been mistress of the younger nuns, and set her in charge of a double monastery at Tauberbischofsheim in the modern Baden. She was a woman of most unusual personal charm, and the affection which Boniface felt for her introduces an element of ordinary human feeling into the record of his austere life. On the eve of his departure for Frisia in 754, he begged her to remain in Germany after his death, and asked that she might be buried with him at last. In later years, while remaining abbess of Tauberbischofsheim, she formed an intimate friendship with Hildegard the wife of Charlemagne, and carried a living memory of Boniface into the heart of the court where the Carolingian renaissance arose. On her death in 780 she was buried near Boniface in his monastery of Fulda, though not, as he had wished, in his own grave.

Boniface was succeeded at Mainz by an Englishman named Lull, whom he had recently consecrated assistant bishop after many years of service as priest and archdeacon. In the last resort, the influence of Boniface had rested on his unique personal qualities, and no less distinguished successor could hope to inherit his ascendancy. Lull never exercised authority over the more ancient bishoprics of Germany; his relations with the Frankish kings were neutral, and he never secured the confidence of the papal court. The one feature of his career which continued the tradition of Boniface was the correspondence which he maintained with the rulers of the English church. Its range is remarkable. Lull received letters from archbishops Cuthbert and Bregowine of Canterbury, Æthelberht, archbishop of York, Milred, bishop of Worcester, Cyneheard, bishop of Winchester, Tyccea, abbot of Glastonbury, Guthberht, abbot of Wearmouth and Jarrow, and Botwine, abbot of Ripon. Eardwulf, king of Kent, and his namesake Eardwulf, bishop of Rochester, jointly commended three deceased kinswomen to the prayers of his church. Alhred, king of Northumbria, and his wife Osgeofu asked him to assist messengers whom they had dispatched to the court of Charlemagne, and Cynewulf, king of Wessex, with his bishops and nobles, renewed with him a treaty of confraternity made with Boniface. Among these eminent correspondents a nameless monk of Malmesbury wrote to remind him that they had been educated together in that monastery, and to send him the greeting of its abbot. The death of Boniface had not affected the attitude of the English church towards its German mission.

As the successor of Boniface in the see of Mainz, Lull was the principal agent through whom communication was maintained between England and the church in Germany. But his position gave him no effective primacy over the other bishops whom Boniface had consecrated, and among the senior members of the German mission there were men of longer and far more varied experience than his own. From the standpoint of general history, the outstanding figure among the men who continued the work of Boniface is Willibald, bishop of Eichstätt, the first of English travellers in the Middle East. It is probable that he was a distant kinsman of Boniface, but he belonged to eastern Wessex, and received his education in an otherwise unknown monastery at Bishop's Waltham in Hampshire. In 720 he set out on pilgrimage from the mouth of the river Hamble, with his father and a brother named Wynbald. The father died at Lucca and the brother remained at Rome, but Willibald with two companions passed on to Syria, touching Sicily, Samos, the coast of Asia Minor, and Cyprus. He remained in the east for more than two years, imperturbably working his way from one holy place to another in extreme hardship and occasional danger. The record of his travels, written long afterwards in Germany, is an important source of information about conditions in Syria some eighty years after the Arab conquest of Jerusalem, but it does less than justice to the quality of what was, in fact, a heroic adventure. Willibald was kindly treated by many individual Moslems, but the temper of the Arab governors was always uncertain, and he was compelled at last to take ship at Tyre in the depth of winter. After a voyage of not less than four months he reached Constantinople, where he remained for two years, returning to Rome before the end of 730. He was still a young man, and he spent the next ten years in retirement at Monte Cassino. In 740 Pope Gregory III ordered him to join the English mission in Germany, where he was ordained priest by Boniface, and in the following year he was consecrated to the new see of Eichstätt. His brother Wynbald was already working under Boniface in Thuringia, and his sister Waldburg came to him soon afterwards from England. Before 750 he had placed his brother and sister in joint charge of a double monastery at Heidenheim in Middle Franconia, which became an important centre of English learning. His own biography was written by an English nun of that house, who was overweighted by her vocabulary, but showed herself capable of sustained and intricate Latin composition. Wynbald died in 761, Willibald appears to have survived until 786, more than sixty years after his return to Europe from Syria. The year of Waldburg's death is unknown, but when, like her brothers, she had become a canonized saint, her feast was kept on 1 May, and the name Walpurgisnacht has preserved her memory in a highly incongruous association.

English interest in the conversion of the Germans was maintained for a generation after the death of Boniface, but its objective was gradually changed. The last English missionaries of this period are associated, not with the tribes of central and southern Germany, but with the Frisians and Old Saxons. As a group they belonged to Northumbria rather than Wessex. The school which Archbishop Egbert had founded in York quickly won a continental reputation, and provided a training for foreign as well as English scholars. The Frisian Liudger, who became the first bishop of Münster, twice came to York for a period of study, and the Englishman Aluberht, who was consecrated bishop of the Old Saxons at York in 767, was his fellow student there. Almost simultaneously the Northumbrian

church produced Willehad, afterwards bishop of Bremen, a
missionary through whom its teaching was carried to the Danish
border. He chose the heathen parts of Frisia as the first scene
of his work, and set out for that country between 766 and 774,
with the approval of King Alhred and a Northumbrian synod.
In 780 he was summoned to court by Charlemagne, who dispatched him to preach to the Saxons in the district between the
Elbe and the Weser. For a short time he was successful, and
some of his followers penetrated into Ditmarsh beyond the
Elbe, but in 782 his work was undone by a rising of the Saxons
under their chief Widukind. Many of Willehad's associates
were killed, and he himself left Germany for Rome, where
Pope Hadrian I entertained and encouraged him. After
leaving Rome he spent two years in Willibrord's monastery of
Echternach, where another Northumbrian, Willibrord's cousin
Beornred,[1] was abbot. In 785 he was able to resume his Saxon
mission and restore his ruined churches. At last, in 787, in a
council at Worms, Charlemagne caused him to be consecrated
bishop of a group of Saxon and Frisian provinces around
Bremen, where he fixed his seat. He died in 789—the last of
the great evangelists who made the eighth century the heroic
age of the Anglo-Saxon church.

[1] Afterwards archbishop of Sens.

VI

LEARNING AND LITERATURE IN
EARLY ENGLAND

AT the middle of the seventh century there was nothing to suggest the imminence of a great English achievement in learning and literature. The strongest of English kings was an obdurate heathen. The country was distracted by wars which destroyed the peace of scholars, and offered little but a succession of well-worn themes to the makers of heroic verse. The Christian faith, which was to carry imagination into new worlds, was only secure in the extreme south-east of the island. Within a hundred years England had become the home of a Christian culture which influenced the whole development of letters and learning in western Europe. The greatest historical work of the early middle ages had been written in a northern monastery, and English poets had begun to give a permanent form to heroic traditions. There is nothing in European history closely parallel to this sudden development of a civilization by one of the most primitive peoples established within the ancient Roman empire.

It was made possible by the political conditions of the second half of the seventh century. The overthrow of Penda in 654 gave a new stability to the relations between the different English kingdoms. There was much sporadic fighting in the next generation, but the time was past when the incalculable resentments of a single king could throw all England into confusion. The comparative security of the following age permitted the cultivation of learning at many different centres, the creation of libraries, the multiplication of books, and a certain amount of intercourse between scholars. The decay of militant heathenism meant that religious men were free to interest themselves in the form as well as the content of literature, to discuss questions of grammar and metrical structure, and to take pleasure in elaborate combinations of exotic words. A great number of teachers, among whom Theodore, Hadrian, and Aldhelm were eminent, made these conditions the basis of an intellectual life which ranged over every field of learning open to investigation in the seventh century.

This English learning represented the interaction of two distinct and sometimes antagonistic influences; the classical tradition of continental schools, and the more artificial scholarship which had arisen in Ireland during the fifth and sixth centuries. The contrast between these influences can easily be overdrawn. Both Irish and continental scholarship were based on the literature of classical antiquity. The writings of Columbanus of Luxeuil, the contemporary of Gregory the Great, show a knowledge of Latin letters and a command of Latin versification which would have been remarkable in fifth-century Gaul. It is often impossible to infer the provenance of a piece of Irish Latin from the style in which it is written; Adamnan of Iona, the biographer of St. Columba, could write as unaffectedly as his younger contemporary, Bede. Nevertheless, there is no doubt that English scholars of the seventh and eighth centuries were affected by the influence of a curiously involved and artificial Latin style, which early Irish men of letters had developed in their isolation. It is distinguished by constant alliteration, and by a vocabulary of rare and ancient words which are often used to disguise rather than express a meaning. In its extreme form it approximates to a secret language of the learned. But it seemed an appropriate medium of expression to many English scholars. It coloured the whole of Aldhelm's writing, and from Aldhelm it passed to his disciples and imitators. Most of the earliest English historians appear to have escaped its influence—Bede, for example, was trained in a school where continental traditions were dominant—but it strongly affected the one historical work which has come down from the ancient Mercian kingdom, the eighth-century life of St. Guthlac by Felix of Crowland. It even survived the collapse of English learning in the ninth century. The clerks who wrote the charters of Athelstan and Edmund reverted to this archaic style for the more formal parts of these documents, and the charter Latin of the next century shows many traces of its eccentricities.

A still clearer proof of Irish influence on the origins of English scholarship is given by certain distinctive types of handwriting current in England before the end of the seventh century. Earlier Irish scribes had developed what were virtually new hands out of the scripts of the texts which had come to them from the Continent. They produced a characteristic 'half uncial' script of great beauty, which was particularly appropriate to the reproduction of liturgical manuscripts, and developed from it a pointed hand, approximating at times to cursive, suitable for the rapid multiplication of less solemn texts. English scribes of the seventh and eighth centuries could give a brilliant reproduction of the best continental writing of an earlier age. The *Codex Amiatinus*, written at Jarrow before 716 for presentation to the pope, is one of the greatest of all uncial manuscripts. But for all except the most solemn purposes, they normally used one or other of the Irish modifications of continental script, with the result that it is sometimes impossible to distinguish between the products of English and Irish *scriptoria* on palaeographical evidence alone. Each of the two great types of Irish hand was firmly established in England within a generation of the death of Theodore. In 704 Waldhere, bishop of London, used the pointed form of Irish script in the solitary letter which has survived from his correspondence with Berhtwald, archbishop of Canterbury.[1] With few exceptions, English royal charters of the eighth century are written in some form of the same hand, and this archaic script continued to be used for such documents until the tenth century. Here, at least the influence of Irish learning survived the ninth-century destruction of ancient Irish culture.

There can be no question as to the reality of Irish influence on the style and script of early English scholars. It is much more difficult to distinguish between the Irish and continental strains in the substance of English learning. There is evidence that a certain number of old Latin texts of the Bible were used by English scholars of this period. These ancient texts were undoubtedly of Celtic origin, and the isolation of the British churches makes it probable that English students derived them from Irish, rather than British, teachers. It is suggestive that Old English religious poets were familiar with a large body of apocryphal literature, discountenanced by the Roman church, but popular in Ireland. There was a strong Irish element in the penitential system of the early English church. But in the last resort, any estimate of English indebtedness to Irish learning must turn on the inferences which can be drawn

[1] *Facsimiles of Ancient Charters in the British Museum*, i, plate 5.

from the recorded visits of Englishmen to Irish schools, from the Irish share in the conversion of England, and from the occasional foundation of Irish monasteries on English soil. The debt has often been exaggerated. The greatest achievements of Irish scholarship belong to a later age. It was not until the eighth century that Irish learning reached its full development and Irish scholars began to play their momentous part in the transmission of ancient literature. Their predecessors were men of narrower range, who had little idea of the co-ordination of knowledge or the discipline of learned inquiry. But the passionate desire for learning which moved them was a new force in the western world.

The origins of organized learning in England lie in the schools established by early missionaries for the instruction of children who might proceed to holy orders. The foundation of such a school in East Anglia is recorded by Bede in terms which prove that the beginnings of an educational system had already been established in Kent. The early history of these schools is utterly obscure, and the learning of the first phase of English Christianity is only illustrated by certain ancient biblical texts which seem to have been brought to England by Augustine. It is no doubt possible that continuous teaching may have been maintained at Canterbury throughout the seventh century; but Bede's description of Theodore's educational work is definitely against the opinion that it was based on any existing school. In the north, Christianity had been obliterated by Cadwallon and Penda before any organization of learning can have developed, and it was restored by Irish monks who were evangelists rather than scholars. The continental influences which dominated English learning in the eighth century have no discernible connection with the original Gregorian mission to England. They represent the ideas of the generation which created the permanent organization of the English church, and are primarily associated with the names of Theodore and Hadrian, Benedict Biscop, and Wilfrid.

Aldhelm, the most illustrious pupil of the school of Canterbury, and Bede, the greatest scholar of the next generation, have each described the teaching of Theodore and Hadrian. It provided an organized body of knowledge, based on the interpretation of scripture, but extending to the sciences which regulated the order of the religious year, the music which was essential in the services of the church, and the metrical rules according to which religious poetry should be composed. It attracted scholars from distant centres of learning. Oftfor, who became the second bishop of Worcester, continued under Theodore the studies which he had begun under the Abbess Hild at Hartlepool and Whitby, and Aldhelm came to Canterbury from the centre of Wessex. Its reputation extended as far as Ireland. One of Aldhelm's few effective metaphors occurs in a sentence which describes Theodore confronted by a crowd of Irish scholars 'like an angry boar surrounded by a pack of grinning Molossian hounds'. No catalogue of Theodore's library has survived, but a letter in which Aldhelm describes his studies at Canterbury brings out the important fact that at least one book of Roman law could be read there. In apologizing to Bishop Hæddi of Winchester for failing to spend Christmas with him, Aldhelm remarks that he has been detained at Canterbury by the difficulties which beset those who, among other studies, wish thoroughly to lay open the decisions of the Roman laws and explore all the secrets of the jurisconsults.[1] The passage, which is an important piece of evidence for the study of Roman law in the Dark Ages, gives a remarkable illustration of the range of learning offered by Theodore's school at Canterbury.

That a knowledge of Greek could be obtained in this school is clear from the testimony of both Aldhelm and Bede. Aldhelm, referring to Theodore and his associates, reproves one of his correspondents for seeking instruction in Ireland as if England contained no masters of Greek and Latin. Bede makes the remarkable statement that in his time there survived disciples of Theodore and Hadrian to whom Latin and Greek were as familiar as their own language, and in the later part of his history he twice refers to the Greek scholarship of their pupil Tobias, bishop of Rochester. It is possible that a considerable number of Greek words and phrases had already been acquired by individual English scholars from Irish teachers. In the sixth and seventh centuries Irish men of learning, as a class, were distinguished from their continental fellows by at least an elementary knowledge of Greek. Latinized forms of Greek words are prominent in their learned vocabulary. But

[1] M. R. James, *Two Ancient English Scholars* (Glasgow University Press, 1931), pp. 13–14, where the book which Aldhelm read is identified with a copy, still extant, of the Breviary of Alaric.

Bede's statement, which implies that Theodore and Hadrian produced pupils who could read and write Greek with ease, claims for the school of Canterbury a proficiency in classical learning rivalled, so far as is known, by no other learned community north of the Alps. It has left few traces in the surviving remains of early English scholarship, but on such a matter Bede's authority deserves respect. He was personally acquainted with at least one leading member of the school of Canterbury. Most of his information about Kentish history was derived from Albinus, a pupil of Theodore and Hadrian, who had succeeded Hadrian as abbot of the monastery of St. Peter and St. Paul outside Canterbury. There is certainly no inherent unlikelihood in the statement that a school of Greek learning arose there in the late seventh century. Theodore is the last known pupil of the schools of Athens. Hadrian, who taught at Canterbury for nearly forty years, was born in Byzantine Africa, and came to England from Byzantine Italy.

All the influences which contributed to the origins of English learning meet in the work of Aldhelm. His first teacher was the Irish scholar Maildubh, the founder of the community which became the abbey of Malmesbury. The fame of Theodore's teaching drew him to Canterbury, and once, at least, he visited Rome. By birth he belonged to the West Saxon royal family, and he was therefore familiar with a mass of floating tradition which later writers were to shape into history. He wrote English verse, now lost, which King Alfred admired greatly. As a man of letters he represents the culture of his age in its most highly developed form, and his writings influenced English and continental scholarship for more than a century. His longest works are a poem, *De Laudibus Virginum*, vaguely addressed 'Ad Maximam Abbatissam', and a closely related prose discourse, *De Laudibus Virginitatis*, written for Hildelith, abbess of Barking, and nine of her nuns. His epistles to Geraint, king of Dumnonia, on the rules which should determine the date of Easter, and to Aldfrith, king of Northumbria, on the different forms of metrical structure, are, in effect, treatises. Historically, although they show the extraordinary range of Aldhelm's reading, these works are less interesting than his shorter letters and poems. A set of verses on a church built by a daughter of Centwine, king of Wessex, corrects

Bede's account of conditions in that country after the death of Cenwalh,[1] and a letter which can have had little purpose except to display Aldhelm's expertise in Latin composition contains a unique contemporary description of Theodore's teaching. Aldhelm was beyond comparison the most learned and ingenious western scholar of the late seventh century, but his ingenuity was expressed in the elaboration of a style which deprives his learning of all vitality. He had an artist's pleasure in the manipulation of words, without a trace of literary feeling, and his influence came to an end as soon as scholars had lost the taste for the eccentric latinity of which he was the master. Few learned men of Aldhelm's power have contributed so little to the ultimate development of their studies.

Aldhelm was not, in fact, the man to lead a younger generation into new paths. None of his pupils was capable of more than a feeble imitation of his style. Boniface, the one great writer produced by the early schools of southern England, turns an occasional phrase in Aldhelm's manner, but the quality of his writing owes nothing to Aldhelm's example. Boniface was a man of individual genius, and his power of expression can easily lead to an over-estimate of the southern English scholarship which he represented. It was the creation of a few highly exceptional men, and their death was naturally followed by a decline in its fertility. Even at Canterbury, the traditions of Theodore and Hadrian do not seem to have outlived the last of their disciples. The principal representative of academic learning among the southern contemporaries of Bede is Tatwine, archbishop of Canterbury from 731 to 734. He had formerly been abbot of Breedon in Leicestershire, and before his election to Canterbury he produced a grammar and a series of Latin riddles which are interesting illustrations of early Mercian scholarship but have little intrinsic importance. The rarity of outstanding scholars in the southern churches of this period does not mean that their inmates were illiterate. The letters which came to Boniface from this part of England prove the scholarship and intellectual curiosity of a number of men and women whose names never enter into literary history. But the learning which gives unique distinction to the English church of this age was centred in a small group of Northumbrian monasteries.

[1] Above, p. 67.

In northern as in southern England the new learning of the seventh century represented a combination of Irish and continental influences. The northern church itself was the creation of Irish monks, and Lindisfarne, where the earliest of English biographies was written, was the original centre of their mission. If the supporters of the Celtic Easter-reckoning had prevailed in 663, the Northumbrian churches would have become permanent outposts of a specifically Irish scholarship. The victory of the Roman party did not undo the work of earlier Irish scholars, whose script survived in the churches of their foundation, but it placed the future of Northumbrian learning in the hands of men trained in the continental tradition. As a result of their predominance, the characteristic style and vocabulary of Irish scholars have left fewer traces in Northumbria than in southern England. No Northumbrian scholar ever applied himself to the combination of strange words with the laborious assiduity of Aldhelm. There is no trace of an author's self-consciousness in the historical literature through which Northumbrian learning lives today.

Among the men who brought Northumbrian learning out of isolation, Benedict Biscop, the founder of Wearmouth and Jarrow, deserves to be regarded as the leader. In the history of his time he is overshadowed by his younger contemporary Wilfrid. But Wilfrid's contribution to the enlightenment of the north was made in the spheres of ecclesiastical observance and regulation; he was too impatient to create a great monastic school, and his churches of Hexham and Ripon were not remarkable for their learning. Benedict devoted the knowledge and experience of half a lifetime to the establishment of two monasteries. By 674, when Ecgfrith, king of Northumbria, gave him land for the foundation of his house at Wearmouth, he had made three separate journeys from England to Rome, lived for two years in retirement on the island of Lerins, guided the newly consecrated Archbishop Theodore from Rome to England, and spent two more years as abbot of the monastery of St. Peter and St. Paul outside Canterbury. His importance in the history of English learning is due to the libraries which his knowledge of southern cities enabled him to bring together at Wearmouth and Jarrow. Before there was any prospect of the foundation of Wearmouth he had accumulated a large collection of purchased books at Vienne. Transported to Eng-

land, these books became the nucleus of the library at Wearmouth, which was increased as a result of a fourth journey to
Rome in 679. Two years later a new grant of land from Ecgfrith
enabled Benedict to found a second monastery at Jarrow on
Tyne, seven miles north-west of Wearmouth, and in 684 he
undertook the last of his journeys to Rome in order to obtain
books and relics for the new house. When he died, in 689, he
had brought into being two neighbouring monasteries, governed
as a single community, which possessed an endowment in relics,
religious ornaments, and books unparalleled in England.

The books collected by Benedict made possible the work of
Bede. The commentaries on scripture and the scientific works,
through which he first became famous, prove his acquaintance
with a singularly wide range of patristic and historical literature.[1] Only a small proportion of his work has been edited in
such a way as to show the exact extent of his debt to his predecessors. Like other ancient scholars, Bede often quotes or
refers to authors whose work he only knew through epitomes,
or through isolated sentences embedded in later texts. His
knowledge of classical literature, for example, was much narrower than has sometimes been inferred from the extent to
which classical reminiscence enters into his writing. Even so,
his work could never have been done without recourse to
libraries of wholly exceptional size and quality. From his
admission to the monastery of Monkwearmouth as a child of
seven until his death at the age of sixty-three he was a member of
the monasteries which Benedict had founded there and in 681
at Jarrow. There is no evidence that he travelled widely in
search of books; he never refers to distant libraries which he has
visited, and the range of his recorded travel does not extend
beyond York and Lindisfarne. Apart from occasional books
which he may have obtained through the favour of learned
correspondents, it is probable that his work rested on the
collections of books made by Benedict, and increased by Bede's
own master Ceolfrith with whom he moved to Jarrow, who was
Benedict's successor in the rule of both his monasteries.

Later generations, considering the long series of Bede's commentaries, placed him in the succession of the great fathers of

[1] On the character of Bede's literary equipment see M. L. W. Laistner, 'Bede
as a Classical and Patristic Scholar', *Trans. R. Hist. Soc.*, 4th Series, xvi (1933),
pp. 69–94.

the church.[1] He himself would certainly have wished to be remembered by these works of exposition. His scientific treatises, which form a link between his commentaries and his *Ecclesiastical History*, arose naturally from his conception of his responsibilities as a teacher. Some scheme of chronology was necessary to the understanding of scripture, and the date of Easter was fixed by astronomical calculation. In 703, early in his literary course, he produced the elementary manual of chronology known under the title *De Temporibus*. It is a meagre work, and it involved Bede for once in a charge of heresy, brought by certain individuals whom he describes as rustics wallowing in their cups. The work through which he ranks as a master of technical chronology, the treatise *De Temporum Ratione*, was written in 725. Its influence is not yet spent, for it established in England the custom of reckoning years from the era of the Incarnation. Bede was in no sense the originator of this system, which formed part of a calculus for determining the date of Easter devised by the computist Dionysius Exiguus early in the sixth century. It was ignored by the Roman church and indeed by all ecclesiastical authorities until 663, when Wilfrid, who had probably become acquainted with it during his first Italian journey, brought it forward at the council of Whitby. There is no unequivocal proof of its employment in English documents before the appearance of the *De Temporum Ratione*, and its rapid adoption thereafter was undoubtedly due to the influence of Bede's historical work.

Through this work Bede emerges at last from the atmosphere of ancient science and exegesis to prove himself the master of a living art. As a historian Bede was singularly fortunate in his environment. An interest in history was one of the features which distinguished the northern from the southern scholarship of the eighth century. Between 698 and 705 a monk of Lindisfarne had described the life and personality of St. Cuthbert in writing which moves stiffly but rises at times to a curious and sinister power.[2] Bede himself never surpassed this nameless

---

[1] Bede's reputation abroad in the Carolingian age is proved by many copies of individual works written on the Continent in hands of this period.

[2] Cuthbert, leaning on his staff, was listening to Wagga the reeve of Carlisle explaining to the queen the Roman wall of the city 'his head bent towards the ground, he then lifted his eyes towards the heavens again and with a sigh said 'Oh! Oh! Oh! I think that the war is over and that judgment has been given against our people in the battle', ed. B. Colgrave, *Two lives of St. Cuthbert*, pp. 122–3. For editions of this and the works which follow see below, p. 695.

writer's description of the sudden sense of disaster which came to Cuthbert as he stood in Carlisle with the queen of Northumbria on the day of the battle of Nechtanesmere. A monk of Whitby had attempted the hopeless task of writing the life of Gregory the Great on the basis of the materials supplied by Northumbrian tradition. Eddi's tendentious life of Wilfrid had been written at the request of Acca, bishop of Hexham, and Tatberht, abbot of Ripon. Within Bede's immediate circle, a monk of Wearmouth had written a life of his master, Abbot Ceolfrith. It is remarkable as a piece of pure biography, without any hagiographical admixture, and it received the compliment of imitation from Bede himself in his Lives of the Abbots of Wearmouth and Jarrow. By 731, when Bede put forth his *Ecclesiastical History*, there plainly existed in Northumbria an audience for a work of erudition devoted to the growth of the English church. Bede's *Ecclesiastical History*, which King Ceolwulf of Northumbria read and criticized in draft, is the response of a great scholar to a great opportunity.

Nevertheless, its essential quality carries it into the small class of books which transcend all but the most fundamental conditions of time and place. Bede was a monk to whom the miraculous seemed a manifestation of the divine government of the world. But his critical faculty was always alert; his narrative never degenerates into a tissue of ill-attested wonders, and in regard to all the normal substance of history his work can be judged as strictly as any historical writing of any time. His preface, in which he acknowledges the help received from learned friends, reads like the introduction to a modern work of scholarship. But the quality which makes his work great is not his scholarship, nor the faculty of narrative which he shared with many contemporaries, but his astonishing power of co-ordinating the fragments of information which came to him through tradition, the relation of friends, or documentary evidence. In an age when little was attempted beyond the registration of fact, he had reached the conception of history. It is in virtue of this conception that the *Historia Ecclesiastica* still lives after twelve hundred years.

One at least of Bede's pupils showed something of his literary quality. Soon after his death, his last days were described by a monk of Jarrow in prose which bears comparison with any narrative in the *Historia Ecclesiastica* itself. The tradition of his teaching was preserved at Wearmouth and Jarrow, and his books were copied there for the benefit of English scholars in continental monasteries. But it was through his influence on the school of York that his work became a factor in the general development of European learning. Egbert, archbishop of York, who founded this school, had studied under Bede, and regarded him with great deference in later life. The last of all Bede's writings is a letter of admonition to Egbert on the duties which he had undertaken as a bishop and the policy which he ought to adopt for the reform of the Northumbrian church. The closeness of their previous relationship as master and pupil is proved by the ninth-century Life of Alcuin, the most eminent of Egbert's disciples. Through Egbert the substance of Bede's teaching was transmitted to a group of scholars who rapidly made York the principal centre of English scholarship.

From an early date they seem to have formed an organized community rather than a fluctuating assemblage of learners around a single teacher. The beginnings of the school undoubtedly lay in the instruction given as a matter of duty by Egbert to the clerks of his church. But his reputation soon attracted other scholars, and an actual course of instruction given to a more general audience seems to survive in his *Dialogus Ecclesiasticae Institutionis*, in which an epitome of ecclesiastical law is presented in the form of answers to specific questions addressed by a pupil to a master. Early in the history of the school Egbert appointed his kinsman Æthelberht to its charge, and Æthelberht, who was himself a great teacher, set himself to form a library for his scholars. In his poem on the saints of York Alcuin names the principal authors whose works were represented in this library, revealing a collection strong in patristic literature and in Christian poetry, but curiously weak in classical texts. Alcuin's verses do not form a catalogue of the library; they give no indication of the extent to which the various writings of a voluminous author were available at York, and they omit the names of authors whose books no eighth-century collector could have ignored. But they prove that Æthelberht had created one of the greatest libraries in western Europe.

Alcuin's career[1] is of peculiar interest as a link between the phase of English scholarship which culminated in the work of

[1] See the discussion by W. Levison, *England and the Continent*, pp. 153–66.

Bede and the revival of western learning under Charlemagne. The first half of his life as a scholar was spent at York. In 767 his master Æthelberht became archbishop, and, apparently, left the immediate direction of his school in Alcuin's hands. For the next thirteen years he was the centre of a notable group of scholars. As a kinsman of St. Willibrord he was intimately connected with the founders of the Frisian church, and the most remarkable of the pupils who came to him at York was a young Frisian noble named Liudger, who afterwards became the first bishop of Münster. During this period he made two journeys to Rome, visiting many local centres of learning in Italy and Gaul, and he was undoubtedly regarded abroad as the leading English scholar when Archbishop Æthelberht resigned his see in 780. Late in that year he undertook a third Roman journey in order to obtain the pallium for the new archbishop. At Parma, on his return home, he was received by Charlemagne, who offered him permanent hospitality at the Frankish court. The second phase of his career began in 782, when he joined the brilliant company of literate men with whom Charlemagne associated on familiar terms. He became the head of the palace school—where he was joined by many of his English pupils—the chief adviser of Charlemagne on doctrinal issues, and his agent in all his relations with England. His first preferment seems to have consisted of the abbeys of Ferrières and St. Lupus at Troyes, but in 796 Charlemagne gave him the greater abbey of St. Martin at Tours, with which he was particularly associated in his closing years. At Tours, where he died in 804, the influence of his scholarship converted a large and wealthy, but undistinguished monastery into a great centre of learning, and contributed to the development of the most beautiful of all forms of script associated with the Carolingian renaissance. He was succeeded at Ferrières by a pupil of his Northumbrian days named Sigulf, and at Tours by a younger Englishman named Frithugisl, who became head of the Imperial Chancery under Louis the Pious. The long series of texts illustrating the relations between England and the Frankish churches ends with the fragments of the correspondence exchanged between Lupus, abbot of Ferrières, and the men who were ruling the school of York at the middle of the ninth century.

Alcuin had nothing of Bede's constructive intelligence, and he was born too late to feel the excitement in the mere use of words which excuses and partly explains Aldhelm's pedantry. At the present day he is chiefly remembered as the writer of many letters, which form one of the principal authorities for the history of his time. They are written with admirable simplicity and show the discretion and restraint which made him an influence for moderation in the Carolingian renaissance of speculative thought. In theology, as in all branches of organized knowledge, Alcuin was the learned and conservative interpreter of the writings of greater men. But his intellectual dependence on his predecessors made him the ideal agent for the transmission of their teaching. He is a great figure in the history of European letters because he and his pupils brought about a continental reception of English learning which profoundly influenced the whole literature of the Carolingian age.

Any account of the early history of English learning tends to become centred round a few great names. The tendency represents the fact that the general course of this history was actually determined by the work of Theodore and Hadrian, Aldhelm, Bede, and Alcuin. But it means that less than justice is generally done to scholars of less pervasive influence, and to schools which never produced an eminent master. It is only through the intensive study of individual manuscripts that it will ever become possible to place the different local centres of English learning in their true relation to the general intellectual life of the eighth and ninth centuries. Nevertheless, it is already possible to foreshadow certain conclusions which future work is likely to confirm. It is probable, for example, that the Mercian contribution to English learning has been undervalued in the past. Cynewulf, the one Old English poet with whom a considerable body of verse is definitely associated, has recently been referred to this region with virtual certainty, and more than one important text which used to be assigned vaguely to Northumbria has now been traced with precision to Lichfield. It is gradually becoming less remarkable that King Alfred found at least four Mercian scholars to help him in his literary work. It is also becoming clear that the concentration of interest on the greatest scholars tends to the neglect of the generations during which their work was continued by lesser, but by no means insignificant, successors. The ascendant phase of English scholarship may end with Alcuin, but it is already apparent that for half a century after his death English religious houses were producing work which may not be original in matter, but represents a living interest in learning and remarkable accomplishment in script. It seems in fact that in Northumbria and Mercia, at least, it was the dislocation of society in the Danish invasions, rather than a weakening of the impulse towards scholarship, which brought the first phase of English learning to an end.

One Northumbrian manuscript of this period, which is a work of supreme excellence, raises questions which affect the whole history of western decorative art in the early middle ages. The most precious of the books belonging to the medieval church of Durham was a codex of the Gospels written in an early Hiberno-Saxon hand. In mere script it is no more than an admirable example of a noble style, and the figure-drawing of its illustrations, though probably based on classical models, has more than a touch of primitive *naïveté*. Its unique importance is due to the beauty and astonishing intricacy of its decoration. The nature of its ornament connects it very closely with a group of Irish manuscripts of which the Book of Kells is the most famous, and it has often been regarded as of Irish provenance, or at least the work of an Irish scribe living in England. But a colophon written in the tenth century by a priest named Aldred, who glossed the whole text of the book in the northern English of that period, states that Eadfrith, bishop of Lindisfarne from 698 to 721, wrote the book, that Æthelwald, his successor, pressed and bound it, and that an anchorite named Billfrith ornamented its binding with metalwork and gems. As it should not be assumed that St. Cuthbert's clergy had forgotten the history of their most sacred text, it follows that the art which is commonly described as 'Hiberno-Saxon' had reached a brilliant phase of development in northern England several generations before the date of the great Irish manuscripts with which it is generally associated. It also follows that this art arose in England, for no Irish examples of this distinctive type of decoration can be referred to a date so early as 721. Even apart from the colophon, there are features of the manuscript which attest its English origin.[1] In text, it is closely akin to the Vulgate of the Northumbrian *Codex Amiatinus*, with little trace of the older Latin readings preserved by

[1] It is an important point that the *capitulare* of the volume has south Italian features which reflect the influence of Hadrian of Canterbury.

Irish tradition. The motives employed in its decoration are all represented in earlier Anglo-Celtic art. There is nothing in its matter, script, or ornament, which forbids its attribution to a bishop trained in the seventh century. The history of English sculpture shows that Anglo-Saxon artists, once set in the way of invention, came very quickly to complete mastery of form. In the decoration of manuscripts, as in sculpture, achievement may well have come through individual genius rather than the slow elaboration of design.

The Christian learning of the seventh-century schools was confronted by a heathen culture which had already given rise to a literature. An elaborate technique of alliterative verse had been developed by a long succession of English poets. Most of the great stories which had arrested the imagination of the Germanic world had received a definite, though by no means stereotyped, form at their hands. Reflection on life and its vicissitudes was already being expressed from the heathen standpoint in verse to which there is no close parallel elsewhere in Europe. To a strict churchman of the period this pagan literature was intensely distasteful, and it was either ignored or discountenanced by the founders of English Christian scholarship. But the bulk of this poetry was addressed to an aristocratic audience, and the English nobility, familiar with the courts of long-descended kings, maintained its interest in heroic tradition. The clergy became more tolerant of this tradition as the danger of a heathen reaction died away, and, indeed, played an essential part in its transmission. The English poetry of the heathen age was first written down by Christian clerks, and most of it only survives in texts which are affected by Christian ideas and imagery. At its height, this influence extends to the permeation of an entire poem with Christian feeling. A poem such as *Beowulf*, in which aristocratic traditions are enveloped in a Christian atmosphere, is an invaluable record of the intellectual outlook of the men under whose protection Christianity was established in England.

In the age of national migrations the various Germanic peoples were conscious of an essential unity which distinguished them from the subjects of the Roman empire to the south and the outer barbarians to the east. It rested on a fundamental similarity of political structure and social convention, and it was expressed from time to time in the great federations created by

overlords such as Eormanric and Theodoric. The heroic narratives which formed the substance of the earliest Germanic
poetry were addressed to men who knew many courts and
peoples, and were acquainted with some, at least, of their
traditions. A good poet could find a patron anywhere. Accordingly, a single heroic story is often preserved independently
in the poetry of many Germanic countries, and conversely,
the heroic poetry of every Germanic country is largely, if not
principally, devoted to stories which have no connection with
its own history. Of the three heroic figures whose names are
attached to extant English poems, Beowulf belonged to the
centre of what is now Sweden, Finn to Frisia, and Waldhere
to the south of Gaul. Much of *Widsith*, perhaps the oldest of all
English poems, consists of mere names of kings and peoples,
inserted on the assumption that an English listener of the
seventh century would be able to associate a story with each
of them. The English heroic poetry which has survived plainly
represents a mere fragment of a body of tradition once common
to the whole Germanic world.

Nevertheless, it is English poetry alone which shows the range
of these traditions and the spirit in which they were treated.
The whole of German heroic verse is now represented by a
single fragment. English poetry of this class includes a long
epic relating the adventures, death, and burial of Beowulf, the
hero of the people living to the south of the great lakes of
Sweden; a composite set of verses purporting to record the
travels of a poet named Widsith, but consisting essentially of a
catalogue of ancient kings and peoples; and a singular piece of
reflective verse, in which a poet called Deor, who has lost his
place to Heorrenda, the master-minstrel of Germanic legend,
recalls the sufferings which others have endured, with the refrain
that his troubles, like theirs, will in time be overcome. In
addition to this very considerable body of verse, fragments of
two other poems have survived; one describing a great battle
in the hall of Finn, king of the Frisians, the other relating how a
hero named Waldhere, encouraged by Hildegyth, his betrothed,
challenged Guthhere, king of the Burgundians, to single combat.
All these poems are preserved in West Saxon English of the
tenth century, but *Beowulf* and *Widsith* contain many ancient
forms of words which show that an Anglian original lies behind
the existing texts. There is no evidence as to the particular

region in which this poetry was first written down, but it is not unlikely that the idea of giving a permanent form to floating poetic tradition was part of the general intellectual activity which created the Latin literature of Northumbria. In any case, it seems clear that the poems took substantially their present shape in a period which may be arbitrarily defined by the birth of Bede in 672 and the final departure of Alcuin from England in 782.

The casual destruction of manuscripts has left *Beowulf* the only poem in which a traditional theme is treated on an epic scale in an ancient Germanic language. It is heroic in spirit and highly wrought, but it does not bear comparison with any of the world's greatest stories. It is not, in fact, so much a story as a series of episodes in the life of a hero, interspersed with many digressions, interesting because of their great age, but often irrelevant. Beowulf himself is represented as the nephew of Hygelac, king of the Geatas, a powerful people whose territory now forms the Swedish provinces of Göta-land. After various youthful adventures Beowulf with twelve companions visits the court of the Danish king Hrothgar, whose hall has been made uninhabitable by the ravages of a monster named Grendel. When Beowulf has destroyed Grendel by his strength and skill as a wrestler, Grendel's mother avenges him by killing one of the king's companions, but Beowulf immediately follows her to her lair in a vaulted chamber under a lake and kills her there. He then returns to his own country, and is honourably received by King Hygelac. The second half of the poem is devoted to an encounter between Beowulf, who is now king of the Geatas, and a dragon which has been ravaging his country, and lives, guarding a treasure, in an ancient funeral barrow. Beowulf kills the dragon, but is mortally wounded, and a long description of his funeral ceremonies forms a kind of epilogue to the whole work. Interwoven with the main story are a number of more normal episodes which undoubtedly belong to the original Beowulf tradition. After his return from the Danish court Beowulf takes part in a disastrous expedition led by Hygelac against the 'Hetware', who lived in the country north of the lower Rhine. Hygelac is killed and his army destroyed, and Beowulf, who has greatly distinguished himself in the battle, is offered the kingdom by his dead lord's widow. Refusing to supplant his kinsman Heardred, Hygelac's son, Beowulf becomes the young king's guardian and adviser. But Heardred is killed in a Swedish invasion which he has provoked by protecting an exiled nephew of the Swedish king, and Beowulf thereupon becomes king of the Geatas, defeats the Swedes, and rules his own people prosperously for a period which the poet estimates at fifty years.

It should not be assumed that the audience to which *Beowulf* was addressed felt any incongruity between these incidents and the folk-mythology of Grendel, Grendel's mother, and the dragon of the barrow. To the thegn or peasant of the eighth century the supernatural world to which these figures belong was in the immediate background of life. Its immanence justified the utmost skill that the poet could bring to its representation. But the historical, as distinct from the literary significance of *Beowulf* lies in the maze of allusion through which the thread of the story runs. It was composed for an audience sufficiently familiar with northern tradition to grasp the meaning of the most casual reference to other stories, and its author lost no opportunity of heightening interest by the introduction of heroic names. The extent to which these stories represent history is the hardest, and perhaps the most important, question raised by the poem. The remoteness of the northern world in which the scene of *Beowulf* is laid means that few of its characters are likely to be encountered in the writings of early Latin historians. The Geatas were unfamiliar to the few ancient authors who knew at least the names of the Danes and Swedes. Nevertheless, Hygelac's unfortunate raid is actually recorded, and placed close to the year 520 by Gregory of Tours. He regarded the raiders as Danes, and he stumbled over their leader's name. But a Gaulish writer of the eighth century, enlarging Gregory's work at this point, represents Hygelac's name accurately as Chocilaicus, and kills him in the land of a people called Attoarii—the classical Chattuarii—who are equivalent to the Hetware of *Beowulf*. A somewhat later author of a book about monsters states that the vast bones of Huiglaucus, king of the Gete, were still preserved near the mouth of the Rhine. This abundant confirmation of a single episode suggests that much of the incidental background of *Beowulf* represents a genuine and accurate tradition. It is still more important as proof that a definite statement of historical fact could be handed down orally in alliterative verse for at least two centuries.

Before the end of the seventh century the technique and some of the conventions of heroic verse were being applied to religious subjects. The main body of English religious poetry seems to fall between 700 and 850. Apart from a few fragments, it has only survived in West Saxon copies of the late tenth century. On the other hand, most of these texts show signs of transcription from Anglian manuscripts, and there is definite evidence that religious poetry was cultivated in Northumbria many years before the death of Bede. Several fragments of the great poem known as the *Dream of the Rood* are inscribed on the decorated cross at Ruthwell in Dumfriesshire, which is one of the outstanding monuments of early Northumbrian art. One of Bede's most famous stories carries the origins of religious poetry in the north back to a date before 680. After recording the death of Hild, abbess of Whitby, in that year, he relates how Cædmon, an oxherd on her land, received the gift of song miraculously in a dream, and afterwards, instructed in scripture and sacred learning by her monks, made many poems, which none who came after him could equal. His verse, as described by Bede, ranged over the creation of the world and the early history of mankind; the journey of Israel from Egypt to the land of promise; the Incarnation and all the cardinal doctrines of the Christian faith; the terrors of judgement, the pains of hell, and the delight of heaven. Most of the English religious poetry which has survived relates to these subjects, and a considerable portion of it has at one time or another been attributed to Cædmon himself. But the only verses which can definitely be assigned to him—nine lines copied into the oldest manuscript of Bede's *Ecclesiastical History*—bear all the signs of unpractised expression in an art which itself was as yet undeveloped. The man who wrote these stiffly moving lines was separated by at least a generation of experiment from even the earliest of the poets whose work is embedded in the Old English *Genesis*, *Exodus*, or *Daniel*.

It was by slow degrees that English poets arrived at a style appropriate to the treatment of religious subjects. The heroic poems which were their only models gave them a large stock of metaphors and many examples of effective narrative. But metaphors which had reflected the life of a pagan aristocracy were often incongruous in a Christian setting, and the loose construction of *Beowulf* shows that the power to give a vivid impression of a self-contained episode might coincide with singular ineffectiveness in the management of a complicated piece of history. The earliest English religious poetry is the work of men who took all revealed history for their province, with a technical equipment which had been developed for the recitation of heroic tales in primitive Germanic courts. More than one early poet mastered his refractory medium and produced great verse. In the *Dream of the Rood* the archaic language in itself contributes to the glamour which transforms the record of a vision into poetry. There were many passages of scriptural history which invited embellishment with metaphors of war. Even so the dead weight of a conventional vocabulary hangs heavily over much of the earliest Old English religious verse. There are signs that individual poets were feeling their way towards a simpler style by the earlier part of the ninth century. Four poems of this period, the signed work of an author named Cynewulf who has only recently been placed in his proper chronological sequence, are profoundly influenced in design and style by classical models.[1] Under normal conditions Cynewulf's work might well have given rise to a new religious poetry, smoother in expression and more regular in form than the experimental verse of an earlier age. But the current of Old English poetry was interrupted when the Danish invasions destroyed English civilization, and it was virtually as a new art that the writing of religious verse was resumed in the tenth century.

Elaborate renderings of sacred history imply an audience enjoying more than a peasant's leisure, and Old English religious poetry, like the heroic verse which preceded it, was addressed to a class which may fairly be described as aristocratic. The verses with which peasants entertained each other have for the most part vanished beyond trace. Some of them may be embedded in Old English riddles, of which nearly a hundred still survive. But learned men also amused themselves with these ingenuities, and the English riddles are too strongly influenced by Latin models to count as popular literature. The only Anglo-Saxon poems for which a peasant origin can reasonably be claimed are two collections of so-called Gnomic verses—sententious observations about the properties of things—which

[1] See K. Sisam, 'Cynewulf and his Poetry', *Proceedings of the British Academy,* xviii, pp. 303-31 reprinted in his *Studies in the History of Old English Literature,* pp. 1-28.

carry a distinctive atmosphere of rustic wisdom. They range from the crudest assertions of simple fact—'frost must freeze, fire destroy wood'—to somewhat elaborate descriptions of persons, or of common incidents of life. They often relate to the virtues, the equipment, or the amusements of nobles, and the finest of them all is the description of a great lady, discreet, generous, and gracious, in her lord's hall. They clearly arose among men who were keenly interested in the aristocratic life, but they always regard it from the outside. A series of them gradually produces the impression of a group of farmers capping alliterative sentences with one another, and occasionally maintaining a sequence of thought long enough to yield a definite picture—two men happily playing at dice on a board, or a sailor returning to his 'Frisian wife'. They deserve more attention from historians than they usually receive, for there is nothing in literature that approaches so nearly to the authentic voice of the Anglo-Saxon *ceorl*.

The bulk of Old English poetry obviously reflects the conditions of the age in which it arose. It presupposes, for example, the existence of a not unintelligent aristocracy, to whom the persons and incidents of sacred history could be made as interesting as the heroic stories of heathen antiquity. Most Old English verse was undoubtedly written to satisfy the demand of such men for instruction or entertainment. But there remain a small number of poems—the first of their kind in Germanic literature—which represent the mood of an author rather than the interests of an audience. They include a description of a ruined city, probably Bath; what appears to be a dialogue between a disillusioned sailor and a youth proposing to take to the sea, and two separate pieces, one realistic, the other devotional, describing the miseries of an exile. As literary experiments, the most remarkable poems of the group are three sets of verses which attempt to tell a story from the standpoint of one of the actors. The simplest is a message from a husband, driven into exile by a feud, to his wife, telling her that he is now prosperous, and begging her to join him. More ambitious but less intelligible is a poem purporting to be the lament of a wife, who has been estranged from her husband by the machinations of his kinsmen. She and her husband are living apart, each in misery; and her chief resentment is directed against a certain young man, whom she regards as in some way the cause of her husband's wretchedness. The third of these poems is a fragment of nineteen lines in which a woman seems to be describing her distress at the absence of her outlawed lover and the end of her love for her tyrannous husband. It is hard to imagine the public for which these poems can have been written. They can never have been sung in a lord's hall, and they seem hardly suitable for monastic reading. They look like the work of a man interested in human relationships, who for his own satisfaction was trying to tell an imaginary story in verse. He was not very successful. Each of these three poems has produced a volume of discussion out of all proportion to its modest length. But they are of extraordinary interest, for they carry the romantic element in English literature back to the very heart of the Dark Ages.

Any estimate of the English achievement in poetry between the seventh and ninth centuries rests essentially on the contents of four manuscript volumes, written during the fifty years between 970 and 1020. One of them, which first appears in the library of Archbishop Usher, consists of the early religious poems associated for convenience of reference with the name of Cædmon.[1] Another, which seems to have been preserved by Laurence Nowell, the sixteenth-century founder of Anglo-Saxon studies, contains the epic of Beowulf and a fragment of a poem on the apocryphal Judith.[2] The third, still preserved at Vercelli, on an ancient pilgrim route across north Italy, includes much of Cynewulf's poetry and a complete text of the *Dream of the Rood*.[3] The fourth—a book given by Bishop Leofric of Exeter to his cathedral and still kept there—is a miscellany comprising examples of all the chief varieties of native verse.[4] With very few exceptions, the poetry contained in these four volumes was already ancient when the earliest of them was written, and apart from these great collections only a few isolated pieces, some of which are mere fragments, survive from the English poetry of this early period. The preservation of so much archaic verse, which no one could have understood

[1] Edited in facsimile by I. Gollancz, *The Cædmon Manuscript*, British Academy, 1927.

[2] Ed. J. Zupitza, *Beowulf: Autotypes of the unique Cotton MS. Vitellius A XV*, Early English Text Society, 1882, ed. 2 with note by Norman Davis, 1959; ed. K. Malone, *The Nowell Codex* (Early English Manuscripts in Facsimile, xii), Copenhagen, 1963.

[3] Facsimile edition by M. Förster, *Il Codice Vercellese*, Rome, 1913.

[4] *The Exeter Book of Old English Poetry*, with Introductory Chapters by R. W. Chambers, M. Förster, and R. Flower, London 1933.

between the twelfth and sixteenth centuries, is one of the fortunate accidents of English literary history. It is clearly unsafe to argue closely from these accidental survivals to the general character and quality of early Anglo-Saxon poetry. The volumes in which the bulk of the surviving verse has been preserved only reflect the taste of a few individuals. But it can at least be said that between Cædmon and Cynewulf a succession of poets, using the traditional formulas of their art as a basis for experiment, expressed a wide range of emotion in verse which at its height belongs to the living literature of the world.

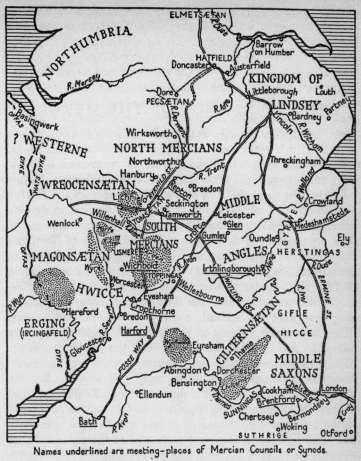

ELMETSÆTAN

NORTHUMBRIA

R. Ouse

Barrow
on Humber

HATFIELD
Doncaster○   ○Austerfield

KINGDOM OF

R. Mersey

Dore   ○Littleborough   ○Louth
PECSÆTAN

LINDSEY

R. Idle   Bardney○
Lincoln   R. Witham

? WESTERNE   Wirksworth   Threckingham

NORTH MERCIANS

Northworthy○
Hanbury   R. Trent

WREOCENSÆTAN   Repton   Breedon
Lichfield   Seckington   MIDDLE   Crowland
Willenhall   Tamworth   Leicester   Medeshamstede
Wenlock   SOUTH   Glen   Ely
MAGONSÆTAN   MERCIANS   Gumley   Oundle   HERSTINGAS
USMERE   ANGLES
Wichbold○   Irthlingborough   R. Ouse
HWICCE   STOPPINGAS   Wellesbourne   ERMINE ST.
Worcester○   GIFLE
Evesham○   HICCE
ERGING   Cropthorne   MIDDLE
(IRCINGAFELD)   Bredon   CILTERNSÆTAN
Hereford   Harford
Eynsham   SAXONS
Gloucester○   Thame   Chelsea○   London
Abingdon○   Dorchester   Cookham
Bensington○   Chiltern   Brentford   Bermondsey
Ellendun○   SUNNINGAS   Chertsey○
Bath   Woking○   Otford○
SUTHRIGE

Names underlined are meeting-places of Mercian Councils or Synods.

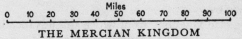

Miles
0   10   20   30   40   50   60   70   80   90   100

THE MERCIAN KINGDOM

VII

THE ASCENDANCY OF THE MERCIAN KINGS

THE fifty years which ended with the resignation of Ine in 726 interrupt the general course of English history. During the first three-quarters of the seventh century the English kingdoms south of the Humber had been tending to develop into a primitive form of confederacy under a common overlord. The supremacies of Edwin, Oswald, and Oswiu of Northumbria foreshadowed a kingdom of all England, and only an unsuccessful battle prevented Wulfhere of Mercia from bringing Northumbria under an overlordship which was already effective throughout the south.[1] For the next half-century no English king was able to establish more than a local ascendancy. There was much fighting in this period. Individual provinces passed by war from one king to another, the younger members of a dynasty occasionally rose against its head, and the entertainment of exiles was a fertile source of trouble. But the period as a whole has little significance in English political history. Northumbria was beginning to fall into isolation, and in the south an uneasy balance of power between a number of independent kingdoms gave no promise of the great advance towards the unity of England which was made before the eighth century was over.

The Mercian kingdom, from which this advance began, was not so much a state as a group of peoples held together by an illustrious dynasty.[2] Its boundaries were ill-defined towards the west, where it marched with the British kingdoms of Powys and Gwynedd, and towards the south, where the country on either side of the middle and upper Thames formed a debatable land, to which the kings of Wessex had a more ancient title. It was not until the reign of Penda that the Mercian kingdom became a great power, and its cohesion must still have been imperfect when Wulfhere, Penda's son, secured recognition as overlord from the other kings of southern England. None of the three kings who followed Wulf here reached this position. The reign of Æthelred, his brother, is more important in ecclesiastical than in political history. He was the benefactor of many churches in the various provinces of his kingdom, and in 704 he retired into the monastery of Bardney in Lindsey. Cenred, son of Wulfhere, who followed him, abdicated in the fifth year of his reign, and early in 709 left England to live in religion at Rome.[1] On his departure the kingdom passed to a son of Æthelred named Ceolred—a dissolute youth, who oppressed monasteries, and according to St. Boniface died insane.[2] He was the last descendant of Penda to rule in Mercia, and his death in 716 ends the first phase of Mercian history.

Æthelbald, his successor, was the grandson of a brother of Penda named Eowa, who had been killed at the battle of Maserfeld in 641. As a possible claimant to the Mercian kingdom, Æthelbald had been driven from his own country by Ceolred. He appears as an exile in the *Life* of his kinsman Guthlac of Crowland, who often sheltered him and his companions.[3] At the outset of his reign he was confronted in southern England by two strong kings of an older generation— Wihtred of Kent and Ine of Wessex. After twenty-five years of independent rule it is unlikely that either of them allowed him precedence. But the death of Wihtred in 725 and the abdication of Ine in 726 left him without a serious rival among the other southern kings, and within five years he had brought all of them to accept him as their lord. Bede, writing in 731, states that all the English 'provinces' south of the Humber were subject to Æthelbald, and in many of his later charters he uses titles which emphasize this supremacy. The most remarkable of these styles occurs in a charter of 736[4] which calls him *rex Britanniae*—a phrase which can only be interpreted as a Latin rendering of the English title *Bretwalda*. At the height of his power Æthelbald was the head of a confederation which included Kent, Wessex, and every other kingdom between the Humber and the Channel.

Between 726 and 802 Wessex passed to five successive kings,

[1] In Cenred's reign there occurred large-scale raids over Mercia by the Welsh, which may have led to the building of Wat's Dyke. See pp. 212–13, below.

[2] *S. Bonifatii et Lulli Epistolae*, ed. Tangl. No. 73.

[3] *Felix's Life of Saint Guthlac*, ed. B. Colgrave, pp. 138, 148.

[4] *C.S.* 154, which is fortunately preserved in a contemporary text.

whose connection with the line of Cerdic is uncertain. For most
of this period Wessex was little more than a large, outlying
province of the Mercian kingdom. Much territory which had
once been West Saxon was annexed to Mercia. In 733 Æthelheard, Ine's successor, lost Somerton to Æthelbald, who
thereupon became the direct ruler of a considerable part of
Wessex beyond Selwood.[1] None of these obscure kings was ever
secure in the possession of the border provinces along the
Thames. Æthelbald's authority in Berkshire was such that he
could give the monastery of Cookham to the archbishop of
Canterbury. The monks of Abingdon regarded him as their
protector.[2] In 752 Cuthred, king of Wessex, revolted against
Æthelbald,[3] and apparently maintained his independence until
his death in 756. But Sigeberht, the next king, was deposed by
his own subjects within a year, and the first recorded act of
Cynewulf, his successor, was to appear at the court of Æthelbald and attest a charter by which he granted land in Wiltshire
to a West-Saxon abbot.[4] It seems clear that Wessex was once
more a Mercian dependency when Æthelbald himself died
a few months later.

Little is known of the relations between Æthelbald and his
other subject kings. There is just sufficient evidence to suggest
that London and Middlesex were finally detached from the
East Saxon kingdom in his time. His predecessors had made
their overlordship felt in this country. Æthelred, Cenred, and
Ceolred had each confirmed the charter by which Waldhere,
bishop of London, obtained Twickenham from Swæfred, king
of Essex.[5] After Æthelbald's reign there seems to be no indication of East Saxon authority in London or in any part of Middlesex. Both he and Offa, his successor, regarded London as their
own town, and dealt as they wished with land in the sur-

[1] A charter recording a sale of land in Somerset by Æthelbald to Glastonbury
abbey was still preserved there in the twelfth century, but is now lost. J. Armitage
Robinson, *Somerset Historical Essays*, pp. 36–7.

[2] F. M. Stenton, *The Early History of the Abbey of Abingdon*, pp. 22–3.

[3] Æthelbald was defeated by Cuthred at a place called *Beorhford*, which has not
yet been identified. Its identification with Burford in Oxfordshire is disproved by
the form *Bureford* under which the latter place consistently appears in early records.

[4] *C.S.* 181. The names of the witnesses show that a number of Cynewulf's
leading subjects attended him on this visit.

[5] *C.S.* 111. Cenred, king of Mercia, and Sigeheard, king of Essex, jointly confirmed the purchase of Fulham by Waldhere, bishop of London, from Tyrhtel,
bishop of Hereford. *Early Charters of the Cathedral Church of St. Paul, London*, ed.
Marion Gibbs (Camden Society, vol. lviii), pp. 3–4.

rounding country. The oldest of Offa's original charters shows
him granting land near Harrow without even asking the king of
Essex to witness his gift.[1]

For nearly thirty years Æthelbald was the dominant figure
in southern England. No other king had ever maintained so
general an ascendancy for so long. Nevertheless, in character
he was the barbarian master of a military household, and the
scandal of his private life embarrassed the leaders of the English
mission in Germany. In 746 or 747 Boniface, at the head of a
group of bishops mostly of English birth, wrote a solemn letter
to Æthelbald, acknowledging his generosity in almsgiving and
the good peace which he enforced, but reproaching him for
his violation of ecclesiastical privilege, his misbehaviour with
women vowed to religion, and the deplorable effect of his
example on a people whose own sins invited a heavy judgement.[2]
One of these charges seems to have been admitted by the king
himself. In the letter Boniface asserted that the privileges of
churches, which Æthelbald had infringed, had been observed
by every English king from the time of Augustine until the evil
reigns of Osred of Northumbria and Ceolred of Mercia. It is
probably more than a coincidence that in 749 Æthelbald issued
a charter to the churches of his kingdom, in which he freed them
from all public burdens except the fundamental duties of
repairing bridges and maintaining fortresses.[3]

In 757, after a reign of forty-one years, Æthelbald was murdered by night by his body-guard at Seckington near Tamworth.
The motive for the crime is unknown, but it may be significant
that a contemporary writer describes him as a royal tyrant,[4] and
that a Mercian abbess received lands from him 'because he had
stabbed—or smitten—her kinsman'—words which would hardly
have been used to describe an ordinary killing in war.[5] A king
of this type could easily become involved in feuds which over-
rode the loyalty of the retainer to his chief. Whatever its explanation, the murder was followed by a civil war in Mercia

[1] *C.S.* 201.

[2] *S. Bonifatii et Lulli Epistolae*, ed. Tangl, No. 73.

[3] *C.S.* 178. The council in which the charter was made was held at Gumley in
the south of what is now Leicestershire. F. M. Stenton, *E.H.R. C.P.*, pp. 1–2.
On the privileges claimed by churches, see W. H. Stevenson, *E.H.R.* xxix (1914),
pp. 699–702. The most important of them was exemption from taxation.

[4] *S. Bonifatii et Lulli Epistolae*, No. 115.

[5] *Pro eo quod percussit . . . cognatum eius*, *C.S.* 535—a long memorandum recording
early gifts to the abbey of Gloucester.

between a certain Beornred, whose connection with the Mercian royal house is obscure, and Offa, son of Thingfrith, who was descended, like Æthelbald, from Penda's brother Eowa. Before the end of 757 Offa had driven Beornred into exile; but the confederacy which Æthelbald had founded fell to pieces on his death, and for the first seven years of his reign Offa seems to have possessed little, if any, power outside Mercia and its dependencies in the southern midlands.[1]

The re-establishment of Mercian supremacy by Offa is the central fact in English history in the second half of the eighth century. But the stages by which it was brought about cannot now be reconstructed. No Mercian chronicle has survived from this period, and charters alone give any definite impression of Offa's place among English kings. They suggest that Kent was the first long-established kingdom to fall under his influence. At the middle of the century Æthelberht and Eadberht, sons of Wihtred, and Eardulf, Eadberht's son, were all reigning together in Kent. Æthelberht died in 762,[2] Eadberht is mentioned for the last time in a charter of that year,[3] and there is no evidence that Eardulf survived him.[4] So far as is known, the dynasty founded by Oisc the son of Hengest ended in these three kings. Even before their disappearance, kings who have no discernible connection with the ancient line had begun to appear in Kent. In 762 a certain Sigered, who calls himself *rex Cantiae*, granted land in Rochester to the local bishop with King Eadberht's consent.[5] A little later Sigered, under the more modest title *rex dimidiae partis provinciae Cantuariorum*, granted an estate at Frindsbury to the same bishop with the consent of a still obscurer king named Eanmund.[6] In 764 Offa appeared at Canterbury in the company of the archbishop and a third ephemeral Kentish king named Heahberht, and made a re-grant of this estate.[7] Heahberht survived as king for

---

[1] During this period Bregowine, archbishop of Canterbury, writes that he has been prevented from sending a letter to Lull by disturbances in Britain and Gaul, but that now peace and protection have been promised by the princes (*S. Bonifatii et Lulli Epistolae*, ed. Tangl, No. 117).

[2] *Chronicle* under 760.   [3] *C.S.* 193.

[4] The correspondence of St. Boniface and Bishop Lull includes a letter from King Eardulf and the bishop of Rochester which must be later than the summer of 754 (*S. Bonifatii et Lulli Epistolae*, ed. Tangl, No. 122), but it cannot be more precisely dated, and none of the charters which mention Eardulf as king can be safely referred to a period after 762.

[5] *C.S.* 193.   [6] *C.S.* 194.   [7] *C.S.* 195.

at least a year, for in 765 he confirmed a charter by which a fourth Kentish king, named Egbert, gave land within the walls of Rochester to the bishop.[1] The text of the charter makes no reference to Offa, but it was submitted to him for confirmation, and at Medeshamstede in his own country he completed it with a postscript giving the bishop power to alienate the land. It is clear that by this time Offa's overlordship must have been generally recognized in Kent, and although Egbert retained the title of king until 779 or later,[2] it is known that Offa treated him as a mere dependant. The most uncompromising assertion of an overlord's authority that has come down from the whole Anglo-Saxon period is Offa's revocation of a grant by Egbert on the ground that 'it was not right for a man to grant away land which his lord had given him, without his lord's assent'.[3] Under these conditions it was natural that Offa should deal at his own pleasure with land in Kent, and two charters of the year 774 have survived, in each of which he grants land to the archbishop of Canterbury without reference to any local ruler.[4]

It is by no means impossible that a reaction against Mercian supremacy occurred in Kent at about this time. In 776, according to the *Chronicle*, the Mercians and Kentishmen fought at Otford.[5] The result of the battle is not recorded, and most historians consider it to have been a Mercian victory. But it is probably significant that Offa cannot be shown to have possessed any authority in Kent during the next ten years, and that at the end of this period he was on the worst of terms with the Kentish people. The enmity that he felt towards them was one of the principal motives which led him to attack the influence of the archbishop of Canterbury by negotiating with the pope for the creation of an independent province of Lichfield.[6] The possibility that the battle of Otford was a disaster for Offa is strengthened by a charter of 784 in which a king named Ealhmund, without any reference to Offa, grants land in Kent to the abbot of Reculver. It is probable that this king was identical with Ealhmund, son of Eafa, of the royal house of Wessex, whose son Egbert succeeded to that kingdom in 802 after a long exile imposed on him by Offa.[7] But in 785 the

---

[1] *C.S.* 196.   [2] *C.S.* 228.   [3] Above, p. 36.   [4] *C.S.* 213, 214.
[5] *Chronicle* under 773 in two manuscripts, 774 in four.   [6] Below, p. 216.
[7] *C.S.* 243. The charter is only known from a thirteenth-century abstract. It represents the king's name in the form *Ealmundus*, which cannot be contemporary. But it contains some ancient features.

series of Offa's Kentish charters begins again,[1] and for the rest of his reign there is no doubt that he was in a position to treat Kent as an ordinary province of the Mercian kingdom.

His success in Kent had been mainly due to the disintegration of the Kentish kingdom which followed the extinction of its dynasty. Sussex, which also became a Mercian province in his reign, had never formed a single kingdom in historic times. It has already been noticed that the country round Hastings, which resembled Kent in dialect and social organization, was still regarded as distinct from the rest of Sussex at the beginning of the eleventh century.[2] The oldest South Saxon charters show that Sussex was divided among a number of kings, and between 757 and 770 Offa confirmed grants of land made by two individuals each of whom bore the royal title in that country.[3] Each of them, however, seems to have belonged to its central and western districts, and there is no evidence that Offa had any power in Sussex east of Pevensey until 771, when, according to a Northumbrian chronicler, he subdued the men of Hastings in war.[4] For the rest of his reign he was the lord of the whole region between Hampshire and Kent. A charter of 772 shows him granting land at Bexhill to the bishop of Selsey in a court attended by Egbert, king of Kent, Cynewulf, king of Wessex, and four South Saxon magnates, to each of whom is accorded the title *dux*.[5] One at least of these *duces* had formerly described himself as a king,[6] and his new style is a good illustration of

---

[1] *C.S.* 247.

[2] In 1011 the *Chronicle* explicitly distinguishes *Suthseaxe* from *Hæstingas*.

[3] *C.S.* 197 records a grant of land near Stanmer made by a king named Aldulf to one of his *comites*. It is attested by a king named Ælhwald, of whom nothing more is known. The attestations of Offa, Cynethryth his wife, and Ecgfrith their son, occur at the end of the witness-list, and are clearly supplementary to it. *C.S.* 206 is a charter of 770 recording a grant of land near Henfield by a king named Osmund to an unidentified church of St. Peter. In this charter Offa's confirmatory subscription occurs early in the witness-list. It is followed by a number of names which appear in Mercian charters of the time.

[4] 'Hestingorum gentem armis subegerat.' *Symeonis Monachi Opera*, ed. Arnold, R.S., ii, p. 44.

[5] *C.S.* 208. This charter is only known from a thirteenth-century copy, and its text has been partly rewritten. But the portion of the witness-list where these names occur includes other names appropriate to the period, which no forger would have been likely to know, and it does not read like a fabrication.

[6] The Osmund *dux* of this charter is certainly identical with the Osmund who in 770 had made the grant recorded in *C.S.* 206 under the title *rex*. (Above, n. 3.) By a similar change of style, the Aldulf *rex* of *C.S.* 197 (ibid.) appears in two later charters (*C.S.* 261, 262) as *dux*.

the process which in the eighth century transformed many local rulers, once capable of choosing a lord for themselves, into the ministers of a sovereign whose authority was felt to be permanent. In itself, this change of style did not mean any real loss of local power. But it certainly implies a movement of thought away from the primitive idea that the mere fact of royal descent gave a man a title to be regarded as a king.

In Kent and Sussex Offa was able to substitute his own authority for that of earlier local rulers. In Wessex, which had been a united kingdom for seventy years before his accession, the local kingship was preserved by the strength of the traditions which had gathered around it. Apart from his isolated appearance at Offa's court in 772[1] there is no evidence that Cynewulf, king of Wessex, ever became Offa's man. There is no doubt that Cynewulf recovered most of the West Saxon provinces which Æthelbald had conquered. He was recognized as king in Berkshire and north Wiltshire as well as in Hampshire and Wessex beyond Selwood. For a time he was master of a stretch of country north of the Thames, but in 779 Offa defeated him at Bensington[2] and reoccupied the debatable land on either side of the river. In 786, after a reign of unusual length, Cynewulf was suddenly attacked by Cyneheard, brother of the Sigeberht who had ruled in Wessex thirty years before. Both Cynewulf and Cyneheard were killed in the course of a struggle which the loyalty of their retainers made famous,[3] and Offa was able at last to bring the West Saxon kingdom under his influence. Cynewulf was succeeded by a certain Beorhtric, whose ancestry, like that of his four predecessors, is unknown. He was opposed by Egbert son of Ealhmund, a descendant of Ingild, Ine's brother, and an undoubted representative of the line of Cerdic. Offa intervened in the struggle on Beorhtric's side, married a daughter to him in 789, and helped him to drive Egbert out of the country—a fact which strongly supports the identification of Ealhmund, Egbert's father, with the man of

---

[1] *C.S.* 208.   [2] *Chronicle* under 777.

[3] The story of the deaths of Cynewulf and Cyneheard gave rise to what seems to be the earliest known piece of English narrative prose. It is inserted out of place in the *Chronicle* under the year 755, and in its written form it can hardly be regarded as earlier than the ninth century. But its character suggests that it took oral shape very soon after the event, and it is good evidence that stories such as formed the staple of heroic verse were circulating in prose already in the pre-Alfredian age. See C. E. Wright, *The Cultivation of Saga in Anglo-Saxon England*, pp. 26–7.

that name who had ruled in Kent, independently of Offa, in the period following the battle of Otford. Egbert found a refuge in the Frankish kingdom, and until 802 Beorhtric ruled in Wessex as a protected dependant, at first of Offa, and then of his successor Cenwulf.

The history of the smaller southern kingdoms is very obscure throughout this period. The East Saxon dynasty survived into the ninth century, but nothing is known of its position in Offa's time beyond the fact that Offa treated its Middle Saxon province as part of his own kingdom.[1] In East Anglia the local dynasty appears to have ended in 749 with the death of King Ælfwald[2]—a man of culture, who had corresponded with Boniface[3] and ordered the compilation of the earliest life of St. Guthlac.[4] The one East Anglian king of the next hundred years who was remembered outside his own country is a certain Æthelberht, whom Offa caused to be beheaded in 794. Like other Anglo-Saxon kings who died unjustly by violence, Æthelberht came to be regarded as a martyr. The centre of his cult was Hereford, where his relics were preserved, and in the eleventh century it was believed that he had been put to death at Sutton Walls near the city.[5] It is natural to assume that Offa killed him because he stood in some way for the independence of his kingdom. But nothing is really known of the circumstances of his death.

The charters which tell most of what is known about Offa's relations with lesser kings have only been preserved by chance. Very few of the documents written in Offa's time have come down, in any form, to the present day, and it is no more than a fortunate accident that some of them show Offa confirming an under-king's gifts, or an under-king in attendance at Offa's court. A late copy of a South Saxon charter, which shows Ealdfrith, king of Lindsey, in Offa's company, is the only

[1] Above, p. 204.

[2] Symeon of Durham, *Historia Regum, sub anno.* He is the latest East Anglian mentioned in the ninth-century genealogies printed by Sweet, *The Oldest English Texts,* pp. 169–71.

[3] *S. Bonifatii et Lulli Epistolae,* ed. Tangl, No. 81.

[4] *Felix's Life of Saint Guthlac,* ed. B. Colgrave, p. 10. It has often been stated that the life was written at the command of Æthelbald, king of Mercia. But the dedication *Aelfuualdo regi Orientalium Anglorum,* which is preserved in an early ninth-century manuscript, proves that Ælfwald was the instigator of the work.

[5] 'Two Lives of St. Ethelbert, King and Martyr', ed. M. R. James, *E.H.R.* xxxii (1917), p. 239.

evidence that the ancient dynasty of the kings of Lindsey survived into the late eighth century.[1] Despite the rarity of these
documents they give a definite impression that Offa was the
effective overlord of the greater part of southern England,[2] and
they prove that his court had become something more elaborate
than a mere concourse of retainers grouped around a king whose
power rested on war. One of the most instructive documents
of the reign is a grant of land by Oslac, *dux* of the South Saxons,
to which Offa, at Irthlingborough on the Nene, added a confirmatory endorsement.[3] The contrast between the crude provincial script of the text and the practised, almost official,
hand of the endorsement represents a real distinction between
the primitive government of the local kingdoms and the beginnings of administrative routine in a court which had become
the political centre of England south of the Humber.

A king who was at the head of such a court could not be
content with a title which merely claimed authority over a
single people. Æthelbald, Offa's predecessor, had expressed
his supremacy in southern England by styling himself 'rex non
solum Marcersium sed et omnium provinciarum quæ generale
nomine Sutangli dicuntur'.[4] In his earliest charters,[5] and from
time to time in the latter part of his reign,[6] Offa called himself
simply *rex Merciorum*. Occasionally, in his central years, he
used a shortened form of Æthelbald's style, describing himself
as 'rex Merciorum simulque aliarum circumquaque nationum'.[7]
But in two documents of the year 774 he adopted styles which
at their face value claimed nothing less than lordship over the
whole English people. In one of these documents he styles
himself *rex Anglorum*[8] and in the other, *rex totius Anglorum patriae*.[9]
The second of these phrases, which seems to represent an
Old English *ealles Englalandes cyning*, carries the conception of a
kingdom of all England back to the eighth century. But the

---

[1] F. M. Stenton, 'Lindsey and its Kings', *C.P.*, pp. 127 ff.

[2] The collection of royal genealogies of Northumbria, Mercia, Lindsey, Kent
and East Anglia in British Museum Cotton MS. Vespasian B. vi, based on a version
compiled in the last years of the eighth century, illustrates the sphere of his overlordship. See K. Sisam, *Proceedings of the British Academy*, xxxix, pp. 290, 309, 324,
329.

[3] *C.S.* 1334. Printed in facsimile as a separate publication by W. de G. Birch,
The Anglo-Saxon Charter of Oslac, Duke of the South-Saxons (London, 1892).

[4] *C.S.* 154.   [5] e.g. *C.S.* 201.

[6] e.g. *C.S.* 257.

[7] e.g. *C.S.* 234.   [8] *C.S.* 213.   [9] *C.S.* 214.

old idea that a king was ruler of a people rather than a country prevailed, and in his later years Offa generally used the style *rex Anglorum* when he wished to indicate his supremacy among English kings.

It would be easy to lay too much emphasis on the experimental titles of an eighth-century king. But the variety of the styles applied to Offa shows that the clerks who wrote his charters were at least trying to express realities, and a modern writer is not entitled to dismiss the style *rex Anglorum* as mere verbiage. There is no direct evidence that Offa had any authority beyond the Humber in 774, when he appears as *rex totius Anglorum patriae*. But his assumption of this style may well be connected with the revolution which in this year made Æthelred, son of Æthelwald Moll, king of Northumbria. The history of Æthelred's reign shows that he had many enemies, and after five years he was driven from his kingdom by a successful revolt.[1] It cannot be proved, but it is by no means impossible that on becoming king he had tried to strengthen his position by joining the confederation of which Offa was the head.

The consolidation of Offa's power in southern England, which gave him influence, if nothing more, in Northumbria, enabled him to define the boundary of his own country against its British neighbours by the greatest public work of the whole Anglo-Saxon period. After nearly twelve centuries the remains of the earthwork known as Offa's Dyke give an impressive suggestion of the power of command which belonged to the greater Anglo-Saxon kings.[2] But the scale of the dyke, which gives it an important place among earthworks of its class, is less remarkable than the skill with which its line was drawn. Over more than seventy miles of broken and sometimes mountainous country its visible remains rarely fail to command the land towards the west, against whose inhabitants it marked the English frontier. Its attribution to Offa rests on the tradition of each of the races which it separated. The Welsh tradition is preserved

[1] Above, p. 93.
[2] The definitive authority on the course and construction of Offa's Dyke is a series of reports upon a minute investigation of this earthwork conducted by Sir Cyril Fox. These reports, appearing each year in *Archaeologia Cambrensis* between 1926 and 1931 inclusive, have been brought together, along with the results of a similar investigation carried out by Sir Cyril Fox on Wat's Dyke, published in *Archaeologia Cambrensis* for 1930 in *Offa's Dyke*, by Sir Cyril Fox, with a foreword by Sir Frank Stenton, London, 1955 (reprinted *C.P.*, pp. 357–63).

in the name Clawdd Offa by which it is still known, and in the statement of Asser, King Alfred's biographer, that Offa ordered a great *vallum* to be made from sea to sea between Wales and Mercia. There is no literary evidence like this from the English side of the frontier; but the local name Offedik, by which the dyke was known in the thirteenth century, stands for an Old English *Offan dic*, which is strictly parallel to the Welsh *Clawdd Offa*. Few, if any, earthworks on the scale of Offa's Dyke are associated so definitely with a particular person.

The northern sections of the dyke have almost disappeared, and it first appears as a continuous line of earthwork near Tryddyn, on the hills between the Alyn and the Clwyd. Its line can be traced along the eastern slopes of these hills past Wrexham to the Dee near Newbridge. After crossing the park of Chirk castle it passes over the lower ranges of the Berwyn mountains, and strikes the Severn six miles below Welshpool. It leaves the Severn at Buttington, passes between the river and the Long Mountain, and from a point some three miles north of Montgomery takes an almost straight course for the heights of Clun forest. For most of the next twenty miles it runs above the thousand-foot contour-line, descending to cross the valleys of the Clun, Teme, and Lugg, but rising after each descent to command again the still wilder country to the west. This great stretch of continuous earthwork ends on the edge of the Herefordshire plain. The country north of the middle Wye was heavily wooded in the eighth century, and in this region Offa attempted nothing more than the construction of short lengths of ditch and bank across open valleys, or lines of local communication. The last of these intermittent earthworks ends above the Wye near Bridge Sollers. Thenceforward, to a point four miles below Monmouth, the Wye itself formed the boundary between Offa's subjects and the independent Britons of the district known as Erging in Welsh and Ircingafeld in Old English. But on the cliffs east of the lower Wye the dyke can be traced in a broken line as far as the widening of the valley above Chepstow, and below that town a short stretch of ditch and bank, showing all the characteristics of Offa's work, strikes away from the river to end on the margin of the Bristol Channel.

There is no direct evidence of the date at which this undertaking was carried out, but it can confidently be assigned to the second half of Offa's reign. It is probable that Wat's Dyke, which runs from Basingwerk on the estuary of the Dee to the Morda Brook south of Oswestry, had been built by King Æthelbald to protect a dangerous part of the Mercian frontier from serious raids such as those which occurred between 705 and 709.[1] These raids may have been part of a more general Welsh revival in the first half of the eighth century,[2] which perhaps influenced Offa in his decision to delineate the frontier. Whoever may have planned the course of the main dyke—and there is no reason for denying the principal share in the work to Offa himself—its execution must have required the constant presence of the king. The course chosen for the frontier north of the Wye seems to have meant the abandonment of English territory to the Britons. Villages bearing names which are very unlikely to have arisen after the eighth century occur in this quarter far to the west of the dyke. The name Burlingjobb, borne by a hamlet within the Radnorshire border, is as ancient in type as any place-name in the western midlands.[3] No subordinate officer could have enforced compliance with the surrender of territory which must have affected the interests of powerful men. It was only in the last years of his reign that Offa's ascendancy was completely established in southern England, and it is very doubtful whether he could have concentrated attention on the delimitation of his western frontier before, at the earliest, 784 or 785. The little that is known of his relations with the British peoples points in the same direction. The decision with which the line of the dyke was drawn, and the general efficiency with which it was carried out, show that it was constructed during a prolonged peace between Offa and the British princes. The Welsh annals record a battle at Hereford between Englishmen and Britons in 760, a harrying of Dyfed by Offa in 778, and an expedition into an unnamed part of Wales in 784. During the long interval of peace between 760 and 778 Offa must have been preoccupied with the establishment of supremacy over the other kings of southern England. After 784 his position was secure, and he remained at peace

---

[1] *Felix's Life of Saint Guthlac*, ed. B. Colgrave, p. 109. See p. 212, n. 2 above, and F. M. Stenton, *C.P.*, pp. 357–63.

[2] The *Annales Cambriæ* s.a. 722 record Welsh victories, and 'Eliseg's Pillar' attributed a recovery of territory from the English to Elise, king of Powys, whose grandson died in 808. See F. M. Stenton, *C.P.*, p. 362, n. 1.

[3] It appears in Domesday Book in the form *Berchelincope*. A name of this type is very unlikely to have arisen as late as the ninth century.

with the Britons until 796, the last year of his life, when he invaded Dyfed again. The making of the dyke probably fell in the latter part of this twelve years' peace.

So far as can be seen the continental relations which give Offa a special place in history also belong to these last twelve years. There were many elements of weakness in the political system which Offa had created, but it was strong enough to carry him into the full stream of European affairs. Between 784 and 796 Offa was the only ruler in western Europe who could attempt to deal on equal terms with Charlemagne. The materials for English diplomatic history begin with the letters which passed between the two kings. Even at Rome Offa seemed a real, though inscrutable, force in the international world. In a deferential letter to Charlemagne, Pope Hadrian I at great length disclaimed belief in a rumour that his deposition and the election of a Frankish pope had been proposed to Charlemagne by Offa.[1] Nothing is known of the origin of this story, but the language in which the pope expressed his confidence in Offa's devotion does not conceal his past anxiety.

This letter is undated, but it seems to have been written in 784 or 785. In 786 Pope Hadrian sent George, bishop of Ostia, and Theophylact, bishop of Todi, as legates to England.[2] The bishop of Ostia was an old man, of long experience in papal business,[3] and his selection for the mission shows the importance which the pope attached to it. In the previous generation the leaders of the English church had looked to Boniface rather than the pope for guidance in the work of maintaining ecclesiastical order. No papal legate had visited England since the mission of Augustine, and the recent rumours about Offa's hostility must have shown the danger of allowing England to pass beyond the range of the pope's direct influence. On his part, Offa had every reason to welcome a reassertion of papal authority over the English church. The most serious weakness in his position was the fact that the archbishop who was the spiritual head of all the Southern English had his seat in the kingdom where resistance to the Mercian supremacy was

[1] *Councils*, iii. 440–2.

[2] They issued a report on their mission, of which the best text, from a Wolfenbüttel manuscript unknown to previous editors, is printed in M.G.H. *Epistolae Karol. aevi*, ii, ed. E. Dümmler, No. 3.

[3] His prominence in negotiations between the Frankish court and the Papacy had caused him to be provided with the see of Amiens (Levison, op. cit., pp. 127–8).

strongest.[1] There can be no doubt that, from the first, Offa regarded the legatine commission as preliminary to the estab-lishment of an independent archbishopric in his own country.

But to the legates themselves, and probably to most English-men, the religious purpose of the mission was more important than its political consequences. A Northumbrian annalist states that the bishops came to renew the ancient friendship between England and the Roman see, and the catholic faith which St. Gregory had taught through St. Augustine.[2] Other evidence shows that the essential duty of the legates was to propose a body of canons for acceptance by the English kings, nobles, and clergy. Before the mission returned to Rome the Bishop of Ostia described the order of its proceedings to the pope in a letter of singular interest. The bishops were first entertained by Archbishop Jaenberht at Canterbury, and after-wards proceeded to the hall of Offa, to whom they showed the pope's letters of commendation. A council was then held at which Offa and Cynewulf, king of Wessex, were present. The bishops laid before it a schedule of the matters which in the pope's opinion needed amendment, and then separated for a more thorough inquiry into the ecclesiastical condition of the country, the bishop of Todi taking Mercia and Wales as his province and the bishop of Ostia passing on to Northumbria. After some delay caused by the king's absence in the north a Northumbrian council was held at which the bishop presented the pope's schedule of matters to be corrected, and a series of canons based on his own recent investigation. Of the twenty canons which he brought forward ten refer to questions of faith and ecclesiastical order—the holding of synods and visita-tions, the behaviour of clergy, and the observance of privileges granted to churches by the Roman see. The remaining ten canons were addressed to the laity. Kings and princes are admonished to obey their bishops, to do justice to the poor, to suppress violence, and to exact nothing more from churches than is allowed by Roman law and the practice of ancient emperors. Illegitimate children are to be excluded from the father's inheritance, and in particular from the succession to

---

[1] Archbishop Jaenberht had previously been abbot of St. Augustine's. He was a supporter of Egbert II, king of Kent, whose allegiance to Offa was uncertain, and the kinsman of Egbert's reeve in Canterbury (*C.S.* 319, 332).

[2] *Symeonis Monachi Opera*, ii. 51. The passage reads like contemporary writing.

the kingdom. Tithes are to be paid and vows performed, irregular marriages and heathen practices are forbidden, and penitential discipline is enjoined on all men. Some of these canons represent the common form of ecclesiastical legislation, but others are original, and the series as a whole was plainly drafted after a careful review of Northumbrian conditions. It was adopted by the Northumbrian council, and then presented to a similar assembly convened in Mercia by Offa, at which its provisions were read out in Latin and English and accepted by the whole company. The bishop of Ostia's report ends at this point.[1] It was not concerned with the political aspect of the mission. Its object was to record decisions taken by English councils in the presence of the legates, and it naturally ignores the informal discussions about the establishment of a Mercian archbishopric in which the legates may be assumed to have taken part. Its historical interest lies in the clearness with which it reveals the deference of English kings, nobles, and clergy towards the representatives of the pope.

The division of the province of Canterbury, which was in the background of the mission, could be defended on the score of expediency. Few, if any, archbishops in Gaul presided, like the archbishop of Canterbury, over twelve suffragans. Offa is known to have represented to Pope Hadrian that the change was made desirable by the extent of his dominions.[2] In reality,

---

[1] It is probable that towards the end of their mission the legates held a general council of the English church. In a letter to Cenwulf of Mercia, written in 797 or 798, Pope Leo III refers to an assembly of this character, at which the legates were present, and Offa promised to send 365 mancuses each year to Rome for the relief of the poor and the maintenance of lights (*C.S.* 288). The text of the letter is bad, but it seems to represent the gift as a thank-offering made by Offa to St. Peter in gratitude for the victories granted to his kingdom. The letter suggests that Offa intended his successors to continue the payment, and it has often been regarded as the origin of the tax afterwards known as Peter's Pence. But an over-lordship such as Offa possessed did not carry the power of imposing a new form of direct taxation on subject kingdoms, and the pope emphasizes the personal character of Offa's gift. It should rather be compared with the gift of 300 mancuses which Æthelwulf of Wessex, by his testament, ordered his successors to send each year to Rome (Asser, *Vita Alfredi*, c. 16). Nothing is known of the circumstances under which Peter's Pence was first imposed. But payments which seem to be identical with the later tax were dispatched to Rome from Wessex at least as early as 887 (*Chronicle, sub anno*) and its extension to other parts of the country may well be due to the authority and influence of Alfred, the first king whom all free English-men voluntarily accepted as their lord.

[2] In a letter to Cenwulf, king of Mercia, who has asked him why Pope Hadrian had consented to the division, Pope Leo III replied 'Rex vester praecellentissimus Offa suis litteris testatus est ut in id omnium vestrum una voluntas et unanima

as Cenwulf, king of Mercia, afterwards admitted to Pope Leo III, Offa desired it because of the hatred which he bore to Archbishop Jaenberht and the men of Kent.[1] In 787 the question was discussed in a council held at Chelsea. It was stormy,[2] but Offa secured its formal assent to the division. Before the end of 788 Hygeberht, bishop of Lichfield, had received an archbishop's pallium from Rome.[3] There is no evidence that Archbishop Jaenberht made any formal appeal to the pope against the division of his province. At general councils of the southern English clergy he was allowed the precedence over Hygeberht to which his seniority by consecration entitled him. In 796, when Offa died, the archbishopric of Lichfield must have seemed an established part of English ecclesiastical organization.[4]

Offa's attempt to secure the ecclesiastical independence of Mercia was followed by a measure intended to provide that the Mercian kingdom should remain in his own branch of the royal house. In 787 Ecgfrith, his only son, was anointed king of the Mercians.[5] The ceremony, remarkable in any case as the formal association of a son in his father's kingship, has a wider interest as the first recorded consecration of an English king. It is

esset petitio, vel propter vastitatem terrarum vestrarum et extensionem regni vestri, necnon et aliis quamplurimis causis et utilitatibus.' *C.S.* 288.

[1] 'Cuius . . . dignitatis honorem primum rex Offa, propter inimicitiam cum venerabili Ianberto et gente Cantuariorum acceptam, avertere et in duas parrochias dissipare nisus.' *C.S.* 287.

[2] *Chronicle* under 785, 'Her wæs geflitfullic senoþ æt Cealchyþe'.

[3] His first attestation as archbishop occurs in *C.S.* 253, a charter of Offa in favour of Rochester cathedral, preserved in the trustworthy *Textus Roffensis*.

[4] The chronology of these events has given rise to considerable discussion. Some scholars have identified the southern legatine council with the 'contentious' synod of 787, and the northern council with a synod held, according to Northumbrian authorities in the latter year at a place called Pincahala. Neither identification is in any way probable. The Northumbrian authorities, which have a contemporary basis, date the synod of Pincahala 2 September 787, and offer no suggestion that it was connected with the legatine mission, which they rightly place under 786. The *Chronicle*, which is the earliest authority for the 'contentious' synod, is two years behindhand in its dates for this period, and the year 785 in which it places the synod can safely be corrected to 787. It is possible, though unlikely, that the legates, who are not mentioned in the original version of the *Chronicle*, may have remained in England until the early part of 787, and that the contentious synod may represent their southern session. But the terms in which Pope Leo III refers to the division of the province of Canterbury (above, p. 216, n. 1) makes this identification highly improbable. His statement that Pope Hadrian had agreed to the division because Offa had said that there was unanimity for it in his kingdom would be a strange distortion of easily ascertainable facts if two legates had been present at the stormy synod where it was actually carried. [5] *Chronicle* under 785.

always hard to prove a negative, but the silence of earlier writers makes it probable that the hallowing of Ecgfrith was the first occasion on which a religious element was introduced into the inauguration of an English ruler.[1] It is also probable that the change was made in direct imitation of Frankish precedents. Offa cannot have been unaware that in 781 Pippin and Louis, sons of Charlemagne, had each been anointed into kingship by Pope Hadrian I.

These events were closely followed at the Frankish court. A Frankish abbot accompanied the legatine mission of 786, and there can be no doubt that Charlemagne was well acquainted with the whole history of its proceedings. His religious policy meant that he could not be indifferent to the opinion of the English church, and he knew enough about the personality of its leaders to be interested in matters affecting its condition. Long before the creation of a Holy Roman Empire had become possible Charlemagne regarded himself as the defender of the faith in western Europe. In this capacity he was at pains to secure the adhesion of the English church to the repudiation of the canons by which the Nicene council of 787 defined the veneration due to sacred pictures and images. English clergy attended the council of Frankfort which condemned these canons and the heresies of the Spanish bishops Felix and Elipandus. Moreover, in the Northumbrian Alcuin, who had been attached to his court since 782, Charlemagne possessed a confidant who understood the complexities of English politics as well as the tendencies of English religious thought. Beornred, archbishop of Sens from 792 to 797, was Alcuin's cousin. Among Frankish ecclesiastics Gervold, abbot of St. Wandrille, was intimate with Offa. Charlemagne was singularly well placed for information about English movements in church and state.

Towards Offa himself Charlemagne always showed formal courtesy. He paid meticulous respect to Offa's rank, and he wished to be regarded as Offa's friend.[2] One of the earliest of English diplomatic records is a letter in which Charlemagne

---

[1] P. E. Schramm, *A History of the English Coronation*, p. 15. The vagueness of the terminology in which the inauguration of a king is described makes it difficult to find any unequivocal early reference to coronation in the literal sense of the word. It would, for example, be unsafe to lay much stress on the statement in the Northumbrian annals preserved by Symeon of Durham, *Opera*, ii (*R.S.*), p. 45 that King Æthelred 'regnum suscepit, qui tanto honore coronatus vix quinque annos tenuit'.

[2] A few months before Offa's death Alcuin wrote to him, 'Sciat veneranda

tells the archbishop of Canterbury and the bishop of Lindsey that in entertaining certain exiles from Offa's country his only object is to reconcile them with their lord.[1] But the relations between the kings were never easy. It cannot have been without Charlemagne's approval that Egbert, the rival of Offa's protégé Beorhtric of Wessex, lived in Frankish territory after Beorhtric and Offa had driven him from England.[2] His exile among the Franks is said to have lasted for three years, presumably from 789, when Beorhtric married Offa's daughter, until 792.[3] Throughout these years there must have been a constant strain in whatever intercourse passed between the Frankish and the Mercian courts. For some time in the early part of this period intercourse was completely suspended as a result of Offa's insistence on his formal equality with Charlemagne. In, or shortly before, 789 Charlemagne proposed that Charles, his son, should marry one of Offa's daughters. Offa refused to agree to the marriage unless Bertha, Charlemagne's daughter, were given to Ecgfrith, his son. Ecgfrith's family was far more ancient than that of Charlemagne, but Charlemagne at once broke off correspondence with Offa, and closed the ports of his territory to English traders. They were only opened again after long negotiations, in which Alcuin and Gervold of St. Wandrille were the chief agents.[4]

The most interesting feature of these transactions is the

---

dilectio vestra quod dominus rex Carolus amabiliter et fideliter sepe mecum locutus est de vobis, et in eo omnino habetis fidelissimum amicum.' *Monumenta Alcuiniana*, p. 290.

[1] *Councils*, iii. 487–8.   [2] Above, p. 209.

[3] *Chronicle* under 836. Many historians have assumed that the three years of this passage is a corrupt reading of an original 'thirteen years' and that Egbert's residence among the Franks lasted from his expulsion in 789 until Beorhtric's death in 802. But the fact that all the MSS. of the *Chronicle* which give the duration of Egbert's exile read 'three years' shows that this reading must have been in the archetype. It is very dangerous to reject a reading which is so well attested.

[4] The quarrel about the marriage negotiations and the closing of the Frankish ports by Charlemagne are placed beyond doubt by the account of the dispute in the *Gesta Abbatum Fontanellensium* (ed. Löwenfeld, pp. 46–7), written within thirty years of Charlemagne's death. There are several references to the dispute in Alcuin's letters, but they are so discreet that there is little to be gathered from them beyond the facts that at the end of 790 the ports were still closed and that Alcuin was expecting to be sent into England to make peace (*Monumenta Alcuiniana*, p. 167). Alcuin's statement in a letter of this date that the dispute had arisen 'lately' makes it unlikely that the daughter of Offa who comes into the story could have been Eadburh the wife of Beorhtric of Wessex, whose marriage certainly took place in 789. The daughter for whom the Frankish marriage was designed was probably Ælfflæd, who married Æthelred of Northumbria in 792.

denial of Frankish ports to English merchants, for it suggests that in normal times there was regular trade between England and the Frankish kingdom. The beginnings of English foreign trade lie in an obscurity which is only broken by occasional grants of freedom from toll to monasteries owning sea-going ships, by discoveries of early English coins on the Continent, and by incidental references to trade or traders in ecclesiastical narratives. It is probable that in the seventh and early eighth centuries the bulk of English overseas trade was in Frisian hands. Many English coins of this period have been found on the sites of early Frisian settlements. Under the year 679 Bede refers casually to a Frisian merchant in London who was prepared to buy an English prisoner of war from his captors.[1] A century later there was an important Frisian colony in York. But there is little evidence of direct trade between England and Gaul in this period, and that Charlemagne regarded its suspension as an effective act of hostility towards Offa is remarkable. It is still more remarkable that, when friendly relations had been re-established a few years later, the two kings proceeded to conclude the first commercial treaty in English history.[2] In 796 they agreed that traders entering Gaul from England or England from Gaul should have the protection of the public authorities in the country which they were visiting, and the right of access to the king in case of trouble. After establishing this general principle, the kings enter into details which show something of the goods which passed between their respective countries. In an earlier letter Offa had asked that certain 'black stones' which Charlemagne had promised to send him should be cut to a required length. Charlemagne agreed that this should be done; but he took the opportunity of remarking that his people were dissatisfied with the length of the *sagæ*—that is the cloths or cloaks—which came from England, and he requested Offa to see that *sagæ* of the accustomed length were sent in future. These provisions are only preserved in a letter which is chiefly concerned with the protection of English pilgrims going to Rome and the dispatch of presents from Charlemagne to Offa and the several bishops of England. But they carry the English textile industry back to the eighth century, and they even imply that an English king of this period might be expected to intervene in its regulation.

[1] *H.E.* iv, 20.   [2] *Councils*, iii. 496–8.

A similar impression of commercial activity is given by the history of the English currency in the eighth century. At its beginning the only coins in general circulation were small silver pieces bearing designs which were determined by the fancy of individual moneyers.[1] In Northumbria this silver currency gradually degenerated into a copper coinage, of no artistic merit, but authenticated by the names of the king and of the person responsible for the issue of each coin. The southern coins of the series are remarkable for the imaginative variety of their designs, and for the most part they are of good silver, but few of them bear the name of any king or moneyer, and the range of their foreign circulation must have depended on the credit of the trader who offered them in exchange for goods. The only examples which can be attributed to any particular town are the specimens inscribed with the name of London, and the names which were once thought to be those of Eorpwald of East Anglia, Penda of Mercia and Æthelred his son have been shown to be more probably those of moneyers.[2] By modern students the coins are generally described as *sceattas*, but the use of the word 'penny' in Ine's laws for the smallest unit of currency suggests that this was the name by which these pieces were then known. The fact that the word was current in northern France in the eighth century provides evidence of English trade with Merovingian Gaul.

In the course of Offa's reign this informal currency was superseded in every part of England but Northumbria by a new type of coin, broader, thinner, and heavier than its predecessors, and bearing almost universally the names of the king and the responsible moneyer. The circumstances of its introduction are uncertain, but it took place in Offa's reign.[3] The series of coins

[1] These coins are described by C. F. Keary, *Catalogue of English Coins in the British Museum, Anglo-Saxon Series*, vol. i; G. C. Brooke, *English Coins*, pp. 5–9; and from the artistic side by G. Baldwin Brown, *The Arts in Early England*, vol. iii.

[2] The names appear in the forms *Epa*, *Pada*, and *Æthilraed*. The identification of *Pada* with Penda was suggested by H. M. Chadwick, *Studies on Anglo-Saxon Institutions*, pp. 3–4; and that of *Epa* with Eorpwald, by B. Dickins, *Leeds Studies in English and Kindred Languages*, i. 20–1. [But see S. E. Rigold in *British Numismatic Journal*, xxx (1961), pp. 13 ff.]

[3] [It includes coins issued by kings of Kent, called Heaberht and Ecgberht, whose existence is also shown by charters. See also F. M. Stenton, *C.P.*, pp. 379 ff.

A rare coin bearing the portrait of a king named Æthilberht, who used to be identified with Æthelberht II of Kent, has been shown by C. E. Blunt to belong with greater probability to King Æthelberht of East Anglia, see *Anglo-Saxon Coins*, ed. Michael Dolley, pp. 49–50 and *B.N.J.*, xxvii (1958), pp. 52–4.]

bearing Offa's name is long and varied, and his earlier issues
are distinguished by portraits showing a delicacy of execution
which is unique in the whole history of the Anglo-Saxon coinage.
His later coins are less beautiful, but in some ways more efficient
as currency; the king's portrait disappears, but his name is
emphasized and the weight of the individual coins is slightly,
but definitely, increased. The fact that these changes were
roughly parallel to a similar development of the Frankish
currency[1] is highly significant in view of the commercial intercourse between England and Gaul at this time. In the history of
the English currency these changes are of fundamental importance, for they resulted in a type of coin which with innumerable variations of design and weight persisted throughout,
and even beyond, the Old English period. From the reign of
Offa to that of Henry III the English currency was based on a
silver penny which showed the king's name on the obverse and
the moneyer's name on the reverse. The continuous history of
the English currency begins in Offa's time.

But the most interesting of Offa's coins stand outside the
main body of his currency. By the middle of the eighth century
the gold coins of the Kaliphate had become familiar in Gaul,
where they passed into unofficial circulation. Later evidence
suggests that they were exchanged at a rate of thirty silver
coins for each gold piece. The 'mancus' of thirty silver pennies,
which often appears as a term of account in English charters
of the ninth century, was derived from these coins. No examples
have been found in English hoards, and it is therefore very
remarkable that copies were made of them in England in
Offa's reign. A single example has been preserved of a gold
coin, imitating a dinar struck by the Kaliph Al-Mansur in 774,
but carrying the legend *Offa Rex* in Roman capitals across the
centre of the reverse.[2] The man who cut the die for this coin
knew no Arabic and made many blunders in the inscription.
But with all its faults of execution, the coin suggests very
strongly that in Offa's time there was sufficient intercourse
between England and the Kaliphate to justify the production of
a gold currency which Arab traders might accept. With this
coin two other gold coins each struck by a moneyer known to

[1] The general relationship between the English and Frankish coinages in this
period is described by C. F. Keary, *Catalogue of English Coins in the British Museum,
Anglo-Saxon Series*, i, pp. xxiii–xxvi.
[2] G. C. Brooke, *English Coins*, pp. 21–2.

work for Offa must be considered although neither bears the king's name. The very beautiful coin struck by the moneyer Pendraed who worked for Offa in his middle period was known to be in the Cotton Collection in the seventeenth century, but, only came to light again in the sixties of the present century. The one struck by Ciolheard should probably be dated a little later, since Ciolheard is known to have worked both for Offa and for Cenwulf. The latest opinion about these coins is that they were struck for ceremonial purposes, such as alms for the Holy See at Rome.[1]

Offa died on 26 July 796, at the height of his power. In 792 he had given a daughter in marriage to Æthelred of Northumbria, and during his last years his supremacy throughout England was unchallenged. But he is the obscurest of the leading figures of Anglo-Saxon history, and it is easy to underestimate his achievement. No contemporary wrote the history of his reign, and of much that he did there is only a faint tradition. King Alfred ranked him as a legislator with Æthelberht of Kent and Ine of Wessex, but no copy of his laws has been preserved. His unification of southern England ran counter to the traditions of all the local kingdoms, and aroused resentments which were factors in English politics for a generation after his death. Alcuin, who admired his strength, saw in his son's untimely death a judgement on his ruthlessness. Nevertheless, as the history of his reign is traced from one fragment of evidence to another, it gradually becomes clear that this formidable and unsympathetic king was a statesman. He grasped the idea of a negotiated frontier. He was the first English king to play an independent part in continental affairs, and he was not overshadowed by the greatest ruler of the whole Dark Ages. He understood that it was the duty of a king to encourage foreign trade. He used the papal authority over the English church for his own political advantage. No other Anglo-Saxon king ever regarded the world at large with so secular a mind or so acute a political sense.

[1] [My husband had the extreme pleasure of seeing and handling the Pendraed coin on one lovely sunny Sunday in the garden of Mr. Blunt's house at Ramsbury. He never forgot that week-end and often spoke of it. For a colour illustration of the coin see Michael Dolley, *Anglo-Saxon Pennies* (the British Museum, 1964, frontispiece). For an account of the two coins by C. E. Blunt and Michael Dolley see *Numismatic Chronicle*, Seventh Series, vol. VIII, 'A Gold Coin of the Time of Offa', pp. 151–9, 1968].

No later Mercian king approached Offa in effective power, or showed any trace of his political quality. Ecgfrith, his son, survived him for less than five months, and before the end of 796 the Mercian kingdom had passed to a distant kinsman named Cenwulf. The first two years of his reign were occupied with a revolt in Kent, which had broken out shortly before Offa's death. On its suppression Cenwulf appointed Cuthred, his brother, king of Kent, and it was not until his death in 807 that Kent became once more a Mercian province. The subordination of Wessex to Mercia, secured by the marriage of Beorhtric, its king, to Offa's daughter, ended with Beorhtric's death in 802. Egbert, son of Ealhmund, whom Offa and Beorhtric had driven into exile, was immediately recognized as king in Wessex. For the first twenty years of his reign Egbert had little, if any, influence outside his own country, but his accession represented a West Saxon revolt against Mercian ascendancy, and there is no evidence that he ever became Cenwulf's man. Mercian influence in Northumbria was ended by the murder of Æthelred, Offa's son-in-law, on 18 April 796. Cenwulf's authority was recognized in Sussex, Essex, and East Anglia as well as in Kent. He was the immediate lord of the ancient West Saxon country which Offa had won to the south and west of the middle Thames. But the independence of the West Saxon court meant that he was not overlord of all the southern English, and in all his numerous charters he never claims this position for himself.

The chief interest of his reign lies in his relations with the two southern archbishops of his time. Archbishop Jaenberht, who had died in 792,[1] was succeeded by Æthelheard abbot of a monastery at Louth in Lindsey. He was on friendly terms with Offa, who gave him a great estate in Middlesex,[2] and he supported Mercian authority in Kent. The men who rose for Kentish independence in 796 naturally regarded him as their enemy, and he abandoned his see. At this moment, when Kent was in revolt and its archbishop in exile, Cenwulf began a correspondence with Pope Leo III which ended in the union of the two ecclesiastical provinces of southern England. The

---

[1] Offa, who consulted Alcuin about the correct procedure for the consecration of Jaenberht's successor, was advised that the act should be performed by the surviving archbishop of his kingdom—that is, Hygeberht of Lichfield (W. Levison, *England and the Continent*, pp. 245–6).

[2] *C.S.* 265.

surviving fragments of the correspondence begin with a letter of 798, in which Cenwulf asserts that his bishops and counsellors have objected to him that the order laid down by St. Gregory for the government of the English church has been broken.[1] It had been originally provided that an archbishop's seat should be established in London and York, but the wise men of the English race considered that Canterbury, where Augustine died, should take the place of London. Through hatred of Archbishop Jaenberht and the men of Kent, Offa had divided the province of Canterbury into two *parochiae*, and Pope Hadrian had consented to the division at Offa's request. Cenwulf now requests the pope to take the advice of his counsellors, so that peace may be restored to the English churches.

This letter shows that Cenwulf was prepared to re-establish the primitive system of government which placed all the southern English churches under the authority of a single archbishop. But it does not follow that he wished this archbishop to have his seat in Canterbury. He admits that the recent elevation of the see of Lichfield to the dignity of an archbishopric was contrary to St. Gregory's plan for the government of the English church. But he also emphasizes the fact that Gregory had intended London, not Canterbury, to be the ecclesiastical metropolis of southern England, and the pope interpreted his insistence on this point as equivalent to a request that London might be the metropolis of the future.[2] There is little doubt that his interpretation was correct. When the letter was written it was doubtful whether Mercian authority would ever be re-established in Kent. The archbishop of Canterbury was a fugitive. The see of London, to all appearance, was vacant. The transference of the seat of the southern archbishopric from Canterbury to London would have made the Mercian king the protector of all future archbishops, and would have given to Cenwulf all the political advantages which Offa had tried to secure by the establishment of the archbishopric of Lichfield. In the event, the plan came to nothing because the pope refused to sanction so great a departure from long-established custom, and the restoration of Mercian authority in Kent made it

---

[1] *C.S.* 287; *Councils*, iii. 521–3. The letter was accompanied by a gift of 120 mancuses to the pope. In the course of the letter Cenwulf states that he had attempted to bring the question to the pope's notice in the previous year, but had failed because of the incompetence of his messenger.

[2] *C.S.* 288; *Councils*, iii. 523–5.

unnecessary. But it is clear that towards the end of the eighth century there was a moment when the removal of the archbishop's seat from Canterbury was under serious discussion.

The pope was anxious to meet the wishes of his English correspondents. At Archbishop Æthelheard's request he anathematized the leader of the Kentish insurgents, an apostate clerk named Eadberht Præn.[1] But the proposal to bring the southern English churches once more into a single province raised issues on which no immediate decision could be taken. The archbishopric of Lichfield had been established by the pope's immediate predecessor in the belief that the English clergy were unanimous in asking for its creation. It was impossible for the pope to reverse at once so recent a decision, and in his reply to Cenwulf's letter he avoided any definite pronouncement. In April 799, before he had taken any further action, he was attacked and maltreated by his enemies at Rome. Until the autumn he was a fugitive at the court of Charlemagne. His position after his return to Rome was insecure, and he cannot have been disengaged from urgent Italian problems until at earliest the spring of 801. In the meantime Cenwulf had suppressed the Kentish revolt, and Canterbury was open to the archbishop. Towards the middle of 801 Æthelheard, who had already been in communication with the pope about the state of the English church,[2] left England for Rome. On 18 January 802, he received a papal privilege, confirming him in authority over all the churches which had ever been subject to the see of Canterbury.[3] On 12 October 803 he held a provincial council at *Clofeshoh*, which decreed that no power in church or state should thenceforward diminish the honour of Augustine's see, and that the privilege of Pope Hadrian establishing the archbishopric of Lichfield should be held invalid, because it was obtained by false representations.[4] Archbishop Hygeberht, who seems to have stood aloof from the controversy about his office, had ceased to hold the see of Lichfield before the council opened. He had been a

---

[1] [He was able to employ five moneyers to strike pennies for him. One of them, Æthelnoth, used the same reverse die with obverses in the names of Offa and Eadberht respectively. See *B.N.J.*, xxxviii, pp. 243 ff.]

[2] In his letter of 798 (above, p. 224) Cenwulf requests the pope to deal with certain questions which had been put to him independently by Æthelheard and the bishops of his province.

[3] *C.S.* 305; *Councils*, iii. 536–7.   [4] *C.S.* 310; *Councils*, iii. 542–4.

bishop since 779, and in 803 he was the senior member of the whole English episcopate. It is probable that he had resigned his see before it was deprived of its dignity, and that he is identical with the abbot bearing the same name who attended the council at the head of the clergy from the Mercian diocese.[1]

One important result of this controversy was the rise of a custom which required each newly elected bishop to make a written profession of Catholic orthodoxy and a promise of obedience to his metropolitan. The custom, which seems to have been confined to the southern province, began at the moment when the Kentish rebellion had thrown the organization of the church into confusion, and it was continued until ecclesiastical order was dislocated again by the Danish invasions. It produced a series of documents which are useful illustrations of the state of learning which prevailed among the higher clergy. Some of them are marked by contortions of phrase and grammatical infelicities which suggest a literary tradition in decay. But, as a whole, they show a competence of expression which cannot easily be reconciled with King Alfred's complaint of the collapse of learning in the generation before his own. The historical information which they yield is meagre, but the first of the series—a profession addressed to Archbishop Æthelheard by Eadwulf, bishop of Lindsey—is of real importance for the history of the crisis which followed Offa's death.[2] After making his confession of faith the bishop, who had been a pupil of Æthelheard, breaks out into a declaration that, whatever others may have done, he at least will give his obedience to the church where he is about to receive consecration, and where the other English bishops have already received it. He adds that not only he himself, but all other bishops, should look with reverence to the see of St. Augustine, from which ecclesiastical order had been spread throughout England. There is no means of determining the date of this singular document, but it clearly reflects the conditions of the time between Offa's death and the papal pronouncement of 802. It was probably written in the latter part of 798, after Æthelheard had returned to Canterbury. It is of historical interest because it suggests that the factor which decided the fate of the archbishopric of Lichfield was the reverence of individual bishops for the traditions of Augustine's church.

[1] C.S. 312.   [2] C.S. 276; Councils, iii. 506–7.

Æthelheard, who died on 12 May 805, was succeeded by Wulfred, his archdeacon. He is an important figure in the history of his church, for he induced the clergy who served it to adopt a communal way of life such as had been systematized in the rule of Chrodegang of Metz.[1] In 816 he held the last of the great ecclesiastical councils which are characteristic of the age of Mercian supremacy.[2] He attested most of the charters which Cenwulf of Mercia issued between 805 and 817, and he received several estates from the king during these years. But in 817 the series of Cenwulf's charters ends abruptly, and it is not resumed until 821. Between these dates a dispute between the king and the archbishop gave rise to a situation which has no parallel in the history of the Anglo-Saxon church. The origin of the quarrel is obscure, but a statement of the archbishop's case[3] suggests that it arose from a claim laid by Cenwulf to various possessions of the see of Canterbury.[4] The quarrel comes into general history because, early in its course, the king brought certain charges against the archbishop to the knowledge of Pope Paschal I. Their nature is unknown, but they were regarded seriously at Rome, and there seems no doubt that the archbishop ceased to exercise his office for at least four years.[5] The dispute was ended in 821, when Cenwulf invited the archbishop to a council at London, and imposed a settlement upon him. As a preliminary to a reconciliation the king insisted that the archbishop should surrender an estate of 300 hides and pay a fine of 120 pounds. He added that, unless this condition were accepted, the archbishop should be despoiled of everything that was his, and exiled from the country, so that he should not be received there again by virtue of any letters

[1] Margaret Deanesly, 'The Familia at Christchurch, Canterbury', in *Essays . . . presented to Thomas Frederick Tout*, pp. 10–13.

[2] *Councils*, iii. 579–84.

[3] Written in 825. *C.S.* 384; *Facsimiles of Ancient Charters in the British Museum*, ii. 18.

[4] In particular to the archbishop's monasteries of Minster in Thanet and Reculver.

[5] The statement of the archbishop's case asserts that through these accusations the English race was deprived of his primatial authority and of the ministry of baptism for nearly six years. But the whole dispute was comprised between the years 817–21, the circumstances of Wulfred's dispossession gave no grounds for the imposition of an interdict on England by the pope, and it is incredible that the English bishops should have taken the extreme step of withholding the sacrament of baptism from their people because they disapproved of the treatment of the archbishop of Canterbury by the king of the Mercians.

from the pope or the emperor. The archbishop unwillingly agreed to these terms, and Cenwulf then promised that he should be restored to the honour and authority of his see, and cleared before the pope from the charges which had been brought against him. It was also agreed that if the king should fail to make the archbishop 'innocent before the pope', the fine which he had paid should be refunded to him. It is unfortunate that this episode, which must have affected every aspect of English public life, is only known from an *ex parte* statement, which deserves the worst that has ever been said about ninth-century English latinity.

Apart from this episode the political history of southern England is almost a blank for the first twenty years of the ninth century. The one recorded conflict between two English kingdoms in this period is the war of 801 between Mercia and Northumbria.[1] On the other hand, there is good evidence from Welsh sources that the Mercian expansion towards the west, suspended by Offa, was resumed under Cenwulf.[2] In 816 the Mercians raided the district between the Clwyd and the Elwy and penetrated into Snowdonia itself. In 818 Cenwulf harried the Britons of Dyfed. It is possible that he was preparing for another Welsh expedition on the eve of his death in 821, for he died at Basingwerk in Flintshire.[3] In any case, the attack on Wales was immediately reopened under Ceolwulf, his brother and successor. Under the year 822 the *Annales Cambriae* state that the 'Saxons' destroyed the fortress of Deganwy at the mouth of the Conway and brought the kingdom of Powys under their power.[4] The *Annales* may have exaggerated this particular disaster, but the severity of the Mercian assault on Powys is beyond question. Welsh poems of the period show that the men of Powys were hard pressed by enemies who can be no other than the Mercians,[5] and within a generation the last male descendant of the ancient kings of Powys left his country for Rome, worn out by age and misery.

[1] Above, p. 94.

[2] J. E. Lloyd, *History of Wales*, i, p. 202.

[3] Gaimar, *L'Estorie des Engles*, line 2240. The statement is unlikely to be an invention, and may well come from the version of the *Chronicle* which Gaimar is known to have possessed.

[4] 'Arcem Decantorum (*sic*) a Saxonibus destruitur, et regionem Poyuis in sua potestate traxerunt.'

[5] Ifor Williams, 'The Poems of Llywarch Hên', *Proceedings of the British Academy*, xviii (1932), pp. 269–302.

The capture of Deganwy proved to be the last important achievement of the ancient Mercian kingdom. King Ceolwulf was deposed in 823, and the kingdom then passed to a certain Beornwulf, of whose family nothing is known.[1] His authority was recognized in Essex, Middlesex, and Kent, and he was the dominant figure in southern England as late as the summer of 825, when he reached a settlement with Archbishop Wulfred in regard to most of the questions left open by Wulfred's forced reconciliation with Cenwulf.[2] But before the year was over Egbert of Wessex defeated Beornwulf in one of the most decisive battles of Anglo-Saxon history, and the ascendancy of the Mercian kings came to an end. The battle was fought at a place called Ellendun, now represented by Wroughton south of Swindon,[3] in country which had long been in dispute between the kings of Wessex and Mercia. Immediately after the battle Egbert sent Æthelwulf his son, the bishop of Sherborne, and the ealdorman of Hampshire, with a large army into Kent, where a certain Baldred was ruling, apparently under Mercian overlordship.[4] Baldred was driven beyond the Thames, and the men of Kent, Essex, Surrey, and Sussex submitted to Egbert. The king of the East Angles and the nobles of his household, who were already in revolt against their Mercian overlord, turned to Egbert for protection. Before the end of the year Beornwulf was killed by the East Angles, presumably in the course of an expedition intended to force them back into his allegiance, and one of his ealdormen, named Ludeca,[5] succeeded him in a kingdom which was now reduced to Mercia, Lindsey, Middle Anglia, and the provinces of the Hwicce and Magonsætan.

Four years later Mercia itself and all its dependencies were

[1] He is probably identical with the *dux*, or ealdorman, named Beornwulf, who witnessed a charter of Cenwulf of Mercia in 812 (*C.S.* 340), and a charter of Ceolwulf in 823 (*C.S.* 373). The low position which he occupies in each charter suggests that he had been one of the less distinguished ealdormen of the Mercian kingdom.   [2] *C.S.* 384.

[3] The identification seems to have been first made by the Rev. C. S. Taylor, and was communicated by him to Dr. Charles Plummer in a letter quoted in *Two of the Saxon Chronicles parallel*, ii, pp. 70–1.

[4] [It has been found possible to list a total of 36 coins of Baldred from (probably) two Kentish mints, struck by eight moneyers, tentatively dated *c.* 823–5. See *B.N.J.*, xxxii (1963), pp. 67–8.]

[5] There are two charters of 824 in which Ludeca appears as a member of Beornwulf's court with the title *dux* (*C.S.* 378, 379), but nothing else is known about him before his accession.

conquered by Egbert. The Mercian kingdom of historic times was the creation of the reigning house. The prestige of this family must have grown during the eighth century, as one after another of the lesser English dynasties became extinct.[1] But the Mercian line itself appears to have ended in King Ceolwulf I,[2] and it is unlikely that the men of outlying provinces regarded any of his successors with the instinctive respect which they had felt for Offa or Cenwulf. Neither Ludeca nor Wiglaf, who succeeded him in 827,[3] was Egbert's equal in birth, or in the wealth which attracted warriors into a king's retinue. The enlargement of Egbert's kingdom in 825 had placed the resources of all south-eastern England at his service. In 829 he threw his whole power into a campaign which made him for a time the immediate ruler of Mercia and enabled him to exact a recognition of his overlordship from the Northumbrians.

The submission of the Northumbrians was made on the border of their country, at Dore near Sheffield, on the divide between the valleys of the Derwent and the Don. The ceremony was probably intended to forestall an invasion, and so far as can be seen it had no political consequences. But the Mercians were reduced to complete, if temporary, subjection. Egbert took the title *Rex Merciorum*,[4] and coins bearing his name were struck in what had been the Mercian port of London.[5] In Wessex the conquest of Mercia was regarded as an achievement which entitled Egbert to a place among the greatest figures in English history. Ignoring the age of Mercian supremacy, the *Chronicle* represented Egbert as next in succession to Oswiu of Northumbria among the overlords of the southern English peoples.

The events of 825 and 829 have always, and rightly, been regarded as marking an important stage in the advance of the

[1] Their disappearance was lamented by Alcuin in a letter which he addressed in 797 to the people of Kent. 'Populi Anglorum et regna et reges dissentiunt inter se. Et vix aliquis modo, quod sine lacrimis non dicam, ex antiqua regum prosapia invenitur, et tanto incertioris sunt originis, quanto minoris sunt fortitudinis.' *Monumenta Alcuiniana*, p. 371.

[2] The ancient Mercian genealogies end with his name, and the names of his successors differ in their initial elements from those which the Mercian royal house is known to have used.

[3] *Chronicle* under 825.

[4] His use of this style is proved by a small number of coins which describe him as *Rex M*.

[5] The legend *Lundonia Civit* occurs on one of the pennies struck for him as king of the Mercians.

English peoples towards political unity. After 825 Kent, Surrey, and Sussex were never separated from the West Saxon monarchy.[1] Essex was only detached from it by a Danish conquest. The annexation of Mercia and the submission of the Northumbrians foreshadowed the appearance of a kingdom of all England. On the other hand, none of Egbert's genuine charters gives him any higher title than 'king of the West Saxons and Kentishmen', no other king acknowledges his overlordship in any written instrument which has survived, and on all grounds it is doubtful whether he exercised any authority outside Wessex and its eastern dependencies during the last nine years of his reign. In 830, according to the *Chronicle*, Wiglaf, the king of Mercia who had been defeated in 829, 'obtained the Mercian kingdom again'.[2] In view of this neutral phrase it is hard to believe that Wiglaf can have received the kingdom from Egbert's hands. No ninth-century writer would have recorded the gift of a kingdom to a dependent ruler in this oblique way. The appropriate phrase occurs in the *Chronicle* itself eight years later, where it is stated that Æthelwulf, king of Wessex, 'gave the kingdom of the Kentishmen . . . to Athelstan, his son'.[3] If Wiglaf had been restored to the Mercian kingdom by Egbert, a West Saxon chronicler, anxious to emphasize Egbert's greatness, would certainly have recorded the gift in some such way as this. Nothing is ever likely to be known about the circumstances of Wiglaf's restoration, but it is probable that he was brought back by a revolt in Mercia such as had ended the supremacy of Oswiu in 657.

In any case, it is clear that Wiglaf had become an independent king at least three years before Egbert's death. An original charter dated 836 shows him holding an assembly of magnates at Croft in Leicestershire, attended by the archbishop of

[1] Egbert's son Æthelwulf held Kent as an under-king during his father's last years (*C.S.* 418, 419). On his own succession to Wessex he gave it to his eldest son Athelstan. In 856, to avoid a civil war (below, p. 245), Æthelwulf resigned Wessex to Æthelbald his eldest son, and confined himself to the rule of Kent, Sussex, Surrey, and Essex. On Æthelwulf's death in 858 these provinces passed to Æthelberht his second son (*C.S.* 496, *Chronicle* under 855), who reunited them to the West Saxon kingdom when he succeeded Æthelbald as king of Wessex in 860. But the kingdom of Wessex, as enlarged by Egbert, was regarded as a unity in spite of these arrangements, and Asser, writing under King Alfred, lays stress on its integrity (*Vita Alfredi*, c. 12).

[2] 'Her eft Wilaf onfeng Miercna rices.'

[3] 'He salde his suna Æthelstane Cantwara rice and Eastseaxna and Suþrigea and Suþseaxna.'

Canterbury and eleven bishops of the southern province —those of Sherborne, Selsey, and Rochester among them.[1] The fact that the members of the assembly are collectively described by Wiglaf as 'my bishops, *duces*, and magistrates' proves, not only the king's independence, but also the revival of Mercian authority over the southern episcopate.[2] Even in mere extent of territory Mercia remained a powerful kingdom after these catastrophes. A charter issued at Wychbold near Droitwich in 831, which Wiglaf calls 'the first year of my second reign', proves that he had authority in Middlesex as well as in the western midlands.[3] London remained a Mercian town until the Danes conquered it, a generation after Wiglaf's time. It is more remarkable that he and his successor Beorhtwulf continued to possess much of the debatable land along the middle Thames which had formed part of the primitive Wessex. In 844 Ceolred, bishop of Leicester, gave an estate at Pangbourne on Thames to King Beorhtwulf in return for a grant of liberties to certain monasteries, of which Abingdon was one.[4] On receiving this land, Beorhtwulf gave it to an ealdorman named Æthelwulf. In later years, when Berkshire had at last become a West Saxon province, Æthelwulf continued to govern it on behalf of its new lords. He led the local forces against the Danes who invaded Berkshire in 870. But his Mercian origin was remembered, and after his death in battle he was carried for burial to Derby in the heart of the Mercian kingdom.[5]

---

[1] *C.S.* 416.

[2] The difficult question of the relationship which existed at this time between the archbishop and the West Saxon court is illustrated by a document of 838, which was apparently drafted at Christ Church, Canterbury (*C.S.* 421, preserved in three contemporary copies). It records that at a council held at Kingston on Thames, which was attended by many bishops and magnates, Egbert and Æthelwulf his son surrendered an estate to the archbishop 'hac vero condicione interposita . . . quod nos ipsi nostrique heredes semper in posterum firmam inconcussamque amicitiam ab illo archiepiscopo Ceolnotho et eiusdem congregatione ecclesiae Christi habeamus et ab omnibus successoribus eius'. The document is so illiterate that it cannot be translated, and its meaning is often obscure, but it shows the archbishop and the West Saxon royal family dealing with each other on equal terms.

[3] *C.S.* 400, a contemporary text relating to Botwell in Middlesex. It is significant that in this charter, issued within a year of Wiglaf's restoration, he makes no reference to any overlordship possessed by Egbert.

[4] *C.S.* 443. F. M. Stenton, *Early History of the Abbey of Abingdon*, pp. 25–7.

[5] *The Chronicle of Æthelweard*, ed. A. Campbell, p. 37. 'Corpus quippe supradicti ducis abstrahitur furtim, adduciturque in Merciorum provinciam in locum qui Northuuorthige nuncupatur, iuxta autem Danaan linguam Deoraby.' The Mercian kingdom was still intact in 870.

From all this it follows that as late as 844 a great part, if not the whole, of Berkshire belonged to the Mercian kingdom and the Middle Anglian diocese of Leicester. Meagre as it is, this evidence all points to a situation in which the kings of Wessex and Mercia stood towards each other on terms of virtual equality. In 839, when Egbert died, he was ruling a territory wider than had belonged to any of his predecessors since Ine, if not since Ceawlin. But his overlordship of the southern English had ended when Wiglaf returned to the Mercian kingdom in 830.

This does not mean that he is an insignificant figure in English history. He was the real creator of the kingdom which formed the basis of the English resistance to the Danish invasion a generation after his death. His annexation of Kent and its adjacent provinces made him the protector of the most venerable of English churches, and brought his dynasty into a new relationship with continental powers. At the other end of his kingdom he completed the long process by which the Britons of the south-west were gradually brought under English rule. In 815, probably in reprisal for a British raid into Wessex, he harried Cornwall from east to west, and made himself so far the master of that country that he was able to devote a tenth part of it to religious uses.[1] His lordship was resented by its inhabitants. There is a record of a British raid into Devon in 825,[2] and in 838 the Britons of Cornwall joined an army of marauding Danes in preparation for an invasion of Wessex.[3] The last recorded event of Egbert's life is the defeat of this force at Hingston Down on the heights to the west of the lower Tamar. It was probably this victory which made Cornwall finally a part of England, for there is no evidence of any later movements for Cornish independence, and fifty years after the battle of Hingston Down King Alfred's will deals as freely with land in Cornwall as with any of the ancient possessions of his house.

Egbert was succeeded by his son Æthelwulf, who had already been reigning for several years as under-king of Kent and the other eastern dependencies of Wessex. On his accession to the

[1] *Chronicle* under 813; *Crawford Charters*, ed. Napier and Stevenson, pp. 18–19, 106–7.

[2] *Chronicle* under 823.

[3] *Chronicle* under 835. The chronology of the *Chronicle* is three years behindhand in this section.

chief kingdom Æthelwulf gave these provinces—Kent, Sussex, Surrey, and Essex—to Athelstan, his eldest son, as an appanage.[1] Of the many kingdoms into which southern England had been divided a hundred years before, Mercia, Wessex, and East Anglia now alone survived. East Anglian history in this period, as always in early times, is utterly obscure. There is nothing beyond a brief series of names recorded on coins to connect King Æthelberht, whom Offa killed in 794, with King Edmund, whom a Danish army killed in 869. None of the intervening kings is likely to have been well known outside his own country. But the East Angles were a compact, and in numbers a formidable people, and it was plainly their revolt which completed the Mercian collapse of 825.

The age of Mercian supremacy has been studied less than any other period of Anglo-Saxon history, and unless new materials come to light, its details will always be uncertain. But its general significance is plain. The great Mercian kings of this age created a political system which included every kingdom in southern England. This system permitted every variety of relationship which could then exist between men of dependent kingdoms and an overlord. At its weakest, it meant little more than occasional hospitality shown by the king of the Mercians to local rulers as well born as himself. But overlordship soon passed into political authority when the overlord was an autocrat like Æthelbald or Offa and, as time went on, more than one insignificant local king exchanged his ancestral rank, and the claim to independence which it implied, for the security of a provincial ealdorman under Mercian patronage. With all its weaknesses the system marks the first advance ever made on a great scale towards the political unity of England. It showed that the particularism of the smaller kingdoms was not an insuperable obstacle to the creation of a greater state.

The emergence of this greater state coincided with the appearance of a new type of deliberative assembly. The affairs of a self-contained kingdom could be settled by discussion between the king, his bishops, the nobles whom he had set in charge of provinces, and his older retainers. In all the early

---

[1] The late MSS. D, E, and F of the *Chronicle* state that the Athelstan who received these provinces was the son, not of Æthelwulf, but of Egbert. But the authority of MSS. A, B, and C and *The Chronicle of Æthelweard*, each of which makes Athelstan the son of Æthelwulf, is conclusive. There does not seem to be any adequate evidence for the existence of a son of Egbert named Athelstan.

English kingdoms from which charters have survived, assemblies of this kind can be seen in session on royal estates, witnessing, and thereby confirming, the king's grants of land and privileges. They passed by natural development into the large and formal conferences at which the later Anglo-Saxon kings met their *witan*, the greater nobles and higher clergy of all England. But the peculiar conditions of the eighth and early ninth centuries led to the evolution of an anomalous type of assembly, in which the king of the Mercians and his nobles were associated with the leading churchmen of every diocese south of the Humber.[1] These assemblies were often described as synods, and their chief work seems to have been the decision of suits relating to property claimed by ecclesiastical persons.[2] They were essentially ecclesiastical councils, reinforced by lay lords for the more effective settlement of pleas.[3]

It is natural to draw a sharp distinction between these councils and the solemn provincial synods which met at rare intervals to reaffirm the doctrinal orthodoxy of the church and to provide for its better discipline. But it is more than doubtful whether the distinction was felt by the men of the period. At *Clofeshoh* in 746 and at Chelsea in 816, the clergy of the southern province were concerned with specific questions of ecclesiastical order, but the king of the Mercians and his principal nobles attended each assembly.[4] The kings of Northumbria and Mercia were present with their nobles at the council which made the legatine decrees of 786 valid in their dominions.

[1] It is a curious and probably a significant feature of these assemblies that, although their jurisdiction covered the whole of southern England, they were rarely, if ever, attended by the kings or nobles of the smaller southern kingdoms. It seems that they relied on the Mercian king for the execution of their judgements,

[2] Their nature is well brought out by the record of a plea decided in a council held at Chelsea in 789 (*C.S.* 256). The council is described as 'Pontificale conciliabulum ... praesidentibus duobus archiepiscopis, Iamberhto scilicet et Hygeberhto, mediante quoque Offa rege cum universis principibus suis.' The company included, beside the king and the two archbishops, nine bishops, six abbots, and eight *principes* or ealdormen.

[3] The habit of summoning such councils seems to have been broken by the Danish wars. It was never resumed, for the *witan* of the later Old English kings included the higher clergy of the whole of England and was competent to deal with every kind of ecclesiastical business.

[4] The acts of the council of 746 are dated 'Anno regni Ædilbaldi regis Merciorum, qui tunc aderat cum suis principibus ac ducibus xxxii.' The corresponding record of the council of 816 is dated in the twentieth year of Cenwulf 'qui tunc tempore praesens adfuit cum suis principibus ducibus et optimatibus'. *Councils*, iii. 362, 579.

The presence of influential laymen at these assemblies was essential if their resolutions were to be more than expressions of opinion. All these synods issued canons which affected lay interests. A single provision of the council of 816 forbidding monasteries to grant leases of their property to laymen for more than the term of one life must have caused anxiety to innumerable noblemen holding monastic lands under arrangements made in an earlier generation. In every set of canons which has come down from this period, such provisions are intermingled with clauses relating to the internal government of the church and the conduct of persons in holy orders. The affairs of church and state were, in fact, interdependent, and no king or bishop of the eighth century would have understood an argument which tried to show that ecclesiastical legislation, or the protection of ecclesiastical interests, was a matter for churchmen alone.

VIII

THE AGE OF ALFRED

AT the end of the eighth century each of the three Scandi-navian peoples of historic times formed a nation, with its own traditions and a clear sense of its difference from its neighbours. The Geatas, Beowulf's people, were now united with the Swedes; their name was remembered, but their dynasty had long since come to an end. The great eastward expansion of the Swedes, through which they became the founders of the Russian state, had not yet begun, and they were chiefly distinguished by the extreme antiquity of their reigning house and the prestige of their sanctuary at Uppsala. The Norwegians were the furthest of the three peoples from any sense of political unity. The narrowness of their habitable lands, which made for their political disunion, was already impelling individuals to seek fortune or settlement oversea, and the first Scandinavian raiders who touched the English coast undoubtedly came from Norway. Between 786 and 802 three ships' companies from Horthaland put into shore at Portland, and killed the reeve of Dorchester, who rode up to ask their business. In 793 Lindisfarne was plundered by raiders from the north, and Jarrow was visited in the following year. But the main body of Norwegian adventurers passed round the north coast of Scotland to Ireland, establishing intermediate colonies in the Shetlands and Orkneys, Caithness and Sutherland, and the Hebrides. It was not until the tenth century that any considerable Norwegian settlements were founded in England, and they were only the result of a secondary migration from Norse colonies previously established in Ireland. The invasions which deflected the course of English history in the ninth century arose from internal movements among the peoples who commanded the entry to the Baltic Sea, and at the court of Charlemagne were regarded as forming a single kingdom of the Danes.[1]

[1] For some forty years after the death of Charlemagne the history of the Danes can be followed in outline in the Frankish annals of the period. The ninth-century life of St. Anskar (*Vita Anskarii auctore Rimberto*, ed. Waitz, 1884) brings out convincingly the power of Horik, the greatest Danish king of the age, and shows that the political confusion into which the Danes had fallen by King Alfred's time was of recent origin.

It was not until the latter part of the eighth century that they became an important factor in European affairs. For more than a century before this period the Frisians had dominated the North Sea, and the Saxons, in their independence, had prevented any but occasional communication between the Frankish kingdom and the Baltic peoples. A new situation arose in the north when Charlemagne completed the long process of Frankish encroachment on Frisia, and brought Saxon independence to an end. His representatives on his new frontier were confronted by a Danish king who regarded himself as the equal of their lord, claimed suzerainty over Frisia and Saxony, and defined his own kingdom towards the south by the first of the great earthworks which limited access from Germany into the Jutish peninsula. It was of still greater importance that the Frankish conquest of Frisia gave the freedom of the North Sea to Danish adventurers. The Frankish kingdom never became strong enough at sea to protect a coastline which, in the eighth century, had been extended from the Rhine delta to the mouth of the Elbe. There is no evidence that any English king between Ecgfrith of Northumbria and Alfred of Wessex had a fleet at his command. With Frisian sea-power reduced to insignificance, the coasts of Britain and the Frankish empire were at the mercy of any Danish expedition strong enough to overcome resistance at its landing-place. One of the most remarkable features of the Danish raids of the ninth century is the fact that more than a third of the century passed before they seriously affected the social order of Britain or the empire.

The delay was primarily due to the well-supported diplomacy of the Frankish court. In his last years Charlemagne was fully conscious of the danger from the north, and was careful to keep himself acquainted with the course of affairs in that region. Historians have not always realized that Louis the Pious, his successor, was equally alert. By keeping in touch with events on the border through *missi* and local officers, by playing off one member of the Danish royal family against another, and by maintaining diplomatic relations with the man possessed of the greatest power among the Danes, Louis kept the Frankish dominions from devastation for twenty years. It was not until the disaffection of Louis's sons threw the empire itself into confusion that its coasts became open to the descent of raiders in force. An annalist of the next generation states that a period of incessant Danish raids on Frankish territory began in 834, and English as well as Frankish sources imply that Danish raiders became a permanent menace to seaboard life at about this time. The series of Danish raids which culminated in the great invasion led by the sons of Ragnar Lothbrok began with a descent of 'heathen men' on Sheppey in 835.

It is highly probable that what Frankish writers regarded as kingship among the Danes was really a suzerainty such as Offa had possessed in England in the previous age. But their language implies that the Danes of this period were not a mere group of independent tribes bearing a common name; and the fact that every Danish king mentioned in the Frankish annals of the ninth century belonged to the same family proves the existence of a predominant dynasty. As in England at an earlier time, every member of the dominant royal family inherited a claim to a share in its lands and prerogatives, and much of the success of Frankish diplomacy was due to the possibility of supporting younger members of the royal house in revolt against their established elders. But the Frankish authorities also show a definite tendency for lordship over the whole Danish people to become concentrated in the hands of a single king. There seems no doubt that Godfred, king of the Danes, Charlemagne's contemporary, ruled over the Danes of the islands and of Scania from the ancient seats of his house in Jutland.

Godfred was murdered by a retainer in 810, Hemming, his nephew and successor, died in 812, and a long war followed in which Godfred's sons ultimately made good their claim to supremacy among the Danes. By 825 they had come to be represented to the outside world by one of their number named Horik, who survived until 854, and at the middle of the century was undoubtedly the effective ruler of the whole Danish people. Apart from an unsuccessful expedition up the Elbe in 844 he generally respected the boundaries of the empire; he was always anxious to avoid a direct attack on his kingdom by Frankish forces, and he was much embarrassed by the irresponsible raids of his men on Frankish territory. A heathen until his death, he acquiesced in the spread of Christianity among the Danes, protected and honoured the great missionary St. Anskar, and by his safe-conduct made possible the expedition to Sweden on which the saint's fame chiefly rests. For a time his court was the link between the Frankish empire and the almost unknown peoples of the farther north. But he never escaped from the enmities aroused in the fighting of his youth; exiled kinsmen were always waiting for an opportunity of revenge, and in 854 he and all the royal house except one boy perished in an invasion led by Guthrum, his brother's son. On his death his kingdom seems to have disintegrated. The life of Rimbert, St. Anskar's successor, and the geographical writings of King Alfred show that there was no strong central power among the Danes of the late ninth century. No genealogical connection can be established between the dynasty to which Horik belonged and the later kings of the Danes who claimed descent from Gorm the Old. The battle of 854 was clearly a turning-point in the history of the Danish people.

It was also a significant event in the general history of Europe. Horik, like every Scandinavian king who rose to a similar position, was anxious to check piracy and unauthorized adventure among his own people. It was not to the interest of such a king that his nobles and fighting-men should escape his control, enrich themselves in war, and return free to give allegiance to any member of the royal house who could attract them to his side. Much of the raiding which complicated Horik's relations with the Frankish court had been carried out by his open enemies, and the nephew who overthrew him had been living abroad as a pirate. After Horik's fall there was no longer a king in Denmark who could even attempt to hold his people back from a prospect of exciting and profitable adventure. Indirectly, the collapse of the Danish kingdom affected many countries, but it is in England that its consequences are most clearly seen. The movement which created the English Danelaw would have been impossible if a king of Horik's quality had been reigning in Denmark.

But in the first phase of Danish enterprise at sea few, if any, of the adventurers were moved by the possibility of winning land for settlement. Louis the Pious had granted territory in Frisia and north-western Germany to more than one exiled member of the Danish royal house, and there was abundant room in these colonies for men to whom life in Denmark was forbidden. The motive behind the voyages of this period was plunder, and the leader of an expedition was quite indifferent whether he landed his followers in Frankish territory or in England. In either country he and they might hope for an adequate return for the labours of the voyage before they met any enemy more formidable than the levies of the countryside. It was not easy for any ninth-century king to improvise an effective programme of resistance to an invader who could disembark more than five thousand seasoned fighting-men at any one of a score of undefended ports.[1] Security, under these conditions, could only be reached through the co-operation of all free men of whatever rank, and in England, at least, there was a stolid resistance to the enforcement of new military duties. So far as is known, King Alfred was the first English ruler to plan an ordered scheme of national defence, and after forty years' experience of Danish ravages there were many of his subjects who refused to work under him for a common end.

The first Danish raiders who are known to have visited England reached Sheppey in 835.[2] During the next thirty years there is evidence of more than twelve separate Danish descents on different parts of the country, and the record is certainly incomplete. Twice at least during this period, in 850 and 854, a Danish army took winter-quarters in England— in Thanet on the first occasion and in Sheppey on the second. Kent seems to have suffered more heavily than any other region during these years, but the *Chronicle* records that in 841 great destruction was done in Lindsey and East Anglia as well as in Kent;[3] Southampton was plundered in 842[4] and a Mercian charter of 855 states that the heathen were then in the country around the Wrekin.[5] Northumbria throughout this period lies almost outside recorded history,[6] but it is known that in 844 a

---

[1] It is impossible to form a clear impression of the size of the ninth-century Danish armies. The number of ships in a fleet is often mentioned, but there is little early information about the number of fighting-men carried by a single ship. It is dangerous to argue back to the ships of this period from the great war vessels of the eleventh century. In this uncertainty it is worth noting that, according to the *Chronicle*, the 23 ships' companies which descended on Devon in 877 lost 840 men in the battle of Countisbury (below, p. 255). This statement, which seems to be contemporary and to come from local knowledge, implies that each ship carried, at the very least, 36 fighting-men. Against the possibility that the numbers of the slain were exaggerated may be set the high probability that a considerable part of the host survived the battle. Without laying any stress on details, it is safe to conclude that the size of a large viking army should be reckoned in thousands rather than hundreds.

[2] *Chronicle*, under 832. The *Chronicle*, in this section, is three years behindhand in its chronology.   [3] *Chronicle* under 838.   [4] Nithard, *Historia*, iv, c. 3.
[5] 'Quando fuerunt pagani in Wreocensetun', *C.S.* 487.
[6] No Northumbrian chronicle has survived from this period in a coherent form. But a number of facts relating to Northumbria are recorded, apparently

king named Rædwulf, who had just come to power, was killed
with one of his ealdorman by a heathen army,[1] It was rarely
possible to intercept a Danish fleet while it was at sea, but the
first naval battle in recorded English history was fought in this
period, when Athelstan, the under-king of Kent, and Ealhhere,
his ealdorman, defeated a Danish force off Sandwich.[2] Responsibility for local defence, when the enemy was once abroad
in the land, rested on the ealdorman of each threatened shire
and its militia. But the danger was too grave for punctilious
attention to county boundaries, and in 845 the combined
levies of Dorset and Somerset defeated a Danish army at the
mouth of the Parret. An occasion of special danger would
bring the king himself into the field at the head of an army
representing the whole of his people. The one decisive English
victory of the period was won, in 851, by King Æthelwulf and
an army drawn from all Wessex over a host composed of 350
ships' companies, which had previously stormed Canterbury
and London and driven king Beorhtwulf of Mercia into flight.[3]

This battle was the most notable event of a reign to which
historians have sometimes done less than justice. On a general
view of Anglo-Saxon history Æthelwulf is naturally overshadowed by his father Egbert. There is, indeed, no evidence
that Æthelwulf reached, or even attempted to win, a position
comparable with that which Egbert held for a short time after
his conquest of Mercia in 829. On the other hand, the annexation
of Kent, Sussex, Surrey, and Essex to the West Saxon kingdom,
which was Egbert's greatest achievement, was never challenged
during Æthelwulf's reign. Before 850 he had settled the ancient

independently, in the *Historia Regum* of Symeon of Durham and the *Flores Historiarum*
of Roger of Wendover. Their nature suggests that they come from a series of brief
annals, primarily concerned with the successions and deaths of kings, which was
compiled at York before the end of the ninth century.

[1] Roger of Wendover, *Flores Historiarum*, ed. Coxe, i. 282–3. [Rædwulf's coins are
far from being as rare as the passing documentary reference would suggest. There
are 30+ in the British Museum and most important collections have specimens.
Their existence helps to confirm the accuracy of the Northumbrian material
available to Roger of Wendover.]

[2] *Chronicle* under 851.

[3] Ibid. The site of the battle is unknown. The *Chronicle* states that it was fought
to the south of the Thames at a place called *æt Aclea*. This common name nearly
always appears in modern times as Oakley. The identification of the battle-site
with Ockley in Surrey is made virtually impossible by the early spellings of the
latter name, which point to an original *Occan leah* (*Place-Names of Surrey*, English
Place-Name Society, p. 276).

dispute between Wessex and Mercia about the lands to the
west of the middle Thames.[1] Berkshire, thenceforward, was a
West Saxon shire. After his victory of 851 there could be no
question of his pre-eminence among English kings. Two years
later Burgred, the new king of Mercia, turned to him for help
against the Britons of Wales, and afterwards received his
daughter in marriage.

Æthelwulf seems to have been a religious and unambitious
man, for whom engagement in war and politics was an unwelcome consequence of rank. Early in 855, after reigning
for nearly sixteen years, he undertook a pilgrimage to Rome,
leaving the government of his kingdom to Æthelbald, his
eldest surviving son. He spent twelve months at Rome, and
he seems to have passed the summer and early autumn of 856
at the court of Charles the Bald, king of the West Franks. On
1 October, at Verberie-sur-Oise, he married Judith, Charles's
daughter. She can only have been thirteen years of age, and
the marriage should probably be regarded as nothing more than
a demonstration of alliance between two kings threatened by
the same enemy. On, if not before, his return to England,
Æthelwulf learned that his eldest son and some of the leading
men in Wessex were resolved that he should not be received as
king, and to avoid a civil war he agreed to a division of the
kingdom, leaving Wessex to Æthelbald and taking for himself
Kent and the other parts of south-eastern England which
Egbert had annexed in 825. On the death of Æthelwulf in
858 these provinces passed Æthelberht, his second son. Æthelbald, who had married his father's young widow, apparently
without raising any scandal among the churchmen of her
country, died in 860, and the West Saxon kingdom was then
reunited under Æthelberht. Five years later he also died, presumably, like Æthelbald, without children, and Æthelred, his
brother, became king.

The accession of Æthelred coincided with a momentous
change in the character of the Danish attacks upon England. The
raids of the previous generation had been isolated enterprises,

[1] [See F. M. Stenton, *The Early History of the Abbey of Abingdon*, pp. 25–7 and also
C. E. Blunt in *Medieval Archaeology* iv (1960), pp. 6–7, where a suggestion by Sir
Frank Stenton is quoted, that a unique coin with the name of Beorhtwulf of Mercia
on one side and that of Æthelwulf on the other may commemorate the transfer of
Berkshire from Mercia to Wessex. The date of this transfer is approximately fixed
by the fact that Alfred, Æthelwulf's youngest son, was born at Wantage in 849.]

carried out by men anxious for a quick return to a friendly
land. But in the autumn of 865 the whole fabric of English
society was threatened by a great army, which landed in East
Anglia, prepared to spend many consecutive years in the
deliberate exploitation of all the opportunities for profit which
England offered. It was a composite host, and it included many
god-descended nobles who were regarded as kings by their
countrymen, and whose rank was recognized even by their
English enemies.[1] Although the names of its leaders are only
recorded incidentally by contemporaries,[2] it seems clear that the
host was brought to England by Ivar, surnamed the Boneless,
and Halfdan, sons of Ragnar Lothbrok, the most famous viking
of the ninth century. The remarkable unity of command implied by its subsequent movements was probably due to the
reputation of the family to which its leaders belonged.

It was the custom of the army to change its quarters each
autumn.[3] Its movements do not suggest that its leaders were

[1] As is shown, not only by the distinction between kings and earls marked in the
Chronicle, but by the arrangement of the English army at Ashdown, where King
Æthelred engaged the Danish kings, and his brother Alfred the Danish earls.

[2] The oldest authorities for the war are vague about the names of the original
Danish leaders. The late eleventh-century manuscript F of the *Chronicle* states that
the chief men in the army which killed St. Edmund in 869 were named Ingware
and Ubba. The statement is too late to have independent authority. In recording
the Danish raid on Devon in 878, all the pre-Conquest manuscripts of the *Chronicle*
describe the leader as 'the brother of Ivar and Halfdan'. The phrase shows that
the relationship between Ivar and Halfdan was generally known in Wessex at this
early date, and implies that they had previously been associated in the command
of the Danish army. Their unnamed brother has often been identified with a son of
Ragnar Lothbrok called Ubbi—the Ubba mentioned in MS. F of the *Chronicle*—
but there is no trustworthy evidence for the identification (see W. H. Stevenson,
Asser's Life of King Alfred, pp. 262–5). The best authority for Ivar's command of the
original Great Army is the *Chronicle* of Æthelweard (ed. Savile, p. 479*b*, ed. A.
Campbell, 1962, p. 35), which speaks of the arrival of the *classes tyranni Igw ares ab
aquilone*. The form *Igwares* proves that the statement comes from an Old English
source, and there is no reason to doubt that Æthelweard derived it from the very
early manuscript of the *Chronicle* which was the basis of his work. The tradition that
Ivar took the chief part in the events leading up to St. Edmund's martyrdom goes
back to the tenth century (*Memorials of St. Edmund's Abbey*, ed. Arnold, i, pp. 9 et
seqq.). Scandinavian sources, which ignore all leaders except the sons of Ragnar,
have a legendary character which impairs their value as evidence.

[3] The chronology of the *Chronicle* is based for this period on a year which, like
that of Bede (above, p. 76, n. 1), began in September before midwinter. It follows
that the movements of the Danish army, which usually took place in the autumn,
are consistently dated a year too late—that, for example, the first descent on East
Anglia, which the *Chronicle* places under 866, really occurred in the autumn of 865.
The chronology of these years was worked out conclusively by M. L. R. Beaven
(*E.H.R.* xxxiii. 328–42), whose reconstruction has been followed in this account of

following anything that can be called a plan of campaign. The history of their first attack upon Wessex, in 870, shows that their method of operation was to seize a defensible position, fortify it, and ravage the surrounding country systematically until its inhabitants bought peace from them. Most of these encampments were placed near a navigable river, by which reinforcements could reach the army easily. But the whole history of the invasion shows that, once established in a base on English soil, the Danes were independent of water-ways. The horses of a great part of East Anglia were at their service after the first year of their operations, and it was as a mounted force that they moved from York to Thetford in the autumn of 869. The cohesion and discipline imposed on the invaders by their life in a hostile country gave them the quality of a standing army, and the initiative in the first ten years of the war was always theirs.

For twelve months after their landing they remained in East Anglia, securing the horses necessary for their further movements, and carrying out raids which compelled the men of the country to buy peace. In the autumn of 866 they moved to York. On 1 November they occupied the city,[1] and they held it for four months before the Northumbrians attacked them. Northumbria at the moment was in a state of civil war. Osberht, its king, after a reign of eighteen years, had recently been rejected by his people in favour of a rival, not of royal birth, named Ælla. The contemporary account of these events in the *Chronicle* shows that he had barely come into power before the Danes were on him, and, if disproof were necessary, would disprove the famous Scandinavian legend that as king in York he had killed Ragnar Lothbrok, the father of Ivar and Halfdan, by throwing him into a pit infested with snakes. It is clear from the course of events that Osberht, Ælla's enemy, was still at the head of a considerable following when the Danes came to York, and that the English assault on the city was postponed until the kings had been brought to the point of uniting their forces. The attack was made at last on 21 March 867.[2] The

the war. The date at which the *Chronicle* reverted to a midwinter beginning of the year is still under discussion. See D. Whitelock, 'On the Commencement of the Year in the Saxon Chronicle' in the 1952 reprint of Earle and Plummer, *Two of the Saxon Chronicles Parallel*, ii, pp. cxli–cxlii.

[1] Roger of Wendover, *Flores Historiarum*, ed. Coxe, i, p. 298.
[2] *Symeonis Monachi Opera*, ii, R.S., p. 106; *Flores Historiarum*, i, p. 298.

Northumbrians forced their way through the ill-repaired Roman walls of the city, but were unable to maintain their ground. Both their kings perished, with eight of their ealdormen, and the survivors bought peace.[1] Later in the year the Danes established an obscure Englishman named Egbert as tributary king of Northumbria,[2] and in the autumn they left that country for a time and took winter quarters in Mercia, at Nottingham.

Burgred, king of Mercia, had married the sister of Æthelred, king of Wessex. It was therefore natural that he should ask for West Saxon help at this crisis. He was joined in front of Nottingham by Æthelred and Alfred, his brother, but the Danes declined a general engagement and in the end the Mercians bought peace from them. In the autumn of 868 the invaders returned to York, and twelve months later they descended again on East Anglia, establishing their winter quarters at Thetford. Within a few weeks of their arrival,[3] at or near Hoxne in Suffolk, they met and defeated an army led by Edmund, the East Anglian king. Either in the battle, or, more probably, as a captive in their hands, Edmund was killed. The contemporary West Saxon author of the *Chronicle* records his death without any sign of interest, but within a quarter of a century he had come to be honoured as a saint in East Anglia,[4] and the early development of his cult suggests very strongly that a basis of fact underlay the legend of his martyrdom.

In the autumn or early winter of 870 the army moved from Thetford to Reading, in Wessex, and established itself in a camp formed by an earthwork drawn between the rivers Thames and Kennet, which meet on the east of the town. Owing to the local interests of the one contemporary chronicler whose work

[1] The statement that 8 Northumbrian *duces* were killed in this campaign, which gives a useful indication of the scale of the fighting, only survives in the annalistic material preserved at York (*Flores Historiarum*, ed. Coxe, I, 298). A late record, but probably based on a good tradition, mentions the flight after the battle of York of two men called Denewulf and Beornwulf (*Chronicon Roskildense*, ed. M. Cl. Gertz, *Scriptores Minores Historiæ Danicæ Medii Ævi*, i, p. 16).

[2] *Flores Historiarum*, ed. Coxe i, 295.

[3] In the tenth century St. Edmund's martyrdom was commemorated on 20 November, and there is no serious doubt that this was the day of his death.

[4] The prevalence of the cult before the end of this period is proved by a large series of coins, bearing the saint's name, and struck, apparently, in East Anglia. There were 1,800+ of these coins in the Cuerdale hoard, the deposit of which may be dated *c.* 903, so that the issue and consequently the recognition of Edmund as a saint is likely to have started no more than a quarter of a century after his death in 869.

has survived, the struggle which followed is the only episode in the war which is known in any detail. It began, three days after the arrival of the Danes, with an engagement at Engle-field, to the west of Reading, in which a raiding party led by two Danish earls was scattered by Æthelwulf, the ealdorman of Berkshire. Four days afterwards King Æthelred and Alfred, his brother, unsuccessfully attacked the Danes in their camp at Reading. The English failure opened the surrounding country again to the Danish army, and during the next four days the greater part of it moved from Reading to the great ridge of chalk, then called Ashdown, which runs across central Berkshire from east to west. In the meantime, Æthelred and his brother had re-formed their army and were keeping in touch with the Danish movements. The Danish leaders decided to await them on higher ground, and drew up their army in two divisions, one led by the kings who were present in the host, and the other by the earls. In answer, the English army was also arranged in two divisions, Æthelred leading the force opposed to the Danish kings, and Alfred engaging the earls. The attack was opened by Alfred, his brother refusing to advance until he had ended the course of prayer with which he had begun the day. The battle was probably decided by the impact of the king's fresh troops on an army already heavily engaged. At the end of the day one Danish king and five earls had fallen, and the Danish army was in flight to its camp at Reading.

The success on Ashdown had no decisive influence on the course of the war. A fortnight later Æthelred and Alfred were defeated by the Danes at Basing, fourteen miles due south of Reading. Two months then passed without recorded incident. In the next general engagement, fought at a place called Meran-tun which cannot be identified, the English had the advantage until late in the day, but before its close the Danes had recovered the ground from which they had been driven. It is not im-possible that through their long experience as an organized force they had come to a point of tactical skill equal to the re-formation of ranks after a flight intended to deceive an enemy. Shortly after the middle of April 871 King Æthelred died. Earlier in the month the Danes had been reinforced by the arrival of a new army at Reading, and it was still uncertain whether the end of the year would not see the combined host in control of Wessex through a dependent king of its own appointment. Only a king of full age could defend the land, and although Æthelred left children, Alfred, his constant companion in the war, was immediately recognized as his successor. The opening of his reign was unfortunate. An English force was attacked and scattered by the Danes at Reading while Alfred was attending his brother's funeral at Wimborne, and within a month of his accession he himself was defeated at Wilton. After a year's fighting which included nine general engagements and innumerable skirmishes, the West Saxons were compelled at last to buy peace from the enemy. But they were still ruled by a descendant of their ancient kings.

Before the army left Thetford for Reading Ivar the Boneless, the most famous of its original leaders, had disappeared from English history. It is possible that he was identical with the viking named Imhar, described as king of the Norsemen of all Ireland and Britain, whose death is placed by Irish authorities in 873.[1] But there are many difficulties in the way of the identification, and nothing can be said with any certainty of Ivar's fate. For the four years after the West Saxon campaign Halfdan, his brother, was the most prominent figure among the Danes in England. In the autumn of 871 the army, leaving Wessex, took winter-quarters in London. The series of coins issued by viking rulers in England begins with pennies and halfpennies, apparently of this date, which bear Halfdan's name. The pennies of this coinage have a monogram representing the name of London on the reverse, and must have been struck within the city.[2] The existence of this currency, and the ease with which the Danes in East Anglia could afterwards co-operate with Danes raiding in Kent, suggest that a Danish force may have remained in London for some years after 872. But to the army as a whole it was no more than a temporary base from which new country could be brought under tribute. Its exactions are well illustrated by a document in which the bishop of Worcester records the sale of land in Warwickshire to a Mercian king's

[1] *Annals of Ulster*, under 872.

[2] Halfdan's London pennies are connected with the Mercian and West Saxon coinage of the period by an obverse type consisting of the figures of two seated emperors, which also appears on pennies of Alfred and Ceolwulf II of Mercia (G. C. Brooke, *English Coins*, pp. 25, 33–4, 44–6). It is hardly possible, as yet, to decide which of the three kings was the first to use this type. [Numismatists are now inclined to think that the Halfdan on these coins cannot be earlier than 886, see *Anglo-Saxon Coins*, p. 80.]

thegn on account of the immense tribute taken by the heathen when they sat in London.[1] It does not follow that Danish raids from London reached any part of the bishop's diocese. He may well have needed the money for a contribution to a general levy raised by the king of Mercia in order to buy peace. What the transaction shows is that the demands of the Danish army might affect the life of districts eighty miles or more from its base.

In the course of 872 the Danish control of Northumbria was threatened by a revolt against Egbert, the English noble whom the army had set up as king in 867. Nothing is known of its history, except that Egbert and Archbishop Wulf here of York were compelled to find refuge with Burgred, king of Mercia.[2] But it supplies a probable explanation of the movement from London to Northumbria with which the army began the campaigning season of 872–3. It can only have remained in Northumbria for a few weeks, for it fixed its quarters for the winter on the Trent, at Torksey, in the Mercian province of Lindsey.[3] Most probably it withdrew from the north because it did not wish to spend an unprofitable year fighting for the reduction of a land already plundered. In any case, it is certain that for the moment the Danes failed to re-establish their control of Northumbria. Egbert died, apparently still an exile, in 873, when, if not before, the Northumbrians chose another Englishman, named Ricsige, as their king, who recalled the archbishop and maintained himself in independence for the next three years.[4]

The plan of controlling a kingdom through a dependent ruler, which had recently failed in Northumbria, was carried through with complete success in Mercia. After the Danes had occupied Torksey for twelve months the Mercians bought peace from them for themselves and the men of their province of Lindsey. From Torksey, late in 873, the army moved to Repton in the centre of Mercia. After a war of which no

---

[1] C.S. 533.

[2] *Symeonis Monachi Opera*, ed. Arnold, ii, p. 110; Roger of Wendover, *Flores Historiarum*, ed. Coxe, i, pp. 323–4. The reception of the fugitives by Burgred in only mentioned by Roger of Wendover.

[3] *Chronicle* under 873 'Her for se here on Norþhymbre and he nam winter setl on Lindesse æt Tureces iege.' Historians have sometimes ignored the original movement into Northumbria. But it was clearly a separate operation from the taking of winter quarters at Torksey, and the Northumbrian rising of the previous year makes it intelligible.

[4] *Symeonis Monachi Opera*, ii, R.S., p. 110; *Flores Historiarum*, i, p. 325.

details are known Burgred, king of the Mercians, left England to spend the rest of his life at Rome. The Danes then appointed as king in his place one of his thegns, named Ceolwulf, upon a condition, secured by oaths and hostages, that the kingdom should be at their disposal whenever they might wish to occupy it, and that he should hold himself in readiness to serve them with all who would follow him. Fulfilment of this condition was exacted three years later, when the army appropriated half the Mercian kingdom for division among its members, and granted the other half to Ceolwulf. In the meantime he reigned in Mercia as a legitimate king, recognized by the church, and served by some, at least, of Burgred's ealdormen.[1]

For nine years the miscellaneous Danish force had acted as a single military unit. In the autumn of 874 it fell apart into two armies which were never reunited. Three kings named Guthrum, Oscytel, and Anund led their own men from Repton to Cambridge, where they remained for twelve months. Halfdan and his followers moved to the mouth of the Tyne. For a year he kept them engaged in expeditions against the Picts and the Britons of Strathclyde. But raids upon such poor and distant enemies can have brought little reward to the lower ranks of the army. England itself was becoming emptied of the wealth which made fighting profitable. The terms imposed on Ceolwulf of Mercia in 874 show that the leaders of the army were already planning a settlement on English soil, and in 876 Halfdan carried out the first of the three great partitions of territory which established Danish armies in more than a third of eastern England. The later history of the north shows that the region in which he planted his men correspond generally with the modern county of York. The numerous Danish placenames of this county, and in particular, those which contain

[1] Two charters of Ceolwulf II are known through copies made in the eleventh century at Worcester (*C.S.* 540, 541). The first of them is witnessed by the bishops of Worcester and Hereford, and by a third bishop named Eadberht who has not been identified. Two at least of the four *duces* who attest *C.S.* 541 appear as witnesses in charters of Burgred. A later charter, also from Worcester (*C.S.* 607), mentions an exchange of lands between the bishop and Ceolwulf, by which the king obtained the village of Water Eaton near Oxford. It is clear that in Ceolwulf's time the Mercian kingdom still came down to the middle Thames. Ceolwulf also issued coins, most of them similar to Alfred's British Museum type V, but there is a single coin of the 'two emperors' type (see above, p. 250, n. 2); nine coins of Ceolwulf are known today, by six moneyers of whom at least three worked for Alfred in the earlier part of his reign. This shows that Alfred was prepared to combine with the man whom the chronicler (annal 874), calls 'a foolish king's thegn'.

personal names not otherwise found in England[1] give some idea of the intensity of the settlement. It was not until the tenth century that there was any considerable Scandinavian immigration into the country north of the Tees or west of the Pennines. For the present, the continuity of life was maintained there under English rulers· such as King Ricsige, who died in this year, his obscure successor King Egbert II, who is known to have reigned beyond the Tyne,[2] and a noble named Eadwulf, who ruled at Bamburgh until 913 and was remembered as a friend of King Alfred.[3] Halfdan himself appears to have left England soon after the establishment of his men in the country around York. There is some reason to think that he joined the Danes who were fighting at the time in northern Ireland, and he may well be identical with the Danish king named Albann who was killed near Strangford Lough in 877.[4]

While Halfdan was dividing out Yorkshire among his men the army of Guthrum, Oscytel, and Anund was attacking Wessex. Late in 875 it moved from Cambridge to Wareham, and devastated the country around.[5] A large part of the original Danish host had followed Halfdan to the north, and in the autumn of 876, after a year of fighting, the West Saxons were able to treat with their enemies on equal terms. The Danes took money from them, but on the other hand surrendered hostages, and swore 'on their holy armlet' that they would leave Wessex—an oath more solemn than any which they had taken in their dealings with other peoples. Their movements

[1] Such as Belgr, Blandr, Feitr, Flatr, Hiarne, Morðr, Nagli, Kausi, Slengr, Skyti, Sprok, Thrylli, which occur in the place-names Bellerby, Blansby, Faceby, Flasby, Harmby, Marderby, Nawton, Cowesby, Slingsby, Skidby, Sproxton, Thirlby. Each of these place-names is mentioned in Domesday Book. There are innumerable Yorkshire place-names which contain personal names recorded in later English sources. Many of these place-names may well have arisen in the ninth century, but they are not, in themselves, evidence of early settlement. See F. M. Stenton, *C.P.*, pp. 308–13.

[2] *Symeonis Monachi Opera*, R.S. ii, p. 111.

[3] His death is recorded by Æthelweard (ed. A. Campbell, p. 53), who describes him as commander at Bamburgh. His friendship with Alfred is mentioned in the mid-eleventh-century *Historia de Sancto Cuthberto* (*Symeonis Monachi Opera*, R.S., i, p. 209).

[4] The *Annals of Ulster*, when recording his death, describe him as king of the Black foreigners, or Danes, and state that he was fighting with the White foreigners, or Norsemen.

[5] The authority for the devastation is Æthelweard (ed. A. Campbell, p. 41), who also says that the Danish army had combined with a 'western army'. See 'The Thriving of the Anglo-Saxon Ceorl', in *C.P.*, p. 387, n. 1.

were watched by a West Saxon army, but they evaded it—by a night march, according to the *Chronicle*—and threw themselves into Exeter. There they were held on the defensive. A fleet, bringing them reinforcements, was destroyed by a storm off Swanage, and in the summer of 877 they moved under something like compulsion from Exeter to Gloucester. Their return to Mercian territory was immediately followed by the dismemberment of the Mercian kingdom foreshadowed in the agreement of 874. Before the end of the year they had divided Mercia and its dependent provinces into two great regions, of which one was left under the rule of King Ceolwulf, and the other partitioned among those in the army who wished for a share in it.

The region thus partitioned cannot be defined closely. In the south of what had been the Mercian kingdom there was much fighting between Danes and Englishmen during the next thirty years, and no evidence bearing on its condition immediately after 877 has survived. In the north the region covered by the division certainly included the medieval shires of Lincoln, Nottingham, Derby, and Leicester. The local nomenclature of this country is intensely Scandinavian and, like that of Yorkshire, contains many Danish personal names not found again in England. The oldest document which illustrates its social organization—a code of Æthelred II—shows that in language and legal custom it was then a Danish rather than an English land. As late as the thirteenth century it contained a large number of independent peasant landowners who were still giving Danish personal names to their children and Danish nicknames to one another. Even without the direct evidence for the division of Mercia in 877 these facts would suggest that this country had at some time been partitioned among the rank and file of a Danish army. To the south of the Welland the evidence for an intensive Danish settlement dwindles rapidly. Danish place-names become rare; and although there were many free peasants in the southern midlands on the eve of the Norman Conquest, they were inferior both in number and in tenacity of status to the men of their class further to the north. On the other hand, the mere rarity of Danish place-names does not disprove Danish settlement, and even in the eleventh century the free peasants of the southern midlands were numerous enough to distinguish the social structure of this region from that of the shires towards the west. There is no evidence of any large-scale Scandinavian immigration into this country later than 877, and it is most probable that the division of that year covered with varying intensity the whole eastern half of the Mercian kingdom.

Not all the army took part in this division. Gloucester was held in force throughout the last months of 877. In the second week of 878 a large army set out from the town and descended on Chippenham. Its leader was Guthrum, apparently the last survivor of the three kings who had occupied Cambridge in 874. In all the fighting of recent years a Danish host had never changed its quarters at mid-winter, and the unexpected occupation of Chippenham restored to the Danes the initiative they had lost during their last invasion of Wessex. Within a few weeks they had received the submission of a large part of the West Saxon people. Others had escaped beyond the sea, and King Alfred himself had fallen back into the more inaccessible parts of Wessex west of Selwood. The stories of his adventures at this time, which first appear in writing in the twelfth century, are only romantic embellishments of a very real state of distress. One important English success was won early in the year. A nameless viking, believed to be the brother of Ivar and Halfdan, who had crossed to Devon from south Wales with twenty-three ships, was killed with more than eight hundred of his men by a company of king's thegns whom he was attempting to besiege on Countisbury Hill. But at Easter 878, when King Alfred withdrew into the Isle of Athelney, there was every likelihood that before the end of the year Wessex would have been divided out among the members of a Danish army.

That it escaped this fate was due to King Alfred. By constantly engaging Danish raiding parties from his base at Athelney he showed that resistance was still possible. After seven weeks of such fighting he was strong enough to begin operations against the main Danish army. At the head of the men of Somerset, Wiltshire, and Hampshire west of Southampton Water, he met the enemy at Edington, fifteen miles to the south of its camp at Chippenham, and won what proved to be the decisive battle of the war. The broken Danish army was able to reach Chippenham, and held out in its camp there for a fortnight. It then agreed to terms in which an undertaking that its king should be baptized was added to an undertaking that it

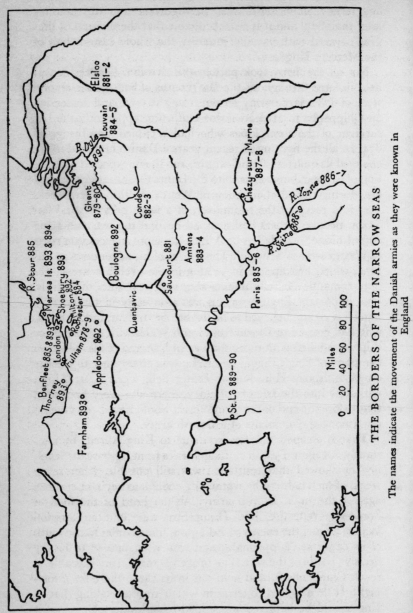

THE BORDERS OF THE NARROW SEAS

The names indicate the movement of the Danish armies as they were known in England

R. Stour 885
Mersea Is. 893 & 894
Shoebury 893
Benfleet 885 & 893
Thorney 893
Milton 892
London
Rochester 884
Fulham 878-9
Appledore 892
Farnham 893
Eisloo 881-2
Louvain 884-5
R. Dyle 891
Ghent 879-80
Condé 882-3
Boulogne 892
Saucourt 881
Amiens 883-4
Quentavic
Chézy-sur-Marne 887-8
R. Yonne 886-7
R. Seine 885-9
Paris 885-6
St. Lô 889-90

Miles
0 20 40 60 80 100

should itself leave Wessex. Three weeks later King Guthrum and thirty of his chief men were entertained by Alfred for twelve days at Aller near Athelney, where Guthrum was baptized, receiving from Alfred, his godfather, the English name Athelstan.[1] In the meantime, and indeed throughout the summer of 878, the Danish army, which was still formidable, remained at Chippenham. But in the autumn it moved to Cirencester, in English Mercia, and twelve months later it turned away from the south and proceeded to a systematic occupation of East Anglia under Guthrum, its king.

The movements of the Danish armies between 865 and 879 open a new phase of English history. In 879, of the four independant kingdoms which had existed at the middle of the century. Wessex alone survived in its entirety. Within the limits of what had been the Mercian, Northumbrian, and East Anglian kingdoms three large armies had now found a permanent settlement. On the surface, the outstanding feature of the next seventy years is the imposition of West Saxon rule on the descendants of these alien colonists. The unrecorded development of an Anglo-Danish society in the parts which they had occupied was of no less significance for the future. The strength of the Danish element in its composition varied widely between one district and another. But it was the dominant strain everywhere, and it was with reason that legal writers of the Norman age described the whole of this country, collectively, as the Danelaw.[2]

Before Guthrum's army had completed the occupation of East Anglia, another viking force was coming together in northern waters. In the autumn of 878 this new army entered the Thames and took winter quarters at Fulham. Nothing is known of its activities at this time, and in November 879 it sailed for the Low Countries. Its subsequent movements on the Continent were closely watched from England, and the local defence did not collapse when a detachment landed in Kent. late in 884. The invaders besieged Rochester, but the town held out until King Alfred relieved it, and part of the Danish army immediately took again to the sea. The remainder gave hostages

---

[1] The ceremony at which he put off his baptismal dress took place at Wedmore, south of Axbridge.

[2] On the social, legal, and linguistic peculiarities of the Danelaw see below, pp. 506–25; also *C.P.*, pp. 136–65, pp. 298–313, and pp. 335–45.

as security that they would keep the peace, but nevertheless carried out two separate raids over the country south of the lower Thames.[1] The situation became dangerous through the support given to the raiders by the Danes of East Anglia. There is no evidence that the raiding touched any part of central Wessex, but the allied armies were still unbeaten when they left West Saxon territory.[2] In reprisal for the part taken by the East Anglian Danes in the war Alfred sent a fleet into their waters. It captured sixteen viking ships off the mouth of the Stour, though it was defeated by a larger Danish force before it returned to harbour. But the events of the year had shown that the chief danger to the security of Wessex now came from the land rather than the sea, and, in particular, that there was urgent reason for an advance of the English boundary in the direction of East Anglia.

The situation was met in 886 by a West Saxon occupation of London. It is possible that the city had contained a Danish garrison ever since Halfdan left it in the autumn of 872. In any case, the observation of a contemporary writer that Alfred obtained it 'after the burning of towns and the slaughter of peoples' proves that a war was necessary for its reduction.[3] With the repair of its walls and the establishment of an English garrison behind them, London, which had counted for nothing

---

[1] The activities of these raiders and the support which they received from East Anglia are only known from the chronicle of Æthelweard (ed. A. Campbell, p. 44). The context of the passage shows that Æthelweard at this point was following a text of the *Chronicle* closer to the original than any of the copies which have survived. (F. M. Stenton, *C.P.*, pp. 106–15.)

[2] According to Æthelweard, pp. 44–5, they descended suddenly on Benfleet in Essex, and then dispersed.

[3] Asser, *Life of King Alfred*, ed. Stevenson, p. 69. The statement of Asser, who was not only contemporary but intimate with King Alfred, is decisive on this point. Asser does not state that London itself was besieged by Alfred; and the *Chronicle* represents Alfred's operations in regard to the city by the ambiguous word *gesette*, which means 'occupied' rather than 'besieged'. The question is complicated by a reference which occurs under 883 in four manuscripts of the *Chronicle* (B, C, D, E) to certain alms which Alfred promised to send to Rome and India when he and his followers 'besieged the army in London'. The statement is not found in the oldest manuscripts of the *Chronicle*, in Asser's *Life of Alfred*, or in Æthelweard's *Chronicon*, and it must be an interpolation in the common original of the four manuscripts which have been mentioned. Even so, the tradition for which it stands must have been current within a short time of Alfred's death, and it is good evidence that at one point in his reign he actually undertook a siege of London. As there is no specific record of any operations undertaken by Alfred against London before 886, it is highly probable that the passage which has been quoted is really a misplaced allusion to the events preceding his occupation of the city in the latter year.

in earlier wars against the Danes, became a national centre of resistance to enemies from every quarter. To Englishmen at the time, the occupation of London gave the first indication that the lands which had lately passed under Danish rulers might ultimately be reconquered. It made King Alfred the obvious leader of all those who, in any part of England, hoped for a reversal of recent disasters, and it was immediately followed by a general recognition of his lordship. In the words of the *Chronicle*, 'all the English people submitted to Alfred except those who were under the power of the Danes'.

The occasion marked the achievement of a new stage in the advance of the English peoples towards political unity. There had been earlier kings, such as Offa and Egbert, whose influence had extended to every English kingdom. But their position had always rested on the force at the disposal of the king who had made his way to supremacy. The acceptance of Alfred's overlordship expressed a feeling that he stood for interests common to the whole English race. As a national leader his authority outside his own kingdom was different in kind from that which had belonged to the lords of earlier confederacies. It was with a sound political instinct that the writer of the *Chronicle*, recording Alfred's death, threw back his mind to the events of 886, and reiterated the statement that he was king of all Englishmen who were free to give him their allegiance.

. He, for his part, respected the traditions of other kingdoms. London was not incorporated into Wessex. For a century and a half it had been a Mercian town, and Alfred now entrusted it to the man who was ruling in English Mercia. King Ceolwulf II, to whom the Danes had given this country, disappears from history in 877. Nothing is known of its government during the next six years,[1] but in 883 an ealdorman named Æthelred suddenly appears as its ruler. There is no good evidence as to his origin, nor as to the means by which he came into power.[2]

---

[1] A Mercian regnal list entered in *Hemingi Cantularium Ecclesiae Wigornensis*, ed. T. Hearne, i, p. 242 assigns Ceolwulf a reign of five years.

[2] On the strength of *C.S.* 537 it is sometimes stated that Æthelred had held high office in Mercia under King Burgred. This purports to be a charter written by order of Æthelred *Deo adjuvante Merciorum dux* to replace an earlier document which the heathen had carried away. King Burgred and his queen appear as witnesses to this new document. As a charter renewed under these circumstances would certainly have been issued in the king's name, it is clear that *C.S.* 537 cannot be genuine in its present form. There is no other evidence that Æthelred had been an ealdorman in Burgred's time.

But already in 883[1] he regarded King Alfred as his lord; he now received London from Alfred; and before the end of 889 he had married Æthelflæd, Alfred's eldest daughter.[2] Until his death in 911 he continued to be the loyal ally of Alfred and Edward his son; content with an ealdorman's title, but presiding over the Mercian council and leading the Mercian armies with an authority which was never challenged. In effect, his attitude made English Mercia a province of Wessex. The enlargement of his sphere of influence by the grant of London enabled Alfred to control a position vital to the security of his own kingdom without risking an annexation of Mercian territory.

It is probable that the terms of the settlement after the war of 886 are preserved in a famous document in which Alfred and all the councillors of the English people record the conclusion of a treaty with Guthrum and all the inhabitants of East Anglia.[3] In form it is a treaty between two equal powers. It begins with a definition of the boundary between their territories, and it ends with a clause forbidding migration from one kingdom to another and stating the conditions to be observed by those who wished to cross the frontier for trade. The line taken by this frontier shows that, although the centre of Guthrum's power undoubtedly lay in East Anglia, he had come to be accepted as king in Essex and in all the districts of the southern midlands which had been occupied by Danish armies after the division of Mercia in 877. The boundary is traced up the Thames, then up the Lea to its spring, then in a straight line to Bedford, and

---

[1] In a grant of privileges made in this year to Berkeley abbey Æthelred states that he is acting with the assent and under the attestation of King Alfred. *C.S.* 551; Harmer, *Select English Historical Documents*, p. 21.

[2] *C.S.* 561; a charter preserved in an eleventh-century copy which includes a number of ancient formulas (W. H. Stevenson, *Asser's Life of King Alfred*, pp. lxvi–vii). A somewhat less reliable charter (*C.S.* 557) suggests that the marriage had taken place before the end of 888. *C.S.* 547, in which Æthelflæd appears as Æthelred's wife, is dated in 880 and in the fifth indiction. These dates are incompatible, and as Æthelflæd was not of marriageable age in 880, the indiction date, which points to 887, is clearly preferable. But a dating clause which shows an inconsistency like this is unsatisfactory as evidence.

[3] There is no direct evidence for the date of the treaty. Some scholars, notably Liebermann (*Gesetze*, iii, p. 84), have taken it to represent an earlier agreement between Alfred and Guthrum which was broken by the Danes in 885. The great obstacle to any theory that would place the treaty before 886 is the statement that on the English side it was concluded by King Alfred and 'the councillors of all the English nation'. It is very difficult to believe that Alfred could have presided over a body which could be described in this way before the English nation, as a whole, accepted his overlordship in 886.

finally along the Ouse as far as Watling Street. Beyond this point it is probable that Watling Street formed the western boundary of Guthrum's country. No indication is given of the distance to which it extended beyond the Ouse, but the later organization of the Danelaw suggests that Guthrum's kingdom was bounded on the north by the upper courses of the Avon and the Welland, and that while Northampton lay within his territory, Leicester was the centre of an independent Danish army. Soon after Alfred's death the boundary laid down in the treaty was superseded by an advance of the Danes into southern Bedfordshire and northern Buckinghamshire, and it has had no discernible influence on the administrative geography of the country through which it runs. But it is of great interest as showing the formidable extent of the kingdom of which Guthrum had become the lord.

The central clauses of the treaty have an interest of another kind. There is nothing to suggest that Alfred claimed any supremacy over Guthrum or his followers. But there is no doubt that he regarded the treaty as an opportunity of securing the interests of the English inhabitants of Guthrum's kingdom. In the second clause of the treaty the complicated Anglo-Scandinavian society of Guthrum's kingdom was divided into two great classes. To the lower, which consisted of the freedmen of the Danes and English ceorls who had taken land at rent from a lord, there was assigned a wergild of 200 shillings, such as belonged to a free peasant in Wessex. The higher class consisted of all men above this social level, and included not only Danish and English nobles but also Danish settlers of peasant rank and English ceorls still farming their own land. The wergild for every man of this most miscellaneous class was fixed at eight half-marks of pure gold.[1] As the relative value of gold and

[1] Liebermann, *Gesetze*, i, p. 126; 'ealle we lætað efen dyrne, Engliscne and Deniscne to viii healfmearcum asodenes goldes, buton ðam ceorle ðe on gafollande sit, and heora liesengum, ða syndan eac efen dyre, ægðer to cc scillingum.' The artificiality of this division makes its interpretation difficult, and different historians have come to different opinions about it. The central problem is the position of the *ceorl ðe on gafollande sit*. Some scholars, notably Vinogradoff (*Growth of the Manor*, pp. 240–1), have regarded him as an ordinary free, landowning, peasant, and his *gafolland*, as land which he holds in his own right, but under tribute to the king. That the ceorl of this passage was a free man is certain. The great difficulty of Vinogradoff's interpretation lies in the strain which it puts on the word *gafol*. It was used in early times to cover both rent and tribute, but even if it is given the latter interpretation here, it still remains a most inadequate description of the complex of renders and services in which the independent ceorl was involved in

silver at this time is unknown, this sum cannot be equated with any wergild then recognized in southern England, but there is some reason to think that it approximated to that of a West Saxon noble. By accepting this clause Guthrum agreed, in effect, that there should be no discrimination of wergilds to the disadvantage of his English subjects. It was a notable concession, which affected the standing of the two races in civil causes as well as pleas of homicide, for the value attached in court to a man's oath depended on his wergild. It was rarely in this period that men of a defeated race received such terms from their conquerors, and their acceptance by Guthrum shows the reality of Alfred's power throughout southern England.

There is no such evidence of his influence beyond the Humber. The history of the Danish kingdom of York, always obscure, is at its darkest in this period. The one certainty is that a Northumbrian king named Guthfrith, who was a Christian, died at York on 24 August 895, and was buried in the minster.[1] It is probable that he was a friend of St. Cuthbert's clergy, and he was remembered with gratitude at Durham. But even before the Conquest a large mass of legend had gathered around his name,[2] and the facts, if any, which lie behind it are probably irrecoverable. The kings who followed him at York are no more than names. A large hoard of coins discovered at Cuerdale, near Preston, which seems to have been deposited in the first years of the tenth century, includes many pieces struck for two Northumbrian kings, named Cnut and Siefred. The coins of Siefred which have the name of a minting-place were all struck at York. Of those issued for Cnut, some were

relation to the king (below, pp. 287–92). It is in every way more probable that the phrase simply means what it says, and that, as Liebermann suggested (*Gesetze*, iii. 85), the 'ceorl who sits on gafolland' was a free-born peasant farming, not his own land, but land which he had taken at rent from a lord. In the eleventh century there were large numbers of free, rent-paying peasants in East Anglia, and there may well have been many men of this type in that country two hundred years earlier. It is a further argument for this interpretation that it brings the ceorl of this passage into line with the *gafolgelda* of Ine's laws, who is there equated socially with the free but economically dependent peasant known as the *gebur* (below, p. 474).

[1] *The Chronicle of Æthelweard*, ed. A. Campbell, p. 51.

[2] It is represented both in the mid-eleventh-century *Historia de Sancto Cuthberto* (*Symeonis Monachi Opera*, R.S. i, p. 203) and in the early post-Conquest chronicle printed by H. H. E. Craster ('The Red Book of Durham', *E.H.R.* xl (1925), p. 524). Versions of the Guthfrith-story current in Scandinavia are discussed and compared with the English evidence by Steenstrup, *Normannerne*, ii, pp. 93–103.

struck at York and others at the ancient port of Quentovic at
the mouth of the Canche. King Siefred is probably identical
with a Northumbrian raider of that name who, according to
Æthelweard, harried the English coast in 893, while Guthfrith
was still alive. Cnut is otherwise unknown.[1] It can only be said
that a king for whom coins were struck at both York and Quentovic must have been the ruler of a genuine viking state, maintained by sea-power.

The Christianity of King Guthfrith did not mean that the
Northumbrian Danes had ceased to feel a community of
interest with those of their race who were still raiding in other
countries. In the autumn of 892 a formidable Danish army,
which had been defeated in the Low Countries in the previous
year,[2] assembled at Boulogne and crossed to England. At the
first rumour of this invasion King Alfred took oaths from the
Northumbrian Danes, and hostages as well as oaths from those
in East Anglia, as security for the peace. But in spite of this
precaution they made common cause with the invaders immediately upon their landing. The long continuance of the war
which followed was chiefly due to this alliance. It more than
once prevented the English leaders from ending a campaign
conclusively, and it created diversions of the English forces at
critical moments. It was through their power at sea that the
Danes of Northumbria and East Anglia chiefly influenced the
course of the war. Already before it began they had been building ships of war much larger than any at Alfred's command.
Raiders from Northumbria and East Anglia continued to harry
the coast of Wessex after the main war had ended, and the
recorded beginnings of the English navy lie in the small fleet
of large vessels built by Alfred in the hope of defeating them
while still at sea.[3]

---

[1] Many historians have identified him with King Guthfrith above, and have
taken 'Cnut' to be a byname of that king. That Cnut was originally a by-name,
meaning 'knot', seems certain. But it is extremely improbable that a king bearing
a name which, like Guthfrith, had ancient, and indeed royal, associations in
Scandinavia, should be represented on his coins by a mere nickname.

[2] At the battle of the Dyle, by Arnulf, king of the East Franks. The difficult
question of the point in the year at which the battle was fought is discussed by
R. H. Hodgkin, E.H.R. xxxix (1944), pp. 505-6.

[3] According to the Chronicle these ships, which were built to Alfred's own design,
were twice as long as those which they were intended to meet, and carried 60 oars
or more. Though smaller than the greatest war-ships of the eleventh century,
they were clearly larger than the vessels provided for the defence of medieval

The building of this fleet was only part of a remodelling of the national defences carried through in Alfred's later years. Already at the middle of the century it was becoming clear that the defence of the land was passing beyond the competence of the local levies of single shires. The systematic ravaging of Wessex by the Danes in 871, and the collapse of the West Saxon defences at the beginning of 878, impressed this lesson on the men of Alfred's generation. The most striking features of the war which began in 892 are the mobility of the English forces and the wide range of their movements. Their composition varied between one set of operations and another. One English army, which kept in touch with a retreating Danish host over a distance of more than a hundred miles, is described in a way which suggests that it consisted of nobles and their retinues.[1] The part played by the peasant militia of the shires is never brought out so clearly, but it was certainly not insignificant. The great weakness of the militia was its objection to service outside the district in which it was raised and its tendency to disperse before a campaign was over. No Anglo-Saxon king was ever strong enough to coerce a recalcitrant peasantry. But by allowing half the men liable for service to remain at home while the other half was out against the Danes, Alfred was able to keep his peasant levies in the field for a longer time and to use them for more elaborate operations than had been possible in any earlier war.

The defence of southern England against earlier invaders had always been hampered by the absence or rarity of fortifications within which the inhabitants of a threatened district could take refuge. By the early part of the tenth century no village in Sussex, Surrey, and Wessex east of the Tamar was distant more than twenty miles from a fortress which formed a unit in a planned scheme of national defence. These fortresses varied widely both in size and design. At Bath, Winchester, Porchester, Chichester, and Exeter the plan was probably determined by whatever then remained of the walls of a Roman town or fort.[2]

Norway, which had only 20 rowing benches on each side (Shetelig and Falk, *Scandinavian Archaeology*, pp. 372–3). [1] Below, p. 266–7.

[2] The defences of the Roman towns had proved inadequate against the earlier viking raids; Canterbury and London were taken by storm in 851, Winchester in 860; York was occupied by a Danish army in 866, London in 871–2, Cambridge in 875, Exeter in 876 and Gloucester in 877. The first *civitas* known to have been held effectively is Rochester in 884–5.

At Wareham, Wallingford, and Cricklade the Saxon fortress consisted of a large rectangular enclosure surrounded by a bank and ditch, and at Lydford in Devon, Christchurch in Hampshire, and Burpham near Arundel a defensible position was created by a line of earthwork drawn across the neck of a promontory. Each fortress was kept in repair, and garrisoned when necessary, by the men of the surrounding country. Responsibility for these duties was distributed among the villages protected by the fortress in accordance with the number of hides which each was reputed to contain. The arrangements for the defence of these fortresses in time of war were based on the principles that four men were needed to hold each perch of wall or earthwork, and that every hide within the district assigned to a fortress ought to supply one man for this purpose. The system was not completed before the reign of Edward, Alfred's son. The Roman fort at Porchester, which was used to fill a dangerous gap between Chichester and Southampton, was not acquired by the Crown until 904.[1] The details of the scheme are known only from the document of Edward's reign which is generally known as the 'Burghal Hidage'.[2] But there is good reason to believe that its outline was laid down by Alfred in the years immediately preceding the Danish invasion of 892. His contemporary biographer states that he was a builder of fortresses. In describing the war which began in 892 the writer of the *Chronicle* refers to the fortifications of Wessex, and to the troops who were detached from the militia for the purpose of holding them. The statement of Alfred's biographer that his subjects were unwilling to labour on these works is curiously borne out by the fact that the only resistance which confronted the invaders of 892 on their landing came from a few peasants sitting in a half-made fort. But the history of the war which followed implies that a new defensive system, based on a series of permanent garrisons, had come into being since the last invasion of England by a Danish army.

The invaders crossed from Boulogne to Kent in two great companies. The larger, which needed 250 ships for its transport,

[1] *C.S.* 613.
[2] Of which a critical edition is given by A. J. Robertson in *Anglo-Saxon Charters*, pp. 246–9. When the text is read continuously it becomes apparent that the organization which it records was brought into being for the sole purpose of providing garrisons for the fortresses. It gives no ground for any theory that the districts assigned to the fortresses were used as administrative as well as military units.

came to land in the mouth of the river Lympne, and entrenched itself at Appledore. The smaller, carried in 80
ships, occupied the royal village of Milton, at the head of a
creek opening into the channel between Sheppey and the
mainland. The larger army was led by a king whose name is
unknown; the smaller by a viking of some reputation in his
time, named Hæsten. Alfred, whose immediate object was to
keep the two armies from uniting, took up a position between
them. Within a few weeks he was able to impose a treaty upon
Hæsten, as a result of which he and his men left Kent for Essex,
and his two sons were baptized. In the late spring of 893 the
larger army, which had avoided any general engagement with
Alfred's main force, set out on a raid which extended as far as
Hampshire and Berkshire. It had turned again towards the
east, with the object of joining Hæsten's army on the coast of
Essex, when it was intercepted and defeated at Farnham by the
West Saxon militia under Edward, Alfred's eldest son. After a
flight of twenty miles it was driven in confusion across the
Thames at a point where there was no ford, and compelled to
take refuge in an island called Thorney, formed by two branches
of the river Colne near Iver, in Buckinghamshire. Alfred, who
was advancing from the west, was recalled by the news that an
army from Northumbria and East Anglia was attacking Exeter.
For the next six months he was unable to take an active part
in the main war. Edward, who was watching the Danes in
Thorney, was joined by Æthelred of Mercia with reinforcements from London. But their army was not strong enough for
an assault, and the Danes could not attempt to force their way
across the river, because their king was badly wounded. The
stalemate was ended by the offer of terms to the Danes which
stipulated that they should leave English territory, but left
them free to join their allies in the east.[1]

The result was a formidable Danish concentration at Benfleet in Essex,[2] where the ships from Appledore and Milton had
already been brought together, and Hæsten's men had made a

---

[1] The part played by Edward and Æthelred in the campaign and the terms on
which the Danes were allowed to leave Thorney Island are mentioned only by
Æthelweard (ed. A. Campbell, pp. 49–50).

[2] According to Æthelweard (ed. A. Campbell, p. 50), the Danes rejoined their
ships at Mersea Island, far to the north of Benfleet. Æthelweard's account of the
campaign, so far as it goes, seems to be well founded, and the movement which he
describes does not conflict with a later concentration at Benfleet.

camp. But an army composed of the militia of eastern Wessex, the garrison of London, and reinforcements from the west, attacked the camp while Hæsten was raiding in Mercia, and captured it, with the ships, the women and children, and the booty which it protected. The defeated army was soon rejoined by Hæsten's men, and the combined force established itself for a time in a new fort at Shoebury, further down the river. But there was no prospect of making good its recent losses by short-distance expeditions from Shoebury, and after it had received reinforcements from East Anglia and Northumbria it set out on a great raid up the Thames valley, then to the Severn, and then up along that river. It was followed by Æthelred, ealdorman of Mercia, with the ealdormen of Wiltshire and Somerset and a force of king's thegns drawn from every fortress in Æthelred's country and in Wessex east of the river Parret. The Welsh princes, who were directly threatened by a Danish raid up the Severn, sent a contingent, and the Danes were held at last by a greatly superior force, in an island in the Severn at Buttington near Welshpool.[1] After a siege which lasted for many weeks they cut their way through the English force drawn up on the east bank of the river. The English claimed a victory, but the Danes still had the semblance of an army when they reached their base at Shoebury.

Before the summer was over they had organized another long-distance expedition. Its objective was Chester, where the deserted enclosure of the Roman city offered a base for operations in English Mercia, and reinforcement from the Scandinavian settlements in Ireland was possible. The army first moved from Shoebury into East Anglia, where it was joined by a large force of Northumbrian and East Anglian Danes. Leaving its women, ships, and booty in East Anglia, it then marched 'at a stretch, day and night' and occupied Chester before any English force could overtake it. But its position was made untenable through the drastic measures taken by the English leaders, who ordered a destruction of all the corn and cattle in the neighbourhood. An attempt to advance into the midlands would have committed the Danes to a general

---

[1] This place has sometimes been identified with Buttington Tump near Chepstow. But the statement of the *Chronicle* that the Danes reached it after moving *up þe Sæferne* is decisive. There are still traces of an island between two branches of the Severn at the northern Buttington, but the construction of a railway across the site has changed its character.

engagement on the edge of a devastated country. When starvation was on them they turned away from English territory into Wales, and remained there from the autumn of 893 until the summer of 894. The *Annales Cambriae*, which place a Scandinavian devastation of Brycheiniog, Gwent, and Gwynllwg five years before King Alfred's death, are probably referring to this expedition, which would therefore seem to have ranged across the whole of Wales down to the northern shore of the Bristol Channel. At its conclusion the Danes, avoiding English Mercia, made their way towards the east deviously across Northumbria, East Anglia, and the territories of the Danish armies of the northern midlands.

Without any delay at their East Anglian base, they returned in their ships to the estuary of the Thames and formed a temporary camp on Mersea island. In the autumn they towed their ships up the Thames and the Lea to a point twenty miles above London, and maintained themselves there, apparently without any organized opposition, until the summer of 895. They were then dislodged by King Alfred, who had taken up a position in the neighbourhood in order to protect the men of the country while they were harvesting. At some point below the Danish camp he obstructed the course of the Lea, so that the Danish ships could not be brought downstream, and planted two forts, one on each side of the river, in order to protect the new work. The Danes then abandoned their camp, sent their women into East Anglia, and, in one of the astonishing marches of which they were capable in an emergency, struck across the midlands to the site by the Severn afterwards known as Bridgnorth. They were followed by an English force, but there is no record of any engagement, and they remained in their camp by the Severn throughout the winter of 895 and the spring of 896. In the following summer they dispersed at last, some joining their allies in East Anglia and Northumbria, while others, who had made nothing by the war, left England in hope of better fortune with the vikings on the Seine.

The initiative had remained with the Danes throughout the war. A Danish movement was generally countered by an English concentration, and it is clear that there was never any serious danger of a collapse of the English defence such as had occurred in 878. But the English leaders were never able to bring a campaign to a decision which left the Danes unable to renew the attack. In all their operations the Danish armies had the advantage of a secure base in the territory won by earlier invaders in the north and east. The alliance between Alfred and Æthelred of Mercia was neutralized by the understanding which existed between the leaders of the Danish armies and the Danish rulers in East Anglia and Northumbria. Their entry into the war was a natural reaction against the ascendancy which belonged to Alfred after his capture of London. Historically it is important, because it opened a new period in which the Danish colonies in the north and east appear as the avowed enemies of the new state formed by the political association of Wessex and English Mercia. Between 896 and 910 there were at least four separate occasions when armies from one or other of these colonies invaded English territory. Three years after the dispersal of their allies from the Continent the country under English rule was thrown again into confusion by raids from Northumbria.[1] The kingdom of Wessex and the ealdormanry of Mercia were still on the defensive when King Alfred died, on 26 October 899.[2]

His place in history is not affected by the inconclusiveness of his later wars. His early victories had saved the elements of English culture and learning from utter obliteration, and the relations which he maintained with Æthelred of Mercia had given a new unity of command to the forces available for their defence. He had created at least a rudimentary organization for the protection of his people, and had made the greatest of English towns an outpost against the national enemy. On any estimate, he was the most effective ruler who had appeared in western Europe since the death of Charlemagne. But beneath his preoccupation with duties, often of desperate urgency, there was always a sense of imponderable values. No other king of the Dark Ages ever set himself, like Alfred, to explore whatever in the literature of Christian antiquity might explain the problems of fate and free will, the divine purpose in the ordering of the world, and the ways by which a man comes to knowledge.

His unique importance in the history of English letters comes

---

[1] *The Chronicle of Æthelweard*, ed. A. Campbell, p. 51.

[2] The date of Alfred's death was established by W. H. Stevenson in 1898 (*E.H.R.* xiii, pp. 71–7) on the basis of an early tenth-century *computus*, which states that the year 912 is the thirteenth year of the reign of King Edward. For a wider survey of the evidence, which points to the same conclusion, see M. L. R. Beaven in *E.H.R.* xxxii (1917), pp. 526–31, and F. M. Stenton in *C.P.*, pp. 79–84.

from his conviction that a life without knowledge or reflection was unworthy of respect, and his determination to bring the thought of the past within the range of his subjects' understanding. The translations of ancient books by which he tried to reach this end form the beginning of English prose literature. In a preface to the first of his own translations[1] Alfred described the condition of English learning at the time of his accession. Very few of the clergy south of the Humber, not a single clerk in Wessex, and not many clerks beyond the Humber, knew the English equivalent of their services or could turn a letter from Latin into English. Even before the churches throughout England had been plundered by the Danes those who served them could make little use of the books which they contained. By 894, the year in which he was writing, there were once more learned bishops in the land, and he had himself become the centre of a group of literate clergy. With their aid he proposed to carry through a scheme for the education of his people which is very remarkable for its range and imaginative simplicity. He himself and his learned helpers would first translate certain books 'most necessary for all men to know', and then all the free-born youth of England who could be supported at the task should be sent to school until they could at least read English writing. Thereafter, those who were needed for another calling should leave school, and those for whom the priesthood was designed should turn to Latin. To Alfred the Latin culture of the century before his own represented the highest achievement of learned endeavour. For his own writings he claimed at most the virtue that, through them, individuals capable of higher things might come to understand the greater scholarship of the past.

In a retrospect extending over more than twenty years details become blurred, and it is probable that Alfred, writing some twenty years later, heavily over-painted the depression of English learning in 871. He certainly did less than justice to the Mercian scholarship of that time. Seven of his literary helpers are known by name, and four of them were of Mercian origin. The highest in rank was Plegmund, a priest to whom Alfred gave the see of Canterbury in 890. The oldest of the group was probably Werferth, bishop of Worcester, who was consecrated

[1] The *Cura Pastoralis* of Gregory the Great, ed. H. Sweet (Early English Text Society), p. 2.

to that see in 873, and whose schooling must have begun some years before the middle of the century. The series of books which was to be the foundation of the new English learning began with a translation by Werferth of the collection of holy legends known as the *Dialogues of Pope Gregory the Great*. With Werferth and Plegmund were associated Werwulf, a member of Werferth's episcopal household, and a priest named Athelstan, of whom nothing more is known. It is unlikely to be through accident that each of these scholars came from Mercia, and that two at least of them came from the Severn valley. So far as is known, western Mercia was never devastated in force by the army of Ivar and Halfdan. It is highly probable that Alfred's four Mercian assistants represented a tradition of learning which had descended to his time without interruption from Mercian schools established in or before the eighth century.

Three of Alfred's recorded helpers came from foreign countries. From Fulco, archbishop of Rheims, the most prominent ecclesiastic of the Frankish kingdom, he obtained a learned monk named Grimbald, whom the archbishop had taken into his service from the monastery of St. Bertin at St. Omer.[1] A less eminent monk named John, from the land of the continental Saxons, was placed by Alfred in charge of a monastic community largely composed of strangers from Gaul, which he had founded in Athelney. It was an unhappy community, planted on a desolate site, and tension between the austere John and certain of his monks broke at last into a conspiracy through which he nearly lost his life. Neither Grimbald nor John has left much impression on literary history. But the third of the foreign scholars, a priest from St. David's named Asser, became Alfred's friend, and described his character and the environment of his life in a very naïve, but sincerely intimate biography.

It was written before any of Alfred's own translations had appeared, but it tells enough about his early life to show the way by which he came to authorship.[2] It is clear that he had a natural intellectual curiosity, which was stimulated by the extraordinary experience of two journeys to Rome,[3] undertaken

---

[1] The difficult questions connected with the life of Grimbald are the subject of a critical study by P. Grierson, *E.H.R.* lv (1940), 529–61.

[2] On all that relates to Asser the definitive authority is the edition of his *Life of King Alfred* by W. H. Stevenson (Oxford, 1904) supported by D. Whitelock, see below p. 696.

[3] In 853 and 855 (*Chronicle* under 853; Asser's *Life*, ed. Stevenson, pp. 7, 9,

before he had reached the age of seven. He was never satisfied with the conventional life of a young West Saxon noble.
On the other hand, through lack of teachers he remained
unable to read even English writing until he had passed his
twelfth year. Asser's description of his later studies, which
relates to the years between 887 and 893, shows that at the
beginning of this period he was still unable to read Latin, and
that his knowledge of works written in that language was gained
by listening to one or other of the scholars whom he had called
to his court. But at Martinmas 887, with Asser's help, he began
to read selected passages of Latin and render their sense into
English. Asser's account of his studies does not carry them beyond this stage. But it was undoubtedly during the years of
peace between 887 and 892 that he acquired the knowledge
of Latin which enabled him to produce English translations of
five elaborate Latin works between 892 and his death in 899.

The series begins with a translation of the famous work
generally known as *Cura Pastoralis*, in which Gregory the
Great, by describing the responsibilities of a bishop, had excused his own unwillingness to accept the papacy. In the ninth
century, as in the age of Gregory the Great, no rigorous line
could be drawn between the pastoral duties of a bishop and
those of the clergy in charge of individual parishes. The *Cura
Pastoralis* was for many centuries regarded as a manual for the
guidance of the parish priest. But to Alfred its chief significance
lay in its insistence on the bishop's responsibility for the instruction of the laity. The success of Alfred's own educational
design depended on the assiduity of his bishops in teaching, and
in seeking out the youths and children from whom the teachers
of the next generation could be drawn. To Gregory the ideal
bishop was both a ruler and a teacher, and to revive the memory
of this ideal in England Alfred sent a copy of his translation to
every cathedral church in his kingdom. The translation follows
its original very closely, though even so it is impressionistic
rather than literal. It was brought into being very slowly,
after Alfred's helpers had explained the Latin text to him,
passage by passage. It is usually regarded as the first of Alfred's

179–85, 193–4). In 853, when he was accompanied by a large retinue of his
father's subjects, Pope Leo IV invested him with the honorary dignity of a Roman
consul—an incident which the compiler of the *Chronicle* afterwards confused with
ordination to kingship. In 855 he was taken to Rome by King Æthelwulf himself.

books, but it is not mentioned by Asser, and therefore most scholars are inclined to attribute it to the year 894.

Although the order in which Alfred's writings are placed depends on internal evidence, it has generally been agreed that after translating the *Cura Pastoralis* he passed immediately to one or other of the two historical works included in the series—Orosius' history of the ancient world and the *Historia Ecclesiastica* of Bede. The organization of English society had undergone few material changes in the period between Bede and Alfred, and there are many passages in which Bede's indications of rank or office become clearer through a rendering into ninth-century English. But intrinsically, the translation of the *Historia Ecclesiastica* is the least interesting of the works which can be attributed to Alfred. In substance, it is simply a close rendering of the Latin text, and it contains little, if any, extraneous matter of the kind which in other works illustrates the character of Alfred's thought. The possibility that the translation may be by another hand than Alfred's is strengthened by traces of an Anglian dialect in the oldest manuscripts of the book, and, more definitely, by peculiarities of style not apparent in Alfred's undoubted writings. That the version was produced under Alfred's influence need not be doubted, but its right to a place in the Alfredian canon is by no means secure.

The authenticity of the translation of Orosius is more firmly established, and it is a work of a different quality. In form, the original is a series of annals. Alfred preserved the annalistic arrangement of his text, but expanded it into what became almost a new book by incidental notes and illustrations. The most interesting of them were drawn from his own experience in war and affairs, and the work as a whole might be described as a representation of ancient history from the standpoint of a ninth-century king. But it is turned into a primary authority for Alfred's own time by a section in which he set down whatever he had been able to learn about the countries and peoples of northern and central Europe.[1] No one before him had attempted such a survey. As a piece of systematic geography it stands alone in the Dark Ages, and at most disputable points its accuracy has been confirmed by modern research. Much of it was obtained directly from men who knew

---

[1] Discussed most recently by R. Ekblom in *A Philological Miscellany presented to Eilert Ekwall* (1942), pp. 115–44.

the North. Alfred learned the trend of the outer coasts of
Scandinavia from a rich Norwegian named Ohthere,[1] who
lived within the Arctic Circle and had sailed from his home as
far as the White Sea in one direction and the port of Slesvig in
the other. Another traveller named Wulfstan came to Alfred's
court and described a voyage from Slesvig to the port of 'Truso'
near the mouth of the Vistula. Their stories were retold by
Alfred in paragraphs which are deservedly among the most
familiar examples of Old English narrative prose.

Towards the end of Alfred's life the character of his work
changes. In his latest books he passes from the representation
of concrete history and geography into the world of ideas.
The most elaborate of the works which he translated—the *De
Consolatione Philosophiae* of Boethius—touched an aspect of life
familiar to all men of Alfred's age. It was written by a statesman waiting for a violent death after a sudden reversal of
fortune. Such vicissitudes formed part of the staple matter of
heroic verse. It was a principle of the morality which poets
shared with men of action that, through the strength of his
will, a man should rise superior to fate. To Alfred it seemed
that Boethius had given a Christian value to this idea, and had
shown that disaster was irrelevant to one whose mind had been
trained to apprehension of the divine wisdom. It cannot be
claimed that Alfred always understood this difficult text. But
by an abundant use of simile and metaphor, and by developing
the Christian implications which underlie the argument of
Boethius, Alfred gave to those for whom he was writing at least
an impression of this last memorial of ancient thought.

The last of Alfred's books stands apart from the rest of the
series. It opens with a fairly close rendering of the first book of
the *Soliloquies* of St. Augustine, and to the end it is dependent
on Augustine's thought. But Alfred himself described it as a
collection of 'blossoms', and although, being cast throughout
into the form of a dialogue, it has an appearance of unity, it is
plainly founded on an anthology of passages relating to the
central problems of immortality, and the way in which the
soul comes to a knowledge of God. As in all Alfred's later
writings, argument is continually reinforced by illustrations
drawn from ordinary life. Some of them are of considerable
historical importance; a passage in which Alfred asks rhetori-

[1] In Old Norse Óttarr.

cally whether a man should not recognize a letter under his lord's seal as an expression of his lord's will is remarkably early evidence for the use of the sealed document in England. But the chief interest of the book lies in its preface, in which Alfred represents his own literary work under the symbol of a man collecting timber in a great wood, where others, like himself, might find materials for every kind of building. The metaphor is the one sustained piece of imaginative prose in Alfred's writings, and it clearly expresses the attitude of a man conscious that his own work is nearly done, who is only anxious that younger men should follow him.

A mere description of Alfred's writings cannot give any true impression of the heroic quality of his work. For the expression of thought and of more than the barest elements of learning, English prose was still an untried instrument when he began to write. The management of an elaborate sentence was an experimental business, and such proficiency as Alfred reached in this art came to him through the example of the Latin authors whose books he was translating. His literate friends made his work possible, but all the books which bear his name give the impression of an individual author struggling with a refractory language. His books remained an isolated achievement, for, as he would have wished, the phase of English learning which they represented came to an end with the development of a new Latin scholarship in the generation after his death. But his work showed the possibilities and limitations of English prose to later writers of greater skill, and his own books were still being copied in Norman England.[1]

In the preface to his translation of the *Cura Pastoralis* Alfred justifies his plan of turning 'necessary works' into English by observing that the Mosaic Law had been rendered into Greek, Latin, and all Christian languages. The passage forms a curious link between his literary work and his laws. Towards the end of his reign he issued a somewhat lengthy code, and he introduced it by the substance of three chapters of Exodus, the so-called 'golden rule' from St. Matthew's Gospel, and the letter sent by the apostolic synod at Jerusalem to the faithful in Antioch, Syria, and Cilicia. But the only object of this introduction was to acquaint his subjects with what Alfred regarded as a piece of model legislation. There is no trace of

[1] The *Soliloquies* has only been preserved in a twelfth-century manuscript.

any extraneous element in the text of his own laws, which are, indeed, remarkably conservative. In a short preface Alfred states that he has collected whatever in the laws of Ine of Wessex, Offa of Mercia, and Æthelberht of Kent he thought to be most just, rejecting many of their enactments, amending others, but not venturing to propose much new legislation of his own. On the other hand, there are important features in his laws which are not derived from any known source and may well be original. They include provisions protecting the weaker members of society against oppression, limiting the ancient custom of the blood-feud, and emphasizing the duty of a man to his lord. A religious king, whose own life had once depended on the loyalty of his men, might be expected to legislate in this spirit, and these provisions may be added to the evidence for Alfred's character which is supplied by his writings.

But Alfred's code has a significance in general history which is entirely independent of its subject-matter. In his preface Alfred gives himself no higher title than King of the West Saxons, and he names his kinsman Ine first among the three kings whose work had influenced his own. But the names of Offa and Æthelberht, which follow in the list, imply that Alfred's code was intended to cover, not only Wessex, but Kent and English Mercia. It thus becomes important evidence of the new political unity forced upon the various English peoples by the struggle against the Danes. Even without this adventitious interest it would still be a landmark in English legal history. It appeared at the end of a century in which no English king had issued laws. Everywhere in western Europe kings were ceasing to exercise the legislative powers which traditionally belonged to their office. In England alone, through Alfred's example, the tradition was maintained,[1] to be inherited by each of the two foreign kings who acquired the English throne in the eleventh century.

[1] This point is emphasized by Pollock and Maitland, *History of English Law* (ed. 2) pp. 19–20.

IX

THE STRUCTURE OF EARLY ENGLISH SOCIETY

THE Germanic peoples who descended on Britain in the late fifth century were not seeking their fortune in an unexplored land. Men who had taken part in the earlier raids upon the Saxon shore must have gained a detailed knowledge of its harbours and of the waterways which led to the interior. They must also have been familiar with the conditions of wind and weather which allowed a favourable crossing of the North Sea. Without such knowledge the migration to Britain, unique in any case among contemporary movements, could never have been attempted. It is significant that the few fifth-century expeditions of which later tradition preserved the memory have the scale of raids rather than migrations. The British coast in the fourth century must have often been visited by chiefs who came, like Ælle, with three ships, or, like Cerdic, with five. The withdrawal of the Roman coastal defences and of the military force behind them gave a new importance to the expeditions of Ælle, Cerdic, and their contemporaries. They could use the knowledge acquired by their nameless predecessors, choose the best harbours, and hold the neighbouring country until reinforcements came. They could prepare the way for a series of national migrations.

That such national movements followed in course of time is certain. An invasion of Britain by a small number of chiefs, each accompanied by his personal followers, might perhaps have conquered the midlands and the south, but would not have produced the social order that is afterwards found there. The earliest text that illustrates the social order of English society—the laws of Æthelberht of Kent—comes from the beginning of the seventh century. It reveals a class of nobles who may well represent the companions of Hengest and Oisc. But the basis of Kentish society in Æthelberht's time was obviously the free peasant landholder, without claim to nobility, but subject to no lord below the king. He was an independent

person with many rights. The laws which refer to him as head
of a family show him entitled to compensation for breach of his
household peace, for misconduct with his maidservant, for the
slaughter of one of his 'loaf-eaters'. If he himself were killed,
his slayer must pay a hundred golden shillings to his kinsfolk,
and fifty to the king, but nothing is said of any lord who might
require compensation for his slaying. If he stole from another
man of his class the king might take a fine from him, or even all
his goods, but he was not the man of a lord with a financial
interest in his misbehaviour. Throughout early English history
society in every kingdom rested on men of this type. Their
appearance in firm establishment upon the soil when Æthelberht was still reigning in Kent proves that the exploits of
chiefs, remembered by tradition, were only preliminary to
national movements of which nothing is told. The origin of the
free peasants of Æthelberht's laws must be sought in free
ancestors who had crossed the North Sea after Hengest and Oisc
had opened a good land for their settlement.

The West Saxon evidence points in the same direction. The
laws of Ine, with which this evidence begins, come from the last
years of the seventh century and reveal a complicated social
order, in which the aristocratic element was already important.
Nevertheless, in Wessex as in Kent, the free peasant formed the
basis of society. As an individual the normal West Saxon ceorl
may well have been of less social consequence than his Kentish
contemporary. His life was valued only at two hundred shillings,
each of five silver pennies, as against the wergild of one hundred
golden shillings—two thousand silver pieces—which belonged
to the Kentish ceorl.[1] But he filled a responsible position in
the state, and the law protected the honour and peace of his
household. He owed personal service in the fyrd, or national
militia; and unlawful entry through the hedge around his
premises, as through the defences around a nobleman's house,
was an offence of especial gravity when the fyrd was out. He
was required to join with others of his class in supporting his
king by contributions to a *feorm*, or food-rent. But it is as the
independent master of a peasant household that he stands out
most clearly in early West Saxon law.[2]

---

[1] On the whole subject of the Old English wergilds see H. M. Chadwick, *Studies
on Anglo-Saxon Institutions*, pp. 78–114.

[2] No early laws have come down from Mercia or Northumbria. But later

In every part of England except Kent the primitive unit of land-division was the tenement of a normal peasant, the holding which supported a ceorl and his household. In English documents such a holding is called a *hīd* or *hiwisc*—words represented by many different Latin phrases, of which *terra unius familiae* approaches most nearly to the true meaning. Everywhere except in Kent the 'hide' formed the basis of social organization. Responsibility for payment of the king's *feorm*, for service in the fyrd, and for all other public burdens was distributed over the country in terms of these peasant tenements. The size of the hide was essentially determined by the peasant's standard of life, and much that is now obscure in early English society would become plain if it were possible to get behind the hide of early documents to the real acres of which it was composed. Despite the work of many great scholars, the hide of early English texts remains a term of elusive meaning. With hardly an exception, documents older than the Norman Conquest ignore the acreage of the hides with which they are dealing, and the evidence which comes from the Norman period is meagre and contradictory. It points with reasonable clearness to the existence of a normal hide of 120 arable acres in Cambridgeshire, and suggests that hides had commonly been formed on this scale elsewhere in the eastern shires.[1] But it is equally clear that the normal hide of central Wessex was far smaller; there is good evidence that it amounted to 40 acres in Wiltshire, and at least approximated to this acreage in Dorset.[2] It is highly unsafe to argue closely from documents of the Norman age to conditions in the seventh century; but the conception of a peasant's normal holding was likely to be stereotyped by its employment as the basis of taxation, and it is hard to avoid the suspicion that the West Saxon ceorls of Ine's day may have been supporting life on far smaller resources than belonged to their contemporaries of similar status in Middle Anglia.

A famous passage in Ine's laws[3] shows the West Saxon ceorl in agricultural association with his neighbours. It may be

statements of custom show that there, as in Wessex, the ceorl's life was valued at 200 shillings, and there is nothing in the literary evidence to suggest that the midland or northern peasant was inferior in condition to his West Saxon contemporary.

[1] F. W. Maitland, *Domesday Book and Beyond*, pp. 476–83.
[2] J. Tait, 'Large Hides and Small Hides', *E.H.R.* xvii (1902), 280–2.
[3] c. 42.

translated: 'If ceorls have a common meadow or other share-land to enclose, and some have enclosed their share while others have not, and cattle eat their common crops or grass, let those to whom the gap is due go to the others who have enclosed their share and make amends to them.' Despite its reference to common crops or grass, this law is not evidence of any common ownership of arable or meadow. The various shares into which the meadows or fields were divided were obviously regarded as the property of individuals, each of whom must be satisfied in person if he suffers loss from his neighbour's default. It is of greater interest that there is no trace here or elsewhere in Ine's laws of any private lord, able to compel observance of the routine of agricultural life. It was necessary for the highest authority in the land—the king and his council—to provide a ruling for the settlement of disputes which in the middle ages would have fallen within the province of a manorial court. The ceorl of Ine's laws was essentially an individualist; owning the land which supported him, though farming it in association with his fellows, and responsible to no authority below the king for his breaches of local custom.

But the unique importance of this law is due to the agricultural system which it implies. Apart from this isolated text, there is no document earlier than the ninth century which throws light on agricultural practice, and the first records which illustrate its minuter details come from the eve of the Norman Conquest. Ine's law about straying beasts proves that an open-field system of agriculture existed in seventh-century Wessex. On more general grounds it is probable that such a system had also arisen by this time in the midlands, Lindsey, and Deira. Throughout this country in the middle ages, under suitable conditions of soil and local contour, the arable belonging to a particular community normally lay in great unenclosed expanses, over which the holding of an individual peasant was distributed in scattered strips. In eastern Yorkshire, Lincolnshire, and the eastern midlands this method of distribution seems to be earlier than the Danish invasions of the ninth century. It may well go back, there and in Wessex, to the beginning of permanent English settlement, for it agrees in general type with the system prevailing in north-western Germany.

A large part of England never came under the open-field system. It is not found in the far north nor the north-west, along

the Welsh border or in Devon. It only came to full development in country which had been settled before the end of the
sixth century, and even there wide regions lay outside its
scope. In Kent a separate race followed a separate agrarian
tradition, and in Essex infertile soil and ancient woodland made
open-field cultivation unprofitable. Nothing is known of the
rural economy of East Anglia before the end of the eleventh
century, and the medieval evidence for that country has been
only partially explored. But it is at least clear that an open-
field system of the midland type never prevailed there, and it
seems on the whole most probable that the first settlers of those
parts held their arable in compact blocks, which were gradually
disintegrated by a long-continued practice of dividing land
among coheirs. The interest of the open-field system, which in
two Nottinghamshire villages still connects the modern world
with Anglo-Saxon antiquity, has led to some exaggeration of
the extent to which it formed the framework of Old English
agrarian life.[1]

The Kentish scheme of land-division, unique in England,
has many points of contact with the agrarian system of the
Rhineland. Its basis was a unit of cultivation known as the
sulung, a term derived from the Old English *sulh*, 'plough', and
meaning simply 'ploughland'. The relationship between the
sulung and the plough-team of eight oxen is shown by the fact
that the quarter of a sulung was called a 'yoke', and is well
illustrated by the association of a bequest of four oxen with a
bequest of half a sulung in the oldest extant Kentish will.[2]
Although a few of the earliest Kentish charters seem to be
estimating land in hides, the Anglo-Saxon conception of a
family-land never gained general currency in Kent. The terms
'hide' and 'sulung' stand, in fact, for two different types of
tenement, one representing the amount of land which would
support a peasant household, and the other the area which
could be kept in cultivation by a single plough-team of eight
oxen. In acreage the sulung was undoubtedly far larger than
the hide. Early in the ninth century a Mercian king and an

---

[1] There is a full account of the open fields of Laxton, Notts., based on 17th-
century surveys, in *The Open Fields* by C. S. and C. S. Orwin (Oxford, 1938).
Eakring, the other open-field village in the county, is less well preserved, but shows
most of the characteristic features of the system. [Regrettably the Eakring open
field is now tractor ploughed and the balks and ridges planed down.]

[2] *C.S.* 412.

archbishop of Canterbury came to an agreement about an exchange of land on terms which show that two hides were then regarded as equal to one sulung. An equation so neat as this may well represent theory rather than fact, but it agrees very well with what is known about the position of the ceorl in early Kentish society.[1] The sulung was a self-contained stretch of arable within definite boundaries, bearing a name by which it could be described in legal documents. Several of these names are recorded in early charters and prove that the sulungs which bore them had once been possessed either by individuals, or by communities each of which regarded a single person as its head. A sulung called Dunwalinglond[2] must once have been either Dunwalh's property or the property of a group of people of whom he was the chief. It would be against the whole trend of Kentish social history to assume that the men who gave their names to sulungs were of noble birth, and the position of the primitive Kentish ceorl was such that even a sulung which was the equivalent of two Mercian hides was not too much for him. A holding of some two hundred acres was not excessive for a man with a wergild of one hundred golden shillings.

It is through their treatment of the arable that different Germanic peoples have left the clearest record of their several customs. But the arable holding, whether sulung or hide, was only the centre of a complex of properties and rights, essential to the maintenance of even the modest standards of life which prevailed in the seventh century. The earliest English charters are often verbose in the enumeration of the various appurtenances of an arable tenement. In a diploma of Hlothhere, king of Kent—the first English charter of which a contemporary text has survived—the arable which passed by the gift is left undefined, but care is taken to indicate that fields, feedings, marshes, little woods, springs, and fisheries went with it.[3] Phrases like these conceal an intensive exploitation of rough ground, forest, and marsh, which was hardly less important in rural economy than the arable cultivation itself. The fundamental necessity of finding food for the plough-beasts was met everywhere by the use of poor land on the edge of the arable. But wherever there were woods or marshes of sufficient extent

---

[1] *C.S.* 341, on which see P. Vinogradoff, 'Sulung and Hide', *E.H.R.* xix (1904), pp. 282–6.

[2] *C.S.* 332.   [3] *C.S.* 45.

there are signs of the pasturage of pigs or sheep upon a large scale; and south-eastern England, in particular, was heavily wooded and fringed with marsh. Already in 697 Wihtred, king of Kent, added pasture for three hundred sheep in Romney marsh to a gift of four sulungs elsewhere which he had formerly made to the monastery at Lyminge.[1] Grants of woodland swine-pastures are often recorded in Kentish charters of the early ninth century. The local names of the Kentish weald and marsh are, in general, of an ancient type, and prove that the intricacies of these regions had been familiar from a very early time.

In Kent and Sussex stretches of woodland pasture, known by definite names, were often attached to important manors. The weald of Kent and Sussex served, in fact, as a great reserve of swine-pasture for the use of communities living in the more open part of the country; and the peculiar manorial economy of these regions could never have arisen without the existence of this forest background. A similar manorial use of ancient woodland can be traced here and there in Wessex. In the tenth century, pastures within defined boundaries in the wooded country between Berkshire and Hampshire were annexed to the bishop of Winchester's estates at North Waltham, in a fold of the Downs, and at Overton in the Test valley.[2] Through the survival of early charters it is possible in Kent to penetrate behind the manorial system to a state of society in which these woodlands were divided between a small number of large 'folks' and used in accordance with their ancient customs. The names *Limenweara wald* and *Weowera weald*, recorded early in the eighth century,[3] prove that the woodlands to which they were applied were then regarded as belonging to the primitive divisions of the Kentish people which afterwards appear as the 'lathes' of Lyminge and Wye. Early spellings of the name Tenterden[4] imply that the surrounding country, although adjacent to the border of Sussex, had originally formed a *denn* or swine-pasture for the men of Thanet. Already under the independent kings of Kent the process had begun by which these ancient stretches of pasture were divided into separate blocks, assigned to individual manors. Before the Norman

---

[1] *C.S.* 97, 98. [2] *C.S.* 625. [3] *C.S.* 141.
[4] Which point unmistakably to an original *Tenetwaradenn*, J. K. Wallenberg, *The Place-Names of Kent*, pp. 355–6.

Conquest this process had obliterated the archaic relation between the lathe and its common weald. A similar process had still more conclusively obscured the ancient common usage of the Kentish Marsh. It is fortunate that the series of Kentish charters begins at a date when the common interest of the folk in its weald was still a reality.[1]

The forest and the laws which preserved it for the king's sport come into the foreground of any picture of medieval English society. The afforestations carried out by the Norman and early Angevin kings give a general impression that a considerable amount of land was lost to cultivation in the generations following the Norman Conquest. Here and there, as in the classical instance of the New Forest, there is medieval evidence for the disappearance of villages, small and poor, but standing for successful encroachment on ancient waste and woodland. But on a closer view the forests of the middle ages appear as the attenuated survivals of vast stretches of wooded or scrub-covered ground, within which patches of cultivation had slowly been brought into permanent existence. The modern forest of Wyre on the border between Shropshire and Worcestershire represents a great tract of woodland which, under the name of *Weogorena leag*, had extended in the ninth century for many miles along the west of the Severn, over against Worcester.[2] In King Alfred's time a thick belt of wooded country connected the district afterwards known as the New Forest with the swine-pastures of western Kent.[3] In the tenth century the forest of Sherwood in Nottinghamshire stretched for at least seven miles to the north of what became its medieval boundary.[4] The primitive English forest can rarely, if ever, have been a continuous expanse of heavy timber. Every royal forest of the middle ages included hamlets, if not villages, of pre-Conquest origin, and it is often impossible to gather from the modern appearance of a tract of country whether it had been a region of primary settlement or of forest colonization. No part of England is less suggestive of an ancient forest than the district once known as Bruneswald, in west Huntingdonshire and

---

[1] For the arrangements by which this interest was carried into effect see J. E. A. Jolliffe, *Pre-feudal England: The Jutes*, pp. 49–59.

[2] *C.S.* 357.

[3] Above, p. 18.

[4] Farrer, *Early Yorkshire Charters*, i, pp. 11–12. In this charter, the boundaries of Sutton, some four miles north-west of Retford, touch 'Scirwudu'.

east Northamptonshire.[1] Most of its villages are mentioned in Domesday Book. But the well-recorded tradition of Hereward's life as an outlaw in Bruneswald shows that a large amount of unbroken woodland still existed in this country at the date of the Norman Conquest.

It does not follow that country attractive to a modern, or even a medieval, farmer was equally attractive to the first English settlers. In particular the heavy clays of the midlands, productive as they became under cultivation in open fields, seem to have been deliberately avoided by the earliest colonists. These clays have yielded remarkably little evidence of occupation in the Roman period, and it is probable that large stretches of them were heavily timbered when the English invasions began.[2] It was not until the settlers had accumulated working capital in the form of plough-beasts, heavy ploughs, and slaves that they could attempt the exploitation of these soils, and by all the signs the process was still in an early stage in the year 600. Along the Trent valley, for example, the archaic place-names and heathen burial grounds which prove early settlement are almost confined to a narrow alluvial tract parallel with the river. Only a few isolated burials have been found in the clays which flank the greater part of its course, and the names of villages on these heavy lands mostly belong to types which are unlikely to have become common before the end of the sixth century.[3]

The main lines of the settlement had certainly been drawn in central and southern England by the middle of the tenth century. Charters of this period prove the existence of innumerable villages, each known by a permanent name and maintained by a territory of which the boundaries could be described in minute detail. A description of England in Edgar's reign, if such an achievement had been possible, would have shown a distribution of villages in the midlands and south differing little from that which is actually recorded in the Domesday Survey. But as the series of charters is followed backwards through the time before the Danish invasions, the outlines of local settlement become blurred. Boundaries are indicated by

[1] Its position is indicated by the place-names Newton Bromswold in Northamptonshire and Leighton Bromswold in Huntingdonshire.

[2] On their significance as a factor limiting the range of early settlement see Cyril Fox, *The Personality of Britain*, p. 71.

[3] *The Place-Names of Nottinghamshire* (English Place-Name Society), pp. xiii–xv.

a bare reference to a few well-known features of the country-side—a wood, tumulus, or stream—and important estates are often conveyed under no name other than that of a river by which they lay.[1] Elementary as they are, these descriptions are often of more than local interest; for they reflect the conditions of a time when river-valleys determined settlement, and village communities had not yet defined their rights in the woodland which overshadowed them. Æthelbald of Mercia, for example, described a property of ten hides near the Worcestershire Stour as lying 'in the province called Husmeræ, near the river called Stur . . . extending in circumference on each side of that river, having to the north the wood called Cynibre, and to the west another wood called Moerheb, of which woods the greater part belongs to the aforesaid land'.[2] A comparison of this vague language with the definite place-names and exact boundaries of a late Old English charter indicates the nature of the unrecorded changes which had come over English country life between the eighth and tenth centuries.

Under these conditions, no single type of settlement can ever have prevailed throughout the whole, even of southern England. On heavy land, and, indeed, wherever there was a prospect of a steady return to co-operative agriculture, ceorls tended to live together in villages. But as late as the eighth century life for perhaps a quarter of the English people was a struggle for existence against unprofitable soil and a scrubland vegetation which would spread again over cultivated fields on any slackening of effort. It was by individual enterprise that these poor lands had been brought into cultivation, and innumerable isolated farmsteads bearing Anglo-Saxon names remain as memorials of the process. Nevertheless, throughout Old English history it was not the farm but the village which formed the basis of social organization. In the eighth and ninth centuries the distribution of public burdens among those who were to bear them, and in particular, the arrangements for the food-rents which supported kings and their ministers, turned on the assumption that the typical ceorl lived in economic

[1] F. M. Stenton, *C.P.*, pp. 76–9. E. Ekwall, *English River-Names*, pp. lxxxiii–lxxxiv.
[2] *C.S.* 154. A West Saxon example of the same practice occurs in a charter of King Cynewulf to Muchelney Abbey, where the land is described as 8 hides 'inter duo flumina Earn et Yle, et ab occidente habet montem qui dicitur Duun Meten' (*Cartularies of Muchelney and Athelney*, ed. E. H. Bates, p. 47).

association with others of his kind.[1] In the eleventh century, when detailed records of taxation first appear, its incidence was spread over the country in a way which implied that England was divided into villages, and that in Wessex and English Mercia the territory of each village would consist of precisely five hides or some multiple of that number. It is not often possible to trace the assessment of an individual village backwards from the eleventh to the eighth or seventh century. But the charters of the earlier period show the same tendency to deal with hides in round numbers—to assume, that is, that whatever may have been the actual number of family-lands within a given territory, they could be regarded from the king's standpoint as exactly five, or ten, or twenty. Different charters, none of which is later than the reign of Offa, refer to five hides, 'being the village called Easttun to the east of the river Salwarpe',[2] to ten hides *æt Onnanforda*,[3] ten hides by the wood called *Toccan sceaga* near to the wood called *Reada beorg*,[4] twenty hides by the river Cherwell,[5] thirty hides to the north of the river Fontmell,[6] forty hides in the places called *Ricingahaam*, *Budinhaam*, *Dæccanhaam*, and *Angenlabeshaam*.[7] Round figures like this are obviously as artificial as the round numbers of hides assigned to villages in Domesday Book, and they were common two centuries before there is any evidence that hundred courts existed for the adjustment of unequal assessments. They show that the men of these early settlements were able by themselves to bring the king's estimate of the number of their hides into some relation to reality when the militia was called out, or a food-rent taken. They supply, in fact, a definite reason for believing in a primitive township-moot.

The king's *feorm* or food-rent, the heaviest of these public burdens, is often mentioned, though rarely defined, in early documents. In its primitive form it consisted of a quantity of provisions sufficient to maintain a king and his retinue for twenty-four hours, due once a year from a particular group of

[1] One of the few pieces of evidence for the plan of the earliest English villages comes from the oldest life of St. Cuthbert (ed. B. Colgrave, p. 90), which describes how an outbreak of fire in a house at the extreme east end of a certain *vicus* was prevented from spreading to other houses by a west wind sent in answer to Cuthbert's prayers. The tale gives a definite impression of a group of houses alined along a village street.

[2] *C.S.* 203. [3] *C.S.* 187. [4] *C.S.* 181.
[5] *C.S.* 57. [6] *C.S.* 107. [7] *C.S.* 81.

villages. It was naturally rendered at a royal village within or near to the district from which it came, and it was applied to the king's use by the reeve whom he had set in charge of this estate. In various parts of England, particularly in the south-west, fragments of this system survived the Norman Conquest; and commuted food-rents probably lie behind the 'hundred pennies' which are mentioned from time to time in the twelfth and thirteenth centuries.[1] According to the one undoubted description of an ancient royal *feorm* which has been preserved, sixty hides at Westbury on Trym were required to supply King Offa two tuns full of clear ale, one 'cumb' full of mild ale, one 'cumb' full of British ale, seven oxen, six wethers, forty cheeses, thirty 'ambers' of rye corn, and four 'ambers' of meal.[2] In themselves, these details can hardly be regarded as a heavy charge on the men of sixty hides. Long before Offa's time lords, and kings among them, were drawing far more burden-some rents from the men of their own villages. An isolated clause in Ine's laws[3] seems to imply that the normal render due to a lord from a ten-hide estate in Wessex amounted to ten vats of honey, three hundred loaves, twelve 'ambers' of British ale, thirty 'ambers' of clear ale, two full-grown oxen or ten wethers, ten geese, twenty hens, ten cheeses, an 'amber' full of butter, five salmon, twenty pounds' weight of fodder, and one hundred eels. Unlike this formidable rent, which clearly represents the management of an estate for a lord's profit, the Westbury *feorm* was derived from the traditional claim of a king to support from his subjects' land. But its details certainly suggest that the economic independence of the ceorl would be insecure as soon as a nobleman or a church had obtained possession of these ancient dues.

The king's *feorm*, archaic as it seems, was a development from a still more ancient system by which the king was entertained by his subjects as he passed over the country. A trace of this system seems to be preserved in one of Æthelberht's laws[4] which provides a double penalty for wrong-doing 'when the king is drinking in a man's home'. Long after Æthelberht's reign the king's servants of every degree were still being quartered on the country as they carried out their duties. The king's fowlers,

[1] E. B. Demarest, *E.H.R.* xxxiii (1918), pp. 62–72.
[2] Together with 6 *lang pero*, of which the meaning is unknown. *C.S.* 273.
[3] c. 70. 1.
[4] c. 3.

huntsmen, and grooms were entitled to this customary entertainment, and in the eighth century there is evidence of a
definite system by which the burden of feeding men in the
king's service was distributed among his people. In 814 King
Cenwulf of Mercia released to the bishop of Worcester the
duty of feeding twelve men which by custom was assigned to
that church and to the other minsters under the bishop's
authority.[1] Strangers with business at the king's court could
claim entertainment on their way, and Beorhtwulf of Mercia, in
releasing a midland monastery from many burdens, was careful
to except the duty of feeding messengers coming from Wessex
or Northumbria, or from beyond the sea.[2] Even the highest of
the king's ministers, the ealdormen in charge of provinces,
lived on the country as they passed over it; and a monastery
when freeing its land from public burdens would sometimes
pay a high price to the local ealdorman in return for an undertaking to abandon this right.[3] A primitive natural economy
lay behind the elaborate phrases in which early charters record
the emancipation of ecclesiastical lands from all service due to
the king or prince.

Besides the duty of entertaining his servants and men seeking
his court, charters of the eighth and ninth centuries mention
a number of services due by custom to the king from the holders
of unenfranchised land. They included the cartage of goods for
his use, and work upon the buildings of his estates. In a charter
of Wiglaf of Mercia, the building of royal villages, the *feorm*
of the king and ealdorman, and hospitality to the king's servants, are the three public burdens expressly mentioned.[4] In
other early documents the duty of erecting buildings for the king
is ignored, but the cognate service of making bridges and strongholds for the defence of the land, appears at the middle of the
eighth century. Already in Offa's reign service in the host and
work upon bridges and fortresses are described as necessary
labours, from which no one might be excused.[5] In a charter
purporting to come from Cædwalla of Wessex, but fabricated
at Canterbury late in the tenth century, these three duties are
described collectively under the phrase *trimoda necessitas*. A
misreading of *trinoda* instead of *trimoda*, for which Selden seems
to be responsible, and a mistaken belief in the authenticity of

---

[1] *C.S.* 350. [2] *C.S.* 454. [3] Cf. *C.S.* 416.
[4] *C.S.* 416. [5] *C.S.* 274.

Cædwalla's charter, have led many writers to use the phrase *trinoda necessitas* as a technical term.[1] No usage of the kind is ever found in genuine Old English documents, but it is clear that in Offa's reign work on bridges and fortresses and service in the fyrd were regarded as standing apart from all other forms of common obligation. Throughout the Old English period they were normally reserved when exemption was granted from all other public burdens, and they are undoubtedly of primitive origin.

Like other archaic forms of service, they were so familiar that few early documents ever attempt to define them. Nothing definite is known, for example, about the system by which the fyrd was recruited, and different scholars have come to very different opinions about the military value of the ceorl. The bare fact that men of this class served in the fyrd is proved by an explicit statement to that effect in Ine's laws.[2] Whatever the basis of their service may have been, it is only reasonable to assume that all able-bodied freemen would fight, or attempt to fight, when their country was invaded. The collapse of its defence meant slavery for the men and women who were worth the taking. The extent to which ceorls were called out in mass for distant expeditions is very uncertain. In the ninth century it was clearly unusual for the fyrd of a particular shire to serve beyond its borders. In all the recorded fighting of Anglo-Saxon history the typical warrior is the man of noble birth, fitted to be a king's companion, with far more than the equipment of an ordinary peasant, and dismounting only for battle. The peasant contingents in the host move very dimly behind this aristocratic foreground. But impressions derived from a few incidents, imperfectly recorded, can easily mislead, and there are facts which suggest that the ceorl may have been by no means negligible as a fighting man.[3] Even in the twelfth century the prosperous freeholder, who was his social representative,

---

[1] W. H. Stevenson, 'Trinoda Necessitas' in *E.H.R.* xxix (1914), pp. 689–703, an article which is of the first importance for the early history of the Old English solemn charter.

[2] c. 51.

[3] Thus St. Cuthbert, whose military service is mentioned by his first biographer, is known to have possessed at least a horse and a spear. There is no conclusive evidence as to his social status, but the well-recorded story which shows him tending his master's sheep *cum aliis pastoribus* makes it unlikely that he was of the class from which kings' companions were drawn. (*Two Lives of Saint Cuthbert*, ed. B. Colgrave, pp. 68, 72, 172.)

possessed an equipment for war comparable with that of the undistinguished knight. The numerous swords and shields found accompanying burials of the heathen period cannot all have belonged to kings' companions and their kin. The Kentish ceorl of Æthelberht's time was certainly rich enough to provide himself with an elaborate military equipment. Above all, the one text which illustrates the composition of the fyrd in the time before the Danish wars shows that kings were interesting themselves in its composition, and suggests that they were attempting to raise its quality by limiting its numbers. Between 799 and 802 Cenwulf of Mercia granted to one of his followers that an estate of thirty hides should furnish only five men when the fyrd was called out.[1]

The duty of building and repairing bridges—the *brycg bot* or *brycg geweorc* of Anglo-Saxon texts—can be traced downwards far beyond the end of the Old English period. It is not mentioned in the earliest laws, but appears under innumerable variations of Latin phrase in charters from the eighth century onwards. In the eleventh century it was still a form of what early documents call 'common labour'. In the time of Edward the Confessor the reeve of Chester had been empowered to call out one man from every hide in Cheshire for the repair of the bridge and wall of the city.[2] By this date social changes had begun to shift the responsibility for these ancient services from the peasantry to their lords. Failure to obey the reeve's summons meant a penalty of forty shillings paid by the defaulter's lord to the king and the earl. But the immediate obligation still lay, as it must have lain originally, on the holders of peasant tenements, and the hide was still regarded as the unit on which common burdens should be thrown. Centuries after the ancient *brycg bot* had everywhere been commuted into a charge on land, the 'pontage' which maintained the Great Bridge as Cambridge was raised by an assessment on the traditional hidage of Cambridgeshire.[3]

For nearly two centuries before the Norman Conquest the *burh*, or defensible centre of population, is often mentioned in contemporary documents. The typical *burh* of the eleventh century was plainly an artificial creation,[4] in which the men

---

[1] *C.S.* 201.   [2] *Domesday Book*, i, f. 262*b*.
[3] Maitland, *Township and Borough*, p. 37.
[4] On the character of the late Old English *burh* see below, pp. 528–38.

of different lords lived together, emancipated in some degree
from the agricultural preoccupations of the peasant, and taking
advantage of such opportunities of trade as the conditions of
their time afforded. They formed a body from which a local
garrison could immediately be drawn in time of need, and their
predecessors had played a very important part in the defence
of the land during the Danish invasions of the ninth and tenth
centuries. There is, in fact, good reason to believe that the
origin of the *burh* as a permanent feature of a national scheme
of defence belongs to the reign of King A!fred. It is at least
certain that no argument as to the nature of the primitive Old
English *burh* can be drawn from the elaborate organization for
the maintenance of local fortifications which existed in tenth-
century Wessex. There is no doubt that the building, repair,
and defence of fortresses had been a burden of general incidence
in the time before the Danish invasions had begun. The 'necessary defence of strongholds against enemies' is mentioned in a
charter issued by Uhtred, under-king of the Hwicce, in 770.[1]
But the nature of these strongholds is utterly uncertain, and it
should not be assumed that the walls of Romano-British cities
had been kept in repair by their English possessors. The walls
of York itself were in decay when the Danes descended on the
city in 866.[2] Two charters of the early ninth century suggest
that the common duty of maintaining places of defence against
native enemies was being extended to meet the new situation
caused by the Danish invasions. In 811 and 822, respectively,
Cenwulf and Ceolwulf I of Mercia speak of service in the host
against heathen enemies, and of the destruction as well as the
building of fortresses.[3] It is highly probable that the fortresses
to be destroyed were the camps of early Danish raiders. But
the development of an organized defensive system out of primitive custom belongs to the next generation.

A similar development can be traced in the history of Old
English local administration. At the beginning of the eleventh
century, England south of the Tees was everywhere divided
into shires, each of which formed a unit in the national administrative system. Except where Danish influences prevailed,
each shire was divided into smaller districts known as hundreds,
for the adjustment of taxation, the maintenance of peace and

---

[1] *C.S.* 203.   [2] Asser, *Vita Ælfredi*, c. 27.   [3] *C.S.* 335, 370.

order, and the settlement of local pleas. Only the barest rudiments of this system have as yet been identified in the pre-Alfredian period. The hundred is not mentioned by name before the reign of Edgar, and there is no direct evidence of its existence before the reign of Edmund. Wessex was apparently divided into shires before the end of the eighth century; but there is no trace of any such division in independent Mercia, and the midland shires, as a whole, have an artificial appearance which in itself suggests that their origin is more recent. The tradition which ascribed the creation of shires and hundreds to King Alfred is of no great age. But it represents the fact that the West Saxon supremacy made possible the establishment of a uniform scheme of local administration throughout southern England.

English historians of the eighth century seem to have known only one kind of territorial unit less than an entire kingdom. They refer continually to districts vaguely described as *regiones* or *provinciae*, which clearly formed the fundamental divisions of the several English peoples. Neither *regio* nor *provincia* was in any sense a technical term, and there is little evidence to show what English word lay behind them. An archaic *gē*, 'district', cognate with the German *gau*, forms the second element of the names Surrey and Ely, each of which is called a *regio* by Bede, and the same word ends the names of the primitive Kentish divisions which came to be known as the lathes of Sturry, Eastry, and Lyminge.[1] But it had passed out of common use at an early date, and no single equivalent was ever found for either *regio* or *provincia* when Latin histories came to be translated into English. Among the various words by which these terms were rendered the most significant is *mægth*, a word originally meaning kindred, which had early developed the wider sense of tribe or people. It would be unwise to infer from this translation that the primitive English *regio* had been the territory of a particular group of kinsmen, but it brings out the important fact that these divisions originated in tribal settlements, and not in any deliberate division of the land for administrative purposes. In the eighth century they were still known by the

---

[1] It occurs again in the Essex place-name Vange, near the Thames, which appears as *Fengge* and *Fænge* in the tenth century, and must originally have meant 'fen-district'. J. K. Wallenberg, *Kentish Place-Names*, p. 291; *Place-Names of Essex* (E.P-N.S.), pp. 174-5.

names of the ancient tribes from whose settlement they had arisen, and their primitive character was remembered. The Gyrwe of the Fens and the Meanware of the Meon valley were obviously real people to Bede. Few of these tribes have any history and their names are often obscure, but they represent the most ancient form of English social organization of which anything definite is known.

By combining the information given by historians and charters, these *regiones* can be traced in every English kingdom. In Kent they formed the basis of an organization which provided for the payment of the king's food-rents, regulated the interest of the peasantry in its communal woods, and administered customary law.[1] Many points of analogy suggest that the rapes of Sussex, like the lathes of Kent, represent ancient *regiones* organized for the maintenance of a traditional form of economic life.[2] There is little direct evidence for so elaborate a system in other parts of the country, and in Saxon territory the *regio* itself is rarely mentioned. In Essex an early *regio* called *Deningei* seems now to be represented by the hundred of Dengie,[3] and in Middlesex the name *Geddingas*, which survives in the place-name Yeading, denoted another local unit of the same type.[4] In Wessex, from the eighth century onwards, local government was organized in shires, distinguished by a strongly marked official character from the popular Kentish *regiones*. No ancient historian throws any light on the original divisions of Wessex, but King Wulfhere of Mercia, when confirming the foundation of Chertsey abbey, mentions that its lands in the 'province' of Surrey extended as far as the boundary of another 'province' called *Sunninges*.[5] The situation of this province is indicated by the place-names Sunninghill and Sonning in east Berkshire. No other example of the primitive West Saxon *regio* is known, but the names of three West Saxon shires show clear traces of an earlier and more popular organization of local government. The names Dorset and Somerset originally denoted, not the districts which were governed from Dorchester and Somerton, but the people who looked to these places for government. 'Wiltshire', which means the district dependent on Wilton, has

---

[1] J. E. A. Jolliffe, *Pre-feudal England: The Jutes*, pp. 39–72.
[2] Ibid., pp. 81–6.
[3] *The Place-Names of Essex* (E.P-N.S.), pp. xxii–xxiii, 213–14.
[4] *C.S.* 182.   [5] *C.S.* 34.

replaced an earlier *Wilsætan*, which simply meant 'the people by the river Wylye'.

There is abundant evidence for the existence of *provinciae* or *regiones* in Anglian territory. The country along the Norfolk river Wissey is called *provincia Wissa* in the eighth-century life of St. Guthlac.[1] The Northumbrian Bede was obviously following common usage in his numerous references to *regiones* and *provinciae*, and the same terms had come naturally to his predecessors. The first biographer of St. Cuthbert speaks of a companion of King Aldfrith who lived in the *regio* called *Kintis*, and of a dwelling-place built for Cuthbert in the *regio* called *Ahse*, midway between Hexham and Carlisle.[2] In the midlands the nature of the primitive *regio* can be illustrated from an actual list of these divisions, which gives in terms of hides the number of tribute-paying families assigned to each. The oldest form of this list, which has already been quoted under the name of the Tribal Hidage, is written in a hand of the late tenth century, when ancient *regiones*, if remembered at all, had become mere names.[3] Its text is extremely corrupt. As it stands, it consists of a series of regional names, each appearing in the genitive plural, and clearly representing tribes or folks rather than districts. The names of famous peoples—the Mercians, West and East Saxons, East Angles, and Cantware—appear among them, accompanied by estimates of hidage which are always generous, and to some scholars have seemed incredible. Some of them, such as the 100,000 hides assigned to Wessex and the 30,000 hides assigned to primitive Mercia, are entirely at variance with other information. The 7,000 hides attributed to Sussex would hardly be taken seriously if Bede had not assigned the same number of families to the South Saxons of his day. That the figures of the Tribal Hidage only approximate most roughly to the actual number of family lands contained in any kingdom is certain. There can have been no accurate counting of hides among the primitive English peoples, and the use of round numbers meant inevitable exaggeration. But it does not follow that these estimates were out of all relation with reality.

[1] *Felix's Life of St. Guthlac*, ed. B. Colgrave, p. 168. It probably took its name from the river.

[2] *Two Lives of St. Cuthbert*, ed. B. Colgrave, pp. 114, 116.

[3] *C.S.* 297. A facsimile of the oldest manuscript is given in the article on the Tribal Hidage by J. Brownbill, *E.H.R.* xl (1925), facing p. 497, and in R. H. Hodgkin, *A History of the Anglo-Saxons*, 3rd edition, 1952, II, plate 53, facing p. 389.

The Tribal Hidage was almost certainly compiled in Mercia, and it is in relation to the provinces of the Mercian kingdom that its details are most convincing. It begins by assigning 7,000 hides to the *Wreocensætan*, the men of the country round the Wrekin, and to a people called *Westerne*, who should probably be sought in Cheshire and north Staffordshire. The *Pecsætan*, or men of the Peak of Derbyshire, and the *Elmetsætan* of south Yorkshire follow, with 1,200 and 600 hides respectively. The men of Lindsey and the district now marked by Hatfield Chase receive 7,000 hides, and the survey then turns southwards and assigns 600 hides to each of the two divisions of the Gyrwe, or people of the Fens. After this, six small peoples are mentioned, with assessments varying from 300 to 1,200 hides. None of them can be identified with absolute certainty, but there is some reason to connect the names appearing in the record as *Herefinna* and *Sweord ora* with the later Hurstingstone hundred in Huntingdonshire, and Sword Point on the edge of Whittlesey Mere.[1] Throughout this section the survey seems to be following a southerly line, for it next comes to two peoples, each of 300 hides, called *Gifle* and *Hicce*, whose names connect them definitely with the river Ivel in Bedfordshire and the district around Hitchin in northern Hertfordshire.[2] At this point the course of the survey becomes uncertain. The *Hicce* are followed by a people of 600 hides whose name appears, in an obviously corrupt form, as *Wiht gara*, and the next two names, *Nox gaga* and *Oht gaga*, borne by large peoples of 5,000 and 2,000 hides respectively, form the most obvious *cruces* in the whole survey. Its compiler seems to have thought that a definite section of his work had closed with these uncouth names, for he proceeded to state incorrectly that the total hidage of the regions which he had covered, assigning 30,000 hides to Mercia itself, amounted to 66,100 hides. The second section of the survey opens with the Hwicce of the Severn valley and the Cilternsætan of Oxfordshire and Buckinghamshire, estimated at 7,000 and 4,000 hides respectively, and followed by an unidentified folk of 3,500 hides whose name appears in the form *Hendrica*. Seven small and obscure peoples, with hidages ranging from 300 to 1,200, bring the survey to the East Angles, estimated at 30,000 hides, and it closes by assigning 7,000 hides to the East

---

[1] *The Place-Names of Bedfordshire and Huntingdonshire* (E.P-N.S.), pp. xviii, xxi.
[2] Ibid. and *Place-Names of Hertfordshire* (E.P-N.S.), pp. xvi, xvii.

Saxons, 15,000 to the men of Kent, 7,000 to the South Saxons, and, probably as a later interpolation, 100,000 to Wessex.

The Tribal Hidage certainly comes from a time before the eastern midlands had been overrun by the Danish armies of the ninth century. There is no reason to think that it covers any part of Northumbria except the border province of Elmet. With this exception, the districts to which it relates are those subject to the overlords of the southern English; its course proceeds outwards from Mercia, and it should probably be attributed to the reign of Wulfhere, Æthelbald, or Offa. Its great age, to which much of its obscurity is due, shows that it must have been intended to serve some practical purpose. No one in the seventh or eighth century can be imagined compiling such a document out of mere curiosity. It only becomes intelligible when it is regarded as an attempt to guide a king's ministers in the exaction of his dues from subject provinces. In this way it becomes primary evidence for the real character of the local divisions—the *regiones* or *provinciae*—mentioned incidentally by early historians. The existence of a primitive Middle Anglian folk bearing the name *Feppingas* is proved by Bede's statement that the first bishop of the Mercians died among the Middle Angles in the region called *in Feppingum*.[1] The Tribal Hidage shows that the *Feppingas* were a small people of 300 hides, forming one of a congeries of similar peoples, each regarded as units in a general system of assessment for the support of a king or overlord.

The existence of this common burden implies that popular courts existed for its local adjustment. Many factors had combined to create such assemblies. Even in the smallest kingdoms the administration of customary law cannot have waited for the occasions when, in King Æthelberht's words, 'the king calls his people to him'.[2] The history of the Kentish lathes illustrates the way in which the popular assemblies of a folk had maintained its primitive interests in common marsh and forest. From the earliest phase of permanent settlement the need must have arisen for local assemblies where, as in the later hundred courts, men might 'defend' their holdings against the king's

[1] *Historia Ecclesiastica*, iii. 21. The late tenth-century list of 'Resting-Places of the English Saints' says he is buried at Charlbury, Oxfordshire. See F. Liebermann, *Die Heiligen Englands*, p. 11.

[2] Laws of Æthelberht, c. 2.

ministers seeking the king's dues. One of the anomalies of Anglo-Saxon history is the extreme rarity of early references to these fundamental institutions. The word *folcgemot* does not appear in the laws before the time of Alfred, when the meetings covered by the term, at which it is assumed that a royal minister will be present, suggest the shire courts of later times rather than the moots of primitive *regiones*.[1] There seems to be only one piece of direct evidence for the existence of popular assemblies in an earlier age, but it is fortunately conclusive. A contemporary memorandum, in which, for once, the liberties of a privileged estate are described from within, expressly states that King Cenwulf of Mercia has freed a retainer's land from the burden of *popularia concilia*.[2]

The fiscal responsibilities of these popular assemblies, and in particular their duty of providing for the maintenance of the local ruler, offer a line of approach towards one of the most difficult problems of Anglo-Saxon history—the origin of the institution known as the hundred. In the eleventh century territorial divisions called hundreds formed the basis of the organization of public justice and the administration of public finance throughout England south of the Thames, and in English Mercia, East Anglia, and the southern Danelaw. These divisions varied very widely in area—there were more than fifty hundreds in Sussex and only five in Staffordshire—and also in the number of hides which each was reputed to contain. In many parts of the midlands the assessment of each hundred approximated to a round one hundred hides, and the correspondence of name and assessment is made more pointed by the existence of divisions assessed at 50 or 200 hides, and described as 'half-hundreds' or 'double-hundreds'. But in southern England this correspondence is exceptional, and within a single county the assessments of different hundreds may range from less than 20 to more than 150 hides. This irregularity does not disprove the theory that in origin the hundred was a district assessed to public burdens at a round hundred hides. The hundred of the midlands was probably the result of a deliberate remodelling of administrative geography carried out in this region in the tenth century. Wessex, and the south of England generally, had never been thus treated. But the contrast between the roughly symmetrical hundreds of the midlands and

[1] Laws of Alfred, cc. 22, 34, 38.1. [2] *C.S.* 201.

the irregular and often minute hundreds of the south shows at least that the hundredal system had not been imposed on the whole country by a single act of state.

In the last century of the Old English kingdom each hundred had a court which administered customary law in private pleas, did justice on thieves and on those who had been slack in their pursuit, and moderated discussion between the king's financial officers and the individual taxpayer. The Old English hundred court has all the features of an ancient popular assembly. It met in the open air, and at regular intervals of four weeks, so that no summons was necessary to compel the attendance of its suitors. The judgements which it gave represented the deliberations of peasants learned in the law, who might be guided but could never be controlled by the intervention of the king's reeve, their president. In the tenth century the hundred received a collective fine from persons convicted of breaking its 'dooms', and in particular from those who disobeyed its orders in regard to the pursuit of thieves. On the other hand, in spite of its many primitive features, it is never mentioned in the most ancient English documents. Some of its functions are carefully described by an anonymous royal ordinance[1] issued between 946 and 961. King Edmund refers to it as an established institution,[2] and its existence in the time of King Edward the Elder is made probable by an enactment in which he speaks of meetings held every four weeks by a king's reeve for the administration of customary law.[3] But the chain of references cannot be carried beyond this point, and there is no direct evidence to connect the hundred courts of the tenth century with the folkmoots mentioned in King Alfred's laws, or with the *popularia concilia* which existed in Mercia in King Cenwulf's time.

Nevertheless, the need for such an institution must have been felt in every part of England for many generations before the reign of Edward the Elder. For a long time, perhaps for a century, after the first occupation of a tract of country, the men of each *regio* may have been able to deal with their own affairs in assemblies at which all were present. But as the law of their country became more elaborate, and as the original arrangements by which they maintained their king were complicated

---

[1] A. J. Robertson, *Laws of the English Kings*, pp. 16–19; Stubbs, *Select Charters*, 9th ed., pp. 80–2. [2] Robertson, op. cit., p. 13.
[3] Attenborough, *Laws of the Earliest English Kings*, p. 120.

by the taking of new land into cultivation, there must have arisen an urgent necessity for some form of assembly intermediate between the meeting of the whole folk and the meeting of a village community. It cannot have been easy for a folkmoot of perhaps seven hundred farmers to administer the intricate and technical West Saxon law of Ine's reign, or to determine the contribution of each local community to public charges such as the king's *feorm*. The round figures of the Tribal Hidage show that in the time before Alfred the unit of one hundred hides had been familiar both to the kings who had imposed these burdens and to the countrymen on whom they fell. They show, in fact, that if a *regio* were to be divided, it would tend to fall into districts each of which would answer for a round one hundred hides when the king took his *feorm* or called out his fyrd. Whatever may have happened in the midlands, it is probable that the hundreds of Wessex came into being by gradual division of the ancient *regiones* along these lines.

That the origin of the hundred should be sought in this direction is strongly suggested by the fact that in the eleventh century a large number of hundreds were annexed financially to ancient royal manors at which the king's *feorm* must once have been paid. In all parts of England many hundreds bore the names of royal manors, and in such cases it is safe to assume that the profits of justice done within the hundred formed, or had once formed, part of the revenue for which the reeve of the manor was responsible.[1] In Wessex beyond Selwood, which was a conservative country, there were still in the eleventh century many royal manors to which were annexed, not only the profits of hundredal jurisdiction, but also sums of money representing the commutation of food-rents once paid at these manors by the men of the neighbourhood. Less remarkable, but equally useful as a clue to hundredal origins, are the numerous cases in which a single royal manor received the profits of jurisdiction from a whole group of hundreds.[2] In 1066 nineteen Oxfordshire hundreds were thus annexed in small groups to seven royal manors, which included Headington, where Æthelred II had possessed a demesne, Kirtlington, where Edward the Martyr had held his court, and Bensington, which had been a place of note since the

---

[1] See H. M. Cam, 'Manerium cum Hundredo', *E.H.R.* xlvii (1932), pp. 353–76.

[2] E. B. Demarest, 'The Hundred-Pennies', *E.H.R.* xxxiii (1918), pp. 62–72.

time of Ceawlin.[1] The antiquity of this grouping of hundreds around royal manors is indicated by the occasional appearance of similar groups in the tenth century, and by the difficulty of imagining the conditions under which they could have arisen in the late Old English period. In the absence of direct evidence the 'six hundreds of Basingstoke' which occur in medieval records are most naturally explained as survivals from a time when Basingstoke had been the administrative centre of a *regio* assessed at six hundred hides to common burdens such as the king's *feorm*. At least three centuries separated the Tribal Hidage from Domesday Book, and it is unlikely that any particular group of hundreds will ever be proved to be the exact representative of an ancient *regio*. But it is at least curious that the medieval 'seven hundreds of Cookham and Bray' in east Berkshire correspond very closely to the probable area of the district which in the seventh century was called the *provincia* of Sonning.

The organization of the folk reflected in the Tribal Hidage implies a state of society in which kings were seeking their rents and services directly from the holders of the ancient family lands. But from an age which was already remote in Alfred's reign, this primitive simplicity had been complicated by the creation of territorial lordships for nobles in the king's service and for churches. Ever since the last quarter of the seventh century kings had been issuing charters which gave a bishop or an abbot authority over a particular tract of land. A century later lay nobles had begun to receive grants by charter; and the number of gifts recorded in this way was certainly much larger than would be gathered from the few early charters to laymen which are now extant. Charters easily disappeared in ancient times—already in 832 Egbert of Wessex made a new charter for three sisters who had lost their *anteriora scripsiuncula*[2]—and all Old English family muniments have perished. Even if they had survived, the early history of many landed houses would still be obscure. There is definite evidence that kings had been granting lands to their followers before ever the foreign device of the charter had been introduced into England. At the middle of the seventh century Benedict Biscop, as a young companion of King Oswiu, was offered an estate appropriate to his rank by his lord.[3] It is probable that in early times it was customary for

---

[1] D.B. i, f. 154*b*.　　　　[2] *C.S.* 410, dated 26 December 833.
[3] Bede, *Historia Abbatum*, ed. C. Plummer, *Bedae Opera Historica*, i, pp. 364-5.

kings to make grants of estates to their gesiths for their lifetime, and that such estates did not pass to their heirs without a fresh grant.[1] There can be no doubt that similar grants had been made by the sixth-century kings under whom the English peoples had been established in Britain. The great ecclesiastical estate is an obvious factor making for the rise of territorial lordship, but its direct influence was confined to a minority of English villages, and was late in coming into effect. It was in the lands which kings had given to their companions that the changes began which created the manorial economy of the middle ages.

Everywhere in the Germanic world the ruler, whether king or chief, was attended by a body-guard of well-born companions. No Germanic institution has a longer history. The phrases in which Tacitus describes the retinue of a first-century chief can be applied to the companions of King Cynewulf of Wessex in the eighth century and to those of Earl Byrhtnoth of Essex in the tenth. Much that is characteristic of the oldest Germanic literature turns on the relationship between the companions and their lord. The sanctity of the bond between lord and man, the duty of defending and avenging a lord, the disgrace of surviving him, gave rise to situations in which English listeners were always interested until new literary fashions of Romance origin had displaced the ancient stories. There is no doubt that this literature represented real life. It was the personal reputation of a king which attracted retainers to his court, and it was the king's military household around which all early fighting centred. The inclusion of foreign warriors among the king's companions and the presence of hostages from other countries in his court went far to cement the great Germanic confederations of early times. The migration to Britain produced no change in the relation of the king to his retinue. There is no essential difference between the king's companions of the heathen age and the nobles who attest the earliest English royal charters. If the *comites* who witness these documents appear as the councillors rather than the military followers of the king, it was certainly their duty to attend him in war, and the seventh century was an age of continual wars. The career of Cædwalla of Wessex shows that late in that century it was still possible for a young noble of royal birth to win a kingdom at the head of a

[1] See F. M. Stenton, *The Latin Charters of the Anglo-Saxon Period*, pp. 60–1.

band of retainers.[1] Some at least of the nobles who saw Cæd-walla devote the great Farnham estate to religious uses[2] must have been his companions in exile. Several charters of Æthelbald of Mercia are witnessed by a *minister* or *comes* named Oba, who appears in the earliest life of St. Guthlac as one of the king's companions in his wanderings before his accession. Even in the early eighth century the bishops and abbots attending a king's court seem incongruous members of an assembly which was still essentially a war-band.

The *comes* of early charters is the *gesith* of the earliest English laws.[3] Originally the word meant simply 'companion', a meaning which gives a valuable clue to the origin of what in the seventh century was by far the most important section of the English nobility. In seventh-century Wessex the fundamental line of social cleavage ran between the ceorl and the man 'of companion's rank'—the *gesithcund man* of Ine's laws. The *gesithcund man's* wergild amounted to 1,200 shillings as against the 200-shilling wergild of the ceorl; and the social distinction implied by this difference was maintained throughout the whole sphere of customary law. It was complicated in Wessex by an intermediate class of men with a wergild of 600 shillings, whose origin is still obscure. But some if not all of these men were nobles of British descent living in Saxon territory, and the disappearance of the class after Alfred's reign was probably due to a gradual intermingling of races in the interior of the kingdom. There is no trace of this class in either Northumbria or Mercia, where the fragments of ancient law which have survived resemble the West Saxon system in distinguishing between the ceorl with a wergild of 200 shillings and the noble with a wergild six times as great. The Northumbrian noble is once expressly called *gesithcund*, and there is little doubt that membership of a king's body-guard had formed the primitive test of nobility in Northumbria and Mercia as in Wessex. In Kent the wergild-system shows the individuality which runs through the whole social organization of that kingdom. There is no trace of any Kentish nobility of British origin, although three classes of men called *læts*, of which the highest possessed much less than a

[1] The account of Cynewulf and Cyneheard in annal 755 of the Anglo-Saxon Chronicle shows that the kingdom could be given by a dead king's retainers.

[2] *C.S.* 72 (above, p. 70).

[3] In the Old English translation of Bede's *Ecclesiastical History* (above, p. 273), *comes* is generally rendered by *gesith*.

Kentish ceorl's wergild, seem to represent a British peasantry surviving under Jutish rule. The most remarkable feature of the Kentish system is the ceorl's great wergild of one hundred golden shillings, contrasted as it is with a noble's wergild only three times as large. The Kentish system, as a whole, is unique in England, and its affinities undoubtedly lie in the Frankish lands where the distinctive culture of Kent had arisen. Even in nomenclature there is a significant difference between the Kentish and West Saxon social system. The *gesithcund man* only appears once in the three surviving codes of Kentish law. The Kentish noble is elsewhere described as an *eorl* or *eorlcund man*, words which point to a state of society where birth, apart from relationship to any lord, had determined personal rank.

This primitive conception of nobility had left little impression on the social order of the other English kingdoms. It is possible, and, indeed, probable that among the many provincial rulers of the eighth and earlier centuries there were some who represented a pure nobility of birth—whose families, though less than royal, had an inherent claim to social distinction. But there is no satisfactory evidence that such families existed in any kingdom except Kent. Even there the members of this class were evidently becoming absorbed into the nobility by service at an early date. Men of obvious social importance, with military households of their own, appear among the companions of early Kentish kings. A charter issued by King Eadberht in 738 is witnessed by seven nobles, explicitly described as the king's companions, each of whom states that he has caused his own *comites* to confirm and attest the king's grant.[1]

In general it would seem that the circumstances of the migration to Britain had disintegrated whatever forms of primitive aristocracy had existed among the continental English, leaving few representatives of a genuine aristocracy of birth, apart from the king and his kinsmen. There can be no doubt that families related to the royal line formed an important element in the society to every English kingdom. Penwalh, the father of St. Guthlac, living in great prosperity in Middle Anglia, and

---

[1] *C.S.* 159. The list of witnesses begins with the statement 'Hanc . . . donationem meam ego Eadberht rex Cantuariorum propria manu confirmavi . . . testes quoque idoneos commites meos confirmari et subscribere feci'. This is followed by 'Ego Vilbaldus commites meos confirmari et subscribere feci', and by six other attestations of the same type.

claiming descent from ancient Mercian kings,[1] stands for a type
of nobility older than the conception of rank earned by service.
But even men of this kind, dominating the country around
their own seats, must have felt the attraction of the courts of
their greater kinsmen, and taken new estates from them.
Eanulf, the grandfather of Offa of Mercia, who could claim an
unchallenged descent from Woden, received extensive lands
among the Hwicce by charter from his cousin King Æthelbald.[2]
There must have been many companions of Ceawlin and
Penda who in birth were the equals of their lords.

The creation of the great Mercian kingdom of the eighth century meant that the heirs of many lesser dynasties were brought
to seek the court of the Mercian king, to take gifts from him, and
to promise him fidelity. It is sometimes possible to trace the
actual course of their decline into subordination. Sigered, the
last king of Essex, attests many charters of Cenwulf, king of
the Mercians; at first as *rex*, then as *subregulus*, and finally as *dux*
or ealdorman.[3] Men of this type may often have been allowed
to rule their own people under their lord's ultimate authority.
But a king who was strong enough could always ignore the
claims of a local dynasty, and in course of time men with no
hereditary title to rule appear as ealdormen of provinces which
had once been kingdoms. The typical ealdorman of the eighth
and ninth centuries was not the heir of a dynasty but a member
of the king's household set in charge of a shire, or *regio*, by his
lord and removable at his pleasure. A king will sometimes refer
to a man, in a single phrase, as his *comes*, or companion, and his
dux, or ealdorman.[4] Even the holder of a definite household
office might be sent to act as the king's permanent representative
in a province. A certain Eastmund, who appears as *dux* in a
charter of Æthelred of Wessex,[5] has been the *pedesecus*, that is,
apparently, the intimate attendant, of Æthelberht, Æthelred's
brother.[6] Only men of this type, with whom the king was well
acquainted, could safely be trusted to lead the fyrd of a district,

---

[1] *Felix's Life of Saint Guthlac*, ed. B. Colgrave, pp. 72–4.

[2] *C.S.* 272.   [3] e.g. *C.S.* 335, 340, 343.

[4] *C.S.* 154, where Æthelbald, king of Mercia, refers to a certain Cyneberht as
fidele duce atque comite meo Cyniberhttæ.

[5] *C.S.* 516.

[6] *C.S.* 496. The place of the *pedesequus* at court is discussed by W. H. Stevenson,
(*Asser's Life of King Alfred*, p. 165). Stevenson illustrated this title from a passage
in *Beowulf* which refers to a courtier of especial importance described as 'sitting at
the king's feet'.

enforce compliance with the judgements of its folkmoots, and impose terms on local nobles who had allowed their own household men to break the peace.[1]

The most admired virtue of an early king was generosity to his followers. It was probably accepted throughout the north that every member of a king's household might expect to receive an endowment in land from his lord.[2] In England, in the very earliest times, the endowment may often have consisted of a stretch of newly conquered land, on which the recipient and his household could be maintained by the food-rents and services of subject Britons and dependent Englishmen. But the gifts which are actually on record have a different character. They were not in the strictest sense grants of lands. Each of these gifts empowered the man who had received it to exact within a definite area the dues and services which the local peasantry had formerly rendered to the king himself. A king's companion thus rewarded received the food-rent which the land of his endowment had previously yielded to the king—the 'tribute formerly due to kings', as Offa describes it in a charter to a Kentish follower.[3] The public duty of repairing the buildings on royal estates passed by such a gift into work upon the new lord's house and farmstead; he, instead of the king, had the benefit of the ancient cartage services, and the entertainment of his servants represented the *feorm* once given to the king's fowlers and huntsmen. In all this there was at first nothing to the detriment of the subject peasantry. Even if the new lord took the fines imposed for their misdemeanours, there was as yet no manorial court to symbolize his authority. Judgement was still given according to ancient custom in the familiar popular assemblies, and the fact that penalties there imposed were taken for the profit of a private lord can have meant little to men preoccupied with the concerns of the passing moment. Even a peasant who was dimly conscious of a new surveillance may well have reflected that in bad times a lord in the village would be a readier protector than a distant king.

The first phase in the history of the private lordship ends with

---

[1] In early West Saxon charters ealdormen are generally called *praefecti*. The description brings out the official character of their position, for *praefectus* was equivalent to *gerefa* or reeve.

[2] On the probability that early English kings made such grants for the recipients' lifetime only, see pp. 301–2 above.

[3] *C.S.* 254.

the establishment of the idea that the possessor of such an estate ought to be able to show a royal charter as evidence of his title. By the time of King Alfred the term *bocland*, 'bookland', had come into common use as a convenient description of an estate secured to its holder by a royal charter or 'book'. Until the tenth century the clerks who composed these documents were free to experiment with formulas of their own choice, and it is only by slow degrees that the Old English charter advances towards precision of style. Being derived in the last resort from Roman private documents of the sixth century, these charters always take the form of a simple conveyance of land, and ignore the fact that the gifts which they record meant, in effect, the alienation of rights by a king for the benefit of a subject. The rights themselves are expressed in the vaguest of words, which often amount to nothing more than a statement that the land at issue is to be free from all earthly service, qualified by certain reservations in the king's interest. A normal charter of the ninth century is careful to insist that, when all other royal rights have passed to the new lord of the land, the king may still exact fyrd-service and work on bridges and fortifications from its inhabitants. For the rest, the king makes no attempt to intervene between the lord and the men who are to be under his authority. His immediate purpose is to show that he has released a particular territory from all except the most fundamental of common burdens. With the social consequences of his action he has, naturally, no concern. The exaction of the ancient food-rents and service by which a new lord will henceforward profit can safely be left to the control of a custom which is none the less valid because it has never been reduced to writing. The king's object is to record what may conveniently be called an 'immunity', to make what in the tenth century would be described as a *freols boc*—a charter of liberties.

Charters of this type generally include a clause stating that the recipient of the estate may alienate or bequeath it in his will. In 778, for example, Cynewulf, king of Wessex, granted a considerable estate at Bedwyn to a certain Bica, whom he calls his *comes* and *minister*, with the liberty of exchanging, giving, selling or bequeathing it to any heir of his choice.[1] In many cases it was obviously intended that the heir should be a religious community.

[1] *C.S.* 225. This is the oldest West Saxon charter of which a contemporary text has survived.

The charter was introduced into England in order to give security of possession to such bodies, and many later documents which on the surface seem to be grants of land to laymen in the king's service were really intended to free an estate from public burdens in order that a monastery might be founded upon it. Even when a noble wished to found a religious house on land already in his possession he would usually obtain a new grant of that land from the king. Nothing but a royal charter could free land from the king's dues and services, and defeat the claims of expectant heirs. It is this aspect of the charter which explains the remarkable fact that an Old English king could make charters purporting to grant land to himself. Under the year 855 the *Chronicle* states that King Æthelwulf granted the tenth part of his land over all his kingdom by charter for the glory of God and his own salvation. One of these charters has surviveded in an original form.[1] It runs in the king's own name, and states that with the advice and permission of his bishops and nobles he has granted twenty hides to himself, so that he may leave it for ever to any one who may be acceptable to him. The real object of the charter is brought out in a long and detailed clause to the effect that the land shall remain thenceforward free from all 'tribute' to king or ealdorman, from all work on royal buildings, and from all invasion of the estate arising through crimes committed within it or through the necessity of arresting thieves. Apart from fyrd-service and bridge-work, which are expressly reserved, the king is, in fact, removing every kind of secular burden from a portion of his demesne in order that it may be devoted without encumbrance to the service of religion. The fact that he could only do this by making a charter granting the estate to himself is a curious illustration of the limited range of conceptions which governed Old English land law in the ninth century.

If ambiguities like these were possible in the reign of Æthelwulf, it is not strange that charters of an earlier age often fail to make their real meaning apparent. On the surface, the Anglo-Saxon land-book is obviously an ecclesiastical instrument. All the earliest of these documents are, in fact, records of gifts to religious persons. In such a context it was only natural that a grantor should open his charter with a contrast between time and eternity, emphasize the religious motives which have inspired his

[1] *C.S.* 451.

gift, and sanction it by an anathema on all who go against it. It is more remarkable that these features sometimes occur in charters of which the religious object, to say the least, is not evident. A charter of 779, in which Offa grants an estate near the Windrush to Dudda, his minister,[1] purports to have been made for the health of the king's soul, and opens with a devout proem. The presumption that Dudda intended to found a monastery on this estate is destroyed by later words, empowering him to bequeath the land to any one of his kin, and providing that if any of his heirs is guilty of a great offence he may purge himself by an appropriate payment without forfeiting the land which Offa has given. That clauses allowing a man to nominate his heir often bore their natural meaning is shown by a law of King Alfred[2] restraining a man from depriving his kin of bookland which his kinsmen had left him, if such alienation had been forbidden by those who first obtained the property or gave it to the existing holder. Before the end of the eighth century there are signs that clerks were feeling their way towards a type of charter which should be an appropriate record of a grant from a king to a noble. At the council of Chelsea in 788 Offa made a charter for one of his *ministri* in terms which, except for a formal invocation, are as secular as those of an Anglo-Norman writ of enfeoffment.[3] But the ecclesiastical traditions of the land-book were too strong for the general adoption of such experiments. In the tenth century the tendency was towards the elaboration rather than the abandonment of the pious formula, and in the generation before the Norman Conquest earls and thegns were receiving royal charters cast in phrases which had been designed to emphasize the sanctity of a gift for religious uses.

This conservatism to some extent disguises the significance of the solemn charter in the development of the Old English land law. Before the end of the ninth century 'bookland'—land exempted from public burdens by a royal charter—had come to be recognized as one of the two great categories into which all land fell. A law of Edward the Elder[4] states that the king has appointed penalties for those who withhold another man's rights 'either in bookland or in folkland',[5] and provides that if the

---

[1] *C.S.* 230.   [2] c. 41.   [3] *C.S.* 254.   [4] Edward, c. 2.

[5] [This phrase may now be compared with one in a little text from the burnt manuscript Cotton Otho B. xi, known from Nowell's transcript, British Museum Additional MS. 43703. It is a reply to a question about the penalty for adultery, and declares this to be the same '*sig swa boclond swa folclond, swaþer hit sie ge cyninges*

dispute concerns folkland the plaintiff shall fix a day on which the defendant shall answer him before the king's reeve. No term in the whole body of Old English law has given rise to more discussion than the folkland of this passage. From 1830 until the last decade of the nineteenth century the view prevailed that folkland meant the land of the people, *ager publicus*; an interpretation which had the great advantage of agreeing with the sense usually borne by *folc* in the numerous compound words of which it forms a part. On the other hand, it could not be applied for long to the known facts of Old English land-tenure without qualifications which destroyed its attractive simplicity; and in 1893 Vinogradoff, reinforcing the theories of seventeenth-century scholars with new arguments, defined folkland as land held under *folcriht*, or common law, in contrast to bookland, or land held in accordance with the provisions of a royal charter.[1] At the present time most scholars would probably accept Vinogradoff's definition, though some at least have felt that it gives a strained interpretation of a simple Old English compound, and that royal charters which are earlier than the tenth century rarely contain any provisions definitely governing the descent of an estate or the conditions of its tenure. It still remains an open question whether the distinction between bookland and folkland may not turn after all on the simple fact that bookland, unlike folkland, was land exempt from the heaviest of public burdens by a royal charter.

Apart from its occurrence in the laws of Edward the Elder,[2] the word *folcland* is only to be found three times in Anglo-Saxon texts. It occurs, unhelpfully, in the poem known as the 'Wife's Complaint', where it simply means 'country'. In a legal sense it appears in the will of a ninth-century ealdorman named Alfred;[3] a document which raises interesting questions, but is obscure at critical points. After bequeathing a large estate, apparently of bookland, to his wife and daughter, the ealdorman bequeathes three hides of bookland to a son named Æthelwald, with the provision that if the king will grant him the folkland as well as the bookland he shall hold it, but that otherwise he shall receive

---

selfes ge ælces monnes.' (be it bookland or folkland, whether it be the king's own or any other man's). See R. Flower, *London Medieval Studies*, vol. I, part I (1937), p. 62.]

[1] *E.H.R.* viii (1893), 1–17; reprinted in the *Collected Papers of Paul Vinogradoff*, i, pp. 91–111.

[2] And in the text mentioned on p. 309, n. 5.

[3] *C.S.* 558; F. Harmer, *English Historical Documents*, pp. 13–15.

another piece of bookland from the testator's wife. These terms show that a nobleman might hold both bookland and folkland, and suggest that while he was free to dispose of his bookland by will, he had no such power over his folkland. A more definite conclusion, that a man's folkland would not descend to his heir without a new grant from the king, cannot be maintained in face of a strong suspicion, raised by the language of the will, that Æthelwald was an illegitimate son. In view of this uncertainty, this famous reference to folkland and bookland does little more than emphasize the contrast between these terms which is generalized in the laws of Edward the Elder.

The remaining reference to folkland is the most instructive. In 858 Æthelberht, king of Kent, brother of Æthelbald, king of Wessex, gave land in a place called Wassingwell to his *minister* Wulflaf in exchange for other land at Mersham, near Ashford.[1] He declared that the land at Wassingwell should thenceforward be as free from all burden of service to the king as the land at Mersham had formerly been. He then indicated the boundaries of the land at Wassingwell, showing incidentally that a stretch of royal folkland held by two men named Wighelm and Wulflaf lay on its western side. This reference to the king's own folkland is interesting; but the importance of the charter lies in an endorsement which states that when the king received the land at Mersham 'he turned it into folkland for himself'. The whole tenor of the document shows that this transaction meant the imposition of public burdens on land which had previously been exempt from them, and that the king was compensating himself for the loss of *feorm* and service from Wassingwell by imposing these burdens on the land at Mersham. The fact that a contemporary could describe his action as 'turning land into folkland' offers at last a definite clue to the real meaning of that term. To the man who wrote this endorsement, folkland meant land from which the king drew food-rents and customary services.

The definition of folkland as land subject to the rents and services by which the whole people had once maintained its king has at least the merit of simplicity. It also brings the term into intelligible relation with other Old English compound words beginning with *folc*. Folkland on this view means no more than 'ordinary land', just as, for example, *folcriht* means ordinary or common law. The current opposition of folkland and bookland

[1] *C.S.* 496.

is most easily explained by the contrast between land subject to
common burdens and land exempted from them by a royal
charter. Exemption from these burdens was frequently granted
by the kings of the eighth and ninth centuries, but it was always
an interference with a traditional distribution of public duties.
All forms of privileged estate were innovations compared with
the ceorl's family land, providing *feorm* and service for the king.
To the end of the Old English period fyrd-service, *brycg-bot*, and
burh bot, from which exemption was hardly ever granted, remained as survivals of the varied obligations which all land had
once carried. The folkland of the ninth century is land still
subject to all the burdens which had once been common to the
whole people.

The distinction between bookland and folkland belongs to the
sphere of what may be called public, if not constitutional, law.
No one but the king can turn folkland into bookland, and he will
rarely, if ever, act without the consent of his council. On such a
matter the council had a natural right to be consulted. The
well-being of the whole kingdom was threatened if kings dissi-
pated the sources of their *feorm* by inconsiderate grants to nobles
or churches. It is more remarkable that, from the seventh century onwards, kings and councils show themselves interested in
the tenurial relationships which were arising between individual
landholders. A lease of lands from a church to a noble, in which
the king has no obvious interest, is sometimes attested by a
formidable assembly of witnesses. In 852 King Burgred of
Mercia, the archbishop of Canterbury, four bishops, two abbots,
and nine ealdormen witnessed an agreement for a lease between
the abbot of Medeshamstede and a Mercian noble.[1] In Wessex
at a much earlier date the king was intervening between the lord
of an estate and men who can only be described as his tenants.
In a series of too concise sentences, Ine provided that a man who
held twenty hides of another must show twelve hides sown if he
wished to leave, that the holder of ten hides must show six, and
the holder of three hides, one and a half.[2] In whatever way these
laws may have been enforced, they were plainly intended to
meet the situation which might arise if a tenant who had fallen
on bad times wished to throw a derelict estate back on to his
lord's hands. They point to a very early development of leasehold tenure in Wessex, and the fact that the king himself would

[1] *C.S.* 464; Robertson, *Anglo-Saxon Charters*, vii.   [2] Ine, cc. 64–6.

often be the lord of the land does not mean that they applied only to cases in which he was interested. Like Ine's definition of the *feorm* which a lord should receive from a ten-hide estate, these clauses represent a state of society in which the economic relations between lord and tenant were regarded as subject to the king's control.

This attitude explains the occasional appearance in Ine's laws of passages intended to govern the relations between a noble and individual peasants who have taken land from him. Immediately after the clauses which have been quoted there comes a sentence which carries the beginning of a manorial economy in Wessex back into the seventh century.[1] 'If a man takes and ploughs a yard of land or more at an agreed rent, and his lord wishes to exact both work and rent from him for that land, he need not take it unless his lord has given him a house, but in that case he must forfeit the crops.' In this passage the 'yard of land' —the quarter hide, or 'virgate', which becomes the normal holding of the medieval villein—makes its first appearance in an English document. At this date the yard of land undoubtedly had its primitive meaning of a tenement formed by detaching one rood—a strip of arable one rod or *geard* in width—from every acre in a hide. The use of this term is in itself proof of the existence of open fields in seventh-century Wessex. But the chief interest of the passage lies in the form of tenure which it implies. The tenant is clearly a freeman, for the conditions on which he takes his holding have been determined by agreement between him and his lord. But the land is plainly regarded as the lord's; he has planted the tenent upon it, and expects it to yield rent or labour at his own discretion. In his economic position the tenant resembles the *gebur* of the eleventh century,[2] who held a yardland, paid rent and rendered service, and received, if not a house, at least its furniture from his lord. The fact that the tenant must abandon the crops if he refuses the lord's claim to service strongly suggests that his yardland, like that of the *gebur*, had originally been sown with his lord's seed. It is, indeed, highly probable that the tenant whom Ine had in mind was actually identical with the *gebur*, who in another of his laws[3] is accorded six shillings as compensation for a breach of the peace in his house. In any case, the passage is of outstanding importance as the first recorded example of a type

[1] c. 67.   [2] Below, p. 475.   [3] c. 6.

of relationship between lord and man which during the next three centuries was to change the whole character of English rural society.

As to the origins of the social order which had just been described, two general conclusions seem to be justified. Its pattern in historic times implies that it arose from mass migrations of free peasants, familiar with life in communities, accustomed to discussion in popular assemblies, and deferential to kingship as part of the natural order of the world. There was little that can properly be called democratic in their conception of society. The institution of slavery was part of the earliest English law, and in view of later evidence there can be no doubt that the primitive English ceorl was usually a slave-owner. Like their descendants in every age, the English peasants of the earliest time were very sensitive to diversities of rank, and in particular to the distinction between themselves and those whose birth entitled them to a place among the retainers of the king. Through grants of rents and services once due to the king, men of this higher class had become lords of innumerable villages long before the end of the seventh century. The beginnings of a manorial economy are clearly visible in Ine's laws. Nevertheless, it is not the manor, but the community of free peasants, which forms the starting-point of English social history.

In the second place, there are few discernible points at which Anglo-Saxon custom has been affected by intercourse with British peoples. There is no reason to think that the Romano-British population of any part of England was deliberately exterminated by its English conquerors. In varying numbers, British river-names survived the Saxon conquest everywhere. Some of them, such as Andover and Wendover, appear in forms implying that the English settlers who adopted them had more than a casual acquaintance with British speech. British names of woods and hills occur sporadically in all parts except the eastern coastlands, and the names of British villages and Romano-British road-stations gradually increase in number as the map of England is read from east to west. But in the parts of England which had been occupied before the end of the sixth century there is nowhere such a concentration of British names as would suggest that the pattern of British life had remained unbroken.

Other lines of inquiry lead to much the same conclusion. In the north-west, beyond the first impetus of the English invasion, the Celtic sheep-scoring numerals of the uplands may be an inheritance from the Britons of Cumbria. Northern records show the prevalence of a type of estate consisting of a central manor with satellite hamlets, which may conceivably have persisted from British days through seven centuries and three foreign conquests. In the south, the *wealas* of the laws of Ine show that men and women of British descent had been incorporated into early West Saxon society. The *lætas* of the laws of Æthelberht have been considered by many scholars to represent a British element in the primitive Kentish people. But this British strain has left no significant impression on English society. Throughout England the essential fabric of the social order, the fundamental technicalities of law, and the organization by which they were administered, are all of obvious Germanic origin. In the economic sphere the units by which a peasant's holding was estimated are Germanic, and it is not in Wales but in Germany that ancient parallels can be found to the technique of English open-field agriculture. Even in Wessex beyond Selwood, where British speech survived for centuries,[1] photography from the air has brought out an illuminating contrast between the rectangular Celtic fields of the Romano-British period and the curving strips of later English arable. In their agrarian routine, as in the principles by which their society was ordered, the Anglo-Saxons in England adhered to their own native traditions.

There remains the difficult, and, indeed, unanswerable, question of the extent to which this society was knit together by the tie of kinship. Of its importance as a protection to individuals there can, of course, be no doubt. Among the English, as among all Germanic peoples, it was a fundamental convention that the killing of a free man brought his kin into immediate action in order to avenge his death, or to enforce the payment of his wergild. It is also clear that the slayer's kin were expected to join with him in paying the wergild or bearing the feud that was its alternative. Many passages in the Old English laws are concerned with the application, which generally meant the limitation, of this principle. On the other hand, unlike most continental codes, Old English legal sources never offer any definition of the kin, and there are no means of determining the limits of

---

[1] On the evidence for this survival in Dorset see W. H. Stevenson's note in *Asser's Life of King Alfred*, pp. 248–9.

relationship to which it extended. There is just enough evidence to show that in King Alfred's time it included maternal as well as paternal kinsfolk, and a legal text of the twelfth century makes it plain that the former paid one-third, and the latter two-thirds, of any wergild which fell on the family group. The association of the father's and the mother's kin in the payment, and, it may be added, in the receipt, of the wergild is an important fact, for it shows that the composition of the family group varied from generation to generation as its range was enlarged by the marriage of its younger members. It was not a clan, and its organization must have been very loose and indefinite.

The free man was entitled to the help of his kinsmen on occasions less formidable than the payment of a wergild or entry into a feud. For a man of good repute, the normal method of rebutting an accusation was to appear in court with a number of companions, each of whom would take an oath in support of the defendant's own sworn denial. It is probable that in the earliest time a man's 'oath-helpers' had been chosen exclusively from among his kin. In any case, the duty of the kin to support the oaths of its members can be traced through all the surviving remains of Anglo-Saxon law. It was a duty that could reasonably be exacted, for a man's kinsmen had a direct interest in the success of his answer to grave charges. By the early part of the tenth century the government had begun to regard the kin as legally responsible for the good behaviour of its members. King Athelstan, for example, orders that the kinsmen of a thief who has been released on payment of a fine must stand surety for his future conduct. The same code provides that a family group which includes a man of bad character must find him a lord and a dwelling-place where he can be attached to appear in court, unless it is prepared to see him treated as an outlaw.[1] At every stage of Old English law it is clear that the kinless man was unhappy in his isolation, and that the state found it hard to deal equitably with him.

This does not mean that respect for the tie of kindred had ever been allowed to dominate the whole administration of English law. It would be expected to appear at its strongest in the rules governing a man's choice of the individuals who were to support him as oath-helpers. On the other hand, even in the earliest English laws, there are passages which ignore or deliberately

[1] ii Athelstan 1, 3; 2.

weaken this primitive function of the kin. Wihtred of Kent[1] provides that a ceorl who wishes to clear himself at the altar must produce, not a group of his kinsmen, but three men who are merely 'of his own class'. Ine of Wessex[2] orders that every person accused of homicide, whatever his status, must include at least one man of high rank among his oath-helpers. King Alfred, in his treaty with Guthrum,[3] insists that a man of lower rank than a king's thegn must produce the oaths of eleven men of his own class and of one king's thegn in order to clear himself from a similar charge. Provisions like these can only mean that the king mistrusts the value of an oath taken by a group of peasants in support of one of their own kind. They must have made it impossible for a ceorl to be cleared from suspicion of the gravest crimes by the mere oaths of his own family circle. It proves a very rapid development of English law that this serious encroachment on the power of the kin to protect its members was made before the end of the seventh century.

As to the influence of the tie of kindred on the tenure and inheritance of land, the pre-Conquest evidence, though fairly copious, is unsatisfactory. Most of it refers to the estates of wealthy persons, who can deal with their properties by devises and testaments. Many of the documents which bear on this subject relate to land held under a royal charter, and therefore exempt from the ordinary rules of inheritance. Little information has been preserved about the customs which regulated the descent of land among the peasantry, and there are questions of great importance, such as the conditions under which a daughter might claim a share in her father's land, on which Old English authorities throw no direct light. Medieval practice suggests very strongly that the holding of the pre-Conquest ceorl had been partible among his sons, or among his daughters if he had no son, and that the conception of the holding as 'family land' was so firmly established that its possessor had no right to alienate any part of it to the disadvantage of his expectant heirs. It seems reasonable to assume that the heirs of a ceorl whose holding was too small for profitable division often remained on their father's land, and cultivated it jointly after his death. But it is clear that the house community of land-owning kinsmen to which such arrangements must often have given rise was in law

[1] c. 21.   [2] c. 54.   [3] c. 3.

a mere group of individuals which could at any time be dissolved by the action of its members. No text of Old English law ever attributes the ownership of land to a family.[1]

[1] Developing a suggestion of J. M. Kemble (*The Saxons in England*, i, pp. 58–64 and Appendix A) historians have often stated that place-names ending in *-ingas*, of which there are many in eastern and south-eastern England, represent a primitive habit of settlement by families. In most cases the first element in these names is a personal name, and the plural form of the second element shows that the names originally denoted, not places, but communities. It has frequently been assumed that the individuals of whom each community was at first composed were connected by kinship with the man whose name was attached to the group. The intensive study which has been given to these names during the past twenty years has shown that this theory cannot be maintained. When combined with a man's name, the element *-ingas* denoted not merely his descendants and other kinsmen but also the whole body of his followers and dependants, free and unfree. There are names of this type, such as Hastings (above, pp. 18, 19) which must originally have covered a large number of separate families. Some names ending in *-ingas*— how many is still uncertain—were derived, not from personal names, but from words or names denoting natural features. Others are philologically obscure. Regarded as a whole, these names are clearly too vague in sense to be of much use for the reconstruction of early society.

X

THE CONQUEST OF SCANDINAVIAN ENGLAND[1]

By the end of the ninth century the Scandinavian attack upon western Europe had lost much of its energy. The Danish invasion of England in 892 was only the ill-planned enterprise of an army which had been decisively defeated on the Continent in the previous year. By the year 900 the great armies which had devastated northern France and the Low Countries between 880 and 890 had disintegrated into a number of small bands, of which one was destined to enter the service of the king of the West Franks, and to receive from him the lands along the Seine which formed the nucleus of the duchy of Normandy. For nearly a generation there had been no Norwegian descent in force on Ireland, and native kings had begun to take the offensive against the foreign settlers along the eastern coast. The future of England was still uncertain, but the possibility of a Danish conquest of the whole country was steadily becoming more remote as the Alfredian organization for the defence of the land was tested and extended.

In 899, when Edward, Alfred's eldest son, became king of Wessex, eastern England from the head-waters of the Tees to the estuary of the Thames was divided between a number of Danish armies. They had been established on the soil by the successive

[1] There are three principal authorities for this period—the main southern version of the *Chronicle*, best represented by MS. A, and two sets of annals, from Mercia and Northumbria, preserved respectively in MSS. B, C, and D of the *Chronicle* and in the *Historia Regum* of Symeon of Durham. The main chronicle ceases to be a continuous record in 920; the Mercian annals (generally called the 'Mercian Register') end in 924; and the Northumbrian annals lose their independence after 945. Materials drawn from other northern sources, of which the relations have not yet been fully worked out, are incorporated in MSS. D and E of the *Chronicle* between 925 and 957. For the period from 939 to 975, the *Flores Historiarum* of Roger of Wendover records a number of facts relating to the north for which there is no earlier authority. They seem to be derived in the last resort from a lost Northumbrian chronicle, probably written at York. Another lost source—a tenth-century poem in praise of Athelstan—is represented by two quotations and an abstract inserted into the *Historia Regum* of William of Malmesbury. The annalistic materials for the reign are so meagre that these fragments are of exceptional historical importance.

partitions of southern Northumbria, eastern Mercia, and East Anglia among the members of the great host which had invaded England in 865, and their hold upon the country had steadily grown firmer with the passage of time. At the very beginning of their settlement they had turned from war to agriculture, and the chief concern of their members was to live their lives in accordance with their own customs on the lands which they had won. But they retained their military organization, so that they were ready at any time to counter an attack on their independence or to use an opportunity of weakening their enemies in the south and west. They had no sense of political unity, and it was nothing but the personal rank of the chief man in each army which determined whether he should be called a king, as in East Anglia and Northumbria, or an earl, as among the armies of the midlands. It was only in an emergency that they ever acted together in war. But their lack of unity made it impossible to reduce them in a single campaign, and it was not until English territory was closed to them by the building of fortresses at strategic points, and their own security was threatened by Norwegian raiders from Ireland, that they were gradually brought to accept the king of Wessex as their lord.

Apart from the kingdom of Wessex, which at the time of Alfred's death included all England south of the Thames and Bristol Avon, the country under English rule fell into two great divisions. North of the Tees and west of the Pennines the surviving fragments of the Northumbrian kingdom were ruled in virtual independence by a number of English ealdormen. The most prominent of them was Eadwulf of Bamburgh, whose country extended along the eastern coast from the Tees to the Firth of Forth. But the early records of the church of Durham[1] show other English lords of equal rank in the region between the Pennines and the western sea. An English minster still existed at Heversham at the head of the Kent estuary. It seems clear that the settled life of this country had not yet been disturbed by the invasions from Ireland and Strathclyde which were to revolutionize the culture and social organization of Cumberland, Westmorland, and Lancashire.[2]

---

[1] Of which the substance is represented in the 'Historia de Sancto Cuthberto', *Symeonis Monachi Opera*, R.S., i, pp. 208–10.

[2] On the general condition of north-western England *circa* 900–25 see F. M. Stenton, *C.P.*, pp. 215–18.

To the south of the Mersey, along the Welsh border, and extending far into the midland plain, lay the region of which Æthelred of Mercia was lord. It included the whole of the district, from Cheshire in the north to Gloucestershire and Oxfordshire in the south, which the Danes of the previous century had left in English hands. But it also included at least the centre and south of Buckinghamshire,[1] and there is definite evidence that Æthelred continued to hold London until his death in 911.[2] Nothing is recorded about the line of his frontier against the enemy forces at Bedford and Northampton. But it is probable that Watling Street, which still divides Mercian Warwickshire from Danish Leicestershire, formed the boundary between the Danes and the English of the southern midlands until, some thirty miles north-west of London, it entered the region commanded by the city.

Before the end of King Edward's reign every Danish colony south of the Humber had been annexed to Wessex. But the campaigns by which this result was brought about belong entirely to the second half of the reign, and there was nothing to foreshadow them in the inconclusive fighting of Edward's first ten years. From 899 until 902 he was kept in unease by an enemy sprung from his own house. Soon after his accession his cousin Æthelwold, son of King Æthelred I, forcibly occupied the royal estates of Wimborne and Christchurch, and declared himself ready to stand a siege in Wimborne. Edward replied by occupying the pre-Roman earthwork now called Badbury Rings, four miles north-west of Wimborne, and Æthelwold thereupon fled by night, leaving behind him a nun whom he had abducted in contempt of the king and his bishops. In the event, his flight made him more dangerous, for he was received by the Danish army of Northumbria. Nothing is known of his movements during the next year, but in 901 he appeared in Essex with a fleet which he had collected over sea, and in 902 he persuaded the army of East Anglia to undertake a great raid over English Mercia and northern Wessex. In reprisal, King Edward ravaged East Anglian territory between the Cambridgeshire dikes and the river Wissey[3] and as far north as the

---

[1] *C.S.* 603.   [2] *Chronicle* under 912.
[3] *Betwuh dicum and Wusan (Chronicle).* On the reasons for identifying the latter river with the Wissey rather than the Ouse see E. Ekwall, *English River-Names*, pp. 315–16, 466.

Fens. He and the men under his own command made good their retreat towards the south, but the Kentish division of the force disobeyed his order to retire, and was intercepted by the Danish army. In the battle which followed,[1] the Danes, as often in Alfred's time, 'kept the place of slaughter', but among their leaders there fell Eohric their king, Æthelwold their ally,[2] and another Englishman of the highest rank, described as Beorhtsige son of Beorhtnoth the ætheling, who was probably a landless descendant of the royal house of Mercia.

This episode had little direct influence on the course of events, but it is interesting as an illustration of the change which had come over the relations between Danes and Englishmen since the early invasions of the ninth century. By the year 902 Danish armies had been established in England for nearly a generation, intercourse on the lines laid down in the treaty between Alfred and Guthrum was making Englishmen familiar with their language and customs, and they had already begun to accept Christianity. The history of Æthelwold's revolt shows the son of an English king using a Danish army for his own interests, without placing himself outside the pale of civilization.

Nothing definite can be said about the terms on which this war was ended, and little is known about the relations between King Edward and the Danish armies during the next seven years.[3] But their general character is indicated by two remarkable private transactions of this period. In 926 King Athelstan made two charters,[4] each confirming to an Englishman of some

---

[1] The battle is said to have been fought *æt þam Holme*. The name is common, and the site cannot be identified with certainty.

[2] The position which he held among them is uncertain. MSS. B, C, and D of the *Chronicle* state that the Northumbrian Danes received him as their king after his flight from Wessex to their country. The statement—improbable in itself—can hardly be accepted in face of the silence of the almost contemporary MS. A. A rare coin of the period bearing the name *Alvvaldu* has often been quoted in support of MSS. B, C, and D, but in view of the form of the name, the attribution of the coin to Æthelwold is unsafe.

[3] Under 906 two independent sources—the *Chronicle* and the northern annals which are preserved in the *Historia Regum* of Symeon of Durham—record a treaty between Edward and the Danes of Northumbria and East Anglia. The *Chronicle* states that it was made at 'Yttingaford'—a site on the river Ousel near Leighton Buzzard—'as king Edward ordained'. The northern annals state that Edward made the treaty 'necessitate compulsus'. It is probable that these discrepant statements refer to the same event, and there is no external evidence to help in a decision between them.

[4] *C.S.* 658, 659. On their significance see F. M. Stenton, 'Types of Manorial

position lands which he had 'bought from the heathen at the command of King Edward and ealdorman Æthelred'. One of these charters relates to the south of Bedfordshire and the other to the north of Derbyshire. It is very unlikely that these transactions stood alone. The purchase of land from the local armies was an obvious means of spreading English influence in Danish territory, and it is possible that the king and the ealdorman had been using their thegns' resources on a large scale for this purpose. In any case, these purchases correct the impression of unqualified hostility between Danes and Englishmen which is produced by the monotonous record of their wars.

The wars began again in 909 when Edward dispatched a combined Mercian and West Saxon host against the Northumbrian Danes. It harried their country for five weeks, and compelled them to accept peace on terms dictated by the king and his council. Next year they took the offensive, and invaded English Mercia. At the moment of their invasion King Edward was in Kent, waiting for the concentration of a fleet which he had summoned from the central and western coastlands of Wessex. The Danes, believing that most of the king's fighting men were on shipboard, extended their operations, and raided over the whole of English Mercia as far as the Bristol Avon. On their return they crossed the Severn, and harried along its western bank until they reached the neighbourhood of Bridgnorth. They then struck east into the midlands, followed by an army drawn for the emergency from Wessex as well as Mercia. They were overtaken at last near Tettenhall in Staffordshire, where the English levies won a conclusive victory.[1] The raiding army was annihilated, and among its leaders three Northumbrian kings were killed.

The battle of Tettenhall opened the way to the great expansion of the West Saxon kingdom which occurred in the following years. The gradual reduction of East Anglia and the Danish midlands by the king of Wessex could never have been brought about if the Danish colonists of that country had been supported by a strong Northumbrian kingdom. In fact, the Danish armies

Structure in the Northern Danelaw', *Oxford Studies in Social and Legal History*, ii, pp. 74-5.

[1] The clearest account of this campaign is given by Æthelweard (ed. A. Campbell, pp. 52-3). He gives a precise date—5 August—for the decisive battle and states that it was fought *in Uuodnesfelda campo*, that is, near Wednesfield, three miles east of Tettenhall, the site named in the *Chronicle*.

in Northumbria never recovered from the disaster of 910, and the chronicles which describe the West Saxon advance against the southern Danes give no hint of Northumbrian intervention. In course of time, the weakness of Danish Northumbria led to a situation which threatened the interests of the West Saxon kingdom. After 910 there remained no power in northern England capable of effective resistance to the Norse invaders from Ireland, who by the year 919 had founded a new Scandinavian kingdom of York. But the king of Wessex had received the submission of every Danish army in southern England before the Irish vikings descended in force on Yorkshire.

In 911, the year after the battle of Tettenhall, Æthelred of Mercia died. The immediate striking-power of the midland Danish armies had not been affected by the Northumbrian defeat, and alliance with Wessex, on whatever terms, was still necessary for Mercian defence. Upon Æthelred's death his widow Æthelflæd, King Edward's sister, was recognized as 'Lady of the Mercians'.[1] With this anomalous title, she ruled Mercia for eight years, kept the loyalty of a formidable military household, and led the Mercian host in person on expeditions which she herself had planned. The record of the fortresses which she built for the protection of Mercia shows that she had an eye for country, and the ability to forecast the movements of her enemies. It was through reliance on her guardianship of Mercia that her brother was enabled to begin the forward movement against the southern Danes which is the outstanding feature of his reign.

As a preliminary to this movement, King Edward took possession of the lands along the Thames which had formed the southernmost extremity of Æthelred's government. The *Chronicle* records that in 911 he occupied 'London and Oxford and the lands that belonged thereto'. Before the year was over he had established an outpost against the Danes of Bedford and Cambridge by building a fortress on the north bank of the Lea at Hertford. With his northern border thus guarded he turned in the summer of 912 against the nearest of his enemies, the Danish army of Essex, and took up a position at Maldon on the

---

[1] It is possible that she was already, in fact, the ruler of Mercia. The best authority for the chronology of the period, the so-called 'Mercian Register', places the building of her first recorded fortress in 910. This, and the fact that Æthelred seems to have taken no part in the campaign of that year, suggest that he may have been incapacitated for some time before he died.

Blackwater estuary. It is probable that he stationed ships in
the river mouth, for without fortifying his base he sent his men
six miles inland to build an earthwork at Witham, on the
Roman road from Colchester to London. In English hands,
this earthwork, of which impressive remains still survive,[1] was
a massive obstacle to any westward movement by the Danish
army based on Colchester, and its construction was followed by
the submission of many Englishmen formerly held subject by the
Danes. In the meantime another detachment of his army had
completed the defences at Hertford by a second fortress, south of
the river. By the end of the year London had been made reasonably secure against any surprise attack by the Danish armies of
the north or the east.

At this point the advance seems to have been suspended for
eighteen months. For the year 913 the *Chronicle* records nothing
but local fighting in the midlands between Danish raiders from
Northampton and Leicester and the men of the country to the
south. Early in 914 all the resources at the king's command
were suddenly needed for the protection of Wessex against a
Scandinavian army which had sailed from Brittany to Wales,
and was harrying beyond the Severn. It was outmanœuvred
by an army drawn from Hereford, Gloucester, and other
Mercian fortresses, and compelled to give pledges for its departure. But it was only kept from a descent on Wessex by an
English force drawn out along the coast from the Cornish
border to Avonmouth, and it was not until the summer, when
the raiders sailed for Ireland, that there could have been any
thought of renewing the attack on the Danes of eastern England.

Thenceforward its course was unbroken. In October the king
appeared with an army at Buckingham, in the extreme north
of his own country, and built a fortress on each bank of the
Ouse. Within a month, apparently by negotiation rather than
force, he secured the submission of Thurketil, the earl commanding the Danish army of Bedford, who was followed by
most of the leading men in that army, and by some of those who
belonged to the more dangerous army of Northampton. In the
campaigning season of 915 he consolidated this success by occupying Bedford itself, and building a new, English, fortress to
the south of the Ouse over against the Danish work on the
northern bank. In 916 the midland campaign was suspended

[1] *Royal Commission on Historical Monuments, Essex.*

in favour of an expedition to Essex, where a new fortress was built at Maldon to protect the garrison of Witham from enemies coming by sea, but before the end of the year the king had reduced the number of the Danish armies in the midlands by helping Earl Thurketil to leave England, with all the men who wished to follow him.

In the meantime Æthelflæd, Edward's sister, was building new fortresses each year in English Mercia. Many of the chief centres of population in that country had been fortified during the earlier phases of the Danish war. Already in Alfred's reign she and her husband had provided Worcester with defences 'for the protection of all the people'.[1] Garrisons had been established in Hereford and Gloucester before 914, and it is unlikely that Shrewsbury, which is described as a city in a charter of 901,[2] was merely an open town. The walls of Chester had been repaired in 907, probably for the protection of the Cheshire plain against a Norse colony lately founded in Wirral.[3] But from her accession to sole power on her husband's death, she carried out year by year a deliberate plan of fortress-building which gave a new solidity to the defences of Mercia. Of the ten fortresses which she is known to have built, three cannot now be identified,[4] but the distribution of the remaining seven shows the way in which the military situation controlled her work. In 912, by a fortress at Bridgnorth she blocked a crossing of the Severn which Danish armies had used twice within living memory. Of the fortresses which she built in 913, Tamworth protected the Mercian border against attack from the Danish army based on Leicester, and Stafford barred entry from the Trent valley into English Mercia by way of the easy passage between the southern end of the Pennines and the high ground of Cannock Chase. Her works in 914 included the repair of a pre-Roman camp on Eddisbury hill in Delamere forest from which a garrison could intercept raiders descending from Northumbria or landing from the Mersey, and a second challenge to the Danes of Leicester in a fortification at Warwick three miles west of the Fosse Way. In 915 she fortified two sites on the extreme border of her country—Chirbury on a tributary of the Severn, which commanded the easiest road from Shrewsbury into central Wales, and Runcorn on the Mersey. Here her work

---

[1] *C.S.* 579.   [2] *C.S.* 587.   [3] Below, p. 331.
[4] *Bremesburh, Scergeat,* and *Weardburh.*

of fortification seems to have ended. It had been carried out
with a thoroughness which allowed her at last to send armies
into her enemies' country, and in the following years she made
her power felt both to the west and the east of her own land.
In 916 the murder of a Mercian abbot by the Welsh was
punished by an expedition which captured the wife of the king
of Brycheiniog by Llangorse lake near Brecon. In 917 Mercian
troops played a great, and in some ways decisive, part in the
general offensive against the midland Danes which King
Edward opened in that year.

The events of 917 are known in more detail than those of any
year since the Danish war of 892–5, and they decided the issue
between Danes and Englishmen which the earlier struggle had
left open. They began in April with an English occupation
of Towcester, the site of a Roman station on Watling Street,
which at that point seems to have formed the southern boundary
of the army of Northampton. The occupation was followed a
month later by the building of a new English fortress at a place
called Wigingamere, which has not yet been identified, but
clearly lay some distance within Danish territory. This advance
of the English frontier led to the concentration of the Danish
armies of Northampton, Leicester, and a region which the
Chronicle vaguely describes as 'the north'. The combined army
attacked Towcester but failed to take it, and then broke away
into an aimless raid towards the south. Simultaneously, the
armies of Huntingdon and East Anglia invaded Bedfordshire,
which was now in English hands, and built a new fortress at
Tempsford on the river Ivel, which they proposed to use as a
base instead of Huntingdon. From Tempsford they moved up
the Ouse valley towards Bedford, but the English garrison of
that place met them in the open country, and drove them back
with heavy loss. A little later a third Danish army, drawn
from East Anglia and Danish Mercia, attacked the English
position at Wigingamere, but failed to take it, and retired
without attempting a siege. The occupation of Tempsford was
the one military success gained by an effort in which at least
five different Danish armies had taken part.

Their obvious lack of unity was only one among the reasons
for their failure. In the latter part of July, while the eastern
and south-midland Danes were closely engaged in the struggle,
Æthelflæd had invaded the territory of their northern allies and

assaulted Derby. The town fell, and was annexed to English Mercia together with the whole region of which it was the military centre. It is probable that Æthelflæd was acting in concert with her brother, and there can be no doubt that the fighting round Derby gave occupation to a large force which might otherwise have joined the Danes in the Ouse valley. The turning-point in the war came when, still before harvest time, an English army drawn from the midland garrisons stormed the Danish fortifications at Tempsford and killed all their defenders, with the Danish king of East Anglia at their head. So far as is known, the king had no successor, and the lack of cohesion between the various Danish armies became steadily more pronounced in the later stages of the war.

Immediately after the success at Tempsford, an army drawn from Kent, Surrey, Essex, and the neighbouring garrisons attacked Colchester. The town was stormed, but no attempt was made to hold it, and the breaches in its Roman walls were left unrepaired. Nevertheless, its fall was a warning to the East Anglian Danes that their southern boundary was insecure, and a little later in the summer they made their last attempt to break the circle of English outposts. A large East Anglian army, reinforced by a company of vikings from the sea, laid siege to Maldon. But the garrison held out until it was relieved, the retreating Danes were heavily defeated, and the kingless army of East Anglia was finally reduced to the defensive.

Up to this point the king seems to have left the campaign to subordinates. But in the early autumn he took the field with the militia of Wessex. Fixing his head-quarters at Passenham, near the point where Watling Street crosses the Ouse, he set his men to surround the fort at Towcester with a stone wall. His display of force led to the immediate submission of Earl Thurferth and the other leaders of the army of Northampton. As soon as the militia divisions with the king had served their term, they were relieved by others, which moved down the Ouse valley to Huntingdon and occupied the Danish fortress there. The fall of Huntingdon left the army of Cambridge the only independent host in the midlands on which the East Anglian Danes could rely for reinforcement. But for all its recent defeats, the army of East Anglia was still formidable, and before attacking it King Edward decided to make certain that the English frontier in Essex was secure. In the event, his decision made an invasion of East Anglia unnecessary. In November, with yet another division of the West Saxon militia, he occupied Colchester and repaired its broken walls. A large number of Englishmen, from East Anglia as well as Essex, came in to him at once. The East Anglian Danes, still an organized army, swore that they would keep peace with him thenceforward by sea and land, and a crowded year ended with the separate submission of the army of Cambridge.

In January 918 there remained south of the Humber four separate Danish armies, grouped around the fortified positions of Leicester, Stamford, Nottingham, and Lincoln. Early in the year Æthelflæd obtained possession of Leicester without any fighting, and most of the local army submitted to her. It is more remarkable that at about this time she received a formal and explicit promise of allegiance from the leading men of the region dependent on York. There is little doubt that this offer was intended to obtain her support against the Norse raiders from Ireland, who are known to have been at large in the north at the time. But before she could act on it she died—at Tamworth on 12 June—and the opportunity of a peaceful annexation of southern Northumbria never returned. So far as is known, no proposal of the kind was ever made to King Edward, her brother, and no English army intervened to prevent the establishment of the Norse kingdom of York.

With the Danes of East Anglia and the eastern midlands in subjection Edward was free to move against the powerful Danish armies beyond the Welland. The direct line of advance into their country was barred by their garrison at Stamford, and his first step was to occupy the high ground to the south of the Welland which overlooked the Danish works to the north. The fortification of his own camp caused the immediate submission of the Danes beyond the river. Their surrender opened the roads to Nottingham and Lincoln, but before he could take either of them he was told of his sister's death, and at once broke off the campaign in order to make sure of his authority in Mercia. It could not be assumed that the Mercian lords would continue to acquiesce in the subordination of their country to Wessex. The sense of danger which had overridden Mercian particularism was steadily becoming less urgent as one Danish army after another fell out of the war. In 918, for the first time in a generation, the Mercian aristocracy was free to give its allegiance to whom it would. The possibility that it might break away from Wessex was ended by King Edward's seizure of Tamworth. All who had been Æthelflæd's subjects at once accepted him as lord. Their wish for a ruler intermediate between themselves and him was met for the moment by the allowance of nominal authority to Ælfwynn, Æthelflæd's daughter. But in the winter of 919, by a violent act of power, Edward caused her to be carried off into Wessex, and thenceforward there remained no formal distinction between Mercia and the other English regions under his rule.

The events of 918 brought Edward into new relations with the Welsh peoples. He had already shown friendship to them by paying the ransom of a bishop of Llandaff who had been captured by the viking raiders of 914. The Mercian ealdormanry, like the older Mercian kingdom, had generally been hostile to the Welsh. Individual Welsh princes are known to have submitted to King Alfred in order to obtain his protection against Æthelred of Mercia,[1] and their successors showed themselves willing, if not eager, to accept Edward as their lord. Immediately after the submission of the Mercians at Tamworth the kings of Gwynedd, Dyfed, and the lands between Merioneth and Gower became his men.[2] Their submission made him the overlord of the whole western half of Wales, and the *Chronicle*, which adds that the whole Welsh people came in to him, implies that they were followed by the less important rulers of the country nearer England.

With a new authority over English Mercia and the British peoples beyond the border, Edward turned to the reduction of the last independent Danish colonies south of the Humber. No part of southern England had undergone a more intensive Danish settlement than the regions of which Nottingham and Lincoln are the historic centres. But the armies based upon those places were now isolated; a Norse army was threatening their natural allies in the country round York, and the main roads leading from their own territory to the west and south were commanded by English garrisons. An overwhelming English force could be brought against them at any time, and

---

[1] Asser, *Vita Ælfredi*, c. 80.

[2] The *Chronicle* merely gives the names of the princes who submitted—Howel, Cledauc, and Ieothwel. For the districts over which they ruled see J. E. Lloyd, *History of Wales*, i, pp. 332-3.

before the end of 918 they surrendered without fighting. The fortifications at Nottingham were provided with a new garrison composed of Danes as well as Englishmen, and the fate of Lincoln is implied by the contemporary statement that after the surrender of Nottingham all the people settled in Mercia, Danes and Englishmen, submitted to King Edward. The English frontier had at last been carried to the Humber.

In the meantime, unnoticed by any southern writer, obscure movements of peoples were changing the character of life in north-western England. In the first years of the century a Scandinavian colony, which has left many distinctive place-names, was founded on the Wirral peninsula by Norsemen from Ireland. Before 915 pirates were visiting the country between the Pennines and the Irish Sea in sufficient numbers to dislodge the local nobles and churchmen. Nothing definite can be said about the date at which the raiders turned from plunder to settlement, but on every ground it is probable that the change began in the first quarter of the tenth century. The ease with which communication was maintained between York and Ireland in the next decades suggests very strongly that the north-west coast of England was in Norse occupation. And a long time is needed for the evolution of the art-forms cut on the pre-conquest sculptured stones of Cumberland, Westmorland, and Lancashire.

The effect of this settlement was to introduce into north-western England a remarkable hybrid culture, in which Norse and Irish elements are inextricably combined. Their interplay has long been noticed in the art of this region. Norse and Irish decorative motives in combination gave rise to new patterns of design, and individual monuments, of which the most famous is the cross at Gosforth in south Cumberland, show a strange association of Christian and Norse imagery. More recently the study of place-names has emphasized the Irish strain in the racial complex of the north-west. Irish personal names, often of an ancient type, are preserved in innumerable local names; Irish loan-words, though less common, are far from rare, and many place-names, such as Brigsteer, 'Styr's bridge', and Gilcambon, 'Kamban's ravine', show the Gaelic habit of forming compounds in which the second element is a definition of the first.[1] Evidence of this kind shows the presence of Norse settlers

[1] E. Ekwall, *Scandinavians and Celts in the North-West of England* (Lund, 1918).

from Ireland everywhere in the coastal region from south Lancashire, where they were in touch with the Norse colony in Wirral, to the estuary of the Solway. It also shows that the central hills of Cumberland were theirs and that they had occupied with the force of a migration Kentdale and the country for many miles on either side of the Cumbrian Derwent.

It is highly probable that the confusion into which their coming had thrown north-western England was increased by an invasion of this country from Strathclyde. The whole plain round the Solway Firth had formed part of the Northumbrian kingdom until its destruction by the Danes. An English abbot of Carlisle is a prominent figure in the legends which gathered round the flight of the monks of Lindisfarne with St. Cuthbert's body in 875. On the other hand, fifty years later, Eamont bridge near Penrith was the point at which King Athelstan chose to meet the king of Scots and his ally, the king of Strathclyde. It was a well-established custom for kings to negotiate with one another on the boundary between their territories, and there is therefore a strong presumption that Athelstan's kingdom ended at the river Eamont. The presumption is strengthened by the fact that in the reign of Edward the Confessor, when for a time the English kingdom had been carried again to the Solway, the lands between the estuary on the north, and the Eamont, the lakeland mountains, and the Derwent on the south, were regarded as lands which had once been Cumbrian—had belonged, that is, to the Britons of Strathclyde.[1] In the absence of direct evidence or early tradition, the early part of the tenth century, when there can have been no coherent English government in this country, seems the most probable time for its annexation by the Britons of the north.

It is also probable that the annexation was carried out without opposition from the English rulers who were in power at Bamburgh. There was a close connection in this period between the kings of Strathclyde and the kings of the Scots, and a common danger from Irish raiders was drawing the kings of Scots into alliance with the English of northern Northumbria. Their most formidable enemy was a viking named Rægnald, who became prominent early in the second decade of the

[1] On this evidence see C.P., pp. 216–19.

century. His career is badly recorded, and at many points its chronology is wholly uncertain.[1] But according to the early records of the church of Durham he descended on the Northumbrian coast between 913 and 915, and defeated at Corbridge an army led by Constantine king of Scots and Ealdred ealdorman of Bernicia.[2] For the next two or three years his movements are obscure, but in 917 he joined forces with a large viking fleet which had assembled at Waterford, and from that base he sailed in 918 on a great expedition against the Scots. A contemporary narrative written in Ulster states that the Scots were prepared for his invasion, 'so that they met on the banks of the Tyne in the land of the northern Saxons', and then describes a battle in which the Scots, successful at first, suffered heavy loss from Rægnald's own men, held until the last moment in reserve.[3] The Durham tradition of the battle places it, like Rægnald's earlier victory, at Corbridge, ignores the presence of the Scottish army, but brings out the interesting fact that there were local Englishmen of rank fighting on Rægnald's side.[4] It seems clear that Rægnald, like his kinsmen in many earlier battles, kept the place of slaughter after a day's indecisive fighting. He certainly remained in Northumbria over the winter, and in 919 he descended on York, stormed the city, and established himself there as king.[5]

His success opened a new field of enterprise to the vikings of the Irish coast. At the beginning of 919 the Mersey, which offered them the easiest entry into the heart of England, was protected only by the isolated fortress which Æthelflæd had built at Runcorn, separated by the deep valley of the Weaver from her garrisons at Chester and Eddisbury. In the autumn of that year King Edward took in hand the strengthening of the threatened frontier; built a new fortress at Thelwall, ten miles upstream from Runcorn, and repaired the Roman fortifications

---

[1] These difficulties have been discussed most recently by A. Campbell, *E.H.R.* lvii (1942), pp. 85–91.

[2] 'Historia de Sancto Cuthberto', *Symeonis Monachi Opera*, R.S. i, pp. 208–9. According to this authority the battle was followed by a division of the country north of the Tees among Rægnald's followers (F. M. Stenton, 'The Danes in England', *C.P.*, pp. 137–8).

[3] *Annals of Ulster*, ed. W. M. Hennessy, pp. 436–7.

[4] 'Historia de Sancto Cuthberto', *Symeonis Monachi Opera*, R.S. i, p. 210. Two Englishmen, Esbrid, son of Edred, and Elstan the *comes*, Esbrid's brother, are said to have been *robusti bellatores* on Rægnald's side.

[5] Symeon of Durham, *Historia Regum*, R.S., under 919.

at Manchester, within the Northumbrian border. But in 920, in spite of these new defences, Sihtric, Rægnald's cousin, with an army from Dublin, invaded north-western Mercia.[1] All that is recorded about the invasion is Sihtric's destruction of Davenport in Cheshire. The scale and ultimate purpose of the invasion are unknown, but it was probably in response to the situation which it had created that in the early summer King Edward undertook the northern expedition which forms the climax of his reign. He first moved to Nottingham, built a new fortress on the south bank of the Trent, and connected it by a bridge with the Danish works which he had garrisoned two years before, thus providing a defensible crossing of the river at the point where the local forces of the midlands could most readily converge for an advance on Northumbria. He then planted a fort and garrison at Bakewell in the Peak of Derbyshire, near a junction of valleys which offered alternative routes towards the north and north-west. Beyond Bakewell there are no traces of his progress, but one of the most famous passages in the whole *Anglo-Saxon Chronicle* records that there then submitted to him the Scottish king and people, Rægnald of York, and Ealdred of Bamburgh with all the Northumbrians —English, Danish, Northmen, and others—and the king and people of Strathclyde.

Each of the rulers named in this list had something definite to gain from an acknowledgement of Edward's overlordship. To Ealdred of Bamburgh, isolated between Britons, Scots, and Norwegians, it meant an assertion that the strongest king in Britain was his protector. The king of Strathclyde gained a confirmation of the lands which his people had annexed from the ancient Northumbria. Rægnald of York gained a recognition of his new kingdom, and the king of Scots gained a temporary security against Rægnald and his viking friends in Ireland. To Edward himself the submission meant that each ruler who became his man promised to respect his territory and to attack his enemies. These are simple obligations, and they no more than dimly foreshadow the elaborate feudal relationship which many medieval, and some later, historians have read into them. But the creation of even this simple bond between King Edward and the rulers of every established state in Britain

[1] Op. cit. under 920. The date is confirmed by the contemporary *Annals of Ulster*, which state that Sihtric left Dublin in this year.

gave to the West Saxon monarchy a new range and dignity which greatly·strengthened its claim to sovereignty in England.

To the West Saxon annalist who wrote the only extant account of Edward's wars they took the form of an inexorable advance, which carried the king of Wessex to supremacy over every power within reach of his armies. The king is the writer's hero, and the narrative ignores whatever might seem to qualify his achievement. Æthelflæd of Mercia is only mentioned when it is necessary to record her death, and nothing would be known of her fortress-building or of her share in the reduction of the Danish armies but for the survival of a set of meagre annals written in her own country. Nevertheless, when all allowance has been made for the short-sightedness of the West Saxon chronicler, King Edward will still be left as the organizer of one of the best-sustained and most decisive campaigns in the whole of the Dark Ages. He showed the ability to plan and the patience to carry out a series of operations which needed years for their completion; and he always had men in reserve for an emergency. In the technique of war he had learned much from his father, who had understood the strategic value of the fortress, and had made the West Saxon militia available for long-distance expeditions. It was the assurance of command with which he used his father's tentative expedients which changed the character of Anglo-Danish warfare in his time.

Little is known about the plan or scale of the fortresses on which the war had turned. Some of these sites are still unidentified, and on others all trace of tenth-century work has been removed by continuous occupation. It is probable that Æthelflæd's entrenchments at Warwick and Stafford are represented by the medieval defences of those towns, and that Edward's fortress south of the Ouse at Bedford consisted of the triangular area surrounded by the river and the two arms of what is still called the King's Ditch. But it is only at Witham and Eddisbury that there survive considerable remains of fortresses which obviously belong to this series. At Witham an outer ditch surrounded an area of 26 acres, roughly oval in outline, within which a scarped enclosure of nearly 10 acres formed a citadel. At Eddisbury, use was made of an ancient hill-spur camp comprising some 20 acres. The size of these works proves that they were intended to receive large garrisons. The massing of men in large numbers behind entrenchments, which is implied by the course of events in 917, shows that Witham and Eddisbury cannot have been of exceptional extent, and dissociates the fortresses built at this time from the castles which afterwards appear on many of the same sites. Some at least of these fortresses were ancient centres of population provided with new defences. Tamworth, which had been the seat of Mercian government until the ninth century, cannot have been deserted in 913. In any case it is clear that the fortresses of this period were intended to be held by divisions of the national militia, and that in area they resembled the medieval town rather than the medieval castle.

Whatever may have been the previous condition of the sites thus fortified, several of them appear as centres of at least a local trade within fifteen years of Edward's death. Coins were struck within this period, not only at Oxford, Gloucester, Hereford, Shrewsbury, and Chester, which had been defensible positions before the advance against the Danes began, but also at Hertford, Maldon, Stafford, Tamworth, and an obscure place called 'Weardburh' which Æthelflæd had fortified in 915. Among the inhabitants whose existence is proved by this currency some, and perhaps many, may have come of their own accord to enjoy the security of the new entrenchments. But in most cases it is probable that the initiative came from the king. No fortress which was intended to form part of an ordered system of national defence could safely be allowed to stand vacant until an emergency caused its occupation. It is significant that both Oxford and Wallingford, which at this date jointly guarded the middle Thames, show signs of deliberate planning for permanent habitation. It is highly probable that there, and in the more recent fortresses of this period, settlers had been encouraged by the king to take up plots on easy terms as his tenants.

By the early part of the eleventh century both English and Danish Mercia had been divided into administrative districts known as shires, each of which derived its name from a defensible town of this kind. In Wessex a group of shires, each organized in dependence on a particular town or important royal estate, had come into being before the period of the Danish wars. The relation between these shires and their capitals is sometimes disguised by peculiarities of nomenclature, but there is no doubt that the 'Dornsæte' and 'Sumorsæte' of Dorset and

Somerset took their names from Dorchester and Somerton. 'Hamtunscir' and 'Wiltunscir' are obviously the districts governed from Southampton and Wilton.[1] There is no trace of any corresponding system in independent Mercia. In the eastern half of the old Mercian kingdom the shires of the eleventh and later centuries represent with little change the districts occupied by the various Danish armies between which this country had been divided. But in western Mercia, where there was no Danish occupation, the shire is most easily understood as a deliberate imitation of West Saxon methods of government, carried out between the reign of Alfred and the year 980, when a reference to Cheshire in the *Chronicle* gives the first indication that the new system was in existence.

Whatever the date at which this system was established, it was certainly the work of a king who had no respect for the ancient divisions of Mercia. Shropshire represents an artificial union of lands which had once been divided between the Magonsætan and the Wreocensætan; Warwickshire was created by joining the most easterly part of the kingdom of the Hwicce to the lands which the Mercians themselves had possessed in and to the south of Arden. The old *provinciae* and *regiones* of the midlands are now so obscure that it is easy to forget that local feeling must once have gathered around them, and that in the west their solidarity had not been broken by the Danish wars. The Wreocensætan are mentioned in a charter of 963,[2] and an incidental passage in the *Chronicle*[3] shows that the name of the Magonsætan was still current in the eleventh century. The division of the western midlands into shires which completely disregarded the boundaries of ancient peoples could only have been carried out by a king strong enough to ignore resentments, and quite indifferent to local traditions. Edward the Elder, who had taken military possession of the chief seat of government in Mercia and destroyed all that remained of Mercian independence, is more likely than any other king to have remodelled the Mercian administration. It is most probable that the artificial shires of the western midlands[4] were created by him in the last years of his reign.

---

[1] Above, p. 295.   [2] *C.S.* 1119.   [3] Under 1016.
[4] Among them, a shire of Winchcombe, which was annexed to Gloucestershire by Eadric Streona during his tenure of the Mercian ealdormanry (Heming, *Chartularium*, ed. T. Hearne, i, p. 280).

The shires of the eastern midlands were no less artificial, but they were not the creation of any external authority. The typical shire of this country came into being through the settlement of a Danish army, such as the armies of Leicester, Northampton, Huntingdon, Bedford, and Cambridge, which are mentioned in the narrative of King Edward's wars. In the tenth century the town which gave the shire its name was not so much the centre of local government as the place where the army met for deliberation in peace, and concentrated in war. The military organization from which the shire arose survived in more than name into an age when the wars of Edward the Elder had become a matter of ancient history. Sixty years after his death a document written in Northamptonshire states that a sale of land was witnessed by the 'army' of Northampton,[1] and in 1013 the southern shires of Danish origin beyond Watling Street made a collective submission as an 'army' to Swein, king of Denmark.[2] Before the Norman Conquest, the lands which must once have belonged to the army of Stamford had come to form part of the great shire which took its name from Lincoln, and the practice of assigning the district known as Rutland to the king's wife in dower had begun the process which in time created the anomalous county of that name.[3] In 1066 Northamptonshire and Bedfordshire extended some miles to the south and Buckinghamshire some miles to the north of Watling Street, which in Edward the Elder's time had probably separated Danish from English territory. But there is no evidence that King Edward or any of his successors had ever attempted any thoroughgoing modification of the boundaries which the Danish armies of the ninth century had drawn between themselves in their own country.

Beyond the Humber Edward had no direct authority. By recognizing the viking kingdom of York in 920 he had abandoned all but a vague protectorate over its English and Danish subjects, and within a year he seems to have lost even this shadow of power. Rægnald, the first Norse king of York, died in 921, but his kingdom passed, apparently without dispute, to Sihtric his cousin. Coins on which Edward's name does not appear were struck at York for Sihtric, and he never acknow-

[1] A. J. Robertson, *Anglo-Saxon Charters*, p. 76.
[2] *Chronicle, sub anno.*
[3] Below, p. 502.

ledged Edward as his lord.[1] In the south after 920 there were
problems of government which left no opportunity for another
Northumbrian campaign. Edward, on the verge of old age, was
responsible for the good order of a composite state twice as
large as the kingdom which he had inherited from his father;
and from many of his subjects in both English and Danish
Mercia he can only have received most unwilling obedience.
In the summer of 924 an alliance between Mercians and
Welshmen called him out on what proved to be his last expedition.[2] Nothing is related of the episode except that the men
of Chester, relying on British support, rose against him; that he
suppressed the rising and placed a new garrison in the town;
and that within a few days he died at Farndon on Dee. The
pretext of the rising is unknown. But it shows that at the end
of Edward's reign the men of a Mercian frontier town were
prepared to make common cause with their hereditary enemies
in the hope of throwing off his rule.

Edward the Elder died on 17 July 924. Before the end of the
year Athelstan, his eldest son, had been recognized as king in
Wessex and probably in Mercia. On 4 September 925 he was
crowned at Kingston. There was a tradition that, as a child,
Athelstan was regarded as the ultimate heir to the West Saxon
kingdom, and that King Alfred had invested him with a scarlet
cloak, a belt set with gems, and a 'Saxon' sword with a golden
hilt as symbols of future dignity. He was brought up in the
household of Æthelred and Æthelflæd, and he must have been
the first king of Wessex who was intimate with the Mercian
aristocracy. His recognition as king of the Mercians was independent of his election in Wessex, and there is no evidence of
any Mercian disaffection in his reign.

The strength of his position in Mercia gave him an advantage
which his father had never possessed in dealing with Northumbrian affairs. Sihtric, king of York, who had ignored King
Edward, proposed an alliance with Athelstan soon after his
coronation, and at Tamworth on 30 January 926 he received

[1] The identification of the Rægnald whose name appears on some coins with
Rægnald the first Norse king of York has been seriously challenged by Michael
Dolley, The Post-Brunanburh Viking Coinage of York, Stockholm, 1958, pp. 41 ff.

[2] William of Malmesbury, Gesta Regum, R.S. i, pp. 144–5. This, and the other
passages from the Gesta Regum referred to in the following pages, are derived from
the lost panegyric which William used for the reign of Athelstan (above, p. 319,
n. 1), and have the authority of a contemporary.

a sister of Athelstan in marriage. But before the summer of 927 Sihtric was dead, leaving by a former wife a young son named Olaf, whom the Northumbrian vikings accepted as his heir. Guthfrith, Olaf's uncle, king of the Irish Norsemen, came over from Dublin to support him, and Athelstan replied by an invasion of Northumbria. After what can only have been a short campaign Olaf and Guthfrith were both driven out of the country; Olaf joining his father's former associates in Ireland,[1] and Guthfrith finding refuge with the king of Scots. Athelstan immediately took the opportunity of obtaining a recognition of his supremacy from the leading rulers of the north. At Eamont near Penrith, on 12 July 927, the kings of Scotland and Strathclyde and the English lord of Bamburgh became his men; each of them undertaking to suppress 'idolatry' within his country—an oblique reference to the practices current among the Norsemen recently settled in Galloway and Cumberland, in the south of English Northumbria, and in northern Scotland. Guthfrith, the fugitive viking leader, whom the king of Scots had promised to surrender to Athelstan, escaped on the way to Eamont, collected a war-band, and began a siege of York. But he was compelled to fall back from the city, and at last, after many miseries, he surrendered of his own accord, spent four days as a guest at Athelstan's court, and was then allowed to return to Ireland. In the meantime Athelstan had taken possession of York, destroyed the fortifications which its first Danish conquerors had built within its walls, and distributed the treasures which he found there. Under conditions which no one in an earlier age could have foreseen, a king supreme throughout southern England had come to rule in York, and in the region of which York was the historic capital.

Within the next four years Athelstan's supremacy had been extended over the western as well as the northern kings of Britain. Either by force or the display of force he brought most of the Welsh princes to a meeting at Hereford, and secured a promise of a yearly tribute, which was said to comprise an unspecified number of hounds and hawks, twenty pounds of gold, three hundred pounds of silver, and 25,000 oxen—figures which verge on but perhaps do not quite reach the incredible.[2]

---

[1] Remaining there until 940, when he joined his cousin Olaf Guthfrithson at York (below, p. 357-8).

[2] *Gesta Regum*, i, p. 148.

A more permanent result of the meeting was an agreement that the Wye should form the boundary between Welsh and English territory in the neighbourhood of Hereford.[1] At the date of the Norman Conquest the Wye between Hereford and Monmouth still separated the English shires of Hereford and Gloucester from the Welsh district of Erging to the west. That the Welsh princes themselves continued to regard Athelstan as their lord is shown by a number of English charters which they witnessed while his guests. Between 931 and 937 Hywel, king of Dyfed, Idwal, king of Gwynedd, and Morgan, king of Morgannwg, visited him many times; Owain, king of Gwent, at least twice; and Teowdor, king of Brycheiniog, at least once.[2] Among these kings, Hywel of Dyfed—the Hywel Dda of Welsh tradition— was strongly influenced by English life and methods of government. He gave an English name to one of his sons, he struck silver pennies of an English model, and it was probably the English conception of the king as legislator which moved him to issue whatever laws are his in the code called by his name. None of his fellow kings showed the same tendency to follow English ways, but all of them had clearly been brought into a new political system of which the English court was the centre.

According to the early writer who recorded the proceedings at Hereford Athelstan set out directly afterwards on an expedition against the Britons of Cornwall. The narrative implies that they were in revolt, and that men of their race in other parts of the south-west were supporting them. It suggests, in particular, that they had many supporters among the Britons who at that date formed an important part of the population of Exeter. The one incident of the campaign which it records is the refortification of the city by Athelstan, and the expulsion of its British inhabitants. In the end the Britons of Cornwall were compelled to accept the river Tamar as their boundary. Nothing is known of any changes in local government after the

[1] It is probably from the years soon after this agreement that there survives a document intended to provide a peaceful settlement of disputes between Welshmen and Englishmen, collectively called *Dunsæte*, on both sides of the Wye, the former in Erging and probably Ewias, the latter apparently in Herefordshire north of the Wye. It includes the appointment of twelve lawmen, six of each race, to declare the rules to be applied when Welshmen and Englishmen were at law with one another. See Liebermann, *Gesetze*, i, pp. 374–7, iii, pp. 214–19; F. M. Stenton, *C.P.*, p. 198; D. M. Stenton, *English Justice 1066–1215*, pp. 6–7.

[2] A list of these attestations is given by J. E. Lloyd, *History of Wales*, i. 353.

campaign, but the definition of British territory by a natural frontier was followed by the creation of a new bishopric for the country thus defined. Before 931 Athelstan had founded a see at St. Germans for the region beyond the Tamar, and placed a bishop of British name in charge of it.

So far as is known the settlement of 927 between Athelstan and the northern kings lasted for at least six years. But in 924, presumably in answer to some unfriendly action by the king of Scots, he attacked Scotland simultaneously by land and sea. The leading members of the expedition by land assembled at Winchester, where Athelstan held a great court on 28 May, attended by a large number of English thegns, by four Welsh princes, and by twelve earls, of whom five bore Scandinavian names and obviously came from the Danish east.[1] On 7 June what was substantially the same company appeared at Notting-ham.[2] The expedition cannot be followed any further in detail, but the king's own route is indicated by the record of gifts which he made at this time to the churches of Beverley, Ripon, and Chester-le-Street. The king of Scots never seems to have offered battle, and the English land-force harried his country as far as Fordun in Kincardineshire, while the fleet ravaged the coast up to Caithness. It was an impressive demonstration of the fact that the collapse of the Norse kingdom of York had brought the heart of the Scottish kingdom within striking dis-tance of an English army.

The sequel came three years later. After the events of 924 it must have been clear throughout the north that Athelstan could only be held within his own country by the union of all his enemies. Among the kings who had a definite cause of quarrel with him the most formidable was Olaf, son of Guth-frith of Dublin, whose father had been expelled ignominiously from Northumbria in the war of 927. Olaf came into power at Dublin in 934, when Guthfrith died; he seems to have been regarded as leader by all the Norsemen of eastern Ireland, and he commanded a fleet which had no rival in Irish waters. It was his natural ambition to recover the northern English kingdom of which his family had been deprived. It was equally natural that the kings of Scotland and Strathclyde, each threat-ened by English domination, should ally themselves with him.

[1] C.S. 702.
[2] C.S. 703; Farrer, Early Yorkshire Charters, i, pp. 1–5.

In 937 he sailed to Britain with a large fleet and united his forces with theirs for an invasion of England. One ancient writer states that the allies penetrated far into Athelstan's country before he engaged them,[1] but all authorities agree that the war ended with their annihilating defeat. From a contemporary Old English poem[2] it appears that they were met by Athelstan and his brother Edmund at the head of an army drawn from both Mercia and Wessex, and that after a long struggle they were broken and pursued until nightfall, leaving among their dead five kings and seven earls from Ireland and a son of the king of Scots. The English loss had been heavy,[3] but the allied force was destroyed; the northern kings reached their own lands with difficulty, and Olaf brought the mere wreckage of an army back with him to Dublin. The site of the battle, which appears in the poem under the name Brunanburh, has not yet been identified.[4]

The battle has a distinctive place among the events which made for the ultimate unity of England. It associated Mercians and West Saxons in the common memory of a great achievement which blurred the traditions of their ancient wars. It was not decisive of the future as Alfred's victory at Edington had been, but it set the seal of a dramatic success on the work which Alfred had begun. In the fighting around Brunanburh Athelstan was defending a state which embraced the descendants of Alfred's Danish enemies, and a civilization which united them to Christian Europe. It was through a sound historical instinct that Ælfric, the greatest of late Old English scholars, writing when civilization was again threatened by foreign invaders, placed Athelstan among the three English kings whose histories might encourage a harassed people. Between Alfred who fought with the Danes until he gained the victory and freed his people, and Edgar, whose enemies sought peace from him without a battle, he sets Athelstan, 'who fought with Olaf, destroyed his army, drove him into flight, and then reigned peacefully'.[5]

The feature which distinguishes the reign of Athelstan from

---

[1] William of Malmesbury, *Gesta Regum*, R.S. i, pp. 151-2.

[2] Critically edited by A. Campbell, *The Battle of Brunanburh* (1938).

[3] It included two sons of Æthelweard, the youngest son of King Alfred, who were taken for burial to Malmesbury. William of Malmesbury, op. cit. i, p. 151.

[4] The literature on this subject is reviewed by A. Campbell, op. cit., pp. 57-80.

[5] *Heptateuch*, ed. S. J. Crawford, p. 416.

the reigns of Alfred and Edgar is the intimacy of his association with the leading western rulers of his time.[1] Between Offa and Cnut there is no English king who played so prominent or so sustained a part in the general affairs of Europe. The Danish invasions had never completely isolated England from the Continent. Alfred had maintained regular intercourse with Rome; foreigners from all parts had visited his court, and the writer of the Alfredian *Chronicle* shows accurate knowledge of the relationship between the different branches of the Frankish royal house. But Alfred and, until his last years, Edward the Elder, could only watch the continental scene from outside. Their part in European history had been to preserve the tradition of effective monarchy in the west. Athelstan's influence in contemporary Europe rested on his position as heir of the one western kingdom which had emerged in greater strength from the Danish wars.

At the time of his accession the English court was already connected with the Continent by two important alliances. Between 893 and 899 King Alfred had married a daughter named Ælfthryth to Baldwin II, count of Flanders. The king and the count had a common interest in preventing the foundation of Danish settlements on the Flemish coast, and the alliance which it brought into being lasted much longer than most relationships of the kind. Sixty years after the marriage Count Arnulf, the eldest son of Baldwin and Ælfthryth, speaks of the established friendship between the kings of England and the counts of Flanders.[2] On her marriage Ælfthryth appears to have received a portion of land in England, and the first recorded grant of an English estate to a continental monastery is her gift of Lewisham to the abbey of Blandinium near Ghent, in 918. Her younger son Adelolf, count of Boulogne, who was obviously named in memory of her grandfather Æthelwulf, king of Wessex, was well known in England. For a generation after Alfred's time there was a personal as well as a diplomatic relationship between the English and the Flemish courts.

The second of these alliances gave the English court a direct interest in the internal politics of France. Between 917 and 919 Charles the Simple, king of the West Franks, the one

---

[1] On the continental marriages of Athelstan's sisters see R. L. Poole, *Studies in Chronology and History*, pp. 115–22.

[2] *Memorials of Saint Dunstan*, ed. W. Stubbs, R.S., p. 360.

descendant of Charlemagne who was still a reigning prince, married Eadgifu, daughter of Edward the Elder. At the date of the marriage the authority of Charles was recognized generally in France, and he had successfully asserted the claim of his house to rule in Lotharingia. But in 922 most of his leading subjects seceded from him in favour of the greatest of their number, Robert, count of Paris, whom they elected king. Robert was killed in 923, and Hugh, his son, declined any title higher than duke of the Franks. But the party opposed to Charles chose Rudolf, duke of Burgundy, as king; Charles fell into his enemies' hands, and apart from a short interval in 927–8, remained in captivity until his death in 929. Neither Edward the Elder nor Athelstan had taken any recorded part in these revolutions; but Louis, Charles's son, was brought to England by his mother, and lived there under Athelstan's protection until an opportunity arose for him to claim his inheritance.

In 926, presumably in order to establish an independent relationship with the king who was protecting the Carolingian heir, Hugh, duke of the Franks, himself proposed a marriage alliance with Athelstan. The mission which he sent to England was headed by Athelstan's cousin, Adelolf, count of Boulogne.[1] It met the king and his council at Abingdon, the site of an ancient monastery then in the king's hand, and offered him rich presents—perfumes, gems, horses, an onyx vase, a diadem set with jewels, and certain eminent relics, namely, the sword of Constantine the Great with a nail from the Cross in its hilt, the lance of Charlemagne with which the centurion had pierced our Lord' side, the standard of St. Maurice the Martyr, and fragments of the Cross and of the crown of thorns set in crystal. On the English side there was a sound political reason for the alliance in the certainty that Louis could never be restored to his father's kingdom without the goodwill, if not the active help, of the duke of the Franks. The mission was dismissed with gifts alleged to be comparable with those which it had brought, and before the end of the year the duke had married Eadhild, Athelstan's sister.[2]

Athelstan's interest in the fortunes of the Carolingian house brought him into relationship with at least one great power outside the French political sphere. Beyond the Rhine Henry the

---

[1] William of Malmesbury, op. cit. R.S. i, p. 150.
[2] Flodoard, *Annales*, ed. P. Lauer, p. 36.

Fowler, the first Saxon king of the Germans, was creating a new state out of the disunited fragments of Carolingian Germany. The imprisonment of Charles the Simple gave him an opportunity of detaching Lotharingia from its connection with the West Frankish kingdom, and in 925 he became for a time the master of that country. But the traditional loyalty of the Lotharingians for the house of Charlemagne was not extinct, and the possibility of its revival made it highly desirable for King Henry to establish friendly relations with Athelstan. The Carolingian heir was at Athelstan's court, he possessed a fleet which, as events were to show, could be mobilized in support of a Lotharingian rising, and his attitude towards such a rising would be likely to decide the action of the count of Flanders. The situation in Lotharingia lies behind the overtures towards an alliance which Henry the Fowler made to Athelstan in 928.

They took the form of a request for a sister of Athelstan as a bride for Otto, Henry's eldest son. According to both German and English tradition, Athelstan replied by sending two sisters between whom Otto might make his choice. Edith, the elder sister, became his wife. The younger sister married a prince who is described so vaguely that it is hard to identify him. It is most probable that her husband was Conrad the Peaceable, king of Burgundy, but her marriage had no political significance, and within two generations the English royal family itself had lost all trace of her. The marriage of Edith and Otto was more important. She died in 946, sixteen years before her husband's coronation as Emperor of the Romans. Liudolf, duke of Suabia, her only son, died in 957, and her husband's dignities passed to a son by a second wife. But her marriage opened a new period of intercourse between England and Germany which had considerable influence on English ecclesiastical history, and in particular on the course taken by the English movement towards monastic reform. The fortunes of her descendants were watched with interest in England. In 982 the death of Otto, duke of Suabia, wounded in battle against the Saracens of south Italy, was recorded by a chronicler at Abingdon with the note that he 'was the son of Leodulf the ætheling, who was the son of Otto the elder and of king Edward's daughter'. The English royal family kept in touch with its German cousins, and the strange chronicle of the ealdorman Æthelweard, a descendant of King Æthelred I, was written for Matilda, abbess of Essen, the grand-daughter of Otto and Edith.[1]

The death of King Rudolf at the beginning of 936 offered an opportunity for the restoration of the Carolingian line in France. Hugh, duke of the Franks, refused the kingdom for himself, and took the initiative in the recall of Louis, son of Charles the Simple, who was still an exile in England. The duke's proposal that Louis should return to France was first presented to Athelstan in a council held at York. After a certain amount of diplomatic correspondence Athelstan sent Oda, bishop of Ramsbury, to France with instructions to obtain security for Louis's reception as king, and when this had been given, provided him with an escort which brought him to Boulogne. The duke and his associates did homage to him on the sands, and on 19 June he was crowned king at Laon.

In the confused warfare which fills the reign of Louis d'Outremer his English kinsmen rarely intervened directly. But their support was behind him in an emergency, and once at least an English force was sent to the Continent on his behalf. In 939 many leading nobles of Lotharingia, the counts of Holland and Cambray among them, offered him their allegiance. The situation had arisen which Henry the Fowler had foreseen when he sought an alliance with Athelstan for Otto his son. In the event it threw an impossible strain on the political system of which Athelstan was the centre, and when Otto, now king of the Germans, invaded Lotharingia, Athelstan sent an English fleet to help Louis. The expedition was a complete failure. The crews ravaged parts of the coast opposite to England, and returned to their own country without ever taking part in the war. Athelstan died before the year was out, and his successor was kept from continental enterprise by a Norse attack on England itself. But the war of 939, ineffective as the English part in it had been, deserves to be remembered as the first occasion on which an English king is known to have assembled a fleet in order to help a continental ally.

In the meantime Athelstan had been taking part in a continental struggle outside the range of his dynastic alliances. In 919, the year in which Edward the Elder completed the reduction of the southern Danes, a horde of Northmen had invaded Brittany, devastated the whole country, and expelled

[1] R. L. Poole, *Studies in Chronology and History*, p. 115.

many of its inhabitants. There are signs of intercourse between England and Brittany in the years of peace before the invasion —when, for example, King Edward had been received into fraternity by the canons of Dol—and many of the expropriated Bretons fled across the Channel. The most important of them was Mathedoi, count of Poher, who had married a daughter of Alan the Great, the last ruler of all Brittany. Alan their son, afterwards known as Alan with the twisted beard, was baptized if not born, in England. Athelstan, not yet king, stood god-father to him, and ever afterwards protected his interests. In 931, after taking part in a disastrous rising of his people against the Northmen, Alan seems to have returned to England. In 936, with Athelstan's help, he brought back many of his exiled countrymen to their own land, and soon afterwards established himself in the counties of Vannes and Nantes, which were the hereditary possessions of his family.

It was mainly through Athelstan's interest in the affairs of Brittany that England first came into contact with the Scandinavian invaders of northern France. The contact was slight. The Northmen against whom he helped Count Alan were the vikings of the Loire, and there seems to be no evidence that he ever had any direct dealings with the much more formidable armies of the country afterwards known as Normandy. Before his death the Normans had occupied every port opposite to England from the Couesnon to the Bresle. Originally established in upper Normandy by Charles the Simple for the defence of the land against other vikings, they had acquired the Bessin in 924 and the Cotentin and Avranchin in 933. But they were still regarded as undesirable aliens by the men who were continuing the traditions of Carolingian government in France, and the confusion of French politics gave them endless opportunities of profitable warfare. The employment which they could offer to all adventurers who wished to join them goes far towards explaining the freedom from viking attack which England enjoyed in the middle of the tenth century.

Among the peoples of the Scandinavian mainland Athelstan possessed a reputation which brought him an offer of friendship from the most famous of their early kings. Long before Athelstan's accession, perhaps before the end of the ninth century, a united kingdom of Norway had been created by Harold, surnamed 'Fairhair', king of Westfold. He and Athelstan had a common enemy in the viking fleets at large in the western seas, and it was probably in order to reach an understanding in face of this danger that Harold dispatched the first recorded mission from Norway to England. It was led by two Norwegians named Helgrim and Osfrid, who brought to Athelstan at York an ornate warship such as was the pride of a northern king.[1] The account of the mission and the description of the ship— which was distinguished by a purple sail, a row of gilded shields along the gunwale, and a gilded stem at prow and stern—have an important place among the few references to Harold Fairhair in early western chronicles. But the fact that Harold, towards the end of his life, was in friendly correspondence with Athelstan has a wider interest in view of the Norse tradition that Hakon, Harold's youngest son, was brought up at Athelstan's court. The tradition is strongly supported by the name 'Athalsteins fóstri' afterwards applied to Hakon.[2] There is no early record of Hakon's presence in England; but surnames of this kind generally represent a genuine popular memory. There is no need to reject this second link between Athelstan and the greatest figure of the Scandinavian foreworld.

Throughout a career thus interwoven with the European history of his time Athelstan's personal interests were centred in southern England. In his royal title he sometimes claimed authority over the whole of Britain. He appears as king of all Britain on one of his coins; and in many of his charters he is described as 'King of the English and ruler of all Britain', or with more unction as 'King of the English, raised to the throne of the kingdom of Britain by the right hand of the Almighty'. But a list of the places where he is known to have held his courts suggests that in the ordinary course of government he rarely travelled far outside his hereditary West Saxon kingdom. He can be traced in the company of his council at Exeter and Lifton in Devon; at Frome in Somerset; at Dorchester in Dorset; at Wilton, Chippenham, Wellow, and Amesbury in Wiltshire; at Winchester, King's Worthy, and Grateley in Hampshire; at Abingdon in Berkshire, Lyminster and Hamsey in Sussex, Thunderfield near Horley in Surrey, King's Milton and Faversham in Kent. In the whole of England north of the

---

[1] William of Malmesbury, *Gesta Regum*, R.S. i, p. 149.
[2] Well recorded in northern literature. E. H. Lind, *Norsk-Isländska Personbinamn*, p. 1.

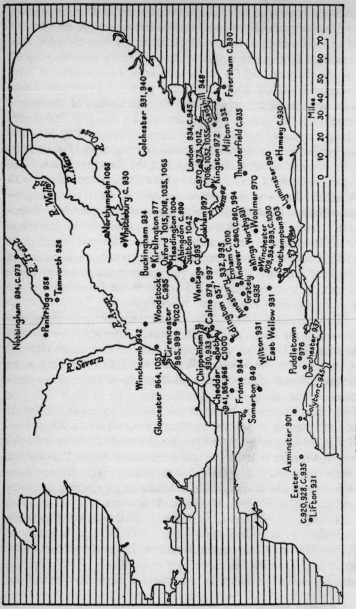

MEETING PLACES OF THE OLD ENGLISH COUNCIL

Thames the only places where he is known to have kept court in time of peace are York, Tamworth, Buckingham, Whittlebury in Northamptonshire, Colchester, and London. His hold on the remoter parts of his kingdom was maintained less by his own travels than by the establishment of a custom that distant magnates should attend him in the south.

One at least of these magnates was himself a landowner in Wessex. Athelstan, ealdorman of East Anglia,[1] afterwards known as the 'Half King', possessed estates in Berkshire and Somerset, and throughout a long life was intimate with the West Saxon royal family. His father, Æthelfrith, who had governed part of Mercia under Æthelred and Æthelflæd, had been known to King Edward, and his own East Anglian appointment was clearly due to the West Saxon associations of his house. Other Englishmen in the king's confidence may have held similar appointments elsewhere in the Danish east. On the other hand, among the provincial rulers who attended King Athelstan's courts a remarkably large number bore Scandinavian names and were obviously of Scandinavian descent. On 12 November 931, for example, no fewer than seven of these strangers were in his company at Lifton in the west of Devon.[2] There is no means of identifying the shires from which they had come, but there is little doubt that they were the successors of the earls who had led the Danish armies of eastern England in the time of Edward the Elder. Whatever their origin, their existence proves that neither Edward nor Athelstan had carried out a deliberate replacement of Danes by Englishmen in the government of the conquered Danish colonies.

Their appearance at the king's courts coincides with an important change in the character of these assemblies. Everywhere in England, until the end of the ninth century, the company which attended the king and witnessed his official acts normally consisted of men with whom he was in constant, if not familiar, association; such as his bishops, the ealdormen who were

---

[1] *Crawford Charters*, pp. 82–4; J. Armitage Robinson, *The Times of Saint Dunstan*, pp. 45–6.

[2] *C.S.* 677. Urm (below, p. 353), Guthrum (O.N. Guðþormr), Haward (O.N. Hávarðr), Gunner (O.N. Gunnarr), Thurferð (cf. O.N. Þorrøðr), Hadd (O.N. Haddr), and Scule (O.N. Skúli). Other Scandinavian earls who witness Athelstan's charters are Styrcær (O.N. Styrkárr), Grim (O.N. Grímr), Fræna (cf. O.N. Fráni) Regnwald (O.N. Rǫgnvaldr), Inwær (O.N. Ívarr), and Healfden (O.N. Hálfdan). J. C. R. Steenstrup, *Normannerne*, iii, p. 70; *Crawford Charters*, p. 75.

governing provinces for him, and his own retainers. From time to time the great Mercian kings had presided over larger and more general assemblies;[1] but their chief purpose had been the maintenance of ecclesiastical interests, and they can be clearly distinguished from the councils in which the ordinary business of the kingdom was transacted. In Wessex the small, intimate, and informal type of council seems to have been adequate for all the work of government until the great enlargement of the kingdom by Edward the Elder. There is no evidence as to the composition of the council during the last fifteen years of Edward's reign. But under Athelstan a new kind of assembly appears in which, even for ordinary business, the bishops, ealdormen, and thegns of Wessex were combined with magnates, lay and ecclesiastical, from every part of the land. On 23 March 931, for example, Athelstan held a council at Colchester which was attended by at least 37 thegns; 13 earls or ealdormen, of whom 6 were Danes; 3 abbots; 15 bishops, including those of St. Germans and Chester-le-Street; and the archbishop of Canterbury.[2] Councils on this scale were frequently held during the middle years of Athelstan's reign, and were summoned, though apparently at longer intervals, by most of his successors. They were national assemblies, in which every local interest was represented, and they did much to break down the provincial separatism which was the chief obstacle to the political unification of England.

Nothing would be known about these councils were it not for the royal charters which have survived in considerable numbers from Athelstan's reign. It is one of the unexplained accidents of Anglo-Saxon history that materials of this kind, which form a main source of historical information for the first three-quarters of the ninth century, become very rare in the reign of Alfred, and come to an end long before the death of Edward the Elder. In style the charters which follow this gap are very different from those of the previous age. In a typical ninth-century charter a clerk is trying to produce a simple record of a grant of land or privilege. The lamentable obscurity of many of these documents is due to the poor Latin of their writers, and not to indulgence in flights of literary composition. Even in the conventional parts of a charter, where it was customary to impute a religious motive to its grantor and

---

[1] Above, pp. 236–8.   [2] C.S. 674.

to denounce a curse upon its breakers, ninth-century clerks are rarely exuberant. When the series of charters begins again under Athelstan style has become the draftsman's first concern. All but a small minority of Athelstan's charters are composed in a highly artificial language, reminiscent of, and partly derived from Aldhelm's stylistic experiments. There were certain matters of fact which not even the most perverse of over-literate clerks could disguise. Place-names and personal names escaped him. But the king's title gave full scope to his ingenuity, and the attractiveness of words like *monarchus, basileus, curagulus*, and *imperator* produced eccentric styles into which many historians have read an assertion of imperial dignity by tenth-century English kings.[1]

For all the absurd elaboration of their language the solemn charters of Athelstan are impressive documents. They were written by clerks who had been trained in the art of formal composition, and whose standards in matters of handwriting and arrangement were remarkably high. In the history of the English administrative system Athelstan's charters are of great interest. The first direct reference to a clerk in the king's service seems to be a grant of land made in 984 by Æthelred II to Ælfwine, his faithful writer.[2] But the employment of identical formulas in charters of Athelstan issued at different dates and for the benefit of different persons shows that a writing-office was attached to the king's court in his time.[3] It should not be said that Athelstan possessed a chancery, if by that word is meant an organized body of clerks with an official known as a chancellor at their head. There is no trace in pre-Conquest England of the French custom that the head of the king's secretariat must authenticate his more important documents, and it is not until the eve of the Conquest, and then doubtfully, that an official described as a chancellor appears in

---

[1] The most interesting of Athelstan's styles—*Angelsaxonum Denorumque gloriosissimus rex*—occurs in a private document written in the New Minster at Winchester (*C.S.* 648). The inclusion of the Danes within Athelstan's kingdom is noteworthy in a record composed in southern England, and the style is one of the earliest pieces of evidence which exist for the use of the compound *Angelsaxones*.

[2] National Library of Wales, Peniorth MS. 390 (formerly Hengwrt MS. 150, f. 355.) The lands lay at Aston Bampton, Lew, and Brighthampton in Oxfordshire.

[3] The original charters of the period 925–75 are studied in detail from this standpoint by R. Drögereit in his tract *Gab es eine angelsächsische Königskanzlei?* He exaggerates the political importance of the king's clerical staff, but places its existence beyond doubt.

this country. But it is at least clear that already in Athelstan's reign a staff of clerks accompanied the king on his progresses, and it is with the appearance of these clerks that the history of the English civil service begins.

Athelstan's charters are the most important memorials of his government. He issued many laws; and some of them are interesting as the product of changing social conditions. He was the first English king to deal in legislation with lords who 'maintained' their men in defiance of right and justice, and his are the first English laws which recognize the importance of the borough as a centre of trade. But most of his laws deal with the suppression of thieves, and their very considerable bulk is largely due to the complexities of what in any early society was an insoluble problem. It was discussed by his council on at least five separate occasions. There was much repetition and reinforcement of individual enactments, with a general tendency towards uncompromising severity. It is more interesting to note that the king himself was inclined to leniency. In what seems to be the last of his laws, he exempts all persons under fifteen from the death penalty[1] 'because he thought it too cruel to kill so many young people and for such small crimes as he understood to be the case everywhere'. It is this suggestion of a humane mind in revolt against the grimmer aspects of government which raises Athelstan's laws above the commonplace.

By a fortunate chance there have been preserved, in addition to the laws themselves, certain documents which illustrate the reaction of the country towards them. The bishops and other magnates of Kent write to thank the king for the laws which he has issued, and to assure him of their obedience.[2] But the most significant of these unofficial texts is a memorandum recording the measures taken for the execution of the king's decrees by a body described as a 'peace-gild', of which the leading members were the bishops and reeves belonging to London.[3] They seem to have belonged to London in the sense that, by virtue of possessions in the city or in the country of which it was the centre, they shared in the responsibility for the maintenance of its defences, and owed suit to a court held

---

[1] Unless they resisted or evaded arrest. vi Athelstan 12, 1.

[2] iii Athelstan: Liebermann, *Gesetze*, i. 170–1; Attenborough, *Laws of the Earliest English Kings*, pp. 142–7.

[3] vi Athelstan: Liebermann, i, pp. 173–83; Attenborough, pp. 156–69.

within them. The ordinary members of the gild were the countrymen of a region which certainly included all Middlesex, and may also have comprised Surrey and part of Hertfordshire. Like later associations of the same kind, this early gild made provision for the spiritual benefit of its members. But its chief object, as its name indicates, was the maintenance of the public peace, and with this object in view an elaborate organization was devised for common action in the pursuit of thieves and for the compensation of injured persons out of the common property of the gild. The constitution of the gild was highly complex. Its members were divided into groups of ten, one of whom acted as headman of his company. The groups of ten members were combined into groups of one hundred, over each of which a separate headman presided. He, with the headmen of the groups of ten, then formed a standing committee, which accounted for the money contributed by the hundred-group to the common stock, and met once a month 'when the butts were being filled' for the gild-feast, to see that the gild statutes were being observed. The system is a remarkable piece of constitution-making, and it shows that the men of the English countryside had a power of organized co-operation which is rarely, if ever, brought out in documents emanating from the king's court. It also reveals, in a very striking manner, the limitations of the central government. Within one of the most civilized parts of England the maintenance of public order clearly depended on the goodwill of a voluntary association of private persons.

There are many obscure passages in the history of Athelstan's reign. One incident, in particular, which was certainly important and may have been momentous, has left no trace in England beyond a vague and distorted tradition. Under the year 933 a Northumbrian annalist states gauntly that 'King Athelstan ordered Edwin his brother to be drowned in the sea'.[1] Anglo-Norman writers expanded this tradition into a pitiful story of Edwin's sufferings and Athelstan's remorse. Fortunately for Athelstan's memory the monks of St. Bertin's in Flanders remembered his gratitude for the burial which they had given to his brother Edwin, drowned in a storm while escaping from England in a time of commotion.[2] The Flemish tradition,

---

[1] Symeon of Durham, *Historia Regum*, R.S., *sub anno*.
[2] *Cartulaire de l'Abbaye de Saint Bertin*, ed. M. Guérard, p. 145.

which was put into writing within a generation of Edwin's death, disposes of the more sinister implications of the Northumbrian annal. It leaves the whole incident obscure, but it strengthens the possibility that a rebellion against Athelstan may have been organized within the royal house itself.

In spite of the unsatisfactory materials for his history, Athelstan is one of the few Anglo-Saxon kings of whose personality a faint impression can be formed. It is known that he was of no more than average height, and that his hair was flaxen, with intermingled golden threads.[1] The record of his movements is hardly needed to show that he possessed the physical energy without which no early king could govern well. More remarkable is the mixture of devotion and intellectual curiosity which made him a collector of relics on a scale approached by no other English king. The devotion appears again in his gifts of books to churches for the recompense of their prayers, and the curiosity found another vent in the entertainment of foreign scholars at his court and in the intercourse which he maintained with foreign monasteries.[2] More unusual, or at least more rarely recorded than any of these qualities, is the touch of humanity shown in the pardon which he granted to criminals willing to make amends, and in his revulsion against the execution of young offenders. In character and cast of mind he is the one West Saxon king who will bear comparison with Alfred.

For the last twelve years of his reign he had held together a composite state which embraced the English peoples of Wessex, Mercia, and further Northumbria; the Britons of Cornwall; the Anglo-Scandinavian population of the Danelaw; and the Norsemen, Danes, and Englishmen of the country around York. The political union of these peoples had been unshaken by the invasion of 937—there is no evidence that Olaf Guthfrithson had found any supporters in England—and at the time of Athelstan's death it probably seemed secure. In reality it was an artificial piece of statecraft, which still depended for existence on the strength and political ability of the reigning king. Edmund, Athelstan's brother, who succeeded him in the autumn of 939, was then a youth of eighteen. He had fought at Brunanburh; and during a short reign he proved himself

[1] William of Malmesbury, *Gesta Regum*, R.S., i, p. 148.
[2] These aspects of Athelstan's character are most fully described by J. Armitage Robinson, *The Times of Saint Dunstan*, pp. 51–80.

to be both warlike and politically effective. But at the moment there can have been little to show his quality. Among the Irish vikings who had survived the defeat of 937 his succession was regarded as an opportunity for a second invasion, and before this new attack Athelstan's kingdom of all England collapsed.

The invading army was led by Olaf Guthfrithson, king of Dublin.[1] Before the end of 939 it had occupied York, apparently without meeting any resistance. Early in 940 Olaf led it on a great raid over the midlands. Repulsed at Northampton, he turned towards the north-west, stormed Tamworth, and then laid waste the surrounding country. On his return towards the north he was met at Leicester by an army under King Edmund. Before the kings had joined battle the archbishops of Canterbury and York arranged a treaty between them. It gave to Olaf the whole region between Watling Street and the Northumbrian border which is now represented by the shires of Leicester, Derby, Nottingham, and Lincoln.[2] The treaty meant, in fact, the abandonment to Norse rule of a large Anglo-Danish population which for more than twenty years had been obedient to the king of England and to local officers governing in his name. It was an ignominious surrender, and it marked the first serious reverse suffered by the English monarchy since Edward the Elder began his great advance against the southern Danes.[3]

In the following year Olaf invaded Northumbria beyond Tees. He must have reached the extreme limits of English territory, for he is known to have sacked the ancient Anglian church of Tyninghame near Dunbar. But he died before the year was over and his kingdom passed into weaker hands. His cousin Olaf Sihtricson, who had been expelled from England in 927, had joined him at York in 940, and was now received

---

[1] The course of the events which followed was first made intelligible by M. L. R. Beaven, 'King Edmund I and the Danes of York', *E.H.R.* xxxiii (1918), pp. 1–9.

[2] The Northumbrian chronicle which is the chief authority for the war (*Symeonis ... Opera*, R.S. ii, p. 94) gives Watling Street as the southern boundary of the ceded territory. Its limits are indicated more clearly by the contemporary poem on its reconquest, on which see below, pp. 358–9.

[3] According to Roger of Wendover (*Flores*, ed. H. O. Coxe, i, pp. 395–6) Olaf owed his success to a *comes* named Orm, whose daughter Aldgyth he married after the treaty. Olaf's ally was probably identical with the *dux*, or earl, named Urm, who witnesses a number of Athelstan's charters. The form *Urm*, which is East Scandinavian, suggests that he was of Danish, not Norse extraction, and his daughter's name implies that he had married into an English family. Unfortunately there is nothing to indicate the part of England to which he belonged.

there as king. He was younger and milder than Olaf Guthfrithson and never equalled him as a viking leader. In 942 he
lost to Edmund the lands between the Humber and Watling
Street which Olaf Guthfrithson had acquired two years before.
In 943 the Northumbrians drove him out, and chose a brother
of Olaf Guthfrithson, named Rægnald, for their king. Within
the year, Olaf and Rægnald separately visited Edmund's court
and were baptized there, the king acting as sponsor to each
of them. In the early part of 944 Olaf seems to have returned to
Northumbria and reasserted himself as king in opposition to
Rægnald. But later in the year Edmund led an army to the
north and expelled both kings, and for the rest of his reign
York remained an English town.

Between the Humber and the Tees, the conquest of York by
the elder Rægnald of King Edward's time had given rise to an
aristocracy of Norse extraction which is unlikely to have welcomed absorption into the English monarchy. Since Athelstan's death it had been reinforced by the followers of Olaf
Guthfrithson, who might quarrel among themselves about the
choice of a king, but were all prepared to resist a government
imposed on them from the south. But between the Humber
and Watling Street Olaf's followers had been ruling by force
a recalcitrant native population to which Edmund came as a
deliverer. Its attitude is expressed in a contemporary English
poem which compresses a remarkable variety of information
into two sentences. The first sentence records that Edmund
conquered Mercia, and in particular the Five Boroughs of
Leicester, Lincoln, Nottingham, Stamford, and Derby, with
their territory as far as the Northumbrian border. The second
states that the Danes of this region, who stand to the poet for
the whole body of its inhabitants, had been held by force under
the Northmen for a long time until Edmund redeemed them
through his valour.[1] The poem is overloaded with clichés, but it
gives a clear impression of conditions in the eastern midlands.
It contains the earliest known reference to the confederation of
the Five Boroughs, which afterwards appears as a separate and
well-defined division of that country.[2] It brings out the highly
significant fact that the Danes of eastern Mercia, after fifteen

[1] On its political significance see A. Mawer, 'The Redemption of the Five
Boroughs', *E.H.R.* xxxviii (1926), pp. 551–7.
[2] Below, pp. 509–11.

years of Athelstan's government, had come to regard themselves as the rightful subjects of the English king. Above all, it emphasizes the antagonism between Danes and Norsemen, which is often ignored by modern writers, but underlies the whole history of England in this period. It is the first political poem in the English language, and its author understood political realities.

There is no direct evidence of the relations between the last three kings of York and the Celtic powers of the north. At Brunanburh, Olaf Guthfrithson had been supported by the kings of Scotland and Strathclyde. But in each of these countries a new ruler came into power between 937 and 944, and the course of events suggests very strongly that while the new king of Strathclyde continued to support the Northmen, the new king of Scots entered into an alliance with Edmund. It is at least certain that in the next campaigning season after his recovery of York, Edmund invaded Strathclyde. The contemporary Anglo-Saxon Chronicle states that Edmund ravaged all 'Cumberland' and gave it to Malcolm, king of Scots, on condition that he should be Edmund's fellow worker by sea and land. That 'Cumbraland' means the land of the Cymre, or Britons of Strathclyde, is proved by an entry in the *Annales Cambriae* recording that Strathclyde was laid waste by the Saxons at this time. A northern English annalist whose work is preserved only in a late copy[1] adds the important facts that Edmund was helped in this campaign by the king of Dyfed, and that two sons of Dunmail, king of Strathclyde, were blinded by Edmund's orders. The devastation was clearly the work of an expedition on a large scale, for which Edmund used the resources of his Welsh allies as well as those of his own kingdom. As a stroke of policy the attempt to create a new relationship with the king of Scots by the cession of Strathclyde was too ambitious to lead to a permanent result. Within a few years Dunmail was reigning again in Strathclyde. But the attempt shows that Edmund was enough of a statesman to realize the necessity of setting a limit to his own kingdom in the north, and it clearly foreshadows the far more important cession of Lothian to a later king of Scots by Edgar, Edmund's son.[2]

---

[1] Roger of Wendover, *Flores Historiarum*, ed. H. O. Coxe, i, p. 398.
[2] For an earlier attempt to establish peaceful conditions on a Celtic border, see p. 341, n. 1 above.

After the recovery of York and the conquest of Strathclyde Edmund was free at last to intervene in continental affairs. His nephew, King Louis d'Outremer, was in urgent need of his help. In the summer of 945 Louis had been captured by the Northmen of Rouen. The duke of the Franks delivered him from their hands, but kept him in the custody of one of his own allies for the greater part of a year. In the first months of 946 Edmund sent a mission to the duke to negotiate for the restoration of Louis to his kingdom.[1] But in May, before he had time for any further action, Edmund was killed[2] while defending his steward against a criminal who had returned from banishment. Neither of his two sons was old enough to succeed him, and the kingdom passed to Eadred, his brother. The first duty of the new king was to secure a general recognition of his authority; for the greater part of his reign he was preoccupied with northern rebellions, and, so far as is known, he never took any part in the internal politics of France.[3]

At first Eadred was received as king in Northumbria without opposition. In 947, at Tanshelf, near the crossing of the Aire afterwards commanded by Pontefract castle, Archbishop Wulfstan of York and the northern magnates swore fealty to him and gave security for their obedience. But before the year was over a new situation was created in the north by the appearance of the most famous viking leader of the age. Some years before, Harold Fairhair had been succeeded as king of Norway by Eric 'Bloodaxe', the best born of his many sons. After a short and extremely violent reign he was driven from Norway by a general rising in favour of his milder brother Hakon, Athelstan's foster-son. He took at once to the sea, led many successful expeditions towards the west, and then descended on Northumbria. To the Norsemen of that country his arrival opened a prospect of independence under a leader descended from the royal house of Norway, and they immediately accepted him as king.

Eadred replied by an invasion of Northumbria. An army which he led in person raided at least as far as Ripon, where it

[1] Flodoard, *Annales*, ed. P. Lauer, p. 101.

[2] At Pucklechurch in Gloucestershire, *Chronicle*, MS. D. A full account of his death, which seems to come from a good tradition, is given by William of Malmesbury, *Gesta Regum*, R.S., i, p. 159.

[3] For the sequence of events in Eadred's reign see A. Campbell, 'The End of the Kingdom of Northumbria', in *E.H.R.* lvii (1942), pp. 91-7.

burned the ancient minster. It seems to have met no organized resistance until it came to the passage of the Aire at Castleford, as it was returning towards the south. There, at the most difficult river-crossing on the Great North Road, it was attacked by an army from York, and its rear-guard was defeated. In spite of this disaster the battle left Eadred in a position to dictate terms to the Northumbrians, and he compelled them to abandon Eric by a threat that otherwise he would utterly destroy their country. For a few months his authority must have been recognized in York. But in 949 Olaf Sihtricson, who had been ruling uneasily at Dublin since his expulsion from England in 944, seems to have been received again in Northumbria as king. His second reign in the north was ended, apparently in 952, by Eric's return. Olaf was driven into flight, and for two years Eric reigned at York in defiance alike of the Irish vikings and the king of England.[1]

The memory of Eric's English kingdom was preserved for centuries in the Scandinavian north. In regard to the chronology of his adventures the Scandinavian tradition is contradicted by English records which are clearly derived from contemporary materials. These discrepancies do not affect the Norse picture of Eric surrounded by his Norwegian followers in the king's garth at York, reigning in great prosperity,[2] but never forgetting his case against those who had injured him as king of Norway. The most significant memorial of his kingdom is the complimentary poem by which Egil Skallagrimsson, the most formidable of his enemies, was allowed to redeem his head,

[1] The chronology of these changes cannot be regarded as certain. MS. D of the *Chronicle*, which gives the fullest account of the period, does not mention the reception of Olaf in 949 or his expulsion in favour of Eric in 952. These events and the dates assigned to them rest on the authority of MS. E, on which see D. Whitelock, *The Peterborough Chronicle* (Early English Manuscripts in Facsimile, IV), pp. 28–9. The political situation in the north is equally obscure. According to MS. D, archbishop Wulfstan of York was arrested by Eadred's orders in 952 'because he had often been accused to the king'. Nothing is known about the charges that were brought against him, but it is at least clear that Eadred could not count on the loyalty of the head of the Northumbrian church. Presumably Wulfstan was able to clear himself, for he had been restored to his archbishopric before Eadred's death (*C.S.* 903).

[2] There is an independent reference to Eric as king in York in the life of St. Catroe which describes a journey of the saint from Strathclyde to Leeds—'the boundary of the Northmen and the Cumbrians'—and then *ad regem Erichium in Euroacum urbem* (A. O. Anderson, *Early Sources of Scottish History*, i, p. 441). The chronology of the life is confused, but the names which come into it seem to be derived from a genuine tradition.

after he had been shipwrecked in the Humber and had found
a friend to bring him before the king. Like all such poems it is
a collection of conventional phrases, and it tells nothing about
the extent of Eric's kingdom or the persons with whom he had
come into contact in England. But its traditional metaphors
and its heathen imagery show that the court which applauded it
belonged in culture to the primitive Scandinavian world.

Nothing is really known about the way in which Eric's kingdom came to an end. The Norse account of his last war is
confused, and reads like reconstructed history rather than tradition. The best English authority for the period[1] simply states
that the Northumbrians expelled Eric in 954, and that Eadred
then took the Northumbrian kingdom. The course of events
is carried a little further by a tradition current at Durham in the
twelfth century that Eric, after his expulsion, was killed by a
certain Maccus, son of Olaf.[2] The tradition reappears in the
statement of Roger of Wendover[3] that King Eric, betrayed
with his son and brother by Earl Oswulf, was treacherously
killed by Earl Maccus on a waste place called 'Steinmor'.
Nothing more is known about Maccus, son of Olaf, though it is
probable that either Olaf Guthfrithson or Olaf Sihtricson was
his father. Earl Oswulf was the leading Englishman of the
north. For at least six years he had been ruling from Bamburgh
whatever lands were English beyond the Tees,[4] and on Eric's
final expulsion he received the whole of southern Northumbria
from King Eadred as an addition to his own northern earldom.[5]
It is possible that Eric may have been attempting an invasion of
his lost kingdom when Oswulf brought about his death, but a
battle on the heights of Stainmore, where the Roman road from
Catterick to Carlisle drops into Edendale, rather suggests the
last stand of a deserted king on the border of his country. Nothing is certain beyond the fact that the manner of his death gained
him the sympathy of those who recorded it.

The battle of Stainmore closed the phase of English history

---

[1] *Chronicle*, MSS. D. E.

[2] Symeon of Durham, *Historia Regum*, *Opera*, ii, p. 197.

[3] *Flores Historiarum*, ed. H. O. Coxe, i, pp. 402–3. The entry recording Eric's
death is wrongly dated 950, but there is no reason to doubt that it comes from the
ancient Northumbrian annals distributed through this part of the *Flores*. (Above,
p. 319, n. 1.)

[4] He is described as 'High-reeve at Bamburgh' in 949 (*C.S.* 883).

[5] Symeon of Durham, *Opera*, R.S., ii, pp. 197, 382.

which began with the division of Northumbria among Half-dan's followers in 876. Throughout this period, with only one considerable interval, every English king had been confronted by an independent Scandinavian power beyond the Humber. Towards the end it was clear that the English monarchy was strong enough to prevent the union of York and Dublin in a single viking state. But the fall of Eric Bloodaxe was an event of much greater significance than the discomfiture of small kings like Olaf Sihtricson and Rægnald II. It meant that a leader who could draw all the landless adventurers of Scandinavia into an army had failed to establish himself in an English kingdom. England still offered the chance of a quick profit to any group of ships' companies which cared to take the risk of an invasion. In his will, which was drafted towards the close of his reign, King Eadred left a large sum of money to be expended, if necessary, in buying peace from a heathen army.[1] But the time was past when an individual adventurer could hope to found a dynasty in England.

[1] C.S. 912; F. Harmer, *English Historical Documents*, pp. 34-5.

XI

THE DECLINE OF THE OLD ENGLISH MONARCHY

THROUGH the work of Edward the Elder and his sons the ascendancy of the West Saxon dynasty was so firmly established that it survived a crisis which threatened the unity of their kingdom. After a long illness King Eadred died on 23 November 955. He had no children, and the members of the royal house who stood nearest to the succession were Eadwig and Edgar, the sons of his brother Edmund. Edgar was only twelve years of age when Eadred died, and Eadwig, who was chosen king, can hardly have been more than three years older. His distant cousin, the chronicler Æthelweard, states that the common people called him the 'all-fair' because of his beauty.[1] The history of his time is chiefly known through the writings of men devoted to monastic saints whom he disliked or ignored. It may be true, as one of them observes, that he could rule neither himself nor others well. But he died at the beginning of manhood, and many things for which they blamed him may fairly be attributed to his extreme youth.

Nevertheless, his reign has some interesting features. It begins a period in which, for the first time since the reign of Egbert, England was free from the imminent threat of foreign invasion. This freedom only lasted for the quarter of a century. In 980 there began a new series of Danish raids which ended in a Danish conquest of the whole land. Writers of the next generation, with rough justice, attributed the happiness of the preceding age to the wisdom of King Edgar, Eadwig's brother. On the other hand, among the small group of men through whom Edgar governed England at least four came to power under King Eadwig. Ælfhere, ealdorman of Mercia, Byrhtnoth of Essex, and Æthelwold of East Anglia all appear as ealdormen for the first time in 956. Ælfheah of Hampshire, Ælfhere's brother,

---

[1] *The Chronicle of Æthelweard*, ed. A. Campbell, p. 55. The phrase 'prae nimia etenim pulchritudine Pancali sortitus est nomen a vulgo secundi' strongly suggests that Eadwig had received the alliterative by-name *eall-fæger*.

reached that dignity a year later. It can at least be said for King Eadwig that he agreed to the promotion of good servants.

The peace of the years between 955 and 980 left a permanent impression on English history in the sphere of religion and culture. It provided the setting for a very remarkable revival of the devotion which in former centuries had carried innumerable Englishmen and Englishwomen into the monastic life. There is no doubt that in the re-establishment of English monasticism, which is the principal achievement of this period, the enthusiasm of King Edgar was the decisive factor. It is unlikely that his brother had been in any way touched by the movement, and he has often been represented as opposed to it. On the other hand, he certainly observed the convention that kings should make gifts for religious purposes. The ecclesiastical persons to whom he gave land range from Oda, archbishop of Canterbury, to the priests in charge of Bampton church in Oxfordshire.[1] It was on an estate granted by King Eadwig that the archbishops of York founded their great minster of Southwell.[2] In view of the shortness of his reign his gifts to monasteries, though few, are numerous enough to show that neither he nor the men who influenced him were hostile to monasticism as an institution. In the last resort, the idea of his opposition to the monastic revival of his time seems to have arisen from the irrelevant fact that for personal reasons he came to regard its leader, Dunstan, abbot of Glastonbury, as his enemy.

From 959 until his death in 988 Dunstan was the central figure in English religious life. In 956, when he came into conflict with King Eadwig, he was already a leader among the men who were working for the establishment of a reformed monastic order in England. By birth Dunstan was connected with the royal family; he had received his abbey from King Edmund, and he had been the close friend of King Eadred. He was naturally at court on the day when Eadwig was anointed king, and before the day was over he had taken part in one of the best-remembered scenes in Anglo-Saxon history. According to Dunstan's earliest biographer[3] the king left the solemn feast which followed his anointing in order to amuse himself with a noblewoman and her daughter, each of whom was trying to entice him into marriage. The absence of the king on such an occasion

[1] C.S. 1347; Ordnance Survey Facsimiles of Anglo-Saxon MSS. ii, Exeter, xvi.
[2] C.S. 1029. 'The Founding of Southwell Minster' C.P., pp. 364-70.
[3] Memorials of Saint Dunstan, R.S., pp. 32-4.

was an insult to the whole English aristocracy, and to avoid serious trouble Dunstan and his kinsman, the bishop of Lichfield, were sent in search of him. They are said to have found him, with his crown thrown aside, in the company of the two ladies; and, apparently, it was only after a violent scene that he was brought back, crowned, to the assembly. The biographer adds that the elder lady, whom he regards as the real mover in the attempt to seduce the king, never forgave Dunstan, and that through her influence he was deprived of his property and compelled to leave the country. In course of time this story, which kept King Eadwig's memory alive for centuries, became embellished with much grotesque detail. Even in its earliest form it has already assumed a scandalous colour which clashes with better evidence. It is known, for example, that the younger of the two ladies married the king and that she was honoured in one of the greatest of English monasteries. In the *Liber Vitae* of New Minster, Ælfgifu, wife of King Eadwig, appears in a list of 'illustrious women, choosing this holy place for the love of God, who have commended themselves to the prayers of the community by the gift of alms'.[1] Churchmen of the highest merit were willing to come to court when both the ladies were present.[2] All that can safely be inferred from the story is the high probability that Dunstan was exiled because he had affronted the king, the woman who became the king's wife, and her mother.[3]

It was probably through mere irresponsibility that within two years of his accession Eadwig lost the greater part of his kingdom. In 955 the West Saxons, the Mercians, and presumably the Northumbrians had separately chosen him king. Between May and December 957 the Mercians and Northumbrians renounced their allegiance to him in favour of his brother Edgar. There is no trace of any particularist feeling behind this revolution, and it was not followed by any important change in the distribution of the great provincial governments. Of the ealdormen whom Eadwig had appointed in 956, Byrhtnoth of Essex,

[1] Ed. W. de G. Birch, p. 57.

[2] *C.S.* 972 is attested by Ælfgifu, the king's wife, Æthelgifu, 'the king's wife's mother', and the bishops of Winchester, Ramsbury, and Worcester. Bishop Cenwald of Worcester, who had commended King Athelstan to the prayers of the churches of Germany thirty years before, was an exemplary prelate who owed nothing to King Eadwig.

[3] MS. D of the *Chronicle*, which states that Archbishop Oda separated Eadwig and Ælfgifu because they were nearly akin, is too late to have authority on a subject which invited legendary accretions.

Æthelwold of East Anglia, and Ælfhere of Mercia remained in office under Edgar,[1] while Ælfheah, Ælfhere's brother, continued to govern Hampshire on behalf of Eadwig. Dunstan's earliest biographer attributes the rejection of Eadwig by the northern peoples to his folly in choosing young advisers as thoughtless as·himself. The probability is that in the society of his West Saxon friends he fell completely out of touch with the local aristocracy of remoter parts.

On Eadwig's death, which occurred on 1 October 959, Edgar was at once accepted as king in Wessex. His accession had little effect on the personnel of the government. But in the ecclesiastical sphere its results were momentous. Archbishop Oda, who had ruled at Canterbury for eighteen years, had died in the summer of 958. Bishop Ælfsige of Winchester who had been designated his successor, died of cold in the Alps while travelling to Rome in order to receive his pallium. In his place Eadwig chose Byrhthelm, bishop of Wells, who has the precedence of an archbishop in Eadwig's latest charters, and had probably been seated at Canterbury for several months when the king died.[2] In the meantime, Dunstan had returned from exile at Edgar's invitation and had been consecrated a bishop in order, as his biographer says, that he might always be present at court to advise the king. Soon afterwards Edgar gave him the see of Worcester, and added that of London to it a little later. On Edgar's accession to power in Wessex, Archbishop Byrhthelm was ordered to return to his former see, on the ground that he was too gentle to maintain discipline in a supreme charge. Dunstan was set in his place at Canterbury.

In history the reign of Edgar has always been coloured by his association with Dunstan. Kings and archbishops have often co-operated in a programme of ecclesiastical reform; but there are few parallels in any country to the enthusiasm with which Edgar brought the whole power of the English state to the furtherance of Dunstan's religious policy. Ancient scholars who inherited the traditions of the monastic revival naturally regarded Edgar with veneration, and modern historians, realizing

---

[1] Ælfheah, Ælfhere's brother, whom Eadwig had created ealdorman of Hampshire in 957 (*C.S.* 1005) continued in that position for the rest of the reign and until his death in 971 or 972.

[2] He appears as *Dorobernensis ecclesiae episcopus* in *C.S.* 1045, and in an ill-preserved charter of 958 in the Athelney Register (Somerset Record Society, vol. xiv (1899), p. 146).

the significance of the ideals to which he gave his patronage, have tended to include him among the greatest of Old English rulers. In part, their praise is justified. It was a notable achievement to keep England secure against foreign enemies for sixteen years, and to maintain a standard of internal order which set a pattern for later generations. But when Edgar is compared with other outstanding members of his house—with Alfred or with Athelstan—he falls at once into a lower class than theirs. He was never required to defend English civilization against barbarians from over sea, nor to deal with the problems raised by the existence of barbarian states within England itself. His part in history was to maintain the peace established in England by earlier kings. It is his distinction that he gave unreserved support to the men who were creating the environment of a new English culture by the reformation of English monastic life.

It is a sign of Edgar's competence as a ruler that his reign is singularly devoid of recorded incident. The first event of his time which made a strong impression upon his contemporaries was his long-deferred coronation, which took place at Bath, on Whit Sunday 973. Up to this period there had been no fixed order for the coronation of an English king, and the form which was observed at Bath was reached only after the archbishop and his associates had produced at least two experimental drafts.[1] In addition to the form which was finally adopted there has survived an account of the actual proceedings, written by an eye-witness.[2] His narrative emphasizes the fact, made clear by the coronation order, that the essence of the ceremony was not the crowning, but the solemn anointing which set the king apart from other men. Dunstan, like many Frankish churchmen of his age, was strongly influenced by the parallel between the anointing of a king and the consecration of a priest, and there is every probability that the king, his pupil in religion, was moved by the same conception. It is by no means impossible that his sense of this parallel caused him deliberately to postpone his coronation until he felt that he had come to full maturity of mind and conduct. It is probably something more than mere coincidence that the year of his coronation was the year in which he reached the age of thirty, below which no one could canonically be ordained to the priesthood.

---

[1] P. E. Schramm, *A History of the English Coronation*, pp. 19–22.
[2] 'Vita Sancti Oswaldi', *Historians of the Church of York*, R.S., i, pp. 436–8.

The most famous incident of Edgar's reign occurred soon after his coronation, and was, in fact, its natural sequel. Ælfric, abbot of Eynsham, who had known many eminent persons of Edgar's time, records that on one occasion all the kings in Britain, eight in number, Cumbrians and Scots, came to him on a single day and acknowledged his supremacy. Three manuscripts of the *Chronicle* state that after Edgar had been crowned he sailed with his fleet to Chester, where six kings came to him and promised to serve him by sea and land.[1] In the Norman age this statement was expanded into a more dramatic form. The west midland annalist known as Florence of Worcester[2] asserts that Kenneth, king of Scots, Malcolm, king of the Cumbrians, Maccus, 'king of many islands', and five other princes named Dufnal, Siferth, Huwal, Jacob, and Juchil swore fealty to Edgar at Chester, and afterwards rowed him on the Dee from his palace to the church of St. John and back again, while he held the rudder. Except for the attempt of later writers to assign kingdoms to these rulers, it was in this form that the story became part of general history. Some, at least, of its details obviously come from a good tradition. Two of the rulers mentioned by Florence are otherwise unknown, but there is no glaring anachronism in the names that can be tested.[3]

Kenneth became king of Scots in 971; Jacob is clearly Iago, king of Gwynedd, who reigned from 950 until 979; Huwel is probably Hywel, son of Idwal, Iago's nephew and enemy; and Maccus, the king of many islands, is presumably identical with Maccus son of Harold, a famous sea-king of the time. Dufnal can safely be identified with Dunmail, king of Strathclyde, who was reigning in that country when Edmund of Wessex ravaged it, thirty years before. Malcolm, who appears in the list as king of the Cumbrians, was Dunmail's son, who only came to the kingdom in 975, when his father went on pilgrimage to Rome, but may well have accompanied him to Edgar's court in the previous year. No Anglo-Norman writer, inventing a list of

---

[1] On the good quality of the evidence for the submission see W. H. Stevenson in *E.H.R.* xiii (1898), pp. 505–6.

[2] *Chronicon ex Chronicis*, ed. B. Thorpe, i, pp. 142–3.

[3] The difficulty of identifying these princes is due, partly to the variant forms in which some of the names appear, and partly to the obscurity of both Welsh and Scottish history in this period. For recent comments upon the submission see A. O. Anderson, *Early Sources of Scottish History*, i, pp. 478–80; J. E. Lloyd, *History of Wales*, i, pp. 349–50; F. M. Stenton, *C.P.*, pp. 218–19.

names with which to garnish an ancient annal, could have come as close as this to fact or probability. Even the rowing of Edgar on the Dee, which gives a fictitious air to the incident, may have been a symbolic act by which these princes had expressed their subjection to their lord. In any case, the core of the story, which is the acknowledgement of Edgar's supremacy by the other rulers of Britain, is not affected by the possibility that legendary accretions may have gathered around it.

There is nothing to suggest that the submission of 973 introduced any new principle into the relationship between the king of England and the Celtic princes beyond his border. By the ceremony at Chester Edgar, like Edward the Elder and Athelstan in similar occasions, became secure against attack from the princes who had become his men, and entitled to their help if others made war on him. The weakness of this relationship was its personal character and its consequent impermanence. At the middle of the century Edmund, Edgar's father, was already feeling his way towards a more stable understanding when he gave Strathclyde to Malcolm king of Scots. There is evidence that shortly after the meeting at Chester Edgar attempted to secure the allegiance of Kenneth, the Scottish king, by a grant of the English lands between the Tweed and the Forth which were then collectively called Lothian. The grant is not mentioned by any contemporary whose work has survived. But a thirteenth-century writer who had preserved much ancient material states that Kenneth was brought to Edgar by Ælfsige, bishop of Chester-le-Street, and Eadwulf, ealdorman of Bernicia, that Kenneth did homage to Edgar, and that Edgar thereupon gave him Lothian and a number of estates in England[1] on which he could reside when he came in future to Edgar's court. The story deserves to be taken seriously. It is set down as a simple matter of fact, and the names which come into it raise no chronological difficulties. As the bare record of a tradition it naturally ignores the historical significance of the grant. The cession of Lothian determined the future of the Scottish kingdom. Within a century it had become an Anglo-Celtic state in which the English element was steadily rising to predominance. But the change was very slow at first, and no Englishman of Edgar's time could have foreseen its consequences.

Even within his own country it was Edgar's policy to limit the

[1] Roger of Wendover, *Flores Historiarum*, ed. H. O. Coxe, i. 416.

reponsibilities of his government. He was the first king to recognize in legislation that the Danish east of England was no
longer a conquered province but an integral part of the English
realm. The recognition took the form of a grant of autonomy to
its inhabitants.[1] In the most explicit of terms Edgar ordains that
in return for the loyalty which the 'Danes' have always mani-
fested, such social and legal customs shall prevail among them
as they themselves may choose. In another passage he expressly
contrasts this liberty of theirs with the subjection of 'Englishmen' to the laws which he and his council have made. When
issuing a set of regulations intended to suppress traffic in stolen
cattle, he is apologetic in insisting that they shall apply in Danish
as well as English territory; and even so, he allows the Danes
themselves to decide what punishment shall be inflicted for the
breach of these regulations in their country.[2] It is not surprising
that within at most a generation after his time the shires of
Danish England had come to be known collectively as the
Danelaw.[3]

This did not mean that his authority in that land was negligible. He appointed the earls and bishops through whom it was
governed, its leading magnates regarded themselves as his men,
and its militia was bound to join him when he went to war in
person. There, as elsewhere, he possessed estates which were
important centres for the administration of justice; and the
breach of his peace, given under his hand and seal, was punished
even more severely in Danish than in English territory. But he
was rarely seen in its more distant parts, and the rights which
belonged to him as king of the whole land left open a vast field
of action within which his Anglo-Danish subjects were free to
govern themselves. It is this freedom which, more than any other
cause, explains their acquiescence in their political subjection.
Here and there, especially in the northern Danelaw, men who

---

[1] F. M. Stenton, 'The Danes in England', *C.P.*, pp. 163–4.

[2] [It may partly have been Edgar's tolerance of Danish customs in the Danelaw
that caused Archbishop Wulfstan in the next generation to write after a panegyric on Edgar in the northern recension of the Anglo-Saxon Chronicle (D, E and
F), *s.a.* 959 the following criticism: 'Yet he did one ill-deed too greatly! he loved
evil foreign customs and brought too firmly heathen manners within the land, and
attracted hither foreigners and enticed harmful people to this country.']

[3] The first undoubted appearance of the name is in the laws of Æthelred II
(vi Æthelred, c. 37). The document known as Edward and Guthrum's Peace,
which mentions the Danelaw, has been conclusively assigned to Æthelred's later
years by D. Whitelock, *E.H.R.* lvii (1942), pp. 1–21.

could trace their descent from companions of Ivar the Boneless may have wished for a king of their own race. But in normal times the feeling never outweighed the solid advantages offered by Edgar's promise of autonomy in return for allegiance.

The unity of Edgar's kingdom was tested immediately after his death by a violent dispute about the succession. Edgar died suddenly, when few of his retainers were at court, on 8 July 975. He had been married twice. By his first wife he left a son named Edward, who in 975 was still a youth on the verge of manhood. In 964 he married as his second wife Ælfthryth, daughter of Ordgar, ealdorman of Devon, and widow of Æthelwold, ealdorman of East Anglia. By her, Edgar had two sons, of whom the elder died in 970 or 971. The younger, a boy named Æthelred, can barely have reached the age of ten in 975. The death of King Edgar before either of his sons was old enough to rule threw the whole country into confusion. According to the best-informed account of the next few years Edward, the eldest son and the natural heir, had offended many important persons by his intolerable violence of speech and behaviour. Long after he had passed into veneration as a saint it was remembered that his outbursts of rage had alarmed all who knew him, and especially the members of his own household.[1] It may have been partly for this reason that a large number of nobles resolved to promote the election of Æthelred, the younger brother. Edward was crowned king before the end of the year, but there are indications of a state of civil war between the partisans of the brothers in the months immediately after Edgar's death.[2]

Little can be gathered about the character of Edward's reign beyond a vague impression of disorder, and the knowledge that a period was abruptly set to the endowment of monasteries which Edgar had encouraged. Ælfhere, ealdorman of Mercia, the most prominent nobleman of the time, was accused of destroying monasteries, and many persons with an hereditary title to monastic lands took advantage of the change of government to assert their claims.[3] It is more doubtful how far this unfriendly

---

[1] *Historians of the Church of York*, R.S., i, p. 449. The passage is incomplete in the only manuscript of this work, but there is no doubt of its meaning.

[2] Ibid., pp. 443, 448-9.

[3] Much of the evidence is contained in Old English memoranda (or in Latin versions of such in the *Liber Eliensis* and the *Historia Ramesiensis*), narratives which set out the *talu*, or statement of a case, from the point of view of one of the parties

atmosphere is a sign of anything that can strictly be called an anti-monastic reaction. There were strong political reasons for a check to the recent drift of land into monastic possession. To judge from the history of houses like Ramsey or Ely, the process of monastic endowment had already been carried to a point at which it might easily give the preponderating weight within a shire to the religious interest. The creation of these large monastic estates inevitably weakened the local influence of the thegns of the shire on whom the king's officers were compelled to rely for the maintenance of public order. It does not prove hostility to the monastic idea if many thegns and some ealdormen resented the sudden appearance of the great monastic landlord.

On the evening of 18 March 978 Edward was murdered at Corfe in Dorset under circumstances of abominable treachery which shocked men who were ready to tolerate any crime of frank violence. On the surface his relations with Æthelred his half-brother and Ælfthryth his step-mother were friendly, and he was visiting them informally when he was killed. According to the earliest account of the murder[1] his brother's retainers came out to meet him with ostentatious signs of respect, and then, before he had dismounted, surrounded him, seized his hands, and stabbed him. He was buried without any service of honour at Wareham, but after a year Ælfhere of Mercia translated his body to the house of nuns at Shaftesbury, where miracles accumulated around it which caused him at last to be regarded as a saint and martyr. So far as can be seen the murder was planned and carried out by Æthelred's household men in order that their young master might become king. There is nothing to support the allegation, which first appears in writing more than a century later,[2] that Queen Ælfthryth had plotted her stepson's death. But no one was punished for his part in the crime, and Æthelred, who was crowned a month after the murder, began to reign in an atmosphere of suspicion which destroyed the prestige of the Crown.

It was never fully restored in his lifetime. He was too young

concerned. On this type of document see F. M. Stenton, *The Latin Charters of the Anglo-Saxon Period*, pp. 43–4, and D. M. Stenton, *English Justice 1066–1215*, pp. 7–13.

[1] Which forms a digression in the early eleventh-century life of St. Oswald, Raine, *Historians of the Church of York and its Archbishops*, R.S., i 449–51.

[2] In the life of St. Dunstan by Osbern, precentor of Canterbury in the time of Archbishop Lanfranc. *Memorials of Saint Dunstan*, R.S., p. 114.

to be an accomplice in his brother's murder. But the crime had been committed for his sake, and he never escaped its consequences. For many years the instinctive loyalty of the common people, on which earlier kings had always been able to rely, was obliterated by the wave of popular emotion which carried King Edward into the ranks of sainthood. Thirty years after the murder, when Æthelred himself ordered the general observation of his brother's festival, the way in which Edward had died must still have been remembered.[1] Much that has brought the condemnation of historians on King Æthelred may well be due in the last resort to the circumstances under which he became king. Throughout his reign he behaved like a man who is never sure of himself. His ineffectiveness in war, which is very remarkable in a king of his line, his acts of spasmodic violence, and the air of mistrust which overhangs his relations with his nobles, are signs of a trouble which lies deeper than mere incapacity for government. They suggest the reaction of a weak king to the consciousness that he had come to power through what his subjects regarded as the worst crime committed among the English peoples since their first coming to Britain.

It is unlikely to be through mere chance that within two years of Æthelred's accession Scandinavian raiding-parties were descending again upon England. Even in Edgar's reign it had been possible for small bodies of adventurers to establish themselves on remote parts of the northern coast. Scarborough derives its name from a viking named Thorgils 'Skarthi'—the hare-lipped—who came to England with his brother Kormak soon after 965, and joined with him in building a fortress on that headland.[2] After Edgar's death the confusion of English politics meant that the defence of the land was weakened at a time when the Scandinavian north was unusually restless. In the middle of the tenth century, after a hundred years of disunion, the various Danish peoples had been brought together

[1] Laws of Æthelred, v. 16. There is a remarkable reference by Æthelred to his brother's death in a charter of 1001 granting Bradford on Avon to the nuns of Shaftesbury (C.D. 706). The king says that he has made the gift 'Christo et sancto suo, germano scilicet meo Eadwardo, quem proprio cruore perfusum per multiplicia uirtutum signa ipse dominus nostris mirificare dignatus est temporibus'. The charter is only known from the late and ill-copied Shaftesbury Cartulary, but it has no suspicious features.

[2] E. V. Gordon, *Introduction to Old Norse*, ed. 2, 1957, pp. 151, 246 f. There is some evidence that Kormak, Skarthi's brother, had the by-name Fleinn, 'arrow', and that this name is preserved in Flamborough.

into a single kingdom. At the moment of Æthelred's accession, the greatest figure in the north was the Danish king Harold 'Gormsson',[1] who, in his own words, 'won for himself all Denmark and Norway and made the Danes Christians'.[2] There is no reason to think that he ever planned an invasion of England. His chief interests lay in the Baltic, and he incorporated many of the most formidable warriors of the north into a highly organized viking community which he planted at Jómsborg by the mouth of the Oder. But a career like his always aroused a long train of resentments. Many of his subjects refused to accept Christianity at his dictation, and shortly before 988 Swein, his son, put himself at their head and drove his father from the kingdom. It is highly probable that among the first raiders who visited England in Æthelred's reign there were men who had left their own country because they hated an autocratic master and an imposed religion.

The earliest raiders of this period descended upon England in small companies, which came to land without warning, and departed before they had met with any but local resistance. Most of the English coast-line was obviously at their mercy. They visited Hampshire, Thanet, and Cheshire in 980, Devon and Cornwall in 981, and Dorset in 982. No raids are recorded during the next six years, but the south-western shires were visited again in 988, when the thegns of Devon met the attack with a gallantry which became famous throughout the country.[3] Disastrous as they were to those who lived in their course, these early raids had little effect on the general well-being of the land. Their chief historical importance is that they brought England for the first time into diplomatic contact with Normandy, where Duke Richard I, the grandson of the founder of the duchy, was nearing the end of a long reign. It was no longer possible for Scandinavian adventurers to found new families in Normandy. But the Norman aristocracy, still conscious of its Scandinavian origin, was well disposed to the men of its own stock who were trying their fortune in the narrow seas, and the Norman ports were open to ships' companies returning from raids in England. By the summer of 990 the English and Norman courts had

---

[1] The by-name *Blátǫnn*, generally rendered 'Blue tooth', by which he is commonly known, is not recorded before the 12th century, but is clearly traditional.

[2] L. F. A. Wimmer and L. Jacobsen, *De Danske Runemindesmærker*, pp. 55–6.

[3] It was commemorated in the earliest life of St. Oswald, which was written at Ramsey (*Historians of the Church of York*, R.S., i, pp. 455–6).

become openly hostile to each other. By the early autumn the news of their enmity had reached Rome, and Pope John XV dispatched an envoy with instructions to arrange a treaty between them.[1] On Christmas day 990 he presented his commission to King Æthelred. Soon afterwards the king and his council drew up a set of terms which could be offered to the duke of Normandy. They provided that in future the king and the duke should accept a peaceful reparation of all the injuries which either might suffer from the other, and that neither of them should entertain the other's enemies, nor any of his subjects except such as could show letters of commendation under his seal. In the early spring the bishop of Sherborne and two king's thegns escorted the envoy to Rouen, where the duke agreed to these terms, on 1 March 991.

Five months afterwards another body of raiders appeared off the English coast. It was larger than any of the forces which had lately harried in England, and to some extent it had the character of an organized army. Its ravages are important in English financial history, for they compelled the government to raise a heavy tax in order to buy off the invaders. The precedent then set was followed on several occasions during the next twenty-five years, and these emergency levies were the prototypes of the recurrent Danegelds imposed by the Anglo-Norman kings. But the war of 991 would be no more than a dim episode in a monotonous succession of disasters were it not for the great poem which describes the death of Byrhtnoth, ealdorman of Essex, in a battle against the raiders.[2] In the second week in August, after a profitable descent on Ipswich, they entered the Blackwater estuary, and occupied Northey island to the east of Maldon. For access to the mainland they depended on a causeway, flooded at high tide, which led from Northey to the flats along the southern margin of the estuary.

[1] The letter which is the only authority for the mission is printed, and the critical questions which it raises are indicated, by Stubbs (*Memorials of Saint Dunstan*, R.S., pp. 397–8; William of Malmesbury, *Gesta Regum*, R.S., i, pp. 191–3). The present form of the letter cannot be authentic, but it is preserved in an early 11th-century manuscript, and its substance appears to be genuine.

[2] The most recent editions of the poem are by E. D. Laborde, *Byrhtnoth and Maldon*, 1936, and E. V. Gordon, *The Battle of Maldon*, 1937. The former is of particular importance for the topography of the battle-site. The latter is based on the copy of the unique manuscript of the poem which was used for the *editio princeps* by Thomas Hearne. The original manuscript was burned in 1731, and this copy is the best authority for the text.

Before they had left their camp on the island Byrhtnoth, with his retainers and a force of local militia, had taken possession of the landward end of the causeway. Refusing a demand for tribute, shouted across the water while the tide was high, Byrhtnoth drew up his men along the bank, and waited for the ebb. As the water fell the raiders began to stream out along the causeway. But three of Byrhtnoth's retainers held it against them, and at last they asked to be allowed to cross unhindered and fight on equal terms on the mainland. With what even those who admired him most called over-courage, Byrhtnoth agreed to this; the pirates rushed through the falling tide, and battle was joined. Its issue was decided by Byrhtnoth's fall. Many even of his own men immediately took to flight and the English ranks were broken. What gives enduring interest to the battle is the superb courage with which a group of Byrhtnoth's thegns, knowing that the fight was lost, deliberately gave themselves to death in order that they might avenge their lord.

To the raiders the battle of Maldon was merely an exciting incident in the course of a successful expedition. During the next four months they compelled the local rulers of Kent, Hampshire, and western Wessex to buy peace from them. Before the end of the year they had entered into a treaty with the English government by which, in return for provisions and a large sum of money, they undertook to keep the peace towards the king and his subjects, and to join them in attacking any other viking host descending on England. The text of the treaty[1] shows that the greatest man among the raiders was Olaf Tryggvason, a descendant of Harold Fairhair, king of Norway, who some four years later made himself master of his own country. It begins by regulating the treatment of merchants and merchant ships falling into the power of either of the parties to the treaty.[2] The next section consists of a series of rules for the settlement of disputes between Englishmen and vikings, and

[1] The treaty was arranged with the raiders by Archbishop Sigeric of Canterbury and Ælfric and Æthelweard, the ealdormen of the two West Saxon provinces. It has sometimes been referred to the year 994, when Olaf descended on England again. But the campaign of 994 did not begin until 8 September, and Archbishop Sigeric died on 29 October (K. Sisam, *Review of English Studies*, vii (1931), p. 10). There is not sufficient time between these dates for a series of events which included an attack on London, the devastation of the coast from Essex to Hampshire, a mounted raid far into the interior of the country, and the settlement of elaborate terms of peace.

[2] On the economic significance of these provisions see below, pp. 541-2.

declares that all the slaughter and ravaging which had taken place before the truce shall be forgotten. The treaty ends with the abrupt statement that 22,000 pounds of gold and silver have been given to the raiders as the price of peace.

In spite of the care with which the treaty was drawn up it is unlikely that it ever came into full effect. The threat of an invasion in 992 caused Æthelred to mobilize all the English ships at his command, but although the operation is described in some detail by the *Chronicle*, no hint is given that Olaf Tryggvason co-operated in it. In 993 the local English commanders were left to their own resources when a hostile fleet descended on Northumbria and Lindsey, and in 994 Olaf appeared again in England as an open enemy. He was accompanied by Swein, son of Harold, king of Denmark. Their combined fleets amounted to ninety-four warships, which probably carried a force of more than two thousand fighting men. It was the most formidable invasion which England had experienced for half a century, and it was made more dangerous by the fact that some English nobles, despairing, it would seem, of Æthelred's government, were prepared to accept Swein as king.[1] Its results were inconclusive; partly because London was stubbornly defended, and also because an alliance between Swein and Olaf Tryggvason was unnatural. Norway, where Olaf's ancestors had ruled, was still a dependency of the Danish kingdom. It was probably their sense of conflicting interests which caused the allies to fall apart after a raid over south-eastern England. Peace was bought from the army for 16,000 pounds. Swein returned to Denmark, and Olaf came to a new understanding with the English court. Hostages for his safety were sent on board his ships, and then Bishop Ælfheah of Winchester and Æthelweard, ealdorman of Wessex beyond Selwood, brought him to King Æthelred at Andover. Already a baptized Christian, he was confirmed at Andover, with the king as his sponsor, and entered into a solemn undertaking that he would leave England and never return to it in war. With this he disappears from English history, and within a few months he had entered on the expedition which ended in his establishment as king of Norway.

After a respite of two years the war began to enter upon a new phase. Hitherto each raid had been the work of a separate

---

[1] On the treason of Æthelric of Bocking, implicated in a plot to receive Swein in Essex, see D. Whitelock, *Anglo-Saxon Wills*, pp. 44, 148–9.

group of ship's companies, which had dispersed as soon as the expedition had produced an adequate return. But in 997 England was visited by an army prepared to devote a number of consecutive years to a systematic plundering of coastal Wessex. In the first year of its operations it harried Cornwall, Devon, western Somerset, and south Wales. In 998 it ravaged Dorset, and extorted supplies from Hampshire and Sussex. In 999 it raided in Kent. In the summer of 1000 it moved to Normandy and remained there until the campaigning season of the following year. Its departure allowed Æthelred to carry out a devastation of Strathclyde, the motive for which is part of the lost history of the north. The return of the vikings in 1001 was followed by a raid in west Sussex, and by something resembling a campaign in south Devon, which was marked by a successful defence of Exeter. But the combined militia of Devon and Somerset failed to hold the enemy in check, and its ships, stationed off the Isle of Wight, were masters of the Channel. In the spring of 1002 an intolerable situation was relieved by a truce for which 24,000 pounds of tribute-money were paid.

A few weeks later Æthelred married as his second wife Emma, sister of Richard II, duke of Normandy. Nothing definite can be said about the political background of the marriage. It is unsafe to assume that the Anglo-Norman treaty of 991 was still in force, and it is possible, though on the whole unlikely, that the raiders who had crossed from England to Normandy in the summer of 1000 had remained there throughout the autumn and winter in the duke's peace. It is also doubtful whether the marriage did much to clarify Anglo-Norman relations. There was a tradition in Normandy that Æthelred soon afterwards became offended with the duke, and sent an army to ravage the Cotentin.[1] It was through events which no one could have foreseen in 1002 that the marriage became important in English history. It entitled Æthelred to hospitality in Normandy when at last the Danes had conquered England. His sons by the marriage were educated in the duchy, and it was with a sense of obligation towards the Norman court that the elder of them ultimately returned to England as king. But in 1002 the idea of conquering England was at most a half-formed ambition in the mind of the Danish king, and the fabric of the English government, though badly shaken by recent disasters, was still intact.

[1] William of Jumièges, *Gesta Normannorum Ducum*, ed. J. Marx, pp. 76–7.

Its collapse was brought nearer by a political crime of which Æthelred was guilty in the autumn of that year. According to the *Chronicle* he ordered all the Danish men in England to be killed on St. Brice's day—13 November—'because he had been told that they intended to kill him and his counsellors, and afterwards to possess his kingdom'. Within more than a third of England no order of this kind could ever have been carried out. York and Lincoln, for example, were Danish rather than English towns. But the fact that a massacre of Danes took place at this time was long remembered, and in a charter to St. Frideswide's minster Æthelred himself refers to the slaughter of the Danes in Oxford.[1] According to a well-recorded tradition the victims included Gunnhild, sister of King Swein of Denmark, then living as a hostage in England.[2] It is highly probable that the wish to avenge her was a principal motive for his invasion of England in the following year.

In 1003 Swein commanded the resources of Jutland, Scania, and the intervening islands; he was intimate with the leaders of the viking community at Jómsborg, and the king of Sweden was his ally. He had recently brought about the overthrow of his formidable enemy Olaf Tryggvason, and either directly or through earls of his own choice he ruled the greater part of Norway. But he was not yet secure enough in the north to attempt the conquest of all England, and although the expedition which he led in 1003 penetrated farther inland than any earlier raiding army, there was nothing unprecedented in its scale. In the first year of its operations a French reeve of Queen Emma, who held Exeter in dower, betrayed the city to the host, and it then harried over Wessex as far as Wilton and Salisbury before it turned back towards the sea. In 1004 Swein and his fleet descended on East Anglia and sacked Norwich. To avoid other disasters an assembly of East Anglian magnates entered at once into negotiations for peace. But while negotiations were pending the army left its ships and struck across country to Thetford. On the morning after it had sacked the town it was met by a force hastily collected by a leading man of the country, named Ulfkell Snilling, whose conduct in this and later years caused East Anglia to be known as Ulfkell's land throughout the

---

[1] *Cartulary of St. Frideswide's*, ed. S. R. Wigram, i, pp. 2–9. The reasons for considering this charter to be authentic are set out by F. M. Stenton, *C.P.*, pp. 226–7.

[2] William of Malmesbury, *Gesta Regum*, R.S., i, p. 207.

north.[1] He was defeated outside Thetford, but the Danes said that they had never met more deadly hand-play in England than Ulfkell gave them. They suffered heavy losses, and it is probable that they were only saved from disaster because Ulfkell's orders to destroy their ships had not been carried out. Without any further devastation that has been recorded, they left England for Denmark in the course of 1005.

In the summer of 1006 they returned, occupied Sandwich, and raided widely in the south-east, evading contact with a force called out against them from the whole of Wessex and Mercia. In the autumn the fleet took up its station off the Isle of Wight, and in the depth of winter the army set out on a raid through Hampshire and Berkshire to Reading, and then across the Chilterns to Wallingford. At this point it was nearly sixty miles from the sea. But out of sheer bravado, instead of returning directly to its ships, it struck out in a great curve along the Ridge Way which follows the line of the Berkshire and north Wiltshire Downs. It halted in order to invite an attack at Cuckhamsley Knob, the meeting-place of the local shire-court, defeated the Wiltshire militia near Avebury, at the point where the Ridge Way crosses the Kennet, and then swept on exultantly past Winchester to the coast. Early in the new year it received tribute-money amounting to 36,000 pounds, and then disappeared from English waters.[2]

Two years passed before England was attacked again. Each of them was marked by an important measure of state. In 1007, after an abeyance of nearly thirty years, the Mercian ealdormanry was revived and given to a thegn named Eadric Streona,[3]

---

[1] His by-name *Snillingr*, which seems to mean 'the valiant', is preserved only by Norse sources. Anglo-Norman and later writers often refer to him as an earl, but he has no official title in contemporary records.

[2] The methods by which these great sums were raised are curiously illustrated by a charter of this period in which King Æthelred records the sale of Beckley and Horton in Oxfordshire to a Dane named Toti for gold which the king needed *ad reddendum tributum*. (Cambridge University Library, Red Book of Thorney, i, fo. v, now published by C. R. Hart, *The Early Charters of Eastern England*, pp. 190–1.) It is possible that many of the Danish families which afterwards appear in southern England were founded by ancestors who had invested tribute-money in English land.

[3] It is uncertain whether this by-name represents an unrecorded noun *streona*, connected with the verb *strienan*, to acquire, or a short form of a compound personal name, such as Streonwald, set in apposition against the main name to which it was applied. The former meaning had been given to it by the end of the 11th century (Heming, *Chartularium Ecclesiae Wigorniensis*, ed. T. Hearne, i, p. 280), but this authority is too late to be conclusive.

whose origins are obscure, and were certainly far from eminent. His later conduct has given him an evil reputation, but his appointment was an intelligent attempt to provide for the better defence of central England by placing the whole of it under a single command.[1] In 1008 the government undertook the formidable task of creating a new fleet of warships, furnished with armour for their crews. The preparations were organized on a national scale,[2] and the fleet had been brought into existence by the early part of 1009. In anticipation of a Danish attack it was stationed off Sandwich, but before the Danes appeared a charge of treason was brought against one of its commanders. Before his trial the accused commander—a thegn of Sussex named Wulfnoth—seduced the crews of twenty ships from their allegiance, and took to piracy along the south coast. His accuser, who was a brother of Eadric Streona, followed him with eighty ships, but a storm drove them all on shore, where they were afterwards burned by Wulfnoth's men. With a fleet thus weakened the king and his council declined to risk a general engagement; the ships which remained to them were brought into harbour at London, and on 1 August the enemy occupied the deserted anchorage off Sandwich.

In fighting quality, and probably in numbers, the Danish army of 1009 was the most formidable host which had visited England since Æthelred became king. It had been joined by many specialized warriors from Jómsborg, and its leaders included men of reputation everywhere in the viking world. It came to England in two separate companies. The leader of the first was Thorkell the Tall, the brother of Sigvaldi the commander at Jómsborg, and the companion of King Swein in many wars. The second and larger division of the host was led by Hemming, Thorkell's brother, and by a chief named Eilaf, whose brother Ulf afterwards married Estrith, King Swein's daughter, and became by her the ancestor of the medieval kings

---

[1] The Chronicle of Florence of Worcester contains what purports to be an earlier reference to Eadric under the year 1006, where he is said to have brought about the murder of Ælfhelm, ealdorman of Northumbria. But Eadric's notorious treasons in later life made him a person to whom mysterious crimes could safely be attributed, and the story told by Florence, which kills Ælfhelm during a hunting-party, does not inspire confidence.

[2] According to the *Chronicle* the country was divided into districts of 310 hides, each of which was required to provide a warship of approximately 60 oars. The armour was obtained through a separate demand of a helmet and a corselet from every 8 hides throughout the kingdom.

of Denmark. For the first six months of their operations the combined armies did little except harry afresh country already scoured by their predecessors. Although the men of Canterbury and eastern Kent bought them off with a gift of 3,000 pounds, London held out against them, and their chief success was the burning of Oxford early in the new year. But in the spring of 1010 their fleet left the Kentish coast for East Anglian waters; they stormed Ipswich at once, and within five weeks they had won what was probably the most hardly fought pitched battle of Æthelred's reign. The defence of East Anglia was still in the hands of Ulfkell Snilling, who had commanded the local forces in 1004, and was now at the head of an army drawn from both East Anglia and Cambridgeshire. Presumably in order to gain time for reinforcement, he had taken up a position far inland, covering Thetford from the north-east. As soon as the Danes had learned this they struck straight across country at his army, and joined battle with it by Ringmere Pit on Wretham Heath, to the north-east of the town.[1] The East Anglians soon took to flight, and although the men of Cambridgeshire kept their ranks for a long time, they were broken at last, and a new raiding ground in north-eastern Mercia was opened to the Danes. They spent the next three months in exploiting it, and then struck out towards the south in a series of raids which by Christmas, when they returned to their ships, had carried them as far as Wiltshire. A chronicler writing in the following year estimated that, apart from East Anglia, they had ravaged the whole or part of fifteen counties in the sixteen months since they came to land in 1009.

Nothing is known about their movements during the spring and summer of 1011. In the last weeks of September they were raiding again in Kent. After a short siege, Canterbury was betrayed to them, and Archbishop Ælfheah, who when bishop of Winchester had escorted Olaf Tryggvason to King Æthelred, seventeen years before, fell into their hands. It is probable that they had already been approached for terms of peace by the English leaders, but the richest parts of England had been drained of wealth by their ravages, and it was not until April 1012 that they received the sum of 48,000 pounds which was the price of their departure. A separate ransom was demanded from Archbishop Ælfheah, and because he would not allow it to be paid, he was killed with revolting barbarity

[1] See W. H. Stevenson, *E.H.R.* xi (1896), pp. 301-2.

in the assembly of the army of Greenwich. The murder was carried out in defiance of Thorkell the Tall, who is said to have offered all that he had except his ship in return for the archbishop's life.[1] A viking commander whose men had once got out of hand was never secure among them afterwards, and the ugly incident at Greenwich helps to explain the remarkable fact that before the end of the year, when the greater part of the army left England, Thorkell came over to King Æthelred with forty-five ships.

The history of England in the next generation was really determined between 1009 and 1012. There was sufficient resilience in Old English society to repair even the heavy material damage suffered in these years. But the ignominious collapse of the English defence caused a loss of morale which was irreparable. The magnates on whom the organization of the defence had turned had shown themselves incapable of concerted action. There was recrimination in high places, and the common man was beginning to suspect the motives of those who were set over him. Above all, there was creeping over every class of society the paralysing sense that defeat was bound to come. And on a people predisposed to accept humiliation the whole strength of the Danish kingdom fell in 1013.

As members of the viking garrison at Jómsborg, the leaders of the army which had invaded England in 1009 owed loyalty to King Swein of Denmark. By becoming Æthelred's man, Thorkell the Tall had given to his former lord what every warrior in the north would regard as ample justification for an attack on Æthelred's country. The wish to punish Thorkell for his defection, and Æthelred, for accepting Thorkell's service, was undoubtedly a principal motive for Swein's expedition of 1013. But it must have been clear at the Danish court that the English capacity for resistance had been broken by the harryings of the last three years, and the history of the expedition shows that from the first it was intended to make Swein king of all England. The rapidity and precision of his movements place him as a general above every other viking leader of his time. His plan of campaign turned on the expectation that the

[1] The archbishop's promise of a ransom and Thorkell's appeal to his men are only known from the German chronicler Thietmar of Merseburg (*Chronicon*, viii, Ch. 42, 43). By a curious mistake he calls Ælfheah 'Dunstan', but his account is strictly contemporary, and based on information which he had received from England.

men of Danish England would be prepared to welcome a Danish king, and that a base established in their country would be secure. But he seems to have been unwilling to risk the direct crossing from Denmark to the Humber, and his first landing in England was made at Sandwich. After a short delay, which allowed straggling vessels to rejoin his fleet, he sailed northwards to the Humber, and finally disembarked twenty miles up the Trent at Gainsborough in Lindsey. His reception showed that he had not mistaken the state of feeling in the northern Danelaw. Without leaving Gainsborough, he was accepted as king successively by the leading men of Northumbria, Lindsey, the whole confederation of the Five Boroughs, and the whole of Danish England south of the Welland and east of Watling Street. As soon as their submission had been secured by hostages, he ordered them to supply his army with horses and provisions, and then set out for the reduction of the shires which still remained faithful to Æthelred. It was not until he had crossed Watling Street into English Mercia that he allowed his men to harry the countryside, and a short display of overwhelming force caused the abandonment of resistance in the districts threatened by his army. Oxford and Winchester surrendered as soon as he appeared outside their defences. With the whole Danelaw, the eastern shires of English Mercia, and the central shires of Wessex firmly held through hostages, he turned from Winchester to a direct attack on London, where the citizen-garrison was supported by Thorkell with the crews of his ships and by King Æthelred with his personal retainers. The attack failed, and many of Swein's men were drowned, apparently because they tried to ford the river. Instead of staying to besiege the city, Swein decided to complete the reduction of Wessex. He marched by way of Wallingford to Bath, where he received the submission of the western thegns, and then returned across central England to his ships at Gainsborough. By this time, according to the *Chronicle*, 'the whole nation regarded him as king in all respects'.[1] and the submission of London

---

[1] His only recorded act as king was to order the levying of a tax. It is mentioned in the *Chronicle*, and a late-11th-century tract on the miracles of St. Edmund remarks incidentally that it was collected in many parts of East Anglia and that the money raised in east Norfolk was brought to Thetford. Owing to the death of Swein before the money had been handed over to his officers, it was returned to those who had paid it. F. Liebermann, *Ungedruckte anglo-normannische Geschichtsquellen*, p. 234.

shortly afterwards deprived King Æthelred of his last strong-hold. For the chance of escape from his lost kingdom he depended on the good faith of Thorkell the Tall, with whom he remained on shipboard until Christmas. He had previously sent his wife into Normandy, and at the close of the year he followed her, leaving Swein in military possession of all England.

A few weeks later the situation was suddenly changed by the death of Swein, which occurred at Gainsborough on 3 February 1014. The crews of the Danish ships in the Trent immediately gave their allegiance to Cnut, the younger of Swein's two sons, who had been left as their commander while Swein was absent in the south. But at the moment they were unready for a new campaign, and, before they were in a condition to take the field, the leading Englishmen outside their power had sent a deputation to Normandy to open negotiations for Æthelred's restoration. The terms on which it was carried out show that many noblemen had submitted to Swein because they were afraid, or at least distrustful, of their own king. It was only on an understanding that Æthelred would rule his kingdom more justly than before that the negotiations were allowed to go forward. In a letter from which a few phrases are preserved in the *Chronicle*, Æthelred promised that in return for the renewed allegiance of his people he would be a true lord to them, reform everything of which they had complained, and forgive all that they had done or said against him. He was received into England on these terms, which are of great constitutional interest as the first recorded pact between an English king and his subjects. Before the end of April, he was in command of an expedition against the Danes in Lindsey.

It gained its object without fighting a battle. Cnut had come to an understanding with the men of Lindsey by which they were bound to supply his army with horses and join it in a great raid over Æthelred's country. But the English army was in motion before the Danish preparations were complete; and Cnut, who in 1014 was a mere youth with no experience of an independent command, decided to withdraw his men from England. As Æthelred entered Lindsey, Cnut and his fleet left the Trent, Before they sailed for Denmark they followed the English coast as far towards the south as Sandwich, where Cnut mutilated and set on shore the hostages who had been given to his father. By his withdrawal Cnut abandoned the men of

Lindsey to a military execution which was carried out ruthlessly by Æthelred. Even in southern England it was felt that Cnut had acted treacherously in leaving his local allies helpless before Æthelred's advancing army.[1] In Lindsey itself, and throughout the Anglo-Danish regions in which the leading thegns of Lindsey had land or kinsmen, Cnut and Æthelred must have been hated with equal intensity. The events of 1014 go far towards explaining the ease with which, a few months later, a son of Æthelred made himself the lord of the Northern Danelaw against his father's will.[2]

From the end of April 1014 until the end of August 1015 the Danish attack on England was suspended. On Swein's death Harold, his elder son, became king of Denmark. Cnut's relations with his brother were friendly. He was allowed to raise an army in Denmark and to bring his ships together in Danish harbours. There is good evidence that Harold joined Cnut during his campaign in England and remained with him for some time after the conclusion of peace.[3] But in Harold's lifetime Cnut could never use the full resources of the Danish kingdom, and after his ignominious return from England he cannot have possessed a reputation of the kind which attracted fighting men into the service of landless adventurers. There can be no doubt that in creating an army adequate to the conquest of England, he owed more than any historian has recorded to the help of his sister's husband, Eric of Hlathir, the greatest nobleman in Norway, who had played the chief part in the overthrow of Olaf Tryggvason, and had ever since been ruling the western coast-lands of his own country as viceroy under King Swein. In 1014 Eric, who had won his first battles thirty years before, was probably the most famous warrior in the Scandinavian world. He was distinguished from the grim figures which fill the centre of the northern scene by a touch of humanity and unselfishness which made it impossible for him to win a kingdom for himself. But he was the best adviser that could have been found for a young prince setting out on a career of conquest, and by joining Cnut he brought to a hazardous enterprise the support of a name familiar throughout the north.[4]

[1] The Abingdon chronicler remarks uncompromisingly that 'the poor people' of Lindsey were 'betrayed' by Cnut.   [2] Below, p. 388–9.

[3] W. H. Stevenson, *E.H.R.* xxviii (1912), pp. 116–17.

[4] The first English writer to bring out the historical importance of Earl Eric was W. H. Stevenson in *Crawford Charters*, pp. 142–8.

Before the expedition had sailed it was joined unexpectedly by Thorkell the Tall, who brought with him nine warships from England. No ancient writer gives any adequate explanation of Thorkell's departure from Æthelred's service. But there was a saga tradition that a corps of professional soldiers which King Swein had established in England under Hemming, Thorkell's brother, perished with its commander through English treachery after Swein's death.[1] It is difficult to fit this story into what is known of English history in this period, but it provides a sufficient motive for Thorkell's conduct, and it is not impossible that Æthelred may have taken Hemming and his men into his service when Swein was dead, and planned, or at least connived at, their destruction when Cnut had left England. Whatever its motive, Thorkell's adherence to Cnut gave him the support of a warrior of great experience, who knew all the leading Englishmen of the day, and had some conception of the political crosscurrents which complicated the problem of national defence.

In the summer of 1015, when Cnut at last landed in England, these currents were unusually intricate. During a great council held at Oxford earlier in the year Eadric of Mercia had procured the murder of Siferth and Morcar, sons of Arngrim, the two leading thegns of the northern Danelaw.[2] The motive of the crime is unknown, but the king made himself accessory to it by confiscating the estates of the victims, and ordering the arrest of Siferth's widow. Within a few weeks, she was carried off by Edmund, the king's eldest surviving son, who married her in defiance of his father and then proceeded to the Danelaw, where he took possession of the property of both Siferth and Morcar. As a rebel against a king who had recently laid waste much of that country, he was sure of a welcome, and before the

---

[1] According to the same tradition, another corps under Eilaf, who had been Hemming's fellow commander in the invasion of 1009, was only saved from massacre because Eilaf had been warned of the plot by his mistress. The tradition as a whole was discussed by Stevenson, *Crawford Charters*, pp. 140–1, who came to the definite opinion that there was a basis of historical fact behind it.

[2] The *Chronicle* describes them as the chief thegns belonging to the 'Seven Boroughs'. This phrase does not occur again, and its exact meaning is uncertain. It clearly includes the five Danish boroughs of Lincoln, Stamford, Leicester, Nottingham, and Derby, and it is more than probable that the two remaining boroughs also lay within the Danelaw. There can be little doubt that one of them was Torksey in Lincolnshire, which fifty years later had a population of more than 200 burgesses. The fact that under Edward the Confessor many thegns belonging to Danish Mercia also held land in Yorkshire suggests that York was the seventh borough of the group.

end of the summer he had been accepted as lord by the whole confederation of the Five Boroughs.

At this moment Cnut appeared off the English coast. After recent events the Danelaw was likely to be hostile, and the fleet, touching briefly at Sandwich, passed on down the Channel to an anchorage in Poole harbour. While the crews were ravaging in Wessex, Edmund and Eadric of Mercia were raising troops in their respective countries. They joined their forces, but separated before they had met the enemy. It was believed at the time that Eadric had been plotting against Edmund. In any case he went over to the Danish side immediately afterwards, seduced from their allegiance to Æthelred the crews of forty ships which had once been Thorkell's, and then did homage to Cnut. Within four months from his landing Cnut was in firm possession of Wessex, and the resources of the Mercian ealdormanry were at his command.

As the year was ending Cnut and Eadric crossed the Thames at Cricklade into country which had formed the under-kingdom of the Hwicce, and was still regarded as a province distinct from Mercia. Nothing is known of the part which Leofwine, its ealdorman, played in the war, but Cnut and Eadric treated him as an enemy, and harried his territory in a raid which extended as far as Warwickshire. Edmund, on his part, raised an army in the Danelaw. But his people seem to have realized that the men of a single district could do little that was effective against the formidable host which was at large in the southern midlands, and they separated, after demanding that the London militia should join them, and that the king himself should take the field. They were soon called out again; and although the king was suffering from an illness which killed him a few weeks later, he brought a contingent of southern troops to their support. Before long, suspecting treason in the army, he returned to London, and the opportunity for a general advance against the Danes was lost. In its place, Edmund joined forces with Uhtred, earl of Northumbria, and carried out with him a devastation of Cheshire, Staffordshire, and Shropshire. They have often been blamed for destroying English villages, but the chief estates of the Mercian ealdormanry lay in the districts which they ravaged, and it was there that the enemy could most easily find remounts and provisions. In reply, Cnut invaded the Danelaw, which Edmund had left unprotected, and then set out for

Northumbria, harrying the country along the line of the Great North Road. Earl Uhtred, who was obviously taken by surprise, hurried back from the midlands to the north, and submitted to Cnut. He was murdered soon afterwards,[1] and Eric of Norway received his earldom from Cnut. With Northumbria in the strongest of hands Cnut was free to begin a direct attack on the south-eastern shires where the English power of resistance was concentrated. Avoiding contact with Edmund and the army of the Danelaw, he marched quickly across English Mercia to his base in Wessex, and began preparations for the removal of his fleet from Poole harbour to the Thames. It was clear that the next phase of the war would turn on the defence of London, and Edmund joined his father in the city. On 23 April 1016, before the Danish fleet had reached the Thames, King Æthelred died, and the men of London, with the magnates who had come in from the country, at once chose Edmund to succeed him.

Within at most a few days after Æthelred's death a more widely representative assembly met at Southampton and swore fealty to Cnut in return for a promise of good government.[2] It included bishops and abbots as well as lay noblemen, and its action showed that most men of position in Wessex regarded Cnut's ultimate victory as certain. Edmund's first task as king was to bring them back to their natural allegiance. In a campaign of which no details are recorded he made himself master of Wessex, and throughout the rest of the war its militia was at his command. But his expedition into the west left the Thames valley ill defended, and allowed Cnut to begin a leisurely siege of London. His fleet took possession of Greenwich in the second week of May. Soon afterwards it moved up stream to an an-

---

[1] The murder was an important event in northern history, but its circumstances are obscure. The *Chronicle* states that Uhtred was killed by the advice of Eadric Streona. The statement is made improbable by northern sources of the Norman age which show that the chief agent in the murder was a nobleman named Thurbrand, known from his rank as Thurbrand the Hold (on this title see below, p. 509). The most detailed of these accounts states that Uhtred and 40 companions who had come with him to treat with Cnut for peace were killed by Cnut's soldiers through Thurbrand's guile *Symeonis . . . Opera*, R.S. i, p. 218. Thurbrand's part in the crime set in motion the most remarkable private feud in English history. Thurbrand was killed by Ealdred, earl of Northumbria, Uhtred's son; Ealdred was killed by Carl, Thurbrand's son; and a number of Carl's sons were killed by Waltheof, son of Earl Siward, whose mother was Ealdred's daughter (op. cit., p. 219).

[2] Florence of Worcester, *Chronicon*, ed. B. Thorpe, i, p. 173.

chorage off the south bank of the river at Bermondsey. Its further progress was barred by London bridge. For the investment of the city which Cnut had in mind it was necessary that his ships should command the whole course of the Thames at London, and he set his men to cut a channel along which ships could be dragged round the southern end of the bridge into the upper river. As soon as the ships were through, their crews began to construct a line of earthwork outside the landward walls of London, and when it was completed they settled down to blockade the city.

Before the end of June Cnut was free to leave London for Wessex. He gave battle to Edmund at Penselwood in Dorset and Sherston in Wiltshire. But neither engagement was decisive, and after the second fight the armies fell out of touch with one another. Cnut seems to have returned to London, and Edmund began to prepare for an assault on the Danish lines round the city. Avoiding all the familiar roads which converged on London from Wessex, he kept to the north of the Thames, and descended on the Danish fortifications by unguarded tracks through the woods behind Tottenham.[1] The Danes, taken by surprise, were driven to their ships and crossed the river. Edmund wished to follow them; but there was no practicable ford across the Thames nearer than Brentford, and the Danes had time in which to establish themselves in a new position. They were defeated in a battle fought on the south bank of the Thames two days after the storming of their lines at London. But the English losses in the campaign were so heavy that Edmund was compelled to retreat into Wessex and begin the work of raising a new army. On his withdrawal the Danes reoccupied their original entrenchments, and London was invested again.

Up to this time the advantage in the war had rested with the Danes. London was the key-point in the struggle; and after a great effort and a brilliant initial success Edmund had failed to drive them from their positions around the city. But the difficulty of obtaining supplies was beginning to make these positions untenable, and Cnut at last decided to throw his whole force into an attack on the city by land and water. It failed, and

---

[1] MS. C of the *Chronicle* states that he came *ut þuruh Clæighangran*. This name has recently been identified with the *Clayhangre extra villam de Totenham* mentioned in a 13th-century Assize Roll, which is now represented by Clayhill Farm in Tottenham (*Place-Names of Middlesex*, E.P-N.S., p. 79).

the host at once abandoned its quarters outside London, sailed to the mouth of the Orwell, and provisioned itself by a great raid over East Anglia and Mercia. The ships, with food and live stock taken in the expedition, sailed from the Orwell to the Medway, and the host, remounted, struck out on an extended course which brought it at last into Kent. Edmund, who had been watching its movements, overtook and defeated it at Otford, and drove it before him into Sheppey.[1] The prospect of a decisive victory, which had seemed within Cnut's reach in the first months of the year, had vanished for the moment with the failure of the attack on London. It is highly significant that Eadric of Mercia, hitherto Cnut's ally, came in to Edmund immediately after the battle of Otford.

The war was ended by one of the many battles which in the Dark Ages unexpectedly reversed the whole drift of a campaign. In the autumn the Danes, to whom the sea was still open, crossed the estuary of the Thames and carried out a raid across Essex and the adjacent Mercian shires. Edmund, commanding an army drawn from every part of southern England, followed them; and overtook them on their return towards the coast at Ashingdon in south-east Essex, where a low hill projects into the flat country between the Thames and the Crouch.[2] Early in the battle which followed Eadric of Mercia took flight, and with him the contingent which he had brought from Herefordshire and south Shropshire. Other detachments followed it; and although the army as a whole continued the battle, it ended in an overwhelming English defeat. Many of the English leaders perished—among them Ulfkell Snilling of East Anglia—and Edmund himself became a fugitive. But he had a reputation of the kind which made a king formidable in disaster; the nickname Ironside by which he is always known shows that he was admired by the common people, and Cnut's advisers realized that it would be well to come to terms with him. On an island in the Severn near Deerhurst the two kings made a solemn compact of mutual friendship, fixed the sum of money that should be given to Cnut's army, and agreed to a division of England which gave Wessex to Edmund and the whole country

---

[1] Florence of Worcester, *Chronicon*, i, p. 177.

[2] On the identification of the battle-site see *The Place-Names of Essex* (E.P-N.S.), p. 177. The battle was fought on 18 October (*Leeds Studies in English*, vi (1937), pp. 20, 21).

beyond the Thames to Cnut.[1] The men of London, who became
Cnut's subjects by this treaty, were required to buy their own
peace from his army, and his ships anchored in the Thames for
the winter. It was a settlement which presaged future trouble.
It imposed a divided allegiance on every nobleman who held
land both in Wessex and Mercia. But before its instability
could be proved, on 30 November 1016, Edmund died, and
the West Saxons accepted Cnut as their king.

[1] According to the *Chronicle*, Wessex alone fell to Edmund in this division.
Florence of Worcester (*Chronicon*, i, p. 178) adds London, Essex, and East Anglia to
his share. But a territory which stretched so far towards the north would not have
been described as 'Wessex' by the chronicler, and the fact that London fell to Cnut
is proved by the separate payment which the citizens made to his army.

XII

ENGLAND AND THE SCANDINAVIAN WORLD

THE reign of Æthelred II is one of the few periods of Anglo-Saxon history which can be studied in a full and contemporary narrative. The anonymous monk of Abingdon who set down year by year his tale of war and misery, the treachery of one leader and the fruitless courage of another, had drawn a picture of life in his generation which may be criticized, but can never be ignored. No one who has followed the sequence of events in his restrained and sardonic prose can fail to receive the impression of an ancient and rich society, helpless before a derisive enemy because its leaders were incapable of government. It is unlikely that the author of these annals knew much about the world, and his criticism of public men is often short-sighted. He was too ready to impute treachery or cowardice to a leader who avoided contact with the enemy. Towards the end of his narrative he becomes querulous instead of ironical, and reckless in his allegations of treason. Nevertheless, men who had a wider knowledge of affairs give the same colour to the age in which they lived. In a famous sermon preached in 1014 Archbishop Wulfstan of York represented the misery of the time as God's judgement upon a treacherous and wicked people. King Æthelred himself, in several charters, speaks of retainers who had proved disloyal. The historians who regard Æthelred's reign as a time of national degeneracy have good contemporary opinion behind them.

It was certainly an age in which a man could betray the state without losing either office or public influence. After changing sides twice in the recent war, Eadric Streona was the central figure among the magnates who arranged the treaty between Cnut and Edmund Ironside in 1016. The weakening of the sense of loyalty and personal duty towards the king, shown in the conduct of many persons less eminent than Eadric, seems to have been accompanied by a general disregard of social obligations. Archbishop Wulfstan describes the oppression of free men by their lords and of slaves by their masters in terms suggesting that the conventions which governed the relations of different classes were breaking down. But the evils which give a sinister complexion to the age were the result of conditions which from their very nature were temporary. They were the effects of a state of war under a king of singular incompetence. Their ultimate cause was realized clearly enough by the unknown man or woman who first described him as 'Æthelred Unræd'—'Æthelred No-Counsel'.[1] In the last resort they all arose from the fact that in a series of crises, each of which demanded a concentration of the national energy, the king could neither give direction to his people nor hold his greater subjects firmly to their allegiance.

But the incompetence of King Æthelred did not mean the collapse of the national administration. Already in Athelstan's reign there is evidence that the king was maintaining a permanent body of clerks in his service. Under Æthelred the necessity of finding vast sums of money at short notice must have increased the importance of the professional element in the group of men through whom the king governed the country. These sums could never have been raised if the king had not possessed at least a rudimentary financial bureau, which could fix the amount to be paid by each shire, and find men of local position to collect it. Even in quiet times the volume of correspondence which passed between the king's court and the shires was steadily increasing. Shire courts were becoming accustomed to the receipt of letters from the king—informal communications, written in English, and authenticated by the impression of his seal hanging from one corner.[2] The king's writ, as such a letter was called, had not yet become an ordinary instrument of government, but a private document of Æthelred's reign mentions a royal precept to the shire court of Berkshire in a way which suggests that written orders from the king often came there.[3] Nevertheless, the chief duty of the king's writing-office was the preparation of the formal Latin charters which were intended to remain as permanent memorials of royal grants or confirmations of land. A considerable number

---

[1] The epithet must have been used in this context as a play upon the king's name, which literally meant 'noble counsel'. H. Bradley, *E.H.R.* xxxii (1917), p. 399.

[2] See F. M. Stenton, *The Latin Charters of the Anglo-Saxon Period*, pp. 89–91 and F. E. Harmer, *Anglo-Saxon Writs*.

[3] A. J. Robertson, *Anglo-Saxon Charters*, p. 136.

of Æthelred's charters still survive in good texts. Their chief
interest lies not in their subject-matter, but in the proof which
they afford that the continuity of the embryo civil service at
Æthelred's command was never broken. Year by year in these
solemn records there recur distinctive phrases and rare words
which had been used by the clerks of earlier kings. The re-
appearance of these words and phrases in charters written for
Cnut shows that the clerks who staffed his writing-office had
learned their business in Æthelred's reign.

Within the framework of the organized state which emerged
from the war the civilization of an earlier age had been preserved. The distinction which belongs to Æthelred's reign in
the history of learning and religion is in singular contast to the
political humiliation of the age. At Cerne Abbas first, and
afterwards at Eynsham, Ælfric, the greatest insular scholar of
the Benedictine reformation, spent a lifetime of study and
exposition, undisturbed, or at least undefeated, by the tumult
around him. Byrhtferth of Ramsey, the most eminent man
of science produced by the English church since the death of
Bede, wrote his most important book in the last decade of
Æthelred's reign. Through the individuality of their script and
the boldness of their execution, a number of manuscripts
written in England during this period have a distinctive place
in the history of European book-production. Few of them can
be dated with precision. Some of the most famous may have
been written before the Danish peril became acute. But the
unbroken development of English handwriting between the
reign of Edgar and the Norman Conquest shows that the activities of English *scriptoria* were never seriously interrupted
during the years of trouble. The Danish ravages must have impoverished many religious communities, and may have brought
permanent destruction to some, but they had no discernible
effect on the intellectual quality of English monasticism.

It is Cnut's distinction as a ruler that from the beginning of his
reign he set himself to win the respect of the English church.
His father Swein, who first appears in history as the leader of a
heathen reaction in Denmark, had behaved as at least a nominal
Christian in later life. He had discountenanced heathenism
in the Norwegian provinces under his overlordship, and it was
remembered that he had given an estate in Scania to a wandering bishop from England, who had used it as a base for mission-

ary work in Norway and Sweden.[1] But Swein's tepid patronage
of Christianity contrasts sharply with Cnut's enthusiastic
devotion to the interests of the church in England. Accepting
from its leaders the traditional English conception of the king
as an agent appointed by God for the promotion of religion
and the protection of its ministers, he identified himself with
them in their task of restoring ecclesiastical authority among a
people demoralized by thirty years of war. Through them he
was brought into contact with the court of Rome, and thereby
into intimacy with the members of a political circle which no
one of his race had ever entered. He was the first viking leader
to be admitted into the civilized fraternity of Christian kings.

There is no reason to doubt the sincerity of his religion. But
beneath it there lay the experience of a king's son, trained
in a barbarian military household, and the barbarian strain in
Cnut's mentality often determined his conduct. At least four
prominent Englishmen—Eadric Streona among them—were
slaughtered without any recorded trial in the first months of his
reign. Eadwig the last surviving son of Æthelred's first marriage, was driven into flight, and afterwards sought out and
killed by Cnut's orders. Two young sons of Edmund Ironside
survived, but only because a refuge was found for them in
Hungary, where Cnut's agents could not reach them. In the
ordering of his own life Cnut ostentatiously disregarded conventions which were beginning to govern the behaviour of
civilized kings. During the war before his accession he had
taken for a temporary wife Ælfgifu, commonly known as
Ælfgifu 'of Northampton', daughter of Ælfhelm, once earl of
Northumbria.[2] In 1017, in order to forestall any action by the
duke of Normandy on behalf of the sons whom his sister Emma
had borne to Æthelred, Cnut entered into an alliance with the
Norman court, of which his own marriage to Emma was the
foundation. His earlier association with Ælfgifu had never been
recognized by the church, and Emma of Normandy was everywhere acknowledged to be his lawful wife. But Ælfgifu was
never dismissed into obscurity. Whatever may have been the

---

[1] Adam of Bremen, *Gesta Hammaburgensis Ecclesiae Pontificum*, Bk. ii. cap. 39, and
ed. B. Schmeidler, ed. 3, Bk. ii, cap. 41.

[2] Her surname is explained by the fact that Ælfhelm, her father, was a considerable landowner in Northamptonshire. He gave Cottingham and other estates in
that county to Peterborough abbey (*The Chronicle of Hugh Candidus, a Monk of
Peterborough*, ed. W. T. Mellows, p. 69).

nature of her personal relations with Cnut in later years, he encouraged her to behave in the north as his queen, and in 1030 he appointed her regent of Norway on behalf of their son Swein. It is perhaps not surprising that the English conception of Cnut as the model of a Christian king, at once the patron and the pupil of the church, was never accepted unreservedly in Scandinavia.

Within each of the countries affected by Cnut's singular career there arose a distinct tradition of his character and achievement. In the north he inherited what proved to be the hopeless task of imposing Danish overlordship on Norway. In Old Norse literature he appears as a great and wealthy king, who attracted potential enemies to his court, overawed them by his splendour, and then disarmed them by bribes. The ordinary Englishman regarded him as a conqueror who had brought peace to a harassed people, given new efficacy to its ancient laws, and honoured its religion. When the first Latin history of Denmark was written, late in the twelfth century, he was chiefly remembered as a great warrior who had vastly enlarged the boundaries of his kingdom.[1] His own poets pile one cliché on another in praise of his ferocious courage. It is the element of truth in the English view which has determined his place in history.

For approximately twelve months after the death of Edmund Ironside Cnut seems to have treated England as a conquered province. It was probably for military rather than administrative reasons that, early in 1017, he divided the whole country into four great districts, within each of which the whole authority of government was concentrated in the hands of one person. Disregarding such traditional units of local administration as the ealdormanries of Lindsey and the Hwicce, he set Eadric Streona in charge of all Mercia from the Humber to the Bristol Avon. East Anglia was given to Thorkell the Tall; Eric of Norway remained as earl of Northumbria; and Wessex, where respect for the native dynasty was likely to be the strongest, was kept by Cnut under his direct control. Historically the division is interesting because it foreshadowed the appearance of the great provincial governments around which English politics turned in the generation before the Norman

---

[1] Swen Aggeson, 'Historia Regum Danorum', in Langebek, *Scriptores Rerum Danicarum*, i, p. 54.

Conquest. It marks an important stage in the development of the Anglo-Saxon ealdormanry, which had always in some degree expressed local self-consciousness, into the Anglo-Scandinavian earldom, of which the boundaries were fixed by the king. But it lasted for less than a year. Within a few months Eadric Streona, guilty or suspected of treason, was killed, and Mercia fell apart again into a number of separate earldoms. In the summer of 1017 the marriage of Cnut and Emma of Normandy removed the danger of foreign intervention on behalf of Æthelred's family. It was no longer necessary for Cnut to keep the West Saxon nobility under close personal supervision, and by the early part of 1018 he had created, or re-created, at least two earldoms in Wessex.

Before the end of that year he was so well established as king that he could dismiss the fleet which had brought him to England. He took command of it for the last time in the spring, when it destroyed thirty ships' companies of vikings which had ventured into English waters.[1] For the payment of its crews a sum of £10,500 was exacted from their old enemies, the citizens of London, and a Danegeld of £72,000 was laid on the rest of England. Forty ships were retained in Cnut's service, and then the remainder of the fleet sailed for Denmark. Its dismissal showed that Cnut intended to reign thenceforward as the chosen king of the English people, and soon afterwards, in a national assembly held at Oxford, his leading followers and Englishmen from all parts of the country came to an agreement about the terms on which they could live together. It was decided that the system of legal relationships which had prevailed in Edgar's reign should form the basis of the new Anglo-Danish state, and an oath to observe 'Edgar's law' was taken by all members of the assembly. It is with the departure of the Danish fleet and the meeting at Oxford which followed it that Cnut's effective reign begins.

It was so successful that contemporaries found little to say about it. The rapid succession of incidents, of which the bare relation makes the *Chronicle* a continuous narrative of Æthelred's reign, ends with the Oxford meeting of 1018. During the next ten years the *Chronicle* shrinks to a series of brief notes, which apart from ecclesiastical matters are nearly all concerned with the king's voyages into foreign parts. Its author knew little

[1] Thietmar of Merseburg, *Chronicon*, ix, c. 7.

THE SCANDINAVIAN KINGDOMS AND SEAS

about their significance, and no coherent account of them can
be gathered from later Scandinavian writers. But the mere fact
that Cnut led four separate expeditions into the north between
1019 and 1028 proves his security in regard to England, and
shows the importance which he attached to his dynastic
interests in the Scandinavian world.

According to a letter which Cnut addressed to his English
subjects after the expedition of 1019,[1] it was undertaken in
order to avert a great danger which threatened them from
Denmark. His words are too vague to show its precise nature.
But there can be little doubt of its connection with the fact that
the Danes were for the moment kingless. Harold, Cnut's
brother, is known to have died in 1018 or 1019. He had no
children, and Cnut was his heir. The leading motive of his
expedition in 1019 was certainly the wish to take possession
of the Danish kingdom. But it is more than probable that in the
interval between the death of Harold and the arrival of Cnut
the more restless of the Danish chiefs, with no king to control
them, had been preparing for the revival of viking enterprise
towards the west.

It is probable that Thorkell the Tall acted as regent of
England in Cnut's absence. He was the most prominent
layman in England. He always has the first place among the
lay magnates who witness Cnut's charters in 1018 and 1019,
and he alone is addressed by name in the letter which Cnut
sent out after his return from Denmark. But in the autumn of
1021 Cnut proclaimed him an outlaw. In the *Chronicle* this
drastic action, of which no satisfactory explanation has been
offered, stands as an isolated incident, but there is little doubt
that Cnut's second expedition to Denmark was one of its
consequences. In 1022, according to the *Chronicle*, Cnut 'went
out with his ships' to the Isle of Wight, and in 1023 he and
Thorkell met in Denmark, and entered into a very remarkable
pact of reconciliation. It was agreed that Thorkell should
govern Denmark in Cnut's name, and that Cnut should give
one of his sons into Thorkell's keeping, and bring one of
Thorkell's sons back with him to England. It is improbable
that an outlawed exile without an armed force behind him
would have received such terms from his former lord. Thorkell,
whose brother had commanded at Jómsborg, could easily

[1] Liebermann, *Gesetze*, i, pp. 273-5.

have raised an army there and in the other Danish colonies along the Baltic. The concentration of Cnut's fleet off the Isle of Wight before his voyage to Denmark is best explained as an attempt to protect the southern coast of England against a raid by Thorkell and his companions.

Thorkell had been prominent in northern warfare for more than a generation, and his reconciliation with Cnut is the last recorded incident in his life. Within the next three years Ulf, the husband of Cnut's sister Estrith, had succeeded him as regent of Denmark, and had been made guardian of Hartha-cnut, the only son of Cnut and Emma of Normandy. Up to the time of his appointment Ulf does not seem to have played any outstanding part in affairs. There is no evidence that he took part in the English war, and he first comes into general history as a rebel against Cnut, his patron. The details of his revolt, as of all northern history in this period, are made obscure by the wealth of conflicting tradition which arose about them. But there is no doubt that at the time when Cnut was threatened by a coalition of his chief enemies Ulf became its ally, and English and Danish authorities agree that he helped to bring about the most signal defeat which Cnut suffered in the whole of his career.

The leader of the coalition was Olaf Haroldson, a descendant of the great Harold Fairhair, who while Cnut was engaged in the conquest of England had made himself the master of the larger part of Norway. His immediate ancestors were the insignificant lords of a small district to the west of the Oslo Fiord, and had been overshadowed for many years by the great family of northern earls to which Eric of Hlathir belonged. The unlikelihood of a career in Norway equal to his rank impelled him out to sea as an adventurer, and although the details of his exploits were ill remembered, there is no reason to doubt that he took service with Æthelred when Swein was about to invade England, and shared in the operations round London in 1013. In the following year he was employed by Richard, duke of Normandy, in a campaign against Odo, count of Chartres, which is the first fixed point in his history.[1] On Æthelred's restoration in 1014 Olaf accompanied him across the Channel. Two years later when Earl Eric, the chief supporter of the Danish interest in Norway, was absent

[1] William of Jumièges, *Gesta Normannorum Ducum*, ed. J. Marx, pp. 85–7.

with Cnut in England, Olaf decided to try his fortune in his own country. Landing with a small force in the west of Norway, he passed quickly to the districts along the Oslo Fiord where Danish overlordship had always been resented. The local kings of that region came in to him, and before long he had defeated Earl Swein, brother of Eric of Hlathir, in a great sea-battle off Nesjar, in the mouth of the fiord. After Swein's defeat Olaf secured acceptance as king in the group of western folk-lands, known collectively as Thrandheim, where the earls of Hlathir had been all-powerful. For the next ten years though he had many private enemies, he had no political rival in Norway.

The king of Sweden was his natural ally. The chief outland interests of the Swedish people lay in their eastern colonies, and their kings had rarely come into direct competition with other northern rulers. But the vast resources which the conquest of England gave to the king of Denmark threatened the rough balance of power which existed in Scandinavia. King Anund of Sweden instinctively associated himself with Olaf of Norway against Cnut, and in 1026 the two northern kings planned a combined attack on the Danish kingdom. For reasons which are quite unknown they were joined by Ulf, the regent of Denmark, and by Eilaf, Ulf's brother, whom Cnut had made an earl in England. Their object seems to have been a systematic harrying of Scania, the richest of the Danish provinces on the Scandinavian mainland. But while Olaf, sailing from Norway, was still off the coast of Sjaelland, Cnut appeared in the Cattegat with a larger fleet and drove him eastwards in confusion. Avoiding a set battle with the Norwegian fleet Cnut sailed on to the mouth of the Holy River in the east of Scania, where most of the Swedish ships were concentrated. It is impossible to reach any certainty about the events which followed. According to Norse tradition many of Cnut's ships were lost through the breaking of a dam which Olaf with that end in view, had built upstream across the river. In Danish tradition Ulf, who is represented as the real founder of the alliance against Cnut, is described as enticing many of Cnut's men to destruction by offering them battle in a position which they could only reach by crossing a decrepit bridge.[1] The *Chronicle*, which gives by far the earliest account of the war, merely states that 'Cnut went with his ships to the battle-place

[1] Saxo Grammaticus, *Gesta Danorum*, ed. J. Olrik and H. Ræder, i, pp. 288–91.

at the Holy River and Ulf and Eilaf met him with a great Swedish fleet and army; and many men perished on Cnut's side, and the Swedes kept the place of slaughter'. No coherent story can be pieced together from these diverse relations. But the agreement of the English and Danish authorities establishes the essential fact of Ulf's treason, and there is no obvious ground for rejecting the further tradition, current throughout the north, that soon after the battle of the Holy River he was murdered by Cnut's orders.

Two years later Cnut made a determined, and for the moment a successful effort to bring Norway once more under Danish overlordship. Under the year 1028 the *Chronicle* states that Cnut 'went with fifty ships of English thegns from England to Norway, and drove king Olaf from that country, and acquired it for himself'. Later Old Norse authorities amplify this outline. They show that long before the expedition sailed Cnut had been working by bribes and promises on the Norwegian noblemen who for any reason were disaffected towards King Olaf. They also make it clear that there was widespread resentment in Norway at the austerity of Olaf's rule, and at the determination with which he set himself to root out heathen practices everywhere in his kingdom. In the event, Cnut became the lord of Norway without fighting a battle. The fifty ships with which he had sailed from England were joined by a large Danish fleet which had assembled in the Liim Fiord. Olaf, declining to risk an engagement, withdrew into the Oslo Fiord, and allowed Cnut to sail unchallenged along the outer coast of Norway. At various stages in his progress he landed in order to secure the allegiance of the local chiefs, and at Nidaros, the most northerly point of his voyage, the men of the all-important Thrandheim country came in to him and acknowledged him as king.

With their submission Cnut reached the height of his power in the Scandinavian world. Olaf was still at large in southern Norway, but he had few supporters, and within a few months he left the country. For the moment Cnut was the unquestioned lord of three kingdoms. As if conscious that his position was in some degree imperial, he held a great court at Nidaros for the declaration of his will regarding the future government of Denmark and Norway. Harthacnut, his son, who had travelled with him to the north, was proclaimed king of

Denmark. In Norway Cnut's authority depended on the loyalty of the men of Thrandheim, and it was necessary that he should show respect to the family of their ancient earls. The great Earl Eric had died some five years previously, but Hakon his son, who had done good service to Cnut in England, was present at Nidaros. He was now set to govern Norway, with an earl's title. Like his father, Hakon was too scrupulous for a successful life in a world ruled by violence. Cnut, who knew him well, doubted his ability to crush the opposition which was certain to arise against the new régime in Norway. But his rank made his appointment inevitable, and the only precaution which Cnut could take was to secure hostages from a large number of Norwegian chiefs before he returned to England.

The settlement reached at Nidaros lasted for less than a year. It was not before the early part of 1029 that Cnut left Norway, and in the following winter Hakon was drowned in the Pentland Firth. There were various rumours about his end, but it is probable that he perished on his return from a visit to England, during which he became betrothed to Gunnhild, Cnut's niece. In his place Cnut sent Swein, his son by Ælfgifu of Northampton, to rule in Norway under his mother's guardianship. Their reception into the kingdom was delayed for a few weeks by the return of Olaf Haroldsson from exile. He had raised a small army in Sweden, and believing that Norway could be won most quickly by a decisive success in the district where his enemies were strongest, he made straight across country for Thrandheim. But the rich peasantry of that region rose against him, and annihilated his army at Stiklestad near the Thrandheim Fiord on 29 July 1030. He fell in the battle, and Swein and his mother were immediately accepted as Cnut's representatives throughout the north.

Their attempt to govern Norway failed miserably. In later generations 'Ælfgifu's time' became a synonym for an age of wretchedness and oppression. Her own behaviour may have been harsh and autocratic, but the real cause of her failure was her determination to impose new forms of taxation, a heavier burden of public service, and severer penalties for violence on the most fiercely independent people in Europe. It was an addition to her offence that the new customs which she wished to introduce were founded on Danish practice. Olaf Haroldsson had been an autocrat; but he had never attempted to change the fundamental relationships which had united king and people in Norway, and as a ruler he stood in the tradition of Olaf Tryggvason and Harold Fairhair. Under what was in effect an alien government, the figure of King Olaf began to attract the popular imagination. Around the central fact of his zeal for the Christian religion legends of his asceticism arose, and a reputation of the kind which predisposed men to expect tokens of his sanctity very quickly gathered around him. A year after his death his body was exhumed in a state of apparent incorruption, and the church at Nidaros into which it was translated became the centre of a cult which spread rapidly throughout Scandinavia. In Norway it was accompanied by an outburst of national feeling which destroyed the authority of Swein and Ælfgifu. By the winter of 1033 it had become impossible for them to live in Thrandheim. For more than twenty months they maintained some vestiges of power in the south, but in the autumn of 1035 they were compelled to escape into Denmark. When Cnut died, a few weeks later, Magnus, St. Olaf's son, was well established as king everywhere in Norway.

Historians have often attributed to Cnut the deliberate intention of founding a northern empire. For a few years he certainly succeeded in uniting Norway with Denmark and England in a composite dominion, held together by his personal supremacy. But there is no evidence that he ever regarded this dominion as an organized state. The most expansive of the titles assigned to him in ancient records—King of Englishmen, Danes, Norwegians, and part of the Swedes—implies that he regarded himself as the lord of a number of separate peoples. The attestations to his charters offer no suggestion that he required nobles from distant provinces to make periodical visits to his court. Above all, it is very doubtful whether he believed that his various kingdoms would remain united after his death. It is safe to assume that he intended Harthacnut to succeed him as king of Denmark and England. But his appointment of Swein as king of Norway clearly foreshadowed Norwegian independence. It is incredible that Cnut can have expected a son of Ælfgifu of Northampton to govern Norway in permanent subjection to a son of Emma of Normandy.

It was not the organization but the geographical position of his dominions which gave Cnut a distinctive place among

European rulers. As king of the Danes he controlled the narrow entry from the Cattegat into the Baltic. The acquisition of Norway, which otherwise brought him little profit and some embarrassment, gave him command of the open waters by which this entry was approached. As king of England he was ruler of a people for whom the freedom of the North Sea was a necessity of life. He dominated the most dangerous portion of the great trade-route which led from the Bay of Biscay to the eastern Baltic, and there fell on him a special responsibility for its peace. No power with commercial interests in the remoter seas of Europe could ignore him, Anxious to enter a world which had been closed to his ancestors, he responded easily to offers of friendship, and his reign marks an important stage in the process which ultimately made the Scandinavian countries an integral part of a European state-system. England, which had relapsed into virtual isolation in the later years of Æthelred II, was brought into new contacts with other lands. So far as is known, the beginnings of diplomatic intercourse between England and south-western France lie in the interchange of courtesies which passed year by year between Cnut and William III of Aquitaine.[1]

His own conception of his place among sovereigns was expressed to all the world in 1027, when he travelled to Rome in order to attend the coronation of Conrad, the Holy Roman Emperor. In part, his journey was a work of devotion. Rome, to him, was the city of the apostles Peter and Paul, and its bishop was the teacher of kings. Early in his own reign he had received a letter from Pope Benedict VIII, exhorting him to suppress injustice, and to use his strength in the service of peace.[2] In the churches which he visited on the way to Rome he appeared as a penitent.[3] But he was also a statesman, and there is no doubt that he regarded the coronation of an emperor as an appropriate moment for a gesture of respect towards the formidable power which threatened his Jutish frontier. It was also an opportunity for negotiations on behalf of traders and pilgrims from northern lands who had long been aggrieved by the heavy tolls levied at innumerable points on the road to

---

[1] Adémar de Chabannes, *Chronique*, ed. J. Chavanon, p. 163.

[2] See Cnut's Letter of 1020 (Liebermann, *Gesetze*, i, p. 273), 3.

[3] The *Encomium Emmae* (ed. A. Campbell, p. 37) contains an often-quoted description of the signs of devotion which he displayed in the monastic church of Saint Bertin.

Rome. Before the company dispersed he had secured valuable concessions from the emperor himself, the king of Burgundy, and the other princes through whose territory the great road ran. From the pope he obtained a relaxation of the immoderate charges hitherto imposed on English archbishops visiting Rome for their *pallia*. In a letter sent to England soon after the assembly Cnut describes these achievements with obvious satisfaction.[1] But there is still more obvious note of pride in his emphasis on the honour with which he was received by 'the princes of all the peoples' between Apulia and the North Sea.

The friendly relations which he had established with the empire were never broken. Towards the end of his reign they brought him an increase of territory which permanently enlarged the Danish kingdom, and as an addition to his effective power more than balanced the loss of Norway. In 1035, or a little earlier, the emperor opened negotiations for a marriage between Henry, his son, and Gunnhild, Cnut's daughter. In return the emperor promised to surrender Slesvig, and a wide stretch of ancient Danish country north of the Eider, which since the time of Harold Gormsson had been organized as a border province of Germany against the Danes. Henry and Gunnhild were not married until the summer of 1036, but the one ancient authority for the cession of Slesvig associates it definitely with the previous negotiations,[2] and there is no reason to doubt that the debatable lands were in Cnut's possession when he died on 12 November 1035.

The only danger which threatened Cnut's essential interests in these later years came from Normandy, where Edward and Alfred, the sons of Æthelred and Emma, had been living since 1016. For the first half of his reign Cnut had been protected against any attempt to restore the line of Æthelred by the goodwill of the Norman court, secured by his marriage to the duke's sister. But Richard II, his ally, died in 1026, and Robert his younger son, who inherited the duchy in 1027 from a colourless elder brother, was an adventurous youth, unlikely to be bound by any understandings to which he had not been a party. To revive the alliance Cnut gave Estrith, his sister, Earl Ulf's widow, to the duke in marriage, but he

---

[1] Florence of Worcester, *Chronicon*, ed. B. Thorpe, i. 185–9.
[2] Adam of Bremen, *Gesta Hammaburgensis Ecclesiae Pontificum*, ed. J. M. Lappenburg, Bk. ii. cap. 54, and 3rd ed. B. Schmeidler, Bk. ii. cap. 56.

soon repudiated her, and there is early though by no means conclusive evidence that he planned an invasion of England on behalf of Æthelred's exiled sons. It is at least clear that there can have been no friendship between the English and the Norman courts for some years before Cnut's death.

But by this time Cnut was sure of the loyalty of his English subjects. If Æthelred's sons had been brought back to England by a Norman army, they would have found the country apathetic, if not hostile. Cnut had given security to the common man, new markets to traders, and the chance of an exciting career to young noblemen. In the active prosperity of his reign memories of the West Saxon dynasty soon lost their political force. Cnut could not, like William the Conqueror, claim to rule in England through inheritance, but from the beginning of his reign he was careful to emphasize the continuity of his government with that of earlier English kings. As an appendix to the history of his desperate struggle with Edmund Ironside, there may be set a charter of 1018 which records the confirmation of certain lands to the bishop of Cornwall, 'when I, King Cnut, succeeded to the kingdom after King Edmund'.[1]

Cnut's attitude towards the task of governing England is perhaps most clearly shown in the great code which is the chief memorial of his reign.[2] It appears to have been drafted by Archbishop Wulfstan of York, who had also produced codes for Æthelred, and whose influence may have played a considerable part in inspiring Cnut to behave as a Christian monarch. It is a lengthy document, and the field which it covers is wide. A long preliminary section, amounting to more than a quarter of the whole, was intended to remind the clergy and laity of their religious duties, and to secure the maintenance of the ecclesiastical interests which permeated the fabric of the Anglo-Saxon state. The remainder, itself a text of more than eighty clauses, deals with secular matters, ranging from the share which the king might claim in the goods of a dead earl to the responsibility of a cottagers' wife for stolen property found in her cupboard. In each part of the code there are chapters which suggest the homilist rather than the king, and in their tone recall certain

---

[1] Ordnance Survey, *Facsimiles of Anglo-Saxon Manuscripts*, ii, Exeter, ix.

[2] Liebermann, *Gesetze*, i, pp. 278–371. On its authorship, see D. Whitelock, *E.H.R.* lxiii (1948), pp. 433–52, lxix (1954), pp. 72–85.

pieces of pseudo-legislation, drafted by Wulfstan, through which Æthelred II had called his subjects to pious works when the country was in danger. These passages scarcely detract from the practical character of the code, which in its length and varied detail gives to Cnut a high place among the legislators of the Dark Ages. But it is in no sense original. At every change of subject Cnut looks back for guidance to the laws of earlier kings. More than a third of his work is demonstrably based on theirs, and there is every reason to think that texts, now lost, lie behind most of what remains. On the surface he comes nearest to an innovation in a rule which brings every free man into a hundred and a tithing, that he may be held to good behaviour under surety. Even this, in which the origin of frank-pledge should probably be seen, is no more than the conversion into an organized system of tentative arrangements which go back at least to Edgar's time. After the Norman Conquest the code acquired fresh importance as the document from which French lawyers could most easily gain a working knowledge of the Anglo-Saxon legal system. The men of Cnut's own time valued it as a restatement of the good customs of the past by a king who was strong enough to enforce them.

The religious strain which colours Cnut's legislation re-appears in two very remarkable letters in which he reminds his English subjects of his care for their interests. In 1020, after his first Danish voyage, and in 1027, while returning to the north from his visit to Rome, he issued proclamations describing his recent activities and indicating their chief results.[1] In the first of these letters he states that the security of England was a principal object of his journey. In the second he emphasizes the freedom he has gained for travellers using the main roads to Italy, and enlarges upon the labours which he has endured and is willing to endure for the benefit of his people. In their form these letters closely resemble the writs which the king was by now accustomed to send down into the shires for the benefit of favoured individuals. Cnut's proclamations dealt with matters in which every free Englishman

[1] The most convenient edition of these proclamations, giving both text and translation, is that of A. J. Robertson, *Laws of the Kings of England*, pp. 140–53. The texts are both printed by Liebermann in his *Gesetze*, i, pp. 273–7, with a full commentary (iii, pp. 186–92). The importance of the proclamation of 1020 in the history of the English charter was shown by W. H. Stevenson, *E.H.R.* xxvii (1912), pp. 1–8.

was interested. They are addressed, not only to the magnates of the realm, but also to the generality of his free subjects, and there is no serious doubt that each of them was intended to be read openly in the court of every shire in England. Their interest is increased by the clearness with which they show the religious element in Cnut's statesmanship. In the letter of 1027 he reminds his bishops and reeves of the good faith which they owe to God and himself, and orders them to see that tithes and ecclesiastical dues are punctually paid. The letter of 1020 represents the fear of God's displeasure as the sanction for the observance of the oaths taken at Oxford, which were the real foundation of the Anglo-Danish state. In each letter, at a moment when he has an especial claim to the gratitude of the English people, he seizes the opportunity to recall them to a sense of their obligations towards God, the church, and its ministers.

There is no reason to assume that Cnut advanced the interests of the English church because he regarded it as an instrument of secular policy. His relations with his bishop and abbots were those of a pupil towards the teachers who had introduced him to the mysteries of a civilization higher than his own. For all their skill in warfare, the intricacy of their decorative art, and the elaboration of their encomiastic verse, the northern peoples of Cnut's age belonged in spirit to a remote, barbaric, world. In Denmark under Swein, his father, Christianity was still an exotic religion, professed by the court, but resisted by a stubborn upland heathenism. From the primitive environment of his youth Cnut suddenly rose to a position in which he was expected to be the protector of an ancient and learned church, venerable because of its traditions, and most impressive as an institution. The responsibilities of his new dignity obviously aroused his imagination. Little as he can have known about the world, it was enough to make him receptive to the ideas which governed western kingship. The rudiments of Christianity were already his. He had been baptized in Germany, and in view of the intercourse which was maintained between the see of Bremen and the Danish court, he must have been aware of the intimate association of church and state in the empire. It was with the imperial precedent in at least the background of his mind that he listened to the churchmen who explained to him the religious duties of an English king.

As a reward for his obedience to their teaching, his rule in England came to be regarded through a haze of kindly tradition, which obscured the fact that he was an alien king with an alien force always at command. Like his enemy St. Olaf, Cnut was surrounded by a large company of specialized fighting-men, which formed the nucleus of his armies, and from which individuals could be dispatched on unpopular or dangerous business. From later Danish evidence it is clear that the members of this body formed a highly organized military guild, united, not only by loyalty to the king, but by a code of behaviour intended to secure that each man respected the interests and, above all, the honour of his fellows. In personal status the king's 'housecarles', as the members of this body were called, corresponded very closely to the thegns of Old English society, and many of them appear as witnesses to Cnut's charters in the company of Englishmen of thegnly rank. But the force as a whole was set apart from other men by the severity of its discipline, its elaborate constitution, and its intimacy with the king. Throughout the reigns of Cnut and his sons its existence must have impressed on every Englishman the truth that the Danish royal house had only come to power in England through conquest.

It was maintained by the proceeds of a new and formidable system of national taxation. On several occasions in Æthelred's reign, peace had been bought from the Danes by large sums of money raised from the country as a whole. After 1012, when Thorkell and the ship's companies which followed him gave their allegiance to Æthelred, a tax of the same general character was imposed each year for their support. Thenceforward until the year 1051 the payment of a standing military force in the king's service continued to be the first charge on the taxable resources of the country. Under Cnut, his sons, and Edward the Confessor the sums thus raised were distributed among the king's housecarles. Throughout this period this charge was distinguished from other public burdens as the 'heregeld' or army-tax. But in 1051 the Confessor ceased to exact it, and the Norman writers by whom it is mentioned, confusing it with the occasional levies raised for earlier Danish armies, refer to it more vaguely as the Danegeld.

By sea as well as by land Cnut's position depended on a standing force maintained at the cost of his English subjects.

Of the great fleet which had brought him to England in 1016 he disbanded all but forty ships two years later. Before the end of his reign he had reduced his permanent fleet to sixteen ships, and it was kept at the same figure by Harold I, his successor. The cost of maintaining even so small a fleet as this added materially to the burden of taxation which the ordinary Englishman had to bear. Under Cnut and his sons the crews of the king's warships were paid each year at the rate of eight marks to each rowlock. The smaller warships of this period needed at least twenty-six oars; the larger at least forty; Cnut's own 'dragon' had 120. The crews of sixteen warships of average size must have taken between £3,000 and £4,000 year by year in wages. Apart from the money required each year for the royal housecarles, it seems clear that the expense of maintaining a fleet of sixteen warships approximated to the sums which the twelfth-century kings of England were accustomed to receive from a levy of Danegeld.

There were other directions in which Englishmen under Cnut were made to feel that they belonged to a conquered country. His victory was not marked by any general expropriation of English landowners such as that which followed the Norman Conquest. But like William of Normandy, Cnut was surrounded by men who expected a reward in land for their service in war, and in churches as far apart as Worcester, Ramsey and Reading there survived tradition of estates which passed at this time from English into Danish hands.[1] In Worcestershire, where Hakon son of Eric of Norway ruled as earl for a short time, there seems to have been a considerable settlement of Danish noblemen. Within seven years of Cnut's death a bishop of Worcester states that 'all the thegns in Worcestershire, both English and Danish' have witnessed a lease of land belonging to his church.[2] Long after the Norman Conquest the chronicler Florence of Worcester shows a knowledge of northern history which is probably derived from members of a local Danish aristocracy.[3] Elsewhere the evidence is less definite. But Domesday Book shows that in 1066 there were

[1] Heming, *Chartularium Ecclesiae Wigorniensis*, ed. T. Hearne, i, pp. 255–6, 277–8; *Chronicon Abbatiae Rameseiensis*, R.S. p. 129 ff.; and W. Stubbs, *The Foundation of Waltham Abbey*, p. 8, which shows that the Dane, Tovi the Proud, was in possession of Reading in Cnut's reign.

[2] A. J. Robertson, *Anglo-Saxon Charters*, p. 180.

[3] *Crawford Charters*, p. 144.

landowners bearing Scandinavian names in every part of England,[1] and it is probable that many of them had inherited their estates from ancestors who had been in the service of Cnut or his sons. One of the Confessor's chief household officers, named Ansger, whose lands extended into at least seven counties, was a grandson of Cnut's follower, Tovi the Proud.[2] The series of Cnut's extant charters, brief as it is, includes two documents which record grants of land by the king to individual housecarles.[3] Each of these men, like his lord, associated himself with the life of his new country. Urk the housecarle founded the abbey of Abbotsbury, and Bovi, his fellow, the abbey of Horton, within the estates which Cnut had given them. The fact that these gifts are only known because they were afterwards turned to religious uses shows that there is a serious risk of underestimating the extent to which the Danish kings endowed their followers with English land.

It is also probable that historians dealing generally with the period have tended to underestimate the significance of the Danish element in the Anglo-Danish state. Cnut was prepared to entrust a wide responsibility in local government to individual Englishmen. But his conception of the relationship between a king and the men thus set in local power ran on Danish rather than English lines. It is significant that before the end of his reign the Scandinavian loan-word 'eorl' had virtually superseded the English 'ealdorman' as the title of these provincial rulers. There was little, if any, difference in power or function between the ealdormen who had governed provinces under Edgar and Æthelred and the earls of the half-century before the Norman conquest. But whereas the earlier ealdormanries had always to some extent represented the distinctive traditions of different parts of England, the Anglo-Danish earldom was simply a district which the king had decided to commit for government to a particular nobleman. The Englishmen of Cnut's reign, who spoke of earls when their ancestors would have spoken of ealdormen, were expressing the truth that the rulers who were set over them were appointed by a king who, as a conqueror, could override local feeling and local interests.

---

[1] O. von Feilitzen, *The Pre-Conquest Personal Names of Domesday Book*, pp. 25–6.
[2] W. Stubbs, *The Foundation of Waltham Abbey*, p. 13.
[3] *C.D.* 741, 1318.

Under these conditions it is impossible to reconstruct the detailed history of the earldoms which at one time or another existed in England between the accession of Cnut and the Norman Conquest.[1] The attestations to royal charters, which reflect the composition of the king's court, give the names of most of the earls who held office in England during this period. The vernacular writs, which become fairly common towards its close, often mention the earl who was responsible for the government of a particular shire. But the artificiality of a system under which, for example, Oxfordshire could be annexed to the earldom of East Anglia, meant that the provincial governments of this age were highly unstable. Under Edward the Confessor new combinations of shires were repeatedly formed in order to provide earldoms for men who enjoyed the king's especial favour, or belonged to families prominent at court. The history of the Anglo-Danish earldoms is further complicated by the possibility that within the larger provinces, such as Mercia or Northumbria, there may have existed subordinate governments held, with an earl's title, by men whose influence was only local. In regard to the period as a whole, although something is usually known about the antecedents and family relationships of individual earls, it is generally impossible to be precise about the geographical limits of their jurisdictions.

The authorities for the reign of Cnut are so meagre that any list of his earls is bound to be incomplete. But it is clear that although the English traditions of local government were unaffected by the Danish conquest, the earls through whom Cnut maintained touch with the shires, with hardly an exception, were either aliens, or Englishmen new to power. Of the sixteen men who witness Cnut's charters with the title *dux*, only six bore English names. Of these Æthelred, who witnesses two charters of the year 1019, and Ælfwine, who appears at court in 1033 and 1035, are merely names; Æthelweard, a member of the Old English royal house, who had been an ealdorman in the south-west, was outlawed in 1020; and Godwine, the famous earl of Wessex, whatever may have been his origin, owed his position entirely to Cnut's favour. So far

---

[1] The attempt was made by Freeman, *History of the Norman Conquest*, ii, Appendix, note G. But as he fully realized, the evidence is far too fragmentary for any continuous account.

as can be seen, Leofwine, who had been ealdorman of the Hwicce under Æthelred II, and Leofric his son, whom Cnut made earl of Mercia, were the only Englishmen whose family remained in power throughout these years.

Of the ten foreigners who are described as earls in Cnut's charters, several are otherwise unknown, Halfdan and Regnold, who witness charters in 1019, and Sihtric, who witnesses between 1019 and 1031, play no part in the recorded history of the time. An earl bearing the outlandish name Wrytsleof, who appeared at court in 1026, is perhaps more likely to have been a visitor from the Danish provinces along the Baltic than the holder of an English earldom. Hrani, who attests at least five charters between 1018 and 1031, must have been a person of some importance at court, though nothing is known about him beyond the facts that his earldom included Herefordshire, and that he took part in a punitive expedition sent by Harthacnut against Worcester in 1041. In contrast to these shadowy figures stands a group of earls, closely associated with Cnut in the general government of the country. The attestations to Cnut's charters point to the existence of an inner circle of counsellors around the king, of which the chief members were Thorkell of East Anglia, from 1018 until 1020, Eric of Northumbria, from 1018 until 1023, Hakon, his son, from 1019 until 1026, and Eilaf, the viking leader of 1009, from 1018 until 1024. From 1018 onwards Godwine of Wessex, though an Englishman, was closely associated with this group. Between 1026 and 1031 there is a gap in the series of Cnut's charters, and a corresponding gap in the recorded succession of his earls. When the series begins again, the Scandinavian earls who had been most prominent in the first part of the reign have all disappeared. Eric of Norway has been succeeded by a Dane named Siward, who was to dominate Northumbrian history for more than twenty years. But apart from Siward, no new Danish earls appear at court in Cnut's last years, and at the end of his reign Godwine, earl of Wessex, and Leofric, earl of Mercia, were apparently his chief advisers.

Through its ultimate consequences the promotion of Godwine and Leofric was of momentous significance for English history. The rivalry of the families which they brought to eminence fatally weakened the possibility of a united English resistance to the Norman invasion of 1066. Leofric himself was regarded by contemporaries as an upright man; he was the son of an ealdorman, and he seems to have maintained himself in power for more than twenty years without violence or aggression. Godwine had no ancestral claim to political influence; he could be unscrupulous in action, and the career of aggrandizement which he opened to his family accounts in great part for the sense of strain and unrest which colours the reign of Edward the Confessor. Of his origin nothing can be said with any assurance. His father's name was Wulfnoth, and it has been conjectured with some degree of probability that he was the son of Wulfnoth, the thegn of Sussex, who had led off a portion of the royal fleet into piracy during the campaign of 1009. There is nothing that can be called an authentic tradition of his part in the war between Cnut and Edmund Ironside, nor of the way in which he came into Cnut's favour. The record of his life begins with the facts that he had been created an earl by Cnut before the end of 1018, and that then, or directly afterwards, he married Gytha, sister of Ulf of Denmark, Cnut's brother-in-law, and of the veteran Eilaf, to whom Cnut had recently given an English earldom. Through his marriage Godwine was brought into a close connection with the court, and this was the basis of his fortunes.

Siward of Northumbria played a smaller part in English politics than either Godwine or Leofric. He was not a statesman, but a Danish warrior of a primitive type, and he was occupied by the double task of defending the northern frontier of England and imposing the rudiments of public order upon the most unquiet of English provinces. From the fall of the ancient Northumbrian kingdom until the conquest of England by Cnut, the country between the Tees and the Scottish border seems to have been ruled almost continuously by the successive heads of the same native Northumbrian family. The fact that late in the tenth century the head of this house bore the Scandinavian name Waltheof suggests that at one point the succession may have passed through an heiress to a stranger, but the personal names borne by earlier members of the family reappear among Waltheof's descendants, and there is no doubt that they were regarded as possessing an hereditary claim to rule in the north. On several occasions the head of this house was appointed earl of Yorkshire by the king, and when Swein of Denmark landed in 1013, Uhtred, son of

Waltheof, was clearly in power to the south as well as to the
north of the Tees. After Uhtred's murder in 1016, Eric of
Norway was set as earl over each of the two Northumbrian
provinces. But the ancient family was not dispossessed, and
from 1016 until 1041, when Eadwulf, Uhtred's younger son,
was treacherously murdered by Harthacnut's orders, it seems
to have been left in power in the farther north, subject to the
general authority, at first of Eric, and afterwards of Siward.
From 1041 until his death in 1055 Siward was the immediate
ruler of all Northumbria, but he allied himself with the native
line by marrying a grand-daughter of Earl Uhtred, and he
showed his respect for its traditions by naming one of his sons
after Waltheof, Uhtred's father.

At the beginning of Cnut's reign the defence of northern
England against the Scots had recently become an urgent
problem. The surrender of Lothian to Kenneth, king of Scots,
seems to have stabilized the Anglo-Scottish frontier for a
generation. But in 1006 Malcolm, Kenneth's son, led a great
army through northern Northumbria and besieged Durham.[1]
Waltheof, the reigning earl, was too old to take action, but
Uhtred, his heir, annihilated the Scottish army in a battle of
which a vivid memory survived the Norman Conquest. Within
a decade, the situation in the north was suddenly changed
through the defeat of Uhtred at Carham on the Tweed, the
northern boundary of his earldom, by the combined armies of
Malcolm, king of Scots, and Owain the Bald, king of Strathclyde.[2] During the years of war which culminated in the Danish

[1] The siege, which is described in the tract commonly called *De Obsessione Dunelmi*
printed among the works of Symeon of Durham (R.S. i, pp. 215–20), can be dated
to 1006 by the *Annals of Ulster* (Anderson, *Early Sources of Scottish History*, i, p. 525).
[2] The date of the battle is uncertain. In the *Historia Dunelmensis Ecclesiae* Symeon
of Durham, *Opera*, R.S. i, p. 84 places it in 1018, 30 days after the appearance of a
comet visible in that year, and a few days before the death of Ealdhun, bishop of
Durham. In the same passage the bishop, who had removed his see to Durham in
995, is said to have completed 24 years in that church—a statement which, interpreted strictly, places his death in 1019, but is perhaps not decisive against the
previous year. On the other hand, in his *Historia Regum*, R.S. ii, pp. 155–6 Symeon
states that the English leader was Earl Uhtred, who is known to have been killed
in 1016. As names are better remembered than dates, this statement outweighs any
argument for 1018 founded on the chronological details given above. It may be
added that there is no evidence for the view that it was the defeat at Carham which
led to the acquisition of Lothian by the Scots. According to Symeon, the English
army was drawn from the country between the Tees and the Tweed, a description
which suggests, as would be gathered from other authorities (above, p. 370), that
the English boundary had already been withdrawn to the latter river.

conquest, Uhtred can have had little opportunity of looking to the defence of his northern border, and for a considerable time after the battle of Carham, northern Northumbria must have lain open to Scottish invasion. There is no evidence that Eric of Norway ever took the offensive against the Scots while he was earl of Northumbria, and the persistence of the danger is shown by the fact that immediately after his journey to Rome, at a time when he was closely preoccupied by Norwegian affairs, Cnut himself led an army into Scotland. He secured a recognition of his lordship from Malcolm, and two lesser kings, but the danger could not be arrested by isolated displays of force, and it was Siward, not Cnut, who restored English power in the North. Siward does not seem to have challenged the Scottish possession of Lothian, but there can be little doubt that he carried through a notable enlargement of his earldom towards the west. At the end of his life he was overlord of all the lands between the Solway marshes and the Cumberland Derwent which had been annexed to the kingdom of Strathclyde early in the tenth century.[1] No tradition of their recovery has been preserved, but none of Siward's predecessors except Eric of Norway commanded resources equal to this task, and Eric's activities were too varied to allow him much time for specifically Northumbrian problems. In Siward, the Celtic powers beyond the English border were confronted by a formidable warrior who had identified himself with Northumbrian interests, and in all their later conflicts the initiative lay with him.

The period immediately following the death of Cnut forms a miserable anti-climax to a reign which for all its weakness in constructive achievement can fairly be regarded as a brilliant age. The kingdoms which Cnut had brought together into the semblance of an empire were, indeed, beginning to fall apart in his lifetime. Norway had become an independent state under Magnus, St. Olaf's son, but in England, Cnut's position was never stronger than at the end of his reign, and the confusion of the next five years is due, not to instability in the Anglo-Danish kingdom, but to the inopportune moment of the king's death. Cnut had clearly intended that when he died England and Denmark should pass to Harthacnut, his

---

[1] A private charter issued within a few years of his death shows that he was in a position to grant peace to the lesser lords of that country; F. E. Harmer, *Anglo-Saxon Writs*, pp. 419–24.

one legitimate son. Harthacnut was already living in Denmark
with the title of king, and so far as can be seen, the English
magnates were prepared to accept him as Cnut's successor.
But the rise of Magnus to power in Norway confronted the
Danes with an enemy who might be expected to take satisfaction for hereditary wrongs by an immediate invasion of
their country. It was therefore impossible for Harthacnut to
leave Denmark in order to take up his English inheritance,
and his absence left the dead king's counsellors with the dangerous task of electing a ruler.

The crisis found them divided in opinion. One party,
headed by Queen Emma and Earl Godwine, was prepared
to take the risk of electing an absent king, and declared for
Harthacnut. The other, led by Earl Leofric and supported by
the seamen of London and by nearly all the thegns beyond the
Thames, wished to postpone a final decision until the situation
in Denmark was clearer, and proposed the novel experiment of
a regency. Their candidate for this position was Harold, son of
Cnut and Ælfgifu of Northampton. In a council held at
Oxford early in 1036 a compromise was reached. Without
prejudicing the question of the future succession to the throne,
it was agreed that Harold should be regent of all England, but
that Queen Emma should live at Winchester, accompanied by
a body of Harthacnut's housecarles, and maintain his interests
in Wessex with their help. It is probable that the royal treasury
was already established at Winchester, for soon after the agreement at Oxford, if not, indeed, before it had been concluded,
Harold sent a force to the city and took possession, against the
queen's will, of all Cnut's best treasures. If he could have
appeared in England within a few weeks of the meeting at
Oxford, Harthacnut would probably have been received everywhere as the rightful heir of Cnut. But three years passed before
it was safe for him to leave Denmark, and by the summer of
1036 Ælfgifu of Northampton was bringing the leading English
magnates into a party of which each member bound himself by
oath to her and her son.[1] Before the end of 1037 Harold was
recognized, formally, as king of all England, and Queen Emma
was driven from the country to find a refuge in Flanders 'against
the raging winter'.

Within the interregnum thus ended, ancient authorities

[1] W. H. Stevenson, *E.H.R.* xxviii (1913), pp. 115–16.

record only one important event. In 1036 Alfred 'the Ætheling', apparently the younger of the two remaining sons of Æthelred II, left Normandy, where he had lived throughout the reign of Cnut, and came to England in order to visit his mother at Winchester. At the time of his landing the party which favoured Harold's election as king was growing rapidly, and a group of leading men, who seem to have felt that Alfred's presence would delay the settlement of the kingdom, prevented him from meeting the queen. Godwine, who had clearly joined Harold's party by this date, was one of these magnates, and probably their leader. He arrested Alfred, dispersed his followers, and put some of them to death. Alfred himself was afterwards taken on board ship out of Godwine's custody, savagely blinded, and brought to Ely, where he soon died of his injuries. Godwine, who had carried out the arrest, and without whose consent the ætheling could never have been given to his tormentors, was justly held responsible for his death by Harthacnut, Alfred's half-brother, by the Norman court which had protected him, and according to a consistent tradition, by Edward, his surviving brother of the full blood.[1]

King Harold I is a dim figure,[2] and it is probable that for part, if not the whole, of his reign, his mother Ælfgifu of Northampton was the real ruler of England. In spite of the fact that he was the child of an irregular union, some, at least, of the English clergy acquiesced in his election as king. In his will, Bishop Ælfric of Elmham refers to Harold as 'my royal lord' and, apparently, to Ælfgifu as 'my lady'.[3] Harold's position was, in fact, so strong that when at last Harthacnut had reached a settlement with Magnus of Norway, he was compelled to collect an army adequate for a large-scale invasion before he could enforce his claim to the English throne. In 1038 or 1039 the relations between Norway and Denmark were stabilized by a treaty which provided that if either Magnus or Harthacnut should die without an heir, his kingdom should pass to the survivor.[4] The treaty set Harthacnut free

[1] The best discussion of the evidence relating to Alfred's death is the note by C. Plummer in *Two of the Saxon Chronicles Parallel*, ii, pp. 211–15.

[2] The nickname 'Harefoot' by which he is generally known is not recorded before the late Middle Ages, but is probably contemporary.

[3] W. H. Stevenson, *E.H.R.* xxviii (1913), pp. 115–16.

[4] Theodric, *De Antiquitate Regum Norwagiensium*, ed. G. Storm, *Monumenta Historica Norvegiæ*, p. 46; *Anonymi Roskildensis Chronicon*, Langebek, *Scriptores Rerum Danicarum*, i, p. 377.

for an expedition to England, and before the end of 1039, he sailed with a detachment from his fleet to Bruges, where Queen Emma was living under the protection of Baldwin, count of Flanders. Even then, he was curiously slow in taking any decisive action. It is possible that Harold was already touched by the illness of which he died on 17 March 1040, and that Harthacnut was biding his time in the hope of a peaceable succession. He was invited to England after Harold's death. But it was not until 17 June 1040 that he landed, and he was brought to England by a fleet of no less than sixty-two warships.

The most serious trouble of his reign arose from the taxation levied for the payment of their crews.[1] He employed his house-carles in the collection of the money, and two of them, whom he sent to Worcester, were murdered by a mob drawn from the city and the shire, 'in the upper chamber of a tower in the minster, where they had hidden themselves'. As a punish-ment Harthacnut dispatched nearly all his housecarles and an army joined by every earl in England with orders to harry Worcester and the surrounding country. There was little slaughter, for the threatened people left their homes, and the men of Worcester defended themselves successfully in an improvised fort on Bevere island in the Severn. But the harry-ing lasted for five days; Worcester was burned, and the episode gives an ugly illustration of the spasmodic violence with which Anglo-Saxon governments reacted to local breaches of public order.

It was the opinion of a contemporary that Harthacnut never did anything worthy of a king in the whole of his reign. He was certainly capable of treachery towards an individual. There must have been a very unpleasant incident behind the statement of the *Chronicle* that he betrayed Earl Eadwulf of Northumbria, who was under his especial peace, and thereby became a breaker of his pledge. But he was something more than a mere degenerate, and there is an unexpected touch of generosity in his attitude towards his half-brothers, the sons of Emma and Æthelred. He regarded the sufferings of the ætheling Alfred as an injury done to one of his own kin, and prosecuted Earl Godwine and Lyfing, bishop of Worcester and Crediton, whom he held chiefly responsible for the ætheling's

---

[1] According to the *Chronicle*, he exacted £21,099 for the 62 ship's companies of his original fleet, and £11,048 for the crews of 32 ships which he kept in his service.

death. Bishop Lyfing was deprived for a while of the see of Worcester. Godwine appeased the king by the gift of a warship carrying eighty fighting men splendidly armed, and then, with magnates from nearly the whole of England as his oath helpers, swore that he had neither wished nor advised that the ætheling should be blinded, but that whatever he had done was in obedience to his lord, King Harold.[1] The prosecution of Godwine and Lyfing was part of a general demonstration against Harold and all his works, of which the disinterment and ignominious disposal of the king's corpse was the supreme event. But the sincerity of Harthacnut's feeling for his half-brothers is shown by his treatment of Edward, the survivor. He invited Edward to England in 1041, adopted him as a member of his household, and, almost certainly, put him forward as his heir. In 1041 Harthacnut cannot have passed his twenty-fourth year. But none of Cnut's children reached middle age, and men about the court may not have been surprised when he collapsed and died 'as he stood at his drink' at the wedding-feast of his father's retainer, Tovi the Proud, on 8 June 1042.

With his death the male line of the Danish royal house came to an end, and the succession to the throne became an open question in both England and Denmark. In England it was immediately settled by a strong movement in favour of the ancient native dynasty in the person of Edward, son of Æthelred II. He was elected king at London by a popular acclamation before Harthacnut was buried,[2] and was crowned at Winchester on Easter day 1043. In Denmark the men who stood nearest to the royal house were Harold, son of Thorkell the Tall, whose wife was Cnut's niece, and Swein, son of Earl Ulf and Cnut's sister Estrith. Before their claims had been settled Magnus of Norway invaded Denmark in order to enforce the right to the Danish kingdom which he had acquired by his treaty with Harthacnut. In 1043 Harold was murdered by

---

[1] Florence of Worcester, *Chronicon*, ed. B. Thorpe, i, pp. 194–5. The incident is not mentioned in any version of the *Chronicle*, but the precision of Florence's account shows that it is based on some earlier written authority.

[2] The popular element in Edward's election, noted by all versions of the *Chronicle*, comes out most strongly in MS. E, which prays that he may hold the kingdom so long as God shall allow it to him. In view of this contemporary evidence, no weight can be attached to the later stories which made Godwine of Wessex the chief agent in Edward's restoration.

Ordulf, son of the duke of Saxony, who had married a sister of Magnus.[1] Harold's widow and sons took refuge in England, and Swein Estrithson became sole leader of the Danes in their struggle for independence. In the meantime, Magnus, claiming to inherit England as well as Denmark under his agreement with Harthacnut, began to prepare for an expedition towards the west, and until his death in 1047 English statesmen were always preoccupied by the fear of an invasion from Norway.[2]

It is very hard to form a clear impression of the course of English internal politics during this period. The king's personality is an enigma, and different historians have come to very diverse opinions about his character and ability. It is probable that he has generally been underestimated, and that there were reserves of latent energy beneath the benign manner which attracted those who knew him, and the asceticism which earned him sainthood. He had been absent from England for twenty-five years when Harthacnut invited him to court. A year later, through Harthacnut's death, there fell upon him the responsibility of governing an unfamiliar country through a group of men firmly established in their respective spheres of influence, and experienced in the elementary statesmanship of their time. Throughout his reign Edward was required to deal with men who at first or second hand represented the traditions of the Anglo-Danish monarchy. Of the earls whom Cnut had set in office, Godwine died in 1053, Siward in 1055, and Leofric in 1057. Their sons inherited their ambitions, their rivalries, and a prescriptive title to their political influence. There must have been virtue in a king who under these conditions upheld the dignity of his crown, and impressed his own conception of Christian sovereignty on the better minds of his age.

For several years his position must have been strangely isolated. From the outset of their reigns all the other kings of his line had been able to rely on the support of a group of courtiers, interested in the royal family, and prepared to give faithful service to its new head. But apart from a few undis-

---

[1] Adam of Bremen, *Gesta Hammaburgensis Ecclesiae Pontificum*, ed. J. M. Lappenburg, ed. 2, Hanover (1876), Bk. ii, cap. 75, and ed. B. Schmeidler ed. iii (1917), ii, cap. 79.

[2] For Anglo-Norwegian relations in this period MS. D of the *Chronicle* is the primary authority. The place where it was composed has not yet been determined, but its author was certainly in a position to obtain good information about northern affairs.

tinguished thegns and one or two ageing bishops,[1] there can
have been no one at Edward's earliest courts who had ever
been in attendance on King Æthelred. The formidable group
of Anglo-Danish warriors and statesmen which accepted
Edward as king by popular choice and right of birth had no
affection for the dynasty to which he belonged. Between
Edward and Godwine, the most powerful of the group, there
can never have been goodwill. Godwine had surrendered
Edward's brother to his death. For nine years Edward bided
his time. In 1045 he married Godwine's daughter. But the
real character of their relations is shown by the energy with
which he set himself to overthrow the earl at the first moment
when an opportunity came his way.

Inevitably under these conditions Edward turned for something more than formal intercourse to men from the country
where his early life had been spent. There is no doubt that
his patronage of Norman knights and churchmen offended
English feeling. A number of Normans held offices in his
household; there were Norman priests in his chapel; and it
is probable that he showed kindness to many individuals of
Norman birth whose names are unrecorded. Some of these
men received his intimate confidence. But the idea that he
surrounded himself with Norman favourites will not survive
an examination of the witnesses to his charters.[2] In its general
character Edward's court, in which the Scandinavian element
is surprisingly strong,[3] closely resembled the court of Cnut.
Moreover, it is dangerous to attribute a Norman origin to every
Frenchman who appears in Edward's company. Only two of
the foreigners at his court were of the first importance as
English landowners, and neither was of Norman extraction.
One of them, whose estates formed the basis of the medieval
honour of Rayleigh, was known from his mother's name as
Robert fitz Wimarch. The name Wimarch is not Norman but
Breton. The second of these magnates, whose lands lay chiefly

[1] Such as Æthelstan of Hereford, who was consecrated in 1012 and died in 1056.

[2] Thus, a representative charter of 1049 is witnessed by 17 laymen below the
rank of earl, all of whom have Old English names except Tostig, Earl Godwine's
son (*C.D.* 787). Even among the king's priests, where the foreign element was
stronger, the total number of Normans was small. On the three Normans whom he
appointed to English bishoprics see below, pp. 464-5.

[3] It is naturally at its strongest in Edward's earliest years. Among the 26 *ministri*
who witness a charter of 1044 (*Ord. Surv. Facsimiles*, ii, Exeter, 12) 7 bear Scandinavian names.

in East Anglia, was Ralf, generally described as the 'staller'—
a word which could be applied to any officer in a king's household. Ralf's parentage is unknown, but it is probable that he
was a Breton by descent, and he is known to have possessed the
barony of Gael in Brittany, which made him one of the greatest
lords of that country.[1] For the rest, the French landowners in
pre-Conquest England, whatever their origin, seem to have
been men of moderate estate, whose influence was rarely more
than local. The information that can be extracted about them
from Domesday Book and other sources gives no ground for the
charge that Edward had been endowing his foreign friends
lavishly with English lands.

It is one of the unsolved mysteries of Edward's reign that
his mother, Queen Emma, appears to have supported the
claim of Magnus of Norway to the English throne. In the
autumn of 1043 the king rode with earls Godwine, Leofric,
and Siward to Winchester, where his mother was living, took
possession of all her property, and confiscated her lands. One
version of the *Chronicle* states that she was thus treated because
she had refused to allow her son an adequate share in her
wealth; another remarks that she had done less for her son than
he wished, both before and after his accession. A hint of some
graver charge in the background is given by the fact that
Stigand, the newly appointed bishop of Elmham, her chief
confidant, was deprived of his see at this time. The suspicion
is confirmed by the definite statement of a well-placed writer[2]
that the queen was accused of inviting Magnus to invade
England and of placing her treasure at his disposal. The
relations between mother and son which are implied by this
charge are hard to understand, but the charge itself is by no
means incredible. For twenty-five years Emma had devoted
herself to the interests of Cnut and her children by him. A
writer who at about this time presented her with a history of
recent events significantly if grotesquely ignores the fact that
she was the widow of Æthelred when she married Cnut.[3] It is

[1] The best account of Ralf the Staller, whom the Conqueror made earl of East
Anglia, is the article by G. H. White in the *Complete Peerage*, ix, pp. 568–71.

[2] Quoted by T. D. Hardy, *Descriptive Catalogue of Materials relating to the history
of Great Britain and Ireland*, I. i, p. 381, [from *Textus Translationis et Institutionis
Monasterii B. Mildrithæ*, and translated in *The Anglo-Saxon Chronicle: a Revised
Translation*, by D. Whitelock, with D. C. Douglas and S. I. Tucker p. 107.]

[3] *Encomium Emmae Reginae* ed. A. Campbell, pp. 33–5.

not impossible that after the death of her only son by Cnut the passage of his kingdom to a stranger seemed to her a lesser evil than its reversion to the dynasty which Cnut had overthrown.

Queen Emma may have offered her own support to Magnus, but few, if any, prominent Englishmen followed her example. No statesman of the older generation seems to have resisted the wave of popular feeling which had carried Edward to the throne. There was general acquiescence in the separation of England from Denmark, which the election of Edward had made inevitable, and on two occasions, at least, public opinion turned uncompromisingly against participation in the northern war. Swein Estrithson, who was the nephew of Godwine's wife, was allowed to feel that the English court was friendly. Beorn, his brother, received an English earldom,[1] and another brother, named Osbern, lived prosperously in England, though without an earl's title. It was probably regard for Swein's interests which in 1044 caused the government to refuse shelter in England to the widow and sons of Harold, son of Thorkell the Tall.[2] But for the rest, English statesmen were content to watch the course of events in the north, and to maintain a fleet ready for sea if Magnus were to attempt an invasion. In 1045 the king took command of thirty-five ships stationed off Sandwich. Twelve months later a much larger fleet was concentrated in the same roadstead in anticipation of an attack which Magnus was too heavily engaged with Swein to deliver. For the greater part of another year Swein continued the struggle, but before the end of 1046 Magnus had become master of Denmark, and early in 1047 Swein asked that fifty ships should be sent to his help from England. Englishmen, alarmed by reports of the great size of the Norwegian fleet, were unwilling to send their ships against it, and the request was refused. Swein was driven into flight, and the Danes, under coercion, accepted Magnus as their king. For a few weeks in the autumn of 1047 England was in greater peril of invasion than at any other time since the accession of Cnut. But on 25 October Magnus died suddenly, and his men, deprived of their leader, were unable to prevent Swein from returning to Denmark.

Magnus was followed as king of Norway by the last heroic

---

[1] It included Hertfordshire (C.D. 826–7), but nothing more is known about it.
[2] Florence of Worcester, *Chronicon*, ed. B. Thorpe, i, p. 199.

figure of the viking age. After many adventures in southern and eastern Europe, and a term of service with the imperial guard at Constantinople, Harold, surnamed Hardrada, a half-brother of St. Olaf, had returned to the north in 1047. On the death of Magnus the Norwegians immediately accepted him as king. For the greater part of his reign he was occupied by an unprofitable war with Swein Estrithson. His first act as king was to make peace with England, and nineteen years passed before he could attempt to realize the western ambitions which Magnus had bequeathed to him. Swein, on his part, sent another appeal to England for ships, which was supported by Earl Godwine. But popular feeling was still opposed to the idea of dispatching a naval force into distant waters; earl Leofric seems to have made himself its spokesman, and Swein was left to maintain the independence of Denmark without English help.

So far as is known, the only enemy which descended on England in these dangerous years was a force of vikings which appeared in the Channel in the course of 1048. It consisted of twenty-five ships' companies, which harried in the Isle of Wight and plundered Sandwich. The men of Thanet prevented them from landing on the island, but they crossed the estuary of the Thames and carried out a successful raid in Essex. They then sailed across the entry to the Channel, pursued ineffectively by 'king Edward and the earls', and sold the men whom they had captured, and their other plunder, in Flanders. The episode, of little importance in itself, led indirectly to one of the few occasions on which an Anglo-Saxon government intervened in the internal politics of the Empire. Count Baldwin of Flanders had recently joined a coalition of disaffected Low Country princes which Godfrey, duke of Upper Lorraine, had formed against the Emperor Henry III. The alliance had held its own for a time, and Baldwin burned the emperor's palace at Nijmegen, but the emperor was in command of the situation by the beginning of 1049. Afraid that Baldwin, defeated on land, would escape by sea, he asked for help from the two powers which could prevent the movement of ships from the Low Country ports. Swein Estrithson, unable to obtain effective English support against Harold Hardrada, put himself under the emperor's protection by becoming his man, and placed himself and the Danish fleet under the emperor's orders. Relations between the English and

Flemish courts, if not hostile, were badly strained; Count Baldwin had been entertaining exiles from England, and raiders who had harried along the English coast had been allowed to sell their plunder in his country. King Edward therefore entered the war on the emperor's side, and concentrated a great fleet at Sandwich, which closed the narrow seas to Flemish ships until Baldwin had been reduced to submission.

Before the fleet had dispersed, the army which had been brought on shipboard was required to pass judgement on a crime of a kind which seemed unpardonable to the ordinary fighting-man of the period. As Earl Godwine's position became stronger after the accession of King Edward, his elder sons were naturally promoted to earldoms. Swein, his eldest son, had received his promotion in 1043, but after three years of respectable government he had offended all responsible opinion by seducing an abbess, and had then abandoned his earldom, apparently because he was not allowed to marry her. Swein Estrithson, his cousin, gave him hospitality for a time, but he was compelled to leave Denmark because of some grave but unspecified crime, and in 1049, while King Edward was at Sandwich with the fleet, he appeared at Bosham with eight ships. Several different versions of the events which followed became current at an early date, and it is difficult, it not impossible, to decide between them when they disagree with one another.[1] But it is at least clear that Swein, finding the king irreconcilable, visited his cousin Earl Beorn, who was in command of a royal warship becalmed off Pevensey, and requested him to act as his friend at court. The two earls set out from Pevensey as if they were about to ride to the king at Sandwich, but on the way Swein induced Beorn to turn westwards, and accompany him to his ships at Bosham. There Beorn was seized by Swein's men and carried on board ship, where he was afterwards killed. When the news reached him, King Edward summoned an assembly of the whole army at Sandwich, which solemnly declared Swein to be 'nithing', that is, a man without honour. He was deserted by the crews of six out of his eight ships, and under a condemnation which would make him an outcast in any part of the northern world, he took refuge with Baldwin of Flanders.

[1] Their substance is set out conveniently in the note by C. Plummer, *Two Saxon Chronicles*, ii, pp. 229–31.

The interest of the story does not lie in the crime, of which no contemporary offers an explanation, but in the action taken against the criminal. Swein could have been adequately punished for a simple murder by a sentence of outlawry. But it was clear that he had been guilty of an act of atrocious treachery, and his condemnation took the form of a judgement by a military assembly that he had outraged its sense of honourable behaviour. The reference of his case to such a body is highly significant.[1] The idea that a man's title to be held in public respect could be destroyed or vindicated by a formal judgement of his fellows is perhaps the chief Scandinavian contribution to the political theory of the Dark Ages. It gave authority to the ordinances which had regulated the lives of Cnut's housecarles, it penetrated deeply into Scandinavian law, and in England it survived the Norman Conquest itself. In 1088 William Rufus called out the English militia with a proclamation that anyone who disobeyed the summons should be declared 'nithing'. The case of Swein Godwinesson is a remarkable indication of the extent to which English society under a native king was still governed by the Scandinavian habit of mind in regard to matters of honour.

The fleet which had been assembled at Sandwich was not exclusively employed in the passive observation of the Flemish coast. There was much unrest at sea in 1049, and twice at least in this year raiding bands appeared in English waters. The royal ship from which Earl Beorn was enticed to his death was part of a large detachment sent from the main fleet against raiders from Ireland who were harrying in the south-west. The dispersal of the fleet was interrupted by rumours that Osgod Clapa, an old companion of Cnut whom Edward had sent into exile, was planning a descent on England, and although Osgod himself was detained in Flanders, his men were able to do much damage on the Essex coast. But the great danger of an invasion in force from Norway was over, and King Edward proceeded to use this relief as an opportunity for a far-reaching change in the character of the English naval defences. Ever since 1012, when Thorkell the Tall placed his forty-five ships at the service of Æthelred II, every English king had possessed a permanent naval force. It consisted of a number of large warships, of the contemporary Scandinavian pattern, manned by

[1] P. Vinogradoff, *English Society in the Eleventh Century*, p. 10.

professional crews who were paid out of the proceeds of a national system of taxation. But on an emergency this nucleus of a fleet was vastly expanded by a levy of ships imposed on the country as a whole. The details of the method by which they were provided, equipped, and manned are lost, but it is clear that the duty of supplying them was a communal obligation to which inland as well as coastal shires were subject, and there are indications that the hundreds within a shire were sometimes combined in groups of three,[1] each group furnishing a single vessel. It does not appear that King Edward made any alteration in this ancient system, and the principle of communal responsibility for the provision of ships for the royal navy survived to raise controversy in the seventeenth century.[2] The king's innovation was to disperse his standing force of warships. At the beginning of 1049 this force consisted of fourteen vessels. Before the end of the year the king had paid off nine crews, who 'went away with the ships and everything'. In 1050 the five remaining crews, who had been promised twelve months' pay in the previous year, were finally discharged. In 1051 the king re-emphasized his sense of security and relieved his people of a heavy burden by abolishing the 'heregeld', the tax which ever since Thorkell had joined King Æthelred had been levied year by year for the payment of retainers in the king's service.

The main reason for these changes was financial. Taxation sufficient to maintain a fleet of warships and a corps of housecarles was a severe strain on a national economy which was still imperfectly developed. In view of the difficulty of raising money from a population with resources barely adequate for its current needs, there is little point in the reflection that in dispersing his warships Edward was taking risks at which a wiser man would have hesitated. There are indications that he tried to minimize the risks by a series of bargains with the men of certain ports which were of exceptional strategic importance. He granted to the men of Sandwich, Dover, Fordwich, and Romney

[1] In the 12th century there are traces of such an arrangement in Buckinghamshire and Warwickshire (*Place-Names of Warwickshire*, E.P-N.S., pp. xix-xx). On the term *sipesocha* applied to some of the Warwickshire groups see Liebermann, *Gesetze*, ii, 2, p. 638.

[2] The function of the shire in the arrangements for the raising of ships is illustrated by a clause in the will of Archbishop Ælfric of Canterbury bequeathing two ships, one to the people of Kent, and the other to 'Wiltshire' (*Anglo-Saxon Wills*, ed. D. Whitelock, p. 52).

the profits of justice in their respective courts on the understanding that each of these ports would provide a specified
number of ships and seamen for his service.[1] It is probable that
he came to similar terms with the men of Hythe and Hastings,
and that in essential features, though not in formal constitution,
the confederation of what were afterwards known as the Cinque
Ports came into being in his reign. Even so, the dispersal of the
king's own naval force left a gap in the national defences which
had a grave, and perhaps a decisive effect on the course of
events in 1066. But in 1049 Harold Hardrada was closely
engaged with Swein Estrithson, and the duke of Normandy was
King Edward's friend.

[1] J. Tait, *The Medieval English Borough*, p. 125.

XIII

THE TENTH-CENTURY REFORMATION

THERE can be no question that the Danish invasions of the ninth century shattered the organization of the English church, destroyed monastic life in eastern England, and elsewhere caused distress and anxiety which made the pursuit of learning almost impossible.[1] East Anglia, the eastern half of Mercia, and southern Northumbria were occupied and colonized by armies of heathen Danes. The bishoprics of Dunwich, Elmham, and Lindsey came to an end, and the see of York was reduced to a state of obscure poverty. Beyond the Tees, the sees of Hexham and Whithorn ceased to exist; the cathedral of Lindisfarne was abandoned, and for seven years its bishop with some of his younger clerks wandered from one insecure refuge to another, preserving the relics of St. Cuthbert from desecration until peace was so far re-established in the north that a new church could be built for them at Chester-le-Street. The continuity of ecclesiastical organization was never broken in the west midlands and the south, but innumerable ancient centres of religion must have perished in the repeated harryings of Wessex between 870 and 878, and the churches of the Severn valley, the safest part of England, must have suffered many evils when the Danes were abroad around the Wrekin or encamped at Gloucester. Throughout England the Danish raids meant, if not the destruction, at least the grievous impoverishment of civilization.

There is no evidence that the Danes who settled in England were fiercely antagonistic to Christianity. In 878 Guthrum and his leading followers were ready to accept the obligation of baptism as the price of a treaty with King Alfred. Guthfrith, the first known king of Danish Northumbria, was a Christian. Here and there among the Scandinavian place-names of the

[1] A very remarkable illustration of the plundering of libraries by the Danes is given by a note inserted in the *Codex Aureus* of the Gospels, now in the National Library at Stockholm. It states that an ealdorman named Alfred and his wife have bought the codex from a heathen army 'because we were unwilling that these holy writings should remain any longer in heathen hands' (F. E. Harmer, *English Historical Documents*, pp. 12–13). Ealdorman Alfred was a contemporary of his namesake, the king of Wessex.

Danelaw it is possible to find traces of heathen cults and heathen practices. The great hill which projects from the north-western edge of Cleveland, and is now called Roseberry Topping, appears in the twelfth century as Othenesberg, and must once have been sacred to Othin, the Scandinavian counterpart of the West Saxon Woden. The village-name Ellough in Suffolk probably represents the Old Scandinavian *elgr*, 'heathen temple'.[1] Place-names such as *Leggeshou*, *Kate-hou*, and *Granehou* seem to commemorate the burial of Danish settlers in heathen fashion under *haugar*, or mounds, to which their names were permanently applied.[2] But in view of the great extent of the region covered by the Danish settlements, the number of place-names which carry a suggestion of Danish heathenism is too small to prove an obdurate adherence to ancient ways of thought. Little is known about the process by which the conversion of the Danelaw was actually brought about.[3] But the fact that no traditions of the work have survived suggests that it owed less to the labours of missionaries than to the example of the Christian social order of Wessex and English Mercia.

Nevertheless, to continental churchmen the Danish occupation of eastern England must have seemed a disaster of the first magnitude. Earlier Danish raids had brought destruction to many ancient churches in each of the Frankish kingdoms. But the Danish settlement in England meant that in the north and east the survival of Christianity itself depended on the tolerance of bands of heathen warriors, and on the influence of the West Saxon court upon their leaders. Through the strength and reputation of King Alfred and his son Christianity was saved from obliteration even in the regions of the densest Danish settlement. Heathenism was never dominant in Northumbria, East Anglia, or eastern Mercia as in the duchy of Normandy in the years immediately after its creation. It was the lack of any provision for a regular supply of clergy which most seriously imperilled Christianity in Danish England in King Alfred's time.

The Roman court must have been well acquainted with the

---

[1] E. Ekwall, *Oxford Dictionary of English Place-Names*, ed. 4, p. 164.

[2] It is significant that in each of these cases the personal name—*Leggr*, *Káti*, or *Græni*—which is associated with the *haugr* reappears in the name of an adjacent village. *Leggeshou*, *Katehou*, and *Granehou* were close respectively to Legsby and South Cadeby in Lincolnshire and Granby in Nottinghamshire.

[3] For a review of the evidence see D. Whitelock, 'The Conversion of the Eastern Danelaw', *Saga-Book of the Viking Society*, xii (1942), pp. 159–76.

condition of the English church. Intercourse between Rome and England was maintained throughout the period of the Danish wars. There is, in fact, some evidence that the papal court was not only familiar with the state of the church in England but anxious to move its rulers to action against the heathenism of the Danish settlers. There has survived what purports to be a letter of Formosus, pope from 891 until 896, in which he blames the English bishops very severely for their past ineffectiveness in this respect, adjures them to continue the work of instructing the heathen which he learns from Archbishop Plegmund that they have begun, and warns them to provide for the maintenance of the episcopal succession in their land.[1] The letter is only preserved in a collection of documents made soon after the Norman Conquest in order to justify the claim of the archbishop of Canterbury to supremacy over the archbishop of York. Most of these documents are forgeries, and the letter of Formosus ends with a paragraph confirming the primacy of the southern archbishop which is probably an eleventh-century fabrication. But the earlier part of the letter may well be authentic. It contains no obvious anachronisms in style or matter, and the pope in whose name it runs, who had been a missionary in earlier life,[2] is likely to have felt more than conventional distress at the retrogression of English Christianity.

Whatever Formosus may have written, neither Alfred nor any of his successors was ever able to re-establish the pre-Danish organization of the church in the north and east. Most of the estates from which its revenues had been derived had passed into alien hands which could not be dispossessed. In the north, the bishop who was the guardian of St. Cuthbert's relics had begun to receive the gifts of land which before the Norman Conquest had made his church the centre of a great lordship. The nucleus of the later palatinate was already in being in 995, when Bishop Ealdhun of Chester-le-Street began to build his new cathedral on the rock of Durham. But the wealth which came to St. Cuthbert's see expressed the veneration felt throughout the north for a local saint of peculiar eminence. No other northern church had this advantage. The ancient church of Hexham sank into insignificance, and no attempt was ever made to re-establish the bishopric of which it had once been the

[1] C.S. 573.   [2] J. Armitage Robinson, *The Saxon Bishops of Wells*, pp. 24–5.

head. The bare continuity of the see of York was preserved.
A certain Æthelbald, who is little more than a name, was
consecrated archbishop in 900,[1] and it is probable that he was
succeeded without any long interval by the Hrothweard who
appears as archbishop in 928, and with whom the history of the
see becomes clear again. But for many years its resources were
unequal to the support of an archbishop's dignity. A memorandum written by St. Oswald, who became archbishop in 972,[2]
includes a long list of outlying properties which had been taken
away from the ancient estates of his see at Ripon, Otley, and
Sherburn in Elmet. It refers to the purchase of other lands by
his predecessor, Archbishop Osketel, but it gives the impression
that a century after the first coming of the Danes to York the
archbishops had not yet repaired the losses which their patrimony had suffered through the Danish invasions. It was
probably in order to increase the archbishop's resources that
Nottinghamshire was added to the see of York at or about
the middle of the tenth century. In 956 Archbishop Osketel
received a large estate at Southwell in the centre of the county
from Eadwig,[3] and in 958 Edgar, as king of the Mercians, gave
him a property hardly less extensive at Sutton and Scrooby
near the Yorkshire border.[4] A few years later a more remarkable innovation at once increased the revenues and lessened
the isolation of the northern archbishops. In 972, when St.
Oswald, who had been bishop of Worcester, was promoted
to the archbishopric of York, he was allowed to retain his
former see. Thenceforward until 1016 the sees of York and
Worcester were always held together. They were reunited for
a short time in 1040, and an attempt to revive the union in
1061, when Ealdred, bishop of Worcester, was translated to
York, was only defeated by the intervention of pope Nicholas
II. The custom was canonically indefensible, but in the tenth,
if not in the eleventh, century there was political justification for
an arrangement which annexed a rich see in a peaceful country
to the ill-endowed archbishopric of a very turbulent province.

In the south as in the north, political and economic diffi-

---

[1] *The Chronicle of Æthelweard*, ed. A. Campbell, p. 52. It is significant that the
ceremony took place in London.

[2] A. J. Robertson, *Anglo-Saxon Charters*, pp. 110–13.

[3] *C.S.* 1029; W. Farrer, *Early Yorkshire Charters*, i, pp. 5–10.

[4] *C.S.* 1044; Farrer, op. cit., pp. 10–12. 'The Founding of Southwell Minster',
see C.P., pp. 364–70.

culties prevented the complete re-establishment of the ecclesiastical organization which had existed before the Danish wars. Of the two ancient East Anglian bishoprics, Dunwich was never revived. Between 870 and 956 there is a gap in the recorded succession of East Anglian bishops. It is known that towards the end of this period Theodred, bishop of London, had episcopal charge of Suffolk, with a cathedral church at Hoxne, served by a community of priests. It is highly probable that Norfolk also was under his jurisdiction and that East Anglia as a whole had been attached to the see of London ever since the conquest of that region by Edward the Elder. Late in the tenth century, when the ecclesiastical history of East Anglia becomes less obscure, Norfolk and Suffolk form a single diocese, with a cathedral at North Elmham, which had been the seat of the bishops of Norfolk from the seventh century until the Danish invasion. Their church had perished, and the modest size of the new cathedral illustrates the meagreness of the resources available to the bishops of the reconstituted see. The series of these bishops begins with a certain Eadwulf, who first appears in 956, and there can be little doubt that the creation of a separate bishopric for East Anglia was part of the general activity which distinguishes the career of Oda, archbishop of Canterbury.

The ecclesiastical history of what had been the eastern half of the Mercian kingdom is very obscure in this period. When the Danish invasions began, this region contained two dioceses; one corresponding to the ancient kingdom of Lindsey, the other comprising the lands which were traditionally regarded as the territory of the Middle Angles. The seat of the Middle Anglian diocese remained at Leicester from the permanent establishment of the see in 737 until the overthrow of the Mercian kingdom by the Danes. Towards the south its boundary advanced or receded in accordance with the success or failure of the Mercian kings in their struggle for the debatable lands along the Middle Thames. In 877, when the Danes took possession of eastern Mercia, the diocese of Leicester was bounded by the Thames, and therefore included the venerable church of Dorchester, which had been the first seat of the West Saxon bishopric. After the Danish occupation of eastern Mercia the see of Lindsey ceased to exist; it was impossible for a bishop to reside at Leicester, and Dorchester became the seat of episcopal authority for the whole region between the middle Thames and the Humber.

These changes made a permanent impression on English ecclesiastical geography. On at least one occasion in the tenth century a bishop was appointed to the special charge of Lindsey. But the ancient see was never re-established, and at the date of the Norman Conquest the bishop of Dorchester on Thames was ruling a diocese which comprised Lindsey and nearly all the eastern midlands. In relation to its vast extent, it was by no means lavishly endowed. In 1066 the bishop possessed twelve demesne manors, of which the richest lay in the south-western corner of the diocese, where Dorchester itself, Thame, Great Milton, Banbury, and Cropredy formed a great episcopal estate of immemorial antiquity.[1] In the Danelaw, apart from Stow in Lindsey, none of the ancient possessions of the see was of outstanding importance. It was through grants received after the Norman Conquest, when the bishop had transferred his seat from Dorchester to Lincoln, that he became a great territorial magnate in this part of England.

It is remarkable that Edward the Elder, who made no attempt to re-establish the ruined bishoprics of eastern England, carried through in his own kingdom a reorganization which increased the number of West Saxon sees from two to five. Its exact circumstances are obscure, and are not made plainer by a very ancient tradition that Wessex had previously been without bishops for seven years, and that the division of the kingdom into five dioceses was the result of a letter addressed by Pope Formosus to King Edward and Archbishop Plegmund.[2] The fact that Formosus died in 896, three years before Edward became king, and the evidence of the *Chronicle* that the succession to the see of Winchester was maintained with at most a year's break throughout Edward's reign, show that the tradition cannot be accepted as history. The reference to Pope Formosus, which is its most interesting feature is most simply explained on the assumption that the letter of that pope to the English bishops of Alfred's time, which has been quoted above, is derived from a genuine text, and that in the tenth century it

[1] Of Histon in Cambridgeshire, Domesday Book states 'Hoc manerium est unum de duodecim maneriis dominicis episcopatus Lincolniensis' i, f. 190.

[2] These statements are made in a letter of Dunstan to Æthelred II, which is preserved in a late-10th-century copy printed in *Crawford Charters*, ed. A. S. Napier and W. H. Stevenson, pp. 18, 19.

was erroneously regarded as supplying the impulse to the division of the two ancient West Saxon dioceses. In any case, it seems clear that the division was a deliberate act of policy, and that the death of Denewulf, bishop of Winchester, in 908 and of Asser, bishop of Sherborne, in 909 gave the opportunity for carrying it into effect. The lines along which the division ran left Hampshire and Surrey to the bishop of Winchester, giving Wiltshire and Berkshire to a bishop whose principal church was at Ramsbury in the former county. The old diocese of Sherborne was subdivided more minutely. Dorset, Somerset, and Devon with Cornwall were formed into three dioceses, of which Sherborne, Wells, and Crediton were the cathedrals. The men who planned the division were clearly influenced by the idea that each of the south-western shires should form a separate diocese, and in Athelstan's reign the symmetry of the design was completed when a see of St. Germans was created for Cornwall.

The ancient dioceses of Winchester and Sherborne had plainly been too large for a bishop's effective supervision. Documents of the ninth century mention the names of several bishops who seem to have been assisting the occupants of one or other of the two great West Saxon sees. Asser, King Alfred's biographer, had received episcopal charge of Devon and Cornwall before his appointment to the full diocese of Sherborne.[1] But the later history of the sees created by Edward the Elder shows that the process of division had been carried beyond the point at which an adequate endowment could be secured for each of the new diocesan bishops. The original endowment of the reduced see of Sherborne seems to have consisted of 300 hides,[2] and that of the see of Wells was much smaller. A patrimony of 300 hides, though sufficient for the maintenance of a bishop and his household, allowed little margin for the temporary grants of land by which an ecclesiastical magnate was accustomed to reward faithful dependants, and provide for the various forms of public service due from his estate. The bishops of Ramsbury seem to have been supported by the revenues of five great manors—Potterne, Cannings, Ramsbury, Old Sarum, and Sonning. These estates were assessed at more than 300 hides in the eleventh century, but large portions of them had been alienated before the Norman Conquest to priests and thegns. It is not surprising that before

---

[1] *Vita Ælfredi*, c. 81.   [2] *C.D.* 708.

the death of Edward the Confessor the sees of Ramsbury and Sherborne had been united, and Cornwall placed once more under the bishop of Devon.

Little can be said with any certainty about the organization through which the late Old English bishops administered their sees. In particular, little is known of the Old English predecessors of the archdeacons and rural deans on whom, in their respective degrees, the administration of a medieval diocese turned. There is no satisfactory evidence of the existence of rural deans in pre-Conquest England. The office of archdeacon had been known there in, and probably before, the ninth century. Wulfred, who became archbishop of Canterbury in 805, had served his predecessor Æthelheard in that capacity. Archdeacons named Cyneheard and Dunning appear in Canterbury charters of 830 and *circa* 850, and in his later years Archbishop Ceolnoth (833–70) seems to have been assisted by a group of four such officials. In 889 an archdeacon occurs in a group of clergy belonging to the see of Rochester. But the archdeacon does not reappear in England until the time of Archbishop Ælfheah of Canterbury (1005–12), and it is unsafe to assume without evidence that the office had existed in the intervening period. Apart from Canterbury, the only diocese in which an archdeacon can be traced between 900 and 1066 is that of York. In the document called the Northumbrian Priests' Law, which appears to come from the time of Archbishop Ealdred (1061–9),[1] fines are imposed on priests who disregard the archdeacon's summons or continue to say mass in defiance of his prohibition. In smaller dioceses the bishop is less likely to have needed an archdeacon's help, and the custom which gave to every bishop at least one archdeacon as his executive and judicial assistant is certainly of Norman introduction.

There is little evidence to show the condition and organization of the bodies of clergy by which the cathedral churches of the tenth century were served. It is clear that the monastic cathedral had ceased to exist in England by the beginning of the century, and it is probable that the canonical association

---

[1] [This was Liebermann's opinion. For reasons for assigning it to the archiepiscopate of Wulfstan (1002–23) see D. Whitelock, *English Historical Documents c. 500–1042*, pp. 434–5 and 'Wulfstan at York,' in *Franciplegius: Medieval and Linguistic Studies in Honor of F. P. Magoun, Jr.*, ed. J. B. Bessinger and R. P. Creed, p. 225.]

of clergy in a communal life, which can be traced here and there in the previous age, had been abandoned in most, if not in all, cathedrals by this date. The services of Winchester cathedral at the middle of the century seem to have been maintained by the establishment of a rota among a group of wealthy clergy, of whom some, at least, were married. On the other hand, the system which assigned separate estates called prebends to the individual members of a cathedral chapter cannot be traced very far beyond the Norman Conquest. Ealdred, the last native archbishop of York, is said to have established prebends in his church of Southwell, which was of cathedral rank.[1] Clerks or 'canons' holding properties which can be identified with the prebendal estates of a later time sometimes appear among a bishop's tenants in Domesday Book. But there seems little doubt that such cases were exceptional, and that the cathedral clergy of the tenth and early eleventh centuries were normally maintained out of revenues common to the whole society of which they were members. Little advance had been made in pre-Conquest England towards the Norman conception of a cathedral chapter; with a dean, a group of principal dignitaries, each with his special duties in the church, and a body of canons for whom a dividend drawn from a common stock was a mere supplement to the proceeds of a separate endowment.

Few remains of the cathedral and other major churches of pre-Conquest England have survived to the present day. The ruined church at North Elmham is the only Anglo-Saxon cathedral of which any portion is visible above ground. But the less eminent churches of the time between the Danish wars and the Norman Conquest are represented by a large number of fragments incorporated into later work, and by a smaller, but still considerable, number of towers and other structures sufficiently extensive to show the principles of design which influenced their builders. In view of the chances of destruction to which they were subject after the Conquest from foreign lords with a taste for grandiose scale and elaborate decoration, the number of Anglo-Saxon churches of which the existence can be proved by architectural evidence is very remarkable. They are not evenly distributed over the country. They are most common in Yorkshire, and in the districts adjacent to

[1] *Historians of the Church of York*, R.S. ii, p. 353.

the important stone-yielding formations which extend from Gloucestershire, through Northamptonshire into Lincolnshire. But their number shows that a strong impulse towards church-building was at work among the English landowners of the tenth and early eleventh centuries. It was not confined to ecclesiastical persons, for some of the finest churches of the time arose in places where there is neither evidence nor probability of religious ownership. It would appear that the bishops of this period had been both diligent and successful in impressing the duty of building and repairing churches upon the ealdormen and thegns of their dioceses.

The development of architecture, as of all other forms of English art, was interrupted by the Danish wars. There is no English building which can be attributed with any show of probability to the years between 850 and 900. For the revival of architecture in the tenth century, inspiration came from a quarter which had contributed little to the constructive arts of pre-Danish England. The builders of the tenth century found their models, not like their predecessors in Italy or Gaul, but in the eastern provinces of what had been the Carolingian empire. Most of the features which give a distinctive character to the second phase of Old English architecture—windows set in the thickness of a wall between an internal and external splay, windows consisting of two narrow arches separated by a mid-wall shaft, triangular-headed openings, the use of the pilaster-strip for the relief of an unbroken wall-surface—are derived from the Rhineland and adjacent regions. In their use of these features English builders as a whole showed considerable technical accomplishment. At their best, they rose to a boldness of conception which gives the quality of a creative achievement to the finest examples of their work. The great tower of Earls Barton shows something more than the competent execution of a borrowed design. The Anglo-Saxon builders of this period could be very inept in details, and the dignity which they generally secured through their adherence to megalithic methods of construction might at any time degenerate into uncouthness when material, or an architect's imagination, failed. But they were the unconscious creators of a style so distinctive that fragments of their work can still be recognized at sight after nearly a thousand years, and so firmly established that in the north it survived the impact of

Norman Romanesque for at least two generations. In Lincoln-shire, Yorkshire, and Scotland individual architects were still designing churches after the Old English manner in the reign of Henry I.

The continental strain in the art and craftsmanship of tenth-century England extended far beyond the sphere of architecture. It was less dominant within the field of the decorative arts, for the great tradition established by earlier English sculptors, though weakened and complicated by Scandinavian influence, was not destroyed by the catastrophies of the ninth century. Even here, however, continental example clearly lies behind the remarkable figure-sculpture, of which examples remain in the winged angels of Bradford on Avon, the draped figure on the cross at Langford in Oxfordshire, and the Virgin and Child at York. The fact that the impulse which produced these works came from Byzantine influence, transmitted to the West through Italy, illustrates the long range of the forces which stimulated the revival of Old English civilization. In regard to the decoration of manuscripts, Old English artists of this period owed much to continental predecessors. The famous Winchester school of illuminators in the tenth century stands in a clear line of descent from the Carolingian schools of the ninth. The Carolingian influence on the art of book-production and in particular on the development of English handwriting, is at once more obvious and more important. The insular script of an earlier time continued to be the basic English hand throughout the tenth century, and indeed, came to its perfection towards the end of this period in volumes such as the magnificent Exeter Book of English verse. But the simple, clear, and beautiful handwriting known as the Carolingian minuscule had appeared in England before the end of Athelstan's reign. Its letter forms influenced the development of the older hand, and it rapidly came to be regarded as the most appropriate medium for the representation of Latin texts. Long before the close of the tenth century English scribes were employing it with absolute mastery and a sense of the decorative value of the script-pattern which it yielded. Its introduction is perhaps the most significant illustration of the play of continental influence on the last phases of Old English culture.

Of the intercourse through which the work of continental scribes and artists became known in England the record is naturally most incomplete. There are a few salient events which must have stimulated English interest in the outside world. One of the most remarkable occurred in 929, when Bishop Cenwald of Worcester set out on a series of visits to the churches of Germany, which brought him to St. Gall, and probably also to Reichenau and Pfäfers. In each of these churches prayers were afterwards offered for King Athelstan. It is clearly significant for the history of English culture that an eminent ecclesiastic of this period should have become acquainted with a region where the achievements of Carolingian architecture were particularly impressive, and the tradition of Carolingian scholarship was strong. Equally suggestive, though more easily overlooked, are certain scattered pieces of evidence that a number of foreign priests and clerks were living at about this time in different English religious houses. Godescalc the priest, whom Athelstan placed in charge of the secularized monastery of Abingdon, bore a German name, which was never current in pre-Conquest England.[1] The name Waltere, borne by a priest of the New Minster at Winchester in Athelstan's time, is much more likely to represent the Old German Walter than the Old English Wealdhere.[2] A little later, Theodred, bishop of London, bequeathed a chasuble to a certain Gundwin, who seems to have been a member of his episcopal household, and whose name is continental Germanic. A reference in the same document to the mass-book which Gosebricht had bequeathed to the bishop is another illustration of the German element in his circle.[3] None of these persons is more than a name, but the names are enough to show that foreign priests and clerks were finding hospitality in England on the eve of the tenth-century revival of English learning.

In any country open to continental influence it was inevitable that there would sooner or later be a response to the movement of monastic reform which early in the tenth century had risen independently in Burgundy and in upper and lower

---

[1] F. M. Stenton, *The Early History of the Abbey of Abingdon*, p. 38.

[2] *C.S.* 648.

[3] D. Whitelock, *Anglo-Saxon Wills*, p. 5. The bishop is known to have travelled in Italy. He refers in his will to chasubles which he had bought in Pavia. The possibility that he was himself a German by birth is suggested rather strongly by his name. Theodred is a very rare Old English name, but the corresponding Old German Theudrad is common.

Lorraine. When all allowance has been made for the scarcity and ambiguity of the available evidence, it seems clear that organized monastic life had expired everywhere in England under the strain of the Danish invasions. King Alfred, who desired its revival, founded a monastery at Athelney, but he was compelled to invite foreign monks to be its inmates, and the little that is known of its early history is unhappy. It is probable that the house of women which he founded at Shaftesbury was more successful, and developed without break into the nunnery which existed there in Athelstan's time. A number of references to religious women in charters of Athelstan and Edmund suggest, in fact, that the conception of the devoted life may have been spread somewhat widely among women at a time when few men felt its appeal. King Eadred's will refers to houses of women at Wilton and Winchester as well as at Shaftesbury. Wilton nunnery, which may have been a ninth-century foundation, was certainly in being in Athelstan's reign. Ealhswith, King Alfred's widow, was the foundress of the Nuns' Minster at Winchester. It is possible that historians have undervalued the contribution made by women to the religious idealism behind the English monastic revival.

In the first quarter of the century there is little, if any, evidence that Englishmen were beginning to turn their minds towards the monastic life. It is significant that the New Minster which Edward the Elder founded at Winchester was not a monastery but a house of clerks. But in 925 a grant of land by King Athelstan on the day of his coronation is witnessed by one of his chaplains, named Ælfheah, who styles himself priest and monk.[1] Neither the date of his profession nor the name of the prelate to whom it was made is recorded, and it is impossible to discover whether the impulse to his vow came to him from abroad or from the traditions of earlier English monasticism. In 934 he became bishop of Winchester, and he died in 951, when the movement of which he had been a forerunner was already a force in English religious life. So far as is known, he never attempted to carry out a reform of his cathedral church. Nevertheless, the part which he played in the English monastic revival was momentous, for it was under his influence, and at his hands, that Dunstan, its original leader, received ordination as a monk.

[1] C.S. 641.

Dunstan had been educated in a part of England where traditions of monastic life were particularly strong.[1] His father was a thegn of Somerset, whose land adjoined the site of the ancient abbey of Glastonbury. It was no longer a house of monks, but a school was maintained there by clerks following some form of common life, and it was visited by many Irish and other pilgrims, attracted by its fame and the relics which it possessed. Dunstan, who had felt the sanctity of the place while still a child, spent his early youth there in study. But his family was related to the royal house, and Athelm, archbishop of Canterbury, who was his uncle, brought him to court early in Athelstan's reign. For some years his life was unhappy. He was unpopular with the other young nobles about the king's household, and as time went on he was fretted by the desire for marriage. During a serious illness he was brought to a decision by his kinsman Bishop Ælfheah, to whom he made a monk's profession, and by whom he was afterwards ordained priest. A monk's vow was not incompatible with attendance at court, and for some time after Edmund's accession in the autumn of 939, Dunstan seems to have been with him continually. But the intrigues of jealous persons brought him into disgrace, and according to his first biographer he was about to leave the country when, as the king was being carried towards the cliffs at Cheddar by a bolting horse, it flashed into his mind that Dunstan had been wronged. The story adds that, to make amends, the king immediately rode with Dunstan to Glastonbury, and installed him there as abbot, promising to supply whatever he might need for the increase of divine service and the fulfilment of the monastic rule. A charter of 940 in which Edmund grants land to Dunstan as an abbot[2] shows that whatever may have been the circumstances of his promotion, it occurred within the first fourteen months of Edmund's reign.

For the next fifteen years Dunstan's life was spent at Glastonbury. By the end of this period he had brought into being the first organized community of monks which had existed in England for at least two generations. He owed much in these years to royal support, and in particular to the friendship of

---

[1] The date of Dunstan's birth is unknown, but convincing reasons for placing it in or before 910 are given by L. A. St. L. Toke, *The Bosworth Psalter*, pp. 133–43.

[2] *C.S.* 752. The charter is only known from a late transcript, but its formulas are of a mid-tenth-century type.

Eadred, who became king in 946. The relations between Dunstan and Eadred were so close that the king entrusted a large number of his own title-deeds and many of his principal treasures to Dunstan's custody. In the assurance of royal protection Dunstan was free to plan for the future, and there is little, if any, doubt that from the first he intended his work at Glastonbury to be the beginning of a movement through which the monastic order might spread in time throughout England. There is no contemporary evidence for the daily routine or the detail of the observances followed at Glastonbury by Dunstan, and although he and his monks were undoubtedly living in accordance with the Benedictine tradition, the exact form in which it came to them is uncertain. But the nature of the customs observed at Glastonbury was of less significance for English monastic history than the spirit in which he ruled his house. His strength lay in the quality which enabled him to control the individualism of his companions so that a common end might be attained. Only a man who could understand a type of character very different from his own could have lived happily, as a monastic superior, with the formidable Æthelwold of Winchester. Through the promotion of monks whom Dunstan had trained the example of his rule at Glastonbury influenced the whole course of the English monastic revival, and it is for this reason above all that he is entitled to be regarded as its leader.

Before the middle of the tenth century there is little evidence that the men who were attempting to revive monastic life in England were in touch with the continental movement towards this end. The first biographer of Dunstan, when describing his early work at Glastonbury, gives no hint of inspiration received from any foreign source. Among English laymen in high position there was sympathy for foreign monks who refused reform. In 944 King Edmund gave the abbey of Bath as a refuge to the monks of St. Bertin who rejected the new discipline of the great reformer Gerard of Brogne.[1] There is no reason to think that the English reformers of this early period learned anything at first hand from Cluny, the original and most famous centre of the continental movement. But at second hand, through the monastery of Fleury on the Loire, which was reformed from

---

[1] *Cartulaire de l'Abbaye de Saint-Bertin*, ed. M. Guérard, 145. The narrative, which dates the gift in 944, wrongly attributes it to Athelstan.

Cluny in 930, Cluniac influence was felt in England long before Dunstan had completed his work at Glastonbury. Oda, archbishop of Canterbury, who died in 958, had taken the habit of a monk at Fleury,[1] many years before his death. Under Oda's direction his nephew Oswald, who afterwards became very prominent as a founder and reformer of monasteries in England, went to Fleury for instruction in the principles of the religious life.[2] Even within Dunstan's own circle Æthelwold, his greatest pupil, came to feel that a wider learning and a more perfect knowledge of monastic discipline could be obtained in monasteries over sea. He was only dissuaded from leaving England by a commission from King Eadred to restore the decayed monastery of Abingdon.[3] It is clear that even in its earliest phases the English monastic revival cannot have proceeded in complete isolation.

Nevertheless, it is also clear that foreign example came to English reformers, not as an incentive to a new task, but as a means of perfecting work which had already been well begun. Unless early writers have failed to record facts in which they should have been interested, the work of monastic reformers in Lorraine and the Low Countries had made no effectual impression on English churchmen before 956, when Dunstan, exiled by King Eadwig, found refuge with the monks of St. Peter's at Ghent. Most of the best evidence for the acquaintance of English monastic reformers with their fellow workers abroad comes from this or an even later time. It cannot have been before 956, and it may have been some years later, that Æthelwold, as abbot of Abingdon, invited skilled chanters from Corbie, and sent Osgar his monk to study the customs observed at Fleury. The contribution of both Cluniac and Lotharingian monasticism to the English revival is proved by the statement in the *Regularis Concordia*—the code of the new English observance—that monks were invited from Fleury and Ghent to advise the council which compiled it. But the *Regularis Concordia* is a document of Edgar's reign, and tells nothing of earlier contacts.

Dunstan's exile was the outcome of Eadwig's resentment at a personal affront. There is no reason to think that Eadwig or his friends were moved by, or indeed capable of forming, any

[1] *Historians of the Church of York*, R.S. i, p. 413.   [2] Ibid., pp. 413–19.
[3] *Historia Monasterii de Abingdon*, R.S. ii, p. 257.

considered opinion adverse to monasticism. But a movement which could not expand without large endowments, and in its expansion was bound to collide with vested interests, needed the support of an enthusiastic king. The future of the English monastic revival was uncertain throughout the years of Eadwig's power. The turning-point in its history came in 959, when Edgar, Eadwig's brother, who had previously supplanted him in England north of the Thames, succeeded him as king of Wessex. From whatever impulse it may have come—tradition traced it back to the sight of a ruined abbey in his boyhood— the ambition to restore the derelict monasteries of England was a dominant interest in Edgar's life. As king he took the earliest opportunity of promoting men who could help him in this work. Dunstan, to whom he had already given the sees of Worcester and London, was translated to Canterbury in 960. Oswald, the pupil of the monks of Fleury, succeeded Dunstan at Worcester, and Æthelwold of Abingdon was raised to the see of Winchester in 963. By these appointments the three wealthiest bishoprics in England were given to men each of whom had proved his devotion to the monastic ideal. The use which they made of their promotion coloured the whole ecclesiastical history of England in the last century of the Old English state.

It is remarkable that Dunstan, to whom the new monasticism owed its inspiration, falls into the background of its later history. As archbishop of Canterbury he was in frequent attendance upon the king, and in precedence, the chief member of his council. It was a position from which even a weak and inexperienced man could draw authority. To Dunstan, a man of power, who had known the leading Englishmen of a time before the reigning king was born, it must have given the opportunity of a decisive voice when a monastery was threatened with vexatious pleas or the immunities of a monastic estate were unjustly challenged. But the initiative in the monastic revival had passed to other men. In the literature which illustrates the time of Dunstan's greatest dignity he appears as an eminent figure, venerable but somewhat remote, an adviser rather than a leader. At the decisive council of Winchester which discussed the customs to be followed in English monasteries, Dunstan does not seem to have been present, and the code which it authorized was the work of

Bishop Æthelwold. There is no reason to think that Dunstan ever retired from the world, or fell out of touch with the men who came to power after Edgar's reign. He crowned both Edward the Martyr and Æthelred II, attended each of Edward's recorded councils, and attested every charter which Æthelred is known to have issued up to the year of his own death. But it is on his pastoral labours, his studies, his visions, and the holiness of his life that his earliest biographer dwells when describing the years of his archbishopric.

It was the energy of Oswald of Worcester and Æthelwold of Winchester which carried the monastic revival to the height of its influence. Oswald's most remarkable achievement was the slow transformation of the body of clerks which was serving his cathedral at the time of his election into a fully organized monastic community. The change, which can be traced through a long series of local documents, was brought about through the gradual replacement of clerks by men who had made or were prepared to make a monk's profession. It was a method which avoided a sudden clash of wills within the church, and it shows that Oswald was a man of infinite patience. But in the generation following his own Oswald's fame was chiefly associated with the great abbey of Ramsey which he founded. It was remembered that he had re-established the decayed abbey of Winchcombe and that in later life, after he had become archbishop of York, he had placed monks at Ripon. But Ramsey was the house of his affection, and it was there that his earliest biography was written. He obtained the site from Æthelwine, ealdorman of East Anglia, as a place in which to settle a little group of disciples for whom he had been unable to provide in his own diocese. In his religious life Oswald owed far more than either Dunstan or Æthelwold to foreign teachers; he had learned monastic discipline at Fleury, and he brought his new foundation at Ramsey into a close connection with that house. An Englishman named Germanus, who had been a fellow pupil with Oswald at Fleury, became the first dean, or prior, of Ramsey, Abbo, the most learned among the monks of Fleury, came to Ramsey at Oswald's request, and taught in the monastic school for two years. The influence of Abbo's teaching was still active in the eleventh century, when one of his former pupils, named Byrhtferth, wrote the most important scientific treatise which had appeared in England since the age of Bede.[1] For a time it is probable that Ramsey was in closer touch with continental learning than any other house of the English revival.

In the earliest biography of Oswald, Æthelwold of Winchester is said to have been the adviser who induced King Edgar to expel clerks from monasteries and set others in their place.[2] The description probably expresses the truth about the most debated episode in the whole history of the revival. A contemporary version of the *Chronicle* states that Edgar drove out the priests from the Old and New Minsters at Winchester, from Chertsey and Milton Abbas, and planted monks in those churches. A member of the New Minster, who may have witnessed the change, when describing the relations of the West Saxon royal family with his house, states that King Edgar cast forth the sluggish crowd of well-born clerks and replaced them by monks.[3] By each of these writers the initiative in what was certainly a drastic and may have been a violent act of power is clearly attributed to the king. On the other hand, Ælfric of Eynsham, Æthelwold's pupil, when writing his master's life, asserts that the clerks were driven from the Old and New Minsters by the bishop with the king's licence,[4] and in one of his English works he refers without any qualification to Æthelwold's expulsion of the clerks from the Old Minster.[5] To apportion the responsibility for the way in which the change was carried out is clearly impossible. It is, perhaps, hardly necessary, for neither Edgar nor Æthelwold would have seen anything reprehensible in strong action against men whom the king regarded as usurpers of holy places, and whose way of life offended the bishop's puritanism.

In any case Æthelwold's reforms at Winchester were only part of a general activity which increased both the geographical range and the territorial strength of the new monasticism. Apart from Oswald's foundation of Ramsey, of which the site was fixed by accident rather than design, Æthelwold's fellow workers had done little to carry the influence of the monastic revival into the Danelaw. Æthelwold formed a deliberate policy of restoring monasticism in this region. He acquired

[1] *Byrhtferth's Manual*, i, ed. S. J. Crawford, 1929.
[2] *Historians of the Church of York*, R.S. i, pp. 426–7.
[3] *Liber Vitae of Hyde Abbey*, ed. W. de G. Birch, pp. 7–8.
[4] *Historia Monasterii de Abingdon*, R.S. ii, p. 260.
[5] *Lives of Saints*, ed. W. W. Skeat, pp. 442, 446.

the sites of a number of decayed monasteries, established monks on some of them, and gave others as sources of revenue to religious houses where the principles of the revival were in operation. His greatest achievement in this direction was the re-establishment of monastic life at Ely, Medeshamstede, henceforward known as Peterborough, and Thorney, but it is significant of his intention that although he did not found monasteries upon them, he also acquired estates at Barrow on Humber, where Bishop Cedd had lived in the seventh century, and Breedon in Leicestershire, which had supplied an arch-bishop to Canterbury in the eighth.[1] Hardly less remarkable than the design itself is the assiduity with which Æthelwold laboured to make it permanent. It was essential that his monasteries should be adequately endowed, and his negotia-tions for this purpose as they are described in the records of Peterborough, Thorney, and above all, Ely, prove his tireless industry and his remarkable competence in affairs. He never forgot a possible claim at law, and he was prepared to plead in local courts far from his own diocese. Unlike Dunstan and Oswald, he has never engaged the affection of historians. He was a strict disciplinarian, and capable of putting the obedience of his monks to extravagant tests. But, in his own day, the crude strength of his somewhat unattractive personality im-pressed men incapable of understanding Oswald's patience or Dunstan's half-mystical devotion.

It is almost inevitable that the history of the English monastic revival should be made to centre upon the names of Dunstan, Æthelwold, and Oswald. The lives of these saints, which were written in the next generation, supply the only means of tracing the course of the movement. But its influence was not confined to men trained by one or other of the three leading reformers. Before the end of Edgar's reign the rapid increase in the number of English monasteries, and the diversity of their observances, had compelled the king and his advisers to take measures for their regulation. Between 963 and 975 Edgar summoned a synodal council to meet at Winchester, and compose a set of customs which should be observed every-where. It seems to have been admitted that the movement was drifting into incoherence, and the council, to which monks from Fleury and Ghent were invited, unanimously

[1] *C.S.* 1270, 1283.

approved a customal, drawn up by Bishop Æthelwold with the other bishops of the southern province, confirmed by Dunstan and King Edgar, and introduced to the world as the *Regularis Concordia*, the Agreement concerning the Rule, of the monks and nuns of the English nation.[1]

It is unlikely that Dunstan at Glastonbury or Æthelwold in his early days at Abingdon had attempted to carry out any elaborate plan of service and devotion. They probably followed a system of monastic observance which adhered very closely to the original rule of St. Benedict. Manuals describing such a system have survived in tenth-century manuscripts, and the early sections of the *Regularis Concordia* are clearly based upon a work of this kind. But the *Regularis Concordia*, as a whole, attempts much more than this, and is profoundly influenced in spirit and detail by the practice of recent continental reformers. Its analysis has not yet been carried far enough to show the precise affiliation of its different parts to earlier continental usages. The task is made difficult, if not impossible, by uncertainty as to the customs observed in some of the most important reformed monasteries on the continent. But, now and then, a remarkable observance points to some particular affinity. It seems clear, for example, that Æthelwold and his associates were acquainted, not only with the customs of Fleury and Ghent, but also with those of the reformed houses of upper Lorraine, and in particular with those of Einsiedeln. It is plain, in fact, that the *Regularis Concordia* is an eclectic code, even if the source of its detail is often uncertain. Its place in the general history of Benedictine monasticism is also well established. In the elaboration of services and prescribed acts of devotion it clearly represents the tradition of Benedict of Aniane, the great reformer who in the ninth century thus amplified the simple rule of St. Benedict. The determination that all English monasteries should follow the same usages was no doubt due to local circumstances, but it is in complete agreement with the desire for a uniform monastic observance which had moved Benedict of Aniane. The one feature which distinguishes the *Regularis Concordia* from all continental customs is the emphasis which it lays on the duty of praying for

[1] See the edition by Dom Thomas Symons, in *Nelson's Medieval Classics*, 1953, and cf. J. Armitage Robinson, *The Times of St. Dunstan*, pp. 143–58, and D. Knowles, *The Monastic Order in England*, pp. 42–8.

MINSTERS AND MONASTERIES *c.* 1035

Miles
0 10 20 30 40 50 60 70 80

+ Monasteries in 1035.
⚜ Cathedral Monasteries
○ Secular Minsters in 1035
⚜ Cathedral Minsters

DURHAM
Hexham
Chester-le-Street
Durham

Y
O
R
K

Ripon
York Beverley

Stow St. Mary

Chester St. Werburg
Chester St. John
LICHFIELD
Derby
Repton
Penkridge   Burton
Shrewsbury St. Alkmund
Shrewsbury St. Chad Lichfield
Wenlock
Morville   Wolverhampton
Bromfield
Leominster
Hereford St. Ethelbert
Hereford St. Guthlac

Southwell

North Elmham
Crowland
Thorney   St. Benet of Holme
Peterborough
Ramsey   Chatteris   Hoxne
Ely
Eynesbury   Bury
Bedford   Stoke by Clare

Worcester
Evesham
Gloucester   Winchcombe
Berkeley   Eynsham   Oxford St. Frideswide
Abingdon
Dorchester   St Albans   Sudbury
Malmesbury Reading
Bath Ramsbury   Sonning
Wells   Chertsey   Westminster   London
Athelney   Glastonbury   Amesbury   Charwelton   Barking
Muchelney   Wilton   Winchester St. Swithin   Rochester   Canterbury
Sherborne   Ramsey   Winchester New Minster   Christ Church
Crediton   Shaftesbury   Winchester Nuns Minster   Canterbury St. Augustines
Launceston   Cranborne   Horton   Bosham   SELSEY
St. Neot   Wimborne   Selsey
Tavistock   Wareham
Bodmin   Cerne Milton
St. Germans   Abbotsbury
St. Buriana

the king and his family. It may not unreasonably be regarded as an acknowledgement of the debt which the leaders of the English revival, and Æthelwold pre-eminently among them, owed to Edgar, the reigning sovereign.

The anti-monastic reaction which followed Edgar's death was due to political rather than religious feeling. Some monastic communities may have been dispersed, and others deprived of property. But although the spread of the movement was checked for a time, its past achievements were not seriously threatened. Whatever its character may have been, the reaction must have lost its energy with the death of Ælfhere of Mercia in 983. Thenceforward there is no sign of any anti-monastic feeling at court, and the reign of Æthelred II is marked by a series of new foundations, such as Cerne Abbas, Eynsham, and Burton on Trent, which prove that desire for the religious life was still strong in England. Each of the three original leaders of the monastic revival survived into Æthelred's reign. Æthelwold died in 984, Dunstan in 988, and Oswald in 992. They had no successors of equal eminence. But the men whom they had trained were ready to carry on their work, and the future of the movement which they had led was secured by the religious houses which had arisen or come to new life under their influence. In 993, the year after Oswald's death, the abbots of eighteen monasteries are known to have attended King Æthelred's court.[1]

On the other hand, the names of these monasteries suggest, what other evidence proves, that the strength of the movement lay almost entirely in the southern half of England. Even here it had made little, if any, impression on the west midland shires which had formed the historic Mercia. Its remarkable progress in the eastern midlands had been made possible by the patronage of a small number of great men, such as Æthelwine of East Anglia and Byrhtnoth of Essex, whose interests were not merely local. The Anglo-Danish noblemen beyond the Welland, engrossed in their own concerns, seem to have

---

[1] *C.D.* 684; *Historia Monasterii de Abingdon*, R.S. i, pp. 358–66. The religious houses are Abingdon, Glastonbury, New Minster at Winchester, St. Augustine's at Canterbury, Ely, Chertsey, Malmesbury, Bath, Muchelney, Milton (Abbas), Exeter, Athelney, Westminster, Ramsey, Peterborough, Thorney, St. Albans, and an unidentified house of which the name appears in the charter as 'Uuind'. A similar list dated 997 (*C.D.* 698) omits Ely, Milton, Athelney, Ramsey, Thorney, and 'Uuind', but adds Cholsey and Evesham.

ignored the new monasticism, and it was not until the twelfth century that the free peasantry of the northern Danelaw began to make gifts of land for religious purposes. Beyond the Humber, Oswald's attempt to restore monastic life at Ripon ended in failure and found no imitators. In this direction little advance was made between the age of Edgar and the Norman Conquest. In 1066 Crowland was the only monastery in the shires of Lincoln, Leicester, Nottingham, Derby, and York.

But the effect of the monastic revival cannot be measured by the mere number of the religious houses to which it gave rise. Through the members of these houses who rose to bishoprics its influence was very rapidly extended over the whole body of the English Church. The series of such promotions, which begins in Edgar's reign, can be traced downwards almost continuously until the eve of the Norman Conquest. It is clear that a living tradition of Dunstan, Æthelwold, and Oswald was preserved among the rulers of the English church for three-quarters of a century. It was in accordance with this tradition that a monastic order was established in at least two cathedrals which had previously been served by secular clergy. By the early part of the eleventh century, and at latest before the death of archbishop Ælfric (995–1005), the community at Christ Church, Canterbury, had become entirely monastic. Wulfsige, bishop of Sherborne (992–1001), replaced clerks by monks in his cathedral. There is no sign of any internal reaction against the work of Oswald and Æthelwold at Worcester and Winchester. The evidence is scanty, but it leaves little room for doubt that the monastic cathedral, which was a unique feature of the medieval English church, was in fact the creation of the tenth-century revival.

The influence of the revival on the parochial clergy was direct and strong. Between 975 and 1066 every English diocese came for a time, if only for a short time, under the rule of a bishop who was a professed monk. Under the conditions of the age a monastic training was the best preparation that a bishop could receive for his pastoral work. It gave him a sense of discipline and order, respect for learning, and the opportunity of knowing men who were capable of sustained enthusiasm for an idea. It is clear that the monastic bishops of this period were anxious to instruct as well as rule their clergy. They held firmly to the ideal that the priest, through his ordination, was set apart from other men, and they regarded it as their duty to move their clergy towards a celibate way of life. In this, like their successors in spirit, the reforming bishops of the twelfth century, they were confronted by the stolid resistance of a clergy unwilling to accept a dictated conception of its calling, and their success was far from complete. The record of their activities is broken, and little is known about the synods which they held and the diocesan visitations which they carried out. But enough has been preserved about their lives to demonstrate the force of their example.

There can, in fact, be no question that the Benedictine reformation of the tenth century brought fresh vitality to the whole English church. But its significance is misunderstood if it is dismissed as one of the many movements which have merely influenced a generation and then passed into history. It opened a new phase of English culture which survived the political catastrophe of the Norman Conquest, and contributed to the distinctive quality of medieval English civilization. The outstanding feature of this phase was the development of a new religious literature in the English language. Although it was demonstrably the outcome of the monastic revival, it was not written for monastic readers. The elaborate treatise on the reckoning of time, written by Byrhtferth of Ramsey,[1] was composed in order to help parish priests in their regular duties. The *Catholic Homilies* of Ælfric, which have been described as 'the classic example of Anglo-Saxon prose', consist of two sets of sermons, suitable for delivery by priests on the chief days of the ecclesiastical year. Ælfric's *Lives of the Saints*, his translations from Scripture, and certain other works were written at the request of laymen. The strongest piece of writing produced in this age was addressed to the whole English people by Wulfstan, archbishop of York, as a call to repentance in the crisis of 1014. Regarded as a whole, these works formed a vernacular literature with a remarkably wide appeal, and the number of manuscripts in which individual writings are preserved shows that it was well received. The fact that some of these manuscripts were written in the twelfth century proves that Norman criticism of the English church had not destroyed the Englishman's respect for his native learning.[2]

The work of Ælfric, the leader of this literary movement,

illustrates every side of its activity. His life was uneventful.
He was educated under Bishop Æthelwold in the cathedral
monastery at Winchester. In or a little before 987, being already
a priest, he was sent by Bishop Ælfheah, Æthelwold's successor,
to a monastery which had recently been founded at Cerne
Abbas in Dorset by Æthelmær, son of the chronicler Æthelweard. At Cerne Ælfric took charge of the monastic school,
wrote most of the English books on which his fame now chiefly
rests, and won a reputation for learning which caused bishops
to come to him for advice. In 1005, when Æthelmær founded a
second monastery, at Eynsham in Oxfordshire, Ælfric became
its abbot. The rest of his life was spent at Eynsham. The year
of his death is unknown.

Ever since the seventh century the English language had
been used for public statements of customary law. In the tenth
century it was often used for private documents. Some clerks
of this period showed remarkable skill in the art of putting a
complicated series of transactions into a narrative form. King
Alfred had proved that English could be a medium for the
expression of thought. It was inevitable that sooner or later, as
the religious revival spread from the monastery over the countryside, the attempt would be made to provide books in the native
language for the instruction of rural clergymen and their
parishioners. Ælfric was not the first to enter this field. He
himself refers to predecessors who had translated portions of
the Bible or written homilies. His work has eclipsed theirs, not
because his mind was original or his learning unprecedented,
but through the distinction of his writing. He was a great
teacher, with a natural gift for exposition. He developed a
highly characteristic prose, often alliterative, which at its best
moves with singular ease. But it was his supreme merit that he
came to the writing of English with a keen appreciation of the
grammatical precision and structural clarity of a Latin sentence. He was interested in the principles of grammar and
syntax, and through the influence of his teaching and the
example of his own works he introduced a new standard of
form into English composition. Nevertheless he was in no sense
a pedant, and he could write with evident sincerity that he
would rather profit his hearers through simple language than
be praised for mastery of an artificial style.

It is impossible to determine the exact sequence of Ælfric's works.[1] But it seems clear that most of his English writings belong to the early part of his career. His *Catholic Homilies*, a collection of the lives and passions of the saints whose festivals were observed by the English nation, were issued in 991 and 992. His *Lives of the Saints*, a similar work dealing with the saints honoured by monks in their services, were written at the request of ealdorman Æthelweard and his son, and are therefore earlier than 998. It was at the invitation of the same ealdorman that Ælfric began the translation of Genesis which forms the first part of his translation of the Pentateuch. All these works clearly belong to his years at Cerne. The series of his so-called 'Pastoral Letters', which form a link between his early and later writings, begins in this period. Soon after 992 he wrote for Wulfsige, bishop of Sherborne, who afterwards became famous as a reformer, a letter which the bishop could read at a synod to his clergy for its instruction in matters of duty, observance, and conduct. After his promotion to Eynsham Ælfric wrote letters of a similar character, but more explicit in their teaching, for Wulfstan, bishop of Worcester and archbishop of York. But, as a whole, the works which are known to belong to Ælfric's later years are of less general significance. From the historical standpoint the most interesting of them are certain pieces of commentary and exposition written for local thegns of Ælfric's acquaintance. They illustrate not only the range of Ælfric's friendships, but also the response which work such as his might find among the lesser nobility of his age.

In the meantime the most highly placed of Ælfric's correspondents, Archbishop Wulfstan, was working towards the same end from another point of departure. As a writer of homilies in the Old English language Wulfstan has earned a reputation only second to that of Ælfric himself. But unlike Ælfric Wulfstan occupied a position which gave him the right to intervene directly in public affairs. One of his chief English works is a discussion of the principles of government in church and state. It seems certain that he took an active part in the work of drafting the later laws of Æthelred II and those of Cnut, for they contain many phrases and constructions which are characteristic of his acknowledged writings. But the work

---

[1] [But see P. Clemoes, 'The Chronology of Ælfric's Works', in *The Anglo Saxons*, ed. P. Clemoes, London, 1959.]

through which he is best remembered is the great homily known from a familiar Latin rendering of his name as the *Sermo Lupi ad Anglos*, which he wrote in 1014.[1] Its object was to convince the English people that its misery was God's judgement upon its misdeeds; it is filled with lamentable details, and it is made very impressive by the fact that Wulfstan obviously knew the world which he was denouncing. Wulfstan had neither the scholarship nor the literary sense of Ælfric. The *Sermo Lupi* makes its effect by sheer monotony of commination. But it is doubtful whether Ælfric could ever have brought himself to address a whole nation with words of power.

To a student of the humanities the chief interest of the tenth-century reformation will probably lie in the process through which, for the first time, English prose became an efficient literary instrument. But to Ælfric and his fellow-workers the writing of learned works in English, the trans-lation of the Scriptures, and the composition of homilies for delivery by rustic priests were all concessions to the needs of men of little knowledge or inadequate scholarship. They were in no way substitutes for the Latin learning through which alone a priest could come to the full understanding of his duty. It was obviously essential that the knowledge of Latin should be kept alive for use in the services of the church. Even apart from this primary necessity, Ælfric, like Alfred a century before him, would have regarded a clerical training based exclusively on the vernacular as disastrous for religion. Ælfric himself, for example, had grave doubts about the wisdom of multiplying translations of the Bible. It is significant that the book which has done most to bring him general fame is a set of imaginary dialogues in Latin and English, written to help his scholars through the early stages of the former language. It was in Latin that he abridged the *Regularis Concordia* for his monks at Eynsham, and wrote the biography of his master Æthelwold.

Nevertheless the Latin literature of the period includes little that is memorable. It is true that the biographies of Dunstan, Æthelwold, and Oswald, which were written between 996 and 1006, are of the first importance for history.[2] Ælfric's life of Æthelwold is an excellent piece of simple narrative.

---

[1] ed. D. Whitelock (Methuen's Old English Library), [ed. 3, 1963].

[2] *Memorials of St. Dunstan*, R.S., pp. 3–52; *Chronicon Monasterii de Abingdon*, R.S. ii, pp. 255–66; *Historians of the Church of York*, R.S. i, pp. 399–475.

But the life of Dunstan, which was written by a foreigner, is not evidence for English scholarship, and the life of Oswald gives a poor impression of its quality. It is a disorderly work, written in a flamboyant prose, studded with strange words, which had to be explained by glosses inserted between the lines. The most interesting Latin work of the time is only indirectly connected with the main revival of English learning. At some point between 975 and 998 Ælfric's friend Æthelweard, ealdorman of the south-western shires, translated the *Anglo-Saxon Chronicle* into Latin for the benefit of Matilda, abbess of Essen, who, like the ealdorman himself, was descended from the royal house of Wessex. Æthelweard's version of the *Chronicle* has exasperated historians ever since the twelfth century. It is very important as a source of information, for it is based on a text of the *Chronicle* different from all surviving copies. But the Latin in which it is written is deplorable. It is the writing of a man who aspired to style without adequate grammatical knowledge, and in many places it is unintelligible. At present nothing can be said to much purpose about the quarter from which Æthelweard derived his eccentric vocabulary and his strange grammatical constructions, for, significantly enough, he has not yet found a critical or a sympathetic editor.[1] But the mere fact that a lay nobleman of the highest rank tried to write a Latin history of his own country is a most remarkable illustration of the general stirring of intellectual life that accompanied the tenth-century revival of English learning.

If the revival failed to produce a distinguished school of Latin authors, it certainly created an atmosphere favourable to the multiplication of Latin books. It was necessary that every monastery should possess the liturgical texts essential to its services, calendars recording the feast-days of the saints whom it honoured, psalters, gospel-books, and writings by the fathers of the church. The need for such volumes, and for more specialized texts, such as the benedictionals or pontificals which contained the offices proper to a bishop, stimulated the development of English penmanship, and resulted in the production of books which in quality of script and excellence of decoration

[1] [The desired edition was produced in 1962 by A. Campbell, who discusses the style on pp. xxxvii, xlv–lx, and claims that it shows no continental peculiarities. K. Sisam, *Proceedings of the British Academy*, xxxix (1953), p. 320, n. 3, suggests that Æthelweard employed a Celtic-trained secretary. Æthelweard's style is defended by M. Winterbottom in *Medium Ævum*, xxxvi (1967), pp. 109–118.]

could not be rivalled in contemporary Europe. The famous manuscripts of this period, such as the Winchester 'Benedictional of St. Æthelwold' and the 'Bosworth Psalter', which was probably written at Canterbury for Dunstan, stand for a large amount of work which, if less ornate, is equally accomplished. By the early part of the eleventh century England was supplying books to foreign churches. In the troubled years before the accession of Cnut, Ramsey abbey repaid something of the debt which it owed to Fleury by the gift of a fine benedictional. A little later another benedictional, written in the New Minster at Winchester, came into the possession of Robert, archbishop of Rouen, and remained thenceforward in his cathedral. The migrations of manuscripts in this period are curiously illustrated by the story of a sacramentary and psalter written by Earnwig, master of the school at Peterborough, given by him to Cnut, sent by Cnut to Cologne, and brought back to England, some thirty years later, by Ealdred, bishop of Worcester.[1] No foreign bishop or abbot of this age could have conceived it possible that a time would come when the isolation and illiteracy of the late Old English church would be accepted as a commonplace by most historians.

It was not only in regard to matters of scholarship and book-production that the English church of this period came into contact with the outside world. In the tenth century, as in the great days of Willibald and Boniface, the advance of English learning was accompanied by an interest in the spread of Christianity over heathen countries. It will never be possible to estimate at all closely the part played by English missionaries in the conversion of the Scandinavian peoples, but there is no question as to its importance. There is no reason to doubt the traditions that Hakon, Athelstan's foster-son, sent for a bishop and priests from England to help him in the establishment of Christianity in Norway, that Olaf Tryggvason was accompanied by an English-born bishop and English priests when he sailed for Norway in 995, and that King Swein of Denmark had allowed a bishop of English extraction to work in Scania. There is certainly a basis of truth underneath the scattered references to English missionaries in Sweden. It is true that traditions like these cannot always be taken at their face value. Within half a century of St. Olaf's death it was recorded

[1] William of Malmesbury, *Vita Wulfstani*, ed. R. R. Darlington, pp. 5, 16.

that he was attended as king of Norway by a number of bishops and priests from England, of whom the most eminent were named Sigafrid, Grimkil, Rudolf, and Bernard. Sigafrid and Grimkil may well have come from the English Danelaw, but Bernard bore a name, common in Germany, of which the English equivalent had long fallen out of use, and Rudolf is known to have been a Norman from Rouen, and a kinsman of Queen Emma. The English claim to credit for a share in the conversion of the north does not really depend on tradition but on details of ritual and organization in which the English and Scandinavian churches resemble each other. Few of them can be traced in Denmark, where the ecclesiastical influence of Germany was always strong. But in Norway and Sweden they are numerous and clear enough to show that the men who founded the national churches knew and respected English practice. Sweden and England, for example, are the two countries where the primitive idea that a man who built a church ought to become its owner had the deepest effect on later parochial organization. The eleventh-century church of St. Peter at Sigtuna on Lake Malar, which shows Anglo-Saxon influence in plan and many details, remains as a memorial of the intercourse by which these resemblances were brought about.

Intercourse between English and continental churchmen was stimulated by the union of England and Denmark under Cnut. If it had not been for the resolute action of Archbishop Unwan of Bremen the Danish church would probably have become dependent on Canterbury. In 1022 Cnut appointed three bishops of German name, and presumably of German birth, to the sees of Roskilde, Fyn, and Scania, Bishop Gerbrand of Roskilde was consecrated by Archbishop Æthelnoth.[1] In the following years political circumstances forced a cosmopolitan outlook on the whole English episcopate, but they also contributed to the promotion of a number of clergy whom Dunstan or Æthelwold would hardly have recommended for the highest office. Between the accession of Cnut and the Norman Conquest political exchanges between the English court and foreign powers were

---

[1] Adam of Bremen, *Gesta Hammaburgensis Ecclesiae Pontificum*, ed. 2, J. M. Lappenburg, Bk. ii, cap. 53; also ed. B. Schmeidler (917) Bk. ii, cap. 55. This statement is confirmed by Gerbrand's attestation of *C.D.* 734, a charter issued in 1022 by Cnut for Ely.

more frequent than at any period since the reign of Athelstan. Churchmen were the natural intermediaries in this business, and a good clerical diplomatist might reasonably expect a bishopric. It is significant that in the reign of Edward the Confessor a number of sees, including both Canterbury and York, were filled by bishops drawn from the circle of the king's priests. There was nothing scandalous in such appointments, and most of the men to whom they fell seem to have left a good name behind them in their dioceses. The bishop who regarded his see merely as a source of income by which he might be supported in the king's service was unknown in England before the Conquest. But the way had certainly been opened for his appearance.

It is probable that the need for information about other states and their rulers accounts in part for the favour shown in this period by English kings to foreign churchmen. It was obviously to the king's advantage that there should be members of his council who knew something at first hand about the continental world and its principal figures. In 1033 Cnut gave the bishopric of Wells to a Lotharingian priest named Duduc, and between this date and 1066 three other priests from the same province were appointed to English sees. There were both political and ecclesiastical grounds for the offer of English preferment to churchmen from Lorraine. In the tenth century the founders of the new English monasticism had learned much from that country, and the traditions of earlier reformers were still alive there. But the political reasons for these appointments were also strong. A king like Cnut or Edward the Confessor, whose policy touched both France and the Empire, could make good use of an adviser who instinctively regarded European affairs from the standpoint of the intermediate lands.

But it is the Norman element in the late Old English episcopate which has attracted most attention from historians. In 1044, two years after his accession, King Edward gave the bishopric of London to Robert, abbot of Jumièges. In 1049 he gave the bishopric of Dorchester to a Norman priest of his household, named Ulf. In 1051, when he was beginning to assert himself against Earl Godwine, the king caused the translation of Robert to the see of Canterbury, and, later in the year, set William, another of his Norman priests, in Robert's

place at London. William, who seems to have been an exemplary bishop, died in possession of his see in 1075, but Ulf,
whose appointment gave scandal at home and abroad, and
Archbishop Robert, whose influence with the king was bitterly
resented, were driven out of England by a popular rising in
1052. The ecclesiastical significance of these appointments
has sometimes been exaggerated. They are too few to give
any basis for the idea that the king was hoping to change the
character of the English church through the promotion of
Norman clergy. But there may well have been a political
motive behind the translation of Robert to Canterbury and
the appointment of William to London. It was almost certainly
in 1051 that Edward made his famous promise that the duke
of Normandy should succeed him as king of England. He is
not unlikely to have felt that the succession would be made
easier by the appointment of an archbishop of Canterbury
who would not hesitate to crown the duke, and the promotion
of a Norman priest to the bishopric of the chief English city.

The events which followed the flight of Archbishop Robert
have sometimes been used as evidence that the leaders of the
late Old English church were indifferent to the movement for
ecclesiastical reform which was rising to influence on the
Continent. The archbishop's place was immediately filled by
Stigand, bishop of Winchester, a close associate of Earl Godwine.
This arbitrary supersession of a lawfully constituted archbishop
ignored canonical principles which high churchmen abroad
regarded as fundamental, and it was never forgiven by the
reforming party in the Roman curia. Archbishop Robert at
once appealed to Pope Leo IX, by whom Stigand was summoned to Rome, condemned in absence, and excommunicated. The process was repeated by Leo's successors Victor II
and Stephen IX. Shortly after the death of Stephen IX,
Stigand obtained the pallium from Benedict X, who held the
papacy uneasily from April 1058 until January 1059. But
the recognition by Benedict, whose own position was regarded
as uncanonical by all strict churchmen, brought no permanent
advantage to Stigand. He was excommunicated again by
Nicholas II, with whose election the reforming party returned
to power at Rome, and by Alexander II, whose support of
William of Normandy in 1066 was partly determined by the
hope of securing Stigand's deposition. On the surface his

continuance in office was a direct challenge to the conception of ecclesiastical order reached by the best opinion of his time.

But Stigand's retention of the dignity, the place in council, and the emoluments of an archbishop of Canterbury does not mean that the English churchmen accepted his metropolitan authority or were indifferent to the sentences which successive popes had passed upon him. Their respect for the attitude of the Roman curia is strikingly shown by the fact that between 1052 and 1066 no English bishop came to him for consecration, except in the months immediately after his recognition by Benedict X. It is in some ways more remarkable that the anomaly of his position was felt by laymen belonging to his own party in the state. Earl Harold invited Cynesige, archbishop of York, to consecrate his newly founded church of Waltham Holy Cross; and the authority of the English evidence that Ealdred of York crowned Harold king[1] outweighs the Norman assertion that he was 'ordained by the unholy consecration of Stigand'.[2] The archbishop himself may well have taken the papal condemnation less seriously. His whole career shows that he was essentially a politician, and he is not unlikely to have regarded the reforming popes who condemned him as the leaders of a party which had come to power only in recent years, and might at any time fall from power again. But there can be no doubt that the representative English churchmen of his age considered him to be archbishop in name only.

Their attitude is only one among many indications of the deference with which the Old English church regarded the papacy. The close connection between England and Rome, which can be traced downwards from the age of the conversion to the early part of the ninth century, was never completely broken in the bad times that followed. A fortified area in Rome inhabited by Englishmen, who formed a section, or 'schola', of the Roman militia as early as the eighth century, was freed from taxation by Pope Marinus (882–4) at Alfred's request.[3] Later in Alfred's reign, money described as the alms of the king and the West Saxon people was sent each year to Rome. These 'alms', which clearly had an official character, may well repre-

[1] Florence of Worcester, *Chronicon*, ed. B. Thorpe, i, p. 224; *Historians of the Church of York*, R.S. ii, p. 348.

[2] William of Poitiers, *Gesta Willelmi Ducis*, ed. Giles, p. 121.

[3] On the 'Schola Saxonum' see W. H. Stevenson, *Asser's Life of King Alfred*, pp. 243–7.

sent the payment afterwards known as Peter's Pence.[1] Among
Alfred's successors, Edmund, Edgar, and Cnut issued laws
enforcing this payment, and money thus raised was sent
annually to Rome during at least the latter part of the Confessor's reign.[2] Meanwhile, the dependence of the English
church on the papacy had received a more formal, but also
a more intimate, expression through the establishment of a
custom that every archbishop of Canterbury must come to
Rome for his pallium. The custom is known to have been
observed by nine out of the fourteen archbishops appointed
to Canterbury between 925 and 1066, and by the reign of
Cnut, at latest, it had been extended to cover the archbishops
of York. The strengthening of the connection between the
English church and Rome was an object of policy to the reforming popes of the mid-eleventh century, and there is both
good and varied evidence for papal influence in England
during the twenty years before the Norman Conquest. The
first occasion on which a pope is known to have rejected a
candidate nominated by the crown to an English see belongs
to this period. In 1051 Leo IX ordered Archbishop Robert
of Canterbury to refuse consecration to Spearhafoc, abbot
of Abingdon, bishop designate of London, and the king
acquiesced in the pope's decision.[3] It was a most remarkable
act of papal authority, but it was isolated, and historically it is
less significant than the success of the same pope in securing
the attendance of representatives from England at his councils,
and the recognition of his right to be consulted about important
changes in the organization of the English church. English
prelates attended him at the council of Reims in 1049, and
at the councils of Rome and Vercelli in the following year,[4]
and his consent was sought before the see of Crediton was
transferred to Exeter.[5] A little later, but within the same
period, the medieval series of papal privileges for English
churches begins with a letter of Victor II in favour of Chertsey
abbey.[6] After the usurpation of Benedict X, marked in relation

[1] Above, p. 217.
[2] Liebermann, *Gesetze*, ii. 2, pp. 609–10; William of Malmesbury, *Vita Wulfstani*,
ed. R. R. Darlington, p. 16.
[3] *Chronicle*, E, under 1048.
[4] *Chronicle*, D, under 1050; E, under 1047.
[5] *Ordnance Survey Facsimiles of Anglo-Saxon Manuscripts*, ii, Exeter, xiii.
[6] W. Holtzmann, *Papsturkunden in England*, i. ii, p. 221.

to England by the gift of a pallium to Stigand, the current of papal influence reaches its height during the short pontificate of Nicholas II. The privilege which he issued for Giso, bishop of Wells, is the oldest papal document which still remains in the English church to which it was directed.[1] Wulfwig, bishop of Dorchester, appealed to him against Ealdred, archbishop of York, who was attempting to acquire ecclesiastical juris-diction over Lindsey, and his judgement, giving the disputed territory to Dorchester, proved to be decisive towards the settlement of a hotly contested issue.[2] But it was in relation to Ealdred himself that his action was of most consequence. Ealdred, who had been bishop of Worcester before his elevation to York, wished to hold the two sees in combination. Ignoring many precedents, the pope made the grant of a pallium to Ealdred conditional upon his resignation of the see of Worcester, and sent two legates to England to settle the questions raised by this condition and other matters affecting the well-being of the English church. Nothing is known of their activities beyond the fact that they selected Wulfstan, prior of Worcester, as a person suitable for appointment to the vacant see.[3] But the dispatch of the commission is the most convincing proof that could be given of the interest felt at Rome in English affairs, and the assurance with which effect could be given to it.

The Anglo-Saxon church has received hard measure from historians. To many writers it has seemed that its individuality meant indifference to the movements of ecclesiastical thought then coming to influence elsewhere in the west. It has been regarded as insular in outlook, ineffective in discipline, and acquiescent in a humiliating subordination to the state. It has too often been judged by an ideal standard to which neither the Norman nor any other part of the western church conformed at the middle of the eleventh century. Through modern research something of its real quality is slowly begin-ning to appear. Much remains to be done, particularly in the analysis of the books which illustrate the Old English concep-tion of canon law. But it can already be seen that there existed in pre-Conquest England a church receptive towards foreign

[1] W. Holtzmann, *Papsturkunden in England*, 2. ii, pp. 131–2.

[2] Lincoln Cathedral, *Registrum Antiquissimum*, ed. C. W. Foster, i, pp. 186–8.

[3] The clearest account of the mission and the events which preceded it is that of William of Malmesbury, *Vita Wulfstani*, ed. R. R. Darlington, pp. 16–18.

influences, and united to the see of Rome by ancient tradition and present reverence. It had recently produced the greatest teacher of the true Dark Ages, and his pupils were continuing his work. It had created a religious literature in the native language. It had not yet lost the inspiration of the revival of religion and learning which had made its recent history illustrious. It was faithful to the memory of its great men.

XIV

ENGLAND BEFORE THE CONQUEST

I. THE PEASANTS AND THEIR LORDS

THE central course of Old English social development may be described as the process by which a peasantry, at first composed essentially of free men, acknowledging no lord below the king, gradually lost economic and personal independence. Like all attempts to reduce a complex piece of history to a formula, the description is, no doubt, over-simple. From the moment when the kings of the migration age began to plant their companions upon the soil there must have existed communities in which expropriated Britons, and Englishmen too poor to be welcomed in settlements of their own people, were working for a lord in return for his protection. At the modern end of the story, although Domesday Book gives the impression that the greater part of southern England was divided into manors inhabited exclusively by serfs and slaves, the terminology of the Survey takes little account of personal status, and leaves room for the existence of many free men who do not appear on the surface of the record. Nevertheless, the general drift of English peasant life in these centuries was undoubtedly from freedom towards servitude, and on the eve of the Norman Conquest, many thousands of Englishmen, each possessing a ceorl's wergild of two hundred shillings, were bound by a strict routine of weekly labour to the estates of private lords.

This depression was the result of several factors, of which the economic insecurity of the primitive ceorl was the most important. In open-field districts his agriculture yielded a meagre return to much effort, and in country broken up by individual enterprise he was living the life of a pioneer struggling with barren, or at least inferior, soil. For the first three centuries after the migration, except, perhaps, in Kent, the resources of the ordinary peasant can rarely have carried him far above the level of subsistence. He had few, if any, reserves from which to re-equip himself after a run of bad seasons or a plague of cattle. A band of raiders could at once reduce him to beggary, and in estimating the conditions of his life it is well to remember that in the pre-Danish period much warfare has escaped the notice of historians. It was during the years of apparent peace at the turn of the seventh and eighth centuries that St. Guthlac, in his unregenerate youth, was accustomed to lay waste his enemies' lands with fire and sword.[1] The compunction which moved him to restore a third of his booty to his victims was regarded by his biographer as a singular proof of grace. Long before the beginning of the Danish wars, which were disastrous enough to affect the whole character of rural society,[2] innumerable ceorls must have been compelled to put themselves and their households at the disposal of lords who could at least offer them food in evil days.

The drift towards subordination was accelerated in the last two centuries of Old English history. No doubt, under the stronger kings of this age, the peasant suffered less than before from the private quarrels of irresponsible noblemen. But this advantage was more than offset by the devastating passage of many Danish armies, the destruction of supplies which might fall into the enemies' hands,[3] and the new burdens laid on the peasantry by governments which were somewhat fertile in measures for national defence, but were often compelled to buy peace. The military expedients introduced by King Alfred— the building and maintenance of fortresses, the reorganization of the West Saxon militia, and its use for long-distance expeditions—cut across the agricultural life of a peasantry slowly recovering after years of war. Under Æthelred II the national economy, which still rested in the main on the taxable capacity of the peasant's holding, was strained by the need of money for the building of a fleet, the payment of Danish crews in English service, and above all, the Danegelds given to victorious Danish armies. In a state that was carrying these burdens the position of the individual free peasant landholder must have rapidly become more and more precarious. The fact that he never became extinct, even under these conditions, proves the strength of the tradition of ancient independence for which he stood.[4]

There is no direct evidence to show the stages by which,

---

[1] *Felix's Life of Saint Guthlac*, ed. B. Colgrave, p. 81.

[2] See 'The Thriving of the Anglo Saxon Ceorl' in *C.P.*, pp. 383–93.

[3] As in 1016, above, p. 389.

[4] It was even possible for individual peasants to prosper to an extent that entitled them to a thegn's rights. See *C.P.*, pp. 388–9.

within any single village, a community composed essentially of independent peasants developed into a community composed essentially of serfs. But the main features of the process seem fairly clear. In what appears to have been the normal case, it began with a grant from the king setting an ealdorman, a *gesith*, a bishop, or an abbot in his own place as the immediate lord of a village, and, in particular, as the recipient of the dues and services which its inhabitants had been accustomed to render to the king himself. The independence of the village group was not threatened at first. But the narrowness of an average ceorl's resources, and the many forms of disaster to which he was exposed, made it almost inevitable that sooner or later the village community would find itself unable to provide the food-rent which its lord had the right to demand. It was generally easier for the head of a peasant household to supply labour than to keep up a regular contribution to a communal food-rent. Most lords had need for labour on the 'demesnes' which they had been acquiring through co-operation with the village community in the extension of the cultivated area, or by the creation of home farms within a ring fence. It seems that, within most villages, the duty of supporting the lord by a communal render in kind gave way, in time, more or less completely, to a system by which each of the regular holdings in the open fields—hides, half-hides, and yardlands—supplied labour for the lord's demesne on a definite number of days in every week. In itself, the change was merely a matter of economic reorganization, which need have had no legal consequences. But in most cases it seems to have formed part of a wider revolution in which the individual peasants surrendered their holdings to the lord of the village and received them back from his hands, acknowledging themselves to be his men, and placing themselves under his protection. When this step had been taken by the whole or the greater part of a village community, the manorial economy of the middle ages was brought within sight.

Unfortunately, there are no means of determining the rate at which this development proceeded. There are no Old English parallels to the private surveys which have survived from Carolingian Gaul, and the oldest documents which describe the services due from English peasants to their lords seem to come from the generation before the Norman Conquest. The most important of them is a treatise on estate management, commonly known as the *Rectitudines Singularum Personarum*.[1] Its object was to set out the dues and services which a lord might expect to receive from the peasants grouped in various degrees of subordination around his home farm, and its author writes, not as a lawyer, but as a reeve or estate agent. After a brief description of the duties of the lord himself towards the state, it proceeds to deal with a class of men known as *geneatas*, who formed a peasant aristocracy. The *geneat* was free from week-work, and his services, though very numerous, were not of a kind that was unbecoming to a free man. He was expected to escort strangers visiting his lord, to ride, carry goods, and 'lead loads', to reap and mow on the demesne at harvest and hay-time, to keep guard near his lord's person or in his lord's stables, to go on errands 'far or near', to join with others in maintaining the hedge around his lord's house, and in cutting and erecting the fences that were necessary when his lord hunted. He paid his lord a rent, which is not described, but was probably in kind, and gave him a swine a year in return for pasture-rights. Like other free men, he paid church-scot and joined in communal alms-giving. It is clear that he does not fit at all neatly into any clear-cut scheme of social classification. He was a peasant with some of the characteristics of a mounted retainer. He is represented in the middle ages by an equally anomalous class of men called radknights or radmen, who in many parts of the country, and especially in the western midlands, formed, like him, a link between the lord's household and the peasantry. There is no doubt that in early times the personal tie between the *geneat* and his lord was much closer than in the eleventh century. The Old English *geneat* originally meant 'companion', and implies that the origin of the class lies in the lord's household. It is probable that in many, perhaps in most, cases, the holding of an eleventh-century *geneat* arose from a gift made by an early lord to one of his servants.

From the *geneat* at the summit of peasant society the *Rectitudines* passes to the *kotsetla*, who, if slaves are left out of the reckoning, may be considered to form its base. It is natural to translate *kotsetla* by 'cottager', but the translation does less than justice to the economic position of the class. Like his successor,

---

[1] Liebermann, *Gesetze*, i, pp. 444–53. The tract known as *Gerefa*, which follows in this edition (pp. 453–5), was shown by Liebermann to be an integral second part of the *Rectitudines*, dealing with the duties of the manorial reeve.

the *bordarius* or *cottarius* of Domesday Book, the eleventh-century *kotsetla* had a small share in the village arable. The compiler of the *Rectitudines* considered that in view of the constant need for his labour, he ought to have at least 5 acres. He paid no rent, but services, which, though not crushing, were certainly heavy. The *Rectitudines*, admitting that they varied from place to place, records that on some estates he must labour on every Monday in the year, and on three days a week, if not on every week-day, in August. As a day's work he was expected to reap an acre of oats and half an acre of other corn, after which the lord's reeve or other servant ought to give him a sheaf as a perquisite. If so ordered he must help to acquit his lord's demesne from such burdens as coastguard duty and services incidental to the king's sport. But he was a free man, even if the most obvious sign of his freedom was the obligation to pay church-scot, and the 'hearth-penny' which every free household sent to the chief minster of its neighbourhood on Holy Thursday.

The *kotsetlan* are followed by a class of men called *geburas*, who were obviously of fundamental importance in the economy of this ideal estate. It is implied that each of them held a yard-land—the quarter-hide which formed the typical villein tene-ment of the middle ages. In return for a holding which can rarely have exceeded 30 acres, the *gebur* was carrying a formid-able burden of rents and services. He was expected to work, as ordered, for two days on every week in the year, and for three days a week at harvest and between Candlemas and Easter. In addition to this basic routine, he was required to plough an acre a week between the first breaking-up of the soil after harvest and Martinmas, and to fetch the seed for its sowing from the lord's barn. He was also expected to plough 3 acres a year as 'boon-work' at the lord's request, 2 acres a year in return for his pasture-rights, and 3 acres a year as rent for his holding. For the last 3 acres he was bound to provide the necessary seed-corn. Between Martinmas and Easter he took his turn as a watchman at his lord's fold. His payments to his lord included ten pence a year at Michaelmas; 23 *sestars*—apparently bushels—of barley and two hens at Martinmas; and either a young sheep or two pence at Easter. Apart from all this, he paid the free house-holder's hearth-penny to the local minster, gave six pence to the swineherd when he drove the village herd to the woods, and joined with another man of his own kind in feeding one of his lord's hounds. On the other hand, the *Rectitudines* makes it clear that as a rule the lord had helped him to start life upon his holding. It is expressly stated that he ought to have received from his lord two oxen, a cow, six sheep, 7 acres already sown upon his yardland, implements for his husbandry, and furniture for his house. It followed as a natural consequence that when he died his lord was entitled to take possession of all his substance.

It seems clear that to the author of the *Rectitudines* the three classes of *geneatas*, *kotsetlan*, and *geburas* covered the great mass of the peasantry with which the reeve of an estate would ordinarily have to deal. He passes from his description of the *geburas* to a series of notes on the humbler estate servants and their perquisites, and his work ends with a long account of the manifold duties of the reeve himself. His tract is the first piece of social analysis attempted by an Englishman, and the problem of bringing his classification into relationship with the facts recorded by other authorities has naturally engaged generations of scholars. Although there has been disagreement at important points, the main results of their work are reasonably well established. There is no doubt that the *kotsetla* is the predecessor of the medieval cottager, who might possess a few acres in the open fields, but eked out his livelihood by working as a labourer for more substantial persons. An origin can easily be found for him among the younger sons of ceorls whose holdings were too small to support more than a single family. The *geneatas* of the *Rectitudines* can safely be identified with the radknights of Domesday Book and later records, and the weight of probability is certainly in favour of their descent from free peasants who had come to a better economic position than their fellows by entering a lord's service. The most difficult and important problems raised by the *Rectitudines* are centred around the peasant trembling on the verge of serfdom who appears in that document as the *gebur*.

The difficulty lies mainly in the fact that the *geburas* of the eleventh century seem to be descended from two very different social classes. Many of them were either themselves emancipated slaves or the representatives of men who had obtained their freedom in an earlier generation. In Wessex and western Mercia a class of men called *coliberti*—freed men who had been emancipated in groups—formed a considerable element in the rural population, and in two separate entries Domesday Book inserts a note to the effect that men thus described were also known as *bures* or *buri*. But a class which played the important part in rural economy attributed by the *Rectitudines* to the *geburas* cannot have been composed exclusively of manumitted slaves, and there is almost contemporary evidence that services very similar to those of the *gebur* were being exacted from men who, in origin, were unquestionably free. The ceorls of Hurstbourne Priors in Hampshire were required to pay 40 pence a year from every hide, to work for three days in every week but three throughout the year, to plough 3 acres of the lord's land in their own time and sow them with their own seed, to mow half an acre of the lord's meadow in their own time, to wash and shear the lord's sheep, and to render four cart-loads of split wood, 16 poles of fencing, two ewes with two lambs, and specified, but now indeterminable, quantities of barley, wheat, and ale.[1] In the aggregate, these services are lighter than those assigned to the *gebur* in the *Rectitudines*. It seems to be assumed that those who render them are holding hides, not yardlands, and no hint is given that the lord has provided the ceorl with an outfit, or that he will take any of the ceorl's substance upon his death. There is no reason to doubt that the Hurstbourne ceorl was farming inherited land with stock and implements that were his own property. But he was as closely involved as the *gebur* of the *Rectitudines* in an agricultural routine organized in relation to the lord's demesne and hall. A short run of bad luck; a series of poor harvests or a new demand from the king for taxes, might quickly reduce a man in his condition to complete dependence upon his lord. It is in every way probable that among the *geburas* of the eleventh century there were innumerable men of free descent, cultivating on unalterable terms family lands which they or their ancestors had been compelled to surrender into the hands of a lord in return for relief from present necessities and in the hope of future security.

The importance of this, and of the other questions of interpretation raised by the *Rectitudines*, lies in their bearing on the real nature of the society which was described, twenty years after the Conquest, in Domesday Book. The social terminology of the great survey is deceptively simple. There is little ambiguity in the terms which it applies to slaves, and to men who

[1] A. J. Robertson, *Anglo-Saxon Charters*, p. 206.

had been recently lifted out of slavery. The *servi* and *ancillae* of Domesday Book are undoubtedly male and female slaves. They are normally regarded as part of the equipment of the lord's demesne, and in most entries they can be distinguished clearly enough from the general body of the manorial peasantry. The *coliberti* can be no other than freedmen who have received holdings from the lord of the estate. But the bulk of the rural population is described in Domesday Book in the most general terms which the compilers of that record could find. In the shires which lay outside the main regions of Danish settlement it was assumed that the mass of the peasantry could be divided into two great classes. The men who fell into the higher and by far the more numerous of these groups were described as *villani*. At a later time this word became restricted to the unfree portion of the manorial peasantry, but in the eleventh century *villanus* meant no more than 'villager', and carried no suggestion of unfree status. Men who belonged to the second, and economically inferior, of the two great classes appear in Domesday Book as *bordarii* or *cottarii*; that is, simply as cottagers. But even in the south and west, where the social order was simplest, Domesday Book recognizes the existence of many men of modest condition who in one way or another stood out above these fundamental peasant masses. It mentions a large number of persons called radmen or radknights, of whom something has already been said, a much smaller number of persons called vaguely 'free men', and a few members of a class which under the name of *sochemanni*, that is, 'men under a lord's jurisdiction', played a great part in the rural economy of Danish England. Apart from the radknights, these classes are almost as vague as the lower orders of *villani* and *bordarii*, and it is very difficult to bring them to a closer definition in the light of evidence contained in Domesday Book itself. No line of research will ever give to Domesday Book the precision of a well-drafted medieval survey. But the vagueness that baffles a modern inquirer is itself a significant fact, for it reflects a society on which historical forces had been playing for many generations to the blurring of class distinctions and the confusion of personal relationships.

The confusion is at its height in relation to the *villani*, who in numbers formed the most important of all the classes recognized by Domesday Book. As a whole, the *villani* of the Survey were clearly the predecessors of medieval villeins, who spent their lives in a state of economic and personal subordination on holdings regarded in law as the property of their lords. Domesday Book, as a national survey, was not concerned with the detail of the economic relations which had arisen between the lords of manors and the peasants on their estates. But in the earliest private surveys which have survived,[1] the successors of Domesday *villani* can be recognized clearly enough in groups of men holding regular shares in the fields of their villages by services of the same order as those attributed to the Hurstbourne ceorls, or the *geburas* of the *Rectitudines*. It is probable that among the men whom Domesday Book describes as *villani*, by far the greater number were rendering labour services, which were already beginning to assume a customary nature, in return for holdings which their lords acquitted from the heaviest forms of public taxation. Within the great class of *villani* there was room for every type of dependent peasant, from the ceorl whose ancestors had lost their economic independence to the freedman planted by his lord on a portion of the demesne. But the word *villanus* was vague enough also to cover men whose absorption into the manorial routine, to say the least, was incomplete, and whose lands were still at their own disposal. In many villages in which Domesday Book mentions no peasant of higher rank than a *villanus*, medieval records reveal the existence of freeholders whose titles, to all appearance, were very ancient. In some cases there is good early evidence that a group of Domesday *villani* included men whom the *Rectitudines* would have described as *geneatas* and Domesday itself in other districts as radknights.[2] It is clear, in fact, that the word *villanus* as used in Domesday Book cannot have been in any real sense a technical term. It is, no doubt, possible to find passages which assume that a normal *villanus* will be bound to labour on his lord's land. The whole scheme of the Survey implies that, unlike the *bordarius*, or cottager, he will be holding one or other of the regular, traditional, shares into which the

---

[1] Such as those in the *Cartulary of Burton on Trent* (William Salt Society, 1916), the *Black Book of Peterborough* (Camden Society, 1849), and the unprinted Register of Shaftesbury (Harl. MS. 61).

[2] Thus, according to D.B., the population of the great manor of Reading consisted entirely of *villani* and *bordarii*. But by a charter of 1130–5 an abbot of Reading releases one of his tenants from 'a certain service called *radeniht*', which is described elsewhere in the charter as *consuetudo*, and was clearly a customary obligation (Cott. Vesp. E. xxv, f. 159 *b*).

fields of his village were divided—a yardland or half-yardland, half a hide, or even a hide itself. But for the rest it can only be said that the Domesday clerks seem to have adopted the word *villanus* as the simplest possible description of the peasant who to them was the typical villager—the man bound to supply customary labour on the lord's demesne as the holder of one of the recognized tenements on which the village economy was based. In view of the circumstances under which the survey was taken, they cannot be blamed severely if they included under this description many men whose labour services, if any, were negligible in amount, and by whom the independent traditions of ancestral ceorls were jealously preserved.

To blame the Domesday clerks for their vague terminology would be unfair for another reason. The Norman Conquest had not been followed by any revolutionary change in the character of the relationships which subsisted between lords and peasantry on their estates. In part, no doubt, this was a result of King William's insistence that the men to whom he gave lands should occupy the legal position of the Englishmen whom they supplanted. But it was much more closely connected with the fact that the Normans themselves had no clear-cut scheme of social relationships which could be applied to the peasantry of a conquered country. There was no Norman stock of well-defined terms which the Domesday clerks could use for the drawing of distinctions between one class of peasant and another. Little is known about the rights and duties of the Norman peasantry in the first half of the eleventh century. There is no Norman parallel to the *Rectitudines*, and the names which Norman charters of this period apply to different classes of peasant are bewildering in their variety. There is, indeed, much to suggest that, at least in the south and west, rural society was at once more stable and organized along clearer lines in England than in contemporary Normandy. That much of the organization was directed to the lord's profit is evident from the *Rectitudines*, and it is unlikely that a Norman lord who took possession of a well-run English estate was often tempted to undertake any drastic remodelling of the system of rents and services in operation there.

It would, no doubt, be easy to show that the economic, and even the legal, position of a large number of peasants was changed in the twenty years after the Conquest. Slavery of the thorough-going English type seems to have been a rare condition in contemporary Normandy, and there are indications that in some parts of England many slaves were emancipated by their Norman masters, and provided with houses and plots of land on which to live as dependent cottagers. There are signs of a tendency towards a fall in the number of *villani* and a corresponding increase in the number of *bordarii*—a tendency which suggests that many small landowners had been ruined by the disorders incidental to the Conquest or by the taxes imposed by the new king. Many peasants who in 1066 had been holding land immediately of the king, or as the voluntary dependants of other magnates, are represented in Domesday Book by *villani* on the estates of Norman lords. Nevertheless, these changes of individual fortune, numerous as in the aggregate they were, took place within a social framework which in all its essential features was well established before the Norman invasion.

It is clear, in fact, that for many generations before the Conquest English society had been moving towards the evolution of a manorial economy. The commissioners who took the Domesday Inquest assumed that England in King Edward's time had been divided into estates which could be described as *mansiones*, and the clerks by whom the results of the inquest were reduced to order were generally able to arrange the materials before them in terms of *maneria* which were believed to have existed in 1066. Their practice shows that it was at least possible to regard the rural economy of pre-Conquest England as organized in relation to the 'residences'—the *mansiones* or *maneria*—of persons who stood outside and above the mass of the peasantry. Englishmen themselves had been feeling their way towards some term which would express this kind of organization. Before the end of the tenth century the phrase *heafod botl*, which in itself meant no more than 'chief dwelling', was being used to cover, not only the house of a lord, but also the adjacent lands which contributed towards his maintenance. The Latin *manerium* and the French *manoir* came into currency in England, not as terms denoting an institution with which Englishmen had been unfamiliar, but because they were the words which the foreign clerks of a foreign aristocracy would most naturally apply to the commonest type of English estate.

Manerium, like *villanus*, is a vague word, and the pre-Conquest estates to which it was applied varied almost indefinitely in regard to size, structure, and internal economy. Some of them covered an appreciable part of a county, and included a large number of dependent villages, hamlets, and farms; others consisted of a few yardlands supporting lords distinguished by rank alone from the peasantry around them. It was not unusual for a pre-Conquest manor to coincide in area with the territory of a single village community; but there was nothing that can be called a general tendency towards this end, and a village of moderate size might well be divided manorially between a considerable number of unrelated lords. Many, even of the largest manors, were geographically compact, but others comprised portions of woodland lying far from the manorial centre, and there are cases in which a number of scattered villages appear in Domesday Book as a single manor because their lord has chosen to treat them as a unit for purposes of seignorial administration. In eastern England, and especially in the districts where the Danish settlement had introduced a new element of freedom into local society, many manors consisted of a central estate at which light rents were paid and occasional services rendered by a large number of virtually independent peasants dispersed in groups over a wide area. It is a further complication that even the small and compact manors which superficially resemble one another did not in fact conform to any single type. On most of them it is probable that the lord's household was maintained by the produce of a demesne on which the local peasantry—the *villani* and *bordarii*—were bound to labour. But there were also manors where no demesne had been created, and on which the peasants supported their lords by rents in money or in kind, and not by service. There are even a few entries in which Domesday Book speaks of a manor without a 'hall', or manor-house.[1] In such cases it would seem that a non-resident lord has been maintaining an estate as an economic unit without keeping up the house which would normally be the centre of its organization. But arrangements of this kind are carefully noted as exceptions to what the Domesday clerks obviously regarded as an almost universal rule. The essential feature of a manor is a lord's house.[2]

[1] e.g. D.B. i, f. 307 *b*.

[2] Thus, in a writ of King Stephen, which speaks of 'domum Walteri de Amunduuilla de Chinierbi et quicquid ad eam pertinet in Chinierbi et in Osgotebi et in Ouresbi et in omnibus aliis locis', the lord's 'house' stands for an estate which extended into more than three villages. *Ancient Charters* (Pipe Roll Society), pp. 39–40.

In several ways the manors which had belonged to Edward the Confessor, and afterwards formed the 'ancient demesne of the crown', stand apart from other estates. It has already been noted[1] that far back in the Old English period the *cyninges tun* or *regia villa*, which was the predecessor of the royal manor, had been a fundamental unit in the organization of justice and finance. It was at the *cyninges tun* that the peasants of the surrounding country had paid the food-rents by which they maintained the king, and in many cases the profits of justice in adjacent hundred courts had been rendered there. It seems that the *cyninges tun* usually contained a prison, and to judge from later evidence, the ceorls on the estate were responsible for the safe keeping of the prisoners. A remarkable law of King Alfred provides that a man who has broken his pledge must go to prison for forty days at the *cyninges tun*, and there do whatever penance the bishop has appointed for him.[2] A man whom the king set in charge of such an estate became at once an important, if subordinate, minister of government, and the reeve of a large royal manor was always a prominent figure in the shire within which it lay. In the course of the tenth century a number of royal manors acquired a new significance in the national life through the settlement of traders attracted by the better order which prevailed in the neighbourhood of a royal residence. Under Æthelred II, for example, coins were struck at places such as Bedwyn and Warminster, where the security which the king could offer to merchants, and the economic needs of communities which the king might visit at any time with a large retinue, had created local centres of monetary exchange. In 1066 many royal manors, especially in the south-western shires, contained in addition to members of the ordinary peasant classes a number of persons described as *burgenses*, whose presence illustrates still more clearly the development of economic life on the king's demesnes.

King Edward's manors, as described in Domesday Book, show other signs of their exceptional history. Most of them cover a wide area, and include farms, hamlets, and even villages, in addition to the group of dwellings around the king's hall which formed the manorial nucleus. As estates, many of them are obviously of high antiquity, and may well represent allotments made to kings in the age of the English settlement.

[1] Above, p. 300.   [2] Laws of Alfred, c. 1, 2.

There is good evidence that in the two centuries before the Conquest kings had been alienating portions of their demesnes, and it is probable that the average royal manor of 1066, for all its size, had been of still greater extent in the recent past. In proportion to their area and population most royal manors were assessed very lightly towards the Danegeld and other public burdens, and in Wessex many of them were exempt from national taxation. It seems clear that their inhabitants enjoyed this privilege because, unlike the men of other lords, they were still required to support the king himself by substantial rents in kind. In Domesday Book these payments were reckoned in terms of a unit called the *firma unius noctis*, that is the amount of provision needed to support the royal household for a single day. In central Wessex there are traces of a somewhat elaborate system by which the king's demesne estates were arranged in groups so that each group provided a day's *firma*.[1] Already before the Conquest many of these rents in kind had been commuted for money payments, and Domesday Book gives figures which show that in King Edward's time the cash equivalent of the *firma unius noctis* might amount to £80, or even more.[2] But the process of commutation was far from complete in 1066, and some ninety years later King Henry II's treasurer recorded that he had known men who had seen the customary supplies of provisions brought up to the king's court from the king's demesne manors at the appointed terms.[3]

The ecclesiastical estates of the Old English period have always interested historians. Many of them can be traced backwards by written evidence to an origin in the grant of some early king, and the documents which illustrate their history throw light on many obscure processes in the development of English society. In size and structure there was a general resemblance between the manors of the church and those of the king. The bishop of Winchester's manor of Farnham and the bishop of Salisbury's manor of Sonning were as large as any but the very greatest estates of Edward the Confessor. In the past, bishops and abbots, like kings, had been accustomed to take rents in kind from their properties, and there are many references to this practice in Domesday Book. Bayston outside

---

[1] Described by Round in *Feudal England*, p. 109 et seqq.
[2] R. L. Poole, *The Exchequer in the Twelfth Century*, pp. 27–31.
[3] *Dialogus de Scaccario*, ed. A. Hughes, C. G. Crump, and C. Johnson, p. 89.

Shrewsbury, for example, is described as belonging to the *victus*
—the *feorm*—of the bishop of Hereford in King Edward's time,
and four columns of the Hampshire survey are devoted to the
lands which in 1066 were still appropriated to the *victus* of
the monks of Winchester cathedral. On the other hand, both the
king and the great ecclesiastical landlords had been in the habit
of creating tenancies which were in effect subordinate manors
within their larger properties. By 1066, on both royal and
ecclesiastical manors, there had arisen a general distinction
between 'inland', which comprised the demesne of the lord and
the holdings of the peasants directly subject to him, and the
parts of the estate which he had granted out on varying terms to
manorial officers, personal servants, priests, or noblemen bound
to him by fealty.[1] On ecclesiastical manors the practice of
granting out portions of the inland to persons whom the lord
wished to reward, or perhaps to placate, began early, and by
1066 it had been carried to a point at which it seriously threatened the integrity of many large and ancient estates.

In early times it was never easy for a community of monks or
clergy to make full use of the property which was nominally at
its command. Its internal economy depended on the punctual
receipt of the food-rents which it was entitled to take from the
peasants on its various estates. It was difficult to organize a
staff of estate servants for this purpose, and it was often the
better course to grant an outlying property on lease to some
individual who would undertake to pay an adequate rent in
money or in kind. In Offa's reign, for example, Beonna, abbot
of Medeshamstede, granted Swineshead in Lincolnshire to a
Mercian ealdorman for his life and the lives of the heirs to whom
he might bequeath it, in return for an initial payment of a thousand shillings and an undertaking to provide the convent with a

---

[1] *Inland* was an overworked term. In addition to the meaning given above, it was
used to denote the portion of an estate by which the lord's household was maintained—a sense in which it corresponded closely to the *dominium* of medieval
records. But the ancient inland of an estate was generally exempt from taxation,
and as this privilege did not extend to peasant land taken by the lord into his own
occupation, a distinction arose between the whole demesne, thus augmented, and
the exempt inland which was its nucleus. The distinction is not often marked in
Domesday Book, but there are passages in the Oxfordshire survey which show that
it was recognized in the eleventh century (*V.C.H. Oxford*, i, pp. 393–4). It is a
further complication that in the Northern Danelaw inland was sometimes used to
cover peasant holdings which were regarded as the lord's property, in contrast to
'sokeland', which was considered to belong to the peasants seated upon it (F. M.
Stenton, *Types of Manorial Structure in the Northern Danelaw*, pp. 5–14).

day's supply of food or its money equivalent every year.[1] But the wish for a steady income was not the only motive for such transactions. They enabled a bishop or abbot to gratify his friends—the first recorded English lease was granted by Bishop Wilfrid of Worcester to a companion of Æthelbald, king of Mercia, 'on account of the old friendship between us'[2]—and to establish a permanent relationship between his church and noblemen whose influence at court might be useful. In course of time churches began to grant leases to men of a lower social rank, and by Edgar's reign the lessee's service was generally at least as important as his rent. During an episcopate of more than thirty years St. Oswald, as bishop of Worcester, carried out what must have been a fundamental change in the organization of the estates of his see by the creation of leasehold tenures.[3] It is often hard to determine the social standing of the lessees, for the word *minister*, by which most of them are described in Latin texts, could be used equally well of a servant with no more than a ceorl's wergild, and a man of noble descent who had done fealty to the bishop. But there is evidence to show that the bishop's tenants included persons of either class, and the fact that many of them received holdings amounting to an entire hamlet, or even a village, establishes the important point that as a whole they were of more than peasant status. Like most Old English leaseholds, the tenures which Oswald created were limited to three lives. But there was always a danger that a lord who had made a temporary alienation of an estate might fail to recover it when the time came, and on this account and for the settlement of disputes which had already arisen, Oswald addressed a long memorandum to King Edgar setting out the terms which he expected his tenants to observe.[4] The bishop's words are often vague, but it is clear that he regarded his tenants primarily as mounted retainers, bound, in a phrase which has become famous, 'to fulfil the law of riding as riding men should'. It was their duty to ride on his errands, to lend him their horses when he needed them, and to make fences when he wished to hunt. They helped him to meet the king's demands for service. They were required to pay him church-scot and other customary

---

[1] *C.S.* 271.　　　　　　　　　　　　　　　　[2] *C.S.* 166.
[3] On the feudal interpretation often given to these and other Old English leases see below, pp. 672–4.
[4] *C.S.* 1136.

dues. But it seems that they were also expected to find lime for the fabric of the church of Worcester and for the building of bridges; and a whole range of services of an agricultural sort may be covered by a general obligation to be obedient to the bishop's commands. In view of the social position of many of the bishop's tenants, they cannot have been subject to any unbecoming forms of personal service, and it is safe to assume that any tedious work demanded from their holdings was done by their slaves, servants, or dependent peasants. On the other hand, it is clearly significant that, as most commentators on the memorandum have observed, the conditions on which Oswald's tenants accepted their holdings strikingly resemble the services due from the *geneatas* of the *Rectitudines*. It is more than probable that Oswald, when framing a scheme of tenure for his own followers, deliberately took for his model the customary obligations of the *geneat*, who, whatever may have been his condition in the tenth century, had originally been the companion, or retainer, of a lord.

For all their variety of detail, the ecclesiastical manors of the Old English period conformed more or less to the same general type, and the development of individual estates can often be followed in contemporary documents. The manors of the lay nobility give no opportunity for any useful generalizations, and in most cases their recorded history begins in 1066. They included a number of what may be called official estates, attached to the more important ealdormanries, which resembled royal manors in size and general character. Aldermaston in Berkshire, of which the name means 'ealdorman's village', was an estate of the same type as the king's manor of Reading, which it adjoined. But in southern and western England it is probable that most of the manors which existed in 1066 go back in the last resort to estates which kings or other great men had granted to members of their households. The retainer of noble birth was at least as important a figure in the ninth and later centuries as in any earlier age. In late Old English documents he is generally described as a *thegn*, and not as a *gesith*, but the change of description did not mean any alteration in his status or in the character of his relationship to his lord. Throughout Old English history it was a social convention that a man of this class should be rewarded for his service by a grant of land, and this custom, which had led to the creation of the first private lordships, was fully operative on the eve of the Norman Conquest.

The thegn's wergild, like that of his predecessor, the *gesith*, was 1,200 shillings, and his rank was hereditary. The division of a thegn's holding between his sons, if carried out in successive generations, could only end in the creation of a number of small properties, on each of which a gentleman could barely live. Through such a process many villages had been divided by 1066 into minute fractions, held as 'manors' by thegns who, economically, were little more than peasants. On the other hand, many families had been careful to preserve the integrity of their individual estates. In the popular mind of the eleventh century the typical thegn was a man with a specific duty in the king's household, who possessed a church and a kitchen, a bell-house, a fortified dwelling-place, and an estate assessed at five hides of land.[1] In 1066 in every shire there were thegns holding manors which to all appearance answer to this description, and the manorial topography of the eleventh century has been perpetuated in innumerable villages where the lord's hall and outbuildings adjoin a church in his patronage and are surrounded by fields representing the hides which had yielded Danegeld to the kings before the Conquest.

Domesday Book rarely enters into details of manorial history, and it is often impossible to tell whether a particular manor had come to its lord from his ancestors or from a king who wished to maintain him in his service. But enough is known to show that many thegns of 1066 were holding inherited estates, and some of them were landowners on a scale which is unlikely to have been reached in a single generation. A thegn of King Edward named Ælfstan, whose chief residence was at Boscombe in Wiltshire, possessed manors not only in that county but also in Somerset, Dorset, Hampshire, Berkshire, Gloucestershire, Hertfordshire, and Bedfordshire. Many important followers of the Conqueror were less well endowed, and Ælfstan's lands formed by far the greater part of the barony which the prominent magnate, William d'Eu, was holding in 1086. Ælfstan had received one of his Wiltshire manors from his lord King Edward, but his property as a whole gives the impression of an estate which had been built up in the course of years by the successive

---

[1] Liebermann, *Gesetze*, i, p. 456. See 'The Thriving of the Anglo-Saxon Ceorl'. *C.P.*, pp. 389-90.

heads of the same family. That such estates could be created a century earlier is shown by a document through which, in 960, King Edgar restored the forfeited property of a West Saxon thegn named Wulfric.[1] It consisted of eight villages in Berkshire, five in Sussex, and two in Hampshire. Wulfric had been in the service of kings Edmund, Eadred, and Eadwig, from one or other of whom he had received six of his Berkshire manors. One of his Hampshire villages had come to him under the will of Bishop Ælfsige of Winchester, and the rest of his property seems to have been ancestral land. The reason for his forfeiture is unknown, but the list of his possessions illustrates very clearly the territorial position attainable by a king's thegn of no outstanding family at the middle of the tenth century.

The distinction between the thegn and the peasant was the fundamental line of cleavage in Old English society. In Wessex and English Mercia the thegn's wergild was six times as large as that of the ceorl. In Northumbria the difference between the wergilds was even wider.[2] It is only in Kent that the word thegn is used before the Conquest to cover men whose life was valued at a ceorl's wergild.[3] Nevertheless, the word *thegn*, which originally meant 'one who serves another', like the word *gesith*, which originally meant 'companion', marked a personal relationship rather than a social distinction, and the standing of the individual thegn was largely determined by the rank of the man to whom his service was done. The leading members of the class were naturally those who served the king himself. They attended him periodically at court, and, at least in Alfred's time, filled its various offices in rotation. They played an important part in the routine of government by keeping the king in touch with the shires, and as individuals they were used for any occasional business in which the king had a personal interest.[4] He, in turn, regarded the maintenance of their dignity as necessary for the honour of the Crown. King Edgar, after claiming for himself all the authority that Edmund, his father, had possessed, declared as a corollary that so long as he lived his thegns should enjoy the status that had belonged to them in his father's time.[5] There were wealthy men within the circle of the

---

[1] *C.S.* 1055. On the history of his lands see D. Whitelock, *Wills*, pp. 115–16.
[2] Below, p. 509.   [3] *C.D.* 731.
[4] [On the increased need for such persons from the time of King Athelstan, see 'The Thriving of the Anglo-Saxon Ceorl'. *C.P.*, pp. 390–3.]
[5] Laws of Edgar, iv, 2 *a*.

king's thegns, and they were well equipped for war. By a law of
Cnut the heirs of a thegn who stood nearest to the king were
required to give him two saddled and two unsaddled horses;
two swords; four spears and shields; a helmet, corselet, and fifty
mancuses of gold, before they took to their inheritance.[1] Something of the warlike quality of the ancient *gesith* still remained to
the king's thegn of the eleventh century.

The king's thegns were a numerous class. A single charter of
Æthelred II might well be witnessed by twenty or more of them.
But other lords than the king might have thegns in their service.
The thegns of a great earl might be an important factor in
a political crisis. One of the measures taken by Edward the
Confessor against the house of Godwine in 1051 was to cause
Earl Harold's thegns to find sureties that they would become
the king's own men.[2] The Old English document which describes the property of a thegn with a special service in the
king's hall shows that he might have thegns of his own, who
attended him when he was on duty at court, rode on his business to the king at other times, and represented him in his
pleas.[3] Domesday Book, which is the chief source of information about these lesser thegns, makes it clear that their number
was very considerable, and that their possessions were often
small. Salden in Buckinghamshire, for example, which was
assessed to Danegeld at no more than 3 hides and half a yardland, was divided in 1066 between four thegns, each of whom
was the man of a different lord.[4] Economically there can have
been little difference between these meagre thegns and the
geneatas of the *Rectitudines*. But in social standing they were sharply
distinguished from even the highest ranks of the peasantry.

Many of these thegns were holding land which they had
received from their lords. Oswald of Worcester was by no
means the only great ecclesiastic of the tenth century to realize
the advantage that might come to his church from the enfeoffment of substantial laymen as its tenants. By 1066 the tenancies
thus created within the estates of a wealthy church were commonly known as its thegnlands, a term which gives a useful
clue to the social position of their holders. The total number
of such thegnly tenants must have been very large—in 1066
fourteen thegns held land within the abbot of Glastonbury's

[1] Laws of Cnut, ii, 71 *a* 1.   [2] Below, p. 564.
[3] Liebermann, *Gesetze*, i, p. 456.   [4] D.B. i, 146 *b*.

manor of Shapwick[1] and they appear on the estates of lay, as well as ecclesiastical, magnates. But in England as a whole they were probably outnumbered by the thegns who were holding lands of their own inheritance in subordination to lords of their own choice. The distinction between these two kinds of thegnly tenure is well brought out by the language of Domesday Book. There are many thegns, generally, though not always, holding land within the ambit of some large estate, who are declared incapable of giving or selling their holdings without the leave of their lords. There are also thegns who are described as the men of greater magnates, but to whom Domesday Book expressly accords the right of alienation. In general, it seems clear that these contrasted forms of tenure represent an essential difference in the character of the relationship between the thegn and his lord. Private arrangements of the most diverse kinds were permissible before the Conquest, but in most cases there is little doubt that the thegn whose holding is inalienable has come to it through his lord's gift, and that the thegn holding land of which he can dispose at will is a landowner in his own right, who has placed himself under a lord's authority.

For more than a century before the Conquest the general trend of social development had been threatening the independence of the lesser thegns. The accumulation of estates by a small number of powerful families, which is one of the salient features of the time, gave a new emphasis to the distinction which must always have existed between the richer and the poorer members of the thegnly class. The business of the shire courts was everywhere falling into the hands of a few great men, and their predominance made the small thegn a person of little account, even in his own country. He was subject to the economic forces which were making for the general depression of the small landowner, and the military obligations implied by his rank increased the anomaly of his condition. It was only natural for a man in such a case to surrender a profitless independence in return for the protection of a lord who could at least help him to maintain his position in life. The process by which this relationship was brought into being is frequently mentioned in Domesday Book under the term *commendatio*. It was created by a ceremony of homage which

[1] D.B. i, f. 90.

bound the man to be faithful to his new lord, and it was kept
alive from year to year by payments in recognition of the lord's
superiority. The lord's reciprocal duty is never defined; but
it can be said in general terms that he was expected to identify
himself with the interests of his man, to support him in pleas,
and to use on his behalf whatever influence he might himself
possess at court or in the shires. The relationship was purely
a matter of personal arrangement, and it might assume many
different forms. The man might or might not pledge himself
to render service to his lord, to wait for his lord's licence before
he alienated his land, or to subject himself and his land to his
lord's jurisdiction. It is more remarkable that public opinion
allowed a man to commend himself simultaneously to more
than one lord. There has survived the text of a writ in which
Edward the Confessor informs the shire court of Norfolk and
Suffolk that Ælfric Modercope, an East Anglian thegn of some
importance, 'may bow to the two abbots at Bury St. Edmunds
and at Ely'.[1]

The practice of commendation was not peculiar to the thegnly
class. It is clear from Domesday Book that in 1066, among the
Anglo-Danish peasantry of East Anglia and the eastern midlands, many hundreds of free men, living on what to all appearance were inherited holdings, were 'commended' to lords whom
they themselves had chosen. The survey gives the impression
that on the eve of the Conquest, even in this unmanorialized
country, society was rapidly moving towards the evolution of a
new order, in which the authority of a lord would supersede the
influence of communal association as the controlling force in
rural life. But in this part of England the new order was still
inchoate, and the lines along which it was developing gave no
promise of the organized cohesion which marked the existing
manorial economy of the west and south, and was to distinguish
the feudal complex of rights and duties. For all the solemnity
of the act of homage by which it was created, the bond of
commendation could easily be broken. Without any breach of
law or social convention, a man who had assumed the obligations implied by commendation might well be free, in the words
of Domesday Book, 'to go with his land to whatever lord he
would'. Here, at least, there was as yet no general feeling that
the various private dues and services that might issue from a

[1] *C.D.* 877.

particular holding should all be concentrated in the hands of a single lord. Above all, there was no anticipation of the momentous feudal tendency towards the association of lordship with jurisdiction.

The origin of private justice is one of the unsolved problems of Anglo-Saxon history. The research of many scholars has failed to find any text earlier than the middle of the tenth century which explicitly assigns the right of holding a court to any lord other than the king. The argument for the existence of private courts at an earlier date than this turns essentially on the interpretation of a number of obscure and often ungrammatical phrases which occur in royal charters of the pre-Alfredian time. It has already been observed that the kings of this period, when granting land by charter, frequently declared that the land should be exempt from all public burdens except the obligation of finding a contingent for service in the national militia, and labour for the repair of bridges and fortresses. There is no doubt that, by virtue of this exemption, land which had formerly been required to furnish a contribution to the king's *feorm*, and to provide entertainment for his servants, was freed from these charges for the benefit of its new lord. The question is whether its inhabitants were still expected to attend the ancient popular assemblies of their country, or segregated into courts where they settled their private disputes, and imposed penalties for the misdeeds of individuals, under the supervision of their lord's ministers.

It is at least clear that the lord of a privileged estate often took the profits of justice arising from cases in which one of its inhabitants was involved. In a series of charters which begins in Offa's reign it is repeatedly declared that nothing is to be paid from an estate 'by way of penalty'. The meaning of this exemption is made clearer by a number of charters which provide that when an outsider has been wronged by a man dwelling within the estate, no fine shall be exacted for the offence by any external power, although the injured party must receive compensation to the value of that which has been taken from him unjustly. As there can have been no intention that theft or the wrongful detention of property should go unpunished, there can be no doubt that a fine will be imposed on the offender, and the purport of the charters makes it plain that the fine will be received by the lord of the estate within which the offender is living. What the charters fail to make clear is the nature of the court before which the offender will be brought for judgement. Some scholars maintain that the lord in such cases is merely the recipient of fines imposed by a public assembly, or folkmoot. To others it seems more probable that a lord who was empowered to receive fines was, by that very circumstance, empowered to hold a court in which they could be imposed. That private courts were, in fact, being held in this period is made almost certain by a group of charters which in everything but explicit statement confer the right of doing justice on the hand-having thief.[1] In a charter of 816 to the bishop of Worcester Cenwulf, king of Mercia, prescribes: 'if a bad man is taken three times in open wickedness, let him be delivered up at a royal village.'[2] It is hard to construe this clause otherwise than as an oblique acknowledgement that a criminal whose guilt is apparent may be allowed to answer for two separate offences in a court composed of the bishop's men before he is surrendered to a royal officer to be held for final judgement in a popular assembly.

But the argument for the existence of private courts in the eighth and ninth centuries does not entirely rest on the interpretation that may be given to these ambiguous texts. Private jurisdiction has many roots, and some of them were closely interwoven into the structure of primitive English society. The authority of the head of a household over the men and women who composed it, and the authority of a lord over his retainers, laid on the lord and the householder at least a measure of responsibility for the good behaviour of their dependants. A passage in Ine's laws[3] shows that in the seventh century a nobleman was expected to keep the members of his household from wrongdoing, and that if he failed in this duty, although he might make terms with the king, the king's ealdorman, or his own lord on their behalf, he would not be entitled to any portion of the fines which were laid on them. The coercive power of a man of position over his dependants, which is explicitly recognized in this law, shades off by imperceptible degrees into the right of holding a court in which they can be restrained from misdoing, and their misdeeds can be corrected before they have come under the cognizance of public authorities. There is no direct evidence that such courts were already

---

[1] i.e., one taken in possession of stolen goods.   [2] *C.S.* 357.   [3] c. 50.

in being in Ine's time, but the situation disclosed by his laws makes it unlikely that another century passed before their appearance. That the private court was a familiar institution before the accession of King Alfred is suggested by a curious passage which forms an historical introduction to his own code.[1] After referring to the spread of Christianity throughout the world, he observes 'Then were many synods of holy bishops and illustrious counsellors assembled over the whole world, and also in England. In the mercy which Christ taught, they ordained that without sin, secular lords, with their leave, might take from first offenders the emendation in money which they then prescribed, saving that they dare not appoint any mercy for the betrayal of a lord since almighty God appointed none for those who despised him.' It has been pointed out that, in describing the 'secular lords' who have the discretion of mercy, the king uses the most general language at his command —language which seems deliberately chosen so as to bring under a single term ealdormen and reeves in charge of public courts and unofficial noblemen administering private justice.[2]

For all their allusiveness, these passages show that the idea of private jurisdiction was at least in the background of men's minds before the age of Alfred. Conclusive evidence that private courts were in existence has begun to appear within sixty years of Alfred's death. Its emergence is due to the fact that, through the exceptional nature of the properties which they were describing, certain clerks writing charters for Kings Eadwig and Edgar found it necessary to supplement the conventionalized Latin of the ordinary land-book by English words of which the meaning could not be in doubt. In the common speech of the period 'jurisdiction', an abstract concept for which there was no familiar English term, was represented by the alliterative pair of concrete words *sacu* and *socn*. Intrinsically, the first of these words denoted a 'cause', or matter in dispute, and the second, the act of 'seeking' a lord, or a formal assembly. But by the tenth century these words had come to be used colloquially without any thought of ultimate derivations, and the statement that a lord of an estate had *sacu* and *socn*—the 'sake and soke' of modern historians—simply meant that he had the right of holding a court which his tenants were required to attend. The phrase is first used in a charter of 956, by which

[1] Liebermann, *Gesetze*, i, pp. 44–6.   [2] Ibid. ii. 2, p. 457.

King Eadwig granted Southwell in Nottinghamshire to Archbishop Osketel of York.[1] Southwell was an estate of a type
common in the Danelaw but comparatively rare in southern
England, in which a number of large but dependent villages
were grouped around a central property. In several of these
villages the lands which were to pass to the archbishop were
intermingled with the lands of other owners, and it was important to find some phrase to express the unity of the whole estate.
The statement 'These are the villages which belong to Southwell
with sake and soke' shows that the entire group of villages was
subject to a court held for the archbishop in Southwell, and
provides the earliest unequivocal reference to the exercise of
jurisdiction by a lord of lower rank than the king.

If the right of private jurisdiction were to be allowed to any
of the king's subjects, the archbishop of York was one of the
first persons who might expect to possess it. But three years
after the grant of Southwell to Archbishop Osketel the same
right was given to a lady who may have been of local importance, but was certainly not a national figure. In 959 Edgar,
when king of the Mercians and Northumbrians, granted Howden in south Yorkshire to a matron named Quen.[2] Howden,
like Southwell, was an estate which included a number of
distinct centres of population. Eight dependent villages were
attached to it, and the charter states that all of them 'belong
to Howden with sake and soke'. Here, as in the Southwell
charter, it is evident that sake and soke are only mentioned
because the peculiar structure of the estate made it desirable
to note the fact that it formed a unit of private jurisdiction.
The unemphatic way in which each of these charters refers to
the privilege of private justice is highly significant. It shows
that neither Eadwig nor Edgar felt that he was creating a
precedent by these grants. It also raises a very strong presumption that the right of keeping a court was already regarded as a
privilege which the holder of an estate under a royal charter
would exercise as a matter of course.[3]

During the century before the Conquest documents written

[1] *C.S.* 1029: see *C.P.* 'The Founding of Southwell Minster', pp. 364-70.
[2] *C.S.* 1052.
[3] [When Edgar states (Liebermann, *Gesetze*, i, p. 200) that a judge who gives a
false judgement is liable to forfeit his 'thegnship', he appears to have in mind the
owner of a private court, not only a royal official; in the latter case one would have
expected him to use a word meaning 'office' (e.g. *folgaþ*), not 'thegnship'.]

in English appear in steadily increasing number, and frequent references to sake and soke, or elliptically, but with the same meaning, to soke alone, show the widespread prevalence of private justice. In a memorandum of approximately the year 975 Archbishop Oswald of York states that his estate at Sherburn in Elmet had lost half the soke which had once belonged to it.[1] His meaning seems to be that half the villages from which suitors had once come to the court at Sherburn had fallen back under the jurisdiction of public courts, or had been annexed for the purposes of jurisdiction to the estates of other lords. In the same document he states that an estate centred at Helperby, which had come to Osketel, his predecessor, through the forfeiture of its owners, included three other villages, and 'soke' over a fourth. Under Æthelred II a northern magnate named Styr, son of Ulf, records that he had prevailed on the king to give Darlington to St. Cuthbert with sake and soke, and that he had himself bought other properties for the saint, of which one, at least, was to be subject to the saint's courts of justice.[2] At the beginning of the eleventh century Wulfric 'Spot', a wealthy thegn of the northern Danelaw, bequeathed to the abbey of Burton on Trent Morton in Derbyshire 'and all the soke which belongs to it'.[3] The fact that all these references come from northern England does not mean that private justice was unfamiliar in Wessex and English Mercia. There is no reason to doubt the tradition that the bishop of Worcester's great judicial liberty of Oswaldslow assumed its medieval shape in the time of King Edgar.[4] What the insistence on soke in northern documents really implies is that in the confusion of relationships caused by the Scandinavian invasions the judicial power of the greater lords was the most effective among the forces which were making in the tenth century for the consolidation of estates.

In all these documents soke is regarded in its territorial aspect, as a right to be exercised over a particular village or group of villages. But in real life jurisdiction is exercised over persons, not places, and the conception of soke as a form of authority possessed by one man over another is brought out clearly in other records. It underlies a law of Æthelred II commanding

---

[1] C.S. 1278; A. J. Robertson, *Anglo-Saxon Charters*, liv.

[2] *Symeonis Mon. Opera*, i, pp. 212–13.   [3] D. Whitelock, *Anglo-Saxon Wills*, p. 48.

[4] F. W. Maitland, *Domesday Book and Beyond*, pp. 267–9.

that no one shall have soke over a king's thegn except the king himself,[1] and it governs the wording of the first known writ issued by an English king for the purpose of granting judicial authority to a subject.[2] In this document Cnut declares that Archbishop Æthelnoth of Canterbury, over his own men, his cathedral church, and such thegns as the king has released to him, shall be entitled to his sake and soke, to the right of doing justice on thieves taken in the act, and to jurisdiction in regard to the harbouring of outlaws, ambush, forcible entry into a house, and breach of the king's special peace. It is probable that jurisdiction of this extensive scope was only allowed to a small number of exalted persons. The last four offences formed the nucleus of the long list of especially grave crimes which medieval lawyers described as pleas of the Crown. In his laws Cnut reserves them to his own jurisdiction[3] unless he chooses to give cognizance of them to anyone as a mark of unusual honour. The writ by which he allowed this power to Archbishop Æthelnoth is a remarkable illustration of the extent to which the mediatization of justice was possible half a century before the Norman Conquest.

The bare statement that a lord has sake and soke over his property or his men tells nothing about the range or the character of the jurisdiction which belonged to him. Its general nature is most clearly shown in an alliterative phrase which is first recorded in the reign of Edward the Confessor, but became in the Norman age the accepted formula for the description of a baron's judicial rights. Old Windsor and Staines, for example, were given by the Confessor to his abbey of Westminster with a declaration that the monks should hold these places 'with sake and with soke, with toll and with team, and with infangenetheof.'[4] These words should not be regarded as an attempt to define the powers which they expressed. They were obviously taken over by the king's writing-office from the speech of common men, and they only give the popular impression of the kind of judicial authority which generally belonged to a great lord. But the common men who attended the courts of great lords were well qualified to speak about the kind of

[1] iii Æthelred, c. 11.
[2] J. Earle, *A Hand-Book to the Land-Charters, and other Saxonic Documents*, pp. 232–3.
[3] Together with neglect of fyrd-service, ii Cnut, c. 12.
[4] *C.D.* 886.

business transacted there, and it is probable that the rhythmic phrase which they evolved gives the essential facts about the private justice which they knew.

Naturally, these facts give only the barest outline of the field which private justice covered.[1] The words 'sake and soke', which, if they need a translation, can best be rendered by 'cause and suit', tell nothing about the functions of the court of which they imply the existence. It is only the practice of later times which suggests that the jurisdiction of an Anglo-Saxon lord covered pleas of land arising among the free peasants on his estate as well as the misdemeanours and the breaches of agrarian routine which formed the staple of manorial justice. 'Toll and team'—the second pair of words—give a more definite impression. They were connected by sense as well as by alliteration, for *toll* in this context denoted the right to take a payment on the sale of cattle or other goods within an estate; *team* denoted the right to hold a court in which men accused of wrongful possession of cattle or goods could prove their honesty; and the best proof was the open testimony of witnesses who had seen the payment of toll when the disputed chattels were acquired. *Infangenetheof*, the word which concludes the formula, has no ambiguity. It simply denoted the right of doing justice on a thief taken within the estate in the possession of stolen property. No society which allowed the intervention of the private lord in the administration of justice could have withheld a privilege of this fundamental kind, and there is something approaching direct evidence that infangenetheof was one of the rights which had belonged to the greater magnates of pre-Alfredian England.[2]

It is difficult to come to any definite opinion about the number of men and women who possessed these rights on the eve of the Norman Conquest. Domesday Book, which is the chief source of knowledge about the landowners of 1066, is very erratic in its reference to their judicial powers. It shows that, in the aggregate, a considerable number of thegns—generally, but by no means always, men of large possessions—held particular manors 'with sake and soke'. But the private landowner's rights of jurisdiction lay outside the main purpose of the Survey, and its compilers recorded them or omitted them

[1] F. M. Stenton, *The First Century of English Feudalism*, ed. 2 (1961), pp. 100–4.
[2] Above, p. 493.

as they pleased when describing individual estates. In regard to Kent, for example, where the body of the county survey never hints that any lay lord of this period had kept his own court, a prefatory note supplies the names of fourteen men and one woman who had possessed sake and soke in the lathes of Sutton and Aylesford.[1] Lists of this kind are rarely given, and the contemporary documents which have come down from the years before the Conquest are far too few to compensate for their absence. It is probable that historians, influenced, perhaps unconsciously, by the meagreness of the information supplied by Domesday Book about the lords of courts, have always tended to underestimate their number.

In this connection, it is essential to distinguish between the lords whose jurisdiction did not reach beyond infangenetheof and those who possessed an interest in the pleas of the Crown. There can be no question that in 1066 many lords were receiving the forfeitures incurred by their own men for offences of the kind which Cnut had reserved for his own justice. Domesday Book frequently refers to certain 'forfeitures' of which, it is implied, the king will normally take the issues, but it also shows that King Edward had allowed this right to most of his greater churches and to many of his greater nobles. The list of offences for which a lord thus endowed might take the forfeitures varies between one district and another. It generally included breach of the king's special peace, ambush and treacherous manslaughter, the reception of outlaws, violent entry into a house, and neglect of a summons to the militia, but it might well be shorter than this. Edward the Confessor allowed the abbot of Abingdon to add only breach of the king's peace, forcible entry, and ambush to the matters of criminal jurisdiction which were covered by the traditional sake and soke, toll and team, and infangenetheof.[2] It is also hard to draw a clear line between the lords who dealt with these more serious offences in their own courts, and those who merely received the forfeitures of their men after they had been tried in the court of a hundred, a shire, or a borough. On the whole, it seems that most of the private courts which handled these graver matters were courts of hundreds or groups of hundreds which had come into the hands of subjects through a royal grant—such as the abbot of Abingdon's hundred of

[1] D.B. i, f. 1 b.   [2] C.D. 888.

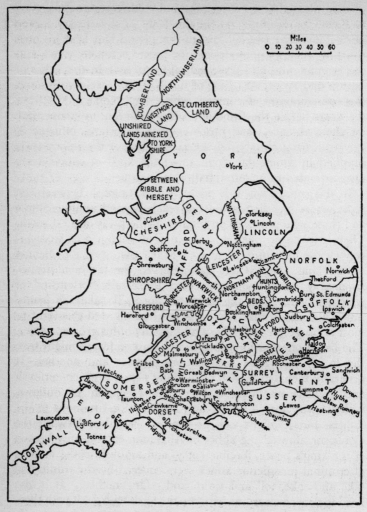

OLD ENGLISH SHIRES AND MINTING PLACES

Hormer in Berkshire,[1] the abbot of Chertsey's hundred of Godley in Surrey,[2] and the bishop of Worcester's triple hundred of Oswaldslow.[3] In many, and perhaps in most, of these cases the lord for whom the hundred court was held was either directly, or through tenants to whom he had given leases, the lord of the various villages of which the hundred was composed. But it was possible for a lord to obtain the right of holding a court for a hundred in which there were independent land-owners of high position. The great pre-Conquest 'liberty' of the abbot of Bury in west Suffolk consisted of a group of eight and a half hundreds within which, as was recorded in the eleventh century, 'Saint Edmund has the whole sake and soke and all royal customs over the land of every man, whoever may possess it.'[4] On the other hand there were hundreds under private lordship from which, so far as can be seen, the king himself had been accustomed to receive, and had therefore been entitled to grant, merely a portion of the forfeitures arising within the jurisdiction of the hundred-court. There are various passages in which Domesday Book assigns to the king two-thirds only of these forfeitures, leaving the 'third penny' to the local earl. It is evident that where this division had once prevailed, a bishop or nobleman who had become lord of the hundred-court cannot have received a higher proportion of its judicial issues than the 'two pennies' which had belonged to the king,[5] and that he must have been closely watched in the exercise of his jurisdiction by men whose duty it was to protect the earl's financial interests. Amid these complications, which become more intricate the more closely Domesday Book is studied, the one generalization that can safely be made about these matters of higher jurisdiction is that no lord—lay or ecclesiastical—could have entertained them save in virtue of an express or implied grant by the king.

It would be unsafe to apply this generalization to the lesser justice which did not stretch beyond infangenetheof. It is probable that many of the thegns to whom Domesday Book attributes sake and soke could have shown a writ of King Edward authorizing them to exercise this right. But the number of persons who are known to have possessed it suggests that it

[1] C.D. 840.   [2] C.D. 849.   [3] D.B. i, f. 172 b.
[4] Feudal Documents from the Abbey of Bury St. Edmunds, ed. D. C. Douglas, p. 9.
[5] As in the Bishop of Lincoln's wapentake of Well, D.B. i, f. 376.

more often came to a man through inheritance, together with
the land within which it was to be employed. To say the least,
it is unlikely that each of the fifteen persons who had sake and
soke in western Kent[1] derived the privilege from a separate
writ of King Edward. In this connection it is significant that
in a pre-Conquest formula composed for the benefit of a man
whose land is claimed by another, he is made to reply that he
himself desires nothing from his adversary, 'neither *læth*[2] nor
land, nor sake nor soke', nor does he intend to give him anything.
In this context sake and soke appears clearly enough as a
privilege annexed to an estate by custom rather than a royal
grant. The common use in the Norman age of the Old English
heall gemot—as 'hall-moot'—to denote a manorial court points,
again, to the familiarity of such courts before the Conquest.
It is probable that under Edward the Confessor, as under the
Norman kings, the jurisdiction covered by sake and soke, toll,
team, and infangenetheof was a privilege which any man of
rank and consequence would naturally enjoy.

2. THE DANELAW

On the eve of the Norman Conquest the local divisions
through which England was governed in the middle ages had
already been drawn in outline in all but the remotest parts of
the land. Everywhere south of the Humber England was
divided into counties. The English frontier towards Wales was
ill defined, but in the midlands, the east, and the south the
counties of 1066, with few exceptions, possessed the boundaries
which they were to keep until the administrative changes of
modern times. The only county which has since arisen in this
part of England is the anomalous shire of Rutland, of which the
southern half, in King Edward's day, was an integral part of
Northamptonshire, and the northern half formed a great
'liberty', detached from the organization of the neighbouring
shires for the benefit of its lady, Queen Edith. The old Northumbrian kingdom had never been divided systematically into
shires. The lands between the Ribble and the Mersey were

---

[1] Above, p. 499.

[2] *Læth* in this passage seems to represent the Old Norse *lap*, 'land', and to be
introduced into the formula for the sole purpose of providing an alliterative pair
of words.

annexed to Cheshire, but were administered separately for the king as dependencies of six great royal manors, at each of which rents were paid and personal services were rendered by a land-owning population of little wealth but more than peasant status, described in Domesday Book as thegns and 'drengs'. Beyond the Ribble the north of what is now Lancashire, the south of Westmorland, and the south-west of Cumberland were attached to Yorkshire, the one part of Northumbria into which the southern institutions of the shire town and the shire court had been introduced by this date. Beyond the Tees a group of liberties within which all manner of pleas and forfeitures belonged to St. Cuthbert's church formed the nucleus of the future county of Durham. Northumberland, the valley of the upper Eden which was the original Westmorland, and northern Cumberland were, in effect, border provinces in 1066, and it is probable that responsibility for their internal order, as for their defence, rested with the great lords of the country.[1]

With the exception of the Danish shires of north-east Mercia every county south of the Mersey and the Humber was divided into hundreds. As an administrative division the hundred was far less stable than the shire. In the middle ages many new hundreds were created, and the boundaries of ancient hundreds were often modified, in the interest of lords who possessed extensive rights of jurisdiction and wished to bring their men together in courts, held in their own names, but carrying the prestige of public authority. The fact that changes of this kind had begun before the Conquest is good evidence of the vitality of the Old English hundredal organization. Here and there in the more populous counties of the south, administrative geography was complicated by the existence of divisions intermediate between the hundred and the shire. The lathes of Kent, of which six are mentioned in Domesday Book, descend, no doubt with many changes of boundary, from the archaic *provinciae* of the independent Kentish kingdom. The development of the Kentish hundreds and the extension of manorial economy and jurisdiction had deprived these ancient institutions of many of their primitive functions, and it is as the unit which governed the

---

[1] Such, at least, is the impression given by the charter of Cospatric to Thorfin mac Thore, *The Ancestor*, vii. 244–7. ([F. E. Harmer, *Anglo-Saxon Writs*, pp. 419–24, 531–6] *E.H.R.* xx (1905), pp. 61–5), which is the most important of the few early documents relating to this region.

assessment of Kent to public taxation that the lathe is of most significance in the eleventh century. There is little, if any, doubt that the division of Sussex into six rapes had been carried out before the Conquest, though the term is not mentioned in any Old English record. The rapes of Sussex have a more artificial appearance than the lathes of Kent, and at the date of Domesday Book each of them was organized as a compact feudal castlery for the defence of the land. On the other hand the term 'rape', which seems to have been derived from the primitive Germanic custom of enclosing the precinct of a court with ropes, suggests that the institution was ancient, and that a popular assembly was its essential feature. Elsewhere in southern England, although hundreds were frequently combined into groups, of which some may well stand for ancient *provinciae*, the grouping was never carried out systematically over an entire county, and the local divisions to which it gave rise are too irregular to be brought into line with the rapes of Sussex or the lathes of Kent.

In the counties of Lincoln, Nottingham, Derby, and Leicester, and in the North and West Ridings of Yorkshire,[1] the local divisions in which villages were combined for the administration of justice were known as wapentakes. In the Scandinavian north the word *vápnatak*, from which the Old English *wæpentac* is derived, denoted the symbolical flourishing of weapons by which a public assembly confirmed its decisions. The extension of the word to cover both the assembly itself and the district from which its suitors came is a development peculiar to the Danish colonies in England. The word first appears in 962, when King Edgar refers in general terms to the buying and selling of goods 'in a borough or in a wapentake'.[2] Before 992 a Northamptonshire document records that 'the whole wapentake' secured the abbot of Peterborough in his title to certain lands,[3] and in an early code of Æthelred II the wapentake court appears as the fundamental unit in the organization of justice throughout

[1] The North, East, and West Ridings of Yorkshire have parallels south of the Humber in the North, West, and South Ridings of the part of Lincolnshire which had once formed the kingdom of Lindsey. The word Riding represents an Anglo-Scandinavian *thrithing*, equivalent to the Old Norse *þriðjungr*, 'third part'. The divisions themselves were clearly of Danish origin. It is evident from Domesday Book and later records that in Lindsey as in Yorkshire they had an important function as units of local government.

[2] Laws of Edgar, iv. 6.   [3] *C.S.* 1130.

the territory of the Five Boroughs.[1] There seems to have been no essential difference of function between the courts of the wapentake and hundred. It is significant that as late as the eleventh century the same district could be described indifferently as a hundred or a wapentake. According to the text of Domesday Book the East Riding of Yorkshire was divided into hundreds, but one of these divisions is expressly described as a wapentake in an appendix of disputed claims.[2] In the Northamptonshire Domesday the district which now forms the southern part of Rutland appears five times as the 'wapentake' and three times as the 'hundred' of Witchley. In the end the question whether a particular judicial district in this part of England would be permanently known as a wapentake or a hundred was settled, not by anything distinctive in the character of its court, but by the relative strength of the Danish and English strains in the local population.

Above the administrative units of the wapentake, the hundred, and the shire, there arose a threefold division of England based on diversities of legal custom. It first appears in the laws of Cnut, where the king, when enumerating the pleas reserved to his own justice, is careful to distinguish between his position as sovereign in Wessex, Mercia, and the 'Danelaw'. It is emphasized in the early Norman compilation generally called the Laws of William the Conqueror, and it is brought into relation to the administrative geography of the age in a number of tracts which name the counties grouped under the law of the West Saxons, the Mercians, or the Danes. According to these lists the sphere of West Saxon law comprised Kent, Surrey, Sussex, Berkshire, Hampshire, Wiltshire, Dorset, Somerset, and Devon; that of Mercian law comprised Oxfordshire, Warwickshire, Gloucestershire, Worcestershire, Herefordshire, Shropshire, Staffordshire, and Cheshire; and the rest of England, beginning with Buckinghamshire, Middlesex, and Essex, and ending with Yorkshire, formed the Danelaw. The debatable land beyond Yorkshire, in which shires of the southern type had never been created, had no place in a scheme which presupposed the existence of public courts, versed in the interpretation of inherited custom; and one of the lists expressly states that

---

[1] Laws of Æthelred, iii.

[2] The *Toreshou Hundred* of i, f. 307 is identical with the *Toreshou Wapentac* of i, f. 373.

Northumberland, Lothian, Westmorland, and Cumberland fell outside the region covered by the three recognized laws.

The recorded points of difference between Mercian and West Saxon law are few and technical. The chief of them is the rule that a man who had undertaken to produce a suspected criminal in court forfeited £2 to the king in Mercia, and £4 in Wessex, if the suspect escaped before trial.[1] There is no reason to think that the structure of society in Wessex and Mercia had ever differed in such a way as to produce any far-reaching distinctions between Mercian and West Saxon law. In private documents of the Norman age it is generally impossible to decide on internal evidence whether a particular estate lay in Wessex or in English Mercia, and Domesday Book, which employs a uniform terminology in relation to each of these countries, suggests very strongly that their social systems were virtually identical. The line of regional distinction which was all-important in eleventh-century England was that which separated Wessex and English Mercia, jointly, from the Danelaw.

Many scholars have urged the unreality of a scheme which unites Buckinghamshire with Yorkshire in a single province. It should be said at once that there were very important differences, both of race and social organization, between one part of the Danelaw and another. Place-names of Scandinavian origin, which prove that the northern half of the Danelaw had been the field of an intensive Danish settlement, are extremely rare in the counties of the south-eastern midlands. The masses of free peasants which give a distinctive character to the Domesday economy of Lincolnshire, Nottinghamshire, and Leicestershire, are represented in the southern Danelaw by a small and insecure minority of the rural population. Nevertheless, these differences do not affect the details of rule and procedure which caused the whole of eastern England, from the Thames to the Tees, to be regarded as the sphere of a distinctive form of customary law.[2] The prevalence of Danish custom within a particular district does not mean that it had been colonized in force by Danish settlers. The establishment of a Danish aristocracy which controlled the course of business in the local courts would be hardly less effective than the settlement of an army

---

[1] *Leis Willelmi*, 3–3.2 (Liebermann, *Gesetze*, i, pp. 494–6).
[2] Liebermann, *Gesetze*, ii. 2, pp. 347–8.

in imprinting a Danish character on the law of a shire. The eleventh-century writers who described the greater part of eastern England as the Danelaw were not theorizing about the racial composition of its inhabitants. They were simply record-ing the fact that the customary law observed in the shire courts of this region had acquired a strong individuality from the Danish influences which had once prevailed there.

The men who drafted compilations of English law under the Anglo-Danish and Anglo-Norman kings were well aware of this individuality. They often state that a particular custom pre-vails 'in the Danelaw' or 'among the Danes'. Many of these customs relate to details of procedure which were highly im-portant to men and women engaged in pleas, but have little significance in themselves. Others reflect distinctive social conceptions. It was not a mere technicality that in the Danelaw the compensation to be paid to a lord for the slaughter of one of his men varied in accordance with the dead man's rank, whereas in Wessex and English Mercia it varied in accordance with the rank of his lord.[1] Among matters of greater moment the most interesting is the high scale of the fines exacted in the Danelaw for offences of the kind which the king considered to be within his own jurisdiction, such as the breach of his hand-given peace, bloodshed on highways, and attacks on houses. For the gravest of these crimes the custom of the Danelaw prescribed fines which were out of all proportion to those imposed elsewhere, and in some cases were so heavy that they must have been laid on districts rather than individuals. Many crimes of less account, for which Saxon and Mercian law appointed specific penalties, were treated in the Danelaw as breaches of the peace at large, and punished as such by a stereotyped fine—the *lahslit* of late Old English codes—which was graded in accordance with the offender's rank. *Lahslit* is a Scandinavian loan-word, and the custom which it denoted is a remarkable illustration of the strength of Scandinavian legal tradition in the local courts of the eleventh-century Danelaw. Now and then some peculiar feature of Danelaw custom attracted the attention of the West Saxon court. In one of the last codes issued in the name of Æthelred II the king is congratulated on abolishing the unjust practice by which 'in the north' a charge of homicide brought against an innocent person could not be rebutted if it had been

[1] *Leges Edwardi Confessoris*, 12.3–12.5 (Liebermann, *Gesetze*, i. 638).

made on oath on the day when the victim died.[1] The author of the code expressed the hope that the king would be able to abolish other northern iniquities. But the invasions which ended in his overthrow were beginning, and there is no sign that any later Old English king ever tried to change the custom of the Danelaw by an act of state.

No general description of this custom has been preserved, and the history of the Danelaw makes it very unlikely that such a statement could ever have been composed. Historically, the Danelaw falls into four main regions: Northumbria; the shires dependent on the Five Boroughs of Lincoln, Nottingham, Derby, Leicester, and Stamford; East Anglia; and the south-eastern midlands. To organize these regions as a single province was beyond the power of any Anglo-Saxon government. Each of them developed its own form of social economy, and the details of the law by which they were governed must have varied widely between one district and another. The only parts of the Danelaw from which pre-conquest custumals have survived are Northumbria and the territory of the Five Boroughs. Northumbrian custom is illustrated by a list of wergilds prevailing within the Scandinavian kingdom of York,[2] a list of penalties imposed on those who broke the peace of the greater northern churches,[3] and a document known as the 'Northumbrian Priests' Law',[4] which contains a set of rules for the conduct of the northern clergy, followed by a code enforcing the payment of ecclesiastical dues and the observance of the canonical law of marriage upon the laity. The custom of the Five Boroughs is known in some detail through a very remarkable code of Æthelred II.[5] It was issued at Wantage in Berkshire, but it is only touched at occasional points by southern influences. Its terminology is essentially Scandinavian, and it was plainly intended to give the authority of a ruler who was universally regarded as king of all England to the existing practice of the local courts between the Welland and the Humber. In the whole of English legal history there is no other document which shows so elaborate a recognition of provincial custom by the central government.

The early list of Northumbrian wergilds shows a grading of ranks to which there is no exact parallel elsewhere. Its singu-

---

[1] v Æthelred, 32. 4.   [2] Liebermann, *Gesetze*, i, pp. 458–60.
[3] Ibid., p. 473.   [4] Ibid., pp. 380–5.   [5] Ibid., pp. 228–33.

larity is increased by the fact that the wergilds are expressed not, as usual, in shillings, but in terms of an ancient unit of account known as the thrymsa, which seems to have been equivalent to three silver pennies. At the bottom of the scale the ceorl's life was valued at 266 of these units—a sum which comes very near to the Mercian ceorl's wergild of 200 shillings of four pence each. Among the nobility the thegn, whose life was usually valued at six times that of the ceorl, is credited with the much larger wergild of 2,000 thrymsas, which is also assigned to the 'mass-thegn' or priest. Above the thegn, a wergild of 4,000 thrymsas is attributed to the king's high-reeves and to noblemen of an exalted class who are described as 'holds'. The wergild of an ealdorman or bishop was 8,000 thrymsas, that of an archbishop or king's son was 15,000 thrymsas, and the king's own life was valued at 30,000 thrymsas, of which half was regarded as his wergild and the other half as reparation for the affront to the royal dignity given by his slaying. The most interesting feature of this very unusual system is the appearance of a class of noblemen intermediate between the thegn and the ealdorman. The term *hold* which is applied to the individual member of this class is of Scandinavian origin. It occurs several times in contemporary narratives of the early Danish wars. Two men thus described were killed at the battle of the Holme, and five others at the battle of Tettenhall. The 'holds' are separately mentioned among the leaders in the Danish army which submitted to Edward the Elder in 914. The class included men of great territorial power. The *hold* whose lordship is recorded in the name Holderness must have been dominant throughout south-eastern Yorkshire. Thurbrand the Hold who murdered Earl Uhtred of Northumbria in 1016 seems to have been the equal of his enemy in everything but rank. It is probable that many of the large and composite estates characteristic of the eleventh-century Danelaw came into existence through the grouping of Danish colonists in village settlements around the residence of a nobleman of this class whom they regarded as their lord.

The Wantage code of Æthelred II was not concerned with the stratification of society. Its purpose was to record the assent of the king and his council to a miscellaneous set of local customs. The most important were those which related to the keeping of the peace, and it so happens that their character

illustrates the organization of the province to which the code
refers. It begins with the statement that no amends could be
allowed for a breach of the peace which the king had given
with his own hand—presumably through the issue of a writ. It
then states the fine for breaking the peace which the ealdorman
or king's reeve had given in the general assembly of the Five
Boroughs, and passes on to the fines for breaking the peace
given—by whom is not said—in the assembly of a single
borough, a wapentake, or an ale-house. The fines are interesting in themselves, for they imply a method of reckoning which
is purely Scandinavian. Its units were the *ora* of 16 pence; the
mark, which at this date, in England as in Scandinavia,
amounted to 8 *orae*; and the 'hundred' of silver, which contained 120 *orae*, and was therefore equivalent to 8 English
pounds. But the chief interest of this section of the code lies in
the assemblies within which peace could be given. The assembly
of the Five Boroughs was not the court of an urban confederation. The Five Boroughs had been the fortified bases of five
Danish armies, which had settled down upon the land and
developed what they remembered of their native law into a
common body of custom. The general assembly of the Five
Boroughs was the court of highest authority in the application
of this custom, and its suitors must have been drawn from the
whole country within which the custom prevailed. The assembly of a single borough was a court of the same character, but
the geographical range of its jurisdiction was narrower. The
wapentakes of the tenth century survived into modern times.
The most difficult problem raised by this list of assemblies is the
nature of the body which could give peace to a man 'in an ale-
house'. The fine for breaking this peace was too heavy to have
been imposed for the mere offence of fighting in an inn. It has
been conjectured that the code is referring to meetings of
villagers for the management of open fields and commons. Whatever their character, these gatherings formed a distinctive, if
enigmatical, feature of the local organization of the northern
Danelaw.

The most interesting feature of this organization is the aristocratic jury of presentment which initiated the prosecution of
suspected persons in the court of the wapentake. The Wantage
code of Æthelred II becomes an important document in English
legal history through a passage which states that the twelve

leading thegns in each wapentake are to go out from the court
and swear on relics taken into their hands that they will neither
accuse any innocent person nor protect any guilty one. They
are also required to arrest all the men of bad repute who are at
issue with the reeve, the king's officer within the wapentake.[1]
The sworn jury is unknown to pure Old English law, and it is
safe to follow the long succession of scholars who have seen in
the twelve leading thegns of the wapentake an institution derived from the juries of twelve familiar in the Scandinavian
north. Although the fate of the suspects was settled by the
ordeal, and not by the judgement of the thegns who had presented them, there is reason to think that these thegns formed
what may be called an upper bench of doomsmen within their
wapentake. A later passage in the code runs: 'Let the judgement
stand on which the thegns are agreed; if they differ, let that
stand which eight of them have pronounced, and let those who
are out-voted each pay six half-marks.'[2] On general grounds
it is highly probable that the thegns of this passage are identical
with the thegns on whom the wapentake relied for the presentment of evil doers. In any case, the passage is interesting as an
illustration of the movement of thought which lay behind the
practice of the Danelaw courts. It is the first assertion in England of the principle that where opinions differ that of the
majority must prevail.

The impression of a powerful Scandinavian influence in the
background of these customs is strengthened by the language in
which they are expressed. Although Æthelred's code for the
Five Boroughs was·issued in Berkshire and composed in the
ordinary West Saxon dialect of the time, it contains a number
of Scandinavian loan-words which appear in authentic Scandinavian forms.[3] But others are anglicized;[4] and from the
linguistic standpoint the Scandinavian strain in the code is
shown more clearly by turns of expression than by the forms of
individual words. The Norse alliterative formula *kvaða and krafa*
has influenced the phrasing of the protection given to the heirs
of a man who has lived and died on his land *uncwydd and uncrafod*,
'uncontested and unchallenged'. The demand that a man who

---

[1] iii Æthelred, 3, 1–4.   [2] c. 13, 2.
[3] e.g. *landcop*, 'purchase of land'; *lahcop*, 'purchase of law'; *sammæle* (cf. Icelandic
sammæli, 'agreement'), 'of one opinion'.
[4] Such as *botleas* for *bótlauss*, 'unamendable'; *sacleas* for *saklauss*, 'innocent';
witword for *vitorð*, 'asseveration'.

has entertained a breaker of the king's peace must clear himself 'with three twelves', that is, with three groups of twelve oath-helpers, is expressed in a Scandinavian manner and has many parallels in Scandinavian law. The conception that a man of bad fame must 'buy law' in order to obtain a standing in the court which will try him is definitely Scandinavian. It is applied in the code to the suspects arrested by the twelve lead-ing thegns of the wapentake, and to moneyers believed to have struck bad coins, and a general statement declares that the posi-tion which a man has secured through *lahcop*, that is, the buy-ing of law, shall not be called into question. There can be no doubt that the men who drafted these customs for presentation to the king habitually thought in a Scandinavian terminology.

Much of this terminology reappears, and further traces of Scandinavian influence can easily be found, in other legal texts of northern or eastern origin. The Northumbrian Priests' Law, for example, takes from the Wantage code the declaration that *lahcop*—the purchase of law—*landcop*—the purchase of land—and *witword*—the formal statement in court which could not be traversed—should never be gainsaid. It adds to these matters beyond debate the *dryncelean*, a term which appears in an Eng-lish form, but represents the Norse *drekkulaun*, a grant of land by a lord to his man as a reward for hospitality. But it is largely a matter of chance whether a particular custom is mentioned in one of the few surviving statements of Anglo-Scandinavian law, and there are many aspects of public life in the Danelaw which are only known from unofficial sources.[1] It is a private memo-randum written in Peterborough abbey in the tenth century which establishes the important point that even in the southern Danelaw the transfer of land was carried out in accordance with Scandinavian practice.[2] The memorandum records the building up of a great estate for the abbey by the purchase of small properties from thegns and peasants. In each purchase the validity of the seller's title is guaranteed by a number of independent sureties who are called 'festermen'. There is no trace of this practice in England outside the Danelaw; the word *festerman* is an anglicized equivalent of the Icelandic *festumaðr*,

---

[1] Thus the 'sacrabar', or public prosecutor (O.N. *sakaráberi*), who appears in medieval Cheshire and Scotland as well as in the Danelaw, is never mentioned before the Conquest. [See D. M. Stenton, *English Justice 1066–1215*, pp. 55–6, 124–31, 136–7.]

[2] *C.S.* 1130.

'surety', and the type of security which the festerman offered can be illustrated from many passages of Scandinavian law.

Facts like these show that in the legal sense the Danelaw was a reality. But from the historical standpoint its legal individuality is chiefly interesting as the reflection of a society which was abnormal in structure and unique in racial composition. Some of its distinctive features—notably the masses of independent peasants who are peculiar to eastern England—became evident as soon as the modern study of Domesday Book began. It has long been realized that, to say the least, the manorial type of rural economy was far less dominant in the Danelaw than in the counties to the south and west. More recently, the study of the personal names which occur in Domesday Book and in the private charters of the early middle ages has made possible a rough estimate of the strength of the Scandinavian element in the different parts of the Danelaw. It will be many years before the society of the Danelaw is known as that of Wessex and English Mercia is known already, but its broad outlines are established, and the Scandinavian strands in its fabric are steadily becoming clearer.

In Suffolk, Norfolk, and Lincolnshire the pre-Conquest Danelaw contained the three wealthiest and most populous counties in England. Much of the country along the fringe of these pre-eminent shires was equally prosperous. The wide-spread prosperity of the Danelaw can fairly be attributed to the impetus given to the work of cultivation by the Danish settlement of the ninth century. Many of the settlers applied themselves to the development of districts which, so far as can be seen, had never before been brought under agriculture—the forests of north-west Nottinghamshire, the marsh of Lincolnshire, the flat lands along the Norfolk broads. On the other hand, the mass of the Danish armies settled in country which had supported an unbroken agricultural life for more than two centuries before their coming, and there is no sign that they attempted to remodel the agrarian pattern in which it had been cast. Its native inhabitants were nowhere exterminated, and in some parts the alien settlers must have formed a small, if ascendant, minority of the local population. It is not improbable that the methods of cultivation which they had known in their own country were similar to those which they found in operation in England. It is at least certain that the layout of a set of open fields is much the same on either side of the line which separates English Mercia from the Danelaw, and there is nothing to suggest that the peculiarities of the later East Anglian field system are due to Danish influence.

But if the Danish settlers accepted the plan of the open fields which they found in England, they introduced new methods of dividing them out. It is probable that at the middle of the ninth century, throughout the country which was to become Danish, the village arable was normally divided into hides, each of which was reputed to contain four yardlands. Two hundred years later this system still prevailed in the southern midlands, but in East Anglia it is hard to discover any standard form of holding, and beyond the Welland the hides and yardlands had been replaced by a division of the arable into units called ploughlands, each of which was composed of eight 'oxgangs'.[1] This northern system was at least founded on an intelligible principle, for in origin the oxgang, of which eight went to the ploughland, was clearly the holding of a man who could contribute one ox to a co-operative eight-ox team. A useful clue to the quarter from which it came is given by the fact that *plogesland*, the oldest recorded form of the word ploughland, is a compound of a Scandinavian type.[2] The substitution of a system based on the amount of work which an eight-ox ploughteam could do in a year for a system based on the amount of land which could support a peasant household marks a radical change in the conceptions by which rural economy was governed. It was only carried out by slow degrees—in eleventh-century Yorkshire it was still possible to speak of 'one hide and five oxgangs'[3]—and it is possible that the division of the northern Danelaw among its original colonists had proceeded on different lines. In Norfolk, Lincolnshire, and Nottinghamshire there are traces of a form of holding called a 'manslot', which might be equivalent to an oxgang, but was generally smaller. The word, which is of Scandinavian origin, means 'man's share'; it is recorded in Nottinghamshire in the middle of the tenth century,[4] and the 'share' which it originally denoted may well have been the portion of land which fell to one of the rank and file of the Danish army at the time of its settlement. It was a familiar unit

---

[1] The Old English *oxangang* is latinized by *bovata* in *D.B.* and later records.
[2] W. H. Stevenson, *E.H.R.* xxvii (1912), pp. 21–2.
[3] A. J. Robertson, *Anglo-Saxon Charters*, p. 166.　　　　[4] *C.S.* 1029.

of land-division in part of Norfolk as late as the thirteenth century. But in the northern Danelaw it only survived as an occasional complication of an economy which by the Norman Conquest was everywhere organized in terms of ploughlands and oxgangs.[1]

The peasants among whom this economy had arisen formed a complex society. It included large numbers of men whose representatives appear in Domesday Book as villeins and bordars. In status and condition they presumably resembled the peasants who are thus described in the surveys of the southern and western shires. There was a considerable amount of downright slavery in the Danelaw, though much less than in most parts of the country. But the social order of Danish England was distinguished from that of other regions by the prominence of what can fairly be called a peasant aristocracy, whose members had escaped absorption into the routine of manorial discipline. Each of them was the man of some lord, but his obligations were neither burdensome nor humiliating. To judge from later evidence, a man of this class was bound to help his lord with labour at the busy seasons of the agricultural year, to attend his court, and to pay him annually a small sum of money in recognition of his superiority. Apart from these requirements the man was his own master; his land was his own; he could alienate it, generally without asking his lord's leave; and he paid to the king the taxes which it was expected to yield. In 1066 peasant proprietors of this kind were to be found in every Danelaw county under the name of sokemen. The word sokeman, which literally meant a man who owed suit to a court, was nearly as indefinite as the word *villanus*, which literally meant no more than 'villager'. In each case it would seem that a miscellaneous class has acquired a general name from a characteristic which might not be distinctive, but was at least salient. The villein was so called because he was the typical peasant, cultivating one of the regular shares into which the arable of his village was divided. The sokeman cannot have been set apart from other men by the mere duty of 'seeking' a court. Suit to some form of court was incumbent on all landholders, whatever their condition. But the personal and economic independence of the

[1] On the *manslot*—a word which like *plogesland* is a Scandinavian formation—see D. C. Douglas, *The Social Structure of Medieval East Anglia*, pp. 50–8; F. M. Stenton, *Danelaw Charters*, p. xxi; A. J. Robertson, *Anglo-Saxon Charters*, p. 441.

sokeman must have given exceptional weight to his judgements, and his importance as a doomsman of the court to which he owed attendance probably goes far to account for the name which became attached to him.

The distribution of these sokemen is significant. They were not confined to the Danelaw.[1] In 1066 there had been small groups of sokemen in Kent and Surrey, though they had lost their status twenty years later. But their sporadic appearance south of the Thames only brings out the more clearly their fundamental importance as an element in the population of Danish England. Many of them, even there, had suffered heavily through the Norman Conquest and the social changes of the next generation. In Yorkshire and Derbyshire they were brought low by the devastation of those counties which followed the English revolt of 1069. In the southern midlands large numbers of sokemen were incorporated as villeins into the manorialized estates created by the Norman lords of those parts. But in the counties of Lincoln, Leicester, and Nottingham, in the north of Northamptonshire, and in East Anglia, they survived to carry their traditions of independence into the heart of the middle ages and beyond. Their mere numbers are impressive. Domesday Book enumerates more than a thousand of them in Northamptonshire, more than 1,500 in Nottinghamshire, nearly 2,000 in Leicestershire, and nearly 11,000 in Lincolnshire. They were widely distributed over the country.[2] Among the thirty-three wapentakes of Lincolnshire there were only four in which the proportion of sokemen to the total population fell below 40 per cent. In two of these wapentakes it reached 70 per cent., and it was higher than 50 per cent. in twelve others. In Leicestershire, as a whole, the proportion falls to 33 per cent., and in Nottinghamshire to 30 per cent., but in each of these counties there was one wapentake in which the percentage rises above 50. Domesday Book gives little information about the holdings of individuals, but later evidence suggests that in Lincolnshire, at least, it was an exceptional sokeman who possessed more than two oxgangs, that is, some 40 acres, of

[1] [On sokemen in Buckinghamshire see 'The Thriving of the Anglo-Saxon Ceorl', *C.P.*, p. 392.]

[2] For the details which follow see F. M. Stenton, 'The Free Peasantry of the Northern Danelaw', Oxford, 1969, pp. 1–191, and B. Dodwell, 'The Free Peasantry of East Anglia in Domesday' (*Norfolk and Norwich Archaeological Society*, xxvii, pp. 145–57).

arable. Whatever may have been the origin of the sokeman's independence, it certainly did not lie in the size of his holding.

This conclusion is supported by what is known about the social economy of East Anglia. East Anglian society was complicated by the fact that the free element in the local population was divided into two classes, one consisting of sokemen and the other of men who appear in Domesday Book as *liberi homines*, free men without qualification. In Norfolk these classes were roughly equal in numbers. It has recently been reckoned that there were 5,544 free men as against 5,651 sokemen. In Suffolk there were only 1,003 sokemen to 8,144 free men. It has so far proved impossible to explain the distinction which was drawn between these classes, and it is a mere surmise that the free men, although peasants, and often of a meagre sort, may have been able to claim an ancestry which gave them higher rank than sokemen. Economically they were on the same level, and they are indistinguishable on any but the closest view of the East Anglian social complex. Taken together they formed more than 40 per cent. of the recorded population in 17 out of 33 hundreds in Norfolk, and in 14 out of the 22 hundreds in Suffolk. It is evident that they were distributed over East Anglia in much the same way as the sokemen were distributed over Lincolnshire, but the holding of the ordinary free man or sokeman was certainly much smaller than that of the same type of peasant in the northern Danelaw. An early survey of the possessions of the abbey of Bury shows large numbers of free men living on holdings which might amount to no more than a single acre, and rarely amounted to more than 20.[1] Free peasants of this humble kind can be traced in all parts of the East Anglian Domesday. Some of them may well have eked out the produce of their acres by finding employment on the farms of noblemen or of wealthier members of their own class. But there were thousands of villeins and bordars and many hundreds of slaves in East Anglia, and the demand for labour must have been limited. It can only be concluded that in this part of the Danelaw large numbers of men were maintaining themselves as independent members of society on resources which can have been little more than adequate for bare subsistence.[2]

[1] D. C. Douglas, *Feudal Documents from the Abbey of Bury St. Edmunds*, pp. 25-44.
[2] The possibility that they may have increased their resources by sheep-farming is not borne out by the information that has been preserved about them.

It was inevitable that the social relationships characteristic of East Anglia and the northern Danelaw should produce types of estate which are never to be found in southern or western England. In the vast majority of cases the tie which united the free man or sokeman to his lord had come into being because the free man or sokeman desired the connection which it created. In East Anglia it had not by 1066 given rise to any stable or coherent form of social organization. A free man or sokeman might commend himself by homage to more than one lord; he could often, perhaps generally, leave the lord whom he had chosen, and seek another; and jurisdiction over him might well belong, by custom or a royal grant, to a lord who had no other interest in his affairs. In Northamptonshire and the northern Danelaw, where freemen in the East Anglian sense do not occur, the relationship between the sokeman and his lord had been stabilized and consolidated before the Conquest. There is nowhere in Domesday Book any hint that the sokemen of this country were free to remove themselves or their holdings from the sphere of their lord's authority, and the whole arrangement of the Survey of this region implies that the sokeman's lord had jurisdiction over him. The relationship had, in fact, become territorialized, and the process had led by 1066 to the development of a remarkable type of estate in which groups of sokemen scattered over many villages, and often associated with a few villeins and bordars, were permanently attached to a central manor for suit of court and the render of such payments and services as custom prescribed. It was through the justice done in the court of the manor that estates of this kind were held together, and many of them appear in later records under the name of 'sokes', a term which emphasizes the circumstances of their origin. Many of these sokes were very large—Earl Harold's soke of Greetham in Lincolnshire embraced men living in thirty-five villages—and some of them had begun to disintegrate before the Domesday Survey was made. It was possible for the Norman lord of a soke to set one of his knights in authority over a particular group of men within its ambit, just as in earlier times it had been possible for a king to set one of his companions in authority over a particular group of independent ceorls. A considerable number of post-Conquest manors arose in this way. But many Anglo-Danish sokes retained their integrity into medieval or even into modern times. Lordship over men, from which they had sprung, steadily hardened down into lordship over land; so that by the twelfth century, although the sokeman was still free to sell, exchange, or give away his holding, no action which he might take could detach it from the estate of which it had now become an integral part.

It cannot be an accident that a social organization to which there is no parallel elsewhere in England occurs in the one part of the country in which the regular development of native institutions had been interrupted by a foreign settlement. There are many unsolved problems in the history of the pre-Conquest Danelaw, and the extent to which the Danish colonists had adapted themselves to the English social framework is one of them. Speculation is dangerous in this obscurity. Nevertheless, the contrast drawn by Domesday Book between Leicestershire with nearly 2,000 sokemen and Warwickshire with none, demands an explanation, and an explanation which is both simple and agreeable to recorded history lies in the fact that Leicestershire, unlike Warwickshire, had been partitioned among the members of a Danish army in the ninth century. It was almost inevitable that the rank and file of this army, who are known to have kept their military organization long after they had turned from war to agriculture, should group themselves upon the soil under the leaders who had brought them to England. There is every probability in a view which sees in such grouping the origin of the sokes characteristic of the Danish shires.

The impression of a strong Danish influence behind the medieval economy of these shires has been greatly strengthened by modern work on the place-names and personal names which occur in their early records. The personal names of the pre-Conquest Danelaw are little known. Only three considerable lists of early names have come down from those parts: one from Northamptonshire,[1] in which about one-third of the names are Scandinavian; another from north Cambridgeshire,[2] in which the proportion of Danish names is approximately 50 per cent.;[3]

---

[1] *C.S.* 1130, discussed by E. Ekwall in *Introduction to the Survey of English Place-Names*, pp. 72–3.

[2] Analysed by D. Whitelock in *Saga-Book of the Viking Society*, xii (1940), pp. 127–53.

[3] This proportion is based on the names which seem to be of local provenance. It would be considerably increased if account were taken of the names in the list which were borne by important persons from other districts.

and a third from south Yorkshire,[1] in which the proportion is above two-thirds. The men who appear in these lists, like those who appear in Domesday Book as holders of pre-Conquest manors, were persons of local importance, and it is unsafe to use their names as evidence for the racial composition of the peasantry. The names of Danelaw peasants are not recorded in large numbers before the middle of the twelfth century, and it is only in recent years that they have been examined in detail. Nevertheless the series of Danish names which the examination has already produced is very remarkable for its variety and for the accuracy with which Old Scandinavian sounds are represented. It shows that as late as the reign of Henry II the traditional names of the Scandinavian world were still remembered, and Scandinavian habits of name-formation were still in use. It includes examples of every kind of name current in the Scandinavian north. There are compound names of an ancient type, like Haward and Agmund, Aszur and Byrgher; single-stem names like Ase and Aki, Thori and Grim; diminutives like Stainke, Akke, and Anke; and many descriptive epithets like Ofram, 'the sluggish', Mole, 'the dull', or Stainbid, 'the stone-biting fish', used in the traditional Scandinavian fashion as independent names. There are many feminine names, usually of a compound type, like Steinware, Ingirith, Siggerith, or Jorild. These names are not isolated curiosities. They can be counted by hundreds in Yorkshire and Lincolnshire, and by scores in Nottinghamshire, Derbyshire, and Norfolk. They also occur in considerable numbers in Leicestershire, Northampton-shire, and Suffolk. On the other hand, they become rare to-wards the south of the Danelaw, and in Wessex and English Mercia most of the recorded examples were borne by burgesses, or by countrymen above the standing of the ordinary peasant. Their distribution agrees remarkably well with the other evidence which shows that the centre of Danish influence lay in the northern Danelaw, and their number and variety suggest that the settlement from which this influence arose was carried out by families as well as by individuals. Above all, they prove that within the vast region covered by this intensive settlement there had been no general assimilation of Danes to Englishmen in the two centuries before the Norman Conquest.

The Scandinavian place-names which are scattered over the

[1] *E.H.R.* xxvii (1912), pp. 12–13.

Danelaw, and concentrated in certain parts of it, are the most obviously significant of all the materials for its history. They establish the fundamental point, that the partitions of southern Northumbria, eastern Mercia, and East Anglia carried out by Danish armies in the ninth century were preliminary to an intensive Danish colonization of at least the northern half of this region. To the south of the Humber the fens along the Witham cause the only important break in a broad sequence of Danish names, which extends from the coast between Grimsby and Saltfleet to the neighbourhood of Leicester. To the north and west of this central belt there are outstanding groups of Danish names in the angle between the Trent and the Humber, in the north-west of Nottinghamshire, and on either side of the border between Derbyshire and Leicestershire. To the south and east the succession of Danish names ends somewhat abruptly on the edge of the Parts of Holland, thins out in Rutland, southern Kesteven, and Northamptonshire, and fades away in the southern midlands. In East Anglia Danish names are distributed widely over Norfolk, and a most remarkable group of them occurs in the extreme east of the county, between the river Bure and the sea. In Suffolk they are rare except in the coastal district to the south of Yarmouth. Beyond the Humber there is no single concentration of Danish names such as occurs along the Grimsby–Leicester line, but in the North Riding, and particularly in its centre, they are as numerous as in most parts of Lincolnshire. In the West Riding, although they are very numerous, there is nowhere any clear tendency towards their concentration, and the groups into which the many Danish names of the East Riding fall here and there have little historical significance. Towards the north there are a considerable number of Danish names in county Durham, but very few in Northumberland. Towards the west, in Lancashire and Westmorland, names which seem to represent a movement of Danish colonists across the Pennines meet and are sometimes indistinguishable from names created by the Irish-Norwegian migrants who invaded this country in the tenth century. The sheer volume of this Danish nomenclature is an important historical fact. Some of these names are ill recorded and many are hard to explain, but there is no mistaking the conclusion to which, as a whole, they point. They are the record of a migration.

Few of these names are mentioned in writings earlier than the eleventh century. But for all their late appearance many of them are recorded in spellings which preserve unmistakable traces of Danish inflexional forms. The Old Scandinavian genitive in *-ar* is shown in such forms as *Scogerbud*, 'booth by the wood', *Lundertorp*, 'hamlet by the grove', and *Herdrebi*, probably 'Herrøð's village', by which Domesday Book denotes Scorbrough in Yorkshire, Londonthorpe in Lincolnshire, and Harby in Nottinghamshire. It still survives in a few names, such as Aismunderby in the West and Helperby in the North Riding of Yorkshire, the villages respectively of a man named Asmundr and a woman named Hialp. In the East Scandinavian languages *ar* was often reduced to *a* before a consonant, and this development accounts for such forms as *Aslocahou* and *Hawardaby*—Aslak's mound and Havarth's village—which are twelfth-century spellings for the Lincolnshire wapentake-name Aslacoe and the Lincolnshire village-name Hawerby. A considerable number of villages, especially in Lincolnshire, owe the modern forms of their names to an Old Scandinavian genitive in *-s*, which has unvoiced a preceding consonant or caused its disappearance. The names Braceby, Rauceby, Laceby, and Winceby, which contain the personal names Breithr, Rauthr, Leifr, and Vindr, are the result of such changes. These details are historically important because they prove the long continuance of Danish habits of speech. They show that at least in the northern Danelaw, where these grammatical peculiarities coincide with a general preservation of Old Scandinavian vowels, the Danish settlers can never have been submerged in the English population around them. They supply another argument against the imagined assimilation of Danes to Englishmen.

The argument is carried further by the existence of a large number of native place-names which have been modified through their adoption by a people speaking a Scandinavian language. There were various English sounds which the Danes could not pronounce. The combination *sc*—that is, *sh*—did not exist in the ancient Scandinavian languages. Its replacement by the northern *sk* has produced such modern names as Screveton in Nottinghamshire, from an Old English *Scirgerefan tun*, 'sheriff's village'. Scandinavian vowels were often substituted for English ones, as in the common Danelaw name Stainton, where the Danish *steinn*, 'stone', has replaced the Old English *stān.* Occasionally a Scandinavian word has been substituted for its Old English equivalent. The place-name Eagle in Lincolnshire represents an Old English *Ācleah*, 'oak wood', in which the native *āc* has been replaced by the Scandinavian *eik*. Modern work on place-names has shown that changes of this kind were far more numerous than was formerly realized. But it has also shown that they were the result of a long-continued, though unconscious, conflict between Danish and English habits of speech which was still in progress at the date of the Norman Conquest. Many names in which the Scandinavian influence ultimately prevailed appear in Domesday Book in spellings which represent Old English forms. It is true that even in the regions of intensest Danish settlement there were English place-names which resisted modification. There are a few cases in which a new Danish place-name came in time to assume an English form. On the other hand, English names which have been modified through the influence of Danish speech can sometimes be found far from the main centres of Danish occupation. The modern form of the place-name Scaldwell in mid-Northamptonshire, which contains the Old English adjective *sceald*, 'shallow', proves that a group of Danish settlers of whom there is no other record were once established in the neighbourhood. As evidence of Danish settlement English names which have been thus changed are at least as important as the names of purely Danish origin, on which the attention of historians has been chiefly concentrated.

Among the vast multitude of these Danish place-names the most interesting from the historical standpoint are those which contain words denoting places of habitation, and in particular, those which end in the terminal *by* or *thorp*. Most of them are recorded in Domesday Book, and therefore throw a faint light on the social organization of the Danelaw in the darkest period of its history. It is impossible to define the words *by* or *thorp* at all closely, but if a generous allowance is made for exceptions, it is broadly accurate to regard *by* as the equivalent of 'village' and *thorp* as the equivalent of 'hamlet'. These names are very numerous—more than five hundred names ending in *by* are mentioned in the Domesday Survey of the country between the Welland and the Tees—and many of them are nothing more than simple topographical descriptions of the sites to which they refer. But on the severest estimate more than half of them have a personal name for the first element, and so many of these personal names are otherwise unknown in England that there can be little hesitation in referring them to a period within at most a generation or two of the original Danish settlement. In the Scandinavian countries *thorp* is normally compounded with a personal name, and many Danelaw names in *thorp* have exact parallels in Sweden or Denmark. But Danish and Swedish names in *by* generally begin with an adjective or noun describing the site, or the condition of its inhabitants, and it is only in districts which, like the Danish colonies in England, were regions of late settlement, that *by* is at all frequently associated with a personal name. On general grounds it is more than probable that many of the Danes whose names are preserved in the village nomenclature of the Danelaw had taken part in the Danish conquest of that country, and that in some degree the individualistic character of this nomenclature reflects the organization of the army which had divided out the land in the ninth century. No doubt, in some cases, a Dane who gave his name to a village in eastern England may have been its lord in the sense in which innumerable English thegns were lords of villages in Wessex and English Mercia. Many of the numerous placenames in which a Danish personal name is compounded with the native word *tūn* may well stand for the replacement of an Englishman by a Dane as the lord of an existing village. On the other hand, the still more numerous names in which *by* or *thorp* is united in a strict grammatical compound with a Danish personal name suggest the foundation of new settlements rather than the establishment of Danish conquerors as lords of old ones. It is also significant that many places thus named were inhabited at the time of their first entry into record by masses of free peasants, who are much more likely to be descended from Danes of the ninth-century settlement than from Englishmen subjected at that time to alien power. The most probable conclusion is that in the division of the land from which these names arose, the rank and file of the Danish armies had settled in groups, under the command of men whose authority was not seignorial nor economic, but military. There is much to suggest that the Dane who left his name to a *by* or a *thorp* had normally been, not the lord, but the leader of the men whose settlement had brought the village or hamlet into being.

It has already been suggested that the planned settlement of an army may underlie the great sokes which are characteristic of the Danelaw. It is a curious, and probably a significant, fact that in most cases the village which was the administrative centre of a soke bore, not a Danish, but an English name. In 1066 Grantham, Bolingbroke, Sleaford, Newark, Mansfield, Rothley, and Melton Mowbray, to name a few famous examples from the territory of the Five Boroughs, were all, in effect, minor local capitals, to which free peasants scattered over a wide area came to hold their pleas and to pay their customary dues to their lord. Each of these names is of English origin, and each place had probably been the centre of an important estate before the Danish conquest. The names of the villages and hamlets dependent on these great manors are by no means always Danish. It was only when a Danish settlement had reached a fairly high degree of intensity that it left any permanent effect on local nomenclature. Nevertheless there is a strong tendency for the various members of a great soke to bear Danish names. Twelve of the nineteen villages which were dependent on Bolingbroke bore names which are Scandinavian in the strictest sense of the word, and eight of them consist of a Danish personal name followed by the termination *by*. Cases like this point clearly enough to an early grouping of Danish colonists in settlements to which their lesser leaders commonly gave their names, under the general authority of a chief—an earl or a *hold*—who took for himself the principal English estate in the neighbourhood. It is easy to over-simplify a complex piece of history like the settlement of the Danelaw, and it should be acknowledged without any reserve that practice must have varied very widely between one district and another. Even so, the impression of a military organization behind the tenurial peculiarities of the eleventh-century Danelaw, faint as it may be, is still too definite to be a mere illusion.

3. TOWNS AND TRADE

No problems in the whole of Anglo-Saxon history are more difficult than those which relate to the origins of the English town.[1] The evidence is fragmentary, and often ambiguous. The

[1] On the origin and development of the Anglo-Saxon borough and on the literature relating to this subject see the definitive study by J. Tait, *The Medieval English Borough*, cc. i–vi.

only documents which give direct information about the beginnings of English urban life come from the south-east, the district
from which communication with the continent was easiest. It
is unwise to assume that places less favourably situated had
come to the point of urban development reached before 850
by London, Canterbury, or Rochester. Now and then a historian or clerk uses phrases which show that a particular place
was something more than an upland village. When Bede refers
to the *praefectus Lindocolinae civitatis* he makes it clear that Lincoln,
if not a city in the medieval sense of the word, was at least a
centre of population of more account than the ordinary *hām* or
tūn of the countryside. But the word *civitas*, which was generally reserved for places known to have been sites of Roman occupation,[1] does not in this period imply any close concentration
of inhabitants. Worcester is called a *civitas* in 803,[2] but some
ninety years later, when the place was fortified as part of a
scheme of national defence,[3] it is clear that no more than a faint
anticipation of urban life had as yet arisen there. There can
be no doubt that York, to which Frisian traders are known to
have resorted in the eighth century, was already an important
centre for the distribution of goods, and that the Danes who
plundered Southampton in 842 knew of the place as a trading
port where stores of movable wealth were likely to be laid up.
It is reasonable to assume that there were merchants sitting
before the gate of Offa's 'palace' at Tamworth. But it is only in
Kent that anything is known about the way in which the
earliest English traders lived together.

The Kentish evidence is derived from a series of early charters
which show that Canterbury and Rochester were divided, more
or less completely, into a number of enclosed holdings resembling, though often larger than, the messuages of a medieval
borough. The individual holding was known from the fence
which surrounded it either as a *haga*—that is, a hedged plot—or
as a *tūn*—a usage which shows this familiar word in its primitive
sense of 'enclosure'. To some, and probably to most, of these
tenements there were attached shares in the common fields and
meadows of the borough, and rights in its common woods and
marshes. A charter of Offa, which includes one of these tene-

---

[1] The list of episcopal signatures at the synod of Clofeshoh in 803 (*C.S.* 312) draws
a consistent distinction between *civitas* when the see was a Roman town, *ecclesia*
when it was not. [2] *C.S.* 312. [3] Below, p. 529.

ments among the appendages of a large estate in rural Kent, gives a curious anticipation of the later practice by which urban properties were commonly annexed to country manors.[1] In some parts of Canterbury dwellings were packed closely together. A private charter of 868 shows that by the customary law of the place two feet must be left empty between houses to serve as 'eavesdrip'.[2] By the early ninth century the population had grown too large to be contained by its walls. Coins were struck in both Canterbury and Rochester, and the hint of commercial activity which they give is borne out by references to the market-place of Canterbury, and by a ninth-century reference to the place as a *port*—that is, a trading centre. But by virtue of its walls Canterbury was not only a *port*, or market-town, but a *burh*, or defensible position, and in the ninth century its inhabitants are described indifferently as *portware* or *burgware*. There is no clear reference to their communal action in any document of this period, but it can certainly be assumed that they held regular meetings for the management of their common agricultural interests. The most remarkable feature of their recorded life is the existence among them of a gild, whose members were known as *cnihtas*.[3] The position of the Old English *cniht* is a difficult question,[4] and it must be left uncertain whether the ninth-century *cnihtas* of Canterbury were young members of landed families maintaining themselves by trade, or resident servants of lords with property in, or adjacent to, the *civitas*. Whatever they may have been, they have a distinguished place in social history as the founders of the earliest gild on record in England.

These details are valuable for two reasons. They show that London was not the only town in ninth-century England. They also show that many of the features which distinguished the typical English borough of the eleventh century had been developed in at least one urban centre before the age of organized town-planning which opened with the Danish wars. Like ninth-century Canterbury the normal county town of the Confessor's reign was a market and minting-place; it was enclosed with walls or an earthen rampart; it was divided into fenced tenements, which Domesday Book frequently describes as *hagae*; and it

---

[1] *C.S.* 248.   [2] *C.S.* 519.   [3] *C.S.* 515.
[4] It is discussed by F. M. Stenton, *The First Century of English Feudalism*, ed. 2 (1961), pp. 132–6.

possessed open fields and meadows, shared out among its leading inhabitants. It had developed a series of local usages,
which, like the Canterbury regulations about eavesdrip, could
fairly have been described as matters of 'customary law'. It was
welded into the economy of the surrounding country by the
attachment of town houses to rural manors. It was at once an
agricultural unit, a trading centre, and a place of defence. The
Canterbury evidence is important because it proves that in this,
its characteristic form, the Anglo-Saxon borough was not a new
conception of the age of Alfred.

Even without the stimulus of the Danish wars economic
forces would in time have increased the number of English
towns. The laws of Alfred give the impression of a considerable
volume of internal trade in the hands of men of substance who
travelled from one district to another with bands of servants.
But the activities of the itinerant trader were hampered by the
necessity of standing as surety for the men who accompanied
him, by the scarcity of places where articles could be stored in
bulk, and by the difficulty of obtaining assurance against the
risk of buying stolen property. The foundation of new boroughs
offered to traders bases for their operations more secure than
could be found in the open country, and the means of establishing the validity of their transactions by the testimony of responsible persons of their own sort. Statesmen, on their part, were
anxious that trade should be restricted to a limited number of
recognized centres. A law of Edward the Elder prohibits trade
outside a *port*, and orders that all transactions shall be attested by
the portreeve or by other trustworthy men.[1] His successors were
unable to maintain this prohibition, but its significance is clear.
By the end of Edward's reign it is probable that every place of
trade which was more than a local market was surrounded by
at least rudimentary fortifications. Like pre-Alfredian Canterbury, the normal *port* of Edward's time was also a *burh*, and the
urgency with which Edward commands traders to resort to it is
explained by its military importance. A derelict *port* was a weak
point in the national defences.

The combination of military and commercial factors in the
history of the Old English borough is well brought out in the
one surviving document which illustrates the internal condition
of a new Alfredian *burh*. Towards the close of Alfred's reign

[1] Laws of Edward, i. 1.

Æthelred and Æthelflæd of Mercia were asked by Bishop Werferth of Worcester to fortify that place for the defence of the people and the security of his cathedral.[1] When the fortifications had been made Æthelred and Æthelflæd, in return for spiritual services, granted to the bishop half the rights which belonged to their lordship 'in market-place or in street', reserving to the king the toll of goods brought to Worcester in wagons or on horses, and to the bishop all the rights which had belonged to his predecessors within the property belonging to his church. The rights which they shared with the bishop included a tax levied for the repair of the borough-wall, a payment vaguely described as *landfeoh*, presumably the rent yielded by tenements within, or close to, the fortifications, fines for fighting, theft, and dishonest trading, and whatever came in to the representatives of the state in respect of offences which could be emended by money payments. The document gives the impression that not only the fortifications but also the market at Worcester was new, and that the rents, dues, and judicial profits which Æthelred and Æthelflæd derived from the borough were regarded as a compensation for the expenses which they had borne in making it defensible.

At Worcester much of the borough belonged to the bishop, and the extent of his property must have narrowly limited the area from which Æthelred and Æthelflæd derived their revenue. In most boroughs the land enclosed by the fortifications had belonged wholly, or in by far the greater part, to the king. Oxford and Wallingford, for example, were each founded on a compact block of royal land regarded as equivalent to eight yardlands, which at Oxford was still known as the king's eight yardlands in the twelfth century. On the foundation of such a borough it seems that the defensible area was divided into plots—represented by the *hagae* and *mansurae* of Domesday Book—which were taken from the king at a money rent by persons wishing to engage in trade. The men who thus became the king's tenants were all personally free. Most of them must have ranked as ceorls, but there was no convention which hindered a thegn from living in a borough as a merchant, and in days when the male inhabitants of a borough might at any time be required to defend its walls, it was desirable that there should be a few men

[1] F. E. Harmer, *English Historical Documents*, pp. 22–3. The document is discussed at length by Tait, op. cit., pp. 19–23.

of rank resident within them. It is also possible that the thegnly element, of which there are clear signs in eleventh-century London and faint traces in some other boroughs, may have been recruited from within, for a well-known English tract states that in the past a merchant who had carried out three voyages at his own charge was regarded as of thegnly status. Whatever their social position may have been, the individuals holding burghal plots from the king were bound by conditions of tenure which, in substance, were the same everywhere. The rents which they paid seem to have been uniform for the same kind of tenement within each borough, and had become stabilized by custom before the Norman Conquest. As a rule the holder of a tenement was free to mortgage or to sell it, often, it would seem, without obtaining the king's licence, but it was regarded as a heritable property, and there is some evidence that the holder's liberty of alienation might be restricted in the interest of his kin. In addition to his rent, the holder of a plot might be liable to a number of personal services, such as the duty of helping to form an escort for the king; his commercial transactions were subject to toll, and he contributed to such payments for special purposes as might be laid upon his borough. It is clear, in fact, that all the essential features which distinguished the burgess tenure of the middle ages had been developed in the Old English borough, and although no more precise term than *burgware*, 'inhabitants of a borough' or *portmenn*, 'townsmen' had been found for men holding burghal plots on these terms, Domesday Book was recognizing a genuine tenurial distinction when it described them as *burgenses*.

The decisive impulse towards the creation of boroughs had been given by the king, and in the eleventh century a majority of the burgesses in any normal borough were his men. Nevertheless long before the Conquest churches and noblemen had been acquiring borough plots, and placing their own men in them. The extent to which the king retained an interest in the 'customs'—rents, dues, and services—which these plots had formerly rendered, varied with the circumstances of each case. The king sometimes allowed a lord of the very highest rank to receive all the customs arising out of his land within a borough. More often the king reserved a portion of them to himself, and in many, if not in most, cases he retained all the customs, leaving to the lord no more than the profits for which he had bargained when he planted out his tenants on their holdings. It might well happen that an eleventh-century burgess paid both a customary rent to the king and a stipulated rent to his lord. Conversely, although the profits of justice done upon or between burgesses were normally the king's, and were in fact included among his 'customs', a lord of sufficient rank often enjoyed the right of sake and soke over his burgess tenants. For all these complications it remains the fact that the essence of burgess tenure lay in the subjection of the individual burgess to the 'customs' of his borough—customs which were always felt to be of royal institution, however completely their origin might have been disguised by royal alienations and private encroachments.

It is clear from Domesday Book that in 1086 a piece of borough property—a messuage, a house, or a group of houses —was often annexed to a manor in the open country. At Leicester, for example, 134 houses were thus attached, singly or in groups, to 27 different manors. So far as can be seen the borough property was treated as a profit-yielding appendage of the manor. It provided the lord with a lodging when he came to the borough on business and with a place of refuge in time of trouble. The elaborate economy of a large Old English manor implied the possibility of access to something more than a mere rural market; and an appurtenant house in a neighbouring borough formed a convenient centre at which goods needed on the estate could be brought together and stored. Most of the evidence which illustrates this practice relates to the time after the Conquest, but it can be traced far back into the Anglo-Saxon period, and Anglo-Saxon kings had encouraged it. In a charter of 958 the boundaries of an estate at Staunton on Arrow which King Edgar had given to one of his thegns are followed by a statement that the king has also given him a *haga* in Hereford.[1] The association of the manor and its burghal appendage is brought out still more clearly by a charter of Æthelred II relating to Moredon near Swindon which refers expressly to a *haga* in Cricklade added by the king to the estate.[2] Other pre-Conquest charters show tenements in Wilton, Winchester, Southampton, Chichester, Worcester, Oxford, and Warwick attached in the same way to rural properties. There can be no serious doubt that such annexations were common already at the turn of the tenth and eleventh centuries.

[1] *C.S.* 1040.   [2] *C.D.* 1305.

It is clear, in fact, that for at least two generations before the Conquest the population of a normal borough must have included the tenants of other lords than the king, and it is probable that in many boroughs this intermingling of tenures goes back to the time of their foundation. Little is known of the institutions through which these artificial communities were governed. But it could not have been easy for groups of men of diverse antecedents to adapt themselves to the conditions of life within borough walls, and at an early date in the history of at least the larger boroughs there must have arisen the need for a court with the authority of the state behind it for the settlement of disputes between individuals and the establishment of a local customary law. Unfortunately, the pre-Conquest documents which refer to borough courts are few, and their language is ambiguous. The ambiguity is chiefly caused by the fact that many boroughs were the meeting-places of shire courts or of courts with jurisdiction over smaller districts such as hundreds or groups of hundreds. It is sometimes hard to decide whether a passage which on the surface refers to a borough court may not actually be referring to one of these courts of wider jurisdiction which had a borough for a meeting-place. From all this confusion there emerges something more than a probability that King Edgar[1] was referring to a borough court, in the strict sense, when he ordered that the shire court should meet twice, and the *buruhgemot* three times, a year. It is certain that in the early eleventh century a distinction was felt to exist between *landriht*, that is 'ordinary law', and *burhriht*, which can only mean the more specialized law of the borough. The fact that this distinction was regarded as a matter of course implies that borough law and borough courts in which it was administered had arisen at least as early as the date of Edgar's ordinance about the meetings of the *buruhgemot*. In 1018 the bishop of Crediton announced to the *burhwitan* of Exeter, Totnes, Lydford, and Barnstaple that he had mortgaged one of his estates to a local thegn, an announcement which suggests that at each of these places the *burhwitan* formed an official body, capable of preserving the memory of a transaction formally brought to its notice. It is not unreasonable to see in these 'borough councillors' the upper bench of a borough court. It is possible that such a bench may have existed in the pre-Conquest court of Chester, where, according

[1] Laws of Edgar, iii. 5. 1.

to Domesday Book there were twelve *judices*, taken from among the men of the king, the bishop, and the earl, who were all bound to attend every session of the court under the penalty of a ten-shilling fine. But the Chester *judices* clearly resemble the bodies of twelve lawmen whose existence is recorded at Lincoln and Stamford and implied at Cambridge and York. These lawmen undoubtedly came into being through Scandinavian influence. Their name connects them at once with the lawmen of the great Scandinavian codes—men with specialized legal knowledge, on whom there lay the responsibility of directing a court in its application of rules to cases. Danish influence was stronger at Chester than in any other borough except London outside the Danelaw, and there can be little doubt that one of its manifestations was the development of a body of doomsmen or lawmen, who, whatever the name by which they were known, took the leading part in the framing of judgements in the local court.

The difficulty of forming a clear impression of the Old English borough court is increased by the fact that the Old English boroughs themselves did not conform to any single type. It would be easy to make a long list of pre-Conquest boroughs, each of which was obviously important in the national economy as the commercial centre of a wide region. A few of them, such as York and Chester, are known to have been in touch with the outside world through trade; others, such as Lincoln, Thetford, Norwich, Ipswich and Colchester, contained populations which could not have been supported by a traffic confined to England; many were administrative as well as commercial centres, and already before the Conquest had risen to the status of county towns. Within most of them there must have been abundant scope for a court of internal jurisdiction co-ordinate with the rural hundred-moot, and it is probable that in 1066 all of them possessed such courts. But in southern, and particularly in south-western England, there were many small boroughs within which the need for a separate court was less apparent. Many of them, such as Bedwyn and Warminster, had arisen on royal manors, where a king, wishing to improve his property, could offer the protection of the special peace around his house to such traders as might be willing to take plots from him. The king's direct influence was naturally paramount in boroughs of this type. Even in boroughs such as Langport or Axbridge, which had once been fortresses in a scheme of national defence, his tenants generally by far outnumbered those of all other lords. In a normal south-western borough there cannot have been the same clash of interests as in the boroughs of the east and midlands. The population of an average borough was much smaller and the volume of trade was less. Life in Bedwyn or Langport was far simpler than in York or Norwich. Under the conditions which prevailed in the south-west a borough could exist for many years without a court of its own. On the eve of the Conquest, so far as can be seen, there were many boroughs in this part of England which had not yet developed courts separate from those of the hundreds in which they were situated. Some of them gave name to hundreds, and in these cases it is reasonable to assume that the court of the hundred met in the borough and that the king's reeve in the borough accounted for the profits of the hundred court. In other cases nothing is known about the relationship of the borough to the hundred in which it lay. All that can safely be said is that although in time all the most prosperous south-western boroughs acquired courts separate from those of the surrounding hundreds, the separation was purely a matter of expediency. An independent court was not inherent in the Anglo-Saxon conception of a borough.

But, for all the vagueness of its constitution, the Old English borough had an official character. Every borough which had arisen in southern or western England since the beginning of the Danish wars had been created by an act of state, and the government continued to be interested in its fortunes. The close-ness of its connection with the king is evident from whatever angle it is regarded. It is more remarkable that at the end of the Old English period the earl, as the king's vice-regent, was accustomed to receive one-third of the public revenue which came in, year by year, from at least a majority of the boroughs within his province. The history of 'the earl's third penny', as Domesday Book calls it, is very obscure. The 'customs of the burgesses', from which it was derived, were highly miscel-laneous, and little is known about the methods by which the earl's part in them was separated from that of the king. Nothing is known at first hand about the origin of the earl's third penny, and in this connection it can only be observed that the ealdor-men of the Alfredian time had played an important part in the work of borough fortification, that their successors had the responsibility of seeing that the fortifications were kept defensible, and that a share in the borough revenues would be an appropriate return for these labours. But it is certain that in 1066 the earl's right to his third penny was derived from public law rather than royal favour. In all places where it was recognized it seems to have passed automatically to each new earl on his appointment, and its operation can be traced in boroughs of the most diverse size and character. It was admitted at Axbridge and Bruton as well as at Ipswich and Warwick. There were important boroughs within which no sign of it has yet been found, and in some of them it is probable that the king had actually kept the whole of the borough revenues in his own hand. But the boroughs within which the earl is known to have taken his third penny are so numerous that the custom may fairly be regarded as a normal feature of Old English borough finance, and as an indication that the idea of the borough as an integral element in the constitution of the state had survived the military urgencies which had brought the Alfredian boroughs into being.

The function of the Old English borough as a minting-place points still more clearly in the same direction. After the fall of the Norwegian kingdom of York the king of Wessex was the only person in England who could authorize the issue of a currency. His servants used his power efficiently, and handed on the tradition of a well-managed coinage to the Norman administrators who replaced them. By establishing a rule that, apart from those of York, all dies must be cut in London, and that every moneyer must come to London for his dies when the design of the coinage was changed, they brought its type and fabric under a very effective supervision.[1] But the need of local markets for a regular supply of coins was fully, perhaps overgenerously, recognized, and in the history of the late Old English coinage an absolute control of design by the government coincided with a decentralization of issue to an extent that has never since been tolerated in England. The first official statement of the attitude of the government towards the currency occurs in the laws of Athelstan.

We declare . . . that there shall be one coinage throughout the king's dominions and that there shall be no minting except in a

[1] D.B. i. f. 172. See R. H. M. Dolley, *The Norman Conquest and the English Coinage*, Spink, 1966, pp. 8–9, for the numbers of moneyers see *ibid.*, pp. 12–14.

port. And if a minter be convicted of striking bad money, the hand with which he was guilty shall be cut off and set up on the mint-smithy ... In Canterbury there shall be seven minters; four of them the king's, two, the archbishop's, one, the abbot's. In Rochester, three; two of them the king's, and one, the bishop's. In London there shall be eight, in Winchester, six, in Lewes, two, in Hastings, one, in Chichester, another, in Southampton, two, in Wareham, two, in Dorchester, one, in Exeter, two, in Shaftesbury, two, in each other *burh*, one.[1]

The passage is made important for the history of the Old English borough by its last words. Declining to attempt a complete list of minting-places, the king shows that he considers, or at least is prepared to allow, that there should be a minter in every *burh*.

The evidence of the coins themselves suggests that at one time or another in the next century a mint was actually set up in every place with a claim to be regarded as a borough.[2] The evidence is fragmentary at first, for it was not until the end of the reign of Edgar that it became the rule for every coin to bear both the name of the moneyer responsible for its quality and the name of the place where it was struck. It is clear that even in Athelstan's time mints were working in boroughs which are unlikely to have been centres of any considerable trade. Coins of his were struck at a place named *Weardbyrig*, which cannot now be identified, and is only known otherwise as one of the *burhs* which Æthelflæd had built for the defence of Mercia. In the reigns of Æthelred II and Cnut, when the evidence has become copious, there is no doubt that moneyers were established, not only in the large commercial centres of the east, the county towns of the midlands, and most of the *burhs* mentioned in the Burghal Hidage, but also in places where the trading community must have been a mere appendage to a royal manor. There cannot have been any large concentration of burgesses and there can hardly have been more than the most rudimentary of fortifications at Aylesbury or Crewkerne or Bruton. Cadbury in Somerset, where coins were struck for both Æthelred and Cnut, and Horndon in Essex, where they were struck for Edward the Confessor, were not even royal manors in 1066,

---

[1] ii Athelstan 14.
[2] The first evidence for the existence of a borough at Bristol comes from coins of Æthelred II minted there.

and Domesday Book gives no hint of anything unusual in their past. Each of them had probably been a short-lived *burh*, like the *novum oppidum* called *Beorchore*, which Æthelred II visited in 1007, but of which there is no other record.[1] Even so, Cadbury certainly and Horndon probably cannot have been important places, and their coins increase the probability that in the first half of the eleventh century every *burh*, whatever its size, had been a centre for the issue of currency.

The fact that every coin of this period bore the name of both moneyer and minting-place provides the materials for a rough estimate of the relative importance of the different boroughs of the Confessor's reign. It is reasonable to assume, for example, that a borough in which at least six moneyers were working simultaneously had a stronger economic life than a borough in which there were no more than three. It would obviously be unwise to use the number of moneyers in a borough as a positive index to its size or urban population, but it must to some extent reflect the significance of the borough as a centre of exchange.[2] London, as would be expected, comes at the head of the list, with more than twenty moneyers working at the same time in the years after 1042. York follows with a round dozen; Lincoln and Winchester had eight or nine; Chester, at least eight; Canterbury and Oxford, at least seven; Thetford, Gloucester, and Worcester, at least six. It is possible that this method of comparison, which rests on the evidence of coins accidentally discovered, does less than justice to Ipswich and Norwich, where a large concentration of pre-Conquest burgesses, revealed by Domesday Book, seems to have been served by no more than four or five moneyers. It is certainly unjust to Hereford, where Domesday Book shows that no less than seven moneyers were at work in 1066, although only five can be identified on local coins. On the other hand, each of the boroughs with six or more moneyers had unusual advantages of situation, each of them served a tract of country which was either unusually large or unusually prosperous, and their names probably approximate to a list of the market centres which were of most consequence in King Edward's time.

[1] *C.D.* 1303.
[2] This line of inquiry has been followed in relation to a large number of mints by G. C. Brooke, *Catalogue of English Coins in the British Museum: The Norman Kings*, i, pp. clx–clxxxviii, and more recently by Michael Dolley, *The Norman Conquest and The English Coinage*, 1966.

It is impossible to form a close estimate of the population of these and other pre-Conquest boroughs. Domesday Book gives many figures which apparently record the number of burgesses living within a particular borough in 1066. But the compilers of Domesday Book were chiefly interested in the king's demesne burgesses, who rendered, or ought to render, full 'customs', and they took less account of the burgesses who were the tenants of noblemen or churches. In regard to many boroughs their figures relate, not to burgesses, but to messuages or houses, and the interpretation of these figures is made difficult by the possibility that a single tenement may have been divided between two or more burgess households. An estimate of the population of a pre-Conquest borough which is founded on Domesday statistics will nearly always tend to be too low. Even so, the figures recorded for a number of boroughs in eastern England amount to totals which sharply differentiate these places from their rural environment. A recent discussion of these figures,[1] which assumes that each recorded tenement was occupied by a single household and that each household comprised no more than five people, has shown that pre-Conquest York must have contained more than 8,000 persons, and Norwich at least 6,600; that the population of Lincoln must have approached the same figure; that Thetford must have included nearly 4,750 inhabitants, and Ipswich more than 3,000. Apart from London and Winchester, which are not described in Domesday Book, the only other borough which seems to have belonged to this class is Oxford, where the Domesday enumeration of houses suggests a pre-Conquest population of more than 3,500. Indefinite as they are, these figures answer one of the fundamental questions raised by the history of the Old English borough. They show that where local conditions were favourable, the accumulation of dwellings within an Anglo-Saxon *burh* might well reach a density which entitles it to be called a town.

Among the English boroughs of the eleventh century a distinctive place belongs to London. In the number of its inhabitants, the range and volume of its trade, and the elaboration of the system by which it was governed, it stands apart from all other English towns. The accidents of war, through which it became for a time the centre of the English resistance to Danish invasion, gave its citizens a lively sense of their impor-

[1] J. Tait, *The Medieval English Borough*, p. 76.

tance to the state, and formed the basis of the singular claim, put forward by their successors, that the men of London had the right of choosing a king for England. In the eleventh century the conception of a capital city had not yet taken a definite shape anywhere in the west. The centre of government in England was the king's mobile court. The king was free to hold a council at any point in his realm, and to lay up his treasures in any place which he considered safe, as Eadred had laid them up with Dunstan at Glastonbury. But half a century before the Norman Conquest London was beyond comparison the largest town in England. It was the principal resort of foreign traders in time of peace, and the base which sustained the defence of the land in war-time. It had the resources, and it was rapidly developing the dignity and the political self-consciousness appropriate to a national capital.

It was inevitable that in a city of this size and importance society should be more complex, and the organization of government more elaborate than in even the largest of provincial boroughs. It is significant that at London men of thegnly rank, who are elsewhere indistinguishable from the mass of the burgesses, appear as a separate class, and probably formed a recognized urban patriciate. Moreover, so far as is known, there is no parallel in any other town to the series of courts through which justice was administered in pre-Conquest London. The folkmoot, which was first in authority, shows all the features to be expected in an ancient popular assembly. It met in the open air immediately to the north-east of St. Paul's cathedral, on the highest ground in the city. It held three sessions a year which every citizen was expected to attend without individual summons; it was, at least formally, responsible for the good order of the city, and it was the only court in London in which a man could be proclaimed an outlaw. The husting, which is first mentioned in England a little before the end of the tenth century, was less august, but of much more importance in the life of the ordinary citizen. In the Norman age, and no doubt earlier, it met once a week for the transaction of civil business. It was well established before the conquest of England by Cnut, but its name, which means 'house assembly', is of Danish origin, and it probably came into being as a court for the settlement of pleas in which Danish and English merchants were involved with one another. By the

Norman period, when the direct evidence for its judicial activity begins, it was entertaining all manner of civil suits, and the commercial side of its business gave it outstanding importance as the body which regulated intercourse between English and foreign traders in the greatest of English ports. A link between the husting and what may be called the police courts of the city was provided by the aldermen, who sat apart in the husting as a bench of persons learned in the law. It was the essential function of the alderman to take charge of one of the wards into which the city was divided, and in this capacity he held a court—the wardmoot of Anglo-Norman records—for the settlement of small disputes and the punishment of minor offences. Many boroughs, such as York and Cambridge, had been divided into wards by the date of the Norman Conquest, but, so far as is known, the wardmoot is peculiar to London. There is little doubt that long before the Conquest, through the acquisition of London properties by persons of high rank, the process had begun which was ultimately to create innumerable enclaves of private jurisdiction in every part of the city. It is in London that the urban immunity, or 'soke', comes to its highest point of development in England. But in 1066, apart from a number of ancient estates in the hands of important churches, the private soke is unlikely to have been much more than an occasional exception to a judicial system which rested on public authority.

London is not described in Domesday Book, and many details of its early constitution are impenetrably obscure. The nature and organization of its government in the years before 1066 would be virtually unknown were it not for the fragments of ancient custom, preserved by the conservatism of its citizens, which are recorded in medieval custumals.[1] But the commercial relations of the city with foreign countries are indicated in a document of approximately the year 1000, which is fundamental in the history of English trade.[2] The document states that the men of Rouen came to London with wine and the larger sorts of fish. It also states that the port was visited by traders from Normandy at large, Flanders, Ponthieu, and France, but its language suggests that they were required to expose their

---

[1] On which see M. Weinbaum, *Verfassungsgeschichte Londons 1066–1268* and *London unter Eduard I and II* (Stuttgart, 1929, 1933).

[2] *Gesetze*, i, p. 232.

goods and pay toll on the wharf or on shipboard. Traders from Lower Lorraine, and in particular from Huy, Liége, and Nivelles, were apparently allowed to enter the city before paying toll, and the 'men of the Emperor', a phrase which covers all other Germanic merchants, are declared to be worthy of such good customs as the men of London themselves enjoyed. The document does not refer to traders from the Scandinavian lands, but a twelfth-century city custumal, which incorporates ancient matter, states that both Danes and Norwegians were at liberty to dwell in the city for an entire year. The probability that this passage relates to the time before the Conquest is strengthened by a statement that while the Danes were free to travel over the country to markets and fairs, the Norwegians were restricted to trade in London. The differentiation between Danes and Norwegians agrees very well with the character of Anglo-Scandinavian relations in the reigns of Cnut and Edward the Confessor, but is unlikely to have arisen at any later time. It would seem clear, in fact, that in the first half of the eleventh century London was a place of frequent resort for traders from every country between Norway and northern France.

Important as it is, the London evidence should not be regarded as more than a general indication of the main lines of English foreign trade. It was written down in order to define the position of foreign traders visiting London, and it naturally takes no account of the travels of English traders into foreign parts. The concessions which Cnut secured for English and Danish merchants from the Emperor and the king of Burgundy prove that his subjects of either race were accustomed to visit Rome for business as well as devotion. An incidental remark by Ælfric to the effect that in his time English traders were in the habit of taking their goods to Rome shows that Englishmen were using the Italian trade-routes a generation before Cnut became king.[1] But the document which gives the clearest impression of active trade between England and the Continent is the treaty concluded between King Æthelred and Olaf Tryggvason in 991.[2] Two of its provisions are especially significant. One of them lays down that every merchant ship of any country brought safely into an English estuary should be immune from

---

[1] *Homilies,* ed. B. Thorpe, ii, p. 120.
[2] Liebermann, *Gesetze,* i, pp. 220–4; *Laws of the Kings of England,* ed. A. J. Robertson, pp. 56–60.

attack, and that even if it had become a wreck, and therefore a lawful object of plunder, its crew with the cargo which they had saved should have peace if they had been able to make their way into a *burh*. The second provides that if the viking fleet should come upon a subject of King Æthelred in any land outside the treaty—a phrase which covers Germany, the Low Countries, and France—he should have peace for himself, his cargo, and his ship, if his ship were afloat, or if he had beached the ship and laid up the cargo in a hut or a tent, but should keep nothing except his life if he had entrusted his goods to a man of the country. In the obscurity that overhangs the whole subject of international trade in the Dark Ages it is useful to have this definite evidence that late in the tenth century the English seas were being traversed by the merchant ships of many countries, and that a viking fleet raiding a continental harbour would not improbably find an English trader there.

It is probable that a considerable volume of trade passed in this period between England and the Scandinavian countries themselves. A well-known passage in the earliest life of St. Oswald states that in the writer's time, that is, shortly after the year 1000, York was filled with the treasures of merchants, chiefly of Danish race, who had come to the city from every quarter.[1] The picture may be overdrawn, but it is good evidence that Danish traders in the tenth century, like Frisian traders in the eighth, had formed a colony in the city. It would be easier to form a definite opinion about the amount of this trade, and about the commercial relations which existed between England and Scandinavia in general, if it were possible to estimate the exact significance of the vast quantities of late Old English money which have been discovered in the northern countries. Most of this money must have reached the north as the proceeds of Danegelds and heregelds taken in England; some of it may well have come from gifts made by Cnut to northern chiefs; and some, from the wages of his housecarles and seamen. But there is a residue which cannot be explained on these lines. Most of the coins belong to the reigns of Æthelred or Cnut, but the series continues through the reign of Edward the Confessor into the Norman period, and it is clear that many of the coins cannot have reached the northern countries until Danegelds had ceased to be levied and the Scandinavian troops in English

[1] *Historians of the Church of York*, i, p. 454.

service had been disbanded. It is also significant that a large number of the coins, including many of Æthelred and Cnut, have been discovered in association with continental coins of the same period, under conditions which show that they had been accumulated gradually, and, to all appearance, in the course of trade.[1] But the clearest piece of evidence for regular commercial intercourse between England and Scandinavia is the remarkable fact that by the beginning of the eleventh century the English currency had come to be accepted everywhere as a model by the Scandinavian peoples themselves. In each of the three northern countries—in Denmark under Swein Forkbeard, in Norway under Olaf Tryggvason, in Sweden under Olaf Skattkonung—the first step towards the introduction of a regular currency was the imitation of pennies of Æthelred II.

The possibility that the northern peoples began simply copying coins brought to their land as spoils of war or in trade is shown by names of English kings, mints and moneyers appearing on coins which are certainly Scandinavian, though there are grounds for thinking that a certain Godwine was a peripatetic English craftsman striking for each of the Scandinavian kings in turn. This employment of at least one English moneyer by northern kings could further suggest that intercourse between England and Scandinavia was based on trade conducted through the medium of a currency.

It is clear that for at least seventy years before the Norman Conquest England had been in continuous relationship through trade with the continental world. Little can be said about the relative importance of the different channels through which that relationship was maintained. Two of the greatest trade-routes of the Dark Ages converged upon England, and there are no means of determining whether the traffic from Italy through the Rhineland to the Low Country ports, or that from Russia along the Baltic to its outlets on the North Sea was of the greater advantage to English traders. As to an earlier time, there is little evidence for the nature or direction of English foreign trade in the century which followed the collapse of the Carolingian empire, when the energy of Mediterranean commerce sank to its lowest point. But even in this impoverished age it is

---

[1] A good example is the great hoard from Stora Sojdeby, analysed in *Fornvännen*, 1915, pp. 53–116; 189–246. It was deposited *circa* 1100.

unlikely that England was ever thrown entirely back on to her own internal resources. It was in the ninth and tenth centuries that the Baltic trade-route, on which Haithaby near Slesvig was the chief distributing centre, became of the greatest consequence. It is more than probable that Englishmen engaged themselves in the commerce which passed along this line, and that the foundations of later English trade with the Scandinavian countries were already laid in this period. That England had shared in the commerce of the Carolingian and pre-Carolingian age is beyond question. In the centuries of Old English history the stream of traffic which reached England was often thin, and it rarely came to a volume at which it could support large masses of population disassociated from the soil. But it would be going against both evidence and probability to suggest that its continuity was at any time completely broken.

XV

THE LAST YEARS OF THE OLD ENGLISH STATE

THE last sixteen years of the Confessor's reign are often regarded as a prologue to the Norman Conquest. The initial Norman success was so conclusive, the victory of Norman ideas within the sphere of government was so rapid and complete, that to many historians the last phase of the Old English state has seemed the mere prelude to an inevitable collapse. The more obvious weaknesses of that state—the instability of its social organization, and the excessive power of a small group of wealthy families, have often been taken as signs of impending dissolution. On the other hand, the ideal of political unity was accepted in every part of pre-Conquest England, and the Old English kings had created a machinery which stronger hands could use for its realization. By law and custom, the powers through which the Conqueror re-edified the English state were inherent in the Old English monarchy. The history of the last years in which these powers were exercised by native rulers deserves to be studied for its own sake.

In the Old English conception of monarchy the king reigned by the grace of God. The idea is continually expressed in the titles attributed to Anglo-Saxon kings by the clerks who wrote their charters. Already before the end of the seventh century Æthelred of Mercia styles himself *Christo largiente rex*.[1] There was no need for a king to wait for his solemn anointing before he assumed a style of this type. Fifteen years before his belated coronation Edgar states that he has obtained the kingdom of the Mercians *divina favente gratia*.[2] It does not seem that Anglo-Saxon churchmen ever set themselves to follow out the implications of the doctrine of the king who rules by God's favour, or that they were embarrassed by the difficulty of reconciling it with the circumstances under which particular kings had actually come to their thrones. Bishop Werferth of Worcester, King Alfred's friend, allowed himself to attest more than one charter in which Ceolwulf II of Mercia, the nominee of heathen

[1] *C.S.* 76.   [2] *C.S.* 1040.

Danes, describes himself as *gratia Dei gratuita largiente rex*.[1] The point on which ecclesiastical opinion insisted was the principle that a king, once constituted, became the representative of God among his people. In one of his latest codes, drafted by the homilist Wulfstan, archbishop of York, Æthelred II is made to state categorically that a Christian king is the vicar of Christ among a Christian folk.[2] Even in the weakest of hands the royal power was upheld by a religious sanction against all other powers in the state.

The boundary between lay and spiritual authority was never defined in pre-Conquest England. The lay and spiritual powers were associated in every action of the Old English state and in the working of all its principal institutions. The bishop sat beside the earl in the shire court, ecclesiastical pleas were heard in the hundred court, and the spiritual element was so strong in the king's council that it is sometimes described as a synod. The effect of this alliance is perhaps most plainly seen in the religious colour which it imparted to Old English legislation, and in particular to that of the period between the accession of Edgar and the death of Cnut. There are many passages in these laws in which the king himself speaks as a homilist rather than a ruler. But the language of contemporary chroniclers leaves no room for doubt that the control of the church through appointments to its higher offices rested, in practice, in his hands.

The *Regularis Concordia* had provided that on the death of an abbot, or of a bishop of a monastic cathedral, his successor should be elected by the monks of the house subject to the king's approval. It is possible that this practice may have been followed during the lifetime of the great tenth-century reformers. But it has left few traces in the contemporary materials for the history of the church, and in the age immediately before the Conquest the king undoubtedly took the initiative in the appointment to bishoprics and abbeys. In the writs by which the king ordered a bishop or an abbot to be put in possession of the rights and property of his church, he naturally represents himself as the giver of the see or the abbey.[3] But the royal patronage of bishoprics and abbeys is brought out no less

---

[1] *C.S.* 540, 541.   [2] viii Æthelred, 2. 1.

[3] As when Edward the Confessor states that he has given the bishopric of Worcester to Wulfstan the monk with sake and soke and toll and team (*Facsimiles of Ancient Charters in the British Museum*, iv. 39).

clearly in chronicles written in monasteries for the use of monks. The Abingdon chronicle repeatedly states that the king has given a particular see to its new bishop. Appointments to abbeys are less carefully recorded, but in 1061 a chronicle written at St. Augustine's, Canterbury, states that when the king was told of its abbot's death he 'chose' a monk of Winchester cathedral to take his place.[1] There is no sign that the king's ecclesiastical patronage was ever contested by English churchmen of the age. They can rarely have been tempted to challenge the religious prerogatives of a king who was a pupil of the church, like Cnut, or a devout ascetic, like Edward the Confessor. But if pressed for a theory that would justify their attitude they would probably have replied that the king, whose highest duty was to protect the church, earned by that service the right of appointing its chief ministers.

Within the sphere of secular government all public authority was ultimately derived from the Crown. Even the earls, who fill the centre of the political stage in the generation before the Conquest, were in fact officers of the king's appointment. There was a natural tendency for a son to succeed a father in his earldom, and by the end of the Confessor's reign the houses which Godwine, Leofric, and Siward had raised to greatness were settled in power beyond the risk of any action that the king might take. Nevertheless, a revolution within an earldom or the disloyalty of its holder might at any time enable the king to demonstrate that in the last resort an earl came to his authority by a royal grant. The principle that an earl brought in by a revolution must be confirmed in office by the king was recognized on the eve of the Conquest in the wildest parts of England. In 1065 the Northumbrians cast out Tostig, son of Godwine, their earl, and chose Morcar, brother of the earl of Mercia, in his place. The last public act of the Confessor's life was to accede to their request that they might have Morcar for their earl.

Within the shires of his government the earl possessed authority and influence which set him above even the greatest of local magnates. By virtue of his office he was entitled to command the shire militia in time of war. It was expected that he and the diocesan bishop would sit together as joint presidents of the shire court, and they are generally addressed by name in royal writs sent down there. The earl seems normally to have received

[1] MS. E, *sub anno.*

the third part of the profits of justice done in the shire court, and the same proportion of the 'customs' rendered by the boroughs within his province. In some parts of England there are traces of estates permanently assigned to his maintenance. But early sources, which tell something of the earl's revenues and prove his importance in the public life of his district, reveal very little about his specific powers. Their vagueness on this matter is one among a number of indications that his essential functions were not administrative, but political. His fundamental duty was to act as the king's representative in the region under his control.

In the century before the Conquest the provincial governments were becoming larger than before, and the political importance of their holders was increasing. The Old English earls never lost touch with local affairs. In 1066 every earl was the lord by commendation of a considerable number of thegns and free men within his province. But the urgency of national politics in the period between the accession of King Æthelred and the death of King Edward inevitably made for the detachment of the great provincial ruler from the life of the district under his charge. This in turn created a need for a new officer of local government, more familiar than the ealdorman or earl with the individual landowners whose co-operation was essential for the conduct of public business. In the end the need was met by the appointment in each shire of a reeve—the *scir gerefa*, or sheriff, of pre-Conquest documents—chosen by the king, and responsible to him alone for the administration of local finance, the execution of justice, and the maintenance of the customs by which the shire was governed.

It was not until the Norman age that the sheriff came to the height of his power, and the early history of his office is very obscure. A document of Athelstan's reign shows a 'reeve' in charge of a district called a *scir*,[1] but in itself, the word *scir* meant no more than 'sphere of office', and it is not until the reign of Æthelred II that the county sheriff of historic times comes plainly into sight.[2] By the end of the Confessor's reign he had become the king's chief executive agent in every branch of

[1] vi Athelstan, 10.

[2] The existence of the sheriff as an executive officer before 1013 is proved by a curious passage in the *Institutes of Polity* (ed. K. Jost, p. 144), in which the bishops, who must take such action 'as the law-books teach' when a priest has forfeited his church for misconduct, are described metaphorically as 'Christ's sheriffs'.

local government. As the title of his office denotes, he ranked as a king's reeve, and his financial activities were only an extension of the duties which normally belonged to royal servants of this type. He was naturally charged with the collection of the payments due by custom to the king from his shire. He had the custody of many of the ancient demesnes of the Crown within his district, and he probably supervised the administration of all of them. In Warwickshire, and doubtless in other counties, he farmed the king's demesnes for a round sum of money to be rendered each year. He was expected to maintain the assessment of his shire to public burdens such as the Danegeld. He already carried, in substance, the financial responsibilities which lay on his successors in Norman and Angevin times.

It was probably as the guardian of the king's interests that the sheriff first became a prominent figure in the shire court. As the king's financial agent he was directly concerned with the ascertainment and collection of the sums which were due to the king from the profits of justice. The relationship in which he stood to the king, and the fact that the king expected him to secure obedience to the decisions of the court, must have given weight to his opinion when he spoke in pleas. In the earl's absence he had a well-founded claim to be accepted as the lay colleague of the bishop in the presidency of the court. The greater earls of the Confessor's reign cannot have been regular in attendance at the courts of individual shires, and much of their business was probably transacted under the guidance of their sheriffs. On the other hand, the earl had an important part to play as soon as ever the routine of the court was crossed by political issues. It was only under the presidency of a great lord with the whole power of the state obviously behind him that a shire court could proceed with assurance against a recalcitrant local magnate. There is no reason to think that the earls themselves regarded the shire court with indifference, and it was certainly not until the Norman age that the sheriff became its regular president.

The historical importance of the Old English sheriff is due to the fact that he was the servant of the king. Within the territory of even the greatest earls he stood for the executive power of the Crown. His presence in the shire is a useful warning against the temptation to regard the pre-Conquest earldoms as autonomous units of government. To the ordinary thegn of the shire the earl was a great lord, to whom a man might commend himself as an insurance against future trouble but with whom he had few contacts in the normal course of life. The sheriff was a man of his own class, with whom he might have official dealings at any time. At every turn the activities of the sheriff must have reminded the common man that whoever might be the earl of his shire, it was governed in the king's name.

The king was expected to rule, and the powers which custom allowed him were sufficient for his needs. But their effective use depended on the co-operation, not only of earls and bishops, but of the wealthy, unofficial aristocracy which led opinion in the shires. The leading members of this aristocracy, at least in southern England, were king's thegns, and the fact that the king was the personal lord of so many gentlemen of local influence was a very important source of strength to the Old English monarchy. Some of these men obtained positions at court, and the king's special favour raised others to earldoms. Odda of Deerhurst, who was appointed earl of western Wessex in 1051, undoubtedly belonged to this class. But in general such men seem to have been content with the position which their lands gave them in their own country, and they only come into history through their right or duty of attending the king at the great council of the realm, the *witena gemot*.

The history of this assembly can be followed through four centuries of development.[1] Throughout this period every king in England had been attended in his public acts by a council, of which his gesiths or thegns, ealdormen or earls, were the essential members. The ecclesiastical element in the council, which had become very prominent before the end of the eighth century and was dominant during part of the tenth, can be traced backwards to a point within a short distance of the age of the Conversion. But at the end of the ninth century it was still possible for King Alfred to grant land by charter in the presence of a company which included no churchmen,[2] and at the recorded councils of Edward the Confessor, though the ecclesiastical order was always powerful, the earls and thegns generally outnumber the bishops, abbots, and priests. Noblemen under

---

[1] The most convenient source of information about the Council is Liebermann's tract, *The National Assembly in the Anglo-Saxon Period* (1913).

[2] *C.S.* 581. The charter, preserved in two copies which seem to be independent, is witnessed by Edward, the king's son, and eight *ministri*.

direct allegiance to the king form the one element which runs through every known council between the reign of Hlothhere of Kent and the eve of the Conquest.

It is only in the most general terms that anything can be said about the number of persons present at a normal council. The only documents which show a council in session are the royal charters attested by its members. So far as they go, the lists of witnesses with which the charters end are good evidence for the composition of the assembly. But the length of a list of witnesses was determined by the size of the parchment on which the charter was written. Few lists‧ can be relied on for a full enumeration of the less important thegns who attended the meeting, and a description of the *witena gemot* which took this evidence at its face value would certainly over-emphasize the official element in the assembly. Even so, meetings are recorded which were certainly large and influential enough for the genuine discussion of political questions.[1] The most elaborate of them belong to the first half of the tenth century. No Old English councils can have been more impressive than the recurrent assemblies at which Athelstan had presided over Celtic princes, Danish earls, and the thegns and ealdormen of all England.[2] Large sessions of the council can be traced at a much later period. The body which confirmed the foundation of Eynsham abbey in 1005 comprised, besides the king, the queen, and the king's seven sons, 14 bishops, 16 abbots, 3 ealdormen, and 44 thegns.[3] But so far as can be seen these later councils included very few of the magnates of northern England, and it is the range of their interests rather than their composition which entitles them to be regarded as national assemblies.

In a sense the king himself owed his position to the council. The feeling that a king ought to be descended from a royal stock was shared by men of all classes in pre-Conquest England, and the instinct of loyalty to the ancient West Saxon dynasty was still a political force in 1066. But the descent of a great

---

[1] The national character of the assembly is well illustrated by a late-tenth-century document which states that a council held by Æthelred II at Cookham in Berkshire was attended by thegns 'from far and wide, both West Saxons and Mercians, Danes and English' (D. Whitelock, *Anglo-Saxon Wills*, p. 46). The reference to the 'Danes' is important in view of the rarity of Danish names in witness-lists of the period. [2] Above, pp. 351–2.

[3] *Cartulary of the Abbey of Eynsham*, ed. H. E. Salter, i, pp. 27–8.

executive office such as the kingship could not be settled by the rules which would govern the devolution of a private estate, and in the past it had often been hard to determine which member of the royal house should succeed to the crown on a vacancy. Of the eight kings who reigned between 899 and 1016 only three—Edmund, Eadred, and Eadwig—came by immediate inheritance to an uncontested kingdom. Under such conditions it was the obvious duty of the late king's council to take the initiative in the choice of his successor, and this, combined with traditions of the time when it had been for a dead lord's followers to proclaim and protect his heir, brought a strong elective element into English kingship. The greatest persons in the land admitted its existence. King Æthelred himself refers in a charter to the election of his brother Edward by the leading men of the lay and spiritual orders.[1] Æthelweard the chronicler, who was himself of royal descent, states as if it were a matter of course that Edward the Elder was 'elected by the magnates'.[2] The great analogy of the empire was at hand to reinforce the idea of elective monarchy, and there can be no doubt of its influence on Old English political conceptions.

The relations between the council and the king whom it had set in power cannot be expressed in any simple phrase. It was the duty of the council to advise the king on any problems which he might choose to bring to its notice. But the line between counsel and consent could never be firmly drawn, and in official documents Old English kings repeatedly use phrases which imply that their *witan* shared in the responsibility for their public acts. There are very few matters of importance to the state on which an Anglo-Saxon king cannot be shown to have consulted his council. During the century before the Conquest its assent is recorded to the issue of laws and the imposition of taxes, to negotiations with foreign powers, and to measures undertaken for the defence of the land. It was in his council that a king would prosecute suspected traitors against whom he felt strong enough to take legal action. That he was expected to secure its assent before creating privileged estates in land is made clear by the innumerable charters which assert that a royal gift of such an estate has been approved by the magnates of the kingdom. It is doubtful whether an Anglo-Saxon king thought it necessary to consult his *witan* before he

---

[1] C.D. 1312.   [2] *The Chronicle of Æthelweard*, ed. A. Campbell, p. 51.

appointed an ealdorman or earl, but he certainly asked for their advice in the use of his ecclesiastical patronage. The intimacy that might exist between a king and his council was shown at an earlier date when King Alfred, intending to dispose of his private property by will, summoned the West Saxon *witan*, and asked that none of them, for love or fear of him, should hesitate to say if there were any rules of common law which limited his power of bequest.[1]

Love or fear must often have hindered individual members of the council from opposing the declared will of the king. In one way or another all of them owed their seats to the reigning king or to one of his predecessors. The bishops, abbots, and earls attended in virtue of offices which they held by a royal grant; the priests belonged to the king's household; the thegns were present in obedience to a royal summons. It was only on rare occasions that an assembly thus constituted could have offered a direct opposition to a policy on which the king had set his mind. On the other hand, it is important to remember that in the lower ranges of the council, among the thegns whose names end witness-lists, there were men whom the king could not easily coerce, and whose influence in the shires could not be ignored. There seems no doubt, for example, that the thegn named Wulfric, whose undistinguished signature occurs in many charters dated between 988 and 1002, was identical with Wulfric Spot, the founder of Burton abbey, whose will disposed of more than seventy villages in northern Mercia and southern Northumbria,[2] and whose loyalty must have been essential for the good order of that country. No doubt he had become the king's own man by an oath of fealty, and there is evidence that the king had given him some of his land. But most of it was clearly inherited property, he held no office which the king could take away, and he was as free as any member of a medieval parliament to speak his mind about public questions. It was in men of his type, who were much more numerous than would be gathered from narrative history, that the potential independence of the *witan* lay.

But the political significance of an assembly should not be measured by the number of its conflicts with its president. Historically, the *witena gemot* is important because it kept alive

---

[1] F. E. Harmer, *English Historical Documents*, p. 50.
[2] D. Whitelock, *Anglo-Saxon Wills*, pp. 46–51, 152–3.

the principle that the king must govern under advice. In late Old English history there are a number of periods during which the government of England must have rested with the council. It alone can have maintained the continuity of administration amid the uncertainty as to the succession after Edgar's death, and in times such as the reign of Harthacnut and the early years of the Confessor, when the king knew little about England. But these brief phases of conciliar government are insignificant in comparison with the generations in which the existence of the council made it impossible for any king to rule as an autocrat. In the nineteenth century the importance of the council was sometimes exaggerated by historians who attributed to it a more positive function, and a stronger political consciousness than the facts warrant. Its history has been encumbered by theories of a democratic origin, which are contradicted both by the derivation of the word *witan* and by the nature of the earliest recorded councils. The natural reaction from these opinions to a belittlement of the council has sometimes been carried too far. Its weaknesses are apparent. Its composition was indeterminate, and gave too little influence to the nobility of northern England. It was dependent on the king for the right to meet, and it cannot have possessed any sense of inherent unity. But in however narrow a form, it gave the character of a constitutional monarchy to the Old English state.

In comparison with England, Normandy in the mid-eleventh century was still a state in the making. For more than a hundred years the whole country between the Couesnon and the Epte had been subject to a ruler who styled himself indifferently the count, the marquis, the prince, or the duke of the Normans. In language and social customs the Normans had become Frenchmen, and on the surface there was little beyond the survival of a few outlandish names to show their alien ancestry. Their dukes regarded themselves as the peers of the greater feudatories of the French Crown, and their loyalty to the dynasty of Hugh Capet is one of the central facts in its early history. But they were not sovereign princes, and the territorial limits of their authority were ill defined. The integrity of the Norman frontier was compromised at many points by the divided allegiance of border families such as the house of Bellême, which held the castleries of Domfront and Alençon of the duke of

Normandy, the Saosnois of the count of Maine, and Bellême of the king of France. It was of more consequence that principles which governed the political association of longer-established peoples could still be defied in eleventh-century Normandy. The recognition of Duke Robert's illegitimate son as heir to his father's lordship would have been impossible in any country where the church, and the theory of the state for which it stood, had their accustomed influence.

It is suggestive of an imperfect political development that the documentary materials for early Norman history are very few.[1] There is no sign that the Conqueror or any of his predecessors issued written laws for the duchy. Their charters are rare, and the series only begins late in the tenth century. In their general lines they resemble the contemporary charters of the kings of France. An official who styles himself Chancellor appears in two charters of Duke Richard II. But the title does not appear again before 1066, and the charters of the intervening years are so irregular in form that they cannot be the work of an organized writing-office fit to be called a chancery. As evidence of a central authority in government the scanty records of the Conqueror's Norman reign are in no way comparable to the long succession of writs and solemn charters produced by the clerks of Edward the Confessor.

This means that little is known about the nature of the company which attended the duke in the ordinary business of his government. There is no need to doubt that the Norman dukes summoned great councils to deal with great occasions. It was remembered that Duke William had held a council of magnates before commiting himself to an invasion of England. But one of the Conqueror's own chaplains, after comparing the Norman council with the Roman senate, said that he had never known it to differ from the duke.[2] The Conqueror's Norman charters suggest that he rarely convened any assembly which in weight or numbers can be compared with the *witan* of Edward the Confessor. The assemblies which William is known to have held as duke resemble courts rather than councils. Of the magnates who commonly attended them some

---

[1] For the condition of Normandy in the generation before the Conquest a general reference may be made to C. H. Haskins, *Norman Institutions*, pp. 1–61.

[2] William of Poitiers, *Gesta Willelmi Ducis*, ed. Giles, pp. 121–2, and also ed. R. Foreville, *Histoire de Guillaume le Conquérant* (Paris, 1952), p. 149.

were his kinsmen and others his personal friends. The chief officers of his household were often present, and a normal session would include one or more of the barons who, with the title of *vicecomites*, were looking after the duke's financial interests, and keeping order for him in the local divisions of the duchy, The ecclesiastical order was generally represented by at least one bishop, and by a small group of the duke's chaplains. But there is nothing to suggest that the Norman bishops, like their English contemporaries, held themselves bound to constant attendance upon the secular ruler, and there is little trace in these assemblies of the unofficial upland barons who corresponded socially to the greater thegns of the English national council. The fluctuating body of advisers which helped the duke of Normandy in his government resembled neither the Old English *witan*, nor the Great Council which continued its functions and traditions under the Norman kings, but the informal *Curia Regis* of the Anglo-Norman state.

The outstanding part which the Normans played in history was made possible by their success in adapting themselves to the new developments in the art of war which arose from the confusion of the Dark Ages. They were eminent as knights and castle-builders. So far as is known, they originated nothing in either direction. The essence of knighthood was ability to fight on horseback. The military value of men thus skilled had been recognized ever since the Carolingian time, and there is nothing to show that the Normans made any original contribution to the training or equipment of the individual warrior. In the early stages of the evolution of the castle Anjou is much more prominent than Normandy. The military distinction of the Normans lies in the mastery with which they used small defensible posts as bases for cavalry action in large-scale warfare outside their own land.

Through the work of modern archaeologists the nature of these defensible posts has been made clear. The earliest Norman castles were structures of earth and timber. The essential feature of such a castle was an earthen mound, or 'motte', surrounded by a ditch, and crowned by a palisaded bank, which enclosed a wooden tower. Beneath the mound a base-court, or bailey, with its own defences of ditch, bank, and palisade, contained the quarters of the garrison, with the stables and other buildings required for their accommodation. It was an elementary device, but it was effective, and it could be repeated quickly, with little expenditure in labour or supervision. It was through castles of this simple type that the Norman conquest of England was secured.[1] In Normandy earthworks of this pattern occur at many places which were the seats of important families, and the ease with which such castles could be raised by individual barons seriously delayed the centralization of the duchy.

Nevertheless there is little doubt that in 1066 most of the greater barons, all the bishops, and the more ancient monasteries of Normandy held their lands of the duke, subject to the duty of providing a specified number of knights for his service when he had occasion to ask for them. The introduction of such a system into England immediately after the Conquest implies that it was well established in Normandy. There are definite traces of it in the Conqueror's early years, and there are indications that it had been in force a generation before. There is also evidence that by 1050, at latest, lords had begun to arrange for the performance of the service which they owed to the duke by granting estates to knights who would undertake to serve in the duke's host. The knight's fee, which was the basic unit of military tenure in post-Conquest England, was undoubtedly a Norman institution. The extent to which the system had been carried out at the time of Duke William's accession is a harder question. There is no reason to doubt that the older baronage of the duchy held itself bound to help its lord, the duke, to do the military service which he owed to the French king. On the other hand, there can have been no precise definition of military service in Normandy before the mass of the Norman fighting-men had accommodated itself to French methods of warfare, and the most ancient Norman families were settled in their possessions before this development can have taken place. The heads of these families regarded themselves as the social equals of their dukes, and their political conduct betrays no consciousness that they owed their lands to a ducal gift. All

---

[1] They are the subject of a definitive study by Ella S. Armitage, *The Early Norman Castles of the British Isles* (1912). Their place in the history of English fortification is shown in detail by A. Hamilton Thompson, *Military Architecture in England during the Middle Ages* (1912), and is indicated in outline by F. M. Stenton, *The Development of the Castle in England and Wales* (Historical Association Leaflet 22, ed. 2, 1933), reprinted in *Social Life in Early England*, ed. G. Barraclough (1960). See also R. A. Brown, *English Medieval Castles* (1954).

this suggests that tenure by military service, in the strict sense of the phrase, was established in Normandy by gradual degrees. It may have been imposed at an early date on the Norman bishops, and a wide field for its introduction was given by the counties—Arques, Eu, the Hiesmois, Évreux, Brionne, and Mortain—which dukes Richard I and II created for their kinsmen. The statement of an eleventh-century writer that Richard II granted the Hiesmois to his brother *ut inde ei militiae exhiberet statuta* clearly represents a good tradition.[1] But the sphere of military tenure must have been greatly enlarged by its extension to lands brought into the duke's power by failure of heirs or confiscation after revolt. Every occasion of this kind allowed the duke to create a new military fee or remodel an old one to his advantage. These occasions were common in the tenth and eleventh centuries. At least four rebellions were suppressed in Normandy between 1047 and 1053. If Normandy in 1066 can be described as a centralized state—and although the description goes too far, it has a basis of fact—it is largely because of the forfeited lordships which the dukes had been able to reconstitute in their own interests.

But it is dangerous to assume that the Conqueror ever controlled the military organization of Normandy with the mastery that belonged to him in his English kingdom. Tenure by military service was introduced into England by his authority. It was for him to determine the number of knights to be provided for his service by each of his followers to whom he had given English land. In general, the service for which he stipulated—the *servitium debitum* of English documents—was so heavy that the ordinary tenant in chief had neither land nor money enough to maintain a force of knights much in excess of the number which he owed to the Crown. In Normandy the institution of knighthood came gradually into being and was first applied by individual lords to their own purposes without reference to the head of the state. Among the fiercely competitive nobility of the duchy every great lord was compelled in self-defence to keep a force of mounted fighting-men in his service. The size of a military retinue bore no relation to the amount of military service which its lord owed to the duke. The burden of this service was much lighter than that which the Conqueror laid on his followers in England, and in

[1] William of Jumièges, *Gesta Normannorum Ducum*, ed. Marx, p. 74.

1066 many lords could discharge it by joining the duke's host with a mere contingent of their household knights.

In the constitution of the early Norman state there was no real check upon the use that a lord might make of his retinue. Towards the end of the Conqueror's reign there was a rule in Normandy that no castle might be built in Normandy without his consent.[1] At its close many baronial castles were being garrisoned by his troops. But his success in England had increased his power in Normandy, and there is no sign that any earlier duke had attempted to interfere with the baronial right of building and manning castles. The custom of private warfare was so firmly rooted that the Conqueror himself could not abolish it.[2] In his father's time, to judge from a story in the Life of Herluin of Bec,[3] it was only with the consent of each party that the duke could impose a settlement on great men in conflict. The story runs that Count Gilbert of Brionne collected a large force of knights in order to avenge himself on his enemies, and in his magnanimity offered to give them battle on an appointed day. On the night before the battle, when the armies were in position, messengers from Duke Robert besought the leaders to swear that they would accept the duke's judgement instead of fighting. They did so, but the narrative makes it clear that they only referred their quarrel to the duke because their numbers were nearly equal, and a battle would have been disastrous to either side.

Over the unattached knights who appear in this and other stories of the time the early dukes had no effective control. No ruler who was master in his own land would have permitted the migration of expert warriors from which the Norman states in Italy rose. Many of these adventurers left Normandy during the minority of William the Conqueror, when the duke's authority was in abeyance. But the movement had already gone far before William's accession, and the volume which it had reached in his father's time shows that it could not be held in check by a duke who was among the strongest of his line. The force behind it was clearly the rise of a large population in a small country, and in particular, a rapid increase in the number of young men qualified for military adventure, for whom there was little scope in Normandy. It is one of the

[1] C. H. Haskins, *Norman Institutions*, p. 282.   [2] Ibid., pp. 278, 283-4.
[3] Ed. J. Armitage Robinson, *Gilbert Crispin*, p. 88.

Conqueror's many titles to statesmanship that he was the first Norman duke to see the use that could be made of this surplus energy for the enlargement of his own power.

The possibility that he might one day become king of England may have been in the background of his mind from the very beginning of his effective reign in Normandy. It was not until 1047 that he was set firmly in his duchy by the victory at Val-ès-dunes won on his behalf over Norman rebels by his lord, King Henry of France. By this date it is probable that well-informed observers at the English court suspected the approach of a problem about the succession to the English throne. The asceticism of King Edward's life, which meant that he would leave no direct heir, must have been known to all who were in attendance on him. William was well placed for information about the English court. A Norman abbot had lately become bishop of London, there were Norman priests in King Edward's chapel, and a lady of the English royal family was married to a member of the duke's immediate circle. Godgifu, King Edward's sister, who had found shelter with her brothers in Normandy while Cnut was invading England, had been married by Duke Robert to his friend Drogo, count of the Vexin.[1] Before 1050 Ralf, her second son, had received an English earldom. After her husband's death in 1035 she married Eustace, count of Boulogne, an independent lord, but William's ally. From one or other of these sources William could learn all that was to be known about the political situation in England. He must certainly have known that the only male representative of the royal family, apart from the king, was his nephew Edward, son of Edmund Ironside, who was living as an exile in Hungary, outside the range of ordinary communication.

It is highly probable that the king himself at this time hoped that William would succeed him. There were several men with a title of some kind to the English kingship, but there was nothing to give him a personal inclination towards any of them. There was no reason why he should encourage Swein Estrithson to reunite England and Denmark. Harold Hardrada of Norway, who believed that the treaty between Magnus and Harthacnut had made him heir to England, must have seemed an outer barbarian to a king with Edward's outlook on the world. The king's natural heir, Edmund Ironside's son, had

[1] J. H. Round, *Studies in Peerage and Family History*, pp. 147-9.

been a young child when he was taken out of England in the early days of Cnut, and little beyond the fact of his survival can have been known about him. William of Normandy had a direct claim on Edward's interest as the son of the man who had protected him in exile. That he carried this interest to the point of recognizing William as his heir is placed beyond serious doubt by the reiterated assertion of Norman writers that there was an occasion when he promised the kingdom to William. They do not agree among themselves about the date of the promise. It could not have been given in Edward's later years, when Harold, son of Godwine, dominated his court. But there is much to suggest that some recognition of the kind was an incident in the episode which is conveniently called the English revolution of 1051.

The story of this revolution is complicated by the existence of two contemporary narratives which take the same facts from different angles. One of them was written at Canterbury by an admirer of Earl Godwine. The other comes from the north or northern midlands, and the attitude of its writer is detached. The whole story cannot be reconstructed, for, apart from the gaps in each writer's knowledge, neither of them had much skill in the management of a narrative, and neither saw far beneath the surface of events. But their stories show at least the general development of a crisis which greatly impressed contemporaries, and through its results became one of the ultimate causes of the Norman invasion of 1066.

At the beginning of 1051 Earl Godwine was the king's most prominent subject. His own earldom extended along the south coast from Kent to Cornwall. His daughter was married to the king. He had recently secured the recall of Swein, his disreputable eldest son, and had obtained his appointment to an earldom which included the Mercian shires of Oxford, Gloucester, and Hereford, and the West Saxon shires of Berkshire and Somerset. Harold, Godwine's second son, was earl of Essex, East Anglia, Cambridgeshire, and Huntingdonshire. In the mere extent of its earldoms the house of Godwine was more powerful at the end of 1050 than at the beginning of 1066. But politically it was isolated. Leofric of Mercia and Siward of Northumbria regarded Godwine, if not with jealousy, at least with complete detachment. The rejection of his proposal to support his nephew, Swein Estrithson, with English ships had shown that they could defeat a policy on which he had set his mind. There is no sign that the king ever forgave him for his share in the death of Alfred the Ætheling. The villainous part which he always plays in Norman tradition proves that the Normans at court regarded him as the betrayer of a prince who by the half blood was of their race. It shows an essential weakness in his position that he was unable to prevent Normans from settling within his group of family earldoms. At a short distance from Hereford, one of Earl Swein's shire-towns, a Norman named Osbern was established in the large manors of Burghill and Hope under Dinmore. A Norman lord who is unnamed, but was probably identical with Osbern of Burghill, had built and garrisoned a castle in Herefordshire,[1] which was a great offence to the men of the country. The suddenness of Godwine's fall in 1051 is perhaps less surprising than it seemed at the time to men who were over-impressed by his appearance of power.

According to the Canterbury writer the trouble began with an affray between the men of Dover and the retinue of Count Eustace of Boulogne, who was returning to France after a visit to King Edward. The count's men, who must have claimed that their lord, while in England, was the king's guest, demanded quarters at Dover overbearingly. In a struggle that followed about twenty men were killed and many wounded, on either side. The count, with the rest of his company, returned to the king, who, without any inquiry that has been recorded, ordered Godwine, as earl of Wessex, to go to Dover and harry the town. A military execution of this kind was the accepted method of punishing offending communities. King

---

[1] Probably Ewias Harold in the Golden Valley (Round, *Feudal England*, pp. 322–4). Domesday Book shows that this castle was built before 1066, though it does not name its pre-Conquest lord. In 1086 it belonged to Alfred of Marlborough, together with Burghill and Hope, which Domesday Book says had belonged to Osbern, Alfred's uncle, when Godwine and Harold were exiled (D.B. i. 186). Osbern was probably identical with the Norman Osbern *cognomento Pentecost* who was compelled to leave England in 1052 (Florence of Worcester, i. 210). The emphasis laid by the *Chronicle* on the building of a single castle makes it probable, though far from certain, that it was the first work of its kind in the county. Two other pre-Conquest castles are recorded in Herefordshire—Hereford itself and Richard's Castle. The first existed on 1055 (*Chron.*, *sub anno*), and the second takes its name from Richard, son of Scrob, a Norman who was settled in Herefordshire in 1052 and left his castle and lands to his son Osbern fitz Richard, who was holding them in 1086. But there is no evidence that either of these castles had been built as early as 1051.

Eadred had dealt in this way with the men of Thetford, where an abbot had been murdered, Edgar had ordered a harrying of Thanet because some traders from York had been killed there,[1] and Harthacnut had caused Worcester to be sacked because its inhabitants had killed two of his housecarles. But, to the lasting benefit of his reputation among the men of Kent, Godwine refused to undertake the expedition. Like many later historians, he may have felt that the king had passed a crushing sentence without knowing all the facts. The Canterbury writer suggests that he refused because he held the count's men responsible for the affair at Dover, and was in any case unwilling to ravage his own earldom. But whatever its motive, an earl's refusal to obey an explicit order from the king came dangerously close to rebellion. Godwine must have known that he was giving grounds sufficient to justify any action which the king might take against him. He seems to have decided that the time had come for a trial of strength with his enemies, and he began at once to mobilize all the forces which his family could command.

The northern chronicler seems to have known little about events in Kent, and his account of them is meagre. But he supplies the important fact that on 1 September Godwine and his sons Swein and Harold assembled a great army on the Cotswolds near Tetbury, some fifteen miles from Gloucester, where the king was then residing. He also states that the army was ready to fight against the king, unless he surrendered Count Eustace and his men, and the garrison of the castle which had given offence in Herefordshire. The Canterbury chronicler mentions the muster of Godwine's army, but he conceals its size, and represents it as demanding to go to its royal lord and his council and obtain their advice and help for the avenging of the disgrace that had been brought on the king and all the people. The words, which avoid particulars, and threaten war discreetly, are probably a quotation from a manifesto actually put forward by Godwine on this occasion. It seems clear that at the moment there was no council in being to which the army could go, for the Canterbury chronicle fortunately states that the assembly which the king convened in order to deal with Godwine was summoned to be at Gloucester on or about 8 September—that is, a week after the date given

---

[1] Roger of Wendover, *Flores Historiarum*, ed. Coxe, i, pp. 414-15.

by the northern chronicler for the appearance of the army on
the Cotswolds. The king, in fact, was taken by surprise. He
was saved from humiliation by Earls Leofric and Siward, each
of whom came to Gloucester with a small force, and sent for
reinforcements when they saw what was happening in the
south. They were joined by Ralf, King Edward's nephew,
with a contingent from his unnamed earldom, and before long
the king was surrounded by an army which was strong enough
to move against Godwine. Each army was ready for an engagement, but neither desired one. Godwine's army, though it
prepared itself to meet an attack, was unwilling to give battle to
the king in person, and there was a feeling among the king's
men that it would be disastrous for the country if the greatest
lords in England were to fight with one another. The deadlock
was ended by an agreement that the armies should separate
without fighting, that hostages should be given by each side
to the other, and that a general meeting of the *witan* should be
held in London on 24 September, when Godwine and his sons
should appear and answer the charges which the king would
bring against them.

The compromise saved Godwine's dignity, but it meant that
he had failed to impose his will on the king by force, and it must
have disillusioned his followers. The king at once proceeded to
make their position impossible. When summoning the *witan*,
he called out the militia of all England. This meant that even
within the earldoms of Godwine and his family the ordinary
thegns and free men on whose backing Godwine relied were
required to join an army levied against him. The three earls
were still at the head of a large force when they appeared at
Southwark for the meeting of the *witan*, but it was outnumbered
and disheartened and it soon began to disperse. The earls were
rapidly falling into the king's mercy, and he set himself to drive
them into exile. For an offence which no chronicle mentions
Earl Swein was once more declared an outlaw. The thegns
who had formerly done homage to Godwine, Swein, or Harold,
were required to find sureties that they would become the
king's men. Godwine and Harold were specially summoned to
make their defence before the *witan*, but they refused to attend
without an assurance, guaranteed by hostages, that they would
enjoy the king's peace there. They were then ordered to appear
with twelve men to support them, but Godwine again insisted

on hostages and a grant of the king's peace. The king's reply was to tell him that he had five days in which to leave the country. Upon this, Godwine and his wife, with their sons Swein, Tostig, and Gyrth, made their way to Bosham in Sussex. Tostig's wife, who was with them, was a kinswoman of Baldwin, count of Flanders, and the whole company spent the winter under his protection at Bruges. Harold and Leofwine, Godwine's youngest son in public life, rode to Bristol, and took ship there for Ireland. The king completed his deliverance by sending his wife away from court to live in retirement at Wherwell abbey.

During the twelve months after Godwine's fall, for the only time in his reign, King Edward was free from the dominance of a strong personality in the background of his court. Neither Siward nor Leofric ever showed any inclination towards the part in national affairs which had been taken by Godwine and was to be taken by Harold. Each of them carried a heavier responsibility of local government than had belonged to Godwine or any member of his family, and neither of them was likely to dictate to the king about the choice of his ministers or associates. The king, on his part, used his new freedom deliberately for the strengthening of the Norman element in the English state. His patronage of individual Normans and his deference to their advice were the principal cause of the reaction which next year brought back Godwine into power. There was no need for the king to squander the resources of the Crown on them. He had more than enough land for their support in the estates forfeited by Godwine and his family. But he certainly gave some of them places at court, and he seems to have appointed others to offices in the country. The English description of the foreigners as men who 'promoted injustice, gave unjust judgements, and counselled folly' suggests a group of Norman sheriffs trying to administer a system of law which they did not understand among people whose ways of life were unfamiliar. Englishmen naturally hated them, and their position in the country can hardly have been improved if, as is probable, the king let it be known that he wished the duke of Normandy to be regarded as his heir. The absence of any reference to such a declaration in the English chronicles of the time proves nothing. Only one out of three contemporary chronicles mentions the important fact that in the winter of

1051 or the spring of 1052 Duke William crossed the sea with a large retinue of Frenchmen and was received by King Edward. Nothing is, or indeed could be, said about their conversation. But it was so unusual for a reigning prince to leave his own dominions that the visit is unlikely to have been a mere act of courtesy. It is in every way probable that the duke came in order to receive a recognition of his standing as successor designate to the crown.

Within a year any prospect of a quiet succession which may have been opened to the duke was closed by the restoration of Godwine. He had failed in 1051 because, in the last resort, the thegns and free landowners on whom he relied had been unwilling to attack the king. In 1052 he avoided this disadvantage by providing himself with a force of seamen who were less scrupulous, and against whom it was less easy for the king to take action. He had come to be regarded as the great enemy of the king's Frenchmen, and there was a genuine movement of popular feeling towards him. But its strength has sometimes been over-estimated, and it was a military enterprise which brought him back to power.

With a few ships collected in Flemish waters he sailed from the mouth of the Yser on 22 June, evaded a small fleet which the king had stationed off Sandwich, and landed at Dungeness. He was in his own country there, and within a short time he obtained promises of support from the men of Kent, Surrey, and Sussex, and in particular from the 'butsecarles', or seamen, of Hastings. The king's fleet was kept by storms from getting into touch with Godwine's ships, and after a wasted voyage it returned to Sandwich and before long was brought to London, apparently in order that it might be provided with more efficient commanders and more trustworthy crews. Godwine took the opportunity of returning to Flanders; still a proscribed fugitive, but with the knowledge that he could at any time cause a formidable revolt in south-eastern England. Before he had been long in Flanders the crews of the king's fleet, tired of the delays in its reorganization, abandoned their ships, and left the whole south coast of England open to attack. As soon as he realized this Godwine sailed with all the force that he could command to the Isle of Wight, which he harried until its inhabitants submitted to his requisitions, and then passed on to Portland, where he behaved in the same way. His object in sailing so far to the west was to join forces as soon as possible with Harold, who was coming from Ireland to help him. The need for provisions, which caused Godwine's outrages, had brought Harold to an engagement at Porlock with the militia of Devon and Somerset, in which more than thirty thegns and many humble men were killed. But he seems to have met no further resistance, and his fleet was intact when he met his father off the south coast, somewhere between Portland and Land's End.

Thenceforward, according to a contemporary, 'they did no great harm', but set themselves to win over the seaboard population to their side. Their force, though large enough for destructive raids, was inadequate to a struggle with the organized power of the state, and their chance of success depended on the speed with which they could increase it. Everything suggests that Godwine, foreseeing this necessity, had made friends in all the south-eastern ports during his first descent upon England. He was now joined by the ships and seamen of Pevensey, Romney, Hythe, Folkestone, Dover, and Sandwich. The men of Hastings are known to have promised him their help, and it is clear that, when he turned towards London along the channel between Thanet and the mainland, he was commanding the naval force of all the towns which were afterwards called the Cinque Ports, and of many lesser harbours. It was this accession of strength which decided the struggle in his favour. The king possessed no more than fifty ships, which were in no condition to meet Godwine's fleet, and were moored on the north bank of the Thames at London, above the bridge. He had sent up country for more troops, but they were late in coming; the Southwark bank of the river was occupied by Godwine's supporters, and the citizens of London, with whom he had been in communication, were ready to declare themselves on his side. The initiative in the events that followed was naturally his. On 14 September he anchored in the river off Southwark at low tide, and before the flood was in he had sent messengers to confirm his understanding with the Londoners. With the incoming tide he and his ships passed through the bridge, keeping close to the Southwark shore, and then put diagonally across the river, so as to surround the king's small fleet. The force around the king was large, but unwilling to fight with its own countrymen. Godwine's ships' companies, sailors by profession and pirates at heart, were ready to fight with anyone, and he could scarcely keep them in hand while the king was being persuaded to agree upon terms of peace. At last through the mediation of bishop Stigand of Winchester and other 'wise men', it was arranged that hostages should be given on either side. Godwine and Harold landed on the north bank with a force sufficient to ensure their safety, and in the morning there was a meeting of the *witan* outside London, where Godwine replied in proper legal form to all the charges which the king had brought against him and his family. By admitting Godwine to his defence the king had virtually conceded the demand for his restoration, and the *witan* had no choice but to declare itself satisfied with his answer. It then proceeded to reverse the whole policy which the government had been following during the past twelve months. It established what it seems to have called 'full friendship' between Godwine and the king, gave him back his earldom, and restored all that had been taken from him and his family. All the Frenchmen who had lately come into England were outlawed, with the exception of those whom the king wished to have about him, and of whose loyalty to him and his people the *witan* were assured. The archbishop of Canterbury and the bishop of Dorchester, who had fled from the city when Godwine entered it, were included in the sentence, and their property was divided between Godwine, Harold, and the queen[1], who was now brought back to court. To mark the end of the crisis, the *witan* issued a conventional promise of 'good law' to the people at large.

The crisis marks an important turning-point in the Confessor's reign. It established the house of Godwine so firmly in power that neither the king nor any rival family could ever dislodge it. It reduced the Normans in England to political insignificance, and thereby decided that if the duke of Normandy were ever to become king of England it could only be through war. By treating Archbishop Robert's see as vacant and setting Bishop Stigand in his place, Godwine and his party made it possible for the duke to appear as the champion of ecclesiastical order when the time came for his venture. But the crisis is no less interesting as an illustration of the attitude of Englishmen and their leaders towards the state. Many historians have taken Godwine's side in his original dispute with the king, and most

[1] *Chronicle*, MS. C.

of them have felt that the king was vindictive towards him. It is natural to sympathize with a man who was so clearly the representative of national feeling against foreign influence at court. But it remains the fact that he brought the country to the verge of civil war at a time when there was grave danger from abroad. The *Chronicle* states that the king's men refused to fight against Godwine in 1052 because they felt that the slaughter of Englishmen would leave the country open to invasion. Their refusal was embarrassing for the king, but their instinct was sound. Every Englishman with any knowledge of the world must have been aware of the peril in which England lay from the ambition of Harold Hardrada. The unwillingness of Leofric and Siward to go to extremities against Godwine is sufficiently explained by their sense of this danger. Against this background, Godwine's conduct is indefensible. As the history of Æthelred's reign had shown, English security against foreign enemies depended on the respect which the king's leading subjects were prepared to show to his authority, and was impaired by any event which lowered its prestige. The campaign by which Godwine forced himself back on a reluctant king was an encouragement to every lord with whom the king was at variance, and, by its revelation of English naval weakness, to every foreign ruler with designs upon the English Crown.

Earl Godwine died on 15 April 1053, within seven months of his restoration. Swein, his eldest son, who would naturally have become the head of the family, had died in exile, while returning from a pilgrimage to Jerusalem. The earldom of Wessex therefore passed to Harold, who was followed in his East Anglian government by Ælfgar, son of Leofric of Mercia. The earldom which Swein had held[1] was divided. Somerset and Berkshire were reunited to Wessex. There is nothing to show the arrangement that was made for Gloucestershire. Oxfordshire and Herefordshire were given to Ralf, King Edward's nephew.[2] He died in 1057, but the four years of his rule in Herefordshire are important in local history, for he made a serious attempt to organize the county as a frontier province. He tried, though unsuccessfully, to convert the county militia into a mounted force; he caused a castle to be built at Hereford, and there is evidence that he encouraged other Frenchmen to

---

[1] Above, p. 561.
[2] For Oxfordshire see F. E. Harmer, *Anglo-Saxon Writs*, no. 55.

plant castles at points where Welsh raiders could most easily be checked. So far as can be seen, he was the real founder of the system of organized castle-building which under the Norman kings made Herefordshire a principal bulwark of the midlands against assault from Wales.

From 1053 until 1055 Harold's earldom of Wessex was the only provincial government which remained in Godwine's family. In the latter year its power was vastly, if precariously, increased when Tostig, Harold's brother, was made earl of Northumbria. Earl Siward, who had held the northern frontier of England for fifteen years, was at the height of his authority when he died, in the spring of 1055. The last of his battles had been fought in the previous summer, when he directed an invasion of Scotland by sea and land, and defeated Macbeth, its king. It is probable that Siward was acting as the protector of Malcolm, son of Duncan, king of Scots, whom Macbeth had killed in battle in 1040. Macbeth was not finally overthrown until 1057, but there are indications in tradition that Malcolm was restored to part of his father's territory as a result of this campaign. The death of Siward's eldest son in the battle affected English history more directly. When Siward himself died in the following year Waltheof, his one surviving son, was probably a child, and certainly too young to rule the most difficult of English earldoms. There were several descendants of the English lords of Bamburgh among whom a successor for Siward could have been found. But it is not surprising that the king and his council took this unique opportunity of governing Northumbria through an earl in close association with the court.

Up to a point the experiment was successful. Tostig secured the friendship of Malcolm, king of Scots, and according to an early tradition became his sworn brother. Their good relations were made apparent in 1059, when Malcolm visited King Edward under the escort of Tostig, the archbishop of York, and the bishop of Durham. No visit of the kind had been paid by any Scottish king since Kenneth I came to Edgar's court, more than eighty years before. The friendship between Malcolm and Tostig did not prevent the king from harrying Northumbria in 1061, when the earl was out of the country; but towards Tostig himself Malcolm seems always to have kept the peace, and their relationship was a rough guarantee of the Northumbrian border in normal times. It was in regard to the govern-

ment of his earldom that Tostig failed. His failure was probably
inevitable. Siward, a Dane by birth and the husband of a
Northumbrian lady, had every qualification for ruling the
Anglo-Scandinavian population of the north. He understood
the people over whom he was set, and the ferocity which made
him a figure of legend to later generations was admired by
men who themselves were always ready for violence. Tostig had
no local connections, and the men of his earldom, regarding him
as an Englishman from the south, were disposed to resent every
display of force to which the state of the country compelled
him. That they endured his government for ten years shows
their respect for the authority of the king who had appointed
him.

The history of southern England in this period is curiously
obscure. Many events are recorded, but different chroniclers
often contradict each other in regard to the same incident,
and a chronicler will sometimes go out of his way to hint that
there is more behind a particular episode than he has cared to
set down. The most important event of the period is touched
by this air of mystery. The fall of King Edward's Norman
friends in the autumn of 1052 had given a new turn to the
problem of the succession. The obvious heir—Edward, the son
of Edmund Ironside—was brought into the centre of the picture,
and in 1054 Bishop Ealdred of Worcester was sent to Germany
to negotiate with the emperor for his return from exile. Edward
had been treated in Hungary as a royal prince and had married
a lady of the Imperial house.[1] It is hardly surprising that when
the way was clear for his return he postponed his journey for at
least two years.[2] There is nothing inherently suspicious in the
fact that he died very soon after he landed in England, and
before he had come to court. But there is a strong suggestion
of intrigue behind the scenes in a chronicler's complaint that
'we do not know why it was so arranged that he could not see
King Edward, his kinsman'.

Dark sayings like this reflect the political uncertainty of the
time. It is doubtful if King Edward ever recovered completely

---

[1] S. Fest (*The Hungarian Origin of St. Margaret of Scotland*, 1940) has argued
that she was a daughter of Stephen, King of Hungary and of Gisela, niece of the
Emperor, Henry II. But the evidence is too vague to establish her precise descent.

[2] A visit of Earl Harold to Flanders late in 1056 was probably connected with
the arrangements for Edward's reception. See P. Grierson, *E.H.R.* li (1936), pp.
90–7.

from his humiliation before Godwine in 1052. He continued to discharge all the formal duties of a king, and he never lost touch with public affairs. But, so far as can be seen, he abandoned the attempt to control them. In his later years his religious interests, and in particular his plans for the abbey which he intended to found at Westminster, seem to have filled the centre of his mind. Under a king whose grip on life was weakening, the decision on every major issue affecting the state fell to the small group of great nobles who monopolized the provincial governments. The rise of Earl Harold to supremacy among them is the most important fact in the political history of England between 1053 and 1066. But it proceeded more slowly than historians have generally realized. Even after the promotion of Tostig to the Northumbrian earldom the house of Leofric was at least as powerful as the house of Godwine. Harold's influence must already have been very strong in southern England, where the centre of national authority lay. But his possessions in that country, though vast, were widely scattered, and he never commanded the resources of any single district comparable to the solid block of country in the northwestern midlands, where the earls of Mercia had no rival. When Leofric, the last of Cnut's earls, died in the autumn of 1057 few people can have foreseen that in little more than eight years Harold would be in a position to secure election to the throne. It was clearly wise for a chronicler to be discreet when his work impinged on politics.

The recorded history of the period is chiefly concerned with the new situation presented to English statesmen by the rise of a formidable power in Wales. The first sign of danger from this quarter was the defeat of a Mercian army near Welshpool in 1039 by Gruffydd ap Llywelyn, king of Gwynedd and Powys.[1] The danger came to a head slowly. It was Gruffydd's ambition to become king of all Wales, but the south Welsh princes resisted him for many years, and it was not until 1055 that he overthrew the last of them. His first opportunity for a serious attack on England came in this year through a sudden turn in English politics. In the spring Ælfgar, earl of East Anglia, son of Leofric of Mercia, was outlawed by the *witan* on a charge of treason. There is nothing that can profitably be added to this statement, for the charge is never described, and of the three

[1] For the details of his career see J. E. Lloyd, *History of Wales*, ii. 357–71.

chroniclers who mention it, one states that Ælfgar was guiltless, another that he was nearly guiltless, and the third that he
admitted his guilt inadvertently. The best evidence of his dis-
affection is his conduct after sentence. On his outlawry he went
to Ireland, raised a force of eighteen ships' companies among
the vikings of the eastern coast, and then allied himself with
Gruffydd ap Llywelyn for an invasion of England. Taking the
easiest road towards the midlands, the allies entered Herefordshire, defeated the local militia, which was preparing to fight
on horseback, burned the town of Hereford, plundered the
cathedral, and killed seven of the canons who were defending
its doors. To deal with this emergency the militia of all England
was called out and placed under Harold's command. It compelled the invaders to fall back on the natural fortress of the
Black Mountain. Harold followed them and encamped on the
western side of the Golden Valley. But no military decision
could be reached in that country, and after a delay, which
Harold used for the entrenchment of Hereford, the leaders in
each army came to terms. At a meeting in the hills above the
Wye to the south of Hereford it was settled that Ælfgar should
be restored to his earldom and all his possessions. Gruffydd is
not mentioned in the only account of the treaty which has survived. He may have been recognized as the lord of the country
known as Archenfield, between the Wye and the Monnow,
which for centuries had been disputed ground between England
and Wales. But his principal gain from the expedition was the
establishment of a close relationship with the heir of one of the
two great families which controlled the English government.

Bishop Athelstan of Hereford, whose church Gruffydd had
ruined, died early in 1056. His successor was a chaplain of Earl
Harold named Leofgar—a militant person, who tried to take
reprisals against Gruffydd without waiting for help from
outside the county. On 16 June he and a number of his priests,
with the sheriff of Hereford and many substantial laymen, were
killed by Gruffydd near Glasbury on Wye. The disaster compelled the government to take action, and the militia of all
England was called out against Gruffydd for the second time
in two years. It was an unwieldy force, wholly unfitted for
mountain warfare, and a contemporary writer enlarges upon
'the misery and all the marching and the hosting and the toil
and the loss of men and horses' which it endured. In the end,

Earls Leofric and Harold and Bishop Ealdred of Worcester arranged that Gruffydd should swear to be a true and loyal under-king to King Edward. A settlement thus confirmed must have been intended to cover every question outstanding between the kings, and there are indications that it included an extensive cession of territory to Gruffydd. A passage in the Cheshire Domesday states that King Edward gave to 'Griffin' all the land which lay beyond the river Dee. Other passages show that Gruffydd, at the height of his power, possessed the whole country between the Dee and the Clwyd, apart from a narrow strip along the Dee estuary. Offa's dyke runs through the middle of this country, and the lands to the east of it seem to have been in English occupation without a break from the eighth to the eleventh century. The Domesday evidence shows that, although Gruffydd may well have overrun this district in unrecorded raids, he was secured in its possession by a gift from the Confessor. The settlement of 1056, by which Gruffydd accepted King Edward as his lord, was probably the occasion when the gift was made.

The settlement appears to have satisfied Gruffydd's immediate ambitions, and he kept the peace towards England for more than a year. The chief interest of English politics in 1057, apart from the mystery connected with the return of Edward, the king's nephew, lies in the readjustment of the southern earldoms which followed the deaths of Leofric of Mercia and Ralf of Hereford. Leofric was succeeded by Ælfgar, his only surviving son. The earldom of East Anglia, vacated by Ælfgar, was given to Gyrth, the fourth son of Earl Godwine, and for some unknown reason Oxfordshire was added to it. Essex, Hertfordshire, Middlesex, and Buckinghamshire, which had been united with East Anglia under Ælfgar, were combined with Kent and Surrey into a new earldom for Leofwine, Gyrth's younger brother. The earldom of Hereford, which Ralf had held, ceased to exist as a separate government, and was merged in Harold's earldom of Wessex. The political ascendancy of Harold was obviously strengthened by these changes. They threatened the earldom of Mercia with isolation. They must have confirmed Earl Ælfgar in his dangerous alliance with Gruffydd ap Llywelyn. They may easily have moved him towards rebellion.

The year 1058 was full of tumult, in which Earl Ælfgar was

the central figure. Unfortunately, its origin and course are obscured by the ineptitude of the only English chronicler who mentions it. His account runs: 'Earl Ælfgar was driven out, but he soon came in again with violence through the help of Griffin, and a fleet came from Norway. It is tedious to tell how it all happened.' No other authority throws any light on the reason for Ælfgar's expulsion, or on the details of the fighting by which he was restored. But it is clear from Welsh and Irish sources that the war was a much more serious business than would be gathered from this annal. The *Annales Cambriae* represent it as a devastation of England carried out by Magnus, son of Harold Hardrada, with the help of Gruffydd ap Llywelyn. Irish authorities show that the Norwegian descent on England, which the English annalist dismisses in a parenthesis, was an expedition on a large scale. The chief Irish chronicler of the period describes it as an attempt at the conquest of England by a fleet drawn from the Orkneys, the Hebrides, and Dublin, led by the king of Norway's son, and only frustrated by the will of God.[1] The fragmentary nature of this information has tended to obscure the fact that a great naval force had been dispatched from Norwegian waters against England eight years before Harold Hardrada sailed on the expedition which ended at Stamfordbridge.

Earl Ælfgar lived for a little more than four years after his second restoration. So far as can be seen, his alliance with Gruffydd lasted for the rest of his life. He is known to have married a daughter to Gruffydd, and the marriage probably belongs to the period after 1058. Apart from an occasional appearance at court nothing is recorded about Ælfgar's last years, and although it seems certain that he died in 1062 no chronicler noted the date of his death. Nevertheless it is one of the determining events of eleventh-century history. If Ælfgar had survived King Edward, it is on every ground unlikely that he would have acquiesced in the choice of Harold as king. He was the head of the one family in England whose members had held high office before the Danish conquest. His interests had always clashed with those of Harold, and he had twice been outlawed by a court under Harold's influence. There is no reason to think that he would have claimed the kingdom, or any part of it, for himself, but he would certainly

[1] *Annals of Tigernack*, quoted by A. O. Anderson, *Early Sources of Scottish History*, ii. 1.

have prevented Harold from obtaining the immediate recognition which gave him the chance of reigning.

Ælfgar was the third successive earl of his house, and his position in Mercia passed, as if by inheritance, to Edwin, his eldest son. But in 1062 Edwin can barely have come to full age. He was too young to use the military resources of his earldom, and his inexperience gave the government an opportunity of breaking the Welsh power which had been his father's ally. At Christmas 1062 Earl Harold, in the first of the rapid campaigns which gave him distinction, struck across country from Gloucester to Rhuddlan, the seat of Gruffydd ap Llywelyn by the Clwyd. He failed to capture the king, but he burned his ships and houses and drove him into unbecoming flight. Towards the end of May he set about the systematic reduction of Gruffydd's country by sea and land. He himself sailed from Bristol round the Welsh coast, landing at convenient harbours and taking hostages from the men of the adjacent regions. In the greater part of south Wales he may well have been regarded as a deliverer, for Gruffydd had no hereditary claim to rule there. In the meantime Earl Tostig, with an army which later writers describe as cavalry, was making his way into north Wales, presumably along the narrow coastal strip which offered the shortest line of approach from Northumbria. Gruffydd was unable to prevent the earls from joining their forces, and Gwynedd itself was conquered. The whole campaign was over in less than three months, for on 5 August Gruffydd, as a fugitive, was killed by his own men. His head and the figure-head of his ship were brought to Harold, who brought them to King Edward. Gwynedd and Powys were given as tributary provinces to two local chiefs named Bleddyn and Rhiwallon, who swore to be faithful to the king and the earl, and to serve them by land and water if their services were needed. The heirs of ancient dynasties came back to power in the south, the border lands which Gruffydd had occupied were reunited to England, and of the united Wales which he had created the tradition alone remained.

For the next two years Harold was at the height of his power and reputation. The Mercian earldom under the inexperienced Edwin was the only considerable part of England outside the direct influence of his family. The campaign of 1063 must have made him popular in all the shires which Gruffydd had threatened, and he was beyond all rivalry at court. No subject of the English Crown had ever been at once so powerful in relation to other noblemen and so great a figure in the country at large. He was bound to realize that, before long, the crown itself might come within his reach. Edward, the king's nephew, had left a son, named Edgar, to whom the kingdom would pass in normal times. But the times were far from normal. The duke of Normandy and the king of Norway were certain to claim the English throne when King Edward died. Edgar, who is known to have lived until 1125, can have been little more than a child in 1063. Harold's chance of obtaining the crown turned on the question whether Englishmen would allow their respect for royal descent to outweigh the advantage of possessing a king who could defend the land.

Before the question was put to them Harold had allowed himself to be drawn into a false position in relation to the duke of Normandy. Within five years from the battle of Hastings Norman writers were asserting that while Edward was still king, Harold had acknowledged the duke as his personal lord. Unfortunately, even the earliest authorities differ from one another about the circumstances of the recognition and the obligations which it imposed upon Harold. Most of them embellish it with incredible details, and none of them is precise about its date. The simplest, and on the whole the most probable, version of the story is the outline drawn before the end of the century by the Bayeux tapestry. According to this work, Harold was sent on a mission to the Continent by King Edward. He sailed before a strong wind to Ponthieu—the tapestry gives no hint that he was shipwrecked—but was arrested by Guy, the local count, and kept under restraint at Beaurain. Ponthieu had recently been brought under Norman overlordship, and the duke was able to obtain the surrender of Harold. After entertainment at William's court Harold accompanied him on an expedition against Conan, duke of Brittany, rescued some Norman soldiers from the quicksands by the river Couesnon, and was present when Conan surrendered the castle of Dinan. At this point the tapestry states that William 'gave arms to Harold'—a statement which was undoubtedly intended to imply that Harold had acknowledged himself to be William's man. The next scene is inscribed 'William came to Bayeux where Harold took an oath to Duke William', and shows Harold standing in William's presence between two reliquaries, with an outstretched hand on each. After this the tapestry makes him return to England, and, apparently, tell the story of his adventures to King Edward.

The tapestry was woven for public exhibition at a time when a number of the minor actors in the story were still alive. It is therefore unlikely to portray any incidents which are entirely fictitious. It is good evidence, not only that Harold became William's man, but that he took a very solemn oath to observe the duke's interests. On the other hand, a piece of stitchwork can only deal with superficialities, and the tapestry gives no information about the reason for Harold's journey or about the nature of his engagement with the duke. No convincing answer has ever been given to the first of these questions. As to the second, it is probably safe to follow the Norman writers who make Harold swear to help William to secure the English throne. His reasons for giving such a promise can only be a matter of conjecture. It is possible that even in 1064—the probable date of the oath—he may have doubted whether his following in England was strong enough to carry his election as king. In a Norman environment he may have felt that, in view of the danger from the king of Norway, his wisest course was to ally himself with the duke and work for his succession. It is perhaps more probable that he simply took the easiest way out of an embarrassing situation, assumed that he could plead duress if he were to break his oath, and left his future conduct to be decided by the course of events in England.

In the autumn of 1065 the political situation in England was suddenly changed by a revolt in Northumbria. So far as can be seen, it was caused partly by resentment at a heavy tax which Tostig had taken from his earldom, and partly by the wish to avenge the death of certain thegns, for which he was held responsible. The rising was made more dangerous by a suspicion that there were sinister influences working for Tostig in the king's own circle. Cospatric, the heir of the native earls of Bernicia, had recently been killed at the king's court, and it was believed that Queen Edith, Tostig's sister, had procured his death in her brother's interest. Tostig himself was visiting the king at Britford near Salisbury when the revolt broke out. It seems to have begun with a descent of some two hundred thegns on York, but it developed almost at once into a general

Northumbrian movement. Tostig's retainers were hunted down and killed, and the rebels seized his stock of weapons and his treasury. Taking on themselves the functions of a public court, they proclaimed Tostig an outlaw. They then invited Morcar, brother of Edwin of Mercia, to be their earl, and when he had joined them they came down as an army into the midlands, drew in a force from the Mercian shires of Lincoln, Nottingham, and Derby, and occupied Northampton. Their numbers were greatly increased by the arrival of Edwin himself, with a host of Mercians and Welshmen, and they felt themselves in a position to dictate terms to the king. Their next movements are uncertain, but it is probable that while the mass of the army remained at Northampton, the negotiations between its leaders and the king were carried out at Oxford. Harold, on whom the work of negotiation fell, tried to bring them into agreement with Tostig, but failed. The king agreed that Morcar should be their earl, and confirmed to them the customs by which they and their ancestors had lived in the time of King Cnut. At last, after continual harrying of the country round Northampton, they retired, taking with them many prisoners and much cattle as spoils of what, in effect, had been a northern invasion of the midlands. Tostig, with his wife and a band of faithful adherents, left England, and, as in 1051, found shelter for the winter with Baldwin, count of Flanders.

That Harold's position was weakened by the revolt is certain. The replacement of Tostig by Morcar brought the Northumbrian earldom to a family which at the very least felt itself the equal of the house of Godwine, and had every reason to oppose its ambitions. The intervention of a Mercian army in the war showed that the Mercian people identified itself with the family of its earls in opposition to the great West Saxon house. On the other hand, the history of the rebellion made it clear that Harold, as the king's chief counsellor, had a claim to influence which was unaffected by the loss of one of the family earldoms, and was admitted in Northumbria itself. For the rising was in no sense a movement for Northumbrian independence. At a time when they were challenging the whole authority of the Crown in order to remove a hated earl, the Northumbrians showed no desire to choose a separate king. It is the combination of strong provincial feeling with respect for the unity of England which makes their behaviour interesting.

On 5 January 1066, ten weeks after his surrender to the rebels, King Edward died at Westminster. His health had been failing ever since the disturbances of the autumn. He was too ill to attend the consecration of Westminster abbey on 28 December, and his death must have been long expected. The course of his illness gave time for the leading members of his council to come together in London and decide who should be the next king. Nothing is known about their discussion, but its outcome was a decision, apparently unanimous, in favour of Harold. The circumstances of the moment made the choice almost inevitable. To the danger of invasion from Normandy and Norway was now added the certainty that Tostig would attempt a landing in the spring and the probability that the king of Scots, his sworn brother, would cross the border to support him. There was an overwhelming case for giving the name and authority of a king to the one Englishman who had shown the ability to plan and carry out a campaign. King Edward himself realized at the end that the claim of his young kinsman Edgar, 'the Ætheling', must give way to military necessities. The only contemporary account of Harold's election expressly states that he 'succeeded to the kingdom as the king granted it to him and as he was chosen thereto'. On the morrow of King Edward's death and the day of his burial, with a haste which shows the urgency of the times, Harold was consecrated in his place, at Westminster'.

---

[1] See *Heremanni archidiaconi Miracula sancti Eadmundi*, ed. F. Liebermann, *Ungedruckte Anglo-Normannische Geschichtsquellen*, pp. 245–6; and cf. *The Bayeux Tapestry*, by Sir Frank Stenton and others (London, 1957), p. 18.

XVI

THE NORMAN CONQUEST

HAROLD was king of England for nine months, in which the national life was overshadowed by the threat of invasion. For more than half this period the forces available for the defence of southern England were kept in a state of readiness for war—on shipboard, or in stations along the coast. It was a time not only of strain and danger but of political unease. The Northumbrians refused at first to accept Harold as king, and were not brought into obedience until he had visited the north, and Bishop Wulfstan of Worcester, who accompanied him, had impressed on them the danger in which the country stood.[1] There is no evidence that Edwin and Morcar, the earls of Mercia and Northumbria, had opposed Harold's election, and there is reason to think that early in his reign he secured their formal allegiance by marrying Ealdgyth, their sister. But the course of events in the autumn showed that they had not identified their personal interests with his, and that the thegns and smaller landowners of their earldoms, to say the least, had no enthusiasm for his leadership.

Few memorials of civil government can be expected from a short reign thus troubled. A solitary writ preserved in a late copy[2] is all that remains to illustrate the work of Harold's writing-office. The best-recorded of his peace-time measures is the issue of a voluminous currency. Coins are known to have been struck for Harold at forty-five different minting-places, ranging from York to Exeter and from Chester to Romney.[3] The regularity of their execution shows that the custom of requiring all moneyers to obtain their dies in London was enforced under Harold. This in turn implies the maintenance of

[1] William of Malmesbury, *Vita Wulfstani*, ed. R. R. Darlington, pp. 22–3. William at this point is closely following a life of Wulfstan written by an English-man named Coleman, who for fifteen years had been the bishop's chaplain. He may have exaggerated the part which Wulfstan played in the reconciliation of the Northumbrians, but he is an excellent authority for the fact of their original dis-affection.

[2] *C.D.* 976.

[3] See Michael Dolley, *The Norman Conquest and the English Coinage*, p. 11.

the centralized control of the currency which had been established by his predecessors.[1] It is good evidence that the continuity of the English administrative system was preserved in
Harold's time.

It was in regard to the defence of the realm that this system
was least efficient. The resources at the king's command were
large but ill organized. At the beginning of 1066 there was
neither a fleet in being, nor any regular arrangement for the
keeping of the sea except the service due by recent agreement
from a small number of southern ports.[2] For a fleet adequate to
forestall an invasion the king relied on an undefined power of
requisitioning ships and impressing crews, and on the contributions in ships or seamen which custom entitled him to demand
from individual shires and boroughs.[3] Given time, he could
bring together a force which was large enough for any ordinary
occasion. But its mobilization was a slow business, and the
period for which it could remain at sea was narrowed by the
absence of any organization for the replacement of the provisions with which it had sailed.

For the defence of the realm by land the king could bring into
the field a composite force, in which a nucleus of professional
soldiers was combined with an aristocratic element drawn from
the thegnhood of the shires, and with peasant levies of varying
quality. The kernel of the host was composed of the military
retainers—the housecarles—of the king and other magnates.[4]
By 1066 it had long ceased to be the custom that a housecarle
should be his lord's companion in time of peace. Many housecarles were living on their own estates. A Domesday reference
to 15 acres of crown land in Wallingford 'where housecarles
used to dwell' suggests that King Edward may have been using
his housecarles for garrison duty at important strategical
points.[5] But wherever he might live, the housecarle was available for instant service in the event of war. It is unlikely that
the corps of housecarles at the disposal of the king or of any
other lord were large enough to be employed as independent

---

[1] Above, pp. 535–6.   [2] Above, p. 432.

[3] The provision of seamen by local communities is brought out by several entries
in Domesday Book. The borough of Warwick, for example, sent 4 sailors or paid
£4 when the king went on an expedition by sea. For traces of the system by which
ships were found communally for the king's service see above, p. 431.

[4] On the housecarles see above, p. 412.

[5] D.B. i, f. 56.

military units. Their essential function, as trained and disciplined troops, was to stiffen the loosely compacted hosts of thegns and peasants with which the recorded campaigns of the age were fought.

The military service of the thegn was a duty which fell on him as a consequence of his rank, and was inherent in the constitution of Old English society.[1] There is evidence in Domesday Book suggesting that every thegn, or at least every thegn possessing rights of jurisdiction, would receive a personal summons to the host, and that if he disobeyed it the king was entitled to confiscate his land. It is also clear from the same authority that each of these greater thegns was expected to cause his own men, whatever their rank, to do the military service which the king required from them. Among the men of the greatest lords a large number were thegns themselves by birth, and members of this class formed a high proportion of the effectives in every English army of the eleventh century.

The military service of the peasant, like that of the thegn, was a personal obligation. The king's right to call on all men for the defence of the land was never abandoned. But so far as can be seen, it was rarely exercised in the last centuries of the Old English state. In eleventh-century Berkshire, for example, one soldier only was required for the host from five hides of land—a group of holdings roughly equivalent in area to the territory of a small village. It is doubtful whether this rule was allowed to prevail in parts of England where the hide was larger than in Berkshire, and it was obviously inapplicable to the northern Danelaw, where land was estimated in ploughlands instead of hides, and to East Anglia, where there was no uniform type of peasant holding. It is of historical interest because it implies that to some extent the militia of the late Old English kings was a body of selected troops, and that its equipment cannot have been contemptible. It suggests that the Englishmen armed with clubs, or with stones tied on sticks, who figure in the battle of

[1] In a charter dated 794, recently printed by H. P. R. Finberg (*The Early Charters of Wessex*, 1964, pp. 118–20), King Beorhtric of Wessex insists on the peculiar responsibility for the defence of the realm which rests on the nobility by service known in his time in Latin as *comites* and in English as *gesithas*. After exempting an estate from most public burdens for the benefit of one of his reeves, the king passes at once to the important reservation *nisi . . . expeditione sola quam omnes comites ad tutelam totius provinciæ et maxime ecclesiarum Dei adire debent*. The military equipment of the late Old English thegns, who as a class represent the *comites* of an earlier time, is indicated above, pp. 488–9.

Hastings, were peasants trying to avenge a fortnight's harrying rather than normally recruited members of the national *fyrd*.

In mere numbers the army which an English king could raise in 1066 was equal to any but the most improbable emergency. But it was difficult for him to concentrate his strength at any given point, or to keep a large force out on service in expectation of an attack. The continental innovation of the castle, which enabled a commander to hold a large tract of country with a small number of troops, had never been adopted in England at large.[1] It was a further cause of weakness that English indifference to foreign developments in the art of war dangerously restricted the tactics open to an English leader in contact with the enemy. Each of the three main classes from which an English army was recruited—the housecarles, the thegns, and the wealthier peasants—used horses in ordinary life, and naturally used them when campaigning. But the art of fighting on horseback, if not entirely unknown, was little practised in England. No attention seems to have been paid to the possibilities of archery as a military instrument. In action, Harold's army could only function as a force of infantry, confined by its nature to a type of warfare which was already obsolete in the greater part of western Europe.

In William of Normandy Harold was confronted by a rival familiar with every device of continental warfare. It was as a knight and a leader of knights that the duke had acquired the reputation which enabled him to recruit an army adequate for the invasion of England. The wars against disaffected kinsmen which had made him the effective ruler of Normandy were an admirable training in the management of small bodies of cavalry and in the art of improvising fortifications. The invasions of the duchy, by which King Henry of France had hoped to reduce him to insignificance, gave him experience in large-scale warfare against superior numbers. From these and the other campaigns of his early life, he emerged with a sense of the value of discipline which sets him apart from other commanders of the feudal age. For his claim to eminence as a general does not rest on the detail of his battles, but on the quality which made the coherent army of Hastings out of a miscellaneous host of feudal tenants, foreign adventurers, and mercenary knights.

The first phase of William's career ends in 1060. Up to that

[1] Ordericus Vitalis, *Historia Ecclesiastica*, ed. A. le Prevost, ii, p. 144.

year he had been chiefly occupied with local interests—the suppression of revolts, the defence of Normandy against the king of France, and the fortification of his southern border. As a force in the politics of northern France he was outweighed throughout this period by Geoffrey Martel, count of Anjou. In 1051 Geoffrey secured control of the county of Maine, and thereby obtained access to many obvious lines of entry into Normandy. Much of William's energy in the following years was given to measures intended to impede an Angevin invasion of the duchy. The one event of this time which shows him in contact with a wide circle is his marriage to Matilda, daughter of Baldwin, count of Flanders.[1] But in 1060 his place among French magnates was completely changed by the deaths of the count of Anjou and the king of France. Philip I, the new king, was a child, and Baldwin of Flanders became regent. Anjou was distracted by a long war between the two nephews of Geoffrey Martel. For the first time in his life William was free to plan far-reaching operations. Within four years he had conquered Maine and effectively reasserted the ancient claim of his house to lordship over Brittany.

At the beginning of 1066 he was admirably placed for an attack on England. From the Scheldt to Finisterre every harbour not under his own control was in the hands of allies, or of men bound to him by feudal obligation. A friendly regency in France and a state of civil war in Anjou meant that Normandy would be secure against invasion in his absence. Even so, many of his barons were alarmed at the risks of the enterprise, and it was only after discussion in a great council of the duchy that he obtained a general assurance of support. It was also clear that the resources of Normandy alone were unequal to the design, and William set himself to the task of enlisting help from other countries. His reputation was so great that he was able to attract volunteers, not only from Brittany and Maine, which were feudally dependent on Normandy, but also from Flanders, central France, Aquitaine, and the Norman colonies in southern

---

[1] The marriage was forbidden by Pope Leo IX at the council of Reims in 1049—apparently on the ground of affinity between the parties—but was solemnized in or before 1053 in defiance of this prohibition. In 1059 William obtained a formal recognition of the marriage from Pope Nicholas II on the condition that he should endow two monasteries, one for men and one for women. The abbeys of St. Stephen and Holy Trinity at Caen were founded in obedience to this requirement.

Italy. There were men of established position among them, but
for the most part they were landless knights, who joined William
for pay because they had heard of his generosity. The maintenance of such an army during weeks of idleness on Norman
soil was a problem which would have defeated most commanders of the age. The organization of a regular supply of
provisions by which William solved it without ruining his
country proves at once his generalship and the efficiency of the
administrative service at his command.

The necessity of raising troops in lands outside his own control
gave much importance to the manner in which William's case
was presented to the world. Pope Alexander II and the Emperor
Henry IV—the two powers which represented international
authority in the west—were each induced to declare themselves
in his favour. From the emperor—or at least from those who
were governing in his name—William obtained a promise of
German help, if it were needed. The pope committed himself
more definitely, after what seems to have been a formal hearing
of William's case. No record of the proceedings at Rome has
survived. It is probable that William's agents asked for a judgement against Harold on the ground that by taking the English
crown he had broken the oath which he had sworn to William
at Bayeux. But there is no evidence that Harold was summoned
to appear at Rome, and the question was clearly treated as a
matter, not of law, but of expediency. The fact which weighed
most heavily in William's favour was the care for the interests
of religion which he had shown in Normandy and could be
trusted to show in England. It was a nice question how far the
better government of the English church and the removal of
Archbishop Stigand, which might be expected to follow from
William's victory, could justify a decision which would give the
approval of the papal court to an aggressive war. Long afterwards Pope Gregory VII, who as Archdeacon Hildebrand had
been William's strongest advocate, wrote that many had
blamed him as one who laboured for slaughter. But in the
end his insistence on William's merits prevailed, and Pope
Alexander sent a banner to the duke as a symbol of St. Peter's
judgement.

The series of events which culminated in the battle of Hastings began early in May when Tostig, Harold's brother,
appeared in some force off the Isle of Wight, and after harrying

the Sussex coast, occupied Sandwich. It was afterwards be-lieved that his attempt had been encouraged by William of Normandy.[1] Harold undoubtedly regarded Tostig's appear-ance as a sign that the Norman invasion was imminent, and at once began to mobilize his fleet and army. But most of Tostig's men were Flemings, and although he may have been in com-munication with William, it is clear that he was not acting under William's orders. There is, in fact, one piece of evidence suggesting that he had already planned the larger enterprise which was to bring Harold Hardrada, king of Norway, to Eng-land as his ally. While still in Kent he was joined by one of his Northumbrian supporters named Copsi, who had been exiled in 1065, and now came to him from the Orkneys with seventeen ships.[2] The Orkneys had recently come under the authority of the king of Norway, and his approval must have been necessary before even so small a force as this could leave the islands.

When the news of Tostig's landing came to London Harold, whose headquarters were in the city, set out at once for Sand-wich. Before he reached the Kentish coast Tostig had taken to the sea again. He had impressed or attracted into his service a number of seamen of Sandwich, and had taken possession of the shipping in the harbour. His fleet at the time of sailing amounted to sixty ships. Making towards the north, he put into the mouth of the Burnham river in Norfolk, and harried the sur-rounding country. He then sailed on to the Humber, and dis-embarked on the southern bank. After more ravaging he was heavily defeated by Earl Edwin and the Lindsey militia; Earl Morcar and the Northumbrians prevented him from landing in Yorkshire, and the seamen whom he had brought from Sand-wich deserted him and took their ships back to Kent. With a fleet reduced to twelve small vessels he made his way to Scot-land, and remained there throughout the summer, accumu-lating resources which he could bring to a combined attack on England in association with Harold of Norway.

His failure had shown that in the spring of 1066 the ordinary English defences were capable of dealing with any private

---

[1] Ordericus Vitalis, *Historia Ecclesiastica*, ed. A. le Prevost, ii, pp. 120–3. The statement that William sent Tostig to England, which is often quoted from the *Gesta Normannorum Ducum* of William of Jumieges (ed. J. Marx, p. 192), occurs in a passage interpolated into this work by Orderic.

[2] Gaimar, *L'Estoire des Engles*, R.S. i. 219. The historical value of Gaimar's work at this point was indicated by W. H. Stevenson, *E.H.R.* xi (1896), pp. 302–4.

adventurer. During the early summer the whole force upon which the king could draw in an emergency was gradually brought into position against the expected attack from France. The militia of all England was called up to stations along the coast, and a large fleet, commanded by the king in person, was assembled off the Isle of Wight. William, in the meantime, was steadily bringing his miscellaneous force into the semblance of an army, and creating a fleet for its transport to England. The work was completed more quickly than had at first seemed possible, but it was not until the beginning of August that he was able to concentrate his men and ships for the invasion. Throughout the last weeks of August and the first week of September his armament, detained by contrary winds in the estuary of the Dives, was confronted by an English fleet ready for action in the Channel. On 12 September, in order to obtain a shorter crossing, he took advantage of a westerly wind to transport his force from the Dives to the mouth of the Somme at St. Valery. In the event, the precaution proved to be unnecessary, for the English defensive system was collapsing at the very time when the movement to St. Valery was in progress. The crews of Harold's ships and the militia guards along the coast had been held to a long spell of tedious duty; their provisions were running out, and their temper was uncertain. Shortly after 8 September the militiamen were sent home, and the decision was taken to bring the ships to London. Many of them were lost on the voyage, and the Channel was left open to William and his overladen transports.

At this moment, amid the confusion of a disbanded militia and a broken fleet, Harold learned that the king of Norway had invaded England with three hundred ships, or more. His descent had been planned in association with Tostig, who joined him, apparently in the Tyne, with all the force that he had acquired in Scotland. Their preparations must have been known throughout the north, but Harold of England had been too closely occupied with the Norman danger to follow their progress, and the attack, when it came, was a surprise. With the aid of a northerly wind, which was keeping William of Normandy land-locked in the Somme, the Norwegian fleet sailed down the Yorkshire coast, throwing off landing-parties which harried in Cleveland, at Scarborough, and in Holderness. The English ships in northern waters were too few to engage it at sea, and it seems that as the Norwegians entered the Humber the English vessels retired before them up the Ouse, and then up the Wharfe as far as Tadcaster. It was probably in order to immobilize them that Harold of Norway anchored his own fleet at Riccall on the Ouse, three miles below its junction with the Wharfe. At Riccall he was within ten miles of York by road, and after placing a guard on his ships he advanced at once upon the city.

It was not until the Norwegians had landed at Riccall that any reliable news of these events reached Harold of England. He set out at once for the north on a forced march, with his own retainers and such elements of the militia as he could collect while on his way. But he was too late to intervene in the campaign before the fate of York was decided, and Edwin and Morcar, with the men of their earldoms, were required to bear the full weight of the Norwegian assault. For the decisive battle they chose a site on the left bank of the Ouse near the village of Gate Fulford, two miles south of York. For the greater part of a hard day's fighting they barred the only road by which the Norwegians could advance, but their lines gave way at last, and large numbers of their men were cut down or drowned. The men of York made peace for themselves on terms which show that the recent northern progress of Harold Godwinson had failed to conciliate them. After receiving food and hostages the king of Norway, instead of occupying the city, led his army back to its ships at Riccall, and arranged a treaty with the citizens which provided that they should join forces with him and march southwards under his leadership to attempt the conquest of all England.

Before attempting to carry out this larger plan the king took the obvious precaution of calling for hostages from the Yorkshire thegns who had survived the battle of Fulford. After receiving an assurance that the hostages would be forthcoming, he decided to await them in the presence of his army at a site seven miles east of York, where roads from all parts of eastern Yorkshire converged on the crossing of the Derwent known as Stamfordbridge. The battle of Fulford had been fought on 20 September, and the negotiations for the capitulation of York, the withdrawal to Riccall, the final arrangement of terms with the citizens, and a march of 12 miles from Riccall to Stamford-bridge must have occupied the army and its commanders for

several days. It can hardly have been before the evening of 24
September that the Norwegians reached their position on the
Derwent. Next day they were attacked by Harold of England.
Hastening from the south, Harold reached Tadcaster, nine
miles short of York, on 24 September, and halted there for the
night, after reviewing the English ships which had taken shelter
in the Wharfe. On the following day he marched through York,
which the Norwegians had left an open city, and came upon
them at Stamfordbridge by the Derwent before they were
aware of his approach. They had encamped on the farther bank
of the river, but they lost its protection by failing to guard
the bridge in force. Its heroic defence by a solitary Norwegian
warrior was remembered in English tradition.[1] In the course of
a long struggle Harold of Norway, and Tostig, who had accompanied him throughout all these operations, were both killed.
The Norwegian army was shattered, and its fragments were pursued to the ships at Riccall. Olaf, King Harold's son, an unnamed Norwegian bishop, and Earl Paul of the Orkneys, who
had been left to guard the ships, received peace from Harold of
England, and sailed home with the remnant of the defeated
army, under oath never to attack England again. It is some
indication of the Norwegian losses that twenty-four ships were
enough to carry the survivors back to Norway.

Of the two general engagements of September 1066 the battle
of Stamfordbridge has always impressed historians. It ended
more than two centuries of Anglo-Scandinavian conflict in a
manner which brought great honour to the last Old English
king. In comparison, the battle of Fulford has aroused little
interest. Nevertheless, it deserves to be remembered in any
attempt to get beneath the surface of the events which followed
it. It is clear, for one thing, that the losses which the Norwegian
army suffered at Fulford must have lessened its power of resistance at Stamfordbridge. But it is equally clear that the far
heavier English losses must have deprived Earls Edwin and
Morcar of any chance of effective action during the critical
weeks of early October. They have often been regarded as un-
patriotic because they held aloof from the campaign of Hastings.
It can at least be urged on their behalf that they had recently
stood for the defence of the realm against the greatest northern

---

[1] Preserved in a late supplement to MS. C of the *Chronicle*, which ends at this
point.

warrior of the age, and that the battle of Hastings had been fought long before either of them could have replaced the men whom he had lost at Fulford.

The battle of Stamfordbridge was fought on Monday, 25 September. On the following Wednesday a change in the direction of the wind offered the chance of a rapid crossing to William of Normandy. Embarkation was immediately begun, and was completed by the late·evening. At nightfall the ships left harbour, and anchored outside the estuary of the Somme to await the duke's directions for the voyage. It was still night when they sailed out into the open Channel. For the early part of the voyage the course was set by the steersman of the duke's own vessel, and given to the other ships by a lantern slung from its mast-head. But in the darkness it gradually outstripped the transports, which were heavily laden with horses as well as men, and when dawn broke the duke found himself in mid-Channel, out of touch with his fleet. It was the most dangerous moment in his career; but the English ships which should have borne down on him were laid up in London river, and he was allowed to ride quietly at anchor until the transports came into sight. At nine in the morning of Thursday, 28 September, the fleet entered Pevensey bay, and the army disembarked at leisure on an undefended shore.

The shell of the Roman fort at Pevensey, within which William constructed an inner fortress of bank and ditch, offered immediate protection to his army on a site adjacent to his ships. But its situation, surrounded on the east and north by marshy levels, made it unsuitable as a base for an invading force. After a few days William transferred his fleet and army to a better strategical position at Hastings, where he caused his men to build a castle of earth and timber, while he set himself to learn the lie of the neighbouring country. From the moment of his landing he was plainly resolved to keep within easy reach of his ships until he had fought a general engagement. At the time of his crossing he can have known nothing of the outcome of the war in the north, and several days may have passed before he could be certain that his opponent would be Harold of England and not Harold of Norway. Even then, he had no sure means of estimating the size of the force which he would be required to meet. The only disinterested information which he received came to him from King Edward's Breton minister, Robert fitz

Wimarch, who told him that his army would be overwhelmed by Harold's vast host, and advised him to keep within his entrenchments. He would have lost his only chance of victory by taking Robert's advice, but it was a matter of elementary prudence for him to remain within a short distance of the sea.

According to a probable tradition Harold was at York when he learned of William's landing. Within thirteen days at most he had completed the settlement of the north, covered the 190 miles between York and London, expanded the force at his command into the dimensions of an army, and brought it by a march of 50 miles to a point within a short ride of Hastings.[1] It was an achievement which has convinced every historian of Harold's energy and determination. But there is not the same unanimity about his generalship. For there is no doubt that he advanced to meet a dangerous enemy before the resources available to him were fully assembled. Even if he dispatched the summonses to the host from York as quickly as they could be written after he was told of the invasion, it was physically impossible for the thegns of distant shires to receive them in time to set out with him for Sussex. No medieval government ever attempted to mobilize a large army with this speed. It is clear, in fact, that the effective part of the host with which Harold fought the battle of Hastings consisted of his own housecarles and those of his brothers Gyrth and Leofwine; thegns and mounted freemen who had joined him on his northward or southward march; and an element representing the men of those classes who lived within a two days' ride of London and were accessible to his messengers. There is every reason to accept the statement of an annalist of the next generation[2] that Harold moved from London before half his army had come together. As to the size of the host which he actually assembled,

[1] The distance from Pevensey to York is 250 miles in round numbers. Without the aid of beacons, of which there is no tradition, the news of William's landing on the morning of 28 September can hardly have reached York before the evening of 1 October. The march from London into Sussex must have begun on 11 October. Even if the preparation of the summonses was taken in hand at York on 2 October, at least a day must have been required for their completion and dispatch. Within the eight days between 3 and 11 October it was impossible for the ordinary thegns of remote counties to receive their summonses from the sheriff, prepare themselves for war, and ride to London. The difficulty is no less if it is assumed that the writs were dispatched from London, for Harold can scarcely have reached the city before 6 October.

[2] Florence of Worcester, *Chronicon ex Chronicis*, ed. B. Thorpe, i, p. 227.

all that can safely be said is that on any probable estimate it cannot have exceeded 7,000 men of all types from housecarles to half-armed peasants.[1]

William's army was probably smaller than that of Harold, but it was composed of picked troops. Every knight, however simple his equipment, had passed through an apprenticeship in the art of fighting on horseback. The apprenticeship was usually served in a great household, and among the lords assembled at Hastings there were many whose retinues were large enough to afford, not only training in horsemanship, but some experience of military discipline. Within the contingents led by such men as Hugh de Montfort, Walter Giffard, Ralf de Tosny, William de Warenne, William fitz Osbern, and William Malet, the individual knights must have known one another intimately, and developed at least a rudimentary capacity for concerted action.[2] It was the internal cohesion of the greater retinues which enabled different divisions of the Norman host to carry out the difficult operation of a feigned flight on two separate occasions during the battle of Hastings. Even in the eleventh century a Norman army was capable of something more than an unco-ordinated series of single combats.

For all the speed of Harold's march, it was William who forced the engagement which decided the campaign. On Friday, 13 October, his scouts told him that Harold was approaching with a great army. In the first daylight of 14 October, after a night of preparation, he ordered his men to advance in the direction from which the enemy had been reported. Before nine in the morning, as he reached the summit of Telham Hill, the highest point on the nine miles of road between Hastings and the modern town of Battle, his outriders reported that they had seen the English force on the rising ground beyond the valley into which his host was about to descend. After a halt which enabled stragglers to join the army, it moved down the hill into full view of the English host, and was formed into battle-order. In the first rank William set his archers and crossbowmen; in the second, his heavily armed infantry; and in

[1] A total English force of 6,000–7,000 men is suggested, after a careful review of the evidence, by W. Spatz, *Die Schlacht von Hastings* (Berlin, 1896), pp. 33–4. No fresh materials for the history of the battle have been discovered since the appearance of this tract.

[2] It is unfortunate that the account of the battle by Spatz, which in most respects is admirable, ignores this aspect of a feudal force.

the third, his knights, arranged in three divisions, with the Bretons on the left, the Normans in the centre, and the French mercenaries on the right. The English host beyond the valley, lacking both archers and horsemen, was unable to interrupt this deployment, and could only close its ranks to await attack.[1]

There is good evidence that Harold had been taken by surprise. A contemporary English narrative expressly states that William came upon him 'unexpectedly, before his army was set in order'.[2] English tradition of the next age adds that many of Harold's men withdrew from the fight because of the narrowness of the position on which the host was drawn up.[3] It is clear from Norman sources that the English army was crowded together,[4] and it is probable that its ranks were set much more closely than was usual in battles of this period. The only certainty that can be reached about its disposition is that Harold and his best men were grouped around a standard set near the summit of the hill at Battle in a place afterwards marked by the high altar of Battle abbey. At a distance of some 200 yards to the east and 400 yards to the west of this point, the ground falls away steeply enough to protect the flanks of an army drawn up

[1] *Senlac*, the name applied to the battle by Ordericus Vitalis in the 12th century (*Historia Ecclesiastica*, ed. A. le Prevost, ii, p. 147, etc.), is a French form of an Old English *Sandlacu*, 'sand-stream', the name of a watercourse near the English position. In the form Sandlake it survived for centuries as the name of a tithing in Battle, but is now obsolete (W. H. Stevenson in *E.H.R.* xxviii (1913), pp. 292–303; *Place-Names of Sussex*, E.P-N.S. 499). The use of the name for the battle-site is peculiar to Orderic. The *Chronicle* merely states that Harold and William fought 'at the grey apple tree', a phrase which seems to imply that the site was then uninhabited. Domesday Book refers to the engagement as the battle of Hastings.

[2] *Chronicle* D: 'Wyllelm him com ongean on unwær ær his folc gefylced wære.' Before 1066 the verb *fylcian*, which is a derivative of *folc*, had acquired the specialized meaning 'to array', or 'set in order'. It clearly has this sense in the account of Harold's northward march given by *Chronicle* C, which states that Harold *his lith fylcade* when he came to Tadcaster on the day before he entered York. The meaning of this passage can only be that Harold set in order the ships which he found in the Wharfe. The equivalent Scandinavian *fylkja* has the same meaning in Norse literature, as in *Egilssaga*, c. 53, and may well have affected English usage. It is significant that Florence of Worcester, who was following a version of the *Chronicle* closely allied to MS. D, describes Harold as joining battle *priusquam tertia pars sui exercitus ordinaretur*. In view of this definite and contemporary evidence that Harold was taken by surprise before his army was arrayed, it is unnecessary to enter into the criticism of the late materials from which Freeman inferred that Harold had fortified his position with a palisade.

[3] Florence of Worcester, *Chronicon ex Chronicis*, ed. B. Thorpe, i, p. 227.

[4] *Cuncti pedites constitere densius conglobati* according to William of Poitiers (*Gesta Willelmi Ducis*, ed. Giles, p. 133 and R. Foreville, p. 186), whose admirable narrative is fundamental for the details of the battle.

along the intervening ridge.[1] Towards the south, the quarter from which William was approaching, the contours are much less pronounced, and on the left front of this position the ground falls little more than 50 feet in the 400 yards between the site of Harold's standard and the lowest part of the road from Hastings. In such a position Harold's only chance of victory lay in the possibility that his army would be able to keep its close formation—its 'shield-wall'—until the Norman host had exhausted itself in attack. He lost the battle because his men were unequal to the stress of a purely defensive engagement too long protracted.

The battle opened with an advance by the archers and cross-bowmen of the Norman front line. Their volleys were effective, but they were severely harassed by the spears, axes, and stones attached to sticks which were flung at them from the English ranks, and they were already in need of a respite when William first sent in his heavy cavalry. In the close fighting which followed, the English at first had the advantage, for the higher ground was theirs, and the two-handed battle-axe—the traditional weapon of the housecarles—easily cut through the flimsy shields and mail covering of the knights. After a fierce struggle the Bretons and other auxiliaries on the left of the Norman line fell back in disorder. The confusion quickly spread to the centre and right; the line gave way as a whole, and a rout was only checked by the appearance of the duke in the path of the fugitives. By his intervention at this moment William gave a new turn to the battle. Once rallied, the knights were able to cut off a large number of Englishmen who had pursued them down the hill, and to begin a new attack on the depleted English ranks. Twice in the following hours groups of knights, remembering this success, deliberately broke away from the battle in pretended flight, and then, wheeling their horses, surrounded their pursuers and destroyed them. In spite of these losses, and of the strain of a long defence without hope of reinforcement, the centre of the English position was held throughout the hours of daylight and the shrunken ranks of the English army, exhausted, and at last outnumbered, were still resisting when Harold fell. Among the stories current about his death the most probable is that which attributes it to an arrow sent

[1] The topography of the site is made clear by the minutely contoured plan and description in F. W. Baring's *Domesday Tables* (London, 1909).

at random into the English lines. His brothers Gyrth and Leof-wine had already fallen; the English host was left without any leader adequate to the command, and in the dusk of evening it broke at last. The fighting ended in the half light, when a body of Englishmen rallied for a final stand in the broken country which lies behind the battlefield. William, who led the pursuit, was in some danger, and many of his followers perished in a ravine of which neither he nor they were aware. But the chance of an English recovery had gone by. The Englishmen who were endeavouring to renew the struggle were dispersed, and in the darkness William returned to the main battleground knowing that his victory was complete.

Events were to show that he had won one of the battles which at rare intervals have decided the fate of nations. But its full significance only appeared slowly. Edwin and Morcar had not been involved in Harold's defeat; the spirit of London was un-broken, and there were ships which could be placed across the line of William's communications with Normandy. It seemed to the English leaders on whom the decision fell that London could be held while a second army was raised for a king whose name would unite the country. Inevitably under these condi-tions they turned for a king to Edgar the Ætheling, the last male of Cerdic's line. It was clear to William that London was the key to the situation, and after resting his army for five days at Hastings he set out on a circuitous but intimidating advance upon the city. His progress can be followed through Romney—where he avenged certain of his followers whom the townsmen had killed in a chance encounter—to Dover, which surrendered on demand. From Dover, after eight days spent on works of fortification, he moved to Canterbury, and remained there or in the neighbourhood for a month. In spite of a sudden illness, he was able to open negotiations for the surrender of other important places, and soon after he left Canterbury he obtained a proffer of submission from Winchester through the influence of Edith, the Confessor's widow, who was holding the city in dower. The Ætheling's men within London offered him no re-sistance until he approached the southern end of London Bridge, and the sortie which they then attempted was beaten back with heavy loss by his advanced guard. But it was evident that the bridge could not be carried by storm, and after burning South-wark he began a movement on a large scale, intended to isolate the city by the reduction of a broad belt of country around it on either side of the Thames. His general course across Surrey, northern Hampshire, and Berkshire can be traced by the abrupt post-Conquest decline in value recorded by Domesday Book for manors lying in his path. He came again to the Thames at Wallingford, where he sent his army across the river by a ford and bridge to encamp on the Oxfordshire bank.[1] The encirclement of London was not yet half completed, but the rate of its progress must have been daunting to the Ætheling's party, and at Wallingford, Archbishop Stigand, its leading member, came in to William and swore him fealty.

From Wallingford the army continued its advance along the line of the Icknield Way beneath the Chilterns. Stigand's defection had shown that the Ætheling's party was beginning to collapse, and William cannot have been surprised when he learned that it had decided to offer submission. His conclusive meeting with the English leaders took place at Berkhamstead, where he received an oath of fealty, secured by hostages, from Edgar himself, Edwin and Morcar, Archbishop Ealdred, Wulfstan, bishop of Worcester, Walter, bishop of Hereford, and the leading men of London. To the Englishman who recorded the meeting it seemed folly that they had not submitted before.[2] William promised to be a good lord to them, but until London was in his hands a display of force was still necessary, and he allowed his army to ravage the whole country along the twenty-five miles of road between Berkhamstead and the city. Of what happened at the end of the march nothing is certainly known. English writers seem to have thought that the occupation of London followed inevitably from the submission at Berkhamstead.

[1] The occupation of Wallingford is mentioned by two writers, each of whom wrote before 1071. William of Poitiers (*Gesta*, ed. Giles, p. 141, and R. Foreville, p. 216) states that after the skirmish at London Bridge the duke 'progrediens dein quoquoversum placuit, transmeato flumine Tamesi vado simul ponte ad oppidum Warengefort pervenit'. As Wallingford is on the right bank of the Thames, this passage presents great difficulty, for it implies that the duke had previously made an unrecorded crossing of the river, and approached the town from the east. That William of Poitiers was in error here is made virtually certain by the statement of his contemporary, William of Jumièges (*Gesta*, ed. Marx, p. 136), that the duke 'ad Warengeforth divertit urbem, transmeatoque vado fluvii, legiones ibi castra metari jussit'. The implication here, which is clearly preferable, is that the duke entered Wallingford from the south or west, and encamped his army on the opposite side of the river. The literary relations of these writers are obscure, but there is certainly no reason to assume the superior authority of William of Poitiers.

[2] *Chronicle* D, under 1066.

Among the French authorities nearest to the event, none of whom mentions the submission, one states that William received the surrender of London as the city came into his sight,[1] another speaks of William's preparations for a siege of the city and of his secret negotiations with its commander;[2] and a third refers to fighting between the citizens and William's advance-guard in an open space within or immediately without the walls.[3] The last two of these stories raise a distinct possibility that there was a party within the city which endeavoured to continue the struggle. But there can be little doubt that the weight of opinion within London was represented by the city magnates who had gone to Berkhamstead, and that most Londoners were anxious that William should take control of the situation with the name and authority of a king.

On Christmas day William was ordained king in Westminster abbey. He had wished to postpone the ceremony until his wife could be crowned beside him, but he had yielded to the urgency of his men that he should assume the rank which had been secured to him at Berkhamstead. Like the kings before him, he swore to rule his people justly. But the later stages of the rite were marked by a significant departure from the accustomed order. William, though he could claim kinship with Edward the Confessor, and acceptance by many leading Englishmen, had come to power through battle. It was thought necessary to ask the assembled people whether they acknowledged him as their lord. The question was put in English by Archbishop Ealdred, and in French by Bishop Geoffrey of Coutances. The shouting that followed was misunderstood by the mounted guard outside the abbey, which thought that the crowd within had turned upon the king-elect. In a panic the knights set fire to the surrounding buildings. But the ceremony went forward to the central point of consecration, and was duly completed by the formalities of coronation and enthronement.

The coronation placed William in the succession of the Old English kings. But it was followed by measures which showed that England was a conquered country. They began with the building of a castle for the coercion of the Londoners—

---

[1] William of Poitiers, *Gesta Willelmi Ducis*, ed. J. A. Giles, p. 141 and R. Foreville, p. 216.

[2] Guy of Amiens, *Carmen de Hastingae Proelio*, ed. Giles, pp. 45–8.

[3] William of Jumièges, *Gesta Normannorum Ducum*, ed. J. Marx, p. 136.

presumably on the site where William afterwards planted
the Tower which is the greatest of his military works. While it
was under construction William stayed at Barking where he
received the homage of many English noblemen, among them
Copsi, Tostig's associate, whom he sent to Northumbria as earl.
From Barking he set out on a progress, during which he raised
other elementary castles and garrisoned them strongly. In the
meantime he had imposed a heavy tax on the country as a
whole, and had taken much money for the redemption of their
estates from individuals who had shown themselves friendly to
his enemies. The lands of the Englishmen who had fallen at
Hastings were naturally subject to confiscation, and there has
survived a writ of the period in which William orders the abbot
of Bury to surrender the holdings of all those under his jurisdiction 'who stood against me in battle and were slain there'.[1]

By the end of March, six months after his landing, he was so
far the master of England that he could pay an overdue visit to
Normandy. He divided the responsibility for the government of
England between his seneschal, William fitz Osbern, whom he
made earl of Hereford, and his half-brother Odo, bishop of
Bayeux, whom he made earl of Kent. To make their task
easier he attached to his train the men of rank around whom
disaffected Englishmen might be expected to gather. They
included Archbishop Stigand, Edgar the Ætheling, Edwin,
Morcar, and Waltheof, Earl Siward's son, to whom King
Edward had recently given an earldom comprising the shires
of Huntingdon, Northampton, Bedford, and Cambridge.[2] It
was Earl William's especial duty to defend eastern England
against invasion from Denmark, where many English exiles had
found refuge, and for this reason his headquarters were fixed at
Norwich. Bishop Odo was set in Dover castle in order to guard
the Kentish ports. But the whole country was in a state of suppressed rebellion, and the bishop with many of his knights was
occupied beyond the Thames when a serious rising broke out in
Kent. Count Eustace of Boulogne, who had been prominent in
the battle of Hastings, had quarrelled with King William. In
the conviction that the native dynasty could never be restored

---

[1] *Feudal Documents from the Abbey of Bury St. Edmunds*, ed. D. C. Douglas, p. 47.
[2] Its boundaries, which contemporaries leave vague, can be reconstructed from
the claims afterwards put forward by Waltheof's heirs, the Senlis earls of Northampton and the Scottish royal house.

a number of Kentishmen decided that the count would be the most tolerable of foreign rulers, and persuaded him that with their help he could seize and hold the port of Dover. He was joined on landing by a considerable English force, but he refused to wait for the reinforcements of which he had been assured, and an ill-conceived attack on the castle was defeated by the garrison. Before the bishop had returned to Dover the count had sailed back to his own country, and his English allies had dispersed.

On 6 December William returned to England. His presence was urgently needed. The military government of the earl and the bishop had alienated all who were within its reach, and in remoter parts, where King William himself was unknown, there was a new determination to check his progress by local resistance. Soon after the king's return the men of Exeter openly defied him. During his absence they had allied themselves with other towns, strengthened their own walls, and persuaded the more warlike of the foreign traders within the city to help in its defence. To a demand from the king for their fealty they replied that they would neither swear fealty nor admit him within the city, but would continue the customary payments which their predecessors had been used to make to the Crown. William's answer was to march into Devon with an army in which, for the first time, English and Norman soldiers were combined. The defence was hampered by the attitude of the thegns of the city, who gave hostages and promised submission to the king while he was on his way. Even so, the city held out for eighteen days; its walls could neither be stormed nor undermined, and in the end it surrendered upon terms. The highest ground in the city was taken for a castle, and a garrison was placed there, but the army was kept from plundering and Domesday Book shows that the customary payments to the Crown were not increased.[1]

With the occupation of Exeter William's power in Wessex seemed to be established. There was fighting in the south-west later in the year, when three illegitimate sons of King Harold, who had collected a raiding-party in Ireland, descended on Bristol, and after the townsmen had beaten them off sailed on to Somerset and defeated the local militia.[2] But this was

---

[1] J. H. Round, *Feudal England*, pp. 431–55.
[2] Near Bleadone Hill, Somerset (*in Breoduna*). Liebermann, *Ungedruckte Anglo-Normannische Geschichtsquellen* p. 9.

merely a private adventure which had no bearing on the course of the Norman Conquest. By Eastertide it was considered safe to bring the Duchess Matilda to England, and she was crowned queen on Whit-Sunday at Westminster. The court which William held for the occasion was attended by many prominent Englishmen. But it was followed by a series of rebellions through which the native aristocracy lost all that remained of its political influence. In the summer Edgar the Ætheling, with his mother and sisters, fled to Scotland, where King Malcolm received them kindly. Earl Edwin, disappointed in the hope of marrying one of King William's daughters, left the court with his brother Morcar for the north, where a strong anti-Norman movement was coming to a head in and around the city of York. The situation created by their departure gave rise to the most extensive campaign which William had so far undertaken in England. It began with the building of a castle at Warwick, which brought the earls to submission. The news that he had raised another castle at Nottingham alarmed the northern insurgents, and he was able to enter York without a battle. His stay in York was marked by the submission of many Yorkshire magnates, by the raising of the castle-mound on which Clifford's Tower now stands, and by negotiations with the king of Scots, which prevented a Scottish invasion of England on the Ætheling's behalf. The campaign ended with the foundation of castles at Lincoln, Huntingdon, and Cambridge in the course of his return towards the south.

His display of power had been impressive, but it had done little to destroy either the will or the capacity of the north for rebellion. In 1069 the whole strength of the Norman hold on England was tested by a second Northumbrian rising and the general war into which it developed. The fighting began in Northumbria beyond Tees. Up to the end of 1068 William had left this region to the government of native magnates, under whom it had fallen into complete disorder. Tostig's ally, Copsi, whom the king had sent to the north from Barking, was regarded as an enemy by the powerful family to which the Bernician earldom had once belonged. After five weeks he was surprised and killed at Newburn on Tyne by Oswulf, son of Eadwulf, the head of that house, who maintained himself as earl until the autumn, when a brigand slew him. His cousin, Cospatric, son of Maldred, then bought the earldom from the king.

But in 1068 he joined the Ætheling's party, and towards the end of the year William at last decided to send one of his own followers with an earl's commission to the north. Robert de Comines, the new earl, was put in command of a considerable force. As he approached Durham the bishop warned him that a large English army was in the field. But he neglected to provide against a surprise, and in the early morning of 28 January 1069 his enemies surrounded the town, destroyed his men trapped in the streets, and burned him in the bishop's house, where he had spent the previous night.

The destruction of the only Norman force on service beyond York was quickly followed by an English attack upon the city. The castellan whom the king had appointed was killed, and the citizens were induced, or compelled, to declare themselves for the Ætheling. But the castle itself held out, and its new commander was able to send an urgent request for help to the king. By a rapid march William relieved the garrison; and then spent eight days in the construction of a second castle, on the right bank of the Ouse, which he committed to Earl William fitz Osbern. After this he returned to Winchester for the Easter festival, where he was joined by Earl William, who in the meantime had completed the discomfiture of the English host.[1] For the next five months the north was quiet, and the only hostilities which troubled the country came from a second unlucky descent of Harold's sons on the south-west.

In the autumn the military situation in England was abruptly changed by the arrival of a Danish fleet. As the heir of Cnut's house and the representative of its traditions, Swein Estrithson, the king of Denmark, had something more than a formal claim to the English throne. It must for some time have been clear to the English leaders that a movement headed by Edgar the Ætheling was unlikely to reverse the Norman Conquest. They had been in correspondence with King Swein at an earlier time, and their recent defeat at York seems to have brought them to the point of offering him the crown. Swein himself was not prepared to use the whole resources of his kingdom in an English adventure. The force which he sent to England was a composite host, which included Norwegians as well as Danes. But it was accompanied by three of his sons, his brother, and

---

[1] His presence at Winchester on 13 April is proved by the charter in Davis, *Regesta*, No. 26.

many Danish magnates, and the fleet which carried it was estimated at 240 ships. In mere numbers it may not have fallen
very far short of the host with which Harold Hardrada had
sailed from Norway three years before.

It first appeared in English waters off the coast of Kent, and
then sailed slowly northwards. Landing-parties which tested
the local defences at Dover, Sandwich, Ipswich, and Norwich
were beaten off from each place, and it reached the Humber
before it found an anchorage where it was unlikely to be attacked. In the meantime, a large English army had been assembled in Yorkshire by the Ætheling, Cospatric, Waltheof,
and other men of influence. After joining their forces the
English and Danish leaders moved at once upon York. The
Norman castlemen, feeling themselves enveloped by a hostile
population, set fire to the city before the host arrived. But they
were too few to hold their own defences against the numbers
coming against them, and most of them perished in open fighting outside the castles. It was the heaviest defeat which the
Normans ever suffered in England, and its consequences might
have been momentous if the allies had not thrown away their
victory in the determination to secure the prisoners and money
in their hands. On the mere rumour that the king was approaching they fell back on the Danish ships in the Humber, crossed
to the Lindsey shore, and entrenched themselves in the Isle
of Axholme. When William appeared before the island they
recrossed to the Yorkshire coast. There, for several weeks, they
remained inert, while the Norman commanders suppressed
the revolts which the news of the Danish landing had encouraged in other parts of England.

It was in Wessex beyond Selwood and western Mercia that
this reaction was strongest. A rising in Devon and Cornwall
gave little trouble, largely because the insurgents wasted their
strength on an attack on Exeter, which had declared itself on
the king's side. A rising in Somerset and Dorset, directed
against a castle newly built at Montacute, was more serious,
and the bishop of Coutances, who suppressed it, was obliged to
draw troops from London as well as from Salisbury and Winchester. But it was the Mercian revolt which gave most anxiety
to the king. Ever since 1067 a Herefordshire thegn named
Edric 'the Wild' had maintained himself in independence at the
head of a large English following, and in alliance with the

Welsh princes of his neighbourhood. In the course of 1069 his
movement spread northwards as far as Cheshire, and eastwards
at least as far as Stafford. It was checked by the castles which
the Normans had planted in this country, and in particular, by
that at Shrewsbury, which held out against a combined attack
by Edric, his Welsh allies, and the townsmen at its gates. But
the suppression of the revolt was clearly beyond the power of
the Norman commanders in Mercia, and the king decided to
deal with it in person. Leaving his half-brother, Count Robert
of Mortain, and his cousin, Count Robert of Eu, to watch the
Danes in the Humber, he set out from Lindsey for Stafford,
where the insurgents were concentrated. After defeating them
in what his admirers called an easy victory, he began the return
march to Lindsey. But at Nottingham he was told that the
Danes were preparing to reoccupy York, and in the hope of
anticipating them he struck off from the Trent valley to the
north.

He failed to reach the city before the Danes had re-entered it,
for he was delayed for three weeks at the passage of the Aire.
The bridge which he expected to use was broken, and the northern bank was held against him. When at last a ford had been
found and crossed, he repeated the strategy which had given
him London, three years before. Instead of attacking York he
drew a wide belt of wasted country around the city on the west
and north, and threatened it with isolation. Before long the
Danes returned to their ships, and soon afterwards were bought
out of the war by the king with an understanding that they
might remain in the Humber for the winter. York was occupied
once more in William's name. But to make an English recovery impossible he continued his harrying, and the Christmas festival which he spent at York was only an interlude in
operations which early in the new year brought him to the Tees.
The submission of Waltheof and Cospatric, which he received
while in camp by the river, was a sign that the resistance of the
north had been broken. The only Englishmen who were still in
arms against him were remnants of the Mercian host which he
had defeated at Stafford, and after arranging for the safe keeping of York he turned at once to deal with them. A march
across the central hills of northern England, in which many of
his soldiers came near to mutiny, enabled him to reach the
Cheshire plain before his enemies were prepared for him. The

last traces of the Mercian rising were crushed without any general engagement; castles were built at Chester and Stafford, and he was free at last to return to Wessex. The crisis of his English warfare was over, and at Salisbury, shortly before the Easter of 1070, he disbanded the mercenary portion of his army.

Any campaign of this length would have desolated the country in which it was fought. But the operations of 1069–70 were distinguished from ordinary warfare by a deliberate attempt to ruin the population of the affected districts. From the eleventh century onwards historians have noted the sustained ferocity with which the king set his men to destroy the means of life in northern England. Their generalities are abundantly borne out by the evidence of Domesday Book, which shows that within the country ravaged at this time vast areas were still derelict after seventeen years. It is in Yorkshire that the desolation is most evident. But the oldest account of the harrying states that it also extended over Cheshire, Shropshire, Staffordshire, and Derbyshire, and Domesday Book proves that the devastation in those parts, though less complete than in Yorkshire, was on the same general scale.[1] The object of the harrying was to secure that neither Mercia nor Northumbria should ever revolt again. It was the most terrible visitation that had ever fallen on any large part of England since the Danish wars of Alfred's time.

There still remained an unquiet year before the conquest was complete. In the spring of 1070 King Swein himself came into the Humber, where the Danish fleet of 1069 was still at anchor. The men of the adjacent country made peace with him, and the seamen whom he had relieved, ignoring their agreement with King William, attempted a diversion in the eastern midlands. Using the Isle of Ely as a base, they were joined by large numbers of Englishmen. The central figure among them was a Lincolnshire thegn of moderate estate, named Hereward, who in history as well as tradition represents the spirit of the native resistance to the Conqueror. His most famous exploit was a successful raid on Peterborough, which he carried out with the help of the Danish seamen. But in the summer of 1070 William and Swein made a treaty which provided that Swein should leave the Humber, and that his men should evacuate Ely. On their departure Hereward took on himself the defence of the

[1] *Chronicon Abbatiae de Evesham*, R.S., pp. 90, 91.

island, and maintained it until far into the following year. In the spring of 1071 many important English leaders came in to him with their men. The most prominent among them was Earl Morcar. Neither he nor his brother Edwin had revolted in 1069, but the king had shown that he mistrusted them and they had taken arms in self-defence. Edwin was killed through the treachery of his own followers while on his way to Scotland, and it was probably as a fugitive that Morcar came to Ely. Soon after his arrival the king began a siege of the island by land and water, which brought most of the garrison to surrender without terms. But Hereward and a few companions cut their way out to further adventures, in which Normans and Englishmen came before long to find a common interest.

For upwards of a year from the summer of 1071, when Ely seems to have fallen, there is little evidence about the king's movements. In the spring of 1072 he was in southern England. But in August he set out on a campaign which was a natural sequel to his recent wars. Throughout the first years of his reign any Englishman who feared or hated him had been sure of a refuge with Malcolm king of Scots. Before the end of 1070 Malcolm married Margaret, the Ætheling's sister, and the Ætheling had come to live again at his court. Relations between the kings were further complicated by the fact that early in 1070 William had restored the great Bernician magnate Cospatric to the earldom which he had forfeited in 1068. Cospatric had spent his exile in Scotland. But as William's man he became Malcolm's enemy, and a local war broke out in the north in which Malcolm harried Cospatric's country along the north-east coast, and Cospatric raided in Edendale and the Solway plain where Malcolm had lately been encroaching on English territory. To stabilize the position on the border, and to deprive the Ætheling of Scottish help, William now invaded Scotland. Without any serious resistance Malcolm did homage to him at Abernethy on the Tay, and gave him his eldest son as a hostage. In treaties made on such occasions it was always an understanding that neither party should harbour the other's enemies, and there can be little doubt that the Ætheling, who next appears in Flanders two years later, left Scotland in consequence of the terms arranged at Abernethy.

The Ætheling's reception in Flanders was the result of a recent change in the character of the relations between the

Flemish and Norman courts. Count Baldwin V, who in 1066 had secured Normandy against invasion from France, died in the following year. Baldwin VI, his eldest son, maintained the tradition of friendship with Normandy, and shortly before his death in the summer of 1070 made William fitz Osbern, earl of Hereford, joint guardian of his heir with Philip, king of France. Before William had taken up the charge a revolt had broken out in Flanders against the government of the count's widow, Richildis of Hainault. The rebels were supported by Robert, the late count's brother, and Richildis was compelled to ask the king of France and William fitz Osbern for military help. William, who hoped to marry the countess, came at once into Flanders, but on 20 February 1071 he and his ward fell in battle against Robert at Bavinchove near Cassel.[1] Within a few months Robert had obtained possession of all Flanders.[2] He never forgave the intervention of William fitz Osbern in the war of 1071; King William was slow to recognize his position in Flanders, and for the next fifteen years the county and the Anglo-Norman state were at least potential enemies.

The loss of the Flemish alliance was one among several indications that King William's predominance in northern France was no longer so secure as it had seemed in 1066. The war of the Angevin succession had ended in that year, and for the rest of his life William was confronted by an aggressive rival in Fulk 'le Rechin', the new count of Anjou. It was Fulk's ambition to destroy the ascendancy which William had achieved in Maine after the death of Geoffrey Martel. In working for this end he was helped by the fact that as count of Anjou he had an ancient claim to suzerainty over Maine, which was admitted by William himself, and hampered his dealings with opponents in the county. It was of even greater advantage to Fulk that William's position in Maine was, at best, anomalous. In charters he sometimes styled himself *comes* or *princeps Cenomannensium*, but in order to secure the Norman possession of Maine he had betrothed Robert, his eldest son, to the sister of the last of the native counts, and although she died before the marriage had taken place, the title of count and the local influence which it carried

[1] J. Tait, *Essays in History presented to R. L. Poole*, pp. 153-4.
[2] In 1071 Robert had for some years been ruling his wife's county of Holland, or West Frisia, as the guardian of her son by a former husband. It is from his connection with this county that Robert's usual surname 'le Frison' is derived.

passed to Robert. In 1069, when Robert was still a minor, there broke out the first of the revolts which gave Fulk the opportunity of supporting armed resistance to the Norman government in Maine. The county was not brought back to the Norman obedience until 1073, when William reduced it in a campaign in which Englishmen and Normans served together. During these four years Robert had come of age; but he proved to be incapable of upholding the Norman interest in his country and it was gradually worn down by Fulk's renewed assaults. It was saved from complete destruction by a compromise arranged in 1081 between Fulk and William, which provided that Robert should keep the county on condition of doing homage for it to Fulk. But the long war had produced conditions in which an important baron could be a law to himself, and for some three years after the treaty Hubert *vicomte* of Maine successfully defied King William from his castle of Sainte-Suzanne, apparently without support from Anjou.

It was a more insidious threat to William's security that in all the warfare of his later years the king of France was behind his enemies. The conquest of England had been accomplished while King Philip was still a boy. Thenceforward there was little that he could do against William except watch for opportunities of embarrassing him. But the opportunities were numerous, and Philip used them with considerable effect. In 1074 he offered Montreuil-sur-mer, an outlying portion of his demesne, to Edgar the Ætheling, as a base for raids over eastern Normandy. It was only by coming to terms with the Ætheling that William avoided the danger. Two years later Philip defeated William in open battle. In reprisal for help lately obtained from Brittany by his enemies in England, William had invaded the duchy and laid siege to Dol. Philip relieved the garrison in person, with heavy loss to William in men and treasure. Early in 1077 the kings came to an agreement. But their fundamental interests were irreconcilable, and within at most eighteen months Philip committed himself to fresh action against William as the ally of Robert, his disaffected son.

The cause of Robert's disloyalty was resentment at a position which gave him the promise of a great inheritance without any immediate power. In 1066, and on at least one later occasion, the Norman baronage had done homage to him as the heir apparent to the duchy. In 1067 he had been associated with his mother as regent of Normandy. But even in Maine, where he had an independent title to rule, he was allowed no real authority, and in Normandy he was denied the means of providing for his own retainers. In 1077 or early in 1078 he broke away in anger from the court.[1] The immediate cause of his revolt was a dispute with his brothers William and Henry which arose while they were campaigning with their father against Rotrou, count of Mortagne, the principal feudatory of the king of France on the southern border of Normandy. After the failure of a wild attempt to seize the tower of Rouen Robert found refuge with his uncle, the count of Flanders. The friends whom he had attracted into the rising joined King William's enemies on the Norman border, and with the approval of the king of France were established in various castles by Hugh, seigneur of the Thimerais, the neighbour of the count of Mortagne. Towards the close of 1078 Philip entered directly into the war. Using Robert as he had hoped to use Edgar the Ætheling, Philip placed him in the castle of Gerberoy, on the border between eastern Normandy and the Beauvaisis. William replied by laying siege to the castle with an Anglo-Norman army. He was badly defeated by the garrison and was wounded, but by negotiations of which no details are known he induced Philip to change sides, and in the last stages of the siege he and Philip were allies. It may be assumed that they were able to take the castle, for Robert returned to Flanders after the siege and finally accepted his father's terms for a reconciliation. From the spring of 1080 until the summer of 1083 he can be traced at court in both Normandy and England. Soon afterwards he went again into exile. His wanderings are obscure, but he was still of potential value to King Philip, and it seems clear that he was living under Philip's protection when the Conqueror died.

These inconclusive wars, in which William never rose above the average generalship of his day, distracted his attention from English affairs. His itinerary cannot be reconstructed, but it is clear that between 1072 and 1084 he spent at least a part of each year in Normandy, and that he was absent from England for nearly three consecutive years between 1077 and 1080. Little is known about the arrangements which he made for the

[1] On the events which followed see C. W. David, *Robert Curthose*, pp. 17–36.

government of England in his absence, and it is probable that
their character varied between one occasion and another. The
regency of William fitz Osbern and Odo of Bayeux in 1067 can
have amounted to little more than the military government of a
half-conquered land. Archbishop Lanfranc of Canterbury was
representing the king in 1075, apparently without any express
commission. At various dates Bishop Geoffrey of Coutances
was ordered to hold individual pleas as the king's deputy. But
towards the end of the reign there begin to appear distinct signs
of a formal viceroyalty. Between 1077 and 1080 Odo of Bayeux
was setting judicial investigations in motion by the use of the
king's authority, confirming private transactions in land which
needed the king's assent, and transmitting the king's commands,
received from abroad, by writs issued under his own name. The
statement of a twelfth-century historian that Odo was justiciar
of England is too precise, but it may well be near the truth.

It is a sign of William's preoccupation with Norman business
that he left his representatives to deal with the most serious
English crisis of his later years. When the native resistance to
the conquest was over, there remained two noblemen of the
highest rank in whom the traditions of King Edward's court
were still alive. Waltheof, Earl Siward's son, was high in the
king's favour. In 1072 he received his father's Northumbrian
earldom, from which Cospatric had recently been deposed, and
then, if not earlier, was allowed to marry Judith, the king's
niece.[1] The second of these outstanding magnates was Ralf, son
of King Edward's Breton minister, Ralf the 'staller'. The elder
Ralf had co-operated with King William in the settlement of
the country after the invasion, and had been created earl of
East Anglia, probably in the first months of the reign. His son
had succeeded him in 1069 or 1070.[2] It illustrates the political
confusion of the period that in 1075 these survivors from the
Old English order suddenly allied themselves in rebellion with
Roger, earl of Hereford, the son of William fitz Osbern.

Their motives are obscure. The king's sheriffs had recently
been holding pleas in Earl Roger's lands,[3] and he probably

[1] Daughter of Adelaide, sister of the Conqueror, by her second husband
Lambert, count of Lens (*Complete Peerage*, i, pp. 351-2).

[2] Ibid. ix, p. 571.

[3] *Lanfranci Opera*, ed. Giles, i, p. 64. The letters of Lanfranc, which are most
easily accessible in this edition, are second only to the *Chronicle* as an authority for
the history of the rising.

believed his feudal liberties to be in danger. But it is hard to find any sufficient ground for the disloyalty of Earls Ralf and Waltheof. It is known that the rebellion was planned at a feast held to celebrate the marriage of Ralf with Emma, Earl Roger's sister. Ralf's conduct would be explained at once if it were possible to accept the assertion of a later annalist[1] that the marriage had been forbidden by the king. It may have been so, but the *Chronicle*, which seems to rest on contemporary materials for this period, expressly states that the king had given the lady to the earl. No early writer gives any intelligible reason for Waltheof's behaviour, and the earliest writer who tries to explain it represents him as acting under duress.[2] It seems clear that Earl Ralf was the chief agent in the rebellion. By inheritance he was a great lord in Brittany,[3] and his connection with that country enabled him to raise a considerable force of Breton mercenaries, and gave him the support of many Breton adventurers who had acquired land in England since the Conquest.

At the outset of their rising the rebels asked for help from Denmark. The idea of an expedition against England was still popular in the north, but effective action was delayed by confusion in the Danish kingdom. King Swein Estrithson had died on 28 April 1074. His death was followed by a prolonged conflict for the succession between Harold and Cnut, his elder sons.[4] Harold, who obtained the kingdom, was an unadventurous person, but Cnut, disappointed of the crown, was anxious for other distinction, and towards the end of 1075 he sailed for England with a fleet of some 200 warships. The threat of a Danish invasion was taken seriously by King William and Archbishop Lanfranc. Durham and probably all the other English castles were garrisoned against it. But the rebels whom it was intended to support had been crushed before their allies sailed, and the Danes returned to their own country with nothing achieved except a raid on York minster.

The rebels had been suppressed without much serious fighting. Most Englishmen were on the king's side, and his representatives were able to prevent the earls from uniting their

---

[1] Florence of Worcester, *Chronicon ex Chronicis*, ed. B. Thorpe, ii, p. 10.

[2] Florence of Worcester, ibid.: 'Waltheofum suis insidiis praeventum secum conjurare compulerunt.'

[3] Above, p. 426.

[4] *Ælnothi Monachi Historia Sancti Canuti Regis*, c. iv; Saxo Grammaticus, *Gesta Danorum*, ed. Olrik and Ræder, pp. 316–17.

armies. Wulfstan, bishop of Worcester, and Æthelwig, abbot of Evesham, co-operated with the Norman barons Urse d'Abitot and Walter de Laci in raising an army which kept the earl of Hereford beyond the Severn. Earl Ralf, advancing to meet him, was confronted near Cambridge by a larger force under the bishops of Bayeux and Coutances, and fell back on Norwich castle. Soon afterwards he escaped to Brittany, but the defence of the castle was maintained by his wife, with whom all the honours of this war remain. It was surrendered at last on terms which allowed the countess and the garrison to leave England. In the meantime Earl Waltheof had abandoned his accomplices, and on the advice of Archbishop Lanfranc had crossed to Normandy in the hope of making peace with the king. Of the three chief conspirators Earl Roger only was at large in England when King William returned from Normandy, and his arrest followed before the year was over.

In accordance with the Norman law of treason, Earl Roger was condemned to perpetual imprisonment and the forfeiture of all his lands. Earl Ralf was out of William's power. His wife was allowed to join him in Brittany, and he never returned to England. Earl Waltheof was treated as an Englishman, subject by his nationality to a law which punished treason with death. On 31 May 1076, after an imprisonment of more than five months, he was beheaded on St. Giles's Hill outside Winchester. So far as is known, he was the only Englishman of high rank whom King William executed. The severity of his treatment caused many to regard him as a martyr, and most writers tell his story with a strong bias in his favour. Within a generation the story had passed into an atmosphere of hagiography and romance,[1] in which facts became of little account. That Waltheof had joined the king's enemies in plotting treason is certain. In the absence of information about the terms on which he came in to the king, it can only be left an open question whether his execution can be justified in morality as well as in law.

The political effects of the rising were important. The earl-doms of Hereford and East Anglia were suppressed, and were not revived for more than sixty years. Waltheof's midland earl-dom of Huntingdon, Northampton, Bedford, and Cambridge

---

[1] It is already apparent in the account of Waltheof's end given by Ordericus Vitalis (*Historia Ecclesiastica*, ed. le Provost, ii, pp. 265–7), which is based on information obtained at Crowland, where Waltheof was buried.

ceased to exist for the remainder of the Conqueror's reign, and
was never re-established in its entirety. The earldom of Northumbria, which Waltheof had held since 1072, was part of the
national organization for the defence of the realm. It could not
safely be abolished while Malcolm, king of Scots, was alive, but,
to keep the authority which it carried in loyal hands, King
William tried the experiment of combining it with the bishopric
of Northumbria beyond Tees. On Waltheof's fall, the military
and civil powers inherent in the Northumbrian earldom were
committed to Walcher, bishop of Durham.

The experiment lasted for a little more than four years. The
bishop himself was anxious to govern his earldom in accordance
with Old English law and custom. His chief adviser in secular
matters was a thegn named Ligulf, who was descended through
his mother from the ancient earls of Bernicia. Ligulf had known
Archbishop Ealdred, he was devoted to the cult of St. Cuthbert,
and was fitted in every way to be the intermediary between the
bishop and the Englishmen of his province. On the other hand,
the foreign knights, on whom the bishop's security depended,
made themselves hated by their violence, and the bishop was
blamed for their misdeeds. In the spring of 1080 the tension
broke in a tragedy precipitated by the murder of Ligulf. The
murder was committed by Gilbert, a kinsman of the bishop,
whom he employed as sheriff in the administration of his earldom. It was believed that Gilbert had been instigated to the
crime by Leobwin, the bishop's chaplain, who had always been
ill disposed towards Ligulf, and had recently quarrelled with
him in the bishop's presence. It was inevitable that suspicion
should spread to the bishop, and it became necessary for him to
send word throughout his earldom that he was prepared to deny
the charge by his oath. For the settlement of terms with Ligulf's
kinsfolk a general assembly of the earldom was held at Gateshead. Refusing to plead in the open air, the bishop withdrew
into the church with Leobwin, Gilbert, and other clerks and
knights. It seems that he hoped for a peaceful settlement, but
the crowd had been excited by the appearance of Ligulf's
enemies in his company, and before long it turned upon the men
whom he had left outside the church. From the moment when
fighting began the bishop and those with him were doomed.
Gilbert and the knights who attended the bishop were killed as
they tried to force their way out of the church, the building was

set on fire, and the bishop and his clerks were cut down one by one as they came out from the burning. Leobwin, whose death the crowd above all desired, was the last to perish. In the hope of destroying all that were left of the bishop's men, the Northumbrians hurried from Gateshead to Durham and attacked the castle. But they failed to carry it by storm, and after spending four days ineffectively before its outworks, they dispersed.

The massacre at Gateshead was punished, as any Old English king would have punished it, by a devastation of the country to which the rebels belonged. The harrying, which was carried out with great severity by Bishop Odo of Bayeux, was followed within a year by an expedition intended to forestall Scottish encroachment on the wasted land. In the autumn of 1080 Robert, King William's son, lately reconciled with his father, was sent to Scotland in command of a large feudal army. The expedition, which penetrated Scotland as far as Falkirk, succeeded in its immediate purpose, and strengthened the permanent defences of northern England by the establishment of a new fortress on the site afterwards known as Newcastle on Tyne. To the vacant earldom of Northumbria the king appointed Aubrey de Coucy, a baron with large possessions in the midlands.[1] It is significant of the state of his earldom that before long he resigned it, forfeiting thereby his whole English estate. For his successor the king chose Robert de Mowbray, a nephew of Bishop Geoffrey of Coutances, who was in office when the reign ended.

The tenacity with which the Conquest was resisted in farther Northumbria affected the security of the whole realm. In itself it was a natural consequence of the remoteness and isolation of the north. The native society which confronted the Normans in this region had been accustomed to defend itself against the Scots without reference to the king of Wessex. It was self-confident, self-contained, and intensely conservative. It regarded the Norman advance as a threat to its familiar way of life, and many of its leaders preferred to make terms with the king of Scots rather than accept subordination to a foreign invader who was likely to impose new customs upon them. As early as 1072 Cospatric, the heir of the Northumbrian earls, went over to King Malcolm. The result of this attitude was that the Norman government could do nothing to advance, and less than was

---

[1] Which afterwards, as the 'Honour of Hinckley', formed part of the great fief of the earls of Leicester.

needed to protect, the English frontier against Scotland. To the end of the Conqueror's reign it placed his forces at a serious disadvantage. On the east the border river of Tweed, unguarded as yet by any fortress, was separated from the new advanced post at Newcastle by fifty miles of country inhabited by a sullen, if not hostile, population. On the west the territory of the Scottish king came down to the Rere Cross on Stainmore, within two days' ride from York. The strengthening of the northern frontier was the most urgent of all the tasks which King William left to his successors.

On the Welsh border the Normans were able to take the initiative. Long before the conquest of England was complete they had begun an invasion of Wales which in twenty years gave them command of all the chief lines of entry into that land. Their original leader was William fitz Osbern, earl of Hereford, who planted castles on the western approaches to his earldom, established outposts at Monmouth and Chepstow, and annexed the Welsh principality of Gwent.[1] But the advance in this direction was checked by the fall of Earl William's son, and it was farther to the north that the Normans of the first generation achieved their most striking success. In 1071 the king set Hugh, son of Richard, *vicomte* of Avranches, as earl in Chester. Except for the ancient possessions of the church, the whole of Cheshire was placed under Hugh's lordship,[2] and provided a base for operations which brought the English frontier to the river Conway, and for a time made the kingdom of Gwynedd a tributary province. The leader in this advance was Hugh's cousin Robert, the castellan of Rhuddlan, who conquered the lands between the Clwyd and the Conway, held them directly of the king, and rendered £40 a year as a rent for whatever he could extort from Gwynedd itself.

The third of the Conqueror's marcher earldoms secured the passes of the upper Severn and upper Dee. In or shortly before 1075 the king created an earldom of Shrewsbury for Roger de Montgomery, a great baron of central Normandy, whom he had previously made lord of Arundel.[3] Towards the north the

---

[1] J. H. Round, *Studies in Peerage and Family History*, pp. 181–7; *V.C.H. Hereford*, i, pp. 270–3.

[2] On his position in that county and the adjacent districts which are now included in Wales see J. Tait, *The Domesday Survey of Cheshire* (Chetham Society), New Series, lxxv (1916), pp. 22–59.

[3] On Roger's earldom of Shrewsbury see J. Tait, *V.C.H. Shropshire*, i, pp. 286–90.

encroachments of Earl Roger on the Welsh of Powys overlapped those of Earl Hugh on the Welsh of Gwynedd, and formed with them a frontier zone which protected the plains of Cheshire and Shropshire. Towards the south Earl Roger's men penetrated into the wild country which rises to Plynlimmon, but their chief work in this quarter was the fortification of the district to the east of these uplands, where the earl's name has become permanently attached to the castle and town of Montgomery. In these activities the king himself took little part. On the northern portion of the Welsh front, where the earls of Chester and Shrewsbury were in command, there was never any need for his intervention. But in the south the Norman forces, uncoordinated, were stationary throughout the second half of the reign. To display the military power that in the last resort was behind them, the king led an expedition to St. David's in 1081 which met no serious opposition and freed many prisoners of war.

The expedition of 1081 was the last military enterprise of the Conqueror's reign in England. For the next four years English chroniclers found few events of any kind to record. The most remarkable incident of this period was the arrest, forfeiture, and imprisonment of Bishop Odo of Bayeux, in 1082. No contemporary writer attempts to explain it, but in the twelfth century it was said that the bishop had been trying to obtain the papacy by distributing money among the citizens of Rome, and that he had induced knights from all parts of England to join him for an expedition to Italy.[1] If this story comes anywhere near the truth, the bishop's arrest was amply justified by his action in recruiting knights who should have been available for the king's service.[2] His motives can only be conjectured. It is incredible that he can have meant to take the papacy by violence. But the pope and the emperor were at war; the emperor had threatened Rome in 1081, and it is not impossible that the bishop may have hoped to earn merit with the curia and citizens by appearing in Rome with an army for the pope's defence.[3]

---

[1] Ordericus Vitalis, *Historia Ecclesiastica*, ed. A. le Prevost, iii, p. 189; William of Malmesbury, *Gesta Regum*, ii, p. 334.

[2] This is the explanation of the arrest offered by William of Malmesbury.

[3] There is no contemporary record of Odo's trial, and later accounts have a dramatic colouring which impairs their value. All that is certain is that Odo was treated in court as an earl and a tenant in chief, and that the fact of his episcopal orders was not allowed to affect the course of the proceedings. It was remembered

The series of uneventful years ended in 1085, when England was threatened for the last time by an invasion from Denmark. In 1081 Cnut, son of Swein Estrithson, succeeded his brother Harold as king of the Danes. It had always been his ambition to win fame in England, and on becoming king he reasserted the family claim to the English throne, which his brother had allowed to lapse. By the beginning of 1085 he had brought Count Robert of Flanders, his wife's brother, and King Olaf of Norway into a coalition which in naval force was overwhelming. On the assumption that a landing could not be prevented, King William removed from the English coast all supplies which might be useful to an invader, and imported a host of mercenaries from France, Maine, and Brittany. In the event the attack never materialized. Cnut assembled a large fleet in the Liim Fjord, but a dispute with his own people delayed his voyage, and in the autumn the ships dispersed. His controversy with his subjects became more violent as time went on, and in the summer of 1086 he was murdered by a band of rebels.

It is by no means impossible that the measures by which the king met this danger gave the immediate impulse to the greatest achievement of his reign—the taking of the Domesday Survey. The mercenaries whom he had brought into England were so numerous that he found it necessary to quarter them upon his barons. According to the *Chronicle* the number of men assigned to each baron was strictly proportionate to the capacity of his land.[1] The assessment of a baron's estate to the Danegeld and other public burdens was well known to the king's financial officers. But the arrangements for the billeting of the mercenaries must have impressed on all who took part in them the vagueness of the information that was to hand about the actual condition of these estates. It may well be more than a coincidence that at the end of the year the king 'held very deep speech with his council about this land—how it was peopled, and with what sort of men'.

It so happens that there has survived a description of the

that the king throughout the trial was careful to address him as 'brother' and 'earl', and not as 'bishop'. The treatment of Odo was quoted as a precedent by Archbishop Lanfranc in the trial of Bishop William of Durham in 1088 according to the tract *De injusta vexatione Willelmi episcopi* (Simeon of Durham, *Opera*, i, p. 184).

[1] *Chronicle* 1085, *be his landefne*. For *efne* see E. Björkman, *Scandinavian Loan-words in Middle English*, p. 209.

Domesday survey written by one who must have been present at that deep speech.[1] In the middle of a tract on technical chronology Bishop Robert of Hereford states that he is writing in the year 1086, in which, by the king's order, a description was made of all England. He observes that it covered the lands of every shire, and the property of every magnate in fields, manors, and men—whether slaves or free men, cottagers or farmers—in plough-teams, horses, and other stock, in services and rents. He adds that the inquiry was made in each shire before commissioners who had no personal interest there, and that the first returns were checked by a second group of commissioners, who made any error the ground of an accusation before the king. He ends by stating that the land was troubled by many calamities arising from the collection of money for the king—presumably by way of amercement for false testimony before the commissioners. The passage gives the impression of an undertaking without precedent, forced upon a reluctant country by the king's will. Of the thoroughness with which it was actually carried out every commentator on Domesday Book has spoken. As an administrative achievement it had no parallel in medieval history. It is a supreme demonstration of the efficiency of those who served the Conqueror, and of the energy with which at the end of his reign he could still enforce the execution of a great design.

The same quality brought into being the remarkable assembly which makes 1086 an important date in feudal history. On 1 August the king held a council at Salisbury, at which, according to the *Chronicle*, all the landowners of any account in England, whosesoever men they were, did him homage, became his men, and swore him fealty, that they would be faithful to him against all other men. The nature of this assembly has been much debated. It is obvious that while it cannot have included all freeholders of substance in England, it was a gathering of wholly exceptional size and importance. It is probable that the king's object in holding it was to obtain homage and an oath of fealty from all the principal tenants of the lords who held of him in chief. It is doubtful whether an ordinary knight who had been enfeoffed in a small estate by his lord would have been considered as a man of any account in 1086, and it is unlikely that many landholders of this sort appeared at Salisbury. The

[1] Printed by W. H. Stevenson, *E.H.R.* xxii (1907), p. 74.

men who fall most naturally under the Chroniclers description are the better-endowed and responsible tenants, without whose co-operation a lord could neither administer his barony nor provide the service that the king expected from him.[1] Men of this type, who were the social equals and the natural counsellors of their lords, were themselves known as barons. They were a numerous class, but they were numbered in hundreds rather than thousands, and a few days would have sufficed for the king to take the homage of them all. Whatever their numbers may have been, the establishment of a personal relationship between these under-tenants and the king was a most impressive demonstration of his power. The precedent which it set was momentous in the development of the English feudal state. For it gave public and solemn expression to the principle that the fealty which the tenant owed to his immediate lord must not be allowed to conflict with the fealty which, like all subjects, he owed to his sovereign.

Towards the end of the year the king left England. Nothing is known about his movements thenceforward until the beginning of the war in which he came to his death. All that is recorded of him during those months is that he allowed Edgar the Ætheling to leave his court and go on an expedition to Apulia with 200 knights. According to the *Chronicle* the Ætheling had little honour from the king. It is doubtful whether there was any motive behind his departure except discontent at a position which steadily became more ignominious as the Norman hold on England became stronger.

The origins of the Conqueror's last war lay far back in Norman history. For a considerable period after the settlement the river Andelle was the boundary of eastern Normandy in the direction of Paris. Between the Andelle and the Oise there stretched the pre-feudal district known as the Vexin. By the beginning of the eleventh century that district had fallen into two portions—the Vexin Normand, between the Andelle and the Epte, which had become an integral part of the duchy, and the Vexin Français, between the Epte and the Oise, which had been acquired by a line of counts holding directly of the king of France. In return for the support of Duke Robert, Henry I of France, early in his reign, placed Drogo, the reigning count,

[1] On these 'honorial barons' see F. M. Stenton, *The First Century of English Feudalism*, ed. 2 (1961), pp. 84–114.

under Norman suzerainty. Drogo himself was Duke Robert's friend, but his successors always resented the Norman overlordship, and in 1077, when the last of the line retired from the world, King Philip of France had no difficulty in uniting the county to the royal demesne. The annexation was a serious threat to the security of Normandy. A direct attack from France upon the duchy was made difficult by the fact that the county of Meulan, on the border between the Vexin and King Philip's land, passed at this time by marriage to the Norman house of Beaumont, which was both strong, and loyal to King William. But Mantes, the capital of the Vexin Français, was now an outpost of the French kingdom, and in 1087 its garrison crossed the river Eure, and harried in the county of Évreux.

King William replied by demanding the cession of the whole of the Vexin Français and, in particular, of Pontoise, Chaumont-le-Vexin, and Mantes. King Philip refused the demand, and William thereupon invaded the province. Mantes was his first objective, and it fell to a surprise assault. But the king, as he rode through the burning town, received an internal injury which compelled him to abandon the campaign, and within a month had brought him to death. He made his way to Rouen, but the noise of the city became intolerable to him as his pain increased, and he caused himself to be carried to the abbey of Saint Gervais, on the hills towards the west. He lived long enough to provide for the immediate future of his dominions. With much difficulty, he was brought to acknowledge that Robert, his eldest son, could not be deprived of his hereditary right to the Norman duchy. England, which had come to him by conquest, he considered to be at his own disposal, and by sending his crown, sword, and sceptre to William, his next surviving son, he designated him its king. To Henry, his youngest son, he gave no land, but a great treasure. Later writers, whom there is no reason to disbelieve, state that he ordered the release of the chief political prisoners in his hands. He died on 9 September, in the twenty-first year of his reign as the crowned king of England, and the forty-first year of his effective rule as duke of Normandy.

His greatness was recognized by those about him. A Norman clerk who recorded his death described him as pre-eminent among kings in wisdom and magnanimity, unshaken by toil or danger, and patient amid all changes of fortune.[1] An Englishman who had lived in his household drew a less conventional picture of a king who afflicted his subjects with taxes and forced labour, and mutilated the disturbers of his sport, but kept the land in peace, and, if stern beyond measure to those who opposed his will, was mild to the good men who loved God.[2] The writer's sympathies were with the ancient royal house of England. But he acknowledges that the Conqueror was stronger and more illustrious than any of his predecessors, and it is with naïve admiration that he sets down the names of the countries which had felt King William's power—Wales and Scotland, Maine, Normandy, his birthright, and Ireland, which his mere reputation would have given him if he had lived for two years longer. Other writers bring out the king's more individual qualities, such as his physical strength and the singular continence of his private life. What no writer of the period could be expected to note is the constructive imagination which directed his government, and in its operation gave a new character to English history.

[1] This simple record, which is printed by J. Marx in his edition of William of Jumièges, pp. 145–8, has been shown to consist largely of phrases borrowed from Einhard's *Life of Charlemagne* (see R. C. van Caenegem, *Studi Medievali*, 3ª Serie, vi. 1, 1965, pp. 307 f.). Nevertheless since the Norman writer would select those attributes of Charles which he saw also in William, it is of much greater authority than the famous account of Ordericus Vitalis (ed. A. le Prevost, iii, pp. 227–49). The long autobiography attributed to the Conqueror by Orderic, interesting as a survey of his reign by an early 12th-century historian, is an elaborate piece of writing, which should not be taken to represent any words actually spoken by the king on the eve of his death.

[2] *Chronicle*, under 1087.

XVII

THE NORMAN SETTLEMENT

THE cardinal principle of the Conqueror's government was
the wish to rule, and to be accepted by Englishmen, as
King Edward's legitimate successor. He claimed the English throne as the heir whom the Confessor himself had selected
from among all his kinsmen.[1] He preserved the constitutional
framework of the Old English state, so that it was without any
breach of continuity that the Old English *witena gemot* developed
under him into the feudal Great Council. His administration was
based on the theory that he had restored the good law of
King Edward's time after it had been overthrown by Harold's
usurpation. Few invaders who have overcome so strong an
opposition have been at such pains to disguise the fact of
conquest.

For himself, William claimed the entire range of powers that
had belonged to any Old English sovereign. They gave him a
weight and variety of authority such as was possessed by no
other king in western Europe. As King Edward's heir he was
entitled to impose taxation on every part of his kingdom, and
on the lands of its greatest magnates. The peace which he gave
to an individual was safeguarded by penalties which varied in
accordance with local custom, but were everywhere intimidating. His writ ran in every shire. There were many occasions on
which he intervened in the relations of his subjects with one
another. Private transactions in land were insecure until he had
confirmed them, and he had a right to be consulted before a
man of any position commended himself to a new lord. The
legislative authority of the Crown, peculiar at this date to England, had not been used by the Confessor, but the issue of Cnut's
great code was still within living memory. In the substance of its
admitted powers the Anglo-Saxon monarchy belonged to another
order than that of France, where the king was struggling to
establish a prerogative against subjects greater than himself,
or of Denmark, where the king could not levy a new tax
without danger to his own life.

[1] William of Poitiers, *Gesta Willelmi Ducis*, ed. J. A. Giles, p. 129, and R. Foreville, p. 174.

It was in keeping with William's desire to rule as King Edward's heir that he made a serious attempt to govern England through men who had held high office in King Edward's day. For the greater part of 1067 the natural leaders of the English people were in eclipse, as hostages with the king in Normandy. But they reappear on the establishment of a regular administration in England after his return, and thenceforward until the summer of 1069 there is no question of their importance in the state. None of the lesser materials for the history of William's reign are more interesting than the charters which show Edwin, Morcar, Waltheof, and Archbishop Stigand associated in council with Odo of Bayeux, Geoffrey of Coutances, Earl William fitz Osbern, and Count Robert of Mortain.[1]

In regard to lower offices than that of earl, the Conqueror showed the same desire to use King Edward's men. At least two of the Confessor's household officers, the 'stallers' Bundi and Eadnoth, attest King William's early charters. Eadnoth, who was one of the few Englishmen to whom William allowed a military command, was killed in 1068 while leading the Somerset militia against King Harold's sons.[2] King Edward's sheriffs of Wiltshire, Somerset, and Warwickshire are known to have been kept in office by the Conqueror, and it is probable that until 1069, at least, most of the sheriffdoms remained in English hands. But the most remarkable illustration of the Conqueror's attitude towards Englishmen willing to serve him is the extraordinary commission which he gave to Æthelwig, abbot of Evesham, in or before 1069.[3] According to a contemporary life of the abbot he received the authority of a royal justice over Shropshire, Herefordshire, Worcestershire, Staffordshire, Warwickshire, Oxfordshire, and Gloucestershire. Like the county justiciars of the twelfth century he combined executive with judicial powers. In one of the Conqueror's earliest writs Æthelwig and the local sheriff were appointed joint guardians of an estate in Staffordshire belonging to Westminster abbey.[4] A few years later the king required him to organize the assembly of the feudal host due from the great lords of his province.[5] That a

---

[1] Three good examples are Nos. 22, 23, and 28 of H. W. C. Davis, *Regesta Regum Anglo-Normannorum*.

[2] Above, p. 600.

[3] On Æthelwig's career see R. R. Darlington, *E.H.R.* xlviii (1933), pp. 1–22, 177–98.

[4] *Monasticon Anglicanum*, i, p. 301.   [5] J. H. Round, *Feudal England*, p. 304.

prelate of King Edward's appointment should have received
such varied authority in so wide a region is the clearest proof
that could be given of the Conqueror's wish to preserve the
English tradition in government.

With this end in view it was essential that William should
obtain the co-operation of the leaders of the English church.
Most of them, if not enthusiastic for his rule, accepted it as inevitable. Æthelwine of Durham is the only bishop who is known
to have joined a rebellion against him. Archbishop Ealdred of
York placed at his service the experience of a man who had
known every person of importance in English life since the days
of Cnut. The one grave complication in William's relations
with the English church was the fact that he was bound sooner
or later to take action which could only end in the deposition of
the senior member of the episcopate. It was certain that, when
occasion offered, the pope would send a legatine commission to
England for the trial and deprivation of Archbishop Stigand.[1]
In return for the moral support which he had received from the
papacy William could do no other than receive the legates and
give effect to their decisions. He was well aware that Stigand's
position was canonically indefensible. But Stigand's influence
in the country was so great that William deliberately left the
initiative in his removal to the Roman curia,[2] and for a time
allowed him uncontested enjoyment of his rank, his place in
council, and the large property which he had accumulated. On
the question of the archbishop's spiritual functions William
seems to have considered that, until a definitive sentence against
him had been published in England, he was entitled to the full
prerogative of his office. In 1067 or 1068 Remigius, almoner of
Fécamp, newly appointed to the see of Dorchester, went to
Stigand for consecration. From first to last William's dealings
with Stigand were purely opportunist, and at the time of his
deposition Stigand bitterly accused him of bad faith.

The first period of the Conqueror's reign ends with the great
revolt of 1069. Up to this point he had apparently succeeded in
his attempt to found a genuine Anglo-Norman state. In more
than two-thirds of England he was represented by earls of
English birth or antecedents. English clerks in his writing-office

---

[1] Who was still holding the see of Winchester in conjunction with that of
Canterbury.
[2] William of Poitiers, op. cit., and R. Foreville, p. 234.

were dispatching writs in the English language to sheriffs of whom most were Englishmen. Except for Remigius of Dorchester, the English episcopate was still as King Edward had left it. No important abbey had so far come under Norman rule. Little is known about the personal relations between Normans and Englishmen in this period, but it is enough to show that they had begun to settle down into an orderly civil association with one another. It is significant, for example, that Roger Bigot, the Norman founder of a house which was to dominate East Anglia, first appears in England as the tenant of a Norfolk manor under Archbishop Stigand.[1]

For all this, the balance of power between the races inclined heavily to the Norman side. The king's respect for the forms of the Old English government could not conceal the fact that his authority rested on the military organization which he controlled. By the beginning of 1069, in the south and east of England, much land had already passed from English into Norman hands. A Norman aristocracy had been planted on the estates of the Englishmen who had fallen in the war of the Conquest, or failed to make terms with the king in the settlement after his coronation. Each of the barons thus enfeoffed was expected to find knights for the king's service when need arose, and each of them kept a military household of knights ready for instant action. A series of royal castles, of which the terminal points were Exeter, York, Lincoln, and Norwich, commanded the main lines of road in southern England and most of its chief centres of population. At opposite ends of this country Herefordshire, under William fitz Osbern, and Kent, under Odo of Bayeux, were organized as military commands. In Sussex the ancient rapes were already in process of conversion into feudal castleries. On every hand the English lords who had survived the Conquest must have felt their insignificance in comparison with the acquisitive aliens on whose support the king in fact relied.

It was from these conditions that the rebellions of 1069 arose. To the Conqueror they meant the collapse of his original plan for the government of England. The ferocity with which he suppressed them was his reaction to a sense of failure. They were followed by a series of confiscations which completed the

---

[1] *Complete Peerage*, ix, p. 575. An equally significant case occurs in the Oxfordshire Domesday, which refers to the gift of a thegn by Earl Edwin to the Norman, Ralf d'Oilli (D.B. i, f. 154 *b*).

depression of the English interest in the south, and opened Yorkshire, the northern Danelaw, and north-western Mercia to an
intensive Norman plantation. It established in those regions
many Norman families which had not yet found land in England,
and it thereby gave rise to a distinction between the northern
and southern baronage which became politically important in
later centuries. Here, as elsewhere in England, few documents
have survived to illustrate the course of the Norman settlement.
But its effects, as shown in Domesday Book, were overwhelming.
In the whole of England south of the Tees only two Englishmen—
Thurkill of Arden and Colswein of Lincoln—were holding
estates of baronial dimensions directly of the king in 1086.

It is a remarkable proof of the Conqueror's statesmanship that
this tenurial revolution never degenerated into a scramble for
land. In every part of England the great redistribution was controlled by the king, and carried out by his ministers on lines
which he himself laid down. From first to last he insisted on
the principle that every Frenchman to whom he gave an
Englishman's estate should hold it with all the rights, and subject
to all the obligations, that had been attached to it at the beginning of 1066. It was with this principle in their minds that the
commissioners who carried out the Domesday Survey approached the innumerable pleas raised by their investigations.
For most of them it provided an immediate solution. The best
reply that a lord could make to a claim upon his property was
the production of sworn evidence that the land or the rights in
dispute had belonged to his *antecessor* on the day when King
Edward was alive and dead.

There were important lords whose manors, with few exceptions, had all belonged to the same pre-Conquest owner. Apart
from two small properties, the entire fief of Geoffrey Alselin,
which extended into every county of the northern Danelaw,
consisted of lands which a thegn named Toki, son of Outi, had
held in 1066. But cases like this are rare. The average Norman
baron had many English *antecessores*. The great fief of Roger de
Busli in Nottinghamshire and south Yorkshire represented the
estates of more than eighty English owners, ranging from Earls
Edwin, Morcar, and Waltheof, to thegns with manors of a
few oxgangs each. Of the process by which these composite
fiefs were created few details are known. But it is clear that the
combination of several thousand small estates into less than

two hundred major lordships must have been an administrative achievement comparable with the Domesday Inquest itself.

The lands which formed a lord's endowment were known collectively as his 'honour'. The word was not a technical term. By derivation it meant no more than 'that which gives a man distinction'. But in practice it came to be reserved for the fiefs of the king's greater tenants, and it was in this sense that it passed into later feudal usage. The lord's chief residence—commonly, though by no means universally, a castle—was known as the head of his honour, and the administrative business by which the integrity of the honour was maintained was usually transacted there. It was natural for an honour to take its name from the place which was, in effect, its capital, and it is for this reason that the lands of Roger de Busli, Ilbert de Laci, and Henry de Ferrars—to name only three examples—normally appear in later records as the honours of Tickhill, Pontefract, and Tutbury.

Geographically, these honours were intermingled with one another in a way which makes it hard to draw a small-scale map of feudal England.[1] None of them formed a compact territorial unit, and many of them consisted entirely of isolated manors or groups of manors scattered widely over the country. On the other hand, it was by no means unusual for the bulk of an honour to be concentrated in a particular district, and it is sometimes clear that the concentration was intended to serve a military purpose. The honour of William fitz Ansculf, for example, extended into twelve counties, but its core was a large block of villages around his castle of Dudley. Domesday Book refers to this block as William's *castellaria*—the contemporary term for a district within which the distribution of land has been planned for the maintenance of a particular fortress. Several other castleries are mentioned in Domesday Book,[2] and the record is certainly incomplete. The compact holdings of Ilbert de Laci in south Yorkshire and Henry de Ferrars in west Derbyshire are known to have been organized as *castellariae* dependent respectively on the castles of Pontefract and Tutbury.[3] Roger

---

[1] The best introduction to English feudal geography is the map of England and Wales in 1086 by J. Tait in the *Historical Atlas of Modern Europe* (Oxford, 1896–1900).

[2] Richmond, Caerleon on Usk, Richard's Castle, Ewias Harold, Clifford, and Montgomery.

[3] F. M. Stenton, *The First Century of English Feudalism*, ed. 2 (1961), pp. 195–6.

de Busli's castle of Tickhill, on the Yorkshire border south of Pontefract, was probably another of these cardinal posts. In Sussex a similar organization was applied to the rapes of Arundel, Bramber, Lewes, Pevensey, and Hastings, each of which was placed under the lordship of a separate baron and named from his chief local castle.[1] The military factor in the Norman settlement was more important than would appear from the sporadic entry of castles and castleries in Domesday Book.

On the other hand even when a lord, for military reasons, received a large group of adjacent manors, they rarely amounted to more than a small proportion of his total honour. Count Alan of Richmond, for example, held a great fee in the eastern counties and many scattered manors elsewhere in England, in addition to his large and highly organized castlery of Richmond-shire itself.[2] The possessions of Earl Hugh of Chester outside the county of his title were sufficient by themselves to make him a feudal magnate of the first importance.[3] In cases like these the outlying properties had a military function as the sources of supply and reinforcement for their lords' chief castles. But there are innumerable instances of dispersal for which no such reason can be found. Some of them arose from the succession of a French lord to one or more Englishmen whose lands had them-selves been dispersed. The position of Ralf Paganel as a land-owner in Devon and Somerset as well as in Yorkshire and Lincolnshire was due to the property which Merleswein, his *antecessor*, held in all these counties. Even so, there remain many scattered honours of which the distribution cannot be explained on either legal or military grounds. Many of them are due, at least in part, to transfers of land from one baron to another during the twenty years between the Conquest and the Domes-day record. But the king had much to gain by extending the influence of the barons in whom he had especial confidence, and it may be significant that the lords whose lands were

---

[1] Chichester, the sixth of the Sussex rapes, was held by Roger, earl of Shrewsbury, the lord of the adjacent rape of Arundel.

[2] On the lords of Richmond, the organization of their castlery, and the holdings of their principal tenants see C. T. Clay, *Early Yorkshire Charters* (Yorkshire Archaeo-logical Society), vols. iv, v.

[3] The history of his fief outside Cheshire and Yorkshire fills more than 200 pages of W. Farrer's *Honors and Knights' Fees*, vol. ii.

scattered most widely are on the whole identical with those who are known to have attended most frequently at court.[1]

The barons of the Conquest formed a miscellaneous company, of which an important part was drawn from lands outside Normandy. It included members of powerful families in the Boulonnais, Picardy, and Flanders—among them Count Eustace of Boulogne himself; William Fitz Ansculf of Dudley, and Ghilo of Weedon Pinkney from the house of the *Vidames* of Picquigny; Geoffrey 'de Cioches' of Wollaston from the *seigneurie* of Choques near Béthune; and Arnulf 'de Hesdin' of Chipping Norton, from the county of Hesdin on the Canche.[2] Gilbert 'de Gand', who obtained a great fief in the northern Danelaw and many possessions elsewhere, was the son of Ralf, count of Alost.[3] The lords who came from Brittany were more numerous, and on the whole more important as individuals.[4] In 1086 Count Alan of Richmond, who was a cadet of the ducal house, was one of the chief landowners in the whole of England.[5] Judhael of Totnes, whose lands owed the king the service of seventy knights, was the greatest magnate in south Devon. Other Breton lords, planted in Lincolnshire and the midlands, ranked high in the second class of English barons. Earlier in the reign the Breton influence had been even stronger. The royal forces which defeated Harold's sons in 1069 were led by Brian, a brother of the count of Richmond, who appears at court in the same year with an earl's title.[6] There is evidence that he had been created earl of Cornwall, and that there, as also in Suffolk, he was holding the extensive possessions which by 1086 had been given to the king's

[1] There is nothing to suggest that the Conqueror regarded compact baronial estates as a danger to public security or that his companions resented the dispersal of their honours. The dubious military advantage of an isolated fief to a lord who meditated rebellion was more than offset by its social inconvenience in normal times. It is suggestive that the holdings in which a baron enfeoffed his leading tenants often extended into every part of his honour. Henry de Ferrars, for example, gave land in six counties to Saswallo, his most important baron.

[2] On the counts of Boulogne and their importance in English feudal history see J. H. Round, *Studies in Peerage and Family History*, pp. 147–80. Other lords from the east are identified in the articles on the Domesday Survey, mainly by Round, in the Victoria County History, and in particular in *V.C.H. Northamptonshire*, vol. i.

[3] Another Flemish lord, Gherbod, *avocat* of St. Bertin, was made earl of Chester on the suppression of the last Mercian revolt, but resigned his command within a year.

[4] On this Breton element in English society see F. M. Stenton, *The First Century of English Feudalism*, ed. 2 (1961), pp. 25–8.

[5] The descent of the early lords of Richmond is set out by C. T. Clay, *Early Yorkshire Charters*, iv, pp. 84 ff.

[6] H. W. C. Davis, *Regesta Regum Anglo-Normannorum*, No. 28.

brother, Count Robert of Mortain.[1] It seems clear that but for
Brian's early death, or departure from England, there would
have arisen a Breton colony in the south-west comparable with
Richmondshire in the north.

But when all allowance has been made for the lords from
Brittany and the east, there can be no question that the Norman strain was dominant among the Frenchmen whom the
Conqueror planted in England. The expedition of 1066 had
been essentially a Norman enterprise, made possible by volunteers from other parts, but based on the resources and the personal support of Norman lords. The brief list of those who are
known to have been present at Hastings includes many of the
greatest names in the duchy. The ducal family and its connections was represented by William, son of Richard, count of
Évreux; Richard, son of Count Gilbert of Brionne; Robert,
count of Mortain; and Odo, bishop of Bayeux. Among the
duke's household officers—each of them an important landowner—there came William fitz Osbern, the *dapifer* or steward;
Hugh de Montfort, the constable; Hugh de Ivry, the butler;
Ralf de Tancarville, the chamberlain; and Girald the marshall.
The unofficial baronage of Normandy supplied Thurstan, son
of Rolf, who carried the Norman standard, Walter Giffard,
Ralf de Tosny, Hugh de Grandmaisnil, Robert de Beaumont,
William Malet, Engenulf de Laigle, and William de Warenne.
Geoffrey de Mowbray, bishop of Coutances, belonged by birth
to the same class. These names have only been recorded
casually, but as a group they represent the families which were
of most account in pre-Conquest Normandy, and afterwards in
feudal England.

It is often hard to identify the Norman seats of these families.[2]
Many of them took their names from their chief manors. But
in Normandy it was not unusual for two or more places to have
the same name, and it is sometimes difficult to decide from
which of them a given family came to England. In general,
identification is only safe when a family can be connected with

[1] J. Tait, *E.H.R.* xliv (1929), p. 86; *Complete Peerage*, iii, p. 427; C. T. Clay, *Early
Yorkshire Charters*, iv, p. 16.

[2] Apart from the remarks on individual families by scholars such as Round, the
literature on this subject at the time this book was originally written was thoroughly
unsatisfactory. In particular, it seriously exaggerated the number of Anglo-
Norman families derived from western Normandy. [Now, however, see Lewis C.
Loyd, *The Origins of some Anglo-Norman Families* (Harleian Society ciii), 1951.]

a particular place by the possession of lands or churches. There is need for much more work along these lines. But it is already becoming clear that an especially large number of important lords came from that part of the original Normandy which is now the department of Seine Inférieure. There were many from Calvados and Eure, but comparatively few from Manche, and very few indeed from the lands along the southern frontier of Normandy which now form the department of Orne. It seems evident that, as might be expected, the duke received most support from the lands around Rouen, his capital.

As a group, the barons of the Conquest were closely inter-related with one another by descent and marriage. Ralf, lord of Tosny in Normandy, who was powerful in East Anglia and the southern midlands, was brother of Robert of Stafford, the greatest landholder of Staffordshire. He seems to have been the nephew of Robert de Tosny, the founder of Belvoir castle. He was a kinsman of Ralf de Limesy, a leading baron of central England, and he married a daughter to Roger Bigot of Norfolk. In rank, and in the range of his family connections, Ralf de Tosny was a typical member of the original Anglo-Norman baronage. Few of the Normans who received large estates in England deserve to be called adventurers, in the derogatory sense of the word. There were doubtless lords of small estate in Normandy, who earned a high place in England by special service during the war of the invasion. But the number cannot have been large. In general, the names most prominent in Domesday Book represent the families around which the previous history of Normandy had centred, and the indi-viduals whose resources had enabled them to support the duke most effectively in 1066.

Their interests, no less than his, required that they should continue their support to him as king of England. Each of them was expected to attend the Christmas, Easter, and Whit-suntide councils which he held, when in England, at Gloucester, Winchester, and Westminster. But the duty of this kind which they paid him went far beyond these formal occasions. The witnesses to his charters suggest that some of the greatest men in the land must have spent an appreciable proportion of their time in his company. In the assiduity of their attendance at court, the counts of Mortain and Richmond, Richard, son of Count Gilbert of Brionne, William de Warenne, the lord of Lewes and Castle Acre, and Henry de Ferrars, the lord of Tutbury, resemble a standing baronial council. Other lords of the first importance repeatedly appear at court—sometimes in numbers which must have given the weight of a national assembly to the meeting. In the last year of his reign, at La-cock, a manor of William d'Eu, the king was attended by the counts of Mortain and Richmond; Roger de Montgomery, earl of Shrewsbury; Richard and Baldwin, Count Gilbert's sons; Henry de Ferrars; Eudo, the king's steward, or *dapifer*, and Robert, his dispenser; Robert of Rhuddlan, the conqueror of Gwynedd; Bernard de Neufmarché from the central march of Wales; Hugh de Port from Hampshire; William de Percy from Yorkshire; Roger de Courselles from Somerset; Roger Bigot from Norfolk; Alfred of Lincoln; and William d'Eu, the king's host.[1] From one or other of these men the king could obtain first-hand information about every part of England, except the furthest north.[2] An association of this kind between the king and his leading barons is shown by every substantial witness-list which has come down from the Conqueror's reign, and the relationship which it implies determined the whole character of his government.

His reliance on the personal service of his barons is perhaps most clearly shown by the personnel of his administration. Bishop Geoffrey of Coutances, whom he made one of the great-est lords in England, was his principal agent in its government, and in particular in the management of the great pleas which were characteristic of his reign.[3] By 1087 Normans of the baron-ial class were in office in all parts of the country as keepers of royal castles and as sheriffs. In some parts, as in Worcester-shire and Devon, these offices were held together. But it was

[1] Davis, *Regesta*, No. xxxii.

[2] It may be noted that in addition to the barons whose local interests are apparent, Richard, son of Count Gilbert, was lord of Clare in Suffolk and of a great fee in East Anglia and the eastern midlands, Baldwin his brother was lord of Okehampton in Devon, Robert the Dispenser was powerful in central England, and Eudo, the steward, in Essex. The company also included a number of bishops; among them William of Durham, who could speak about conditions beyond the Tees.

[3] Bishop Geoffrey's importance does not appear until the scattered memoranda of the reign have been brought together, and it has usually been underestimated. His activities as bishop are described in the almost contemporary life printed in *Gallia Christiana* xi, Instrumenta, cols. 217–24. A modern study of his whole career is badly needed. (See E. H. R. vol. lix, pp. 129–61 (1944) where J. H. le Padowrel has written an article on the bishop, whose career spans almost the whole of the second half of the eleventh century, 1049–93).

unusual for the civil and military administration of a district
to be thus united, and the military duties of the typical Anglo-
Norman sheriff were confined to the summoning and command
of the local militia. Even so, his office gave him the dominant
influence within his shire. Most of his specific functions had
belonged to his pre-Conquest predecessor. But the abolition
of the great Old English earldoms made him the immediate
representative of the king's government, and, unlike the shire-
reeves of King Edward's day, he was usually the social and
territorial equal of the strongest magnates with whom he had
official contact. Among the Conqueror's sheriffs, Edward 'of
Salisbury', the sheriff of Wiltshire, Roger Bigot of Norfolk and
Suffolk, and Geoffrey de Mandeville of London and Middlesex, were the heads of families which two generations later
obtained earldoms. Peter de Valognes of Essex and Hertfordshire, Hugh fitz Baldric of Yorkshire, Nottinghamshire, and
Derbyshire, and Hugh de Port of Hampshire were landowners
of hardly less importance. Haimo of Kent, who was a royal
seneschal, and Robert d'Oilli of Oxfordshire, who was a royal
constable, had the prestige which came from constant association with the court. None of these men is likely to have been
disinterested in his attitude towards his duties. The financial
perquisites of a sheriffdom were enough to attract the richest
barons, and there were sheriffs who seem to have been completely unscrupulous in the use which they made of their
opportunities.[1] In 1076 or 1077 the king appointed a strong
commission—comprising Archbishop Lanfranc, the bishop of
Coutances, Count Robert of Eu, Richard, son of Count Gilbert,
and Hugh de Montfort—with instructions to summon his
sheriffs and command them to restore the lands which they had
acquired through the folly, timidity, or greed of his bishops and
abbots, or through their own violence.[2] But for the future of

[1] Picot of Cambridge and Eustace of Huntingdon have perhaps the worst
reputation of all King William's sheriffs. But there is abundant evidence in Domesday Book that sheriffs in most parts of England were using their official powers for
their own advantage.

[2] The terms of this commission are given by a document printed in Rymer's
Foedera, i. 3 from a manuscript in Canterbury cathedral. Writs issued in the course
of the investigation are printed in *Historia Monasterii S. Augustini* (R.S.), p. 352,
and *Feudal Documents from the Abbey of Bury St. Edmunds*, ed. D. C. Douglas, pp. 56–7.
The date of the commission is approximately fixed by the fact that the writ
relating to St. Augustine's was issued at the dedication of Bayeux cathedral,
which seems to have taken place in 1077.

English local government it was a momentous fact that in relation to his office even the most formidable of the Conqueror's sheriffs was content to regard himself as the king's minister.

The sense of a common interest with the king was certainly a main reason for the acquiescence of his barons in the heavy military obligations with which he charged their lands. They were all familiar in their own countries with the principle of tenure in return for military assistance to a lord. On becoming English landowners, they naturally accepted the condition that each of them should hold his fief of the king, under an engagement to find a specified number of knights for the royal host whenever they might be required. But the Anglo-Norman state was threatened by so many enemies that the king needed a great reserve of knights, and in the Conqueror's reign, when much of England was impoverished by war, the provision of his contingent must have been a serious drain on the resources of the average baron. So far as can be seen, the amount of each baron's service was fixed by the king himself at a round number of knights, without any investigation into the value or productive capacity of the lands for which it was to be rendered. It is impossible to reach precise figures for the total number of knights which King William required from his followers, but it cannot have been less than 4,000, and it may have been much greater. The number of barons responsible for the appearance of these knights cannot easily be brought above 180. It is clear that the production of what by feudal standards was a large army was imposed on a group of barons which in comparison was remarkably small.

The size of this feudal army was much increased by the imposition of knight-service on bishoprics and abbeys. The amount of this service, as of that demanded from lay barons, was determined arbitrarily by the king.[1] The wealthy sees of Canterbury, Winchester, and, apparently, Worcester were each required to find him 60 knights. The bishop of Lincoln, whose estates had been utterly inadequate to the size of his diocese, was made a territorial magnate by new grants of land, and a service of 60 knights was placed on him also.[2] The lands of the

[1] For the details, see Helena M. Chew, *The English Ecclesiastical Tenants-in-Chief and Knight Service*, pp. 1–36.

[2] Nearly all the numerous manors acquired by Bishop Remigius had been used for the enfeoffment of knights by 1086, and it is probable that most of them had been granted to him for this purpose by the king.

archbishop of York had been too heavily wasted to carry any additional burden, and although he received other estates from the king, which he used for the enfeoffment of knights, the service of only 7 was required from him. The services of the remaining bishops varied between 40 demanded from the bishop of Thetford and 2 demanded from the bishop of Chichester. Among the abbeys, Peterborough, which was assessed at 60 knights, was treated most severely. Glastonbury and Bury were each assessed at 40; Abingdon at 30; New Minster at 20; Tavistock, Westminster, and St. Augustine's, Canterbury, at 15 each; and Coventry at 10. Fifteen other abbeys, including wealthy houses such as Ramsey, St. Albans, Chertsey, and Evesham, received assessments varying from 7 knights to 1. It is impossible to trace any general principle behind these figures except a vague idea that the wealthier institutions ought to be burdened the more heavily. It has been suggested that a wish to penalize houses which had opposed him explains the heavy service which the king set on the abbeys of Peterborough, Abingdon, and New Minster. But the heavy service laid on Bury, where the abbot was on the best of terms with the king, cannot be explained in this way, and in general the theory of a political discrimination between one abbey and another becomes less probable the more closely it is examined. The essential fact remains that by bringing the English bishops and abbots within the scope of feudal obligation, the Conqueror secured the service of some 780 knights—a force roughly equal to that which he obtained from the lay and ecclesiastical baronage of all Normandy.

For some years after the Conquest it was usual for both lay and ecclesiastical lords to maintain in their own households the knights whom they needed for the king's service. It is significant that the Anglo-Saxon word *cniht*, which became the normal English term for a mounted soldier, meant 'servant' or 'household retainer'. Military households, composed essentially of men trained or in training to fight on horseback, were a permanent feature of Anglo-Norman society. But as the risk of an English rebellion died down, it became unnecessary for a lord to keep the whole body of his knights ready for instant war, and by the date of Domesday Book the creation of tenancies to be held by military service had gone far on most baronial fiefs. With the details of this process the king had little concern.

There are cases which show that he sometimes took a personal interest in the military tenancies created on the lands of the church.[1] But as a rule, he seems to have allowed his barons, lay or ecclesiastical, to make whatever provision each of them might choose for the military service imposed upon his fief.

The ordinary knight of the eleventh century was a person of small means and insignificant condition. His equipment was elementary, and his only title to distinction was his proficiency in mounted warfare. A large number of these meagre knights can be traced in Domesday Book—many of them grouped in small holdings around the chief residences of their lords. But on every great honour, lay or ecclesiastical, there appear tenants holding considerable estates, of which the integrity was preserved far into the middle ages. Many of these holdings bore the service of three or more knights, and some of them were highly important units of feudal administration. To judge from later evidence the men who held them usually possessed the rights of jurisdiction—sake and soke, toll, team, and infangenetheof—which had belonged before the Conquest to the wealthier Anglo-Saxon thegns.[2] In social position men of this standing were indistinguishable from the lords who held immediately of the king, and in the language of the time they, like the king's own military tenants, were recognized as barons.[3]

The honorial barons, as tenants of this class may conveniently be called, have received less attention from historians than is their due. On a general review of feudal society they tend to be overshadowed by their lords, the tenants in chief of the Crown. But their function within the honours to which they belonged was identical with that of the king's own barons in the realm at large. Every important honour was a state in miniature governed, as was the kingdom, by its lord with the help of tenants whom he convened to form a court. No honour of any size could have avoided disintegration without some recognized means of adjusting the tenurial relationships by which it was held together. In the honorial court, by which this object was secured, the lord's baronial tenants played a leading part. They shaped its decisions and became the keepers of its precedents. They preserved a collective memory of transactions

---

[1] Such as the enfeoffment by the abbot of Bury described by D. C. Douglas, *E.H.R.* xlii (1927), pp. 245–7.   [2] Above, pp. 497 et seqq.

[3] For some illustrations of their place in society see F. M. Stenton, *The First Century of English Feudalism*, ed. 2 (1961), pp. 84–114.

within the honour, and thereby gave the character of an institution to what had been, in origin, an accumulation of
separate estates.

About the holdings which were created for the provision of
knight-service—the 'knights' fees' of feudal records—little can
be said in general terms. There were knights' fees which consisted of single villages, and here and there, especially on the
ancient possessions of the church, it is possible to find fees which
coincided with the holdings of pre-Conquest thegns. But cases
like these are exceptions, on which no theory should be founded.
It is equally difficult to reach any general conclusions about the
value of the normal fee. Knights' fees worth £20 a year were
known in the twelfth century. But fees of half this value were
commoner, and there can be no question that a large number
of the knights enfeoffed in the Conqueror's reign had accepted
holdings framed on a much smaller scale than this. It would
seem, in fact, that in most cases a knight's fee was the result of
a bargain between a lord and his prospective tenant, and represented nothing more significant than a holding for which a
particular individual at a particular date had been prepared
to undertake a knight's service. The typical knight's fee is as
elusive a conception as the typical barony.

It was from these simple origins that there arose the elaborate
system of military tenure which governed the legal relationship
of the aristocracy to the Crown throughout the middle ages. Its
main features are discernible clearly enough in the Conqueror's
reign. The proved descent of innumerable estates shows that
knights' fees were already, as a general rule, hereditable.[1] Norman
practice suggests, and medieval evidence implies, that English
custom allowed the lord of a tenant by knight-service to act as the
guardian and supervise the military education of an infant heir,
to take a relief from an incoming heir of full age, and to give an
heiress in marriage. With comparatively few exceptions, the
holdings which the Conqueror had formed for his leading
followers passed as recognizable units into the 'baronies' of
medieval feudalism.[2] The military responsibilities which they

[1] For an early military enfeoffment limited to a single life see V. H. Galbraith,
E.H.R. xliv (1929), pp. 353–72.
[2] The chief exceptions are due to the forfeitures incurred by a small number of
very great lords, notably Bishop Odo of Bayeux, Count Robert of Mortain, Earl
Robert of Northumbria, who had inherited the vast fief of Bishop Geoffrey of
Coutances and Robert de Bellême, earl of Shrewsbury.

carried in later generations had already been laid down in outline by the king. The structure of society in its higher ranges, had assumed the character of an organization for the defence of the realm.

Among other forms of tenure, the most interesting are those which centre around the administration of a lord's household, and in particular the household of the king. Records of the twelfth and later centuries mention a large number of small estates held by the performance of some specific service to the king—in his hall or chamber, his pantry, buttery, or kitchen, his kennels or his stables, or the woodlands where he found his sport.[1] The number of these holdings which can be traced back to Domesday Book is sufficient to prove that this kind of tenure was well established in the Conqueror's time. It was not confined to persons serving the king himself, for households resembling that of the king were maintained by all his leading barons, and some at least of them had begun to make provision in land for their servants. But the process was carried much further by the king than by any other lord, and the men who took holdings from him on these terms were of many sorts and conditions. Domesday Book tells little about their services, but it records their names, and thereby shows that some of them were Englishmen.

The size and elaboration of a royal household increased the responsibilities of its leading members, and their constant attendance upon the king gave them under some conditions the character of ministers of state. At the court of Philip I of France the steward or *dapifer*, the butler, the chamberlain, and the constable regularly witness the king's official acts. The Conqueror's Norman court had been much less strictly organized, and although his steward, butler, and chamberlain frequently attest his ducal charters, there was no rule or custom which required their presence. In pre-Conquest England the prominence of the great earls made the king's household officers of little account in politics. In this respect, the Conqueror followed Old English tradition, and he never allowed any official functions in government to become attached to any of the places in his court. The organization of the court itself is obscure at many points, for no complete list of its members can be compiled, and al-

---

[1] The best introduction to the study of these tenures is *The King's Serjeants and Officers of State* by J. H. Round (1911).

though it is known that a number of persons bore the same official title at the same time, it is often hard to determine their relative positions in the ministerial scale. The large fief of Robert *Dispensator*, which afterwards formed the honour of Tamworth, sets him apart among the king's dispensers. On the other hand, the office of chief butler seems to have been shared by two brothers, Hugh and Roger d'Ivry, of whom the latter was a considerable landholder in England, and at one time, somewhat incongruously, commander of the tower of Rouen. There is direct evidence that Robert Malet, the lord of Eye, was the chief of the king's chamberlains, and virtual certainty that Hugh de Montfort, the lord of Haughley, was the chief of his constables. There can be no doubt that William fitz Osbern was the chief steward, or *dapifer*, until his death in 1071, but there is nothing to show whether at a later time Eudo *dapifer* or Haimo *dapifer*, each of them an important tenant in chief, was considered to hold the higher place. These names, to which others could easily be added, prove that the ministers of King William's household included men of high rank, great possessions, and heavy military responsibilities. They imply that even in the first decades of the Anglo-Norman court its central offices were beginning to take on an honorary cast.

Two hundred years, or more, before the Conquest an honorary element had begun to appear in the households of the Old English kings. Oslac, the father of King Æthelwulf's first wife, though a man of most noble birth, served in court as butler.[1] But for some reason this element failed to develop in England, and the offices which can be traced at the courts of Alfred and his successors seem all to have been realities. They cover most of the duties which were necessary to the life of a primitive noble household, and in many respects they anticipate the curial organization of the Norman age. The will of King Eadred, which is the chief authority for the pre-Conquest royal household, shows that the principal officers at his court were the 'discthegns', responsible for the service at his table; the 'hræglthegns', who kept his clothes; and the *birele*, or butlers.[2] A continental writer of the time would have described these men as *dapiferi*, *camerarii*, and *pincernae*. Their functions must have closely resembled those of the *dapiferi*—whom English historians

---

[1] Asser, *Vita Ælfredi*, ed. W. H. Stevenson, p. 4.
[2] F. E. Harmer, *English Historical Documents*, pp. 34-5.

generally call 'stewards'—the chamberlains, and the butlers of the Anglo-Norman court. The officers whom King Eadred knew as stewards were of a humbler sort.[1] There are glossaries in which the Old English *stigvveard* is equated with the Latin *oeconomus*, and it seems probable that the officers whom Eadred thus described resembled the dispensers of a medieval household.[2] The marshal, whose place was in the stables, is not mentioned among King Eadred's servants, but he can be recognized clearly enough in the king's 'horse-thegn' who appears twice in the Alfredian section of the *Chronicle*. The conservatism of English tactics explains the absence of any pre-Conquest reference to an officer corresponding to the French constable, who in this period was the commander of his lord's household knights. The later development of the Old English royal household is obscured by the indiscriminate use of a word *staller*, apparently borrowed from the Norse *stallari*, as a term which could be applied to anyone with a permanent and recognized position in the King's company.[3] But it is unlikely that Duke William, when he visited King Edward's court in 1051, can have noticed much that was unfamiliar in its arrangements.

The group of household officers which attended the king, in Normandy as in England, was the nucleus of the central institution of the Anglo-Norman state, the king's court or *Curia Regis*. A number of the leading men in each country belonged to it in virtue of their household offices, and the presence of other barons visiting the king made it competent to deal at any time with most forms of public business. For pleas of exceptional importance, for the settlement of matters affecting the greatest families, and for the preparation of royal ordinances, it could easily be expanded into a body which was informally representative of the entire lay and spiritual baronage.[4] In the Conqueror's time it never lost the character of a gathering of men whom the king knew personally and with whose

[1] Eadred bequeaths only 30 mancusses to each of his *stigweards*, as against 80 bequeathed to each *discthegn*, *hrægithegn*, and *birele*.

[2] There are indications that the *stigweard* was rising in the ministerial scale during the 10th century. There are late glossaries which identify him with the *discifer* or *discthegn*. But his position was still far from eminent in 1066.

[3] In regard to the staller, as to all the officers of the Old English court, a general reference may be made to the details collected by L. M. Larson, *The King's Household in England before the Norman Conquest* (1904) especially pp. 149–52.

[4] Such as the court at Lacock described above, p. 632.

own affairs he was familiar. Fundamentally, the ordinary
meetings of this primitive *curia* were social occasions, and the
atmosphere in which they were held permitted an interchange
of ideas between the king and individual lords impossible at
the general assembly of all magnates which formed the Great
Council of the realm.

The Great Council was the Anglo-Norman equivalent of
the Anglo-Saxon *witena gemot*. Its sessions were more regular
than those of the *witan*. So far as can be seen, the Conqueror's
practice of meeting the great lords of England at Christmas,
Easter, and Whitsuntide was an innovation.[1] But the business
of the Great Council, though equal in range, was certainly less
in volume than that with which the *witan* had dealt. For all
except the greatest matters of state, it was the Conqueror's habit
to use his court rather than his council. It does not follow
that the Great Council was an insignificant appendage to his
government. He is known to have consulted it on special
occasions. The decision to take the Domesday Survey was the
outcome of a discussion in the Christmas Council of 1085. Even
when no great matters were on hand, the meetings of the council
were politically useful as opportunities for ceremonial display.
A twelfth-century historian lays stress on their value as a means
by which the king could impress foreign ambassadors with the
splendour of his company and the lavishness of his entertainment.[2] It was more important that they enabled the king to
keep in touch with the individual members of the baronage, and
to assure himself of their loyalty. In the first part of the Conqueror's reign, when a competitive aristocracy was uneasily
settling down into possession of the lands that were its reward,
there was especial value in a custom which required the whole
baronage to assemble three times a year under the king's eye.
It must have brought to his attention innumerable disputes of
a kind which in France would have led to private war. But
it was to his court that he referred the business of their settlement.

Within this informal court, developments were taking place
which led in time to the appearance of definite and organized
departments of state. Before the Conqueror's death they had
already produced a royal chancery. It is possible that the staff

---

[1] Liebermann, *The National Assembly in the Anglo-Saxon Period*, pp. 48–50.
[2] William of Malmesbury, *Gesta Regum*, R.S. ii, p. 335.

of the Confessor's writing-office passed as a whole into King William's service. In any case, the forms of his earliest documents show that the clerks of his chapel included men trained in English conventions of draftsmanship.[1] His earliest writs are composed in English, and in style are indistinguishable from writs of King Edward. As late as 1069 his clerks were producing solemn charters which in all respects conform to the traditional Old English type.[2] Soon afterwards the character of his writs and charters begins to change. Latin gradually replaces English as the language of writs, and charters are drafted on French, rather than English, lines. But there was no sudden breach of continuity. It was through a writ in English that Bishop Maurice of London, appointed in 1085, obtained possession of his castle of Bishop's Stortford.[3]

These changes in the style of the king's writs and charters coincided with the establishment of a new order in his writing-office. In or before 1068 the king appointed Herfast, his chaplain, to the supervision of his household clerks, with the title of chancellor. He is the first person who can be proved to have held this office in England, for although some authorities give the title to a foreign priest of King Edward, named Regenbald, they are either unsatisfactory in themselves or too late to be good evidence.[4] Herfast was appointed bishop of the East Angles in 1070, and the next chancellor who can be identified with certainty[5] is a clerk named Osmund, who was made bishop of Salisbury in 1078. On his promotion he was followed as chancellor by Maurice, archdeacon of Le Mans, to whom the see of London was given in 1085. The last chancellor of the reign was Gerard, afterwards bishop of Hereford and archbishop of York, who attests one of the Conqueror's latest writs, and attended him during his last illness.[6] It is clear from these

[1] The proof of this continuity was first set out by W. H. Stevenson, in *E.H.R.* xi (1896), pp. 731–44.

[2] The best example is the charter for Bishop Leofric of Exeter, of which a contemporary text is reproduced in *Ordnance Survey Facsimiles* ii, Exeter, 16.

[3] *Early Charters of St. Paul's Cathedral*, ed. M. Gibbs, p. 12.

[4] R. L. Poole, *The Exchequer in the Twelfth Century*, p. 25, note 2.

[5] A certain Osbert is described as chancellor in a charter of William I to St. Augustine's Canterbury, which, if genuine, is not later than 1075 (*Historia Monasterii S. Augustini*, R.S., p. 350). He has usually been identified with Osbern, afterwards bishop of Exeter. But the form of the charter is anomalous, and the name needs confirmation from some other source.

[6] Gerard was first shown to have been chancellor to William I by V. H. Galbraith, *E.H.R.* xlvi (1931), pp. 77–9. The presence of Gerard, as chancellor, at the

details that in the Conqueror's time tenure of the chancellorship was merely a stage through which a clerk might come to higher preferment. Then, as for long afterwards, the chancellor was simply an officer of the king's household, the head of his secretariat, and the keeper of his seal. His duties, as yet, were purely ministerial. The creation of the office is important because, for the first time, it placed the unorganized body of the royal clerks under the control of a permanent chief appointed by the king.

There was no comparable change in the organization of the king's finances. The Conqueror inherited from his Old English predecessors a considerable revenue, derived in the main from crown lands, the customary payments of shires and boroughs, and the profits of justice. By 1066 the renders in kind which had once supported the king had generally been converted into money rents, and Domesday Book shows that the king's officers had already begun the practice of assaying the money, in order to make sure that the silver content of a payment corresponded to its nominal amount. The practice was widely extended by the Norman kings, but there is no doubt that its essential features are of Old English origin. There are traces of an organized financial system in England at a date unexpectedly remote. As far back as the ninth century Asser's life of Alfred shows that the king was able to deal with his income as a whole, and to appropriate definite portions of it to specific purposes in a manner which presupposes the existence of a central treasury.[1] In the early part of the eleventh century it is probable that the treasury was fixed at Winchester, the most convenient place for a king whose chief interests were in Wessex.[2] But it was closely attached to the royal household, and the meagre evidence that bears on the subject implies that the custody of the king's money, as of his clothes, jewels, records, and muniments, was the duty of his hræglthegns or chamberlains.[3] There are faint signs that

---

king's death-bed is mentioned in the tract *De Obitu Willelmi ducis Normannorum regisque Anglorum* printed by J. Marx in his edition of the *Gesta Normannorum Ducum* of William of Jumièges, pp. 145–8.

[1] Ed. W. H. Stevenson, pp. 86–9, where the king's revenues are carefully described as 'divitiae . . . quae annualiter ad eum ex omni censu perveniebant et in fisco reputabantur'.

[2] Cnut's treasures were laid up at Winchester at the time of his death (above, p. 420).

[3] On the pre-Conquest hræglthegn see R. L. Poole, *The Exchequer in the Twelfth Century*, pp. 22–4.

the Conqueror may have slightly modified these simple arrangements. One of his Hampshire serjeants appears in Domesday
Book as Henry 'the Treasurer'. But the smallness of his holding proves that his official rank was low, and the later history
of the treasury shows that his appointment can have made little
difference to an institution which after the Conquest, as before, was controlled by unspecialized officers of the court. In
the twelfth century the exchequer, in which the Old English
treasury had been incorporated, was in essentials the king's
household acting as a financial bureau.[1]

From the time of Æthelred II, at latest, the Old English
kings had been accustomed to meet any occasion for special
expenditure by levying a general land-tax, or 'geld'. The right
naturally passed to their Norman successors. The Conqueror is
known to have imposed gelds on 1066, 1067, and 1083,[2] and
there is evidence of an undated levy in the central years of
his reign.[3] In many, if not in most, shires the collection of the
geld was based on an assessment which was already ancient in

[1] In the introduction to the Oxford edition of the *Dialogus de Scaccario*, which is
the principal modern authority on the early exchequer, its staff is described as
'the staff of the king's household put to financial tasks and slightly influenced by
their duties' (p. 13).

[2] The collection of this geld in the five south-western counties produced the
series of records generally known collectively as the *Inquisitio Geldi* of 1084 (printed
as part of the Exon Domesday in D.B., vol. iv). The title is misleading, for the
documents are not records of an inquest, but of the amount of geld which the king
has obtained from the several hundreds of these shires. The arrangement of the
returns varies between one set and another, but the features common to all are a
record of the hidage of each hundred, a detailed statement of the number of hides
exempt from geld because they were cultivated as demesne for the king's barons
within the hundred, and a note of the money which the king has actually received
from the hundredal geld.

[3] The document known as the *Northamptonshire Geld Roll* (A. J. Robertson,
Anglo-Saxon Charters, pp. 230–7) records the collection of a geld during the period
between the provision of an estate for Queen Matilda in or after 1068 and her
death in 1083. It is written in English, and is of great interest as an indication of the
type of record that must have been made when gelds were taken for Old English
kings. Like the *Inquisitio Geldi*, it is drawn up hundred by hundred. Within each
hundred it records the number of hides at which it was assessed, and sets against
this total the number on which geld had been paid, and the number which yielded
nothing because they were either waste or exempt from geld as 'inland', that is
baronial demesne-land. In some of its features, such as the special exemption
allowed to persons in the king's service, the document resembles the Danegeld
accounts entered on the early Pipe Rolls. If, as is probable, Osmund 'thes kynges
writere', whose holding is thus exempt, is identical with Osmund the chancellor,
the roll must be earlier than his election to the bishopric of Salisbury in 1078.
That it is later than 1072 is suggested by a reference to land owned by the king of
Scots, which had probably come to him under the treaty of Abernethy.

1066. Its details, as they are known from Domesday Book, illustrate with remarkable clearness the traditional agrarian conceptions which still prevailed in different parts of the country. On a wider view their interest is greater, for they are relics of the first system of national taxation to appear in western Europe.

In relation to these matters of assessment England falls into four well-defined regions: East Anglia; Wessex, with English Mercia, Essex, and the southern Danelaw; Kent; and the northern Danelaw between the Welland and the Tees.[1] In its assessment, as in most features of its early history, East Anglia stands apart from the rest of England. There, as elsewhere, the burden of taxation was distributed over the country in terms of villages. But whereas in other parts the amount which a village paid was determined by the number of hides, ploughlands, or sulungs which the king's financial officers attributed to it, the liability of an East Anglian village was measured by the number of pence which it was required to contribute when the hundred where it lay paid 20 shillings. It was a further peculiarity of this region that the villages within a hundred were arranged in a number of groups, each of which contributed an equal number of pence towards the 20 shillings charged upon the hundred. In the Suffolk hundred of Thedwestry, for example, there were six of these groups, each containing three of four villages, and each assessed at 40 pence towards the hundredal 20 shillings. These groups of villages were known as 'leets', a term of which the derivation is still uncertain. For all their artificial appearance, the leets were not merely a device for the collection of gelds.[2] There is evidence that each of them had a court in early times, and some of them, which had come under ecclesiastical lordship, appear as units of economic organization as late as the thirteenth century. Their part in local administration

[1] Northumbria beyond Tees, a border province containing many large exempt estates, is not described in Domesday Book, and seems to have lain in this period outside the national fiscal scheme. The country north of the Ribble, which is now included in Lancashire, was assessed, like southern Westmorland, in the same way as the northern Danelaw. The country between the Ribble and the Mersey, which is associated with Cheshire in Domesday Book, was assessed on the same general lines as English Mercia, though the details of the assessment have distinctive features.

[2] Their character is brought out most clearly in two books by D. C. Douglas— *The Social Structure of Medieval East Anglia*, pp. 191–204, and *Feudal Documents from the Abbey of Bury St. Edmunds*, pp. cli–clxxi.

was clearly important, and it is probable that their origin lies in the time of settlement after the Danish occupation of East Anglia in the ninth century.

In the rest of England assessment to gelds was based on the theory that every county contained a definite number of taxable units—hides, ploughlands, or sulungs—which was well known to the king's financial officers. In Wessex, English Mercia, Essex, and the southern midlands the unit in this assessment was the hide. From a date which lies far back in English history a large round number of hides had been attributed by the king's ministers to each county in this region, without any but the most general reference to its true agricultural condition. It was assumed, for example, that Northamptonshire contained exactly 3,200 hides: Bedfordshire and Worcestershire, 1,200 each; Staffordshire, 500.[1] The date at which these assumptions were first made is unknown, but one at least of them can be traced back to the early part of the tenth century.[2] By the reign of Edward the Confessor, within each county, and apparently by its court, the hides assigned to it had been divided in round numbers among its constituent hundreds, and the quota of each hundred had been distributed, generally in blocks of five or ten hides, among the villages of which it was composed. As the number of hides assigned to a village for purposes of taxation can rarely have coincided with the number of arable tenements which it contained, it must often have been hard to ascertain the amount which each landowner ought to pay when a geld was taken. In the twelfth century it was in the hundred court that the final incidence of the geld was settled and it was presumably there that such questions were decided before the Conquest.[3]

The fact that assessment to gelds proceeded from above downwards—from the king's court, through the county and hundred, to the village—was established long ago by scholars such as Round and Maitland. But more recent work has produced a significant number of cases in which the Domesday assessment of a village is identical with the hidage assigned to it

[1] These figures are given, with others of the same type, in the early 11th-century list generally called the 'County Hidage', on which see F. W. Maitland, *Domesday Book and Beyond*, pp. 455-7.

[2] 1,200 hides are attributed to Worcester in an early addition to the 'Burghal Hidage', on which see above, p. 265.

[3] See J. H. Round, 'The Hundred and the Geld', *E.H.R.* x (1895), 732.

by some pre-Alfredian charter.[1] These correspondences raise the possibility that, here and there, the hides allotted to the counties of historic times may represent the assessments of the same districts to the food-rents of early kings. It is always hard to penetrate behind the county organization of the united English state to the *regiones* and *provinciae* of the first English kingdoms, but the attempt has led to significant results in the one district for which the evidence is adequate. In Kent, where the unit of eleventh-century assessment was the archaic sulung, there is reason to think that the distribution of these units recorded by Domesday Book preserves the outline of the system by which the local rulers of that kingdom had been maintained in the time of its independence.[2]

In the northern Danelaw, the district between the Welland and the Tees, the system of assessment which prevailed in 1066 was comparatively recent. Like most of England outside Kent, this region had originally been divided into hides, or family lands. But the unit on which the pre-Conquest assessment of this country was based was not the hide but the Anglo-Danish *plogesland*, the *carucata terrae* of Domesday Book, the 'carucate' of modern writers.[3] Like the hides of Wessex and Mercia, the ploughlands of the Danelaw assessment had at some time been distributed, county by county, in large blocks which the counties had divided among their wapentakes, and the wapentakes among their villages.[4] But in the northern Danelaw the division proceeded, not as in the south by fives and tens, but by sixes and twelves, and it was carried out on these lines with a consistency which gives a distinctive character to an average set of assessment-figures from those parts.[5] Its exactitude is shown by the

---

[1] Thus Sedgeberrow in Worcestershire appears as a village of 4 hides in Domesday Book and in *C.S.* 223, a charter of Offa.

[2] J. E. A. Jolliffe, *Pre-Feudal England, The Jutes*, pp. 43–7.

[3] On the agrarian background of the Danelaw assessment see above, pp. 506–9.

[4] A number of facts suggesting that this assessment is unlikely to be earlier than the eleventh century are brought together in F. M. Stenton, *Types of Manorial Structure in the Northern Danelaw*, pp. 87–9.

[5] The existence of this 'six carucate unit', as it is generally called, was first pointed out by J. H. Round in *Feudal England*, pp. 69–90. Since Round wrote, detailed work on the Domesday Survey of the Danelaw shires has abundantly confirmed his argument. Many illustrations of the system are set out in *V.C.H. Nottinghamshire*, i, pp. 208–11, *V.C.H. Leicestershire*, i, pp. 278–80, and *The Lincolnshire Domesday and the Lindsey Survey*, ed. C. W. Foster and T. Longley, pp. xi–xiv. There can now be no question that the system extended over the whole of the northern Danelaw and that it is a distinctive peculiarity of that region.

fact that in Lincolnshire, Nottinghamshire, and Derbyshire the wapentakes were divided into a number of districts, each assessed at precisely twelve carucates, which under the name of 'hundreds' served, like the East Anglian leets, for minor purposes of local government.[1] That this system of assessment was an innovation is shown, not only by its details, but by the impossibility of correlating it with what is known about the early fiscal organization of the same country. There is no discernible connection between the 7,000 hides assigned to Lindsey with Hatfield Chase by the Tribal Hidage and the sum of roughly 2,000 carucates at which Lindsey was assessed to gelds in 1066.

Historians have often written severely about the Old English system of assessment. It has been described as cumbrous, overelaborate, and inequitable. It may be admitted that its details are extremely complicated. The intricate combinations of assessment-units into neat blocks of five hides or six carucates sometimes look like the result of a game with figures, played by clerks with no interest in realities. Nevertheless, as a piece of large-scale financial organization, it has no parallel in the Dark Ages. For all its apparent rigidity, it enabled the king to vary the weight and incidence of his demands as the needs of the moment required. The number of shillings to be charged on each hide, carucate, or sulung was in his discretion, and a district which had fallen on evil days, or the estate of a favoured church or individual, could be permanently relieved by a reduction of its assessment. The best proof of its practical convenience is the fact that it served the purposes of a new government, fertile in administrative expedients. The Conqueror handled it freely. In the course of his reign most villages in Sussex, Surrey, Hampshire, and Berkshire obtained reductions of hidage as a compensation for their losses in the war of the Conquest. But he never attempted to set up a new system in its place.

On the judicial side of his administration the changes which he introduced were more important. Apart from Domesday Book, the most interesting documents of his time are those which record the discussion or the settlement of pleas. The series begins with the report of an inquiry made between 1071

---

[1] No detailed account of these hundreds has yet been written, but the chief facts at present known about them are brought together in F. M. Stenton, *Danelaw Charters*, pp. lxiii–lxx.

and 1075 about the losses of lands and jurisdiction which the
monastery of Ely had suffered since 1066.[1] The commissioners
who held it included the bishops of Coutances and Lincoln,
Earl Waltheof, and the sheriffs of Cambridge and Hertford.
They obtained the facts 'from the testimony of men knowing the
truth', and they found evidence of wholesale encroachment at
the abbey's expense. The rebellion of 1075 must have delayed
the settlement of the questions thus raised, and in 1080 the
inquiry was reopened. The first step on this occasion was to
ascertain the truth about the liberties which the church had
possessed in 1066.[2] For this purpose Odo of Bayeux, in the
king's name, summoned a large assembly to Kentford, on the
border between Cambridgeshire and Suffolk. It was attended
by four abbots, of whom three were Englishmen,[3] by at least
four sheriffs, with many French and English landowners from
the neighbouring shires, and on the king's behalf by Richard,
son of Count Gilbert, Haimo, the king's *dapifer*, and Tihel de
Helion, a Breton lord with much land in Essex. The bishop of
Coutances was its president. In support of its liberties the abbey
produced the charters of Old English kings, and their evidence
seems to have been taken as conclusive. The questions affecting
the abbey lands, which the assembly also considered, were
more difficult, and it proved impossible to decide them all in a
single meeting. The king therefore resummoned the assembly,
and ordered that a number of Englishmen who knew how the
lands lay at King Edward's death should be chosen and put on
oath as to the facts.[4] But for all his insistence, many of these
questions were still open when the Domesday commissioners
came round the eastern shires in 1086.

In 1075 or 1076 a more famous inquiry of the same kind
had been held in Kent.[5] It arose from a complaint by Archbishop Lanfranc that Bishop Odo and his men had been encroaching upon the estates of the see of Canterbury, but its
scope was extended to cover the more delicate question of the

[1] *Inquisitio Comitatus Cantabrigiensis*, ed. N. E. S. A. Hamilton, pp. 192–5. Its
interest was first observed by J. H. Round, *Feudal England*, pp. 459–61.

[2] *Inq. Com. Cant.*, p. xvii.

[3] The fourth was Baldwin of St. Edmunds, who had been intimate with King
Edward.

[4] *Inq. Com. Cant.*, p. xviii.

[5] The date seems to me to be fixed to 1075 or 1076 by the presence of Ernost,
bishop of Rochester, who died in July 1076 after he had been bishop for only half a
year.

king's judicial authority within those lands.[1] To reach a settle-ment the shire court of Kent, reinforced by important persons from other parts, sat for three days on Pinnenden Heath near Maidstone under Bishop Geoffrey of Coutances. The procedure that was adopted is far from clear, but it is certain that at every point appeal was made to Old English practice and to indi-viduals familiar with it. By the king's order the aged Bishop Æthelric of Selsey, who had lately been deposed, was brought to the meeting in a cart, in order to answer the questions of Anglo-Saxon law that were expected to arise. The incident symbolized the king's wish to maintain what King Edward had sanctioned, and although the rights which Lanfranc asserted left few sources of judicial profit to the Crown within his demesnes, his claims were admitted on the ground of accepted custom.

The most detailed illustration of procedure in this age relates to a dispute between the bishop of Worcester and the abbot of Evesham about their rights over the Worcestershire villages of Bengeworth and Great Hampton.[2] The bishop admitted that these places were of the abbot's demesne, but claimed that for purposes of justice and ecclesiastical taxation they belonged to his own hundred of Oswaldslow, that their contingents to the militia should serve in his division of the host, and that his officers should collect the royal gelds which fell on them. The case was heard by the inevitable Geoffrey of Coutances, who was ordered to ascertain the customs in force 'on the last occa-sion in King Edward's time when a geld was taken for the fleet' —an instruction which presumably refers to the final levy of the 'heregeld' in 1051.[3] The case was opened at Worcester before an assembly comprising the leading men of the neigh-bouring shires. The bishop announced that he was ready to produce a number of witnesses, prepared, from their own knowledge, to give sworn evidence in his favour. As the abbot was unable to produce witnesses the plea was adjourned, and the abbot was instructed to bring whatever relics he might choose into court and take his own oath upon them. On the

---

[1] M. M. Bigelow, *Placita Anglo-Normannica*, [p. 9 in a footnote to his edition of the plea. A bibliography of the modern literature relating to the plea is prefixed to the translation in *English Historical Documents 1042–1189*, ed. D. C. Douglas and G. W. Greenaway, London, 1953, pp. 449–51.]

[2] Most easily accessible in *Monasticon Anglicanum*, i, p. 602, and Heming's *Chartularium Ecclesiae Wigorniensis*, ed. T. Hearne, i, pp. 77–83.

[3] Above, p. 431–2.

appointed day the bishop appeared with his witnesses, and the abbot, with the body of St. Ecgwine, the founder of his church; but before the oaths were taken the abbot, on the advice of his friends, admitted the justice of the bishop's claim.

It is probable that many lawsuits of this period proceeded along these lines. But the king's justices, burdened with a multitude of pleas, needed a simpler method of ascertaining facts, and it seems clear that for this purpose they were already beginning to use juries. It may be that a jury, in the sense of a group of men appointed by a court to give a collective verdict on oath, lies behind the reference in the great Ely plea to the Englishmen who were to be chosen and sworn to testify about conditions in King Edward's time. In any case, there is conclusive evidence that the principle of the collective verdict was familiar at the time in the king's court. During his viceroyalty Odo of Bayeux, mistrusting a judgement of the shire court of Cambridge, ordered it to choose twelve of its number to confirm or deny on oath what all had said, and afterwards caused the sheriff to summon a second group of twelve to confirm or reject the verdict of the first.[1]

In spite of the vague reporting of early pleas, it is clear that the Norman kings established the jury as a regular part of the machinery of English government. In the opinion of most scholars the jury was introduced into England as a Norman institution, ultimately derived from the sworn inquests which the later Carolingian sovereigns had used for the determination of their rights. That the jury, in this sense, had been known to the early Norman dukes is possible, though it has not yet been proved.[2] On the other hand, the 'twelve leading thegns' of the wapentake,[3] who swore that they would neither protect the guilty nor accuse the innocent, were members of a society which had grasped the essential principle of the jury seventy years before the Norman Conquest. So far as can be seen, these benches of superior thegns were peculiar to the district between the Welland and the Humber, but their existence must have

---

[1] *Textus Roffensis*, ed. T. Hearne, pp. 149–52; M. M. Bigelow, *Placita Anglo-Normannica*, pp. 34–6.

[2] There does not seem to be any clear case of the employment of a jury in Normandy between the Norman Settlement and 1066 [; nor, indeed in the period covered by the recently published volume of ducal charters ed. Marie Fauroux, *Receuil des Actes des Ducs de Normandie* (911–1066) Memoires de la Société des Antiquaires de Normandie, Caen (1961)].   [3] Above, pp. 510–11.

been known and their example may have affected the practice of local courts far outside this region. Domesday Book shows[1] that a leading thegn of a Lindsey wapentake might also be a leading thegn of a Devon hundred. In view of these facts it becomes difficult to regard the jury simply as a Norman device transplanted by an act of state to England. That the Conqueror vastly enlarged the scale of its employment is beyond dispute. But although many links in the chain of development are missing, the trend of the evidence suggests that the Anglo-Norman jury may well have owed as much to English practice as to Carolingian reminiscence.[2]

Before the Conqueror's death Englishmen in all but the remotest parts of the land had become familiar with the jury through its employment in the Domesday Inquest. In every shire the facts which it was the purpose of the inquiry to secure were confirmed on oath by an assembly which may be described untechnically as an enlarged shire-court. If a contemporary account of the proceedings may be trusted, this gathering comprised the sheriff, the king's barons enfeoffed within the shire, with their foreign tenants, the court of every hundred, and the priest, reeve, and six *villani* from every village.[3] But the information relating to each hundred was separately attested, and was probably presented to the commissioners, by its own jury. In Cambridgeshire, the only county for which sufficient evidence has been preserved, the hundredal jury usually consisted of eight persons, four of them Englishmen and four Frenchmen.[4] The jurors were drawn from the middle classes of the rural population. Most of the Englishmen seem to have been substantial freeholders, and although a few military tenants can be identified among the Frenchmen, none of them was of outstanding rank or wealth.

[1] As in the case of Merleswein, above, p. 628.

[2] As Vinogradoff remarked (*English Society in the Eleventh Century*, p. 7): 'It seems . . . that this is emphatically a case when the growth of an institution has to be traced to different roots.'

[3] *Inq. Com. Cant.*, p. 97. The passage is concise, and its wording in part ambiguous. Round was of the opinion (*Feudal England*, pp. 118–20) that the commissioners went on circuit through each of the hundreds within each shire, and that the people described above appeared before them in the course of this progress. Maitland (*Domesday Book and Beyond*, p. 11) believed that the commissioners held one session in each shire, which all these people attended. The probabilities of the case, and the natural sense of the passage taken as a whole, [as well as later judicial itineraries] make Maitland's view preferable.

[4] *Inq. Com. Cant.*, *passim*.

The instructions which the commissioners received have survived in an abstract preserved by the monks of Ely.[1] They were
framed on the assumption that England was divided into
manors, and they were drafted from the standpoint of estate-
management rather than public economy. They begin with a
demand for the name of each manor, and the names of those
who were holding it at the beginning of 1066 and at the time of
the inquest. The last demand was understood to mean not
only the name of the tenant in chief to whose honour the manor
belonged, but also that of any tenant to whom he might have
granted it. The instructions then pass to statistics, and require
in the first place a statement of the number of hides within the
manor. It is now clear that this inquiry referred, not to the
number of real, arable, hides which the manor contained, but
to the number at which it was assessed to the king's gelds. The
agrarian side of the inquest begins with the next question, which
asks for the number of plough-teams belonging respectively
to the demesne and the manorial peasantry. There is no ambiguity about this question, but it is immediately followed by
one which cannot have been easy to the commissioners themselves. With a specious appearance of precision it attempts a
classification of rural society, and requires the jurors to report
how many *villani*, cottagers, slaves, free men, and sokemen
there were within the manor. The meaning of these terms, and
of the figures which were produced by this question, is the
central problem of Domesday study. On the first point, it is
virtually certain that the free men and sokemen were separated
from all other classes by the fact that their holdings were regarded as their own property, on which they, and not the lord
of the manor, paid taxes.[2] On the second point, later evidence
indicates that while the slaves may have been counted as individuals, the *villani*, cottagers, free men, and sokemen were
heads of households, occupying tenements from which the lord
of the estate derived rents of services. Domesday Book is not
the record of a census.

The remaining articles are simpler. They begin by asking
for the amount of woodland, meadow, and pasture within the
manor, and for the number of its mills and fish-ponds. They

[1] Printed in their context in *Inq. Com. Cant.*, p. 97. Most readily accessible in
Stubbs, *Select Charters* (9th ed.), p. 101.
[2] F. W. Maitland, *Domesday Book and Beyond*, pp. 24–5.

then inquire more vaguely how much has been added to or
taken from the manor—a question which would cover, among
other matters, the innumerable encroachments brought out by
contemporary pleas. The next question asks for the 'value' of
the manor in 1066, and at the taking of the inquest. It is probable that the men who framed the question wished for an
estimate of the sum at which the manor could have been leased
at each of these dates. It is also probable that the figures supplied in answer often stand for rents actually paid under the
terms of such a lease. The amount of land within the manor
but outside the lord's direct control was clearly relevant to this
question of manorial values, and the next article appropriately
asks for a statement of the holding of each free man and sokeman
in 1066 and at the moment of the inquest. At this point the
questionnaire is rounded off by a demand that the details which
had been required should be supplied in relation to three
periods—the time of King Edward, the time when King
William gave the manor to its new lord, and the year 1086—
but a postscript makes an additional demand for an opinion
whether more could be had from the manor than it was actually
yielding. In view of the character of the previous questions,
it is probable that this last inquiry refers, not to the taxable
capacity of the estate, but to the possibility that its lord might
be able to improve it by better management.

Detailed as they are, these instructions only give the main
lines along which the inquiry proceeded. It is clear, for example,
that the livestock on each manor was brought into the actual
survey. The author of the *Chronicle* was scandalized that the
king should have descended so low as to order the counting of
oxen, cows, and swine. Account is taken of the farm stock in
the survey of the south-western counties contained in the so-
called 'Exon Domesday',[1] and in the survey of the eastern
counties which forms the second volume of Domesday Book
itself. On the other hand, it is doubtful whether the idea of
obtaining a minute description of every manor in England at
three separate dates was fully carried out. The manorial
values of 1066 and 1086 are consistently recorded in Domesday
Book, but there are many sections in which nothing is said

---

[1] Preserved in Exeter cathedral, and printed in volume iv of the Record Commission edition of Domesday Book. These details are omitted from the version
incorporated in the official Domesday Book laid up in the king's treasury.

about the value of an estate at the time when its new lord received it. In the survey of the eastern counties, where the information given by the jurors is preserved more fully than elsewhere, materials are generally given for a comparison between the conditions of 1066 and 1086, but information about the intermediate date is provided less systematically. It is also doubtful how far the jurors were expected to answer the embarrassing question whether the yield of estates could be increased. In so far as their answers can be traced in Domesday Book, they seem to be represented by a statement of the number of plough-teams for which an estate had land at the time of the inquest. It is probable that this statement, which is not expressly demanded by the articles of the inquiry, was intended to be compared with the number of working teams, and thus to give some indication of the extent to which the agricultural capacity of the estate was realized in practice. On the whole, a comparison of the articles with the returns that were made to them suggests that the commissioners had a free hand in the management of the inquiry, and that their first concern was to prevent it from degenerating into an accumulation of useless facts.

The decision that the inquiry should be made had been taken at the Christmas council of 1085. Before the end of 1086 it had been completed, and the returns had been brought to the king.[1] For a time they were laid up in the treasury at Winchester, where they were consulted during the reign of William II.[2] But a mass of separate rolls was an unsatisfactory record of a description of all England, and it is probable that before the Conqueror's death work had already begun on the two volumes which since the twelfth century have been known as Domesday Book.[3] In their compilation the material contained

[1] It may reasonably be assumed that the 'writings', as the *Chronicle* calls them, were presented to the king before his departure from England, late in the year.

[2] A writ of William II which is later than 1093 (H. W. C. Davis, *Regesta*, No. lxxx) states that certain land claimed by the abbey of St. Benet of Holme 'inbreviata fuit in meis brevibus . . . qui sunt in thesauro meo Wyntonie'. The use of the word *breves* implies that the original returns to the inquest had been inspected.

[3] The date of Domesday Book is a difficult question. The Old French sound-changes which appear in the Domesday forms of place-names are useless for this inquiry owing to the extreme scarcity of contemporary French material. The volumes have not yet been analysed palaeographically. It is uncertain how many hands were employed on them, and therefore hard to estimate the speed at which they could have been produced. The handwriting as a whole points definitely to a late-11th-century date for the manuscript. On general grounds, there is an overwhelming probability that the volumes were written before the information which

in the returns was rearranged so as to bring out more clearly the way in which the land was divided among the magnates of the country. The inquest had been taken, and the returns had been drawn up, by counties and hundreds. It followed that the fiefs of the king's own barons, which it was a primary object of the inquiry to ascertain, could only be pieced together from the rolls by the combination of many scattered and often small particulars. In the preparation of Domesday Book the county, as the largest and most stable division of the kingdom, was adopted as the unit of arrangement, but within each county the lands of each tenant in chief were brought together under separate headings. It would be incorrect to call Domesday Book a feudal record, for it contains no account of the obligations by which the higher social orders were bound in service to the king.[1] But its arrangement was deliberately planned so as to reveal the territorial basis on which English feudalism rested.

Of the two volumes into which Domesday Book is divided one is devoted to the counties of Essex, Norfolk, and Suffolk; the other to the rest of England. The former, though generally called the second volume of the complete work, seems to have been the first to appear. It shows many signs of hurried compilation, and includes much detail, chiefly relating to live stock, which the so-called first volume does not contain. It may well have become apparent, as the volume on the eastern shires took shape, that a survey of all England on the same scale would be too bulky for convenient use.[2] However this may be, there is no doubt that the details relating to other parts were drastically curtailed and systematized in the final abstract. The result was a volume which as an efficient digest of information will bear comparison with any official record of any period. As the ordered description of a national economy it is unique among the records of the medieval world.[3]

---

they contain was seriously out of date; that is, before, at latest, the confiscations after the revolt of 1088.

[1] There is a fundamental difference in this respect between Domesday Book and the great feodaries of the 13th century, which were compiled for the express purpose of ascertaining the details of feudal service.

[2] This was Round's opinion (*Feudal England*, pp. 140–2), and it is borne out by all recent work on the Survey.

[3] The inquest as a whole is called a *descriptio* in the colophon of vol. ii of Domesday Book itself, and in a writ of William I which is dated *post descriptionem totius Angliae* (T. Madox, *Formulare Anglicanum*, plate I, No. 1).

The object for which the Survey was undertaken is a question to which more than one answer can be given. A generation ago, when the modern study of Domesday Book began, the tendency of scholars was to regard it as primarily a fiscal record—a collection of facts which would enable the king to correct anomalies in the assessment of the country to his gelds. In recent years more attention has been given to the wider aspects of the inquiry, and in particular to its significance as an opportunity of settling outstanding pleas. That the commissioners had the authority of royal justices is certain, and enough of their decisions has survived to show that their work in this capacity was an integral part of their conduct of the inquest. On the other hand, there are signs in the text of the Survey of haste and urgency which cannot easily be reconciled with the carrying out of long-term financial or judicial purpose. In the background of the inquest, the king's officers had been faced with the operation of distributing a large force of fighting men among the king's barons in proportion to the productivity of their demesnes. In searching for the purpose of the Survey, it seems pointless to go beyond the fact that the recent threat of an invasion had impressed on the king and his council the inadequacy of their knowledge of the economic resources at their immediate command in an emergency. It was urgent that the king should know more about England—'how it was peopled and with what sort of men.'

XVIII

THE REORGANIZATION OF THE ENGLISH CHURCH

IN his attitude towards the ecclesiastical politics of his day the Conqueror took the position that it was the duty of the secular ruler to supervise the government of the church within his dominions. The reconstruction of the Norman church after the disasters of the tenth century had been the work of his predecessors. From them he inherited an ecclesiastical supremacy which enabled him not only to appoint bishops and abbots and to summon councils, but to intervene in diocesan administration. William of Poitiers, his first biographer, records that he took action as duke against bishops and archdeacons who dealt too leniently with offenders convicted in their courts.[1] In 1066 there was no part of the Continent where the ecclesiastical authority of the ruler was more firmly established than in Normandy.

Since his coming of age William had always shown himself anxious to use his powers for the furtherance of religion, and it was with the reputation of a reformer that he began his English reign. But his conception of reform was strictly practical, and, from the Roman standpoint, old-fashioned. His lifetime coincided with the first phases of the revolution through which the pope became the effective sovereign of the western church. With many of its objects William was in sympathy. But he never admitted that the pope was entitled to impose a religious policy on secular princes, and in the actual business of reform he regarded himself not as the pope's minister, but as his collaborator and ally. Throughout his life he resisted every papal act from which he foresaw danger, not merely to his political interests, but to the integrity of his ecclesiastical powers.

As king of England he became the sovereign of a country where respect for the papacy was a matter of national tradition. It was compatible with extreme insularity in thought and

[1] *Gesta Willelmi Ducis*, ed. Giles, pp. 114–15 and R. Foreville, pp. 124–7.

custom, but it was a genuine feeling which coloured the whole of English religious life. King Edward himself had regarded the see of Rome with guileless veneration. The Conqueror, whose attitude towards the papacy was far more independent, had no wish to bring the English church into closer subjection to Rome, and the reforms which he attempted to introduce were simply intended to establish a better ecclesiastical order. At his accession the chief obstacles to such an order were the anomalous position of Archbishop Stigand, the confusion of lay and ecclesiastical jurisprudence in the practice of the local courts, and the virtual autonomy of the individual bishops. Within ten years Stigand had been deposed, a royal writ had separated the justice of the bishop from the justice of the hundred-court, and under the king's authority an archbishop who styled himself primate of all Britain was holding councils which represented the whole English church.

In all these changes William was moving along lines approved at Rome, and in regard to the first of them, it is probable that the immediate impulse came from the papacy. The deposition of Stigand was carried out by a council held under papal authority by Ermenfrid, bishop of Sion, and two cardinal priests at Winchester, in April 1070. Throughout the summer and autumn of 1069 the king had been engaged in a campaign which can have allowed him few opportunities of beginning a correspondence with Rome about the dispatch of a legatine commission. It is much more probable that the news of the death of Archbishop Ealdred, which left the excommunicated Stigand the only metropolitan in England, had caused the pope to demand that the way should be opened for a new appointment to Canterbury.[1]

Of the fifteen English bishoprics which existed in April 1070, York was vacant, and Durham in a state of extreme confusion.[2]

[1] Ealdred died on 11 September 1069. It is safe to assume that the news had reached Rome within eight weeks; that is by 6 November. Deliberations in the curia may well have occupied another three weeks, that is, until 27 November. If four weeks are allowed for the dispatch of the summonses and the assembly of the council on 7 April 1070, it follows that the legates must have reached England not later than 10 March. There is ample time between November and March for a papal messenger to travel to England, obtain the king's approval of the mission, meet the legates at a prearranged point in France, and conduct them across the Channel.

[2] Bishop Æthelwine, who had at first shown himself friendly to the Normans (above, pp. 601–2), had been alarmed by William's northern campaign of 1069. He

Stigand of Canterbury and Winchester, his brother Æthelmær
of Elmham, Æthelric of Selsey, and Leofwine of Lichfield were
for different reasons certain or likely to be unseated by the
council. There remained eight bishops whose position was not
open to challenge—William of London, Remigius of Dorchester,
Herman of Sherborne, Giso of Wells, Walter of Hereford,
Leofric of Exeter, Wulfstan of Worcester,[1] and Siward of
Rochester. The first five of these bishops were of foreign birth,
and Leofric of Exeter, though possibly an Englishman, had been
educated abroad.[2] Of the two bishops who represented the
native religious tradition, Siward of Rochester was the incon-
spicuous occupant of the smallest of English sees, and Wulfstan
of Worcester, who was to come to great eminence in the future,
had not wholly freed his diocese from its ancient dependence on
the church of York.[3] The abbots who came from each diocese in
the company of its bishop gave a majority on the council to its
English members. But few of the abbots were men of distinction,[4] and, like the rest of the assembly, they seem to have
accepted as inevitable the direction which they received from
the legates.

No report of the proceedings at Winchester has survived, and
their course cannot now be followed. One of the bishops
against whom the legates were bound to take action abandoned
his see before the council opened. Leofwine of Lichfield, who
was a married man with sons, refused to attend the council, but
came to the king's court, resigned his bishopric into the king's
hands and then retired into the monastery where he had been
educated.[5] The legates excommunicated him, but took no steps
towards the filling of his see. According to later writers Stigand
appeared in the council; but his condemnation was a foregone

had left Durham with the relics of St. Cuthbert as William was approaching the
Tees. He had returned by 25 March 1070 (Symeon of Durham, *Opera*, R.S. i,
p. 101), but he had left England before the winter (ibid., p. 105), and was outlawed
before the end of the year. In view of his recent attitude towards the king, it is
certain that he cannot have attended the council.

[1] The legend that the removal of Wulfstan was at some time under consideration
is disproved by R. R. Darlington, *Vita Wulfstani*, pp. xxxi–xxxiii.

[2] The difficult question of Leofric's origin is discussed by R. W. Chambers,
The Exeter Book of Old English Poetry, p. 5.

[3] On the Worcester–York connection see above, p. 436. The York tradition
represented Wulfstan as a mere *vicarius*, or suffragan, of Ealdred (*Historians of the
Church of York*, R.S. ii. 98–9).

[4] Æthelwig of Evesham was the great exception.

[5] *Lanfranci Opera*, ed. J. A. Giles, i, pp. 22–3.

conclusion, and it does not seem that he attempted any formal defence to the charges that were brought against him.[1] His brother, Æthelmær of Elmham, was deposed on grounds which are nowhere stated. Beyond a vague report that certain abbots were degraded, nothing is recorded of the other business before the council, except for a tradition that Wulfstan of Worcester put forward a claim to a number of villages which Archbishop Ealdred had annexed to the see of York.[2] After the session at Winchester the cardinal priests went back to Rome, but at Whitsuntide, Bishop Ermenfrid held a second council at Windsor, where Bishop Æthelric of Selsey was deposed on charges which in the pope's opinion were inadequately proved.[3]

The work of the commission ended with a remarkable episode in Normandy. Returning across France, Ermenfrid held a council of Norman bishops which imposed a set of penances on all ranks of the Conqueror's army.[4] There was nothing anomalous in the issue of such a code, for the moral discipline which the Church administered required a penance from every man who of set purpose killed or wounded another, even in a pitched battle under his own king. The interest of the code lies in its particularity. On everyone who had fought at Hastings as a matter of duty it sets a year's penance for each man whom he had killed, with separate provisions for those who had killed or injured some but could not tell the number, or, wishing to injure some, had failed to injure any. To such as these it allows commutation of penance by alms or the building of a church. On all who served the duke for hire it imposes penance as for homicide; it punishes clerks who had fought or armed themselves for the battle 'as if they had sinned in their own country'; and it relegates monks to the judgement of their abbots. On the archers it sets a penance equivalent to a triple

---

[1] The legend that Stigand was imprisoned closely at Winchester after his deprivation is contradicted by the fact that he held the large manor of East Meon, worth at least £40 a year, until his death, D.B. i, f. 38. According to a late Winchester authority he died in 1072. *Annales Monastici*, R.S. ii, pp. 29, 30.

[2] Florence of Worcester, *Chronicon*, ed. B. Thorpe, ii, pp. 5, 6. But the claim is referred to a later time by the older sources for Wulfstan's life, *Vita Wulfstani*, ed. R. R. Darlington, p. xxviii.

[3] *Lanfranci Opera*, i, p. 31.

[4] Wilkins, *Concilia*, i, p. 366. In view of its conformity to the penitential system of the time, and the early date of the manuscript which contains it, there is no reason to doubt its authenticity.

Lent. In regard to other killings before William's coronation it appoints a year's penance for the death of a man killed while resisting the seizure of food, and three years for the death of one resisting wanton plunderers. The killing of a man after the coronation was adjudged homicide, unless the victim had been slain in arms against the king. The penance for less violent crimes was fixed at the rate prescribed for them in Normandy. The code ends with an order that goods taken from English churches should be restored, and that if they were retained, the Norman bishops should place a ban upon their sale. The realism of the decrees is admirable.

In the meantime the king was taking his own measures for the better order of the English Church. For the succession to Canterbury he found a scholar, already eminent, who was of one mind with himself on most questions of ecclesiastical politics. Lanfranc, abbot of the monastery of St. Stephen at Caen, to whom he offered the archbishopric, was a teacher with a European reputation.[1] Born at Pavia, probably in the second decade of the century, he had spent his early youth in the study and practice of the civil law.[2] Turning from law to theology, he became a pupil of Berenger, archdeacon and master of the school of Tours—an association which Berenger's unorthodoxy made embarrassing to him in later years. After leaving Berenger, Lanfranc taught for a time in the cathedral school of Avranches, but shortly after 1040, desiring to enter religion, he joined the company of enthusiasts which formed the nucleus of the abbey of Bec. Three years later he was appointed its prior. Herluin, the founder of Bec, was an individualist of genius, and, departing from the monastic custom of the age, he allowed Lanfranc to open a school for all comers. He attracted to Bec many pupils who afterwards rose to high places in the

---

[1] The details of Lanfranc's early life are lost. No attempt was made to write his biography until he had been dead for more than thirty years. The *Vita Lanfranci* by Milo Crispin, which was then produced (ed. J. A. Giles, *Lanfranci Opera*, i, pp. 281–313), is vague and uncritical. It can be supplemented from the references to Lanfranc in the *Vita Herluini* by Gilbert Crispin (ed. J. Armitage Robinson, *Gilbert Crispin, Abbot of Westminster*, pp. 87–110), but the result is insufficient for a coherent story. The first episode in Lanfranc's career which can be precisely dated is his attendance at the Councils of Reims, Rome, and Vercelli in 1049–50 ('De Corpore et Sanguine Domini' in *Lanfranci Opera*, ii, pp. 154–5).

[2] The fact that Lanfranc was in full possession of his energy until shortly before his death in 1089 makes it improbable that he was born before 1010 (D. Knowles, *The Monastic Order in England*, p. 107), and virtually precludes his identification with the famous Lombard jurist of the same name.

church—Pope Alexander II among them—and the intellectual distinction of Bec in the next generation is primarily due to his teaching.

The beginnings of his long association with Duke William are obscure. After some ten years at Bec he appears as one of the duke's closest advisers. According to the oldest tradition of his life the accusations of certain informers caused the duke to order him into banishment.[1] But the same tradition states that the duke restored him to favour after an interview by the roadside before he had gone far on his journey. Thenceforward their intimacy was never broken. There is no serious doubt that Lanfranc was William's agent in the negotiations with the papal court which ended in the recognition of the duke's marriage.[2] In 1063 he was summoned from Bec to become abbot of the duke's new foundation at Caen. There is every reason to accept the statement of a contemporary that the promotion of Lanfranc to Canterbury was already in William's mind at the time of his own coronation.[3]

It is more doubtful whether Lanfranc himself was prepared to accept the proposal. He had found happiness in the monastic life, he was indifferent to promotion, and he had no conception of his own capacity for government. He had already refused to accept a place in the Roman curia which Nicholas II and Alexander II had offered him, and in 1067 he declined election to the archbishopric of Rouen. It was only in obedience to a direct command from the pope that he accepted the see of Canterbury three years later. The prospect of ruling a distracted church in a foreign land was intensely distasteful to him, and after experience of its realities he found them almost insupportable. He was consecrated archbishop on 29 August 1070. A few months later he addressed a letter to Pope Alexander in which, with obvious sincerity, he asked for release from office on the ground of his own inadequacy.[4] That he survived these troubles was due partly to the pope's firmness, but essentially to the support and understanding which he

---

[1] *Vita Herluini* in J. Armitage Robinson, *Gilbert Crispin*, pp. 97–8.

[2] On a point like this, which is likely to have been a matter of common knowledge, it seems safe to follow the tradition recorded by Milo Crispin (*Lanfranci Opera*, i, p. 289).

[3] William of Poitiers, *Gesta Willelmi Ducis*, ed. J. A. Giles, p. 147, and R. Foreville, p. 234.

[4] *Lanfranci Opera*, ed. Giles, i, pp. 19–21.

received from the king. Lanfranc and William belonged to
different worlds of thought and action, but an instinct for order
was common to them both, and on the means by which a better
order might be established in the English church they were of
one mind. Lanfranc, who could remember the time when the
papacy had been incapable of religious leadership, believed,
like William, that responsibility for reform in any local branch
of the church lay in the first instance on the secular ruler.

The most urgent problem which confronted him in England
was the relationship between the archbishoprics of Canterbury
and York. At Whitsuntide 1070, before Lanfranc had accepted
William's invitation to England, the king had given the northern archbishopric to Thomas, a canon of Bayeux. The consecration of Thomas was reserved for Lanfranc, and before the
ceremony Lanfranc demanded that Thomas should make him
a written profession of obedience. With a proper regard for the
dignity of his church Thomas refused at first, but was ultimately
brought to make a profession to Lanfranc himself, reserving the
right to protest if any successor to Lanfranc should assert a
similar claim. In the autumn of 1071, when the two archbishops went to Rome for their *pallia*, Thomas reopened the
matter of the profession, and also asserted that the dioceses of
Lichfield, Worcester, and Dorchester rightly belonged to his
province. The pope referred each of these questions to an
English council, and sent the cardinal deacon Hubert to
preside over it as legate. At Winchester in April 1072 Lanfranc
set out a case for his primacy based on the *Ecclesiastical History*
of Bede, on the acts of early English councils, on the professions
of early English bishops, on the testimony of living witnesses,
and on a series of papal letters confirming the precedence of
Canterbury over all other English sees. It is now recognized
that these letters were either forgeries or, if founded on genuine
documents, interpolated in the interest of Canterbury. The
responsibility for their production in council rests on Lanfranc,
but the theory that he was himself the forger is contradicted by
all that is known about his character, and by the extreme
unlikelihood that one who had recently called himself a new
Englishman[1] should have possessed the knowledge of English
history needed for the fabrication. It is far more probable that
in using these dubious materials Lanfranc was following,

[1] *Lanfranci Opera*, i, p. 23.

without personal investigation, a case prepared for him by the monks of his cathedral.[1] The council, for its part, seems to have accepted Lanfranc's documents at their face value. It ruled that the church of York ought to be subject to the church of Canterbury, and to its archbishop as primate of all Britain; that the archbishop of York and his suffragans should come to councils summoned by the archbishop of Canterbury; and that the dioceses in dispute between Lanfranc and Thomas should belong to the southern province, leaving to York only the see of Durham and such bishoprics as existed in Scotland.[2] The council also expressed the opinion that the right of the archbishop of Canterbury to a sworn profession of obedience from the archbishop of York had been established as a matter of custom, but recorded that 'out of love for the king' Lanfranc had released Thomas from the obligation to take an oath. It was declared that the release was not to form a precedent, and it in no way detracted from the force of a judgement which at every essential point was uncompromisingly in Lanfranc's favour.

While the question of the primacy was still under debate Lanfranc was holding the first of the great synods which distinguish his government of the English church.[3] In the spring of 1072 he held what is described as a 'general council' at Winchester. It deposed Wulfric, abbot of the New Minster at Winchester, and accepted a number of canons, of which the headings only have survived.[4] Most of them appear to have

[1] Z. N. Brooke, *The English Church and the Papacy*, pp. 118–26, where the question is discussed in relation to the modern literature which it has produced.

[2] The decision on these points, taken and recorded at Winchester in the chapel of the castle (*Palaeographical Society Facsimiles*, iii, plate 170) was reaffirmed at Whitsuntide by a larger assembly at Windsor (Wilkins, *Concilia*, i, pp. 324–5). The autograph signatures of the legate, the two archbishops, and four bishops give especial interest to the record of the Winchester session.

[3] The series, dated by the years of Lanfranc's episcopate, is given in the Latin record of his acts printed by Thorpe, *The Anglo-Saxon Chronicle*, i, pp. 386–9, by Plummer, *Two Saxon Chronicles*, i, pp. 287–92, and in facsimile by the Early English Text Society, *The Parker Chronicle*, ff. 32, 32 *b*. The manuscript was written after Lanfranc's death, but apparently before 1100. The fragmentary records of these councils are printed by Wilkins, *Concilia*, i, pp. 362–8, but the edition is uncritical, and it is sometimes difficult to assign a particular set of canons to a particular assembly. Until a new edition has been produced, the history of Lanfranc's archbishopric will always be obscure at important points.

[4] In the thirteen *capitula* printed by Wilkins, p. 365, under the title 'Concilii Wintoniensis capitula et injunctiones'. There seems no serious doubt that H. Boehmer was right in assigning these canons to the council of 1072 (*Kirche und Staat in England und in der Normandie*, pp. 63–4).

dealt in general terms with elementary matters of ecclesiastical order, but there are two which have a more immediate significance. One is a decree that every bishop shall hold a synod twice a year; the other enjoins all bishops to appoint 'archdeacons and other ministers of the holy order' in their churches. The words are vague, but it is at least probable that they foreshadow the creation of organized chapters in non-monastic cathedrals.

The second of Lanfranc's councils, and the only one of which a formal record exists, met at London in 1075.[1] Its main purpose was to declare the adherence of the English church to certain ancient canons which the interruption of the custom of holding councils in England had caused to fall out of mind. Its decrees refer at every point to the acts of former popes and synods, and most of them are directed against abuses recurrent everywhere—simony, the vagrancy of clerks and monks, the participation of clerks in judgements touching life and limb, marriage within prohibited degrees, and the use of spells and divinations. The only articles which refer specifically to English problems are a decree regulating the precedence of bishops at future councils, and an ordinance providing, agreeably to the canon law, for the transference of certain sees from villages to towns. In the absence of the king, who was then in Normandy, it was impossible to carry out all the changes of this kind which the council had in view, but authorization was given for the removal of the sees of Lichfield, Selsey, and Sherborne to the urban centres of Chester, Chichester, and Salisbury.

The effect of this ordinance was to accelerate a process which had begun already in King Edward's time. In 1050, with the approval of Pope Leo IX, the see of Crediton had been transferred to Exeter.[2] The bishops whom the Conqueror appointed

---

[1] Wilkins, i, pp. 363–4. The subscriptions show that the council included the archbishops of Canterbury and York; 11 English bishops; Geoffrey, bishop of Coutances; Anschitil, archdeacon of Canterbury; and 21 abbots. The fact that 12 of the abbots were Englishmen is noteworthy. It is probable that Geoffrey of Coutances attended because as the king's chief executive minister it would fall on him to supervise any redistribution of property that might follow from the council's decisions.

[2] R. W. Chambers, in *The Exeter Book of Old English Poetry*, pp. 5–9. On the English side it was hoped by the change to give the bishop security against raiders. A similar motive had caused the transference of the Bernician see in 995 from Chester-le-Street to the rock of Durham.

to rural English sees were naturally in favour of such changes. Three years or more before the decision was taken about the sees of Sherborne, Lichfield, and Selsey, Herfast, the new bishop of East Anglia, had removed his seat from North Elmham to Thetford.[1] Before 1086 Remigius of Dorchester took the urban minster of St. Mary in Lincoln for his cathedral.[2] The local organization which these changes made necessary was carried out slowly. The East Anglian see was moved again to Norwich before a cathedral establishment had been created at Thetford. Bishop Remigius died in 1092, before the consecration of the new church which he built in Lincoln, and it was not until 1089 that Bishop Osmund was able to establish a college of canons at Salisbury.[3] But it is clear that by 1087 the rural cathedral had become an anomaly in the English diocesan order.

It was in his third council, held at Winchester on 1 April 1076, that Lanfranc came nearest to a comprehensive review of the major issues affecting the English church.[4] It was a suitable moment for the attempt. The election of Pope Gregory VII in the spring of 1073 had brought fresh energy to the continental movement towards ecclesiastical reform, and the Winchester canons of 1076 are the English counterpart to the great decrees which had lately been coming forth from Rome. But their moderation and the respect for existing conditions which they display are in singular contrast to the uncompromising tenor of the papal ordinances. For Lanfranc was not an enthusiast, and his decrees reflect the attitude of a statesman, prepared to sacrifice consistency if he could thereby secure his more essential aims.

The method of his approach is most clearly seen in his treatment of the question of clerical celibacy. Like all reformers of his age Lanfranc disapproved of clerical marriage, and in this he was in line with a strong tradition within the English

---

[1] He uses the style *Tetfortensis episcopus* in his autograph subscription to the decree of 1072 about the primacy of Canterbury. *Palaeographical Society Facsimiles* iii, plate 170.

[2] D.B. i, f. 336.

[3] M. O. Anderson, *The Chronicle of Holyrood*, p. 110.

[4] The abstract which contains the only extant record of the acts of this council is printed by Wilkins, *Concilia*, i, p. 367. Wilkins's text was ultimately derived from the copy printed by Matthew Parker, *De Antiquitate Britannicae Ecclesiae* (Hanau, 1605), p. 114. The decrees are probably more accessible in this edition than in that of Wilkins.

church itself. On various occasions during the previous century the Anglo-Saxon witan had legislated for a celibate priesthood,[1] and in Lanfranc's own time Wulfstan of Worcester was requiring the married clergy in his diocese to abandon either their wives or their churches.[2] On the other hand, clerical marriage was so common that a general condemnation of the practice would have meant a challenge to English social custom, which, for the sake of peace, Lanfranc was anxious to avoid. The legislation which he introduced in 1076 was intended to make such marriages impossible thereafter. The council decreed that no canon should keep a wife, that no unmarried parish priest should take a wife, and that no bishop should ordain anyone to the priesthood or diaconate without a previous declaration of a candidate's celibacy. But it also decreed that parish priests who were already married should not be compelled to put away their wives.

This has often been described, with truth, as a compromise. The principle of clerical celibacy was left for full realization to the future. Even so, it was a notable achievement to secure its recognition without any audible conflict. It is, moreover, probable that historians have sometimes underestimated the positive significance of these decrees. The 'canons' to whom married life was forbidden were not only the members of cathedral chapters. In all parts of England, and especially in the north-west midlands, there were collegiate foundations, representing 'old minsters' of the Anglo-Saxon time, of which the clergy would come under the rule of celibacy.[3] Sixty years before Lanfranc came to England King Æthelred II had tried to impose a celibate life on such communities by a law that canons whose collective property would maintain a dormitory and refectory should live unmarried.[4] The constitution of many important local churches must have been affected by Lanfranc's revival of this ancient legislation.

The clauses which follow were intended to secure the parochial organization of the church against the invasion of

---

[1] Æthelred II, probably under the influence of Archbishop Wulfstan, is particularly explicit on this subject. Liebermann, *Gesetze*, i, p. 238.

[2] *Vita Wulfstani*, ed. R. R. Darlington, pp. 53–4.

[3] Such, for example, as the churches of Bromfield and Morville in Shropshire (D.B. i, ff. 252 *b*, 253), of which the history is traced by R. W. Eyton, *Antiquities of Shropshire*, v, pp. 210–11; i, p. 32.

[4] v Æthelred, c. 7 (Liebermann, *Gesetze*, i, p. 238).

vagrant monks and clergy, and to protect the parish priest against oppression by the patron of his living. The council first ruled that no clerk or monk should be admitted into another diocese without letters dimissory from his own bishop, and that no monk, even if he were provided with such letters, should be allowed to serve a parochial cure. It then proceeded to decree that no parish priest should render any service for his benefice other than that which he had been accustomed to render in King Edward's time. The regulations about migrating clerks and monks concerned the internal discipline of the church and barely touched its relations with the secular world. But the decree about the service to be rendered by the parish priest affected the interests of every lord with a church upon his property. Old English society had held firmly to the idea that a manorial church was the property of the manorial lord,[1] and that the lord was entitled to bargain with the priest who was to serve his church for a share in the revenues attached to it. There are innumerable entries in which Domesday Book includes a church among the profit-yielding appurtenances of an estate.[2] In the years after the Conquest there was a real danger that foreign lords set in possession of English manors would deal harshly with the native incumbents of their churches. Without provoking a direct conflict with lay opinion, it was impossible for Lanfranc to challenge the custom which allowed the patron of a church to regard himself as its owner. It was a simpler method of protecting the parish priest to reinforce by the act of a solemn council the Conqueror's known insistence on respect for the conditions prevailing in the time of King Edward.

The dependence of Lanfranc's legislation upon the king's policy appears again in his treatment of the question of ecclesiastical justice. The most permanent achievement of the council of 1076 was to complete the process by which, under royal sanction, courts of ecclesiastical jurisdiction were established in England. The intimate association of the Old English church and state had delayed the appearance of courts specifically assigned to the hearing of spiritual pleas. Before the

---

[1] On the origins of this idea see above, pp. 148–9.

[2] The evidence bearing on the legal position of the English parish church in this period is set out by H. Boehmer, 'Das Eigenkirchentum in England', in *Festgabe für Felix Liebermann*, pp. 301–53.

Conquest suits of this kind formed part of the miscellaneous business transacted in the hundred court, and were decided by a traditional law on which the new canonical jurisprudence had little influence. In or shortly after 1072[1] the Conqueror issued an ordinance[2] withdrawing spiritual pleas from the hundred court, and providing for their termination before the bishop in accordance with the 'canons and episcopal laws'. By this ordinance a fine was appointed for every failure to obey the bishop's summons; he was empowered to excommunicate contumacious persons; and the king promised to secure that the excommunication should be effective. The disciplinary provisions of the ordinance appear in the acts of the council of 1076, and it was clearly at this time that the English church, through its general synod, recorded its acceptance of the new system.

From its formal recognition of the new ecclesiastical courts the council passed by a natural sequence of thought to the marriage law which they were to administer. It does not seem to have put forth any general legislation on the subject, but it issued a decree forbidding anyone to give his daughter or kinswoman in marriage without the blessing of a priest, and declaring that such marriages should not be taken as lawful but as fornicatory.[3] From the little that is known about Old English marriage customs it seems that Lanfranc was here attempting an important modification of English practice, and was endeavouring to impose a religious character on what had been in essentials a secular contract. It is possible that the close association between Lanfranc and the king gave practical effect, for a time, to this innovation. But there is no trace of it in later records, and at the middle of the twelfth century, when the marriage law of England at last becomes clear, English churchmen were plainly committed to the canonical doctrine that a valid marriage is contracted by the mere declaration of

---

[1] C. H. Walker in *E.H.R.* xxxix (1924), pp. 399–400.

[2] Most easily accessible in Stubbs, *Select Charters*, 9th ed., pp. 99–100. A critical text is given by A. J. Robertson, *Laws of the Kings of England*, pp. 234–6.

[3] The decree, which is based on earlier canons, is brought into relation with the general development of the English marriage law by Pollock and Maitland, *History of English Law*, ii, pp. 370–4, where its significance is minimized. But it is obviously connected with the preceding decree recognizing the new ecclesiastical courts and, if the decrees are read consecutively, they give a strong impression that the bishops' courts are being instructed to deny the validity of marriages which a priest has not blessed.

a man and woman that they take each other as wife and husband.[1]

The councils which Lanfranc held were impressive symbols of his authority.[2] But the factor which made that authority effective was his personal ascendancy among the English bishops of his time. With few exceptions the men whom the Conqueror appointed to English sees were competent in affairs, blameless in conduct, and versatile enough to address themselves to the Englishmen as well as the Frenchmen of their dioceses. One of them—Osmund of Salisbury—came in time to be honoured as a saint. Gundulf of Rochester and the unfortunate Walcher of Durham were remembered for the holiness of their lives; Remigius of Lincoln and Walchelin of Winchester seem to have possessed unusual gifts for organization; Robert of Hereford was a distinguished scholar. But in breadth of learning, power, and knowledge of the world, no other bishop in England could be compared with Lanfranc. The nature of his primacy appears most clearly, not in the record of his councils, but in the surviving fragments of his correspondence with individual bishops and abbots. His letters, which are models of lapidary concision, show him advising his correspondents on details of diocesan or monastic administration, restraining them from inconsiderate action, and intervening on their behalf with the king. They prove that long before his death he had come to a knowledge of the English church, its leading ministers, and their problems, such as none of his predecessors can have surpassed. They prove no less clearly that he used his knowledge in a way which made him not only the ruler of the church, but also its protector.

But for all his eminence as an ecclesiastical statesman, it was in relation to the monastic order that Lanfranc made the sharpest impression on English religious life. The most considerable

[1] The council of 1076 transacted other important business, but the record of it is imperfect. The acts of the council begin with a statement that the case of Bishop Æthelric of Selsey has been canonically decided, and end with a decree forbidding the *supplantationes*—presumably the destruction or spoliation—of churches. But nothing more is known about the case of Æthelric beyond the fact that his deposition was confirmed, and the exact meaning of the forbidden *supplantationes ecclesiarum* is uncertain.

[2] It is known that Lanfranc held three other councils in addition to those which have been mentioned—at London in 1077 or 1078, at Gloucester in 1080 or 1081, and at Gloucester again at Christmas 1085. But their acts are unrecorded, and all that can be said about their proceedings is that Æthelnoth, abbot of Glastonbury, was deposed in the council of London, and Ulfketel, abbot of Crowland, in the Gloucester council of 1085.

of his later writings is the set of *Consuetudines* which he composed for the monks of Christ Church, Canterbury.[1] They
represent a collection of continental usages, selected for their
applicability to English conditions, and although they were not
intended to form a code of universal observance, their influence
can be traced in a number of important English houses. In the
routine which they prescribe there is nothing that clashes
abruptly with the customs set out in the *Regularis Concordia* or
would be likely to offend English monks trained in the native
discipline. The one aspect of English monasticism of which
Lanfranc is known to have disapproved was the veneration
paid to saints, mostly of English birth, whose merits seemed to
him inadequately proved. On this point the monks of his
own cathedral met him with an opposition which he only surmounted by an act of authority. The revised calendar which he
imposed on them omitted the names of many saints whose cult
had been traditional in that Church.[2] Among the earlier archbishops who had been thus honoured, Augustine and Ælfheah
alone survived his scrutiny. Even so, it is significant of respect
for English practice that the list of festivals which he authorized
was based, not on that of any continental church, but on the
calendar which had been in use at Winchester in King Edward's time.

It was a characteristic feature of Lanfranc's primacy that his
friendship with the king gave him what amounted to a general
oversight of the monastic order in England. The Conqueror
regarded the right of appointing abbots as part of his inheritance, and there are cases in which he interested himself in the
choice of an individual for a particular post.[3] But as a rule he
seems to have left the choice to Lanfranc. Some of Lanfranc's
appointments were commonplace, and one of them was disastrous. At Glastonbury, the wealthiest of English monasteries,
the misgovernment of Abbot Thurstan drove the monks into
rebellion, and, to the disgust of responsible persons from the

[1] Wilkins, *Concilia*, i, pp. 328–61. On the character of the *Consuetudines* see D.
Knowles, *The Monastic Order in England*, pp. 123–4.

[2] Lanfranc's revision of the Christ Church calendar is the central theme of
F. A. Gasquet and E. Bishop, *The Bosworth Psalter*. The main conclusions of the
book are set out on pp. 27–39.

[3] A good example is his correspondence with Abbot John of Fécamp about the
promotion of Vitalis to the abbey of Westminster; Mabillon, *Vetera Analecta*, ed. 2,
pp. 450–1.

king downwards, the abbot allowed his men-at-arms to harry the community in the monastic church itself.[1] But the Glastonbury scandal stands alone. For most of the greater English houses Lanfranc was able to find in Normandy abbots who were at once eminent in religion and competent in affairs. Gundulf of Bec, whom he appointed to the dependent see of Rochester, established the monastic order in that church, and lived in austere devotion to a religious ideal, but was so effective in business that he was used by Lanfranc as a suffragan, and by the king as supervisor of the works at his new Tower of London.[2] Such abbots as Paul of St. Albans, Serlo of Gloucester, Scotland of St. Augustine's, Canterbury, and Gilbert Crispin of Westminster, brought to those houses a conception of the monastic life which, if not more spiritual, was more widely informed and more insistent in its appeal than the tradition inherited by Englishmen from the age of the great revival. Without depreciating the intrinsic merits or the surviving force of that tradition, it is safe to say that the English monastic order as a whole received fresh vitality, and that many venerable communities were brought to a stronger life than they had ever known, through Norman abbots of Lanfranc's choice. The full results of their work were not seen in his lifetime, but their debt to his encouragement, advice, and, at dangerous moments, his protection, is beyond dispute. It was of vital importance for the future of English monasticism that in the critical years of the Norman settlement, the king's most intimate adviser should have been an archbishop whom an English chronicler could describe as 'the father and consolation of monks'.[3]

It does not appear that Lanfranc made any systematic attempt to enlarge the English monastic order by the foundation of new houses. Among the Anglo-Norman lords of the first generation there were few whose resources were equal to the endowment of a large monastery. The only great English foundations of Lanfranc's time were the king's commemorative abbey of Battle, and a priory at Lewes for which William de Warenne obtained a colony of monks from Cluny. The

---

[1] The most recent account of the case is that of D. Knowles, *The Monastic Order in England*, pp. 114–15.

[2] The main authority for Gundulf's life is the biography by a monk of Rochester printed by H. Wharton, *Anglia Sacra*, ii, pp. 273–92. The curious incident of his employment on the Tower comes from a document in the *Textus Roffensis*, ed. T. Hearne, p. 212.   [3] *Chronicle*, under 1089.

characteristic benefactions of this age are gifts of land in England
to monasteries in France. To Englishmen there can have been
nothing strange in such gifts. A number of Norman houses had
received grants of land from King Edward, and the cathedral
church of Reims had acquired land in Staffordshire from Earl
Ælfgar of Mercia.[1] The Conquest led to a large increase in the
number of these alien properties, and it seems clear that by 1086
many of them were supporting small communities of foreign
monks. But the future of alien priories was to be undistinguished, and it is unlikely that those who brought them into
being received much encouragement from Lanfranc.

In all that concerned the internal order of the church the
Conqueror seems to have left both initiative and direction in
Lanfranc's hands. But in matters of ecclesiastical politics
Lanfranc merely followed a course prescribed by the king. In
his relations with Rome he was content to act as the minister of
a sovereign who regarded the papacy with complete detachment. The Conqueror's need of papal support ended with the
deposition of Stigand and the establishment of Lanfranc's
primacy. For the claim of Gregory VII to universal dominion
William had no respect, and the whole tendency of his later
government was to emphasize his own supremacy over the
English church. According to a writer of the next generation
he insisted that no pope should be recognized and no papal
letters received in England without his command or permission;
that no legislation should be proposed without his approval in
any council of the English church; and that no bishop should
implead or excommunicate any of his barons or ministers without his leave.[2] As a further safeguard he forbade his bishops to
go to Rome, even when summoned by the pope, and thereby
caused some embarrassment to Lanfranc himself.[3] At the end
of his reign a sudden turn in the struggle between the pope and
the emperor enabled him to free the English church, for a time,
from all effective papal authority. In the situation caused by
the expulsion of Gregory VII from Rome, and the consecration
of the anti-pope Clement III, William, with Lanfranc and the

[1] D.B. i, f. 247 b. On the priory of Lapley which was supported by Ælfgar's
gifts see *Monasticon Anglicanum*, vii, pp. 1042–3.

[2] Eadmer, *Historia Novorum*, R.S., p. 9.

[3] Z. N. Brooke, *The English Church and the Papacy*, pp. 137–8. In spite of great
urgency on the part of Gregory VII, there is no satisfactory evidence that Lanfranc
ever visited Rome after his return from the journey for his pallium in 1071–2.

entire English church, observed a strict neutrality.[1] It was a situation which would have seemed incredible to Edward the Confessor, and it is a most singular illustration of the range which the Conqueror attributed to the powers inherent in the English Crown.

William's relations with the Papacy, which would not have been easy under any circumstances, were complicated by the fact that he had come to the English throne in a way which gave the pope an opportunity to claim his feudal allegiance. By submitting his case to the curia in 1066 he had accepted a position which superficially was that of a litigant maintaining his right in the court of a superior. He afterwards denied that he had made any proffer of fealty to the pope, and there is no reason to doubt that the papal decision in his favour was given honestly on the facts as they were understood at Rome. But it was inevitable that the Hildebrandine papacy, in the interest of its claim to secular dominion, should make a political use of William's application, and although it was never put forward as the pretext, it was certainly the ultimate basis of the demand for fealty which Alexander II and Gregory VII made upon him.[2] As presented by Alexander II the demand was supported by a tendentious piece of reconstructed history, which asserted that the English state had formerly been subject to the Roman see, that Peter's Pence had been its tribute, but that evil men had lately seduced it from the pope's obedience. William's reply to Pope Alexander has not been preserved, but to Gregory VII, who renewed the demand, apparently in 1080, he addressed a masterly letter defining his position. On the feudal question he refused fealty outright, saying that he had never promised it, and that none of his predecessors had entered into such a relationship with any former pope. On the question of Peter's Pence, acknowledging that its collection had been interrupted while he was in Normandy, he assured the pope that arrears should be sent to Rome as soon as possible. No statesman has ever settled a major issue in fewer words, or more conclusively.

The significance of the Norman Conquest in the history of the English Church cannot be expressed in any simple phrase. In a

[1] Ibid., pp. 144–5.
[2] On this, see Z. N. Brooke in *E.H.R.* xxvi (1911), pp. 225–38, and *The English Church and the Papacy*, pp. 140–5.

sense it was the prelude to a revolution. It opened the church at once to the full impact of foreign influences which, though present in pre-Conquest England, had been kept there within a narrow range. By 1089, when Lanfranc died, an uninterrupted sphere had been provided for the operation of the canon law through the creation of separate ecclesiastical courts. Under Lanfranc's direction copies of the leading texts on which that law was based had been transmitted to the greater English churches. Chapters on a Norman model had been established, or were on the point of establishment, in the chief cathedral minsters. By the introduction of the territorial archdeaconry the first step had been taken towards the remodelling of diocesan administration on continental lines. The church as a whole had been brought by Lanfranc into a state of constitutional unity as effective as that of any province in western Europe. In regard to all matters of external activity, the ecclesiastical changes which followed the Conquest were drastic and far-reaching.

It is much more difficult to trace the effect of the Conquest on the state of the English clergy. The enforcement of the legislation of 1076 against clerical marriage proved to be beyond the power of the ecclesiastical authorities. A century after the Conquest married clergy were still common in England, and it was by no means unusual for a benefice to pass by inheritance from father to son. The ownership of churches by laymen, and the right of the lay proprietor to a yearly payment from the clerk whom he appointed to serve his church, continued to be recognized in law. The parish priest of the twelfth century derived his living from the same sources as those which had maintained his Anglo-Saxon predecessor. His attitude towards his calling is hard to determine. As a class, the parochial clergy of Norman England were inarticulate. It can only be said that the Old English teaching on the priesthood and its duties survived the Conquest for at least a hundred years. The pastoral letters which Ælfric had written for Wulfstan of York in King Æthelred's time were still being copied in the reign of Henry II.[1]

As to the relations between the new French prelates and their English subjects, there is little contemporary evidence. It is more than probable that the relations were often strained, and that some abbots and bishops were long in coming to easy

[1] On the manuscripts of these letters see B. Fehr, *Die Hirtenbriefe Ælfrics* (Bibliothek der Angelsächsischen Prosa), pp. x–xxii.

terms with their conservative monks and clergy. Lanfranc was not the only foreign churchman who criticized the English conception of sainthood; and in matters of ritual, as in those of cult, there were peculiarities of insular custom which must have displeased men trained in continental observances. On the other hand, these grounds of division were offset by two factors which worked with especial force in the years immediately after the Conquest. One of them was the king's determination to preserve the conditions of King Edward's time, which meant that a Norman abbot or bishop needed the advice of English monks or clerks whenever the interests of his church were threatened with encroachment.[1] The other was the veneration felt in Normandy as well as England for King Edward himself. There was a living memory of him in the Conqueror's own circle. Osbern, brother of his friend Earl William of Hereford, who was made bishop of Exeter, had been a priest in the Confessor's chapel. Until he died, a pattern of antique virtue, in 1103, he continued to observe 'the customs of his lord king Edward', and to commend others who also observed them.[2] His example is a warning against attaching much importance to the generalizations of later writers about Norman contempt for English barbarism.

That Englishmen and Frenchmen could work together for a religious end is proved by the remarkable movement which revived monasticism in northern England.[3] Its leaders were a Norman knight named Reinfrid, who had felt the desolation of the north while campaigning with the king, and an English monk of Winchcombe named Ealdwine, who had learned from Bede the history of the Northumbrian saints, and wished to live in religious poverty in their land. Desiring to leave the world, Reinfrid made profession as a monk to the great Æthelwig of Evesham, who was then holding Winchcombe in charge. By Æthelwig, Reinfrid and Ealdwine were brought together, and formed, with one of his own monks, into an authorized

[1] For example, Athelhelm of Jumièges, abbot of Abingdon, used the legal knowledge of his English monks in disputes between the abbey and the king's officials. *Historia Monasterii de Abingdon*, R.S. ii, p. 2.

[2] William of Malmesbury, *Gesta Pontificum*, R.S., pp. 201–2. The bishop's attitude helps to explain the survival of the great collection of English books left to Exeter by Bishop Leofric through the dangerous period after the Conquest.

[3] On this movement and the materials for its history see D. Knowles, *The Monastic Order*, pp. 164–9.

mission to the north. Bishop Walcher gave them Bede's roofless church at Jarrow, with the wilderness around it, where they were soon joined by followers, both French and English, mostly from the south.[1] Within two years Earl Waltheof had given them the church of Tynemouth, and Bishop Walcher had resolved to transfer the whole community to his cathedral.[2] But before he had taken action the original leaders of the movement had separated for new adventures. Reinfrid went into Yorkshire, where he acquired land at Whitby near Hild's ruined house. Ealdwine went into Scotland and tried to found a religious settlement at Melrose. King Malcolm at once demanded his fealty, and he was only delivered from a dangerous situation by Bishop Walcher, who recalled him to England and re-endowed him and his companions with the ancient monastic site at Wearmouth. They remained there during the unhappy years before Walcher's murder, and it was not until 1083 that Bishop William de Saint Calais, his successor, was able to receive them at Durham. Their numbers were still small. The united communities of Jarrow and Wearmouth which took possession of the church of Durham amounted to twenty-three persons. But they had opened a new chapter in English monastic history.

To the wider questions affecting the relations of church and state there was little reaction at this time in England. The dominance of a religious king, insistent on his prerogatives, gave no opportunity for the discussion of innovations, or for public debate on the Gregorian claim to the lordship of the world. The practical demands subsidiary to that great challenge were inappropriate to English conditions. It would have been unprofitable as well as indiscreet to raise the issue of lay investiture against an autocratic ruler, who regarded the bestowal of ecclesiastical office as a matter of personal responsibility.[3]

[1] The names of the monks who came to Durham from Jarrow and Wearmouth show that, although most of them were English, the French element in those societies was by no means inconsiderable (Surtees Society, cxxxvi, p. 42). Their most distinguished member was Turgot, afterwards prior of Durham and bishop of St. Andrews.

[2] The bishop's intention is proved by the terms of Earl Waltheof's charter (Surtees Society, vol. ix (1839), pp. xviii, xix). The charter itself shows that the first stage of the movement had been completed before Waltheof's fall in 1075.

[3] In what has every appearance of an original charter, the Conqueror himself speaks of a manor which he had formerly given to Bishop Remigius of Lincoln *cum episcopali baculo. The Registrum Antiquissimum of the Cathedral Church of Lincoln*, ed. C. W. Foster, i, Plate 4.

There can be no doubt that English bishops and abbots were well aware of the conflict on this point that was beginning abroad. But they had no reason to desire its extension to England, and they contributed nothing to the literature of its earliest phases. It was not until the Conqueror's power had passed to heirs less scrupulous than himself that the realities behind the symbolism of investiture were forced upon the consciousness of English churchmen.

EPILOGUE

THE ANGLO-NORMAN STATE

By the end of the Conqueror's reign all directive power within the English state had passed from native into alien hands. In 1087, with less than half a dozen exceptions, every lay lord whose possessions entitled him to political influence was a foreigner. The English church was ruled by men of continental birth and training. No Englishman had been appointed by the Conqueror to any English see and, when he died, Wulfstan of Worcester and Giso of Wells alone survived from the episcopate of King Edward's day. Ramsey and Bath were the only abbeys of more than local importance which remained under the authority of Englishmen. The leading members of the king's household were all Frenchmen; a French clerk presided over his chancery, and French sheriffs controlled the administration of all but an insignificant number of shires. It would never be gathered from Domesday Book or from the witness-lists of King William's later charters that he had begun his reign in the hope of associating Frenchmen and Englishmen in his government on equal terms.

There was more than one reason for the disappearance of the great English landowner. In the twenty years between the coronation of King William and the completion of the Domesday Survey a considerable number of English families must have become extinct in the course of nature. Several of the Conqueror's barons are known to have married Englishwomen, who, presumably, were the heiresses of native houses. Other prominent families suffered forfeitures which compelled their younger sons to find new careers in foreign parts. Within twenty years from the battle of Hastings, Englishmen in large numbers were serving the Eastern Emperor as guardians of his palace, or in operations against the Normans of south Italy and the Turks of Asia Minor. But it is also probable that many families which escaped forfeiture and extinction fell into insignificance because no place could be found for them in the new order which was developing in England. It was essential to the stability of the government that provision should be made in England for the endowment of a powerful military force. It would have been impossible for the Conqueror to leave a large number of important Englishmen in possession of their estates without requiring them to enfeoff knights for his service. But it must have been clear to him that an English thegn was ill fitted to be the lord of men whose conception of warfare was fundamentally different from his own, and Domesday Book shows that the number of Englishmen to whom he allowed this responsibility was remarkably small. So far as can be seen, most of the prominent Englishmen who survived the wars of the Conquest were deprived of the greater part of their estates, retaining no more than was sufficient to maintain them in modest prosperity. Their fate was hard, but in the circumstances of the time it was inevitable. They were the victims of a social revolution.

A hundred years ago most writers would have been inclined to define this revolution as the introduction of the feudal system into England. It is still hard to find a better definition. Here and there in pre-Conquest England there are signs of an approach towards a form of society which can loosely be described as feudal. Many scholars have used the remarkable leases granted by St. Oswald and other Old English bishops as an indication of this tendency. If feudalism is regarded merely as a form of social order which recognized the principle of tenure in return for service, there is no reason to quarrel with this opinion. St. Oswald's tenants were bound to him by fealty, and he would undoubtedly have maintained that their tenure was conditional on the performance of the services which he expected to receive from their holdings. But to regard these leases as evidence of a social organization which might have produced a tenurial system like that of medieval England is to go beyond anything that the facts warrant. In any scheme of social relationships to which the word feudal can profitably be applied the tenant's service was specialized and defined exactly. Its amount was determined by a bargain between the tenant and his lord, in which the size of the tenancy was a secondary consideration. Pre-Conquest leasehold tenure has none of these features. The stipulated services are many and various, and their amount was decided, at least in part, by the size of the tenant's holding. It is perhaps more important that these leases contain no demand for services of a military character. The riding-service which some of them required was not the duty of going on military expeditions, but service to a lord as his escort or messenger. It can safely be assumed that the king would expect the tenants of a bishop, or of any other magnate, to serve in the levies of their shires, mounted and equipped in a way appropriate to their several degrees. But it is no less clear that their liability to military service was a personal obligation, independent of any contract with the lord of whom they held their lands. They were not in any sense the predecessors of medieval knights, and the men who were holding land on similar conditions in the Norman age could never be fitted into any accepted category of feudal tenure.

In contrast to these various and indeterminate conditions the services which governed post-Conquest tenures were limited in range and definite in amount. It is true that after the Conquest, as before, it was possible for an individual to owe more than one form of service for the same piece of land. Of Ditton in Surrey, held by Wadard of Bishop Odo, Domesday Book says 'He who holds it of Wadard renders him 50 shillings and the service of one knight'. But such cases were exceptional, and the services which they comprised were always defined with precision. It is of more significance that immediately after the Conquest military tenure of a kind which was not even foreshadowed in the Confessor's time becomes of universal and paramount importance. It is now half a century since Round made what was then the daring claim that, in England, tenure by knight-service was a Norman innovation. After a generation of research Round's theory has been confirmed at every point. What remains to be done is to demonstrate, by work on individual fees, the extent to which tenures of this new model had been created by the Conqueror's companions. That the process was gradual is certain. But it is already clear that the system of military tenures revealed by the feodaries of the Angevin age had been laid down in outline before the Domesday Inquest was taken.

The partition of England among a foreign aristocracy organized for war was the chief immediate result of the Norman Conquest. After all allowance for the sporadic survival of English landowners and the creation of new holdings for the household servants of great men, the fact remains that an overwhelming majority of the manors described in Domesday Book were held by some form of military tenure. The provision of knights for the king in adequate numbers was the first charge upon the baronage of the Norman settlement. The arrangements devised for this purpose gave to the upper ranges of Anglo-Norman society a stability and cohesion unknown in the pre-Conquest state. They substituted for the fluctuating relationships which had connected lords and their men in Old English times a system which held the higher social classes permanently together in a definite responsibility for military assistance to the king. There was no place in Norman England for the man of position who claimed the right to 'go with his land to whatever lord he would'.

It was the outstanding merit of this aristocracy that it set itself to use the institutions which it found in England. The chief administrative divisions of the country—shires, hundreds, and wapentakes—were accepted as a matter of course by its new lords. They for their part applied Old English methods to the management of their estates, and they were remarkably tolerant of the varied and often inconvenient types of manorial structure which had come down from King Edward's time. The institutions which they found it necessary to create were few in number and specialized in purpose. The honorial court, which was the chief of them, came into being for the settlement of the internal business of a great fief. The castlery, which never became of the first importance in English life, was a tract of country organized by a series of planned enfeoffments for the maintenance of a particular fortress. Neither of these innovations interfered at any essential point with the accustomed course of local government. The framework of the Old English state survived the Conquest.

The innovation which touched the common man most nearly was the formidable body of rules and penalties which the Norman kings imposed on the inhabitants of the districts reserved for their hunting. The French origin of the Anglo-Norman forest law has now been placed beyond dispute, and the Conqueror's severity towards those who broke the peace of his deer is recorded by one who had known him.[1] That he enlarged the borders of King Edward's forests is certain, and there is no need to doubt the early tradition that the New Forest was converted

[1] *Chronicle*, under 1087.

into a royal preserve by his orders, to the destruction of many peasants who were struggling for existence in that unfriendly land. Nevertheless even within the forest sphere there was no absolute break with the past. The idea of a royal forest, jealously preserved, had been familiar to Englishmen for forty years at least before the Conquest. Cnut had laid a heavy fine on anyone who hunted in a district which he had set apart for his own pleasure.[1] Forest wardens had been maintained by Edward the Confessor. It is more important that the new forest legislation, which was intended for the protection of the king's deer, never interrupted the operation of the common law. The forest courts brought the peasant within their jurisdiction under a new surveillance in the interests of the king's sport, but left him in all other matters to the familiar justice of shire and hundred.

In these ancient institutions the Anglo-Saxon tradition was never broken. The virtue of the Old English state had lain in the local courts. Their strength had been due to the association of thegns and peasants in the work of justice, administration, and finance, under the direction of officers responsible to the king. The memory of this association survived all the changes of the Conqueror's reign. To all appearance, his barons and their men accepted as a consequence of their position the share in local business which had fallen to their English predecessors. As early as 1086 the feoffees of Norman lords can be seen on the hundredal juries which swore to the information collected for the Domesday Survey. Their successors carried the aristocratic element in local government down to the heart of the middle ages, and beyond. There is a genuine continuity of function between the thegns of the shire to whom the Confessor addressed his writs and the knights of the shire whose co-operation made possible the Angevin experiment in centralization.

In some, and perhaps in many, cases there was also continuity of descent. The number of thirteenth-century landed families which can be traced backwards to an ancestor bearing an English or a Danish name is by no means inconsiderable. It includes some families of baronial rank, such as Berkeley, Cromwell, Neville, Lumley, Greystoke, Audley, Fitzwilliam of Hinderskelfe and Fitzwilliam of Sprotborough,[2] and many others of less prominence which were influential in their own

---

[1] Laws of Cnut, ii. 80, 1.

[2] For the descents, see *Complete Peerage* under these titles.

districts. Isolated families of position with such an ancestry can be found in most parts of England, but they were especially numerous in the far north, where they were indistinguishable from the English aristocracy of southern Scotland, in Yorkshire and Lancashire, and in the northern midlands. A few families of this type are known to have been descended from English landowners of 1086, and a small minority of these families are carried back by Domesday Book to the time of King Edward. But there are many which cannot be traced beyond the first half of the twelfth century, and of which the origin must be left an open question. Their distribution suggests that some at least of them were founded by Englishmen who had been planted by the king or by some Norman lord on lands devastated in the wars of the Conquest. It may be hoped that more descents of this kind will be worked out in the future, for every established case helps to reduce the abruptness of the transition from the English to the Norman order.

In the law and practice of the local courts few changes of the first importance had been made by the end of the Conqueror's reign. The most far-reaching was the withdrawal of ecclesiastical pleas from the jurisdiction of the hundred. Of the king's other innovations the chief was the institution of a device for the protection of the Frenchmen who had come to England since 1066. It was ordered that if any of them were killed, and his lord failed to arrest his slayer within five days, the lord must pay 46 marks to the king, the hundred in which the murder took place being responsible for any portion of this sum which the lord was unable to produce.[1] The regulation probably belongs to an early part of the Conqueror's reign, when most of the Frenchmen in England were attached to the households of knights or barons, and it gives no more than a point of departure for the mass of custom which rapidly developed round the murder fine and presentment of Englishry. For the orderly settlement of disputes between Frenchmen and Englishmen the Conqueror provided that if a Frenchman accused an Englishman of perjury, or of one of the commoner sorts of violent crime, the Englishman might choose for his defence either the native ordeal of iron or the foreign method of the judicial combat.[1] Here the advantage was clearly with the English defendant. For the rest, there is little in the remains

[1] Liebermann, *Gesetze*, i, p. 487.   [2] Ibid.

of William's legislation which might not have been prescribed by an Anglo-Saxon king; and the only enactment[1]
which reads like a deliberate modification of English practice is
an order that offences formerly punished by death should in
future be punished by mutilation. In most of its details the law
observed by Englishmen in 1087 was the law of King Edward,
and, for that matter, the law of Cnut and Æthelred II.

But in spite of these and many other points of continuity,
the fact remains that sooner or later every aspect of English life
was changed by the Norman Conquest. The conclusions which
different historians have reached about its significance have
naturally varied with their personal interests and with the line
of approach which each of them has chosen. By some, impressed
with the Old English achievement in art and letters, the Conquest has been lamented as the destruction of a civilization.
Others have regarded it as a clearance of the ground for a
cosmopolitan culture of which Anglo-Saxon England gave no
promise. Some have stressed the survival of English institutions
and ideas; others, the novelty of the social order to which the
Norman settlement gave rise. There will never be unanimity
on the degree to which, in the historian's balance, the efficiency
of the Norman government should outweigh the havoc done by
the Conqueror's armies. On all the problems connected with
the Conquest opinion is continually changing as the attention
of students shifts from one type of evidence to another, as fresh
materials come to light, and as old theories are tested by a new
grouping of familiar facts.

For all this, it can at least be said that to the ordinary
Englishman who had lived from the accession of King Edward
to the death of King William, the Conquest must have seemed
an unqualified disaster. It is probable that, as a class, the
peasants had suffered less than those above them. Many individuals must have lost life or livelihood at the hands of Norman
raiders, and many estates may have been harshly exploited in
the interest of Norman lords anxious for ready money; but the
structure of rural society was not seriously affected by the
Norman settlement. To the thegnly class the Conquest brought
not only the material consequences of an unsuccessful war, but
also loss of privilege and social consideration. The thegn of
1066 who made his peace with the Conqueror lived thence-

[1] Liebermann, *Gesetze*, i, p. 488.

forward in a strange and unfriendly environment. The political system of his youth had been destroyed, he had become the subject of a foreign king, and he must have felt at every turn the dominance of a foreign aristocracy which regarded him and his kind, at best, with tolerant indifference. It was as the depressed survivor of a beaten race that he handed on the Old English tradition of local government to the men who had overthrown the Old English state.

To such a man there can have been little satisfaction in the strength of the Anglo-Norman monarchy or the scale of its executive achievement. But it is hard to believe that he can have been wholly unconscious of the new spirit which had entered into the direction of English affairs at the Conquest. The gallantry of individuals in the crisis of 1066—of Edwin and Morcar at Fulford, of Harold at Stamfordbridge and Hastings—tends to conceal the troubled insecurity of the preceding years. Throughout the reign of King Edward England had been a threatened state, relying for existence on a military system which recent events had shown to be insufficient for its needs. The initiative had always been with its enemies, it had never found an effectual ally, and before King Edward's death it had ceased to count as a factor in European politics. The Normans who entered into the English inheritance were a harsh and violent race. They were the closest of all western peoples to the barbarian strain in the continental order. They had produced little in art or learning, and nothing in literature, that could be set beside the work of Englishmen. But politically, they were the masters of their world.

BIBLIOGRAPHY

I. ORIGINAL SOURCES

I. ANNALS

THE fundamental authority for Old English history is the
series of annalistic compilations known collectively as the
Anglo-Saxon Chronicle. Seven of these compilations have survived in manuscript, more or less completely, to the present
day. In each manuscript the annals begin with an outline of
history from the invasion of Britain by Julius Caesar to the
middle of the fifth century. In this introduction, and in the
chronicle which follows down to the year 891, all these manuscripts are ultimately derived from a set of annals written in
English in King Alfred's reign. Soon afterwards the manuscripts
begin to diverge from one another, presumably because they
represent continuations of this chronicle made in a number of
different churches. Down to the year 915 a large amount of
material is common to most of these manuscripts, but the
question of their mutual relations had already become a serious
critical problem, and it increases in complexity as the annals
are followed downwards towards the Norman Conquest. The
most elaborate attempt at its solution is the Introduction by
C. Plummer to the second volume of *Two of the Saxon Chronicles
Parallel* (Oxford: vol. i, 1892; vol. ii, 1899; reprinted 1952,
with an appendix 'On the Commencement of the Year in the
Saxon Chronicles' and a Bibliographical Note by D. Whitelock).
Vol. i of this edition contains the texts of the chronicles generally
known as 'A' and 'E' (for these symbols see below), supplemented by the passages of most importance in other versions.
Nearly all the information which they supply is incorporated
into this edition. But it is hard to estimate its value when, as
here, it is broken up and dispersed, so that for the critical study
of the *Chronicle* and the appreciation of its several versions it is
necessary to use the six-text edition by B. Thorpe (*The Anglo-
Saxon Chronicle*: R.S. 1861, vol. i, Texts, vol. ii, Translation).
The translation is unsatisfactory, and there are omissions from
the texts and infelicities of arrangement which make a new
edition desirable. [G. N. Garmonsway has made a new trans-

lation for Everyman's Library, ed. 2, 1960. *The Anglo-Saxon Chronicle: a Revised Translation*, ed. D. Whitelock with D. C. Douglas and S. I. Tucker (London, 1961) is arranged to make it easy to distinguish the main version from parts peculiar to individual manuscripts or groups of manuscripts and contains the most recent discussion of problems of transmission, and a full bibliography.]

For convenience of reference the manuscripts of the *Chronicle* are generally distinguished from one another by letters of the alphabet. MS. A (Corpus Christi College, Cambridge, MS. 173) contains a series of annals which are substantially consecutive to the year 924, and are continued, though with many gaps, to the year 1070. The portion which ends in 1001 was written at Winchester. The remainder was written at Christ Church, Canterbury, and the manuscript ends with a Latin record of Lanfranc's primacy which is the chief authority for his official acts. The peculiar value of this manuscript lies in the early date at which the first part of it was written. From the beginning to 891 the script may be dated *circa* 900. Thenceforward to 924 the manuscript is in various hands of approximately the latter date, and the section which ends in 955 is unlikely to be later than King Eadred's death in that year. The important Alfredian section has been separately edited, with full notes, by A. H. Smith (*The Parker Chronicle*, London, 1935). The whole manuscript has been published in facsimile by the Early English Text Society (*The Parker Chronicle and Laws*, London, 1941). A copy of this or a closely related manuscript, made *circa* 1025 (Cotton, Otho B XI), formed the basis of the first edition of the *Chronicle*, by Abraham Whelock (*Venerabilis Bedae Historia Ecclesiastica*: Cambridge, 1644, pp. 492–562). From its editor's initial it is generally known as MS. W. It was almost completely destroyed by fire in 1731. [A transcript by Lawrence Nowell is now in the British Museum Additional MS. 43703, on which see R. Flower, *Proceedings of the British Academy*, Vol. xxi (1935) pp. 47–73.]

MS. B (Cott. Tiberius A VI), in one hand of *circa* 1000, ends in 977. MS. C (Cott. Tib. B I), in various mid-eleventh-century hands, ends in 1066. Down to 977, MSS. B and C are independent copies of a chronicle, now lost, written, to all appearance, at Abingdon, where it was certainly continued by the scribes who wrote the latter part of MS. C. The early part of

this continuation is the chief authority for the reign of Æthelred
II. It has been well edited by M. Ashdown in *English and Norse
Documents relating to the reign of Ethelred the Unready* (Cambridge,
1930). [MS. C is also edited by H. A. Rositzke, *Beiträge z. engl.
Phil.* xxxiv, Bochum-Langendreer, 1940.] The history of MS.
D (Cott. Tib. B IV) is more complicated. It also is in various
hands, of which the oldest can hardly be earlier than 1050,
while the latest may be of the early twelfth century. The
emphasis, peculiar to this manuscript, which is laid on the
English descent of Queen Margaret of Scotland suggests that
its final form may have been destined for the Scottish court.
The consecutive run of annals ends in 1079, but a late addition
records the defeat of Angus, earl of Moray, in 1130, and
strengthens the possibility of a Scottish destination for the
manuscript. The provenance of the version from which it is
derived has been much discussed, but is still uncertain. It has
generally been attributed to either Worcester or Evesham,
mainly because of the points of resemblance between this text
and the twelfth-century chronicle attributed to Florence of
Worcester. But the indications of such an origin are by no
means convincing. The most prominent figure in the later part
of the *Chronicle* is Archbishop Ealdred of York, and it is at least
possible that this section was originally composed by a member
of his circle. The version is especially important for the period
after 1042. It gives an intelligent account of Anglo-Scandinavian
relations under Edward the Confessor, and an invaluable
English narrative of the Norman invasion and the events which
followed it. The manuscript has been edited separately by E.
Classen and F. E. Harmer (*An Anglo-Saxon Chronicle*, Manchester,
1926).

MS. E (Bodleian Library, Oxford, Laud MS. 636) is written
in one hand as far as the year 1121, and continued in various
hands to 1154, where it ends. It was written in Peterborough
abbey, and contains much local matter of interest to that house.
It is founded on a chronicle which in its earlier portion has a
close affinity with the text behind MS. D. But from 1023 to
1066 MS. E is clearly based on a chronicle written at St.
Augustine's, Canterbury, and it is probable that this text
covered the whole period from 1023 to 1121. MS. E is particularly valuable for the reigns of the Norman kings, and its
description of the Conqueror's personality and achievement is

of unique importance. [The manuscript has been published in facsimile by D. Whitelock, *The Peterborough Chronicle* (Early English Manuscripts in Facsimile IV, Copenhagen, 1954) and the latest portion has been excellently edited by Cecily Clark, *The Peterborough Chronicle, 1070–1154*, O.U.P., 1958.]

MS. F (Cott. Domitian A VIII) is a bilingual text in Latin and English, written at St. Augustine's, Canterbury, *circa* 1100. It extends to 1058, and is founded on a chronicle closely resembling that which forms the basis of MS. E. For historical purposes it is the least important of the series, but it is an interesting link between the vernacular chronicles of the Old English period and the Latin chronicles of the later Norman age. [The manuscript has been edited by F. P. Magoun, Jr. in *Mediaeval Studies of the Pontifical Institute of Mediaeval Studies*, vol. ix (1947), pp. 235–95; see also his articles 'The Domitian Bilingual of the *Old English Annals*: The Latin Preface', *Speculum*, vol. xx (1949), and 'Notes on the *F*-text', *Modern Language Quarterly*. vol. vi (1945).]

Three Latin versions of the *Chronicle* are of special importance for its history. The annals between 851 and 887 were translated into Latin by Asser in his biography of King Alfred. An early version of the annals to the end of 892 was translated by the ealdorman Æthelweard (above, p. 461) soon after 975 (ed. H. Savile, *Rerum Anglicarum Scriptores post Bedam*, London, 1596; ed. H. Petrie, *Monumenta Historica Britannica*, 1848). The copy which Æthelweard followed was at some points nearer to the original than any extant text, and no definitive account of the *Chronicle* will be possible until Æthelweard's work has been edited in a form which can be compared sentence by sentence with the Old English versions. From 893 to 975 Æthelweard's chronicle, though meagre, is an independent authority. The surviving fragments of the unique manuscript, burned in 1731, are in a hand little, if at all, later than 1000. [This chronicle is now available in an adequate edition, with translation, *The Chronicle of Æthelweard*, ed. A. Campbell (Nelson's Medieval Texts), London, 1962.] The third of these early translations is of uncertain authorship, but is generally attributed to a monk of Worcester named Florence, who died in 1118 (*Florentii Wigorniensis Monachi Chronicon ex Chronicis*, ed. B. Thorpe, London, vol. i, 1848; vol. ii, 1849). Whoever he may have been, the author of this work derived his information from many different sources, among them a version of the *Chronicle* resembling, but distinct from, MS. D. He preserves what seems to be a genuine west-midland tradition of events in the eleventh century which he may well have derived from English land-owners in the country round Worcester. The miscellaneous character of his materials, which increases the positive value of his work, makes it difficult to reconstruct the version of the *Chronicle* which he followed. A new edition of this important text is badly needed.

The most important problems in the history of the *Chronicle* relate to its Alfredian section. The chief of them concern the materials on which its author drew. Bede supplied a chrono-logical framework for the history of the conversion, which was a primary interest of the compiler. Beyond this the nature of his sources can only be conjectured, and no account of them can claim, in any sense, finality. The remarkable fullness of the annals between 670 and 750 suggests that he used a chronicle composed, probably in Latin, within that period (H. M. Chad-wick, *Origin of the English Nation*, p. 26). It may well be that the annals referring to the conquest of Kent, Sussex, and Wessex came to him from this source. Between 750 and 800 his own record is so meagre that it is doubtful whether any written materials can have lain before him. Between 800 and approxi-mately 839 it is probable that he was following a second set of contemporary annals. Between 840 and 865 the entries in the *Chronicle* are inconsecutive, and some of them must have been written appreciably later than the events which they relate. It is probable that they are the work of the man who wrote the subsequent 'Alfredian' section from 865 to 891.

Many scholars have identified this author with King Alfred himself. The only definite evidence for the identification is the frequent resemblance between the wording of the *Chronicle* and that of Alfred's translation of Orosius. This resemblance, natural enough between two works of an annalistic character, is offset by the statement under 853 that Pope Leo consecrated Alfred king when he first came to Rome as a child, It is in-credible that Alfred himself should have confused decoration, or even the rite of confirmation, at the pope's hands, with an anointing to kingship. Moreover, when compared with the great Frankish annals of the ninth century, which seem to descend from an official record, the *Chronicle* has definitely the character of private work. The focus of its interest lies in the south-western shires, and it was most probably composed in that country. That in its present form it reflects the example of Alfred's English writings need not be doubted, and it is probable that the dispatch of copies to different centres of study, soon after 892, was an imitation of the practice which the king is known to have adopted for the circulation of his own works.

The literature bearing on this problem is extensive. An impression of its complexity may be gathered from C. Plummer, *Two Saxon Chronicles*, ii, pp. civ–cxii, and R. H. Hodgkin, *History of the Anglo-Saxons*, ii. 624–7, 706–8 (both definitely for Alfredian authorship), F. M. Stenton in *Essays presented to T. F. Tout*, pp. 15–24 (suggests local origin in the south-west)[1], and R. W. Chambers, *England before the Norman Conquest*, pp. xii–xx (a singularly clear account which suspends judgement) [see also introduction by D. Whitelock to *The Anglo-Saxon Chronicle: a Revised Translation* (cited above p. 689].

Meanwhile a second line of annalistic tradition was being developed in the north. Its starting-point was the chronological summary with which Bede ended the *Historia Ecclesiastica*. This development produced two valuable eighth-century chronicles—the so-called *Continuatio Bedae* which ends in 766 (*Bedae Opera Historica*, ed. C. Plummer, i. 361–3) and a more important set of annals, consecutive to 802, which can be read most conveniently in the *Historia Regum* of Simeon of Durham (*Symeonis Monachi Opera*, ed. T. Arnold, R.S. ii. 38–66). For most of the ninth century northern historiography shrinks to a few disconnected annals mostly recording the succession of kings (above, pp. 243–4). In the tenth century there are traces of at least two sets of northern annals. One of them (*Symeonis . . . Opera*, ii. 92–4) was composed in St. Cuthbert's church at Chester-le-Street. The other, which apparently comes from York, is only known through entries amalgamated with other matter by the thirteenth-century chronicler, Roger of Wendover (*Flores Historiarum*, ed. H. O. Coxe, vol. i, London, 1841). [These have been conveniently extracted and translated by D. Whitelock, *English Historical Documents* c. 500–1042, pp. 255–8.] From texts related to these a considerable amount of northern detail for this century was incorporated into MSS. D and E of the *Chronicle*. The Cuthbertine annals appear to have ended in

[1] [An opinion to which he adhered to the end.]

the reign of Eadred. The York annals cannot be traced beyond the death of Edgar.

2. HISTORY AND BIOGRAPHY

Among the materials which may be brought together under this head the *De Excidio Britanniae* of Gildas and the *Historia Brittonum* of Nennius were edited by Mommsen in the *Monumenta Germaniae Historica, Auctores Antiquissimi*, xiii, Part I, 1894. The exact date at which Gildas wrote is uncertain, but there is no doubt that the *De Excidio* is a genuine work of the first half of the sixth century. At present there is no general agreement about the authority of the different parts of the work which passes under the name of Nennius (for references see vol. i of this *History*, and add the article by F. Liebermann in *Essays presented to T. F. Tout*, pp. 25–44). Much that has been written about Nennius is hypercritical, but it is clear that no section of his work should be used without extreme caution and many reservations. For Anglo-Saxon history in the strict sense the most important feature of the work is a series of notes, mainly on Northumbrian history, which Nennius or another has added to a set of English royal genealogies. There are obvious mistakes in the notes, but they seem to represent an authentic tradition.

The fundamental *Historia Ecclesiastica* of Bede was edited with copious annotation by C. Plummer (*Venerabilis Bedae Opera Historica*, 2 vols., Oxford, 1896). The chief point on which the notes need revision is the dating of events falling, in any year, between 1 September and 25 December (on which see R. L. Poole, *Studies in Chronology and History*, Oxford, 1934). [The two oldest manuscripts of the work have been published in facsimile in Early English Manuscripts in Facsimile; II *The Leningrad Bede*, ed. O. Arngart, 1952 and IX *The Moore Bede*, ed. P. Hunter Blair, 1959. There is a new edition, *Bede's Ecclesiastical History of the English People*, ed. B. Colgrave and R. A. B. Mynors (Oxford Medieval Texts), 1970.] Plummer's edition also includes Bede's Epistle to Archbishop Egbert, his lives of the abbots of Wearmouth and Jarrow, and the anonymous biography of Abbot Ceolfrith. Of Bede's two biographies of St. Cuthbert, that in prose has been edited by B. Colgrave (*Two Lives of St. Cuthbert*, Cambridge, 1940), and that in verse by W. Jaager (*Bedas metrische Vita sancti Cuthberti*, Leipzig,

1935). For Bede's scientific writings it is still necessary to refer to unsatisfactory editions such as that of J. A. Giles (*Venerabilis Bedae Opera*, vol. vi, London, 1843), but the list has been freed from much spurious matter by C. W. Jones (*Bedae Pseudepigrapha*, New York and London, 1939) [The same author has published *Bedae Opera de Temporibus*, Mediaeval Academy of America, 1943]. For the study of Bede's commentaries, which are essential to any estimate of his thought and learning, there is now a foundation in the edition of the *Commentary and Retractations on Acts* by M. L. W. Laistner (Medieval Academy of America, Cambridge, Mass. 1939). [The monks of St. Peter's in Steenbrugge are bringing out the works of Bede in *Corpus Christianorum: Series Latina* (Turnhout, Belgium). The following volumes, ed. D. Hurst, O.S.B. have appeared: cxix (1962) *In primam partem Samuelis Libri iiii*, and *In Regum Librum xxx Quaestiones*; cxx (1960), *In Lucae Evangelium Expositio* and *In Marci Evangelium Expositio*; cxxi (1955), [*Opera Homiletica* and *Opera Rythmica*].

The shorter historical writings of the age of Bede have all been published in reliable texts. The anonymous life of St. Cuthbert has been edited by B. Colgrave (*Two Lives of St. Cuthbert*, Cambridge, 1940), The Life of Gregory the Great by an anonymous monk of Whitby, ed. B. Colgrave, University of Kansas Press, 1968, and Eddi's life of Wilfrid, by W. Levison (*Mon. Germ. Hist., Scriptores Rerum Merovingicarum*, vi, 1913). There is another good edition of the latter work by B. Colgrave (Cambridge, 1927). The biographical record of the northern church is carried down to a later time by two long contemporary poems, the *Carmen de Sanctis Eboracensis Ecclesiae* by Alcuin (ed. W. Wattenbach, *Monumenta Alcuiniana*, 1873; ed. E. Dümmler, *Mon. Germ. Hist., Poetae Latini*, i, 1881), and the history of an unidentified monastery by a certain Æthelwulf (ed. T. Arnold, in *Symeonis Monachi Opera*, R.S. i; ed. Dümmler, *Poetae Latini*, i). [This poem has been edited with translation and full apparatus by A. Campbell, *Æthelwulf, De Abbatibus*, Oxford, 1967.] The life of St. Guthlac by Felix, valuable as an example of early Mercian hagiography, is available in a sound text, ed. W. de G. Birch (*Memorials of St. Guthlac*, Wisbech, 1881). [It has also been edited with translation and notes by B. Colgrave, *Felix's Life of Saint Guthlac*, Cambridge, 1956.] Among the leaders of the English mission to Germany, Willibrord, Boniface, Willibald, and Willehad were each the subject of an early biography (*Vita Sancti Willibrordi*, ed. Wattenbach, *Monumenta Alcuiniana*; ed. W. Levison, *Mon, Germ. Hist., Scriptores Rerum Merovingicarum*, vii, 1920; *Vita Sancti Bonifatii*, ed. P. Jaffé, *Monumenta Moguntina*, 1866; ed. W. Levison, *Mon. Germ. Hist. Scriptores in usum Scholarum*, 1920; *Hodoeporicon Sancti Willibaldi*, ed. O. Holder-Egger, *Mon. Germ. Hist., Scriptores*, xv, 1887; *Vita Sancti Willehadi*, ed. Pertz, *Mon. Germ. Hist., Scriptores*, ii, 1829). Each of these lives is primarily concerned with its hero's work abroad, but the series throws much incidental light on English history.

In the second half of the period there is no dominant history such as that of Bede, and biographical materials become, relatively, more important than before. Asser's *Life of King Alfred* (ed. W. H. Stevenson, Oxford, 1904) [a new impression with an article by Professor D. Whitelock on recent work on Asser appeared in 1959. She has recently delivered the first Stenton lecture at Reading University on 'The Genuine Asser' demonstrating that there is no foundation for recent suggestions that Asser is a forgery. The lecture was delivered in 1967 and published in 1968 by Reading University.] Asser gives a unique picture of an Old English king in his relations with his court and household. Stevenson's notes are invaluable for the study of contemporary events and institutions. The *Gesta Regum* of William of Malmesbury (ed. W. Stubbs, R.S., 1887-9, i. 144-52) contains two quotations and an abstract derived from a tenth-century panegyric of Athelstan which is otherwise unknown. Between 995 and 1005 lives were written of Dunstan, Æthelwold, and Oswald, each of which illustrates the general history of their age. That of Dunstan, by the priest 'B', was edited, with later lives and illustrative correspondence, by W. Stubbs (*Memorials of St. Dunstan*, R.S., 1874). The life of Æthelwold, by Ælfric, was published as an appendix to the *Chronicon Monasterii de Abingdon* (ed. J. Stevenson, R.S., 1858, ii. 255-66.) An expansion of this work by a monk of Winchester named Wulfstan is printed in *Patrologia Latina*, cxxxvii. 84 et seqq. The life of Oswald was edited by J. Raine in *Historians of the Church of York* (R.S., 1879-94, i. 399-475). The life of Wulfstan of Worcester by William of Malmesbury (*Vita Wulfstani*, ed. R. R. Darlington, R. Hist. Soc., 1928) is essentially a Latin version of an English biography by Coleman, Wulfstan's chaplain, and is therefore a primary authority for its period. A unique fragment of autobiography by Bishop Giso of Wells is printed in *Ecclesiastical Documents* (ed. J. Hunter, Camden Society, 1840).

There are early biographical materials for three of the eleventh-century rulers of England. The so-called *Encomium Emmae* (ed. G. H. Pertz, *Mon. Germ. Hist.*, *Scriptores*, xix, 1886, pp. 509–25) is in effect a panegyric of Cnut [; a new ed., with translation has been produced by A. Campbell in the Camden Society third series, lxxii, 1949]. It is almost contemporary, but completely unreliable on points of fact. The *Vita Æduuardi Regis* (ed. H. R. Luard, *Lives of Edward the Confessor*, R.S., 1858, pp. 387–435), formerly dated between 1066 and 1075, has been referred to the early part of the twelfth century by M. Bloch (*Analecta Bollandiana*, xli, 1923). This dating has been effectively challenged by R. W. Southern (*E.H.R.* lviii (1943), pp. 385–400), but the *Vita* contains too many demonstrable mis-statements to serve as an authority for the Confessor's reign. [It can now be used in a new edition with translation ed. Frank Barlow (Nelson's Medieval Texts, 1962) who supports the traditional view that the author was contemporary. His suggested date is 1065–7, although the obvious errors seem to suggest a wider period. Professor Darlington prefers 1066–75, *E.H.R.* lxxix (1964), p. 147.] The early and middle life of William the Conqueror is described in the *Gesta Willelmi ducis Normannorum et regis Anglorum* of William of Poitiers (ed. J. A. Giles, *Scriptores rerum gestarum Willelmi Conquestoris*, London, 1845). [Guillaume de Poitiers, *Histoire de Guillaume le Conquérant*, ed. Raymonde Foreville (Les Classiques de l'Histoire de France au Moyen Age), Paris, 1952.] This book, which was written in or soon after 1071, has generally been undervalued. The author's unreserved admiration for his hero colours the whole of his work, but does not seriously affect his record of facts, about which his information was sound. On the battle of Hastings he can be supplemented by the *Carmen de Bello Hastingensi* of Guy of Amiens (ed. Giles, as above), and on the Conqueror's early life by the *Gesta Normannorum Ducum* of William of Jumièges (ed. J. Marx, Société de l'histoire de Normandie, 1914).

For the personal relations between William and Harold and for the whole campaign of Hastings the Bayeux Tapestry is a primary authority. Its detail can conveniently be studied in the series of photographs published by F. R. Fowke in *The Bayeux*

Tapestry (London, 1898). The scale of the plates is small, but the reproduction is admirably clear. [*The Bayeux Tapestry*, ed. F. M. Stenton, Phaidon Press, 1957, is a comprehensive survey by leading modern authorities on various aspects of the work.] The date of the work has given rise to much discussion, but no external evidence has been brought forward to affect the conclusions suggested by the simplicity of the military equipment which is represented, and by the prominence given to Bishop Odo of Bayeux and certain knights who are known to have been associated with him. On the essential point that the tapestry was made, probably by command of Bishop Odo, at a time when the war of the Conquest was well remembered, Round, writing in 1915 (*E.H.R.* xxx. 109–11), was in complete agreement with Freeman, writing in 1869 (*Norman Conquest*, iii. 570–5). [Professor Wormald examined all possible comparative material for his article in *The Bayeux Tapestry*, *supra*, and concludes that it is most probable that the work was made to the order of Bishop Odo and begun very soon after the events it celebrates, probably by an English artist at Canterbury.]

No other memorial of the kind has survived from this period, but in a poem addressed by Baudri, abbot of Bourgueil, to Adela, King William's daughter, there is a description of a tapestry representing the course of events between the Norman council which decided on the invasion of England and the capture of a town immediately after the battle of Hastings. The poem has been edited with excellent notes by P. Abrahams, *Les Œuvres Poétiques de Baudri de Bourgueil*, Paris, 1926. Baudri's verses do not seem to have been intended, and should not be taken, for a precise description of a real piece of stitchwork, but they show that such representations of history were possible at the date when he was writing—that is, between 1099 and 1102. There is no reason to think that Baudri had seen the Bayeux Tapestry itself. His account of the battle of Hastings reflects the language of William of Poitiers, but he was not exclusively dependent on William's narrative. The early date of the poem gives importance to a definite statement that Harold was killed by an arrow. But, on the whole, Baudri adds remarkably little to the information supplied by contemporary writers.

Of the Anglo-Norman historians who wrote in the twelfth century the most important for the period covered by this book is Ordericus Vitalis (*Historia Ecclesiastica*, ed. A. le Prevost,

Paris, 1838–55). He preserved, in substance, the lost conclusion of the work of William of Poitiers, and is the main authority for the Conqueror's later wars. He gives much information about a number of leading Norman families, especially those connected with the monastery of St. Évroult, where his life was spent. But he was inaccurate in matters of rank and genealogy, he was inclined to give a dramatic colouring to events, and his book is ill arranged. William of Malmesbury, the finest scholar of the group, contributes less than could be wished to the history of periods earlier than his own. His two chief works, the *Gesta Regum* (ed. W. Stubbs, R.S., 1887–9) and the *Gesta Pontificum* (ed. N. E. S. A. Hamilton, R.S., 1870), each composed *circa* 1125, supply a number of isolated facts, a few documents, and many stories, mostly of a legendary or romantic kind. He was an assiduous collector of materials, but the only major work, now lost, which he possessed seems to have been the panegyric on Athelstan noted above. The other general histories of the period are chiefly interesting for the study of the *Chronicle*, on which most of them are founded. For this purpose, and for occasional pieces of concrete information, the most important are the *Historia Anglorum* of Henry of Huntingdon (ed. T. Arnold, R.S., 1879) and Geoffrey Gaimar's *L'Estoire des Engles* (ed. T. D. Hardy and C. T. Martin, R.S., 1888–9).

Chronicles written from a local standpoint are in some ways more valuable as sources of fact. Most religious houses preserved traditions of their history, and in some of them the traditions were written down within a century of the Conquest. The *Chronicon Monasterii de Abingdon*, for example (ed. J. Stevenson, R.S., 1858) contains an account of local events in the Norman age, written by a monk who entered the house before 1117 (F. M. Stenton, *Early History of the Abbey of Abingdon*, Reading, 1913). The great monasteries of eastern England produced much matter of this kind, which often shades off indistinguishably into general history. It is the subject of a detailed analysis by F. Liebermann (*Ueber ostenglische Geschichtsquellen*, Hannover, 1892). [See also *The Chronicle of Hugh Candidus a monk of Peterborough*, ed. W. T. Mellowes, Oxford, 1949.] But the most important of all these local compilations are the memoranda and narratives which come from the church of Durham. The *Historia de Sancto Cuthberto*, of *circa* 1050 (ed. T. Arnold, *Symeonis Monachi Opera Omnia*, R.S., 1882–5, i.

196–214), the early post-Conquest chronicle reconstructed by
H. H. E. Craster in *E.H.R.* xl. 504–32, and the *Historia Dunelmensis Ecclesiae* of Simeon of Durham (ed. T. Arnold, as above,
i. 1–135), are fundamental for the history of northern England
in the tenth and eleventh centuries. The *Historia Regum* of
Simeon (ed. T. Arnold, ii. 1–283) is a national chronicle, partly
based on northern materials and continually reinforced from
them. [There is a good study of this compilation by P. Hunter
Blair, 'Some observations on the "Historia Regum" attributed
to Symeon of Durham', in *Celt and Saxon*, ed. N. K. Chadwick,
Cambridge, 1963, pp. 63–118.] The cultivation of history at
Durham is further illustrated by a number of short pieces, not
yet completely analysed, which are included in the R.S.
edition of Simeon's works. The most valuable for this period
is a strange fragment inappropriately headed *De Obsessione
Dunelmi*, which relates the history, feuds, and marriage alliances
of the family of the earls of Bernicia (i, pp. 215–20).

The Norse materials bearing on English history, and in particular the sagas of the kings of Norway, raise special problems.
Their literary merit is often great. They bring out the importance of a number of individuals, such as Earl Eric of Hlathir,
who are underestimated by English writers. They bear witness
to an intense vitality of tradition, which kept in vivid memory
the leading figures and salient incidents of northern history. But
their innumerable mistakes on points of fact show the weakness
of a tradition which is uncontrolled by written record. They
can only be followed with peril for the sequence of events, and
the imaginative power which keeps them still alive is continually
used to heighten the colour of the history which they relate.
For a judicious estimate of the historical value of this literature
see M. Ashdown, *English and Norse Documents* (Cambridge, 1930).
The conditions under which it can be employed to supplement
the English evidence are well illustrated in the notes to the
Crawford Charters (below, p. 702), pp. 139–49. Information rele-
vant to English affairs can occasionally be obtained from Latin
histories written in the north, such as the Norwegian history of
Theodric the Monk and the *Historia Norwegiae* (ed. G. Storm,
Monumenta Historica Norvegiae, Kristiania, 1880), the *Historia
Regum Daniae* of Sven Aggeson (ed. J. Langebek, *Scriptores
Rerum Danicarum*, vol. i, Copenhagen, 1772), and the *Gesta
Danorum* of Saxo Grammaticus (ed. J. Olrik and H. Ræder,

Copenhagen, 1931). The *Vita Sancti Anscharii* of Rimbert (ed. Waitz, *Mon. Germ. Hist.* 1884) is invaluable for conditions in the north immediately before the great Danish expeditions of the ninth century. The *Ortus, Vita et Passio Sancti Kanuti* of Ailnoth of Canterbury (ed. Langebek, *Scriptores,* vol. iii) is important for the projected invasion of 1085, and has intrinsic interest as a biography written in Denmark, early in the twelfth century, by a monk of English birth and education. The *Gesta Hammaburgensis Ecclesiae Pontificum* of Adam of Bremen (ed. J. M. Lappenberg, ed. 2, Hanover, 1876) [and B. Schmeidler in *Scriptores Rerum Germanicarum in usum Scholarum,* ed. 3, Hanover and Leipzig, 1917] contains information derived by its author from Swein Estrithson, king of the Danes.

3. LETTERS, CHARTERS, AND LAWS

i. *Letters*

Apart from the papal correspondence bearing on the mission to England, on which see below, three collections of letters are of outstanding importance for the history of this period. The correspondence of Boniface and Lull has been edited by P. Jaffé (*Monumenta Moguntina,* Berlin, 1866) and M. Tangl (*Mon. Germ. Hist.,* Berlin, 1916). It is elucidated in a valuable monograph by H. Hahn, *Bonifaz und Lul; ihre angelsächsischen Korrespondenten* (Leipzig, 1883). The letters of Alcuin (ed. Wattenbach, *Monumenta Alcuiniana,* Berlin, 1873 [and E. Dümmler, *M.G.H.: Epist. Karol. Revi,* II (1895)] are principally concerned with his continental interests, but include much that bears directly on English history in the obscure age of Mercian ascendancy. Little correspondence has come down from the last centuries of Old English history, but the post-Conquest reconstitution of the English church is illustrated at countless points by the letters of Lanfranc (ed. J. A. Giles, *Lanfranci Opera,* Oxford, 1844, i, pp. 17–81). They also bear on the wider questions at issue between William I and Gregory VII, for which the main authority is the correspondence of Gregory himself (*Gregorii VII Registrum,* ed. E. Caspar, *Mon. Germ. Hist.,* 1920, 23).

ii. *Charters*

There are several phases of Old English history of which no reconstruction could be attempted without the use of charters. For most of the period after 700 the charter evidence is full and fairly consecutive. There are two main collections of these documents. Those issued before the death of King Edgar are printed in the *Cartularium Saxonicum* of W. de G. Birch (3 vols., London, 1885–93). The *Codex Diplomaticus Aevi Saxonici* of J. M. Kemble (6 vols., London, 1839–48) includes charters of all periods down to 1066. A selection of documents chosen for their historical interest was printed by B. Thorpe under the title *Diplomatarium Anglicum* (London, 1865). None of these editions offers much help towards the elucidation of the texts, and in the *Codex Diplomaticus* the texts themselves are often normalized. Birch does not attempt any distinction between genuine and spurious charters. Kemble marked with an asterisk the charters which he thought spurious, but his condemnation is erratic, and should not be allowed to prejudge the authenticity of any document. [The Royal Historical Society has issued a very useful complete list of *Anglo-Saxon Charters*, ed. P. H. Sawyer, London, 1968, which includes references to all important discussions on the individual texts. It thus supersedes the catalogue sections of H. P. R. Finberg, *The Early Charters of the West Midlands*, 1961 and *The Early Charters of Wessex*, 1964, and C. R. Hart, *The Early Charters of Eastern England*, 1966; each of these works, however, includes some texts not printed elsewhere.] There is a model edition of a small number of charters in *The Crawford Collection of Early Charters and Documents* (ed. A. S. Napier and W. H. Stevenson, Oxford, 1895), and much attention has lately been given to the important group of documents written in Old English. Good and well annotated texts of most of these records are provided in *Select English Historical Documents* by F. E. Harmer (Cambridge, 1914), *Anglo-Saxon Wills* by D. Whitelock (Cambridge, 1930), and *Anglo-Saxon Charters* by A. J. Robertson (Cambridge, 1939). Each of these volumes includes a translation of the selected documents. [An unpublished vernacular will of unusual length and interest has been edited in facsimile for the Roxburghe Club by D. Whitelock, with Lord Rennell of Rodd and N. R. Ker, 1958.] The necessity of caution in the use that is made of vernacular records has been emphasized by F. E. Harmer; 'Anglo-Saxon Charters and the Historian' (*Bulletin of the John Rylands Library*, xxii (1938), pp. 339–67). [In the *Latin Charters of the Anglo-Saxon Period*, Oxford, 1955, F. M. Stenton provides an introduction to the solemn charter.] Most of the pre-Conquest charters preserved in texts written on single sheets of parchment have been reproduced in the *Facsimiles of Ancient Charters in the British Museum* (4 parts, London, 1873–8), and the Ordnance Survey *Facsimiles of Anglo-Saxon Manuscripts* (ed. W. B. Sanders, 3 parts, Southampton, 1878–84). [A facsimile of one of the most important cartularies, *Textus Roffensis, Part II* has been edited by P. H. Sawyer (Early English Manuscripts in Facsimile, xi, Copenhagen, 1962).] For the period 975–1016 considerable additions could now be made to the texts collected in the *Codex Diplomaticus*, and a new edition of all the royal charters issued between these years is much to be desired. [F. E. Harmer's definitive edition of *Anglo-Saxon Writs*, Manchester 1952, is the work of many years and is of particular value to the historians.]

There is at present no collective edition of the charters of William I. The *Regesta Regum Anglo-Normannorum* of H. W. C. Davis (vol. i, Oxford, 1913) contains abstracts of nearly 300 charters from the Conqueror's reign, of which nearly 50 are printed in full from manuscript sources. For general historical purposes, such as the reconstruction of the king's court at different periods, the collection is very useful. But there are many problems of diplomatic, and, indeed, of history in the strict sense of the word, which will never be settled until complete texts of all the known charters of the Conqueror have been brought together. There is a still more urgent need for a new collection of the private charters of the period. At present they are most conveniently approached through the abstracts in J. H. Round's *Calendar of Documents preserved in France* (London, 1899), and the texts in Dugdale's *Monasticon Anglicanum* (London, 1846, vol. vii). Their importance may be gathered from the examples critically edited by D. C. Douglas (*E.H.R.* xlii (1927), pp. 245–7) and V. H. Galbraith (ibid. xliv (1929), pp. 353–72).

iii. *Laws*

The laws of the Old English kings and the private statements of custom which have descended from that age are included with the laws and juristic compilations of the Norman period in the great edition of F. Liebermann (*Die Gesetze der Angelsachsen*, Halle, 1903–16: vol. i, Texts; vol. ii, part 1, Glossary, part 2, Commentary; vol. iii, Introduction and notes to individual texts). The annotation in vol. iii is exhaustive, and the commentary

which occupies part 2 of vol. ii is indispensable for the study
of Old English social history. The only important contribution since made to the history of the text is the demonstration
by K. Sisam that the Old English version of Athelstan's
'Ordinance on Charities' and one of the three Old English
versions of Athelstan's first code are translations by the Eliza-
bethan scholar Lawrence Nowell from the twelfth-century
Latin rendering known as the *Quadripartitus* (*Modern Language
Review*, xviii (1923), pp. 100–4, xx (1926), pp. 253–69, re-issued
in *Studies in the History of Old English Literature*, Oxford, 1953.
On the other hand there are many points, some of them important, on which Liebermann was not prepared to offer a
final opinion, and the scale and elaboration of his edition makes
it difficult to use for ready reference to single passages. A useful
supplementary edition and translation of the laws put out by
royal authority is provided in *The Laws of the Earliest English
Kings* (ed. F. L. Attenborough, Cambridge, 1922), and *The
Laws of the Kings of England from Edmund to Henry I* (ed. A. J.
Robertson, Cambridge, 1925). [One of the two main early
twelfth-century collections of Anglo-Saxon law has been edited
in facsimile by P. H. Sawyer, *Textus Roffensis, Part I* (Early
English Manuscripts in Facsimile, vii, Copenhagen, 1957)].
The Old English documents edited by F. E. Harmer, D.
Whitelock, and A. J. Robertson (listed above) contain many
references to pre-Conquest suits at law [: as does the *Liber
Eliensis* ed. E. O. Blake with a valuable foreword by D. White-
lock, Camden Society, third series, vol. 92 (London, 1962)].
M. M. Bigelow's *Placita Anglo-Normannica* (London, 1879)
includes a useful collection of materials illustrating the pleas of
the Conqueror's reign. [The first chapter in D. M. Stenton's
English Justice 1066–1215, Philadelphia, 1964, demonstrates how
much the Norman and Angevin legal system depended on the
Anglo-Saxon inheritance.]

There remains under this head one composite volume which
is primarily devoted to ecclesiastical matters, but illustrates
most aspects of English life between the sixth and ninth centuries. In vol. iii of *Councils and Ecclesiastical Documents relating
to Great Britain and Ireland* (ed. A. W. Haddan and W. Stubbs,
Oxford, 1871) letters, charters, and laws are combined into
what is in effect a handbook of materials for the period 590–870.
The materials begin with the letters of Gregory the Great

relating to the English mission, and include every outstanding text which illustrates the internal order or the external relations of the English church. The charters are criticized with a scholarship far stricter than that of Kemble, and the leading texts of ecclesiastical law and ordinance are presented in a form which on all major points is definitive. For the acts of English councils in the century after Bede this edition is never likely to be superseded, and it provides a text of the penitentials of Theodore and his followers adequate for all but the most subtle purposes. It is unfortunate that Stubbs, by whom all the editorial work was done, never treated the later conciliar records of the Old English church in the same manner. For these, and for the memorials of Lanfranc's legislation, it is still necessary to use the unsatisfactory edition of D. Wilkins (*Concilia Magnae Britanniae et Hiberniae*, vol. i, London, 1737). [Mention should be made of Sir Henry Spelman's *Concilia, Decreta, Leges, Constitutiones in re ecclesiarum orbis Britannici*, London, vol. i, 1639, a first attempt to produce a carefully edited edition of *Concilia* in which Spelman edited a manuscript which provided a text of a council held at Rome by Pope Agatho in the autumn of 679 to settle disputes within the church in England. It preserved a genuine record of the decision taken, but the text was bad, p. 150. Stubbs could only quote Spelman adding 'that the MS. from which these Acts were printed has not been identified'. See 'Sir Henry Spelman and the Concilia' by F. M. Powicke, *Proceedings of the British Academy*, vol. xvi, p. 359 (1930). The most convincing feature of the text is the list of 18 bishops and 35 priests with which the record opens, on which see R. L. Poole, *Studies in Chronology and History*, 1934, pp. 51–3.]

4. RECORDS

The earliest English public records of which the text has survived are the Northamptonshire Geld Roll and the South-Western Geld Inquests of 1084 (above, p. 644–7). The earliest record of which the official copy has always remained in public custody is Domesday Book. The text of its two volumes, transcribed with astonishing accuracy by Abraham Furley, was published at the expense of the Government in 1783. No title-page was provided for either volume, and no comment of any kind was made upon the text. In 1811 the first Record Commission issued an index to these volumes, and in 1816 it printed a supplementary volume containing, with later matter, the text of the Exon Domesday and the *Inquisitio Eliensis*. Between 1861 and 1864 a photozincographed facsimile of Domesday Book was issued, in sections each covering a county, by the Ordnance Survey. In 1833 the Record Commission published a *General Introduction to Domesday Book* by Sir Henry Ellis, which is still of value for its lists of tenants-in-chief and under-tenants holding in 1086. For the landholders of 1066 it is now superseded by O. von Feilitzen, *The Pre-Conquest Personal Names of Domesday Book* (Uppsala, 1937). [During Sir Hilary Jenkinson's Deputy Keepership of the Public Record Office the two volumes of Domesday Book were rebound in the Record Office and the process fully reported on in *Domesday Rebound*, H.M.S.O. 1954.] The identification of places, which was not attempted in the index of 1811, has been carried out for most counties in the Domesday sections of the *Victoria County History*, which comprise a translation of the survey of each county, an introduction and a map. Many of these introductions [Bedfordshire, Berkshire, Essex, Hampshire (also the Winchester Survey), Herefordshire, Hertfordshire, Northamptonshire, Somerset, Surrey, Warwickshire and Worcestershire], were written by J. H. Round. Among those by other hands may be mentioned Norfolk by C. Johnson, Yorkshire by W. Farrer, and Shropshire by J. Tait. There is a separate edition of the Cheshire Domesday by Tait (Chetham Society, New Series, vol. lxxv), which is supplemented by the same author's *Flintshire in Domesday Book* (Flintshire Historical Society's Journal, vol. xi). *The Lincolnshire Domesday and the Lindsey Survey*, ed. C. W. Foster and T. Longley (Lincoln Record Society, vol. xix), is important for its notes on the numerous extinct villages of this county, [introduction by F. M. Stenton, who also dealt for the *V.C.H.* with Derbyshire, Huntingdonshire, Leicestershire, Nottinghamshire, Oxfordshire and Rutland. Cambridgeshire was done by L. F. Salzman. Staffordshire by C. F. Slade. The Wiltshire Domesday Book and Geld Rolls have been exhaustively treated by R. R. Darlington, who ends his long and satisfactory introduction by saying that 'on some matters it is unlikely that any two scholars will ever reach agreement.'] The statistics of Domesday Book cannot be fully understood until the details supplied for each village have been brought together, as by F. H. Baring in

Domesday Tables (London, 1909). More work of this kind is urgently needed, especially for eastern England, where many villages were minutely subdivided. [In six vols. H. C. Darby with the help of other scholars has dealt with Domesday Geography in uniform style with maps, Cambridge, 1952–69. The concluding volume is awaited.] On the interpretation of these details the fundamental books are J. H. Round's *Feudal England*, F. W. Maitland's *Domesday Book and Beyond*, and P. Vinogradoff's *English Society in the Eleventh Century* (below, pp. 718–19). There is no large-scale description of Domesday Book which incorporates the results of modern research, but the main features of the survey may be gathered from *Domesday Book* by W. de G. Birch (London, 1887) and *The Domesday Inquest* by A. Ballard (London, 1906). There is a brief but admirable introduction to the modern literature on Domesday problems in 'The Domesday Survey', by D. C. Douglas (*History*, xxi, 249–57), which is also of value for its just appreciation of the work of seventeenth- and eighteenth-century scholars.

The interpretation of Domesday Book is assisted by a number of subsidiary materials, most of which are now available in good editions. The most important of these 'Domesday satellites' are the *Inquisitio Comitatus Cantabrigiensis*, edited with the contemporary *Inquisitio Eliensis* by N. E. S. A. Hamilton (Royal Society of Literature, 1876), *An Eleventh Century Inquisition of St. Augustine's, Canterbury* (ed. A. Ballard, British Academy Records Series, vol. iv, 1920), the 'Feudal Book of Abbot Baldwin' (ed. D. C. Douglas, *Feudal Documents from the Abbey of Bury*, British Academy Records Series, vol. viii, 1932), and a survey of seven manors in Somerset belonging to the church of Bath printed in *Two Chartularies of the Priory of St. Peter at Bath* (ed. W. Hunt, Somerset Record Society, vol. vii, 1893). [P. Sawyer, 'Evesham A, a Domesday Text', Worcester Hist. Soc. 1960 Miscellany I.] A facsimile edition of the *Domesday Monachorum* of Christ Church, Canterbury, ed. D. C. Douglas [for the Royal Historical Society, 1944]. At the present time much attention is being paid to the relation which these materials and the Exon Domesday bear to the completed volumes of Domesday Book. The problem is the subject of articles by V. H. Galbraith ('The Making of Domesday Book', *E.H.R.* lvii (1942), pp. 161–77 [and a book of the same title, Oxford, 1961]) and R. Lennard ('A Neglected Domesday Satellite', ibid. lviii. 32–41), and is also discussed by D. C. Douglas in the article on the Domesday Survey listed above. [Mr. Weldon Finn has been working on the making of Domesday Book, for many years; 'The evolution of successive versions of Domesday Book', *E.H.R.* lxvi, pp. 561–4; 'The immediate sources of the Exchequer Domesday', *Bulletin of J.R.L.* xl, pp. 47–78; 'The Exeter Domesday and its Construction', ibid. xli, pp. 260–87; 'The Teamland of the Domesday Inquest', *E.H.R.* lxxxiii, pp. 95–101.]

5. SOURCES OF INCIDENTAL INFORMATION
i. *Coins*

The basic authority for the Old English coinage is the *Catalogue of English Coins in the British Museum: Anglo-Saxon Series* by C. F. Keary (London, vol. i, 1887; vol. ii, 1893). But large numbers of late Anglo-Saxon coins have been discovered in Scandinavia, and for any approach to a complete view of this currency it is necessary to consult the earlier work of B. E. Hildebrand, *Anglosachsiska Mynt i Svenska Kongliga Myntkabinettet* (Stockholm, 1881). This in turn needs to be supplemented from studies of special collections such as S. Holm's *Studier öfver Uppsala Universitets Anglosaxiska Myntsamling* (Uppsala, 1917) and B. Schnittger's analysis of the Stora Sojdeby hoard in *Fornvännen* (Stockholm, 1915, Parts 2 and 4). Keary's catalogue does not refer systematically to coins in private English collections, and should not be regarded as a full record of the mints and moneyers known from coins found in England. There is useful supplementary information on this subject in G. C. Brooke's *English Coins* (London, 1932). [Successive volumes of the *Sylloge of Coins of the British Isles* published by the British Academy of which the first volume appeared in 1958 is essential for this study, in progress. *Anglo-Saxon Coins, studies presented to F. M. Stenton on his 80th birthday*, ed. R. H. M. Dolley, 1960, contains many valuable articles, particularly the article on 'The Coinage of Offa' by C. E. Blunt. See also articles in the *British Numismatic Journal* for Anglo-Saxon and Anglo-Norman coins.] For the Anglo-Norman currency reference should be made to Brooke's *Catalogue of English Coins in the British Museum: The Norman Kings* (2 vols., London, 1916). The introduction contains a valuable estimate of the number of moneyers working at the same time in each minting-place. The Old English coinage illustrates the state of English proficiency in the decorative arts at different periods and the early sceatta series is surveyed from this point of view in G. Baldwin Brown, *The Arts in Early England*, vol. iii (London, 1915). [The tract on *Anglo-Saxon Pennies* by Michael Dolley published by the British Museum (1964), is a most satisfactory attempt to illustrate some of the most beautiful pennies which have entered the National Collection since the end of the nineteenth century. The frontispiece of gold pennies is particularly valuable. The tract on *The Norman Conquest and the English Coinage* by Michael Dolley published by Spink (1966), must be mentioned although it covers a longer period than is dealt with in this book.]

ii. *Archaeology and Architecture*

[There is now an authoritative study of the most important Anglo-Saxon earthwork, *Offa's Dyke* by Sir Cyril Fox, with a foreword by Sir Frank Stenton (published for the British Academy, 1955.] The archaeological materials for English history shrink rapidly in volume with the abandonment of heathen burial customs. The significance of this material for earlier periods is discussed by J. N. L. Myres in vol. i of this History. The one outstanding discovery which has been made since the appearance of that volume is the richly appointed ship-burial at Sutton Hoo in Suffolk. A valuable interim report on its contents, by various hands, has been published in *Antiquity* (ed. O. G. S. Crawford, vol. xiv, 1940). [See also C. Green, *Sutton Hoo: The Excavation of a Royal Ship Burial*, London, 1963. No satisfactory conclusion about its date can yet be reached and excavations in the vicinity are still in progress.] After the Conversion, apart from coins and isolated discoveries such as the ninth-century 'Alfred Jewel', there is little evidence which illustrates the decorative treatment of small objects, and the history of English pottery is virtually a blank from the seventh century until the Norman Conquest. For finds relating to this period reference may be made to the articles by R. A. Smith in the *Victoria County Histories*, and to separate studies such as R. E. M. Wheeler, *London and the Saxons* (London, 1935) and *London and the Vikings* (London, 1927). [Some important studies are included in *Dark Age Britain: Studies presented to E. T. Leeds*, ed. D. B. Harden (London, 1956);

see also *The Relics of St. Cuthbert*, ed. C. F. Battiscombe (O.U.P., 1956); D. M. Wilson and C. E. Blunt 'The Trewhiddle Hoard', *Archaeologia* xlviii (1961); and D. M. Wilson, 'Anglo-Saxon Ornamental Metalwork 700–1100, *Catalogue of Antiquities of the Later Saxon Period*, I (British Museum, 1964).] The northern background of viking culture is described at length in H. Shetelig and H. Falk, *Scandinavian Archaeology* (trans. E. V. Gordon, Oxford, 1937). The development of Old English art-forms is traced downwards to the age of Alfred by T. D. Kendrick, *Anglo-Saxon Art* (London, 1938)[; and the period from Alfred to the Conquest is covered in his *Late Saxon and Viking Art* (London, 1949)]. [An exhaustive study of all the remains of Saxon churches is contained in the two-volume work *Anglo-Saxon Architecture* by H. M. and Joan Taylor, Cambridge, 1965.]

From the historical standpoint the main interest of post-conversion archaeology lies in the parallel arts of sculpture and manuscript decoration. On their relationship in early times with one another, and with the ornamental metal-work of the heathen age, see A. W. Clapham in *Antiquity*, vii. 43–57. There is no general survey of Anglo-Saxon book-ornament, and reference is necessary to studies of individual works, such as *The Lindisfarne Gospels* by E. Millar (London, 1923). [This manuscript has been published in a beautiful facsimile, *Evangeliorum quattuor codex Lindisfarnensis*, ed. T. D. Kendrick and others, Oltun and Lausanne, 1956–60.] On the illustration of books in the latter part of the period see O. Homburger, *Die Anfänge der Malschule von Winchester in X. Jahrhundert* (Leipzig, 1912). Old English sculpture has been treated on a broad scale by many scholars—among them G. Baldwin Brown, *The Arts in Early England*, vol. vi, Part ii (London, 1937); J. Brønsted, *Early English Ornament* (London and Copenhagen, 1924); W. G. Collingwood, *Northumbrian Crosses of the Pre-Norman Age* (London, 1927); and A. W. Clapham, *English Romanesque Architecture*, vol. i (Oxford, 1930). For the development of English architecture, which cannot be followed without reference to changing forms of sculptured decoration, there are two essential modern authorities. Baldwin Brown's *Arts in Early England*, vol. ii (ed. 2, 1925) contains a list naming every church in which remains of Anglo-Saxon work are visible. Clapham's two volumes on *English Romanesque Architecture* (i, Before the Conquest, 1930; ii, After the Conquest, 1934) trace the whole progress of architectural design, structure, and decoration from the beginning of the seventh to the end of the twelfth century. His more general volume, *Romanesque Architecture in Western Europe* (Oxford, 1936), brings English and continental developments into a coherent historical relationship. [Since this book was written the history of Anglo-Saxon art has been enormously advanced by the writings of Francis Wormald, especially in 'Decorated Initials in English MSS. from A.D. 900 to 1100', *Archaeologia*, xli (1945); *English Drawings of the Tenth and Eleventh Centuries*, London, 1952; *The Benedictional of St. Ethelwold*, London, 1959; and 'An English Eleventh-century Psalter with Pictures', *The Thirty-Eighth Volume of the Walpole Society*, 1960–2. Also his article in *The Bayeux Tapestry* referred to above, p. 698. See also G. R. D. Dodwell, *The Canterbury School of Illumination 1066–1200*, Cambridge, 1954.]

iii. *Place-names*

There are two periods for which the evidence of place-names is particularly valuable as a supplement to the facts recorded by historians. For the beginnings of Anglo-Saxon history they can be used, with caution, to illustrate such problems as the progress of the English occupation, the relations between the English settlers and the Britons, the character of Anglo-Saxon heathenism, and the structure of the earliest English society. Their value is even more obvious for the age of Alfred and his immediate successors. They indicate the varying degrees of intensity with which different parts of the country were colonized by the Danish invaders of the ninth century, they reflect in some degree the nature of that colonization, and they bring into sharp contrast the distinction between the Danish settlement in eastern England and the Norse settlement in the north-west. The general significance of place-name evidence can be gathered most readily from the *Oxford Dictionary of English Place-Names*, by E. Ekwall (ed. 4, Oxford, 1960), and their bearing on specific questions, from the same author's *Scandinavians and Celts in the North-West of England* (Lund, 1918), *The Place-Names of Lancashire* (Manchester, 1922), *English Place-Names in -ing* (Lund, 1923 [ed. 2, enlarged, 1962]), and *English River-Names* (Oxford, 1928). The publications of the English Place-Name Society (vols. i–xliii, Cambridge, 1924–67) provide material

from which the place-names of twenty counties and the three
Yorkshire ridings can now be studied in detail. [F. M. Stenton's
The Place-Names of Berkshire as long ago as 1911 set out the
essential value of place-name studies for the historian.] A.
Mawer's *Place-Names of Northumberland and Durham* (Cambridge,
1920) is important for the Anglian settlement of Bernicia, and
B. G. Charles, *Non-Celtic Place-Names in Wales* (London, 1938),
for the history of the Anglo-Welsh border. A number of points
at which place-name studies bear on historical questions are
discussed by A. Mawer, *Problems of Place-Name Study* (Cambridge, 1929) and F. M. Stenton, 'The Historical Bearing
of Place-Name Studies' (*Trans. R. Hist. Soc.*, 4th Series, vols.
xxi–xxvii, 1939–45, now republished in his Collected Papers
1969). [An excellent popular work on *English Place-Names*, by
K. Cameron, now Director of the English Place-Name Society,
was published by Batsford (London, 1961).] The bibliography
in the *Oxford Dictionary* includes all the leading books related
to the subject and most of the principal sources from which
early forms of place-names are derived.

iv. *Literature and Learning*

In a general history it is impossible to attempt even the most
summary bibliography of Old English literature. The volume of
this literature is great, and the discussion to which it has given
rise is minute and often controversial. A serviceable bibliography of the texts and principal commentaries will be found
in *The Cambridge Bibliography of English Literature*, volume I (ed.
F. W. Bateson, 1940)[, vol. v Supplement, ed. George Watson,
1957. Several important articles are contained in K. Sisam,
Studies in the History of Old English Literature (Oxford, 1953)].
Reference has been made above in footnotes to editions of the
prose writings which are of most significance for historical
purposes. *Widsith* and *Beowulf*, the most important of the Old
English 'heroic' poems, are available in many editions, among
which may be mentioned K. Malone, *Widsith* (London, 1936),
and F. Klaeber, *Beowulf and the Fight at Finnsburg* (London, ed.
3, 1936). R. W. Chambers, *Beowulf, an Introduction to the Study
of the Poem* (Cambridge, ed. 3, with a supplement by C. L.
Wrenn, 1959), illustrates the whole complex of archaeological,
literary, and historical problems which centres upon the story.
[Two works published since 1947 are of outstanding value in

Beowulf studies. D. Whitelock, *The Audience of Beowulf*, Oxford, 1951, and K. Sisam, *The Structure of Beowulf*, Oxford, 1965.] A. Campbell, *The Battle of Brunanburh* (London, 1938), and E. V. Gordon, *The Battle of Maldon* (London, 1937), are good editions of the two chief historical poems of the period.

The contribution of Anglo-Saxon scholars to the Latin literature of the Middle Ages is indicated, with an analysis and appreciation of individual works, in the fundamental *Geschichte der lateinischen Literatur des Mittelalters* of M. Manitius (München, 1911–31). For the period before 900, in which Anglo-Saxon scholarship reached its height, there is an admirable recent guide in M. L. W. Laistner's *Thought and Letters in Western Europe* (London, 1931). Each of these books includes a full series of bibliographical references.

[N. R. Ker's *Catalogue of manuscripts containing Anglo-Saxon* (Oxford, 1957) is a valuable and comprehensive survey of manuscripts written in Anglo-Saxon. It also includes those which contain even brief Old English notes. The publication of *The Diary of Humfrey Wanley 1715–1726*, ed. C. E. and Ruth C. Wright (London, The Bibliographical Society 1966), marks the completion of a formidable task and enables the modern scholar to estimate the extent of the debt he owes to the great collectors of the eighteenth century.]

II. MODERN WORK

I. BOOKS OF REFERENCE

The *Dictionary of National Biography* is still useful for Anglo-Saxon history. Most of the articles relating to this period were written by W. Hunt, and represent the best-informed opinion of the late nineteenth century. They need much revision, particularly on points of chronology, and they give undue prominence to statements by Anglo-Norman writers, but they have not been superseded as an introduction to the leading figures of the age. For the period before 800 the earlier *Dictionary of Christian Biography* (ed. W. Smith and H. Wace, 4 vols., London, 1877–87) is in some ways of greater value. It includes a number of articles by Stubbs, which incorporate the results of his researches for the *Councils* (above, p. 705), and still retain the freshness of original work. The article on Theodore of Tarsus, which runs to some 7,500 words, is the best account of

Theodore's work which has yet appeared, and the article on Offa of Mercia, though much slighter, is a notable appreciation of a king whom most historians have underestimated.

Among other works of reference the *Handbook of British Chronology* (R. Hist. Soc., 1939 [ed. 2, 1961]) contains lists of kings and bishops, with a valuable account of the sources from which the information is derived. In the preparation of this work the dates of the Old English kings were checked and, where necessary, revised in the light of modern research. For the dates of the bishops the *Handbook* follows W. G. Searle's *Anglo-Saxon Bishops, Kings and Nobles* (Cambridge, 1899), which for this period supplements the *Registrum Sacrum Anglicanum* of W. Stubbs (Oxford, ed. 2, 1897). The annotated genealogies of royal and aristocratic families which occupy the second half of Searle's book are valuable, though spurious material is occasionally used in their construction. Searle's earlier work entitled *Onomasticon Anglo-Saxonicum* (Cambridge, 1897) 'aims at being a fairly complete list of Anglo-Saxon names and of the men and women who bore those names'. It is of great value for the identification of individuals mentioned in Old English documents; and as a well-attested record of the personal names current among the Anglo-Saxon peoples it has been fundamental in the development of place-name studies.

For the bibliography of the period, C. Gross, *The Sources and Literature of English History* (ed. 2, London, New York, and Bombay, 1915) covers all the more important articles, books, and editions of texts published before that year. For later work the bibliographies in the *Cambridge Medieval History*, vols. i–iii and v, should be consulted. They can be supplemented from the lists of books in more recent specialized works such as D. Knowles, *The Monastic Order* (below, p. 728). [See also Wilfrid Bonser, *An Anglo-Saxon and Celtic Bibliography* (450–1087) 2 vols., Oxford, Basil Blackwell, 1957.] The care with which ancient editions of texts are recorded is one of the most valuable features of Gross's bibliography, for it is often desirable to get behind the conclusions of modern editors to those of their sixteenth- or seventeenth-century predecessors. The manuscripts of the chief narrative and biographical sources for the period are reviewed in T. D. Hardy's *Descriptive Catalogue of Materials relating to the History of Great Britain and Ireland* (3 vols. in 4 parts, R.S., 1862–71)—a great book, which made possible much of the history written in the next generation, and of which the practical value is by no means yet exhausted.

2. PERIODICALS

Among periodicals the *English Historical Review* is indispensable, and there are many relevant articles in the *Transactions of the Royal Historical Society* [and the *Bulletin of the Institute of Historical Research*]. *History*, the journal of the Historical Association, includes occasional studies on general questions. The *Saga-Book of the Viking Society* is a periodical miscellany containing many articles which illustrate the Scandinavian background of late Old English history. The major archaeological journals, on which see vol. i of this *History*, p. 472, are less important for this than for the Romano-British age, but are valuable for notices of discoveries relating to the period, and essential for the history of architecture and the allied decorative arts. [To these may now be added *Medieval Archaeology*, 1957– .] The transactions of local societies contain many useful communications. The work of G. B. Grundy on the boundary-clauses of Anglo-Saxon charters will be found in the proceedings of the *Bristol and Gloucester Archaeological Society*, the *Berks., Bucks. and Oxon. Archaeological Society*, the *Somersetshire Archaeological and Natural History Society*, the *Oxfordshire Record Society*, the *Birmingham Archaeological Society*, and the *Dorset Natural History and Archaeological Society*, as well as, for Hampshire and Wiltshire, in the central *Archaeological Journal*. Publications of this nature include valuable articles bearing on the problems of early genealogy and feudal descent. The important researches of G. Wrottesley into the details of Anglo-Norman feudalism were concentrated on Staffordshire, and published by the *William Salt Archaeological Society* in its *Collections* for the history of that county. Many characteristic studies by J. H. Round appeared in the *Transactions of the Essex Archaeological Society* and the *Sussex Archaeological Society's Collections*, and L. C. Loyd's definitive article on the origin of the family of Warenne was communicated to the *Yorkshire Archaeological Society's Journal* (1933). [When the present work was published L. C. Loyd's *Origins* of some Anglo-Norman families was in a series of manuscript notes and tables now ed. by Charles T. Clay and David C. Douglas for the Harleian Society, vol. 103, Leeds, 1951.] Most of the known documents relating to this period have been published in large-scale collections (above, p. 691), but the publications of local societies should not be ignored in the search for such materials. The *Cartularies of Muchelney and Athelney Abbeys* published by the Somerset Record Society (ed. E. H. Bates, 1899) contain the Latin texts of seven pre-Conquest charters otherwise unknown, and English versions of six others. The modern approach to Old English conditions through the study of medieval documents would have been impossible without the material which county record societies have made available.

3. GENERAL HISTORIES

The period between the end of Roman rule in Britain and the death of King Alfred has been surveyed, with constant reference to modern work in related fields, by R. H. Hodgkin (*History of the Anglo-Saxons*, 2 vols., Oxford, ed. 3, 1952). [This ed. has an appendix on Sutton Hoo by R. L. S. Bruce-Mitford and some small changes in the text.] For the period from 899 to 1066 there is no modern authority of comparable range. The whole period is covered, as part of a general survey of Romano-British and Anglo-Saxon history, by Sir J. H. Ramsay in *The Foundations of England* (2 vols., extending to 1154, London, 1898), T. Hodgkin in *The Political History of England*, vol. i (London, 1906), and Sir Charles Oman, *England before the Norman Conquest* (ed. 8, revised, 1937). The reign of William I is treated by Sir J. H. Ramsay (see above), by G. B. Adams in *The Political History of England*, vol. ii (London, 1905), and by H. W. C. Davis, *England under the Normans and Angevins* (ed. 8, London, 1924). The period from 500 to 1087 occupies four chapters of the *Cambridge Medieval History*—vol. i, pp. 382–91, by F. G. M. Beck; vols. ii, pp. 543–74, iii, pp. 340–408, and v, pp. 481–520, by W. J. Corbett. The last of these chapters contains a valuable summary of its author's unpublished analyses of Domesday Book. The bibliographies to these volumes give the best available survey of recent work on Anglo-Saxon and early Anglo-Norman history.

[Since 1947 there have been many histories aimed essentially at students and general readers. Vols. ii and iii of the Penguin History of England, *The Beginnings of English Society* by D. Whitelock, 1952, and *English Society in the Early Middle Ages* by

D. M. Stenton, 1951, both of which have been several times revised. Two books by P. Hunter Blair may also be referred to: *An Introduction to Anglo-Saxon England*, Cambridge, 1956, and *Roman Britain and Early England 55 B.C.–A.D. 871*, Edinburgh, 1963. Both are illustrated. Also *Feudal Britain* by G. W. S. Barrow, London, 1956; *Anglo-Saxon England and the Norman Conquest* by H. Loyn, Oxford, 1962, may be noted. The anniversary of the Norman Conquest produced a flood of books, not all of much value, but mention should be made of *The Norman Conquest, its setting and impact* compiled by the Battle and district Historical Society, with articles by D. Whitelock, D. C. Douglas, C. H. Lemmon and F. Barlow.]

There is an admirable modern survey of Welsh history in J. E. Lloyd's *History of Wales* (London, 1911, ed. 3, 1939, pages unchanged). For the details of early Scottish history W. F. Skene's *Celtic Scotland* (Edinburgh, 1876–80) is still useful. But it underestimates the complexities of the evidence, and it should be corrected by the critical digest of the materials provided by A. O. Anderson in *Scottish Annals from English Chroniclers* (London, 1908) and *Early Sources of Scottish History* (Edinburgh, 1922).

[*English Historical Documents c. 500–1042*, London 1955 ed. D. Whitelock provides not only a valuable account of the more important sources for this period but also a full translation of the texts or of the more valuable parts of them, whether verse or prose.]

4. POLITICAL HISTORY

Among older narratives J. R. Green's *Making of England* and *Conquest of England* (London, 1881, 1883) still belong to the living body of historical literature. They were written before the criticism of documents and the sciences of archaeology, language, and ecology had provided a basis for historical reconstruction. The *Making of England* was strongly influenced by the pioneer essays of E. Guest (collected in *Origines Celticae*, 2 vols., London, 1883), which are at once uncritical and highly speculative (see W. H. Stevenson, 'Dr. Guest and the English Conquest of South Britain', *E.H.R.* xvii (1917), 625–42). But in relating the course of early English history to the nature of the ground on which it was worked out Green was anticipating the methods of later inquiry, and for sixty years his narrative has never ceased to arouse the interest of numerous readers.

The importance of E. A. Freeman's *History of the Norman Conquest* (5 vols. and index, Oxford, 1867–79) is of another kind. It provides a detailed narrative of events for the period 975–1087, supported by quotations from the original authorities and by a series of appendixes dealing with problems of especial difficulty. As an introduction to the sources for the political history of the period the book is of great and permanent value. The criticism of the sources is less satisfactory. Freeman gave little attention to the internal history of his materials; he was unwilling to reject the statement of any writer whom he regarded, on general grounds, as authoritative, and there are many points at which his narrative forces discrepant pieces of information into an unreal synthesis. Much of the criticism to which his own work has given rise was caused by his reliance on evidence which will not bear a close examination. In the literal presentation of this evidence he was painfully exact, and the charges of 'inaccuracy' which have been brought against him (as by J. H. Round, *Feudal England, passim*) are heavily overstrained. If the book has failed to hold a reading public it is partly because of its length, partly because of changes of literary fashion, but essentially because interest in history has shifted to fields which lay outside Freeman's view. With the development of religion, learning, society, law, and administration he had no concern, and his account of political history is coloured throughout by the presuppositions of his own age.

The next generation of scholars made the details of this history more precise, and vastly increased its perspective both in time and space. Under the first of these heads the work of W. H. Stevenson is of primary importance. He never attempted a large-scale piece of historical representation and, apart from his edition of Asser and his collaboration with Napier in producing the Crawford Charters (above, p. 702), the main results of his research on this period are scattered in articles and reviews contributed to the *E.H.R.* between 1887 and 1914. Stevenson was the first scholar to use modern methods of diplomatic for the criticism of Old English charters; he set a new standard of accuracy in the identification of Old English place-names, and he indicated, though he never worked out, the lines along which a reconstruction of the earliest English history might be possible. He was one of the first English historians to appreciate the strength of the Scandinavian element in pre-Conquest England.

The quality of his work gives it a significance in the study of Anglo-Saxon England comparable with that of Haverfield's achievement in the study of Roman Britain.

In the meantime J. H. Round was clarifying the history of the Norman Conquest by work of a similar kind. As a scholar Round, like Stevenson, was critical rather than constructive, and the studies by which he was most widely known were directed against points of detail in Freeman's narrative of the battle of Hastings. These essays, with others of much greater consequence, were brought together in the remarkable miscellany called *Feudal England* (London, 1895 [re-issued with a Foreword by F. M. Stenton, 1964]), which includes his principal contributions to the history of the period before 1087. The main conclusions established in this volume—the artificiality of the pre-Conquest system of assessment, and revolutionary character of tenure by knight-service—supplied a new point of departure for work on Domesday Book and English feudal society. Round's other collections of studies (*Geoffrey de Mandeville*, 1892; *The Commune of London*, 1899; *Studies in Peerage and Family History*, 1901; *Peerage and Pedigree*, 1910; *The King's Serjeants and Officers of State*, 1911) deal, in the main, with later periods, but contain much matter relevant to the eleventh century, particularly in the form of genealogy, of which he was the greatest English master. For a complete view of Round's work, of which only a small proportion was collected into books, reference should be made to the bibliography in his posthumous volume *Family Origins* (ed. W. Page, 1930).

Contemporaneously with Round's later writings work on materials of another sort was giving a new extension to the English historical scene. Until the beginning of the present century comparatively little had been done to bring Old English history into organic relationship with what could be gathered from literary sources about the society of the Germanic foreworld. English heroic poetry had been used by many earlier scholars, notably by J. M. Kemble in his *Saxons in England* (ed. 2, London, 1876), but as the decoration rather than the substance of history. Its bearing on the origin of such basic political conceptions as kingship, overlordship, and nobility by service was demonstrated in three books by H. M. Chadwick—*Studies on Anglo-Saxon Institutions* (Cambridge, 1905), *The Origin of the English Nation* (Cambridge, 1907), and *The Heroic Age*

(Cambridge, 1912). Other illustrations of its direct historical value were given by R. W. Chambers in *Beowulf, an Introduction* (above, p. 712–13). As a result of such work as this the English peoples can now be envisaged against the background of a common Germanic civilization, which went far to determine both the structure of their society and the ideas which informed it.

The influence of Scandinavian ideas and institutions on this society was first shown in convincing detail by J. C. H. R. Steenstrup in the final portion of his *Normannerne* (4 parts, Copenhagen, 1876–82). The strength of this influence was underestimated by English historians of the age of Green and Freeman, and has only of recent years been adequately recognized. There is no modern large-scale study of its effects, but many illustrations will be found in Liebermann's commentary on the *Gesetze* (above, p. 707), and its importance was stressed by P. Vinogradoff in his *Growth of the Manor* (ed. 2, London, 1911) and *English Society in the Eleventh Century* (Oxford, 1908). The most obvious signs of its persistence are the loan-words and personal names which occur in early sources. [For the settlement of Danish armies in the midlands see F. M. Stenton, *The Free Peasantry of the Northern Danelaw* (Oxford, 1969).] There is an admirable review of this evidence in two books by E. Björkman—*Scandinavian Loan-Words in Middle English* (Halle, 1900), and *Nordische Personennamen in England*, with its supplement *Zur englischen Namenkunde* (Halle, 1910, 1912). The Danish colonization of eastern England is illustrated in many publications of the English Place-Name Society (above, p. 698) and its intensity is becoming clearer as more early documents relating to this country are published. Among the larger collections of this material may be mentioned *Early Yorkshire Charters* (ed. W. Farrer and C. T. Clay, 12 vols. (and vol. III of index), 1914–65, see below p. 708), *Danelaw Charters* (ed. F. M. Stenton, British Academy, 1920), and *The Registrum Antiquissimum of the Cathedral Church of Lincoln* (ed. C. W. Foster and K. Major, 9 vols., Lincoln, 1931–68). The significance of the Danish colonies as a factor in English politics is discussed by F. M. Stenton in *The Danes in England* (British Academy, 1927) [; and the contrast between 'The Danish settlements in England and in Normandy in 'The Scandinavian Colonies in England and Normandy', *C.P.*, pp. 335–47. For the Danes in Normandy see

Les Noms de Personnes Scandinaves en Normandie de 911 a 1066 by
J. Adegarde des Gautres, Lund, 1954].

In relation to the length of this period the number of special
studies devoted to its political history is by no means large.
The Life and Times of Alfred the Great, by C. Plummer (Oxford,
1902), *Alfred the Truth Teller* by B. A. Lees, *Canute the Great* by
L. M. Larson, and *William the Conqueror* by F. M. Stenton (New
York and London, 1908, 1912, 1915) and treat three outstanding figures in some detail; [D. C. Douglas produced a
large scale life of *William the Conqueror* in 1964, on which he had
spent many years, London;] but there are statesmen of the first
rank, such as Offa and Athelstan, of whom no full-scale biography has ever been attempted. [Offa's foreign relations are
well-treated by J. M. Wallace-Hadrill, 'Charlemagne and
England', *Karl der Grosse: Lebenswerk und Nachleben*, ed. W.
Braunsjels, i, 1965–6, pp. 638–98.] The charter evidence for
the age of Mercian ascendancy is used by F. M. Stenton in
'Lindsey and its Kings' (*C.P.*, pp. 127–37 (1927), 1970 and
'The Supremacy of the Mercian Kings' *C.P.*, pp. 48–66
(1918) 1970. The substantive history of the time has not yet
attracted many students. On the other hand, the history of
the fifty years after Alfred's death has been revolutionized
by modern work. Three essays by M. L. R. Beaven, whose
early death was a grievous loss to Anglo-Saxon studies,
resolved many problems in the light of a revised chronology ('The Regnal Dates of Alfred, Edward the Elder, and
Athelstan', *E.H.R.* xxxii, 1917, pp. 517–31; 'King Edmund
I and the Danes of York', *E.H.R.* xxxiii, 1918, pp. 1–9; and
'The Beginning of the Year in the Alfredian Chronicle', ibid.,
pp. 328–42). 'The Redemption of the Five Boroughs' by A.
Mawer (*E.H.R.* xxxviii, 1923, pp. 551–7) demonstrated the
antagonism between the Danish colonists and the Norwegian
invaders of Mercia; 'The Chronology of the Reign of Edward
the Elder', by W. S. Angus (*E.H.R.* liii, 1938, pp. 194–210) has
established the main sequence of events for the period which it
covers; 'Wulfstan and the so-called Laws of Edward and
Guthrum' by D. Whitelock (*E.H.R.* lvii, 1942, pp. 1–21) has
made the early history of the Danelaw more intelligible; 'Two
Notes on the Norse Kingdom of Northumbria' by A. Campbell
(*E.H.R.* lvii, 1942, pp. 85–97) has clarified the relationship
between the northern and southern rulers of the time. Most

modern work on the later part of the period has been given to social rather than political history, but R. R. Darlington's 'Æthelwig, Abbot of Evesham' (*E.H.R.* xlviii, 1943, pp. 1–22, 177–98) [and his 'Anglo-Norman Historians' an inaugural lecture, 1947] illustrate the results which can be obtained from a closer examination of the authorities for the Conqueror's reign. There is important new material in P. Grierson's 'Relations between England and Flanders before the Norman Conquest' (*Trans. R. Hist. Soc.*, 4th Series, xxiii, 1941, pp. 71–112), and 'A Visit of Earl Harold to Flanders in 1056' (*E.H.R.* li, 1936, pp. 90–7). S. Fest's *The Hungarian Origin of St. Margaret of Scotland* (Debreden, 1940) throws light on the marriage of Edward the Ætheling. B. Wilkinson's 'Freemen and the Crisis of 1051' (*Bulletin of the John Rylands Library*, vol. xxii, pp. 368–87) and 'Northumbrian Separatism in 1065 and 1066' (ibid., vol. xxiii, pp. 504–26) deal with problems bearing on the nature of English politics in the generation before the Conquest. The obscure continental warfare of the Conqueror's later years has been made as clear as the evidence will allow by C. W. David, *Robert Curthose* (Harvard, 1920).

5. CONSTITUTIONAL HISTORY

The foundation of modern research in this field is the massive *Constitutional History of England* by W. Stubbs (3 vols., Oxford, 1874–8; last ed. of vol. i, 1897). The book is at its strongest where it draws upon its author's intimate knowledge of Old English documentary sources; at its weakest where it adapts the conclusions of German historians to English conditions. As an editor of original materials Stubbs had no illusions about the quality of the evidence for Anglo-Saxon institutions, and his unwillingness to theorize about them gave his work a solidity on which scholars of the next generation were able to rely. Unfortunately Stubbs never revised the *History* systematically, and there are important points at which it has long been superseded. A number of them are indicated in *Studies and Notes supplementary to Stubbs' Constitutional History* by C. Petit-Dutaillis (translation by W. E. Rhodes, Manchester, 1908). But it is through a shifting of emphasis rather than the correction of details that the *History* has been most affected by modern work, and it is still of authority as a record of ascertained fact.

Among later studies of separate institutions may be mentioned
L. M. Larson, *The King's Household in England before the Norman
Conquest* (Madison, 1904); F. Liebermann, *The National Assembly
in the Anglo-Saxon Period* (Halle, 1913); W. A. Morris, *The
Frankpledge System* (New York, 1910) and *The Medieval English
Sheriff to 1300* (Manchester, 1927). The Old English conception
of monarchy is illustrated by the ceremonies described by P. E.
Schramm, *A History of the English Coronation* (Oxford, 1937). An
almost contemporary continental version of the order used at
Edgar's coronation is printed by P. L. Ward, *E.H.R.* lvii, 345–
61. The character of Old English and Anglo-Norman legislation can be gathered most clearly from the first four chapters of
the *History of English Law* by F. Pollock and F. W. Maitland
(ed. 2, Cambridge, 1898). The legal ideas underlying the
various types of document in use before the Conquest are
elucidated by H. D. Hazeltine in the General Preface to D.
Whitelock's *Anglo-Saxon Wills* (above, p. 691). The most recent
survey of the whole constitutional field is *The Constitutional
History of Medieval England* by J. E. A. Jolliffe (London, 1937).
The book is original, and based throughout on ancient materials,
though Anglo-Saxon scholars have shown that the texts will
not always bear the interpretation put on them. Joliffe's
earlier book *Pre-Feudal England: The Jutes* (Oxford, 1933) contains a valuable demonstration of the economic factors underlying the organization of Old English local government. On
the constitutional history of early Normandy C. H. Haskins,
Norman Institutions (Harvard, 1918), is a masterly synthesis of
scattered evidence, an appreciable part of which was brought
to light by the author's own researches. The feudal organization of Anglo-Norman society is described by F. M. Stenton,
The First Century of English Feudalism (Oxford, 1932)[; ed. 2,
1961. A number of recent writers have endeavoured to revive
'views which have been refuted many times' and to repeat
'statements which have been shown to be baseless', as Professor
R. R. Darlington says in his excellent Creighton Lecture, 1962,
on 'The Norman Conquest'. Sir Frank Stenton was not convinced by the work on this period of G. Warren Hollister, E.
John, Miss M. Hollings or Mr. Richardson and Professor Sayles,
whose books and articles are therefore here omitted. Professor
Darlington's lecture should be referred to, also the articles of
Professor J. Holt, 'Feudalism Revisited,' *Economic History Review,*

2nd series, xiv, 1961 and ibid. xvi, 1963]. The Conqueror's imposition of military service on the lands of bishops and abbots is the starting-point of Miss H. M. Chew's *The English Ecclesiastical Tenants-in-chief and Knight Service* (Oxford, 1932). *La Monarchie féodale en France et en Angleterre* by C. Petit-Dutaillis (Paris, 1923) is a valuable comparative study of French and English constitutional developments. The difficult problems connected with the emergence and essential nature of the feudal order have recently been discussed, with full reference to earlier studies, in two valuable articles by C. Stephenson, 'The Origin and Significance of Feudalism' (*American Historical Review*, xlvi. 788–812), and 'Feudalism and its Antecedents in England' (ibid., xlviii. 245–65).

The character of English feudalism as a permanent form of social order can be seen most clearly in the internal history of the fiefs created by the Conqueror. The most important work so far carried out in this field is W. Farrer's *Honors and Knights' Fees* (3 vols.: i and ii, printed for the author, 1923–4; iii, London and Manchester, 1925). [Sir Charles Clay has continued the work of Farrer for many of the Yorkshire fees. Farrer had published three volumes of Yorkshire charters, unindexed; Sir Charles Clay has published an index of Farrer's volumes and nine further volumes of Yorkshire charters dealing with the honours of Richmond, Paynel, Skipton, Warenne, Stuteville, Trussebut, Percy and Tisun, identifying the individuals and their lands.] Farrer's notes on the large honour of Wallingford were edited by H. E. Salter in the *Boarstall Cartulary* (Oxford, 1930) and there is much relevant, though less well-organized, material in his *Feudal Cambridgeshire* (Cambridge, 1920). Among earlier examples of this type of work the most valuable is R. W. Eyton's *Antiquities of Shropshire* (12 vols., London, 1854–60), which traces the feudal history of a compact earldom from the Conquest to the death of Henry III. Studies of this kind rest on the accurate identification of undertenants and their holdings—a form of research which has been in progress ever since the seventeenth century. Sir George Sitwell's *Barons of Pulford* (printed for the author, Scarborough, 1889) may be quoted as an outstanding illustration of its historical value. The local persistence of the feudal divisions of 1086, which is itself a fact of social importance, appears in the history of countless villages. The *History of Aisthorpe and Thorpe in the Fallows* by C. W. Foster (Lincoln, 1927) is an excellent example of modern research applied to these ancient complications. The work of all inquirers into feudal history has been greatly facilitated by the modern official edition of the *Book of Fees* (3 vols., Stationery Office, 1920–31), and in particular by its vast, and almost impeccable, index.

6. SOCIAL AND ECONOMIC HISTORY

Social and constitutional history are so tightly interwoven in this period that any distinction between them is bound to be arbitrary. P. Vinogradoff's *Villainage in England* (Oxford, 1892) may be regarded as the starting-point of modern work on the structure of Anglo-Saxon society. The book relates primarily to medieval conditions, but the introduction contains a valuable résumé of earlier controversies about the origins of the Old English social order. Vinogradoff's later books—*The Growth of the Manor* and *English Society in the Eleventh Century* (above, p. 705)—are often hard to follow in detail, but they have the great merit of relating English problems to continental evidence, and they have influenced the direction of much subsequent inquiry. There is a full bibliography of his articles and reviews in *The Collected Papers of Paul Vinogradoff*, ed. H. A. L. Fisher (Oxford, 1928), ii. 479–99. *The Social Structure of Medieval East Anglia* by D. C. Douglas (Oxford, 1927) is an admirable example of later work on the lines which he laid down. But the book which has done most to bring other students into this field is F. W. Maitland's *Domesday Book and Beyond* (Cambridge, 1897). It was the object of the book to ask questions rather than answer them. It may be admitted that many of the answers which Maitland himself proposed have been proved inadequate to the facts. But the vitality of Maitland's writing, the acuteness of his mind and, above all, the interest which he could impart to the austerest of technical problems, have made *Domesday Book and Beyond* a source of inspiration which is hardly affected by changes of opinion about its subject-matter.

Economic history in this period cannot be regarded as an independent subject. The economy of the village community and the manor can only be approached, and that tentatively, through the general study of social organization. The history of the currency cannot be disassociated from the numismatic study of the coins themselves, on which, moreover, the reconstruction of pre-Conquest trade-lines in great part depends. The interaction of economic and social development is repeatedly illustrated in the recently published *Cambridge Economic History* (ed. J. H. Clapham and the late Eileen Power, vol. i, 1941 [ed. 2 by M. M. Postan, 1966]). In addition to articles on individual countries the volume contains important chapters on general problems, notably the 'Settlement and Colonization of Europe' by R. Koebner and the 'Rise of Dependant Cultivation and Seignorial Institutions' by M. Bloch. These articles are mainly based on continental materials, but they throw light on many features of the English agrarian order—especially, perhaps, through the points of contrast which they reveal [; the chapters commented on here are retained in the 2nd ed.]. The fragmentary nature of the evidence for vital features of the Old English economy is well brought out in the discussions which have centred around the origins of the English borough. The agricultural basis of its life was described and related to the Old English agrarian system by F. W. Maitland in *Township and Borough* (Cambridge, 1898). On the other hand, it has been possible to maintain, as by C. Stephenson in *Borough and Town* (Cambridge, Mass., 1933), that English urban development was essentially due to the new conditions created by the Norman Conquest. The minute survey of the problem by J. Tait in *The Medieval English Borough* (Manchester, 1936) has traced the beginnings of this development back to the pre-Alfredian age, but the fact that so fundamental a question should have been so long at issue illustrates the general obscurity of the Old English economic scene.

The field-systems in operation in pre-Conquest England are so obscure that recourse is continually necessary to comparative material from other countries and to later evidence from England itself. The classical survey of the comparative evidence is A. Meitzen's *Siedlung und Agrarwesen der Westgermanen und Ostgermanen, der Kelten, Römer, Finnen und Slaven* (3 vols. and Atlas, Berlin, 1896). It needs to be controlled by the results of later work, but is still of great value as a storehouse of facts. The various types of agrarian pattern which prevailed in England are described by H. L. Gray, *English Field Systems* (Cambridge, Mass., 1915). A realistic description of the English open-field system is given by C. S. and C. S. Orwin in *The Open Fields* (Oxford, 1938). The book relates primarily to the village of Laxton in Nottinghamshire, where the system is still in operation, but it contains practical observations of general applicability which bring the distribution of land in the open fields into connection with the technique of co-operative agriculture. The book throws light upon the system in every phase of its development. The complicated problems of open field origins are discussed by J. N. L. Myres in vol. i of this *History*, 441–4. The methods of aerial survey, which have provided a new line of approach to these questions, are made clear by O. G. S. Crawford in *Air Survey and Archaeology* (Ordnance Survey, ed. 2, 1928). [In *Rural England 1086–1135*, Oxford, 1959, R. Lennard has described the economic state of rural England during the Norman period.]

7. ECCLESIASTICAL HISTORY

The most recent detailed account of Anglo-Saxon ecclesiastical history is the volume by W. Hunt in the *History of the English Church*, ed. W. W. Stephens and W. Hunt (London, 1907). For the connection between English and continental movements it can be usefully supplemented by Miss M. Deanesly's *History of the Medieval Church* (London, 1925). There are periods, such as the age of Bede and the third quarter of the tenth century, in which the ecclesiastical interest is central, and it is treated at length in every general history of the age. The enterprise of English Churchmen on the Continent between the seventh and ninth centuries, which most of these histories have under-estimated, has been described on a scale commensurate with its importance in W. Levison's *England and the Continent in the Eighth Century* (Oxford, 1946). This book is valuable, not only for its treatment of outstanding figures, such as Willibrord, Boniface, and Alcuin, but also as a source of information about persons of less fame, whose work consolidated the achievement of the great leaders. There is a brief but masterly survey of the same field in S. J. Crawford's *Anglo-Saxon Influence on Western Christendom* (Oxford, 1933). Most of the intensive study that has been devoted to the pre-Alfredian church has been spent on editions and annotations of texts, and on technical discussions of individual problems. The most elaborate recent survey of this work is J. F. Kenney's *Sources for the Early History of Ireland, Vol. I: Ecclesiastical* (Columbia, 1929), of which the scope is much wider than would be gathered from its title. Among books and

articles of more than specialist interest may be mentioned
Mary Bateson, 'Origin and Early History of Double Monasteries' (*Trans. R. Hist. Soc.*, 1899); M. Deanesly, 'The Familia
at Christchurch, Canterbury' (*Essays . . . presented to T. F. Tout*,
1925), and 'The Archdeacons of Canterbury under Archbishop
Ceolnoth' (*E.H.R.* xlii, 1927); W. Levison, 'Bede as Historian'
in *Bede, his Life, Times, and Writings*, ed. A. Hamilton Thompson
(Oxford, 1935); R. L. Poole, *Studies in Chronology and History*,
chapters 1–4 (Oxford, 1934); J. A. Duke, *The Columban Church*
(Oxford, 1932); R. A. L. Smith, 'The Early Community of St.
Andrew at Rochester' (*E.H.R.* lx, 1945). *The Bosworth Psalter*
by F. A. Gasquet and E. Bishop (London, 1908), though
primarily concerned with the tenth and eleventh centuries,
illuminates the whole subject of the commemoration of saints
in the Old English church. The history of patronage is traced
from the age of Theodore to the eleventh century by H.
Boehmer in 'Das Eigenkirchentum in England' (*Festgabe für
Felix Liebermann*, Halle, 1921).

   The later phases of Old English church history centre upon
the monastic revival of the tenth century. The subject can best
be approached through the work of J. Armitage Robinson, of
which preliminary results appeared in *The Saxon Bishops of Wells*
and *St. Oswald and the Church of Worcester* (British Academy
Supplement Papers, 1919), and a consecutive account, in *The
Times of St. Dunstan* (Oxford, 1923). Since this book was first
issued Dom Thomas Symons has published an edition of
The Regularis Concordia, in Nelson's Medieval Classics
[1963]. Other valuable articles by him on points of detail
have been published in the *Downside Review* (vols. xl, 1922;
xliv, 1926). The significance of the revival as the beginning of continuous English monasticism has been shown
by D. Knowles in *The Monastic Order in England* (Cambridge,
1940), which reinforces the best account of subsequent
religious history with a full list of both original and secondary materials. There is no biography of Ælfric which in
any way corresponds to his importance, but his methods of
work have been displayed by K. Sisam in three articles in the
Review of English Studies (vols. vii–ix, 1931–3), and there is useful
information about his canonical learning in B. Fehr's introduction to his pastoral letters (*Die Hirtenbriefe Ælfrics*, Hamburg,
1914). The importance of Ælfric's contemporary, Wulfstan II,

archbishop of York, has been made clearer by D. Whitelock in her edition of his *Sermo Lupi ad Anglos* (London, [ed. 3, 1963]) and her article 'Archbishop Wulfstan, Homilist and Statesman' (*Trans. R. Hist. Soc.* 4th Series, xxiv, 1942 [revised and reprinted in the anniversary volume 1968. Wulfstan's genuine homilies have been published by D. Bethurum, Oxford, 1957, and his *Institutes of Polity, Civil and Ecclesiastical*, a work of particular interest for historians, by Karl Jost, Berne, 1959.]). The most interesting feature of recent work on the late Old English church is a strong tendency to challenge the criticisms passed on it by earlier writers. The closeness of its relations with the Continent has been stressed by R. W. Chambers in *The Exeter Book of Old English Poetry* (London, 1933), and R. R. Darlington has shown its fidelity to the principles of the tenth-century reformation ('Ecclesiastical Reform in the Late Old English Period', *E.H.R.* li, 1936). A similar view is taken by Knowles in *The Monastic Order*.

The effect of the Norman Conquest on the English church is treated most fully by H. Boehmer, *Kirche und Staat in England und in der Normandie* (Leipzig, 1899). Boehmer's knowledge of the sources was profound, but his book suffers from the assumption that the Old English church must have been isolated and ineffective. A similar combination of great learning with inperfect judgement is shown in Boehmer's later work *Die Fälschungen Erzbischof Lanfrancs von Canterbury* (Leipzig, 1902), which brings an unqualified charge of forgery against Lanfranc without any adequate consideration of the other evidence for his character. A better balanced view of his conduct is taken by A. J. Macdonald in his *Lanfranc* (Oxford, 1926). This, and the wider question of Lanfranc's standpoint in relation to the king and the papal curia, are discussed in Z. N. Brooke's *English Church and the Papacy* (Cambridge, 1931), which on these essential problems is definitive.

8. MAPS

Among the many maps which illustrate different aspects of Anglo-Saxon history, four are of outstanding importance. The *Historical Atlas of Modern Europe* (ed. R. L. Poole, Oxford, 1896–1900) includes a map of 'England and Wales before the Norman Conquest' by W. H. Stevenson, which is indispensable for the identification of place and regional names, and a map of 'England and Wales in 1086' by J. Tait which provides an admirable introduction to English feudal geography. The earlier part of the period is illustrated in minute detail in O. G. S. Crawford's *Map of Britain in the Dark Ages*, published in two sheets by the Ordnance Survey (South Sheet, Southampton 1935; North Sheet, Southampton 1938). The South Sheet covers the period down to 871, the North Sheet down to *c*. 850. These maps are particularly valuable because they indicate not only the chief historical sites of the period, but also its principal archaeological monuments, and the physical features of hill and woodland which controlled the distribution of settlements. [A new edition in a single sheet on the scale of 16 miles to the inch was published by the Director General of the Ordnance Survey in 1966. The officer of the Survey particularly responsible for it was C. W. Phillips, now retired.]

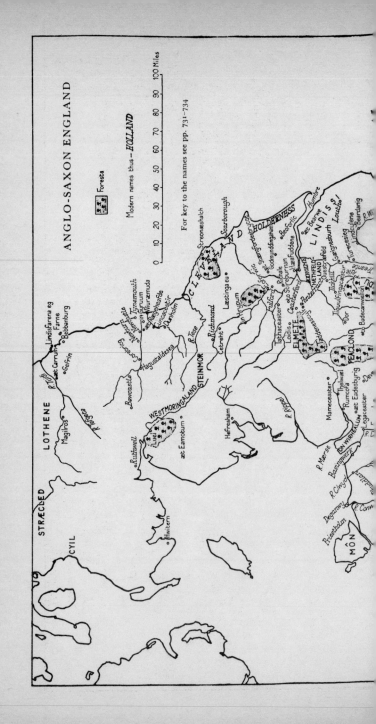

ANGLO-SAXON ENGLAND

Modern names thus — *HOLLAND*

Foresta

For key to the names see pp. 731–734

0 10 20 30 40 50 60 70 80 90 100 Miles

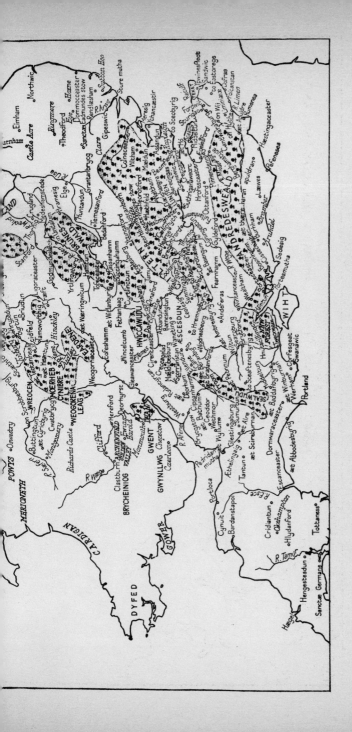

KEY TO ANGLO-SAXON PLACE-NAMES

Names in italics have no recorded Anglo-Saxon form.

Abbandun. Abingdon, Berks.

Abbodesbyrig, æt. Abbotsbury, Dors.

Ægelesburg. Aylesbury, Bucks.

Ægelesford. Aylesford, Kent.

Æscesdun. Berkshire Downs.

Æthelingaig. Athelney, Som.

Afene. Avon, R.

Alre, æt. Aller, Som.

Ambresbyrig, æt. Amesbury, Wilts.

Andeferas. Andover, Hants.

Andredesweald. The Weald of Sussex.

apuldran, æt. thære haran. Battle, Suss.

Apuldre, æt. Appledore, Kent.

Archenfield. S. Heref.

Arundel, Suss.

Arwe. Orwell, R.

Assandun. Ashingdon, Ess.

Axholme, Isle of, Lincs.

Bænesingtun. Bensington, Ox.

Baddanbyrig, æt. Badbury Rings, Dors.

Badecanwiellon, to. Bakewell, Derby.

Bancornaburg. Bangor on Dee, Denbigh.

Bardanstapol. Barnstaple, Dev.

Basengum, æt. Basing, Hants.

Basingwerk, Flint.

Bathum, æt. Bath, Som.

Beamfleot. Benfleet, Ess.

Beardanig. Bardney, Lincs.

Bearwe, æt. Barrow-on-Humber, Lincs.

Bebbanburg. Bamburg, Nhumb.

Bedanford. Bedford.

Beoforlic. Beverley, Yorks.

Beorhhamstede. Great Berkhamstead, Herts.

Beranbyrg, æt. Barbury Hill, Wilts.

Berecingas. Barking, Ess.

Berghamstyde. Bearsted, Kent.

Bewcastle. Cumb.

Bosanhamm. Bosham, Suss.

Bradanforda, æt. Bradford-on-Avon, Wilts.

Bramber, Suss.

Bregentford. Brentford, Midd.

Briudun. Breedon-on-the-Hill, Leic.

Bruneswald. Bromswold Forest, Hunts.

Brycgstow. Bristol.

Brycheiniog, Brecknock.

Brytford. Britford, Wilts.

Buccingahamm. Buckingham.

Burhham. Burpham, nr. Arundel, Suss.

Burnham River, Norf.

Buttingtun. Buttington, Montgomerysh.

Byrtun. Burton-on-Trent, Staffs.

Cælichyth. Chelsea.

Caerleon, Mon.

Calne, Wilts.

Cantwaraburg. Canterbury.

Cardigan.

Carrum, æt. Carham, Nhumb.

Castle Acre, Norf.

Ceasterford. Castleford, Yorks.

Ceoddor. Cheddar, Som.

Ceolesig. Cholsey, Berks.

Cerotæsei. Chertsey, Surr.

Cetreht. Catterick, Yorks.

Chepstow, Mon.

Ciltern. Chiltern Hills.

Cippanhamm. Chippenham, Wilts.

Cirenceaster. Cirencester, Glouc.

Cisseceaster. Chichester, Suss.

Clare, Suff.

Clæighangra. In Tottenham, Midd.

Clastburh. Glasbury, Brecon.

Cleveland, Yorks.

Clifford, Heref.

Clwyd, R.

Cocham. Cookham, Berks.

Colneceaster. Colchester, Ess.

Conway, R.

Corebricg. Corbridge, Nhumb.

Corfesgeat. Corfe, Dors.

Cræft. Croft, Leic.

Creccagelad. Cricklade, Wilts.

Crecganford. Crayford, Kent.

Cridiantun. Crediton, Dev.

Crugland. Crowland, Lincs.

Cuncacestir. Chester-le-Street, Dur.

Cwatbrycg. nr. Bridgnorth, Sal.

Cyil. Kyle.

Cynibre. Kinver Forest, Staffs.

Cyningestun. Kingston, Surr.

Cynuit. Countisbury Hill, Dev.

Cyricbyrig, æt. Chirbury, Sal.

Cyrtlinctun. Kirtlington, Ox.

Dean Forest of.

Dee, R.

Deganwy, Caernarvon.

Deoraby. Derby.

Deorham. Dyrham, Glouc.

Deorhyrst. Deerhurst, Glouc.

Devennport. Davenport, Ches.

Dofras. Dover, Kent.

Dommocceaster. Dunwich, Suff.

Dor. Dore, Derby.

Dorciccæstræ. Dorchester-on-Thames, Ox.

Dornwaraceaster. Dorchester, Dors.

Dudley, Worcs.

Dunholm. Durham.

Dyfed, S. Wales.

Eadesbyrig, æt. Eddisbury, Ches.

Eamotum, æt. Eamont Bridge, Westm.

Eardene. Arden, forest of.

Eastorege, to. Eastry, Kent.

Egonesham. Eynsham, Ox.

Elge. Ely, Cambs.

Ellendun. nr. Wroughton, Wilts.

Elmete. Elmet, Yorks.

Elmham. North Elmham, Norf.

Englafeld. Englefield, Berks.

Eofeshamm. Evesham, Worcs.

Eoforwic. York.

Escanceaster. Exeter.

Esce. Exe, R.

Ewias Harold, Heref.

Eye, Suff.

Farne. Farne Island.

Fearndun. Farndon-on-Dee, Ches.

Fearnhamm. Farnham, Surr.

Fethanleag. In Stoke Lyne, Ox.

Folcanstan. Folkestone, Kent.

Fordwic. Fordwich, Kent.

Froom. Frome, Som.

Fulford, Yorks.

Fullanhamm. Fulham, Midd.

Gæignesburh. Gainsborough, Lincs.

Gefrin. Yeavering, Nhumb.

Gipeswic. Ipswich, Suff.

Gleawanceaster. Gloucester.

Glestingaburg. Glastonbury, Som.

Godmunddingaham. Goodmanham, Yorks.

Godmundeslæch. Gumley, Leic.

Golden Valley, Heref.

Gower, S. Wales.

Grantanbrycg. Cambridge.

Grenewic. Greenwich, Kent.

Gwent, S. Wales.

Gwynedd, N. Wales.

Gwynllwg, West Monmouthshire.

Gyldeford. Guildford, Surr.

Gyruum. in. Jarrow, Dur.

Hæafuddene. Howden, Yorks.

Hægel. Mouth of R. Camel, Corn.

Hæstingaceaster. Hastings, Suss.

Hæthfeld. Hatfield, Herts.

Hæthfeldland. Hatfield Chase, Yorks.

Hagustaldesea. Hexham, Nhumb.

Hamtun. Northampton.

Hamtun. Southampton.

Heantune, æt. Wolverhampton, Staffs.

Hearge, æt. Harrow, Midd.

Hefresham. Heversham, Westm.

Hengestesdun. Hingston Down, Corn.

Heorotford. Hertford.

Hereford.

Hinckley, Leic.

Hlydanford. Lydford, Dev.

Hnutscillingc. Nursling, Hants.

Hó, æt. Hoo, Kent.

Holderness, Yorks.

Holland, Lincs.

Hoxne, Suff.

Hramesig. Ramsey Hunts.

Hremnesbyrig, to. Ramsbury, Wilts.

Hrofesceaster. Rochester, Kent.

Hrypadun. Repton, Derby.

Hrypum, in. Ripon, Yorks.

Humbre. Humber, R.

Huntandun. Huntingdon.

Hwiccawudu. Wychwood Forest, Ox.

Hwitern. Whithorn, Wigtownsh.

Hythe, on. Hythe, Kent.

Idle, R.

Kesteven, Lincs.

Læstingaeu. Lastingham, Yorks.

Læwes. Lewes, Suss.

Legaceaster. Chester.

Liccidfeld. Lichfield, Staffs.

Ligoraceaster. Leicester.

Limen. R. Lympne, Kent.

Liminiææ. Lyminge, Kent.

Lindcylene. Lincoln.

Lindisfarena eg. Lindisfarne.

Lindissi. Lindsey, Lincs.

Loidis. Leeds.

Lothene. Lothian.

Louth, Lincs.

Luel. Carlisle.

Lunden. London.

Lygeanburh. Limbury, Beds.

Mældubesburg. Malmesbury, Wilts.

Mældun. Maldon, Ess.

Mærse. Mersey, R.

Magilros. Old Melrose.

Mameceaster. Manchester, Lancs.

Medeshamstede. Peterborough, Northants.

Meresig. Mersea Island, Ess.

Merioneth.

Middeltun. King's Milton, Kent.

Middeltun. Milton Abbas, Dors.

Miodowæge. Medway, R.

Moerheb. Morfe Forest, Sal.

Môn. Anglesey.

Monmouth.

Montgomery.

Nen. Nene, R.

Newburn, Nhumb.

Newcastle on Tyne, Nhumb.

New Forest, Hants.

Northwic. Norwich.

Okehampton, Dev.

Oswestry, Sal.

Ottanford. Otford, Kent.

Ouestræfeld. Austerfield, Yorks.

Oxnaford. Oxford.

Passanhamm. Passenham, Northants.

Peaclond. The Peak, Derby.

Pedridanmutha. Mouth of R. Parret, Som.

Pefenesea. Pevensey, Suss.

Peonnum, æt. Penselwood, Som.

Pinnendenn. Penenden Heath, Kent.

Pontefract, Yorks.

Porteceaster. Porchester, Hants.

Portesmutha. Portsmouth, Hants.

Portland, Dors.

Portlocæ. Portlock, Som.

Powys, Wales.

Priestholm, Anglesey.

Puclancyrcan, æt. Pucklechurch, Glouc.

Rægeheafde, æt. Gateshead, Dur.

Rayleigh, Ess.

Readingum, to. Reading, Berks.

Reculf. Reculver, Kent.

Rendlæsham. Rendlesham, Suff.

Rhuddlan, Flint.

Richards Castle, Heref.

Richale. Riccall, Yorks.

Richmond, Yorks.

Ringmere. Ringmere Pit in E. Wretham, Norf.

Rippel. Ribble, R.

Rumcofa. Runcorn, Ches.

Rumenea. Romney, Kent.

Ruthwell, Dumfriessh.

Sæfern. Severn, R.

Sanctæ Albanes stow. St. Albans, Herts.

Sanctæ Eadmundes stow. Bury St. Edmunds, Suff.

Sanctæ Germane. St. Germans, Corn.

Sandwic. Sandwich, Kent.

Scarborough, Yorks.

Sceaftenesbyrig, to. Shaftesbury, Dors.

Sceapig. Sheppey, Kent.

Sceobyrig, to. Shoebury, Ess.

Scireburnan, æt. Sherborne, Dors.

Scireburnan, to. Sherburn in Elmet, Yorks.

Scirwudu. Sherwood Forest, Notts.

Scorranstan. Sherston, Wilts.

Scrobbesbyrig, on. Shrewsbury.

Sealwudu. Selwood.

Searoburg. Salisbury.

Seolesig. Selsey. Suss.

Snotingaham. Nottingham.

Stængfordesbrycg, æt. Stamfordbridge, Yorks.

Stæthford. Stafford.

Stanford. Stamford, Lincs.

Steinmore. Stainmore, Yorks.

Stræcled. Strathclyde.

Streonæshalch. Whitby, Yorks.

Sture mutha. Mouth of R. Stour, Suff.

Sturigao. Sturry, Kent.

Sumurtun. Somerton, Som.

Sunningas. Sonning, Berks.

Suthriganaweorc. Southwark.

Suthwellan, æt. Southwell, Notts.

Sutton Hoo, Suff.

Swanawic. Swanage, Dors.

Taddenesscylf. Tanshelf, Yorks.

Tame, R.

Tamoworthig. Tamworth, Staffs.

Tamu. Thame, Ox.

Tamur. Tamar, R.

Tantun. Taunton, Som.

Tathaceaster. Tadcaster, Yorks.

Tefgeta. Teviot, R.

Temesanford. Tempsford, Beds.

Temes. Thames, R.

Tenet. Thanet, Kent.

Teotanheale, æt. Tettenhall, Staffs.

Tese. Tees, R.

Thelwæl. Thelwall, Ches.

Theodford. Thetford, Norf. and Suff.

Thornig. Thorney, Cambs.

Thornig. Thorney Island near Iver, Bucks.

Tickhill, Yorks.

Tiouulfingacæstir. Littleborough, Notts.

Tofeceaster. Towcester, Northants.

Tottaness. Totnes, Dev.

Treante. Trent, R.

Tuidi. Tweed, R.

Turecesieg. Torksey, Lincs.

Tutbury, Staffs.

Tweoneam. Christchurch, Hants.

Tynemouth, Nhumb.

Undalum, in. Oundle, Northants.

Use. Ouse, R.

Wæge. Wye, R.

Wæringwicum, æt. Warwick.

Waltham. Waltham Holy Cross. Ess.

Waneting. Wantage, Berks.

Wealingaford. Wallingford, Berks.

Wealtham. Bishop's Waltham, Hants.

Wege. Wey, R.

Weogorenaleag. Wyre Forest, Worc.

Weogornaceaster. Worcester.

Weolud. Welland, R.

Werham. Wareham, Dors.

Westburg. Westbury-on-Trym, Glouc.

Westmoringaland. Westmorland.

Westmynster. Westminster.

Wethmor. Wedmore, Som.

Wiht. Wight, Isle of.

Wii, on. Wye, Kent.

Wiltun. Wilton, Wilts.

Winburnan, æt. Wimborne, Dors.

Wincelcumb. Winchcombe, Glouc.

Windlesora. Old Windsor, Berks.

Wintanceaster. Winchester, Hants.

Wirhealum, on. Wirral, Ches.

Witham. Witham, Ess.

Withma. Witham, R.

Witlanbyrig, æt. Whittlebury, Northants.

Wiuræmuda. Monkwearmouth, Dur.

Wodnesbeorg. in Alton Priors, Wilts.

Wreocen. The Wrekin, Sal.

Wyllum, æt. Wells, Som.

Ypwinesfleot. Ebbsfleet, Kent.

Yrtlingaburg. Irthlingborough, Northants.

Ythancæstir. Bradwell-on-Sea, Ess.

Yttingforad. in Linslade, Bucks.

INDEX